PROPERTY TAX IN AFRICA

PROPERTY TAX IN AFRICA
Status, Challenges, and Prospects

Edited by

Riël Franzsen and William McCluskey

Cambridge, Massachusetts

Library of Congress Cataloging-in-Publication Data

Names: Franzsen, R. C. D. (Riël C. D.), editor, author. | McCluskey, William J., editor, author.
Title: Property tax in Africa : status, challenges, and prospects / edited by Riël Franzsen and William McCluskey.
Description: Cambridge, MA : Lincoln Institute of Land Policy, 2017. | Includes bibliographical references and index.
Identifiers: LCCN 2017002416 (print) | LCCN 2017003809 (ebook) | ISBN 9781558443631 (pbk. : alk. paper) | ISBN 9781558443648 (prc) | ISBN 9781558443655 (epub) | ISBN 9781558443662 (ibook) | ISBN 9781558443679 (pdf)
Subjects: LCSH: Property tax—Africa. | Tax administration and procedure—Africa.
Classification: LCC HJ4127.A35 P76 2017 (print) | LCC HJ4127.A35 (ebook) | DDC 336.22096—dc23
LC record available at https://lccn.loc.gov/2017002416

Designed by Jeff Miller

Composed in Janson by Westchester Publishing Services in Danbury, Connecticut.
Printed and bound by Puritan Press Inc., in Hollis, New Hampshire.
The paper is Rolland Enviro100, an acid-free, 100 percent PCW recycled sheet.

MANUFACTURED IN THE UNITED STATES OF AMERICA

Contents

PART III African Countries by Region

PART IV The Future of the Property Tax in Africa

List of Tables and Boxes

Foreword

The Lincoln Institute of Land Policy completed its identity change from an international organization to a global organization at the United Nations Conference on Housing and Sustainable Urban Development (Habitat III) in October 2016. This transition hinged on our recognition that land policies play an essential role in global efforts to address critical challenges, such as adapting to or mitigating climate change, or establishing sustainable, municipal fiscal systems. As we've grappled with climate change, global policy makers and analysts have come to a surprising conclusion: urbanization is an answer to global efforts to reduce the human carbon footprint. But this conclusion will be validated only if we get urbanization right. To get urbanization right, cities will need sufficient, reliable, and sustainable revenues. How else will we pay for the green infrastructure that will protect us from more frequent and severe weather events? And how will we pay for the transition to efficient, compact urban settlements that reduce reliance on carbon for transport or heating and cooling buildings?

While it might not seem obvious, the challenges of climate change and municipal finance are related, and more importantly, they both connect to our emerging global practice in property taxation. This book is the first comprehensive academic exploration of the property tax in Africa. It is rigorously researched and provides in-depth reviews of the property tax systems in half of the countries on the continent. Alongside our recently published volume on the property tax in Latin America, *Property Tax in Africa* fills an important gap in our global library.

Over the last seven decades, the Lincoln Institute has built, tested, and shared a broad arsenal of land policy tools. Within our arsenal, no tools are more important than those that support land-based revenue generation. These include the land tax, the property tax, land value capture, computer-assisted mass appraisal, and cadasters. These tools help to harness the value of land to invest in our places and ourselves. They have the potential to mobilize the resources needed to meet two seemingly insurmountable future challenges: (1) delivering lifeline goods and services to all urban residents; and (2) making annual investments of trillions of dollars globally in urban infrastructure.

This volume comes at an opportune time. Nowhere are the fiscal challenges of urbanization more pronounced than in Africa, the second most populous, largest geographically, and poorest continent in the world. Africa is urbanizing faster than any continent. Cities that rely heavily on insufficient intergovernmental transfers as their major revenue source are struggling to identify their own revenues to pay for basic goods and services for new urban residents. At the same time, they are searching for capital to build new infrastructure and to maintain their roads, sewers, and water systems. In the chapters that follow, sobering assessments are provided for the state of play of property tax systems in numerous African countries. Clearly, establishing high-functioning systems capable of delivering reliable annual revenue flows to help cities make ends meet will require a lot of work. But there is plenty of room for optimism.

Although property tax revenues across the continent are an abysmally small share of GDP, African cities are outperforming their countries in growing annual property tax revenues. As they begin to enjoy the virtuous cycle of tax base growth through infrastructure investments, their commitment to and success at using the property tax will only improve. Moreover, African cities and countries can benefit from new technologies that were not available when OECD countries built their local fiscal systems. New GIS technology will help cities and countries adopt digitized cadasters and land registries, leap-frogging the paper-based systems of more developed countries. Soon, computer-assisted mass appraisal will be implemented in cities beyond Cape Town as land markets mature and exchange prices are disclosed more transparently.

The Lincoln Institute has benefited greatly from its partnership with the African Tax Institute at the University of Pretoria. This volume is only one illustration of the scope of our work together. We look forward to continuing this important work and helping to buttress the use of the property tax across the continent as one answer to the challenge of getting urbanization right.

George W. McCarthy
President and CEO
Lincoln Institute of Land Policy

Preface

This book is the final outcome of a collaborative research project between the Lincoln Institute of Land Policy (Cambridge, Massachusetts, United States) and the African Tax Institute (the University of Pretoria, South Africa) that commenced in 2007 and ambitiously explored the current status of recurrent property taxes in all 54 countries in Africa.[1] The project began primarily as a mapping exercise undertaken by 14 research fellows who were tasked with gathering data in four to six countries each (Franzsen 2007). They were asked to prepare an overview of property-related taxes in these countries, focusing on recurrent taxes (Franzsen and Youngman 2009).

Africa is the second-largest continent, with a total area of more than 30 million km². With more than a billion inhabitants, it is also the second most populous continent (UNICEF n.d.).[2] Because of its size and diversity, its variety of languages, and data and capacity constraints, as well as political instability in some countries or regions, even a mere mapping exercise was challenging. From the outset, it was unlikely that detailed reports on all 54 countries could be written. Country reports based on available primary or secondary data were prepared for those countries the research fellows were able to visit.[3]

Language barriers are common within the 2,000 languages spoken on the African continent. There are four official languages widely used in African countries: Arabic (twelve countries), English (twenty-two countries), French (twenty countries), and Portuguese (five countries). There are countries with other official languages: in Ethiopia, the official language is Amharic; in Rwanda, it is Kinyarwanda; and in Somalia, it is Somali. There are 15 countries with more than one official language.[4]

Finding reliable data was challenging. In some countries, simply locating copies of relevant laws was difficult, and even in countries where legislation could be accessed, it became apparent that law and practice may differ, in some instances significantly. Given the quality and quantity of available source data, the scope and depth of the country reports differ widely. Also, for a variety of reasons, not all countries were visited,[5] and not all country reports were posted as working papers on the Lincoln Institute's web page.

Multiparty democracies have mostly supplanted the one-party systems that marked the onset of independence in many countries; since the 1990s, democratization and decentralization have been gaining momentum. However, political instability and in some instances civil war have characterized the postcolonial era in many sub-Saharan African countries. The so-called Arab Spring of 2011 also resulted in political instability in North Africa. Its legacy is still evident in Egypt, Libya, and Tunisia.[6] According to the 2015 Fragile States Index (FSI 2016), 22 of the most fragile states globally are African countries.[7] This has a direct impact on land tenure security and property markets and thus indirectly affects the taxation of real property, as is discussed in some detail in chapter 1. African countries generally fare poorly in various other international comparative indexes,[8] such as the corruption perception index, the doing business index (e.g., property registration and paying taxes), the transparency index, and the international property rights index. Although the overall picture from these indexes seems rather bleak, it must also be stated that on the whole, African countries have experienced significant economic growth in recent years, albeit in many instances from a low base (African Economic Outlook 2016).

Over time, the scope of the project was broadened to include a comprehensive qualitative overview of policies (e.g., tax base options) and administrative issues (e.g., assessment and collection practices), as well as the prospects for property taxes across Africa. This necessitated a much more hands-on approach to individual country reports, as well as reliance on our professional experience in various African countries.[9] Not all the country-specific working papers could be revised and incorporated as country chapters in this book. We believe, however, that the 29 country-specific chapters selected all contain valuable information, as do the four regional chapters. Furthermore, it was not feasible to update all the country chapters in all respects. Although basic country data, such as population, urbanization, and per capita GDP, were updated in all cases, some property tax data may be out of date, as indicated in the relevant chapters. Except for per capita GDP data in U.S. dollars, references to monetary amounts are in the local currency. A currency exchange table (as of June 15, 2016) is provided in table A.3 in the appendix.[10]

In discussing property taxes, classifying or regionalizing African countries is difficult because both can be based on various factors. For the purposes of this book, colonial history and language were primarily used to classify sub-Saharan countries where it was necessary to regionalize the discussion. This broad group of countries can be divided into predominantly English-speaking (Anglophone), French-speaking (Francophone), or Portuguese-speaking (Lusophone) countries. This division was used throughout this book, but especially in the discussions in chapters 1 and 2, chapters 32 to 34, and chapter 36. Although Arabic is predominant in the countries in North and Northeast Africa, a simple language-based classification does not necessarily fit neatly. Hence, a rather arbitrary classification based on geographic location was used for the countries in North and Northeast Africa, especially in chapter 35.

This book reviews developments in policies, laws, and administrative practices pertaining to the property tax in African countries and examines revenue importance, tax bases, valuation and assessment, tax rates, and property tax administration. Although it focuses primarily on reviewing current policies, laws, and practices, it also comments on the prospects for property taxes on the African continent if sufficient information and data are available. If only one lesson is to be learned from this book, it is that one size does not fit all in regard to property taxes in Africa.

In conclusion, we wish to express our gratitude to the board and staff of the Lincoln Institute of Land Policy, especially the current president and CEO, Dr. George "Mac" McCarthy; the former president and CEO, Dr. Greg Ingram; and Joan Youngman, Semida Munteanu, and Emily McKeigue. We also thank Professor Roy W. Bahl, Dr. Peadar Davis, Dr. Frances Plimmer, who acted as critical reviewers at various stages of the process.

Riël Franzsen and William McCluskey
September 2016

Notes

1. The fifty-four countries include the six island states, Cabo Verde, Comoros, Madagascar, Mauritius, São Tomé and Príncipe, and the Seychelles. The disputed territory of Western Sahara (also referred to as the Sahwari Arab Democratic Republic), annexed and administered by Morocco, is not regarded as an African country.

2. Other basic statistics on the countries in Africa are provided in table A.1 and table A.2 in the appendix.

3. The 42 countries visited are Angola, Benin, Botswana, Burundi, Cabo Verde, Cameroon, the Central African Republic, Chad, Comoros, Congo, Côte d'Ivoire, Democratic Republic of the Condo, Egypt, Equatorial Guinea, Eritrea, Ethiopia, Gabon, The Gambia, Ghana, Guinea-Bissau, Kenya, Lesotho, Liberia, Libya, Madagascar, Malawi, Mauritius, Mozambique, Namibia, Niger, Nigeria, Rwanda, São Tomé and Príncipe, Senegal, Seychelles, Sierra Leone, South Africa, Sudan, Swaziland, Tanzania, Uganda, and Zambia.

4. Table A.1 includes a list of official languages.

5. The 12 countries not visited by research fellows are Algeria, Burkina Faso, Djibouti, Guinea, Mali, Mauritania, Morocco, Somalia, South Sudan, Togo, Tunisia, and Zimbabwe.

6. For example, there have been military uprisings (the Central African Republic), coups (Burkina Faso, Comoros, Mali, and Niger) and attempted coups (Burundi and Chad). Varying degrees of political instability are currently experienced in Algeria, Burundi, the Central African Republic, Chad, Comoros, Côte d'Ivoire, Democratic Republic of the Congo, Egypt, Guinea, Libya, Madagascar, Mali, Niger, Nigeria, Somalia, South Sudan, Sudan, and Zimbabwe, among other countries.

7. In September 2016, in descending order of fragility, these countries were South Sudan (1), Somalia (2), the Central African Republic (3), Sudan (4), Democratic Republic of the Congo (5), Chad (6), Guinea (10), Nigeria (14), Côte d'Ivoire (15), Zimbabwe (16), Guinea-Bissau (17), Burundi (18), Niger (19), Ethiopia (20), Kenya (21), Liberia (22), Uganda (23), Eritrea (24), Libya (25), Mauretania (26), Cameroon (28), and Mali (30).

8. The most recent rankings of African countries on these indexes are reflected in table A.8 in the appendix.

9. Botswana, Cameroon, Egypt, The Gambia, Kenya, Lesotho, Liberia, Malawi, Mozambique, Rwanda, South Africa, Swaziland, Tanzania, Uganda, and Zambia.

10. Given the volatility of most currencies in Africa, this table provides only rough guidance. For accuracy, current exchange rates should be consulted.

References

African Economic Outlook. 2016. *www.africaneconomicoutlook.org/en/outlook*.

Franzsen, R. C. D. 2007. "Property Taxation in Anglophone Africa." *Land Lines* 19(2): 8–14.

Franzsen, R. C. D., and J. M. Youngman. 2009. "Mapping Property Taxes in Africa." *Land Lines* 21(3): 8–13.

FSI (Fragile States Index). 2016. "Fragile States Index 2015." *http://fsi.fundforpeace.org/rankings-2015*.

UNICEF. n.d. "Generation 2030—Africa." *http://data.unicef.org/gen2030/index.htmlUN*.

PART I

Current Status
and Challenges

1

Introduction

RIËL FRANZSEN AND WILLIAM McCLUSKEY

A recurrent property tax is levied in almost all countries in the world (McCluskey, Bell, and Lim 2010).[1] Although the property tax is the mainstay of local taxes in many developed and industrialized countries, it is only beginning to gain a foothold in developing and transition countries. Many comparative reviews of property taxes have been published in the past three decades.[2] The breakup of the former Soviet bloc and the fragmentation of Yugoslavia created opportunities for the new democracies to reestablish private ownership rights and to develop land registration systems to support legal and fiscal cadastres (Malme and Youngman 2001; Dale, Mahoney, and McLaren 2010). Real property markets emerged along with associated reforms in the financial and banking sectors. These developments were coupled with and necessitated by the revision of real property taxes in these transition countries.[3] Over the past 25 years, property tax reforms have also received attention in Asia,[4] as well as in Latin America and the Caribbean.[5] Although property tax reform has also occurred in African regions and countries during the past 25 years, little has been written on the subject.[6] Therefore, a comprehensive review of property taxes in Africa is both needed and timely.

This book addresses the following questions:

- How important is the recurrent property tax in African countries?

- What property tax bases are currently used, which are performing best, and why?

- What assessment techniques are used, and to what extent are computer-assisted mass appraisal (CAMA) and geographic information systems (GISs) used?

- How are tax rates determined, and how common is the use of differential (classified) rates?

- Who is responsible for the key aspects of property tax administration: property data collection and tax base coverage, valuation and assessment, and billing, collection, and enforcement?

- Is the property tax properly managed? Are there success stories?

- What are the key issues of property tax reform?

To answer these questions, it is important to define the concepts *property-related taxes* and *property tax*.

Terminology

Terminology is important. In comparative research on property taxation, care must be taken to ensure that the terminology used is understood and applied uniformly across various countries or jurisdictions. Specific statutory and common-law terms may have different meanings in different jurisdictions. Countries may use different terms for the same concept; for example, in Anglophone African countries, the recurrent property tax levied at the local level is referred to as *rates*, sometimes with an added descriptive noun (*compound* in The Gambia, *local* in Mauritius, *property* in South Africa, or *tenement* in Nigeria).

Property taxes are often broadly defined, especially for purposes of national country statistics, to include property transfer taxes, stamp duties, and death and gift taxes (IMF 2014). In some countries (Armenia, Georgia) and some states in the United States, the property tax may also include personal property (movable assets) or intangible property.

For the purposes of this book, the term *property-related tax* refers to any tax on the transfer, ownership, or occupation of real estate or immovable property (Franzsen and McCluskey 2005; Martinez-Vazquez, Noiset, and Rider 2010). Taxes on the transfer (acquisition, alienation, or both) of property include stamp duties, real estate transfer taxes, capital gains taxes, gift taxes, and death and inheritance taxes.

Hereinafter, the terms *recurrent property tax* or simply *property tax* will be used to describe only a recurrent tax on real estate (immovable property), whether land or buildings or both. This type of tax is the main focus of this book. However, other property-related taxes are discussed when their interaction with the property tax is important.

In an attempt to overcome at least some of the problems with terminology, the following terms are used as defined below unless the contrary is explicitly indicated:

- *Annual value* or *annual rental value* is the basis of the property tax where the taxable value is related to an estimate of the rental value of the taxable property.

- *Capital improved value* is the market value of a property, that is, the value of the land plus all improvements as a single taxable object.

- *Immovable property* is land, as well as buildings and all permanent fixtures affixed to land, and is synonymous with the term *real property* used in some countries.

- *Land rent* or *ground rent* is a charge for occupation or lease of land owned by the national government or held under terms of customary tenure.[7]

- *Land tax* is a recurrent tax on the ownership of unimproved or improved land, excluding buildings and all or most of the other improvements made to the land.

- *Land value taxation* is a property tax system in which land is the only taxable object, and the value of improvements is ignored. This system is often called *site value taxation* or *unimproved value taxation*.

- *Property tax* is a recurrent tax levied on the ownership or occupation of immovable property, whether land only, land and buildings, or buildings only.

- *Rates* is the term for the property tax levied at the local-government level in many of the member states of the Commonwealth of Nations and former British territories, such as Australia, Hong Kong, Kenya, Singapore, South Africa, and Zimbabwe.

- *Rating* is a term used to depict the local property tax system in the United Kingdom and in many former British colonies where the property tax is referred to as *rates, assessment rates, property rates,* or *tenement rates.*

- *Site value rating* is a property tax system in which the tax is levied on the value of the land only, often including some types of improvements to the land itself, such as leveling, but excluding the value of any improvements on the land (Dowse and Hargreaves 1999; Franzsen 2009; Franzsen and McCluskey 2013).

- *Split rate taxation*, also referred to as *composite rating* or *differential rating*, is a property tax system in which the land and the buildings (and possibly other improvements) on it are valued separately and are taxed at different rates.

- *Unimproved value* describes the tax base of a land-only property tax. The term is used especially in Australia and the Pacific region and is sometimes synonymous with *site value*. However, unimproved value is sometimes defined to exclude all improvements, such as site clearance, filling, and leveling (Dowse and Hargreaves 1999).

Recurrent Property Taxes

A recurrent property tax is a general feature of the overall tax systems of most of the countries in Africa. Like countries elsewhere in the world, African countries use a variety of tax base options (Franzsen and McCluskey 2013; McCluskey and Franzsen 2013a).

Tax Bases

Determining an appropriate tax base is a key policy decision discussed in chapter 2 (Kelly 2000). This decision is usually made at the central-government level in unitary countries (Czech Republic, South Africa) and at the state or provincial level in federal countries (Canada, India, Nigeria, and the United States). In some countries, legislation explicitly allows local authorities to select an appropriate tax base from two or more options (Australia [at the state level], Kenya, Malaysia, Namibia, New Zealand, and Swaziland), and municipalities are allowed, at least in theory, to choose a tax base that will suit their needs. In some instances, legislation indirectly allows for the use of a different base (India and Tanzania). A number of countries prescribe different tax bases for different property use categories (Côte d'Ivoire, Niger, Thailand, and the United Kingdom). Other countries, however, prescribe a single tax base by law (Brazil, Estonia, Indonesia, the Philippines, South Africa, and Zambia). Undeveloped and developed property may have different tax bases (Côte d'Ivoire).

There are three broad categories of property tax bases: a per-unit tax, an area-based tax, and a value-based tax (Franzsen and McCluskey 2013; McCluskey and Franzsen 2013a). In countries where property markets are efficient and the valuation skills and capacity exist to determine credible property values on a significant scale and on a regular basis, capital value or rental value approaches are generally preferred. Not surprisingly, capital and rental value systems are most common in industrial countries. Real estate market evidence usually determines the choice of one or another of these three bases. The Republic of Ireland is an interesting example. When it became necessary to reintroduce a property tax on residential property, the lack of data on property size and value left the government with no choice but to introduce a rudimentary flat tax per property unit in 2012.[8] Area-based taxes are common in low- and middle-income countries (Burundi, Czech Republic, Democratic Republic of the Congo, Slovakia, and Sudan). Value-based property taxes can be annual-value taxes (Egypt, France, Ghana, Hong Kong, India, Israel, Malaysia, Thailand, and Uganda), unimproved land value or site value taxes (Australia, Estonia, Jamaica, Kenya, and New Zealand), or capital improved value or market value taxes (Brazil, Canada, Colombia, Denmark, South Africa, and the United States). Given the rich comparative literature on property tax bases, only a brief discussion of area-based and value-based taxes follows.

Area-Based Systems

An area-based approach is generally used where insufficient market data exist to implement a value-based system. It can be applied to land only (as a rate per unit of area) or to buildings only (a rate per unit of actual or usable floor area). There are basically two approaches: a simple or strict per-unit assessment without any adjustment for factors such as location or use, and a unit-value assessment with adjustments for location, use, or other factors, such as building age and quality.

Simple area-based systems, without any adjustments for use or location, are uncommon. Most countries that use an area-based system adjust the tax base by one or more factors, usually location and use, but in some cases also the quality and age of buildings and other improvements. These factors account for value, and although they complicate an otherwise simple system, they generally increase equity and introduce some progressivity. For example, in Kinshasa, Democratic Republic of the Congo, properties are categorized by neighborhood and are taxed accordingly. Most cities in Tanzania use both an area-based system (flat rates) and a value-based system. A simplified area-based system is used for properties that are not yet on a valuation list (McCluskey and Franzsen 2005a). In the three municipalities in Dar es Salaam, some adjustments are made for use, size, and location. In 2002, for example, the relevant property tax bylaw in Temeke Municipality provided classified tax amounts for more than 60 property categories (McCluskey and Franzsen 2005a).

Various Indian cities, including Ahmedabad in Gujarat State, have introduced a so-called calibrated area-based system (Brzeski 2005; U. A. V. Rao 2008). This simplified system uses adjustment factors, such as location, building size, usage, age, and occupancy. Because there are no clear provisions for future changes to these factors, there is little buoyancy in the system other than the increase in property numbers (Cornia 2008). This is confirmed by the stagnation of revenues in Delhi and Patna (M. G. Rao 2013). Bangalore in Karnataka State implements a slightly different system, the Self Assessment Scheme (SAS), that can best be described as a hybrid of an area-based system and a value-based system. The city has been classified into value zones based on published guidance values produced by the Department of Stamps and Registration, and these are adjusted regularly by "expert judgment" (McCluskey and Franzsen 2013b; U. A. V. Rao 2008). Until at least 2011, property tax revenues were steadily increasing. Over a three-year cycle, the increase is mandated to be at least 15 percent. This provides some buoyancy to the system, which means continued growth of revenue, given proper collection efficiency (McCluskey and Franzsen 2013b). There are no appeals of valuations under this system.

Capital Value Systems

CAPITAL IMPROVED VALUE SYSTEMS

Most developed countries and many developing countries use some form of capital improved value system. However, assessment of the capital value of taxable property can vary significantly. In South Africa, the property tax is levied on "market value." Latin American countries levy the property tax on "assessed value" (De Cesare 2012).

In Namibia, the Philippines, and Swaziland, land and buildings are valued and taxed separately. In the Philippines, land assessments are based on market transactions, while assessments of buildings and other improvements are based on depreciated replacement costs. This approach is also used in most Latin American cities and is to some extent a solution to the scarcity of valuers. However, in Bogotá, Colombia, the assessment process is becoming more market related (McCluskey and Franzsen 2013b). Indonesia uses a somewhat simplified system of assessment for both land and buildings. Land is categorized into approximately 100 land value zones according to use and location, whereas buildings are categorized into 40 classes, each of which has a prescribed unit price per square meter. Therefore, properties are not valued individually but are assessed according to the prescribed land zone and building class rates (Lewis 2003). Macedonia, Montenegro, and Serbia follow a similar approach. Another novel approach, a simplified system based on capital improved values, is found in Great Britain and the Republic of Ireland. In 1991, England, Scotland, and Wales replaced the politically unacceptable poll tax with the council tax. This residential property tax combines assessment and taxation by allocating all dwellings to one of eight value bands and setting a tax rate for each band. The advantage of this system is that a discrete value does not have to be determined for each individual property (see chapter 36).

A key question in many developing countries where property markets are informal or do not work efficiently, and where valuation skills are often lacking, is whether a value-based system is the best option. A dated or incomplete system relying on individually determined property values may be more inequitable than a pragmatic alternative based on adjusted area values (the *arnona* in Israel) or value bands (Great Britain and the Republic of Ireland).

Unimproved Land or Site Value Systems

A land or site value system ignores existing improvements on the land and therefore requires significantly less information and skill to set up and maintain. However, it requires proper legal definitions of *unimproved value of land* or, in some instances, *site value of land*. Some improvements (such as leveling, clearing, and underground drainage) may over time have merged with land to such an extent that it becomes difficult and artificial to disregard them in determining the value of the relevant land parcel (Franzsen 2009; Oldman and Teachout 1979).

It is appropriate for land value systems to define the tax base to include site improvements. Various studies in Jamaica have researched the feasibility of a system based on improved values. Mostly, they have recommended retaining the system of unimproved land value (Franzsen and McCluskey 2008; Holland and Follain 1991; Sjoquist 2005). It also may provide a simple solution in rural areas (Bahl, Cyan, and Wallace 2015). With few exceptions (e.g., subdivisions and amalgamations), the physical attributes of land remain constant, and thus a land value tax system is less costly to maintain than one that includes valuation of buildings and other improvements (Franzsen and McCluskey 2008). Furthermore, landowners should bear a heavier tax burden, so a land value tax is more progressive (Bahl 2009). However, because the base is narrower and less buoyant, and because significant wealth inherent in buildings is excluded, higher nominal tax rates are required, which may be politically problematic (Bahl 2009). Furthermore, a land value tax is not consistent with the property transfer tax, which is based on total values (Bahl and Wallace 2010).

Systems based on unimproved land values or site values are presently used extensively by local authorities in various Australian states and territories (New South Wales, Northern Territory, Queensland, and Western Australia) and some local authorities in New Zealand. Estonia introduced a land value tax in 1993, and coverage is excellent. However, the land tax is not an important source of tax revenue in Estonia. An unimproved land value system is also encountered in developing countries, such as Fiji, Jamaica, and the Solomon Islands (Franzsen and McCluskey 2005). In Africa, Kenya and Namibia levy a tax on unimproved land, as do a number of Francophone countries, such as the Central African Republic and Côte d'Ivoire.

IMPROVEMENT VALUE SYSTEMS

Where land cannot be taxed for political, social, or cultural reasons, buildings constitute a viable tax base (Anguilla, Bermuda, Ghana, Mozambique, and Tanzania). Given the high levels of development in urban centers in many developing countries, the value of buildings is a considerable percentage of total property value, and thus, the tax base is relatively large. However, determination of the value of buildings is much more complex, time consuming, and costly than that of land values (Franzsen and McCluskey 2013).

Separate Valuation of Land and Improvements (Split Rating)

Under a split-rate system, land and buildings are valued separately, or the total market value of the property is determined and the assessed value of either the land or the building is deducted to determine a residual value for the other component. The cost of valuation is high because credible and defendable values must be determined for both the land and the building components (Franzsen and McCluskey 2013). The attractiveness of the split-rate system lies in the rate differentiation. A high rate can be applied to land, encouraging development, but the building stock, which represents significant capital wealth, is also taxed. Split-rate systems are used in various countries, including Namibia and Swaziland.

Annual Rental Value Systems

A rental value assessment approach imposes a tax on the annual rent that taxable property would command in the marketplace, based on current patterns of property use. Whereas a capital value approach generally reflects the value of the highest and best use of the property and therefore tends to tax gains in value that the owner has not yet realized, the annual rental value approach typically does not. It is also a tax on occupation rather than ownership (although in Pakistan it is indeed the owner). Determining a notional market rent for owner-occupied property may also be difficult (Bahl and Wallace 2010). A rental value system relies on obtaining credible evidence from an active rental market with sufficient arm's-length transactions for all relevant property use types. In some instances, the tax base is net rental value (Melbourne, Australia); in other cases, it is gross rental value (Perth, Western Australia). A third option may be simply to allow for a specific percentage deduction from gross rental to determine the assessed value. In developing countries, however, the relevant laws can lack clarity on how vacant land should be accommodated. Where there is rent control, the question will arise whether market rent or regulated rent should be used as the tax base (Bahl and Wallace 2010; Franzsen and Mc-Cluskey 2013).

Many countries, especially former British colonies (Egypt, Hong Kong, Malaysia, Sierra Leone, Singapore, and Uganda) and former French colonies (Algeria, Côte d'Ivoire, Mali, Mauritania, Morocco, and Niger), use an annual value property tax system. In stark contrast to the rather static annual rental value systems in Egypt and Uganda, Hong Kong and Singapore operate vibrant, well-administered rental value systems under which all taxable properties are revalued annually.

Area-Based Versus Value-Based Approaches

Scholars generally agree that value-based approaches provide a better tax base than area-based approaches. First, the benefits from local-government services (public transport, schools, police stations, and recreational facilities) are more closely related to the value than to the size of property. Second, the value of local infrastructure (such as surfaced roads, pavements, storm-water drainage, and street lighting) can be capitalized into property values. Third, market value provides a naturally buoyant tax base, whereas an area-based system tends to be static (Cornia 2008) unless value-approximation coefficients are used, but these must be regularly adjusted. Determination and adjustment of these coefficients are usually subjective and nontransparent, whereas market values can generally be determined more objectively and more transparently, especially if a credible objection and appeal process exists.

Land Tenure, Information Management Systems, and Governance

A proper land titling or deed registration system is important for a well-developed property market and a well-functioning property tax. It is essential that the registration of land titles be comprehensive, efficient, and transparent. However, the lack of comprehensive registration has not precluded the imposition of a property tax in most African countries. For example, in both Cameroon and Rwanda, formally registered land constitutes less than 1 percent of total land parcels. The property tax can be levied on leasehold rights (Zambia) and other types of limited property rights, such as *emphyteusis* (Burundi, Democratic Republic of the Congo, and Rwanda),[9] concessions (Cameroon, Democratic Republic of the Congo),[10] or usufruct (Benin, Burundi, and the Central African Republic).[11] For property taxation, the same database used for the land rent or ground rent can be used. What is required, though, is a broad definition of *owner* that includes, for example, leaseholders, absentee landlords, tenants, and other occupiers.

The problems with land administration in Africa include (1) the multiplicity of land tenure systems; (2) a land administration system for the transfer of property held under formal tenure alongside an informal land administration system managed by traditional (or tribal) authorities; (3) a deed registration system that runs parallel to a title registration system; and (4) outdated and poorly maintained manual land record systems, although this is changing (World Bank 2015).

Duality of Tenure

Property rights to land play a fundamental role in governing the patterns of its use, management, and taxation. The way in which land is owned or occupied in African countries often limits the revenue potential of the property tax. In many countries, land belongs to the state and cannot be privately owned (Ethiopia, Lesotho, Mozambique, Swaziland, Tanzania), or private ownership is greatly limited (Cameroon, Rwanda, Sierra Leone, and Zambia). However, state ownership of the land does not preclude levying a property tax.

In some countries, large tracts of land are held under traditional or customary tenure and are used for communal grazing and subsistence agriculture. For example, in Botswana, 6 percent of the land is owned freehold, 23 percent is state owned, and 71 percent is customary land. In Uganda and Mozambique, customary tenure accounts for 62 and 90 percent, respectively, of the land area. Dual or even multiple tenure systems are prevalent in many countries in Anglophone, Francophone, and Lusophone Africa. Dual tenure systems sometimes are contentious. In South Africa, for example, it is reported that in many rural communities, there is conflict between the elected, formal local government and traditional leaders, which can hinder local development and service delivery.

Traditional forms of land tenure are a problem for property taxation (Macmillan 1997; Ramodibedi 2000). There are three issues: (1) Who is the taxable person? (2) How is the land to be valued? (3) How are formal local-government structures and traditional leaderships or chiefdoms to coexist? On the first problem, one can argue that the person with paramount control of the land, that is, the tribal chief or village elder, should be the taxpayer. He can then apportion the tax bill among the users of the land.

Land valuation is difficult because the land is typically rural and is used for basic subsistence farming or low-value residences. Taxable value is difficult to determine, and the income of the taxpayers is very limited. Such communal rural land is typically exempt (Kenya and Nigeria) or falls below the value threshold at which properties are taxed (South Africa). Therefore, large rural areas of land are not part of the tax base, although rural land that is commercially farmed should constitute a taxable object and is indeed taxed in several African countries (Namibia, South Africa, Sudan, and Zimbabwe). However, even small-scale farming may be taxed (Egypt and Eritrea). In Kenya, however, freehold agricultural land, including commercial farms, is typically not taxed. In South Africa, the property tax legislation provides for a temporary exemption that could be repealed once all the legal requirements and the administrative capacity to maintain the system are in place. Communal land is not only a rural issue in South Africa; it is also a problem in at least two of the eight metropolitan municipalities, eThekwini Metropolitan Municipality and the City of Tshwane (Franzsen 2003).

The third problem may be the most difficult to resolve. In Niger, traditional chiefs play an important role in local governance and the collection of local taxes, but in Ghana, the Local Government Act of 1993 clearly states that customary bodies do not have any power to raise revenue through property taxes. The South African constitution of 1996 also implies this. Communal (tribal) land is excluded from local-government property tax bases in Botswana, Lesotho, Namibia, and Swaziland. In certain instances, tribal authorities have powers to levy property-related charges for tenure rights on members of the tribe. It is not surprising that many traditional authorities are therefore opposed to any form of formal, democratic local government that undermines their powers and functions, especially in regard to land (Franzsen 2001; Macmillan 1997).

Although the taxation of tribal land is problematic, it is not impossible. In Zimbabwe, a so-called development levy is imposed on all persons who are heads of households within any communal or resettlement ward of a rural district council. Although this is more akin to a poll tax, it does relate to the occupation of land. The head of a household is defined as a person who occupies or uses communal land or resettlement land for agricultural or residential purposes (other than occupancy by a spouse, child, or dependent of such a person). This levy is typically imposed on a family unit occupying land under the terms of a traditional right of occupation or use. It may be uniform throughout an area or differential (Brakspear 1999). There are also examples in Canada and New Zealand where tribal land is taxed (Franzsen 2001).

Land policies and tenure reforms directly affect a country's economy and investor confidence and can become very contentious political issues, as in Lesotho (Ramodibedi 2000), Namibia, South Africa, and Zimbabwe. Land reform in Zimbabwe over the past two decades indicates how controversial it can be.

Land Information Systems

Since 2000, African countries have made dramatic improvements in developing their land information systems (LISs). For example, Uganda began its involvement with an LIS in 2007 with a project funded by the World Bank and has now launched the National Land Information System Infrastructure, in which some 70 percent of all land titles are registered. Ghana's Land Administration project began in 2004. In 2012, Tanzania began the Integrated Land Management Information System and followed with the Zanzibar Land Information System in 2014.

Developing a modern LIS can take a decade or more. This makes the process susceptible to loss of support unless it is underpinned by strong political commitment and donor backing (Burns 2007). To reduce the risk that the government will lose interest in the project, countries should develop a long-term strategy and realistic goals and objectives. The LIS should have strong support from a lead ministry, such as a ministry of lands, with buy-in from other ministries, such as finance and local government. The advantages of having a national LIS must be articulated in a way that shows that they include both fiscal and nonfiscal benefits.

A critical element in any LIS is the institutional arrangements within which the system operates. Typically, countries must deal with multiple organizations, each with legislation empowering it to participate in the delivery of some part of the land administration process. Powers often overlap and add to bureaucratic red tape, which allows agencies to remain self-serving, with scant regard for the efficiency of services to the public and community. Overcoming such conflicts is important in developing a successful LIS.

Development and implementation of an institutional vision, strategy, assessment, and operational plan for institutional reform are essential. Key reform principles include operational independence, financial sustainability, accountability, and customer orientation. Other component outputs are (1) an analysis of sound practices in legislation and regulatory framework improvement; (2) structures to enhance the accountability of the land registry to key stakeholders; (3) training and capacity building within the registry and other sectorial stakeholders; and (4) public outreach activities to improve public perceptions of the registry.

To support the property tax, a land administration system should include a process for determining, recording, and disseminating information about tenure, ownership, value, and use of land. The LIS is composed of textual records that define rights or information and geospatial data that define the space over which these rights and information apply. An important motivation for land administration projects throughout the developing world is the facilitation of transparent and efficient land markets, on which the property tax relies.

Advances in spatial data systems through geographic information systems have led to improvements in cadastral mapping and LISs. Paper-based LISs often suffer from misplaced or lost documents and inconsistent record keeping and are seldom linked or integrated nationwide. In addition, they often fail to detect multiple, duplicate, or ambiguous ownership claims. Geospatially enabled digital LIS systems can help resolve most of these information failures. Moreover, geospatially based LISs can specify property rights and community boundaries more precisely and can eliminate many disputes between customary and statutory law. Land administrations in Burkina Faso, Ghana, and Mozambique, for example, have turned to geospatial cadastral surveys to create more accurate national land tenure systems.

Land Registration and the Cadastre

The cadastre is closely linked with land registration. A cadastre is a systematically organized database of property data along with associated maps within a jurisdiction or country (FIG 1995). This information delineates a property's boundaries, determined by a survey, and includes a map that indicates the boundaries. Although cadastres were originally established for property tax purposes, they are used for land registration purposes in many countries. When a cadastre is used for tax purposes, it is a fiscal cadastre; when it is used for land registration purposes, it is a legal cadastre. However, modern cadastres are typically multipurpose (Mozambique).

Bogaerts, Williamson, and Fendela (2002) consider the cadastre the core or basis of a land administration system and emphasize that the establishment of modern land administration systems is not possible without an effective cadastre. Dale and McLaughlin (1999) conclude that the basic building block of land administration systems is the cadastral parcel and that land administration can be divided into four functions: juridical, regulatory, fiscal, and information management. The Bathurst Declaration (UN-FIG 1999) states that land administration systems, and in particular their central cadastral components, are essential elements of a country's national infrastructure. However, the link between a cadastre and a legal land register continues to differ among countries. Some countries have fully integrated systems, but many, such as Kenya and Mozambique, have land registration systems that are not linked to the cadastre.

It is important to note, however, that a cadastre, or even a cadastral survey, is not a prerequisite for having a land or property tax system, although it will affect the nature and sophistication of the system. A problem often associated with coverage of valuation rolls in value-based systems is the poor state of the land registration and titling systems because the registration of titles or deeds and the availability of comprehensive fiscal, legal, and multipurpose cadastres are important to the effective administration of full-fledged property tax systems. Property registrations include information on the current owner, which is important for the administration of the property tax. However, the land registry must share this information with the billing department to ensure that the correct person is billed. This will instill confidence in the ownership and other limited rights pertaining to land and buildings and thus will provide increased tenure security. More secure tenure rights should result in improved levels of formality in property markets and better property tax compliance. This also could increase access to and reduced costs of mortgage finance and have an overall positive effect on market values.

Although a land registration system is important, it should not be used as an excuse for failing to tax all properties irrespective of their registration. In Rwanda, for example, only properties with a freehold title are presently liable for property taxation. For the vast number of properties that are not in freehold, a leasehold fee must be paid. Arguably this is a fee for the right to occupy, not a tax. This is also the case for the ground rent or land rent in Burundi, Kenya, Lesotho, Mozambique, Tanzania, and Zambia. In Lesotho and Kenya, only properties in urban areas covered by a land registry are taxable. Landowners can evade the property tax by not registering, but they then have limited legal protection of the land they own. In Botswana, insufficient and incomplete records on land parcel use or ownership in areas practicing customary land tenure have been the biggest obstacle in developing a land information system. Although land information in these areas has improved greatly, it still is not good enough to provide a sound basis for land administration.

Many administrative problems beset property registration, such as expensive surveying, time-consuming and costly legal processes (Chad), lack of competent personnel in registry departments, manual and paper-based systems, and the absence of local, decentralized registry offices. A major part of the problem is a lack of understanding by property owners of the benefits of registering their property. Often the process is voluntary. The lack of a comprehensive property registry results in transactions within the informal market, which in turn adversely affect the operation of the property market (Mozambique). However, several countries have good registration practices, including Burkina Faso, Cabo Verde, Malawi, Mozambique, Namibia, Rwanda, South Africa, Zambia, and Zimbabwe.

Many countries have ongoing land titling and registration projects funded by donors (Cabo Verde, Lesotho, Mauritius, Uganda, and Zambia).

However, in many places, the process is lengthy and expensive, and progress is slow (Kenya). The lack of a land registry creates difficulties for the property tax because of the lack of clarity about who owns what. Tying property tax liability only to registered properties significantly reduces coverage. The solution is to speed up the registration process, as was done very successfully in Rwanda. However, this is costly and presupposes the necessary capacity to administer self-declaration procedures. The benefits to the national government of comprehensive land registration often outweigh the cost of initial or first registration. By ensuring that the first registration is mandatory, the process can be made regular at low or no cost. Apart from providing an improved basis for taxation, registration can result in efficiencies in other areas, such as planning land use, providing a base for secured lending to owners, and developing a national land information system.

Recognition of customary tenure in land administration systems varies. In some countries, such as Mali, customary rights are explicitly recognized, but these administrative systems often operate in a very complex legal and institutional environment. In other instances (Mozambique and Uganda), there is a unified legal system based on customary law. The 1997 Land Law in Mozambique, promulgated under a socialist administration, uses the term *family law* rather than *customary law*. Customary land use tends to dominate in Burundi, Chad, Côte d'Ivoire, Niger, and Togo. In the Central African Republic, traditional land tenure is restricted to land use rights rather than ownership. Land can be either state owned or freehold in Côte d'Ivoire. In Equatorial Guinea and Gabon, all land is owned by the state, but it can be allocated and "owned" by individuals provided it is put to productive use.

Many developing land administration systems distinguish between urban and rural systems. In Mozambique, urban municipalities have the power to develop their own cadastres, while a national land information cadastre is being developed for rural land.[12] The existence of separate land registries and cadastral offices frequently leads to problems with inconsistent and duplicated records. In Mozambique, for example, the Ministry of Justice is responsible for the legal land registry, but the Ministry of Lands Environment and Rural Development has responsibility for the rural cadastre. In Kenya, the land registry has been decentralized to counties, which operate as independent entities with little national oversight or control.

In several Francophone countries, such as Burundi, Madagascar, Mali, and Niger, land-related policies have had to recognize and embrace tenure dualism, that is, both customary and statutory tenure (Durand-Lasserve, Durand-Lasserve, and Selod 2015). Hence, they allow customary law and practice to continue alongside statutory law. Current land policies and laws in the region are deeply influenced by the colonial legacy.

Land tenure security is weak in both informal and formal markets in many African countries (Congo, Côte d'Ivoire, Equatorial Guinea, and Mali). One of the primary causes is postwar disputes between returnees and current occupiers (Burundi, Rwanda). Refugees are a major challenge not only for host countries but also for their country of origin when they return (Democratic Republic of the Congo, Rwanda). Land grabbing, illegal occupation, and conflicts over land hinder efforts to establish proper and defensible rights to land (Congo, Mali). Corruption and speculation (Mali) also affect tenure security and the value of property. Many land parcels are undocumented, and many of the existing land records are out of date, as in Chad and Côte d'Ivoire. Burundi and Niger are examples of countries that have land codes or similar laws that seek to address ownership and occupation rights to land while in some instances also recognizing the legitimacy of customary and legal rights.

In many countries, for example, the Congo and Madagascar, only land that has been registered has the full protection of the law. Registration processes tend to be centralized, complex, and cumbersome (Allassembaye 2010; Monkam 2010) and are often associated with high transfer taxes and fees (Chad, Côte d'Ivoire, Equatorial Guinea, Madagascar, Mali, and Togo), which discourage property registration (Monkam 2010). Lack of registration also affects the property tax because ownership rights are indeterminate, and in some countries, such as Equatorial Guinea, only registered land is liable for the property tax. Generally, recording fees, transaction taxes, and stamp taxes are detrimental to transactions that facilitate efficient allocation of resources between economic actors (Fossat et al. 2013).

Often, several ministries are involved in land-related matters, again creating complexity and confusion, as in Burundi. A further property-related issue that significantly affects property taxation is the lack of street addresses, which makes it very difficult to match taxable properties with owners or occupiers. In several countries, significant progress has been made in some pilot cities, such as Quagadougou (Burkina Faso), Bobo-Dioulasso (Mali), and Lomé (Togo) (Farvacque-Vitkovic and Kopanyi 2014). Programs to upgrade and digitize land registers and cadastres and other projects to increase efficiency have been ongoing in various Francophone countries, including Burkina Faso, Burundi, Cameroon, Côte d'Ivoire, Guinea, Madagascar, Niger, Rwanda, and Senegal (World Bank 2015).

Security of tenure and the settling of land disputes should be priorities. The benefits of increased market values and more formalized markets, especially for a value-based property tax, are obvious. Formalizing markets and removing disincentives to legal transfers by, for example, revisiting high transfer taxes and expensive regularization of informal tenure should also be priorities. It is heartening to note the simplification and cost reduction in this sphere in recent years in many African countries. The process in Rwanda is described in box 1.1.

The Food and Agriculture Organization of the United Nations (FAO 2012, 20) declares: "States and other parties should ensure that information on market transactions and information on market values are transparent and widely publicized, subject to privacy restrictions." In addition, the FAO (2012, 29) also states: "States should provide systems (such as registration, cadastre and licensing systems) to record individual and collective tenure rights in order to improve security of tenure rights." Many countries have embarked on ambitious land registration systems and cadastral efforts that are supported by donor agencies. These initiatives are largely based on the need to know who owns what.

Box 1.1 An Example of Good Land Information Management

Ten years ago, transferring property in Rwanda took more than a year. Today, as a result of the Land Administration Information System, the process takes only a month.

The system of land tenure and the provision of land rights in Rwanda are important components of the reformed property tax system. Rwanda has made significant progress in digitally recording all individually owned parcels. The Constitution of the Republic of Rwanda recognizes state and private property and grants every citizen the right to private property. To provide security of land rights, the government introduced the National Land Policy (Government of Rwanda 2004) and the Organic Law on Land (Law No. 08/2005), which constituted the first comprehensive governance framework for land ownership, use, and management in Rwanda. The Organic Law on Land recognizes rights to land obtained under customary law as equivalent to rights obtained under formal law and requires land registration. Under this law, all rural land previously held under customary tenure is now registered and granted an emphyteutic lease. Land registration provides for two types of certificates of land rights: the certificate of registration of full title (broadly equivalent to freehold ownership) and the certificate of registration of emphyteutic lease, that is, leasehold. Emphyteutic leases are long-term leases available to the general public and require the lessee to use and develop the land in accordance with its classification or zoning requirements. The term of emphyteutic leases can be up to 99 years with entitlement to renewal as long as the land is used in accordance with the law (Government of Rwanda 2006, 2007).

The Land Tenure Regularization process under the Rwanda Natural Resources Authority (RNRA) began formally in 2008 and has been completed. An estimated 10.3 million parcels have been demarcated, adjudicated, and digitized. Parcel data are contained in the Land Tenure Regularization Database, which contains 8.4 million titles, 6.1 million of which have been physically collected by the "new" owners; approximately 90 percent of the titles have been collected by owners within the three districts of Kigali.

The digitization of all parcels throughout the country represents an invaluable resource for the administration of the property tax. The land tenure system in Rwanda is a modification of the Torrens system that is used in Australia and New Zealand. The Register of Titles records the certificates of registration, which identify the object that is owned, the owner, and the legal ownership rights. The Lands and Mapping Department within the RNRA has primary responsibility for the registration of land titles. The objective is to have a decentralized office of the department within each district linked to the Land Administration Information System.

There is no doubt that comprehensive land information systems and their integrated mapping provide a useful resource for property tax administration. Aerial maps are powerful tools for viewing properties that are taxed or are not taxed. But it is also important to note that land registration systems can also be used to limit the property tax base, as is pointed out in this chapter. In some countries, only registered land and properties are taxable. This situation opens the door for tax avoidance or evasion since registration is largely voluntary. In some countries, registration also incurs additional costs that property owners would like to avoid. As we will argue in later chapters, this will strengthen the case for including all properties, registered or not, in the property tax base.

Notes

1. The property tax has been well studied in a substantial body of research. The seminal contribution of Dick Netzer (1973) began the modern era of property tax research work in the United States (Youngman 2016). Surveys of the practice in less developed countries include Bahl (1979, 2009), Bahl and Martinez-Vazquez (2008), Bird and Slack (2004), Kelly (2014), McCluskey and Franzsen (2005b), Norregaard (2013), and UN-Habitat (2011). The literature on property taxation in cities in developing countries includes Bahl and Linn (1992), Bird and Slack (2006), and McCluskey and Franzsen (2013b).

2. There have been various studies with a regional focus (e.g., Brown and Hepworth 2002; Franzsen 2003; Malme and Youngman 2001; Maurer and Paugam 2000; Sulija and Sulija 2005; Trasberg 2004). However, there are also many comparative studies with a broader, global focus on the recurrent property tax (Bing, Connelly, and Bell 2009; Bird and Slack 2004; Franzsen and McCluskey 2005; McCluskey 1999; McCluskey,

Bell, and Lim 2010; McCluskey, Cornia, and Walters 2013; OECD 1983; Rosengard 1998; UN-Habitat 2011; Youngman and Malme 1994).

3. Since the early 1990s and especially since 2000, there has been significant property tax reform in the countries of Central and Eastern Europe, for example, in Armenia (Almy and Abrahamian 2001), the Czech Republic (Rohlícková 1999), Estonia (Tiits 2008; Tiits and Tomson 1999), Hungary (Péteri and Lados 1999; Tassonyi 2004), Latvia (Bird 2004d), Lithuania (Aleksiene and Bagdonavicius 2008), Poland (Bird 2004a; Brzeski 1999), Russia (Malme and Kalinina 2001; Timofeev 2004), Serbia (Levitas, Vasiljevic, and Bucic 2010), Slovakia (Bryson et al. 2001), and the Ukraine (Bird 2004c).

4. For example, India (Bird and Slack 2004; M. G. Rao 2013; U. A. V. Rao 2008), Indonesia (Kelly 1995, 2015; Rosengard 1998), Laos (Visounnalath, Stevenson, and Burns 2002), Malaysia (Hizam et al. 1999), Pakistan (Keith 1999), the Philippines (Baraquero 1999; Kelly 1995), and Thailand (Kelly 1995; Varanyuwatana 1999).

5. For example, Argentina (Rezk 2004), Brazil (De Cesare and Ruddock 1999), Chile (Rosengard 1998), Colombia (Ruiz and Vallejo 2010; Uribe 2006), Jamaica (Lyons and McCluskey 1999; McCluskey 2005; Sjoquist 2005), and Mexico (Bird 2004b).

6. For example, in Egypt (Amin 2010), Gabon (Monkam 2009a), Ghana (Jibao 2009a), Kenya (Kelly 2000; Olima 1999; Rosengard 1998), Rwanda (Almy 2004), Senegal (Monkam 2009b), Sierra Leone (Jibao 2009b), South Africa (Franzsen 2005; Slack 2004), Tanzania (McCluskey et al. 2003; McCluskey and Franzsen 2005a), and Uganda (Olima 2010). See brief country reviews of Botswana (Franzsen 2003; Monagen 1999), Guinea (Vaillancourt 2004a), Kenya (Rosengard 1998; Olima 1999), Lesotho (Franzsen 2003), Namibia (Franzsen 2003), South Africa (Franzsen 1999, 2005; Slack 2004), Swaziland (Franzsen 2003), Tanzania (Kelly 2004), Tunisia (Vaillancourt 2004b), and Zimbabwe (Brakspear 1999). There are regional reviews of Anglophone East Africa (UN-Habitat 2013), Southern Africa (Franzsen 2001), and Anglophone West Africa (Jibao 2009c). See also Fjeldstad and Heggstad (2012), Franzsen (2003), and Franzsen and McCluskey (2005).

7. Land rent should not be viewed as a tax, because it is a fee payable for the right or privilege to occupy state-owned or customary land. It is described in more detail in chapter 2.

8. This flat tax system was replaced by a value-banding system in 2013.

9. *Emphyteosis* is the right to full usage of uncultivated land belonging to the state on condition of improving and maintaining the land and payment to the state of a fee in cash or in kind.

10. A concession is a contract by which the state recognizes that an individual, a legal person, or a group of persons (e.g., a community) has the right under private or public law to use real estate subject to the conditions and methods prescribed by the law.

11. A usufruct is a limited real right in property under which the usufructuary (the holder of the usufruct) has the right of use of the property and the fruits of the property.

12. Colombia has a similar system.

References

Aleksiene, A., and A. Bagdonavicius. 2008. "Value-Based Property Taxes in Lithuania." In *Making the Property Tax Work*, ed. R. W. Bahl, J. Martinez-Vazquez, and J. M. Youngman, 411–435. Cambridge, MA: Lincoln Institute of Land Policy.

Allassembaye, D. 2010. "North Central Africa Appendix 1: Chad." Working paper WP10NCA2. Cambridge, MA: Lincoln Institute of Land Policy.

Almy, R. 2004. *Manual on Administering the Rwandan Fixed Asset Tax*. Kigali: MINALOC, ARD. Inc./FDP.

Almy, R., and V. Abrahamian. 2001. "Property Taxation in Armenia." In *The Development of Property Taxation in Economies in Transition: Case Studies from Central and Eastern Europe*, ed. J. H. Malme and J. M. Youngman, 85–95. Washington, DC: World Bank Institute.

Amin, K. 2010. "Property Tax System in Egypt." Paper presented at the ATI/Lincoln Institute of Land Policy fellowship workshop, Stellenbosch, South Africa (December 4–5).

Bahl, R. W., ed. 1979. *The Taxation of Urban Property in Less Developed Countries*. Madison: University of Wisconsin Press.

———. 2009. *Property Tax Reform in Developing and Transition Countries*. Washington, DC: U.S. Agency for International Development.

Bahl, R. W., M. Cyan, and S. Wallace. 2015. "Underutilized Land and Property Taxes." In *The Role of Taxation in Pakistan's Economic Revival*, ed. J. Martinez-Vazquez and M. Cyan, chapter 8. Oxford: Oxford University Press.

Bahl, R. W., and J. F. Linn. 1992. *Urban Public Finance in Developing Countries*. New York: Oxford University Press.

Bahl, R. W., and J. Martinez-Vazquez. 2008. "The Determinants of Revenue Performance." In *Making the Property Tax Work*, ed. R. W. Bahl, J. Martinez-Vazquez, and J. M. Youngman, 35–60. Cambridge, MA: Lincoln Institute of Land Policy.

Bahl, R. W., and S. Wallace. 2010. "A New Paradigm for Property Taxation in Developing Countries." In *Challenging the Conventional Wisdom on the Property Tax*, ed. R. W. Bahl, J. Martinez-Vazquez, and J. Youngman, 165–201. Cambridge, MA: Lincoln Institute of Land Policy.

Baraquero, O. 1999. "Decentralizing Property Taxation: The Philippine Perspective." In *Property Tax: An International Comparative Review*, ed. W. J. McCluskey, 248–265. Aldershot: Ashgate.

Bing, Y., K. Connolly, and M. E. Bell. 2009. "A Compendium of Countries with an Area Based Property Tax." Working paper WP09BY1. Cambridge, MA: Lincoln Institute of Land Policy.

Bird, R. M. 2004a. "Land and Property Taxes in Poland." In *International Handbook of Land and Property Taxation*, ed. R. M. Bird and E. Slack, 253–258. Cheltenham, UK: Edward Elgar.

———. 2004b. "Property Taxes in Mexico." In *International Handbook of Land and Property Taxation*, ed. R. M. Bird and E. Slack, 292–297. Cheltenham, UK: Edward Elgar.

———. 2004c. "Property Taxes in Ukraine." In *International Handbook of Land and Property Taxation*, ed. R. M. Bird and E. Slack, 246–252. Cheltenham, UK: Edward Elgar.

———. 2004d. "Real Estate Tax in Latvia." In *International Handbook of Land and Property Taxation*, ed. R. M. Bird and E. Slack, 259–261. Cheltenham, UK: Edward Elgar.

Bird, R. M., and E. Slack, eds. 2004. *International Handbook of Land and Property Taxation*. Cheltenham, UK: Edward Elgar.

———. 2006. "Taxing Land and Property in Emerging Economies: Raising Revenue . . . and More?" ITP paper 0605. Toronto, ON: International Tax Program, Rotman School of Management.

Bogaerts, T., I. P. Williamson, and E. M. Fendela. 2002. "The Role of Land Administration in the Accession of Central European Countries to the European Union." *Land Use Policy* 19: 29–46.

Brakspear, G. 1999. "Property Taxation in Zimbabwe." In *Property Tax: An International Comparative Review*, ed. W. J. McCluskey, 216–232. Aldershot: Ashgate.

Brown, P. K., and M. A. Hepworth. 2002. "A Study of European Land Tax Systems." Working paper WP02PB1. Cambridge, MA: Lincoln Institute of Land Policy.

Bryson, P. J., G. C. Cornia, S. Capkova, and M. Koncek. 2001. "Land and Building Taxes in the Republic of Slovakia." In *The Development of Property Taxation in Economies in Transition: Case Studies from Central and Eastern Europe*, ed. J. H. Malme and J. M. Youngman, 51–66. Washington, DC: World Bank Institute.

Brzeski, J. 1999. "Real Property Taxation in Poland." In *Property Tax: An International Comparative Review*, ed. W. J. McCluskey, 411–418. Aldershot: Ashgate.

———. 2005. "Bringing Area-Based Formula Closer to Market." Paper presented at the eighth annual conference of the International Property Tax Institute, Prague, Czech Republic (August 23–24).

Burns, T. 2007. "Land Administration Reform: Indicators of Success and Future Challenges." Agriculture and Rural Development Discussion Paper 37. Washington, DC: World Bank.

Cornia, G. 2008. "Commentary." In *Making the Property Tax Work*, ed. R. W. Bahl, J. Martinez-Vazquez, and J. M. Youngman, 307–312. Cambridge, MA: Lincoln Institute of Land Policy.

Dale, P., R. Mahoney, and R. McLaren. 2010. *Land Markets and the Modern Economy*. London: RICS Research.

Dale, P., and J. McLaughlin. 1999. *Land Administration*. Oxford: Oxford University Press.

De Cesare, C. 2012. "Improving the Performance of the Property Tax in Latin America." Policy Focus Report. Cambridge, MA: Lincoln Institute of Land Policy.

De Cesare, C., and L. Ruddock. 1999. "The Property Tax System in Brazil." In *Property Tax: An International Comparative Review*, ed. W. J. McCluskey, 266–282. Aldershot: Ashgate.

Dowse, G., and B. Hargreaves. 1999. "Rating Systems in New Zealand." In *Property Tax: An International Comparative Review*, ed. W. J. McCluskey, 283–312. Aldershot: Ashgate.

Durand-Lasserve, A., M. Durand-Lasserve, and H. Selod. 2015. *Land Delivery Systems in West African Cities: The Example of Bamako, Mali*. Washington, DC: Agence Française de Développement and World Bank Group.

FAO (Food and Agriculture Organization). 2012. *Voluntary Guidelines on the Responsible Governance of Tenure of Land, Fisheries and Forests in the Context of National Food Security*. Rome: Food and Agriculture Organization of the United Nations.

Farvacque-Vitkovic, C., and M. Kopanyi. 2014. *Municipal Finances: A Handbook for Local Governments*. Washington, DC: World Bank. *https://openknowledge.worldbank .org/handle/10986/18725*.

FIG (International Federation of Surveyors). 1995. *FIG Statement on the Cadastre*. Copenhagen.

Fjeldstad, O.-H., and K. Heggstad, K. 2012. "Local Government Revenue Mobilisation in Anglophone Africa." Bergen: CMI working paper WP 2012:6.

Fossat, P., G. Montagnat-Rentier, P. Petit, G. Parent, G. Chambas, and J. Russell. 2013. "Continued Modernization of the Malian Tax System and Administration August." International Monetary Fund Technical Report. Washington, DC: IMF. *https://www.imf.org/external/pubs/ft/scr/2013/cr13355.pdf.*

Franzsen, R. C. D. 1999. "Property Taxation in South Africa." In *Property Tax: An International Comparative Review*, ed. W. J. McCluskey, 337–357. Aldershot: Ashgate.

———. 2001. "Property Taxation in Botswana, Lesotho, Namibia and Swaziland." *Journal of Property Tax Assessment and Administration* 6(3): 3–17.

———. 2003. "Property Taxation Within the Southern African Development Community (SADC): Current Status and Future Prospects of Land Value Taxation, Botswana, Lesotho, Namibia, South Africa and Swaziland." Working paper WP03RF1. Cambridge, MA: Lincoln Institute of Land Policy.

———. 2005. "Property Taxation in South Africa." In *Land Value Taxation: An Applied Approach*, ed. W. J. McCluskey and R. C. D. Franzsen, 147–189. Aldershot: Ashgate.

———. 2009. "International Experience." In *Land Value Taxation*, ed. R. Dye and R. England, 27–47. Cambridge, MA: Lincoln Institute of Land Policy.

Franzsen, R. C. D., and W. J. McCluskey. 2005. "An Exploratory Overview of Property Taxation in the Commonwealth of Nations." Working paper. Cambridge, MA: Lincoln Institute of Land Policy. *www.lincolninst.edu/pubs/pub-detail.asp?id=1069.*

———. 2008. "The Feasibility of Site Value Taxation." In *Making the Property Tax Work*, ed. R. W. Bahl, J. Martinez-Vazquez, and J. M. Youngman, 268–306. Cambridge, MA: Lincoln Institute of Land Policy.

———. 2013. "Value-based Approaches to Property Taxation." In *A Primer on Property Tax: Administration and Policy*, ed. W. J. McCluskey, G. C. Cornia, and L. C. Walters, 41–68. West Sussex: Wiley-Blackwell.

Government of Rwanda. 2004. *National Land Policy.* Kigali.

———. 2006. *National Land Tenure Reform Program.* Kigali.

———. 2007. *Strategic Road Map for Land Tenure Reform Program.* Kigali.

Hizam, R., F. Plimmer, A. Nawawi, and S. Gronow. 1999. "Rating in Malaysia." In *Property Tax: An International Comparative Review*, ed. W. J. McCluskey, 86–115. Aldershot: Ashgate.

Holland, D., and J. Follain. 1991. "The Property Tax in Jamaica." In *The Jamaican Tax Reform*, ed. R. Bahl, 605–640. Cambridge, MA: Lincoln Institute of land Policy.

IMF (International Monetary Fund). 2014. *Government Finance Statistics Manual.* Washington, DC.

Jibao, S. 2009a. "Property Taxation in Anglophone West Africa Appendix 2: Ghana." Working paper WP09AWA8. Cambridge, MA: Lincoln Institute of Land Policy.

———. 2009b. "Property Taxation in Anglophone West Africa Appendix 5: Sierra Leone." Working paper WP09AWA11. Cambridge, MA: Lincoln Institute of Land Policy.

————. 2009c. "Property Taxation in Anglophone West Africa: Regional Overview." Working paper WP09AWA1. Cambridge, MA: Lincoln Institute of Land Policy.

Keith, S. 1999. "Real Property Taxation in Pakistan." In *Property Tax: An International Comparative Review*, ed. W. J. McCluskey, 130–147. Aldershot: Ashgate.

Kelly, R. 1995. "Property Tax Reform in Southeast Asia: A Comparative Analysis of Indonesia, the Philippines and Thailand." *Journal of Property Tax Assessment & Administration* 2(1): 60–81.

————. 2000. "Designing a Property Tax Strategy for Sub-Saharan Africa: An Analytical Framework Applied to Kenya." *Public Budgeting and Finance* 20(4): 36–51.

————. 2004. "Property Rates in Tanzania." In *International Handbook of Land and Property Taxation*, ed. R. M. Bird and E. Slack, 189–198. Cheltenham, UK: Edward Elgar.

————. 2014. "Implementing Sustainable Property Tax Reform in Developing Countries." In *Taxation and Development: The Weakest Link? Essays in Honor of Roy Bahl*, ed. R. M. Bird and J. Martinez-Vazquez, 326–363. Cheltenham, UK: Edward Elgar.

————. 2015. "Strengthening the Revenue Side." In *Fiscal Decentralization in Indonesia a Decade After the Big Bang*, ed. Directorate General of Fiscal Balance, Ministry of Finance, Government of Indonesia, 168–200. Jakarta: University of Indonesia Press.

Levitas, T., D. Vasiljevic, and A. Bucic. 2010. "Property Taxation—Analysis of the Current Situation and Reform Perspectives." In *Tax Policy in Serbia—Looking Forward*, ed. M. Arsic, 97–125. Belgrade: USAID and Foundation for the Advancement of Economics.

Lewis, B. D. 2003. "Property Tax in Indonesia: Measuring and Explaining Administrative (Under)Performance." *Public Administration and Development* 23: 227–239.

Lyons, S., and W. J. McCluskey. 1999. "Unimproved Land Value Taxation in Jamaica." In *Property Tax: An International Comparative Review*, ed. W. J. McCluskey, 385–410. Aldershot: Ashgate.

Macmillan, H. 1997. "Tradition, Tribes, Chiefs and Change in Southern Africa." In *Traditional Leadership in Southern Africa*, 135–145. Johannesburg: Konrad-Adenauer-Stiftung.

Malme, J. H., and N. Kalinina. 2001. "Property Tax Developments in the Russian Federation." In *The Development of Property Taxation in Economies in Transition: Case Studies from Central and Eastern Europe*, ed. J. H. Malme and J. M. Youngman, 67–83. Washington, DC: World Bank Institute.

Malme, J. H., and J. M. Youngman, eds. 2001. *The Development of Property Taxation in Economies in Transition: Case Studies from Central and Eastern Europe*. Washington, DC: World Bank Institute.

Martinez-Vazquez, J., L. Noiset, and M. Rider. 2010. "Assignment of the Property Tax: Should Developing Countries Follow the Conventional View?" In *Challenging the Conventional Wisdom on the Property Tax*, ed. R. Bahl, J. Martinez-Vazquez, and J. Youngman, 299–349. Cambridge, MA: Lincoln Institute of Land Policy.

Maurer, R., and A. Paugam. 2000. "Reform Toward Ad Valorem Property Tax in Transition Economies: Fiscal and Land Use Benefits." World Bank. *http://documents.worldbank.org/curated/en/544251468762625226/pdf/253930Urbanbackground13.pdf.*

McCluskey, W. J., ed. 1999. *Property Tax: An International Comparative Review*. Aldershot: Ashgate.

McCluskey, W. J. 2005. "Land Taxation: The Case of Jamaica." In *Land Value Taxation: An Applied Analysis*, ed. W. J. McCluskey and R. C. D. Franzsen, 19–63. Aldershot: Ashgate.

McCluskey, W. J., M. E. Bell, and L. C. Lim. 2010. "Rental Value Versus Capital Value: Alternative Bases for the Property Tax." In *Challenging the Conventional Wisdom on the Property Tax*, ed. R. Bahl, J. Martinez-Vazquez, and J. Youngman, 119–157. Cambridge, MA: Lincoln Institute of Land Policy.

McCluskey, W. J., G. C. Cornia, and L. C. Walters, eds. 2013. *A Primer on Property Tax: Administration and Policy*. West Sussex: Wiley-Blackwell.

McCluskey, W. J., and R. C. D. Franzsen. 2005a. "An Evaluation of the Property Tax in Tanzania: An Untapped Fiscal Resource or Administrative Headache?" *Property Management* 23: 45–69.

———. 2005b. *Land Value Taxation: An Applied Analysis*. Aldershot: Ashgate.

———. 2013a. "Non–Market Value and Hybrid Approaches to Property Taxation." In *A Primer on Property Tax: Administration and Policy*, ed. W. J. McCluskey, G. C. Cornia, and L. C. Walters, 287–305. West Sussex: Wiley-Blackwell.

———. 2013b. "Property Taxes in Metropolitan Cities." In *Metropolitan Government Finance in Developing Countries*, ed. R. Bahl, J. Linn, and D. Wetzel, 159–181. Cambridge, MA: Lincoln Institute of Land Policy.

McCluskey, W., R. Franzsen, T. Johnstone, and D. Johnstone. 2003. "Property Tax Reform: the Experience of Tanzania." In *Our Common Estate*, i–iv, 1–51. London: RICS Foundation.

Monagen, N. 1999. "An Analysis of Local Government Finance in Botswana." In *Property Tax: An International Comparative Review*, ed. W. J. McCluskey, 33–39. Aldershot: Ashgate.

Monkam, N. 2009a. "Property Taxation in Two Francophone Countries in Central Africa: Case Study of Gabon." Working paper WP09FAA2. Cambridge, MA: Lincoln Institute of Land Policy.

———. 2009b. "Property Taxation in West Africa: Case Study of Senegal." Working paper WP09FAA3. Cambridge, MA: Lincoln Institute of Land Policy

———. 2010. "Mobilising Tax Revenue to Finance Development: The Case for Property Taxation in Francophone Africa." Working paper no. 195. Pretoria: University of Pretoria, Economic Research Southern Africa (ERSA).

Netzer, D. 1973. *The Property Tax*. Washington, DC: Brookings Institution.

Norregaard, J. 2013. "Taxing Immovable Property—Revenue Potential and Implementation Challenges." IMF working paper. Washington, DC: IMF.

OECD (Organisation for Economic Co-operation and Development). 1983. *Taxes on Immovable Property: Report by the Committee on Fiscal Affairs and the Ad Hoc Group on Urban Problems*. Paris.

Oldman, O., and M. Teachout. 1979. "Some Administrative Aspects of Site Value Taxation: Defining 'Land' and 'Value'; Designing a Review Process." In *The Taxation of Urban Property in Less Developed Countries*, ed. R. Bahl, 207–237. Madison: University of Wisconsin Press.

Olima, W. H. A. 1999. "Real Property Taxation in Kenya." In *Property Tax: An International Comparative Review*, ed. W. J. McCluskey, 358–374. Aldershot: Ashgate.

———. 2010. "Property Taxation in Anglophone East Africa: Case Study of Uganda." Working paper WP10NEA8. Cambridge, MA: Lincoln Institute of Land Policy.

Péteri, G., and M. Lados. 1999. "Local Property Taxation in Hungary." In *Property Tax: An International Comparative Review*, ed. W. J. McCluskey, 419–439. Aldershot: Ashgate.

Ramodibedi, M. M. 2000. *Report of the Land Policy Review Commission*. Maseru: Kingdom of Lesotho.

Rao, M. G. 2013. "Property Tax System in India: Problems and Prospects of Reform." Working paper no. 2013-114. New Delhi: National Institute of Public Finance and Policy.

Rao, U. A. V. 2008. "Is Area-Based Assessment an Alternative, an Intermediate Step, or an Impediment to Value-Based Taxation in India?" In *Making the Property Tax Work*, ed. R. W. Bahl, J. Martinez-Vazquez, and J. M. Youngman, 241–267. Cambridge, MA: Lincoln Institute of Land Policy.

Rezk, E. 2004. "Taxes on Land and Property in Argentina." In *International Handbook of Land and Property Taxation*, ed. R. M. Bird and E. Slack, 281–285. Cheltenham, UK: Edward Elgar.

Rosengard, J. K. 1998. *Property Tax Reform in Developing Countries*. Boston: Kluwer Academic Publishers.

Rohlíčková, A. 1999. "Property Taxation in the Czech Republic." In *Property Tax: An International Comparative Review*, ed. W. J. McCluskey, 440–454. Aldershot: Ashgate.

Ruiz, F., and G. Vallejo. 2010. "Using Land Registration as a Tool to Generate Municipal Revenue: Lessons from Bogota." *http://siteresources.worldbank.org/EXTARD/Resources/336681-1236436879081/5893311-1271205116054/RuizVallejoPaper.pdf*.

Sjoquist, D. 2005. "The Land Value Tax in Jamaica: An Analysis and Options for Reform." *Bulletin for International Fiscal Documentation*, November, 489–497.

Slack, E. 2004. "Property Tax in South Africa." In *International Handbook of Land and Property Taxation*, ed. R. M. Bird and E. Slack, 199–204. Cheltenham, UK: Edward Elgar.

Sulija, V., and G. Sulija. 2005. "Reform of the Property Tax and Problems of Real Estate Appraisal for Taxation Purposes in Transitional Economies of Central and Eastern Europe." Working paper WP05VS1. Cambridge, MA: Lincoln Institute of Land Policy.

Tassonyi, A. 2004. "Land-Based Taxes in Hungary." In *International Handbook of Land and Property Taxation*, ed. R. M. Bird and E. Slack, 219–235. Cheltenham, UK: Edward Elgar.

Tiits, T. 2008. "Land Taxation Reform in Estonia." In *Making the Property Tax Work: Experiences in Developing and Transitional Countries*, ed. R. W. Bahl, J. Martinez-Vazquez, and J. M. Youngman, 395–410. Cambridge, MA: Lincoln Institute of Land Policy.

Tiits, T., and A. Tomson. 1999. "Land Value Taxation in Estonia." In *Property Tax: An International Comparative Review*, ed. W. J. McCluskey, 375–384. Aldershot: Ashgate.

Timofeev, A. 2004. "Land and Property Taxes in Russia." In *International Handbook of Land and Property Taxation*, ed. R. M. Bird and E. Slack, 236–245. Cheltenham, UK: Edward Elgar.

Trasberg, V. 2004. "Property and Land Taxation in the Baltic States." *Journal of Property Tax Assessment & Administration* 1(2): 208–220.

UN-FIG (United Nations and International Federation of Surveyors). 1999. *United Nations–FIG Bathurst Declaration on Land Administration for Sustainable Development*. International Workshop on Cadastral Infrastructures for Sustainable Development, International Federation of Surveyors and United Nations, Bathurst, New South Wales, Australia.

UN-Habitat. 2011. *Land and Property Tax—A Policy Guide*. Nairobi: United Nations Human Settlement Program. (Principal author: Lawrence Walters.)

———. 2013. *Property Tax Regimes in East Africa*. The Global Urban Economic Dialogue Series. Nairobi: UN Human Settlements Program.

Uribe, M. C. 2006. "Property Tax in Colombian Municipalities: Tax Base and Institutional Issues." Working paper WP06MU1. Cambridge, MA: Lincoln Institute of Land Policy.

Vaillancourt, F. 2004a. "Land and Property Taxation in Guinea." In *International Handbook of Land and Property Taxation*, ed. R. M. Bird and E. Slack, 205–209. Cheltenham, UK: Edward Elgar.

———. 2004b. "Land and Property Taxation in Tunisia." In *International Handbook of Land and Property Taxation*, ed. R. M. Bird and E. Slack, 210–216. Cheltenham, UK: Edward Elgar.

Varanyuwatana, S. 1999. "Property Tax in Thailand." In *Comparative Property Tax Systems: An International Comparative Review*, ed. W. J. McCluskey, 148–162. Aldershot: Avebury Publishing Ltd.

Visounnalath, O., R. Stevenson, and T. Burns. 2002. "Lao People's Democratic Republic: A Practical Review of Land and Property Valuation in the Context of Land Administration." *Journal of Property Tax Assessment & Administration* 7(3): 3–17.

World Bank. 2015. "Registering Property." *www.doingbusiness.org/data/exploretopics/registering-property/reforms*.

Youngman, J. 2016. *A Good Tax: Legal and Political Issues for the Property Tax in the United States*. Cambridge, MA: Lincoln Institute of Land Policy.

Youngman, J. M., and J. H. Malme. 1994. *An International Survey of Taxes on Land and Buildings*. Boston: Kluwer Law and Taxation Publishers.

2

Policy and Practice

WILLIAM MCCLUSKEY, RIËL FRANZSEN, AND ROY BAHL

The property tax is levied in all African countries except Burkina Faso and Seychelles. In some countries (Ghana, Kenya, Nigeria, South Africa, Swaziland, and Uganda), it is a constitutionally guaranteed source of revenue for local governments. In all cases, it is levied by local or national law. But almost everywhere in Africa, it is underused and badly administered. Colonial heritage does not seem to be a factor in the weak performance of the property tax, nor does the level (national or local) at which the tax is levied. Some factors plague property tax performance in developing countries throughout the world, but other reasons for this immaturity of the property tax are specific to individual African countries or to the continent as a whole.

Property taxation has much of the same appeal in Africa as it does in other low- and middle-income countries (Franzsen and McCluskey 2016; McCluskey and Franzsen 2016). The property tax is the academic's choice for the principal local-government source of revenue in developing countries (Oates and Schwab 2009). This is mostly because a tax on immovable land or property distorts resource choices less than any other tax (Norregaard 2013). However, there are many other reasons to champion the property tax. Bahl and Martinez-Vazquez (2008) elaborate on several of these advantages: (1) revenue growth is potentially income elastic because the market value of real estate is growing rapidly; (2) the property tax is often a progressive tax because much of the burden falls on the owners of land, who tend to be in higher income brackets; (3) it may be seen as a benefit charge for the use of services and thus give a sense of fairness; (4) local-government authorities have an easier time taxing a base that is immovable and located within their jurisdiction; and (5) the property tax is familiar to local residents and is one that many higher-level governments are willing to devolve. Perhaps most important, it is almost always referred to, rightly, as having significant untapped revenue potential.

For all these reasons, one might expect that the property tax would be an important revenue source for local governments. However, in practice, this is not the case even in many developed countries and certainly not in less developed countries (Blöchliger and Kim 2016; Norregaard 2013; Bahl and Martinez-Vazquez 2008). Nevertheless, support for the property tax as a local-government revenue source remains strong, and interest in its reform continues (Kelly 2014; UN-Habitat 2011). Especially since the 2008 financial crisis, there has been a global move to reinvigorate the property tax, led by international development banks and bilateral donors. The reasons for this renewed interest in the property tax are the increased revenue needs of urban local governments and the possibility of reducing the dependency of local governments on central-government transfers and donor funding (Norregaard 2013).

The specific reasons that the property tax has not developed in Africa vary from country to country but almost always involve some combination of counterproductive policies and weak administration. The structural and administration problems with the property tax have been studied for a long time, and there is no shortage of recommendations for reform.[1] Yet, as we discuss in this chapter, progress in adopting and implementing reforms has been very slow.

The Importance and Potential of Property Tax Revenue

International comparisons of revenues raised from property taxation are difficult because comparable data are not readily available. In this book, our focus is primarily on the annual, recurrent property tax. Our view is that the property tax includes the annual recurrent property tax, the property transfer tax, and special assessments on real property. All of these are taxes levied on real property; in most cases, they are value based; and the incidence patterns are similar. The International Monetary Fund (IMF), which is the standard source for comparative fiscal data, takes a broader view. It defines the term *property tax* for statistical purposes to refer to "taxes payable on the use, ownership, or transfer of wealth" (IMF 2014, 417). Besides recurrent property taxes, this category includes capital transfer taxes (e.g., stamp duties and property transfer taxes), estate and inheritance taxes, gift taxes, and net wealth taxes. There are problems with reporting the data. Sometimes budgetary classifications are not consistent from country to country; sometimes only budgeted amounts are reported; and sometimes data for local-government property taxes are not reported at all.

Global Comparisons

Even if one takes these data problems and definitional issues into account, the observation that the property tax produces little budget revenue seems valid. Research by Bahl and Martinez-Vazquez (2008) and Norregaard (2013) highlights the poor revenue performance of the property tax in developing countries.

The best comparable data on the revenue yield of the property tax in developing and transition countries as sourced by the IMF over various years suggest an average yield of only about 0.6 percent of gross domestic product (GDP), versus 2.2 percent for industrial countries (Bahl and Martinez-Vazquez 2008). The true average for developing countries is probably even lower than this estimated amount because many countries with negligible property tax revenues do not report data and are not counted in this average. Bahl and Bird (forthcoming) have assembled a comparison of property tax revenues relative to GDP for 25 countries, drawn from various sources.[2] The results show a concentration of countries in which property tax revenues are below 0.5 percent of GDP, reinforcing the conclusion that the property tax is normally an inconsequential source of revenue. By comparison, the average ratio of total tax revenue to GDP is about 16 percent for developing countries (Bahl 2014). Given the relatively low effective rate of property taxation, the continued public resistance to it is all the more surprising.

In general, rich countries make more use of property taxes than poor countries. Property taxation is a kind of luxury good that wealthier places can afford and manage better. But there is much more to the story about the demand for more property taxation. Bahl and Martinez-Vazquez (2008) conducted an econometric analysis of the determinants of variations in the property tax share of GDP. Using panel data for 70 developed and developing countries and treating the property tax share as endogenous in the model, they found that higher levels of expenditure decentralization increase the use of property taxation. The implication of this for fiscal planners, and for those who would provide assistance to them, is that the demand for property tax financing will increase with the demand that local governments play a larger role in service delivery.

Norregaard (2013) finds an average revenue yield of more than 2 percent of GDP in the 34 member states of the Organisation for Economic

Table 2.1 Property Taxes as a Percentage of GDP in
Selected OECD Countries

Country	Year	All Property Taxes as % of GDP	Recurrent Property Taxes as % of GDP
Australia	2009	2.48	1.45
Belgium[1]	2010	3.00	1.24
Canada	2010	3.49	3.04
France	2010	3.65	2.46
Germany	2010	0.85	0.46
Greece[2]	2009	1.24	0.17
Ireland[3]	2010	1.56	0.88
Israel	2010	3.12	2.32
Japan	2010	2.70	2.14
Luxembourg	2010	2.65	0.07
Mexico	2009	0.30	0.19
New Zealand	2010	2.16	2.11
Switzerland	2010	2.22	0.09
United Kingdom	2010	4.23	3.42
United States	2010	3.21	3.07

Source: OECD Revenue Statistics (2011) as reported by Norregaard (2013).

[1] In Belgium, property transfer taxes, levied within a range of 10 percent to 12.5 percent, are very high.

[2] Until 2014, Greece relied heavily on property transfer taxation (Norregaard 2013). In 2010, the recurrent tax was dilapidated, base erosion was problematic, and tax collection was poor.

[3] Ireland abolished its residential property tax in the 1970s. In 2012, as a response to the aftermath of the 2008 financial crisis, it reintroduced a property tax on residential property.

Co-operation and Development (OECD).[3] However, this may be somewhat misleading. In 2010, only seven countries (Canada, France, Israel, Japan, New Zealand, the United Kingdom, and the United States) raised more than 2.0 percent of GDP from the recurrent (annual) property tax (table 2.1). In 2010, twenty-two member states, including Germany, Luxembourg, and the three upper-middle-income countries, Chile, Mexico and Turkey, raised less than 1.0 of GDP through recurrent property taxes. Luxembourg, the country with the highest per capita income in 2010, and Switzerland, also with a high per capita income, raised 2.65 and 2.22 percent of GDP from "property taxes," but only 0.07 and 0.09 percent of GDP from recurrent property taxes. Both countries focus more on the taxation of net wealth. In Germany, the recurrent property tax is important, but there is also a heavy reliance on transaction, estate, and gift taxes. The country that raises the most from recurrent property taxes as a percentage of GDP is the United Kingdom, where the council tax on residential properties and uniform business rates on nonresidential properties together account for 3.42 percent of GDP. Only in Canada and the United States did recurrent property taxes also exceed 3 percent of GDP in 2010.

Using data for 2009 and 2010, Norregaard (2013) estimates that the average yield from recurrent property taxes in high-income countries is 1.06 percent of GDP, more than 2.5 times the average level of 0.40 percent of GDP that he finds for middle-income countries. However, there are large variations within both groups. The yield of recurrent property taxes on average represents about 4.5 percent of total taxes in high-income countries and 2.1 percent in middle-income countries. Again, the conclusion is that the level of property tax collection increases sharply with income level (Norregaard 2013).

Revenue Performance in African Countries

With a few exceptions, the property tax is an unimportant contributor to total revenues in African countries. To be fair, we must note that unreliable data limit the conclusions that can be drawn about this. In many instances, budgetary data are reported only for the central government. Local-government revenue data are generally not available (or are too negligible to report) for many of the 40 African countries covered in the IMF *Statistics Yearbook*. The picture we get from the data in table 2.2 is dismal. For the 32 countries that report property tax data, the average share of GDP is 0.38 percent. The share of the property tax exceeds 1 percent in only three countries: Mauritius, Morocco, and South Africa. In both Mauritius and Morocco, property transfer taxes are significant. Only in South Africa does the recurrent property tax exceed 1 percent of GDP.

When we look at the property tax as a percentage of total taxes, the picture is still bleak. The property tax exceeds 1 percent of total tax revenues in only nine African countries. The conclusion is clear: property tax revenues in Africa are well below the average in other low-income countries.

The recurrent property tax is a local tax in almost all Anglophone countries in Africa. Although it is not a significant revenue source in general, with the notable exception of South Africa, it can be an important source of local-government revenue. In Accra, Ghana, the property tax contributes approximately 21 percent of own-source revenues, but only 8.6 percent of total revenue because of the heavy reliance on central government transfers.

Table 2.2 Total Tax Revenue and Property Taxes as a Percentage of GDP in African Countries

Country[1]	Total Taxes as % of GDP (2012)	Fiscal Year	Property Taxes as % of GDP	GDP per Capita in USD (2012)	Income Level (2016)
Algeria[2]	37.4	2011	0.00	5,584	Upper-middle
Angola	43.8	2012	0.15	5,532	Upper-middle
Benin	15.5	2012	0.24	808	Low
Botswana	26.9	2011	0.06	6,936	Upper-middle
Burkina Faso	15.6	2012	0.10	673	Low
Burundi	13.6	–	No data	244	Low
Cabo Verde	18.3	–	No data	3,498	Lower-middle
Central African Republic	9.9	2012	0.10	470	Low
Comoros	11.8	–	No data	750	Low
Congo	9.5	2008	0.32	391	Lower-middle
Côte d'Ivoire	16.0	2013	0.07	3,191	Lower-middle
Democratic Republic of the Congo	10.2	–	No data	1,281	Low
Djibouti	18.5	–	No data	1,587	Lower-middle
Egypt	13.2	2012	0.83	3,226	Lower-middle
Equatorial Guinea	11.9	2009	0.03	23,278	Upper-middle
Ethiopia	9.7	–	No data	470	Low
Gabon	15.1	–	No data	10,642	Upper-middle
The Gambia	14.5	2008	0.53	505	Low
Ghana	15.4	–	No data	1,642	Lower-middle
Guinea	19.2	–	No data	487	Low
Guinea-Bissau	7.9	–	No data	559	Low
Kenya	15.6	2012	0.01	1,185	Lower-middle
Lesotho[3]	54.8	2011	0.70	1,159	Lower-middle
Liberia	21.1	2012	0.15	414	Low
Libya	1.2	–	No data	13,035	Upper-middle
Madagascar	9.1	2010	0.06	445	Low
Malawi	21.4	–	No data	270	Low
Mali	14.2	2011	0.70	642	Low
Mauritania	17.4	–	No data	1,283	Lower-middle
Mauritius	18.9	2012	1.39	9,114	Upper-middle
Morocco	24.5	2010	1.75	2,931	Lower-middle
Mozambique	19.1	2011	0.70	565	Low
Namibia	31.0	2012	0.15	5,680	Upper-middle

Table 2.2 (*continued*)

Country[1]	Total Taxes as % of GDP (2012)	Fiscal Year	Property Taxes as % of GDP	GDP per Capita in USD (2012)	Income Level (2016)
Niger	14.5	2010	0.06	394	Low
Nigeria	10.2	–	No data	2,740	Lower-middle
Rwanda	13.6	2011	0.1	667	Low
São Tomé and Príncipe	14.2	2012	0.32	1,488	Lower-middle
Senegal	19.3	2012	0.10	1,019	Low
Seychelles	29.6	–	No data	12,845	High
Sierra Leone	10.7	2010	0.05	619	Low
South Africa	23.2	2013	1.60	7,592	Upper-middle
Sudan	5.4	–	No data	1,662	Lower-middle
Swaziland[3]	36.0	2012	0.05	3,989	Lower-middle
Tanzania	11.6	2011	0.08	828	Low
Togo	15.4	2010	0.24	581	Low
Tunisia	21.0	2012	0.53	4,188	Lower-middle
Uganda	10.5	–	No data	656	Low
Zambia	15.0	2008	0.03	1,687	Lower-middle
Zimbabwe[2]	26.3	2012	0.00	851	Low

Sources: IMF (2015, 2016); Jibao (chapter 25); *http://data.worldbank.org/about/country-and-lending-groups.*

[1] Insufficient data were available for Cameroon, Chad, Eritrea, Somalia, and South Sudan.

[2] The property tax as a percentage of GDP is 0.001 percent in Algeria and 0.002 percent in Zimbabwe, hence 0.00 in the table.

[3] The high percentages of total tax revenue as a percentage of GDP for Lesotho and Swaziland can be explained by the customs duties and excise tax shares received from the Southern African Customs Union (SACU).

In Freetown, Sierra Leone, the property tax accounts for about 42 percent of own-source revenues. In Botswana, South Africa, and Swaziland, the property tax is an important source of local-government tax revenues, although in Botswana, grants from the central government remain the most important source of revenue for urban municipalities. In Lesotho, the property tax is the most important own source of revenue in Maseru (the only jurisdiction currently empowered to levy property tax). In Namibia and South Africa, profits on so-called trading services (e.g., provision of electricity and water) and the property tax are the most important sources of revenue. However, for all the other Anglophone countries in this region, electricity and water are not provided by municipalities, so these services cannot be a source of budgetary revenue. However, government grants are becoming more important in both South Africa and Zambia. The property tax remains the most important source of revenue in Swaziland, at least in Mbabane and Manzini (Franzsen 2003; Mbabane 2013; Steffensen and Trollegaard 2000).

The importance of the property tax as a revenue source is minimal in the Francophone countries (Monkam 2010), even though it is usually a national tax. In Niger, for example, property tax revenues amount to less than 1 percent of total tax revenues and less than 0.1 percent of GDP (Hassane 2009). Furthermore, 70 percent is retained at the national level, and only 20 percent is remitted to local governments. Various factors contribute to the poor performance of the property tax in Francophone countries, including highly centralized tax administration, poor discovery and capturing of data on properties, poor billing and collection practices, weak or no enforcement, and very generous exemptions. The situation is similar in Lusophone countries (Nhabinde 2009) and the countries in North and Northeast Africa, where the property tax contribution to total revenue is very low. Although property taxes in São Tomé and Príncipe contributed 0.32 percent of GDP in 2012, the lion's share is from the transfer tax. Despite an increase since 2000 in nominal terms, the recurrent property tax in Addis Ababa, Ethiopia, contributed less than 1 percent of municipal revenue in 2004 (Soressa and Gebreslus 2009). In Algeria, the contribution of property taxes to GDP in 2011 was only 0.001 percent.

An interesting and encouraging trend is the importance of the property tax in various metropolitan cities in developing countries, including a number of cities in Africa (McCluskey and Franzsen 2013). The data in table 2.3 illustrate the importance of property tax in some important African cities. In 2009 in South Africa, the four large metropolitan municipalities mentioned in table 2.3 raised almost 50 percent of the total property tax collected by more than 240 municipalities countrywide. In 2015, the eight metropolitan municipalities raised more than 70 percent of the recurrent property tax in South Africa. In the 2014 financial year, Gaborone's share of the total recurrent property tax in Botswana increased to 65.1 percent.

This is consistent with what has been happening elsewhere in the world. In the 36 largest cities in India, the property tax accounts for 28 percent of own-source revenue (Mathur, Thakur, and Rajadhyasksha 2009). De Cesare (2012) reports a survey of 64 municipalities in Latin America that shows that the property tax accounts for an average of 24 percent of local-government tax revenue. This gives a different perspective on the issue:

Table 2.3 Importance of the Property Tax in Selected Cities in Africa

Country	City	Year	City Percentage of Total Country Property Tax
Botswana	Gaborone	2011	47.20
Ghana	Accra	2007	51.74
Kenya	Nairobi	2014	23.00
Liberia	Monrovia	2012	92.65
South Africa	Cape Town	2009	12.23
	Durban	2009	14.77
	Johannesburg	2009	12.57
	Pretoria	2009	8.52
Tanzania	Dar es Salaam	2010	55.57
Uganda	Kampala	2008	11.50

Source: Adapted from McCluskey and Franzsen (2013).

the property tax in developing countries is an important part of the strategy for local-government finance even if it is not an important part of the strategy for overall government revenue mobilization (McCluskey and Franzsen 2013).

Revenue Potential in Africa

A sense of the revenue potential of property taxation for African countries might enable countries and donors to chart a better reform plan. Although there is no really good way to estimate this potential, and the data supporting any estimate will be dreadful, two approaches can be suggested.

The first is comparison with averages for developing countries. From table 2.2, we estimate that the average ratio of property tax to GDP is about 0.38 percent in Africa versus an average for all middle- and low-income countries of 0.6 percent of GDP (Bahl and Martinez-Vazquez 2008). Seventeen of the thirty-two African countries reporting such information had property tax ratios below the international average. One problem with this comparison is that it is benchmarked against weak performance by other low-income countries. Still, this calculation suggests a significant potential for increased revenue, especially given the growth rate of African GDP.

The second approach, developed by Norregaard (2013), uses the average revenue ratios of the best performers among countries grouped by income level as a benchmark for the revenue potential of all countries in that group.[4] When the African countries for which data are available are considered in this manner, the results confirm the hypothesis that there is considerable untapped property tax potential in Africa. Property tax revenue in the 17 middle-income countries included in table 2.2 averaged 0.47 percent of GDP, but the average for the highest countries was 1.25 percent; for the 13 low-income countries, the average rate was 0.20 percent, but for the five best in this group, it was 0.45 percent. This rudimentary benchmarking exercise suggests that a doubling of property tax revenues over present levels in Africa might be feasible.

So why is revenue not increasing? What factors obstruct the use of the property tax? The answer, as we show in this chapter, is a combination of counterproductive tax policies and weak administration, almost always overlaid by unwillingness to enforce the tax. But the environment within which the property tax must operate in Africa also plays a part. The continent includes some of the poorest countries in the world. In these countries, there is little capacity to sustain a property tax with broad coverage at a high level. Political uncertainty and protracted civil wars are also prevalent in many African countries. These events have displaced many tens of thousands and even millions of people and have damaged or destroyed infrastructure, homes, and commercial buildings, with adverse consequences for property markets and the revenue potential of the property tax. In short, trust and good governance are sadly lacking in many countries on the African continent.

The Institutional Environment

The institutional environment includes the structure of government, the legal authority to levy and collect the tax, and the fiscal autonomy that has been given to subnational governments in deciding how to spend the money. These institutions result from culture, colonial heritage, topography, natural resource endowment, and even historical accidents. They are important influences on the way in which the property tax functions, and they typically change very slowly.

Whether governance is unitary or federal, and whether it features strong third-tier local governments, can affect the implementation of a strong and well-founded property tax. Normally, we would expect more decentralized countries to be more aggressive about reliance on the property tax. In this regard, there is great variation in Africa. Botswana, The Gambia, Ghana, Kenya, Lesotho, Liberia, Malawi, Mauritius, Namibia, Sierra Leone, Swaziland, and Tanzania have only two levels of government. Nigeria, South Africa, Zambia, and Zimbabwe have three levels. (The Comoros, Ethiopia, Nigeria, and Sudan are the only federal countries in Africa.) Uganda has a unique and intricate system of local government consisting of five tiers, but the Seychelles has only a central government with local administration on some of the individual islands. There are also some special arrangements for property and land taxation that lie outside the normal government structure. Some form of regional or district government exists for rural areas in a few countries (Namibia, South Africa, Uganda, and Zimbabwe). However, there are significant differences in the way in which these regional governments are financed. For example, in Uganda, district councils are legally entitled to levy property tax, but in practice, they generally do not have the capacity to implement this tax. In South Africa, some district municipalities may have the capacity to levy property tax, but they are prohibited from doing so by law because the lower-tier local municipalities have been given the legal power to levy the property tax.

Most Francophone African countries have a two-level government structure, although the Democratic Republic of the Congo has a provincial level as well. In Lusophone Africa, the three small countries have a two-level structure, but Angola and Mozambique have three levels of government. The geographically vast countries of North and Northeast Africa generally have three levels of government. Algeria, for example, has 48 provinces, Egypt has 27 governorates, Ethiopia has 9 states and 2 self-governing territories, Mauritania has 15 regions, and Sudan has 18 states.

In summary, we can say that most Anglophone countries in Africa have an institutional structure in place that can allow for decentralized administration of the property tax, but the extent to which they take advantage of this varies widely. The Francophone and Lusophone structures are much more centralized. Despite decentralization efforts in Sudan, the institutional capacity of local governments remains weak.

"Ownership" of the Property Tax in Africa

There are several ways to answer the question "Who owns the property tax in Africa?" Technically, the owner is the level of government that writes the property tax law and sets the tax rate. In the transition countries of the former Soviet bloc, the owner is the level of government that receives the revenue. But Casanegra de Jantscher and Bird (1992, 1) remind us that "tax administration is tax policy." This suggests that the revenue from the property tax is determined mostly by the government responsible for the administration. The intention that local governments own the property tax is more or less clear in industrial countries, but it is ambiguous in middle- and lower-income countries. Patterns are insufficiently regular in Africa for us to argue that this ambiguity is due to low overall rates of revenue mobilization, weak administration, or low rates of economic development.

National governments impose most property taxes in Africa. The recurrent property tax base is determined and the tax rate is regulated by national legislation in nearly all Anglophone countries. The exceptions to this general rule are Nigeria and, more recently, Kenya. In Nigeria, each of the 36 states, as well as the capital territory of Abuja, has its own property tax legislation. In Kenya, the property tax has always been a local-government tax, although under the new constitution, there is some debate about the distribution of lawmaking power between the national government and the county governments (see chapter 15).

Administration of the property tax (identification of properties, database updating, valuation, and collection) is a local responsibility in most Anglophone countries. The notable exceptions are Liberia, where the property tax is levied and collected by the central government, and Namibia, where the land tax on commercial farms is levied nationally and administered almost entirely within the Ministry of Land Reform. In some Anglophone countries, tax administration is a shared responsibility, but there is much variation from country to country.

The property tax is typically levied and administered under the national tax code in Francophone countries, for example, Burundi, the Central African Republic, Chad, Côte d'Ivoire, Equatorial Guinea, Madagascar, and Niger. The tax codes in these countries are generally quite comprehensive, especially regarding collection and enforcement. However, application of these laws is generally weak (Monkam 2010). In Cameroon, the property tax is also a central-government tax, but it is administered at the local level by officials of the central-government tax administration.

In Lusophone Africa, the property tax is levied under national laws and collected by the central government in Angola, Guinea-Bissau, and São Tomé and Príncipe. In Cabo Verde and Mozambique, the recurrent property tax has been a local tax since the early twenty-first century. In Cabo Verde, the *imposto unico sobre o patrimóno* (*IUP*), or unique tax on property, is indeed unique because it taxes the ownership of property and the transfer of ownership under the same law. Municipalities collect the ownership component, levied annually, whereas the transfer of property is taxed centrally. This requires significant coordination and cooperation between municipalities and the national government. The recurrent property tax in Mozambique was decentralized in 2003, but only to municipalities deemed to have sufficient capacity to administer this tax.

In North and Northeast Africa, countries differ greatly in how the property tax is levied. The imposition and administration of the real property tax and the agricultural land tax in Egypt are centralized within the Real Estate Tax Authority. To the extent that it still exists, the property tax is also administered centrally in Libya. In Ethiopia, Somalia, and Sudan, however, the tax, or at least its administration, has been devolved to the local level. In Morocco, the General Tax Administration in the central government collects the residence tax (*taxe d'habitation*), the municipal service tax (*taxe de services communaux*), and the business tax (*taxe professionnelle*) on behalf of local authorities and retains a 10 percent collection fee on the residence tax. The tax on vacant urban land (*taxe sur les terrains urbains non-bâtis*) and the tax on building operations (*taxe sur les opérations de construction*) are collected locally.

The property tax revenues that are reported in local-government budgets may come through the front door by rate setting or greater coverage of the tax base, or they may come through the back door by not administering the tax according to the law. In this, we may expect the African Anglophone countries to have a comparative advantage because of their propensity to give greater administrative discretion to local governments, so their relatively stronger performance as described in table 2.2 is not surprising. The property tax is levied under a central-government law, but it is usually collected by local governments, and an old adage states that money sticks where it hits.

National laws may allow for local options to set the tax base or determine the tax rate, and this can determine the level of revenue mobilization. In Kenya, Namibia, Swaziland, and Zimbabwe, for example, the national law provides for a choice of tax bases, whereas in Uganda, the central government determines the base, and the law provides for limited rate setting by local authorities within nationally determined limits. In South Africa, there is only one tax base, market value, but municipalities set their own tax rates and decide on exemptions and rebates.

Even though the property tax is centrally imposed and collected in most Francophone and Lusophone countries, local governments often share in the revenues. In most Francophone countries, the property tax is administered at the national level, but it is usually not viewed as an important tax and typically accounts for a very small share of national revenues. The result is often weak collection and lax enforcement. This appears to be an issue in, for example, Burundi, Cameroon, the Central African Republic, Congo, the Democratic Republic of the Congo, and Guinea. The issue becomes especially important in countries where the revenue is formally shared with local governments, as in Niger, or is entirely distributed to local governments, as is legislated in Cameroon, Côte d'Ivoire, and Equatorial Guinea. The property tax is administered only locally in a few Francophone countries. In Madagascar, one of the goals of the 2008 tax reform was to strengthen the resources of district authorities through a genuine process of decentralization. The Burundi Revenue Authority assesses the property tax and has the authority to collect it, but it currently does not collect the tax since this function is devolved to communes. In Burundi, the approach seems to be pragmatic given that some administrative capacity exists in the capital city, Bujumbura (Nti-batingeso 2015).

In Guinea-Bissau, the revenue is distributed to local governments. In Cabo Verde, the tax rate is determined nationally, but the recurrent tax component of the unique tax on property is administered locally. Revenue from this tax is shared between the central government and local governments. In North and Northeast Africa, the property tax is usually centrally administered, although in Egypt the revenue is distributed to local governments. Tax rates are determined nationally in Algeria, Egypt, and Morocco.

Some countries have defined the property tax as a shared revenue source. In Cameroon and Gabon, it is viewed as a "local" tax because revenues are allocated to local governments, but the base, exemptions, and rates are fixed nationally. In Cameroon, the tax rate is 0.1 percent, collected by regional units of the national Tax Directorate. In Niger, the central government determines the tax rates and collects the tax, but the revenue is shared between the national government (80 percent) and the communes (20 percent). The limited funding available to local governments and the lack of visibility of property taxes at the local level affects local development and service delivery. In the Democratic Republic of the Congo, the national government administers and collects the tax but remits the revenue to local-government authorities. In Côte d'Ivoire, the revenue from the tax on income from real property goes to the state, but all the proceeds from the various real property taxes are allocated to local authorities under a fixed formula: regions, 17 percent; *départements*, 28 percent; districts, 6 percent; towns, 6 percent; and communes, 43 percent. In Benin, the revenue from the tax on undeveloped land is fully distributed to the communes, while 10 percent of the revenue from the tax on developed property and the (new) urban property tax introduced in some communes is retained by the center, and 90 percent is distributed to the communes. In Cabo Verde, some of the taxes collected nationally (including the comprehensive property tax) are shared with the Municipal Financing Fund and are distributed from this fund to the various municipalities.[5]

Fiscal Decentralization

Fiscal decentralization means giving discretionary tax and expenditure powers to elected subnational governments and holding local officials accountable for the public service outcomes (Bahl 2008; Bahl and Bird forthcoming). Comparative analysis has shown that higher-income and more populous countries have decentralized more rapidly than poorer countries (Bahl and Wallace 2005), so it is not surprising that the budget structure of many African countries has remained highly centralized (Dickovick and Riedl 2010). Still, there has been some progress in strengthening subnational-government finances in Africa (Smoke 2003).[6] Most African countries hold subnational elections (Burkina Faso, Kenya, Mali, Morocco, Mozambique, Namibia, South Africa, Tanzania, and Uganda). Important expenditure responsibilities have been devolved, and local governments have been given access to various revenue resources, including the property tax (Kenya, Madagascar, Nigeria, South Africa, and Uganda), needed to meet these responsibilities.

However, local-government revenue mobilization remains a weakness in most countries. Continued and significant reliance on intergovernmental transfers generally increases central-government control over how the revenue is spent (Botswana and Uganda). Monrovia (Liberia) and Kampala (Uganda) are striking examples. Both these cities are burdened with unfunded mandates and have little control over the manner in which they can use their own sources of revenue, including the property tax. Although central governments transfer resources through an intergovernmental fiscal transfer system, these transfers are often unpredictable and inadequate to fund local services. It is essential for local councils to enhance their own-source revenues in order to ensure local autonomy, promote accountability, enhance economic governance and local ownership, and realize the efficiency gains of decentralization by linking their revenue and expenditure decisions to support local economic and social development in their jurisdictions.

Fiscal decentralization could provide an incentive for increased revenue mobilization from property taxation. History and practice have shown that central governments have been willing to devolve the property tax. Bahl and Martinez-Vazquez (2008) provide empirical evidence that is consistent with the argument that the demand for property taxation is driven by the level of decentralization. This supports the notion that increased reliance on property taxation should ideally be part of a properly formulated strategy for strengthened decentralization (Norregaard 2013). In fact, property tax reforms over the last 20 to 30 years have generally been part of a broader decentralization agenda in Kenya, Rwanda, Sierra Leone, and Sudan and are part of the ongoing reform agendas in Ethiopia, Somalia, and South Sudan.

Issues in most African countries are the legal underpinnings and the technical capacity to implement a property tax (Dickovick and Riedl 2010). For example, Sierra Leone introduced the Local Government Act of 2004 without a decentralization policy. A formal decentralization policy could have helped inform the intent of the new law and might have helped minimize some of the overwhelming administrative challenges experienced in its implementation. This untenable situation was rectified only after the event when the Decentralisation Policy was adopted in 2010 (Tommy, Franzsen, and Jibao 2015). A similar problem has arisen in Kenya, where the 2010 constitution clearly states that county governments may impose the recurrent property tax, but does not provide clarity about what the term *impose* entails (Franzsen 2013). Some counties are now arguing that under the new constitution, they can draft and introduce their own property tax laws. From a policy perspective, this could be problematic. South Africa's constitution is quite clear in this regard. Although the property tax is a local tax, it is regulated by a national law.

Taxes on Real Property Transfers

The annual property tax is usually coupled with a tax on the sales price of real property transfers. Although most countries levy both taxes, they usually administer them separately. The transfer tax may be levied as a stamp duty on the transfer document, as a separate property transfer tax, or as a capital gains tax. Legal liability for payment may rest with the buyer or the seller or may be split between them. Property transfer taxes are widely used in Africa.

Advantages and Disadvantages of Taxes on Real Property Transfers

There are several reasons that real estate transfer taxes have become part of tax systems in developing countries, and that their staying power is so great. First, a tax on real property transfers is easy to administer because most buyers and sellers desire a legal record of ownership and therefore will voluntarily comply. Second, it generates revenue but appears to have a very low cost of collection. For a low-income country, even a yield as low as 1 percent of GDP can be hard to give up. In some countries, the property transfer tax generates much more revenue than the annual property tax (Mauritius, Morocco, and São Tomé and Príncipe). Third, if property ownership is concentrated in the higher-income classes, and if turnover is greater for higher-income properties, a property transfer tax will be progressive.[7] Fourth, the number of payers of the tax in any given year is much smaller than in the case of most general taxes, so there is likely to be less voter opposition. Fifth, a property transfer tax might reach that part of the taxable capacity (property wealth) that is not captured by most income and value-added taxes. Sixth, third parties, such as attorneys or notaries, can collect the tax and remit it to the appropriate ministry. Finally, some governments have used the property transfer tax to cool down an overheated investment market in real property.

There also are major disadvantages of the property transfer tax (Alm, Annez, and Modi 2004; Bahl 2004, 2009; Norregaard 2013; Wallace 2008). The most important problem is that the cost of properly administering a property transfer tax is very high in low- and middle-income countries because the tax base is heavily influenced, if not determined, by taxpayer declaration of the sales price. Levies on taxpayer honesty do not work anywhere, and so a backup valuation system is needed to verify the declared sales prices and revalue them when necessary. In Kenya, the Ministry of Lands and Physical Planning undertakes a valuation in most instances. In industrial countries, this problem is solved by the combination of more arm's-length transactions and the involvement of several parties in the transfer (buyers, sellers, real estate agents, banks and mortgage companies), along with homeowner insurance requirements. Such arm's-length sales do not occur in most low- and middle-income countries. In most of these countries, there is a shortage of trained valuers. Declared values are not routinely checked for accuracy, and underdeclaration is commonplace. For example, Alm, Annez, and Modi (2004) studied Indian states with different stamp duty rates and found that underdeclaration of sales prices tends to rise with the stamp duty rate. They report that in Maharastra State, nearly 70 percent of declarations were undervalued by at least 20 percent. Very high transfer tax rates (13 percent in Jamaica) are an open invitation to underdeclaration and a signal that monitoring will not be vigorous. In Jordan, it has been estimated that only about 10 percent of all declarations are checked (Bahl 2012).

Because of the low probability of being detected, and because the property transfer tax often is levied at a high nominal rate, property owners have a significant incentive to understate taxable values. Understatement of taxable value leads not only to revenue loss but also to a weakening of the database that is necessary for objective assessment of the annual property tax. The shortage of trained valuers is seldom discussed, but it is a very great drawback to levying a property transfer tax at a high rate.[8] It forces the use of third-party data and subjective estimates for appraisal, and it all but rules out the possibility of computer-assisted mass appraisal.

Another problem is that the property transfer tax is structured as a gross sales tax. This means that a tax will be assessed on expenditures that enhance the value of a property. Compared with a capital gains tax, this will discourage investments in improvements. Finally, property transfer taxes impose a cost on property transactions and thereby reduce the volume of formal transactions and slow the development of the real estate market.

Property Transfer Taxes in African Countries

Almost all African countries use property transfer taxes. Although the tax is usually a central-government tax (Kenya, Lesotho, South Africa, and Zambia), the tax base can easily be shared between levels of government, or it can simply be a local tax, as in The Gambia and Sudan. In many countries, the tax rate is significantly higher when nonnationals or foreigners acquire property, for example, in Equatorial Guinea and Seychelles (any property) and in Botswana (agricultural land). This is also common in many countries in the Caribbean region (Bahl 2004; Franzsen 2016).

In some Anglophone countries, a property transfer tax is levied as a transfer tax on contracting parties (Namibia, South Africa, and Zambia); in others, it is levied as a stamp duty (The Gambia, Kenya, Tanzania, and Uganda); and in still others, it is levied in both forms (Lesotho). Tax rates range from a relatively low 1 percent (Uganda) to as high as 10 percent (Lesotho) and even a maximum rate of 13 percent in South Africa, where a sliding scale applies.

Property transfer taxes are also significant in non-Anglophone countries. In Burundi, the tax rate is 3 percent; in Guinea, 5 percent; in Togo, 6 percent; in Mali, 7 percent; in Burkina Faso, 8 percent; and in Chad, 10 percent (in some instances, 15 percent). In the Comoros, it ranges between 2 and 9 percent for sales transactions. In several Francophone countries, more than one transfer tax or stamp duty is levied (the Central African Republic, the Comoros, Congo, and Madagascar).

Lusophone countries levy property transfer taxes at varying rates. In Cabo Verde, the transfer tax is 3 percent, and the stamp duty is 1 percent. Guinea-Bissau and São Tomé and Príncipe levy transfer taxes at high rates of 10 percent and 8 percent, respectively. In São Tomé and Príncipe, the revenue from the transfer tax significantly exceeded the revenue from the recurrent property tax from 2001 to 2007. All countries in North and Northeast Africa levy a tax (or taxes) on the transfer of real property. Egypt has the lowest tax rate on property transfers, 2.5 percent. Algeria, Morocco, and Tunisia (three former French colonies with similar transfer tax systems) levy rates in excess of 5 percent. The rate in Djibouti is 10 percent; in Mauritania, it can be as high as 15 percent (see table A.5 in the appendix).

Many African countries have been reducing their registration costs, including the costs resulting from high transfer tax rates. In many instances, registration processes and practices have also been streamlined (World Bank 2015), which should lead to a reduction of informality in property markets and an increase in title security. Notably, many Francophone countries have decreased transfer taxes or registration fees, for example, Benin, Chad, the Comoros, Guinea, Madagascar, Mali, and Senegal (World Bank 2015). Senegal reduced registration fees for several types of transactions in its 2012 reforms, particularly the fees on real estate transactions, which were decreased from 15 percent to 10 percent. Senegal also overhauled its stamp tax in 2012. The Central African Republic did the same in 2011, reducing the rate from 15 percent to 7.5 percent. (Fossat et al. 2013). In Lusophone Africa, Guinea-Bissau has reduced the tax rate from 10 percent to 5 percent. These developments may lessen the incentive to underdeclare sales prices.

Only a few countries have increased the rates of their transfer taxes, most notably Zambia, where the rate increased from 3 percent to 10 percent in four years, although it fell to 5 percent in 2016. Increases have also been enacted in the Congo and Gabon (World Bank 2015). Although South Africa (where progressive tax rates apply) increased the maximum rate from 11 percent to 13 percent on March 1, 2016, this was partly offset by a significant increase in the zero-rate level.

Options for Reform

Given the negative features of a high transfer tax, theory suggests that tax rates should instead be reduced significantly. The best approach is to rethink the basic objectives. Property transfer taxes are now levied as sales taxes on gross receipts. If the underlying goal is to tax the increase in property values at the time of a transfer, why not abolish the property transfer tax in favor of a capital gains tax on real property (Bahl 2004; Blöchliger and Kim 2016; Norregaard 2013; Wallace 2008)? If capital gains are taxed, the buyer has a genuine interest in declaring the actual market value because underdeclaration will negatively affect the asset's base cost when it is resold. In other words, a capital gains tax would have a self-checking feature that could lead to more accurate self-declaration of sales values and thus strengthen valuation for the annual property tax (Bahl and Wallace 2010).

In the short run, assessment of capital gains would be notional, but the present approach of declaration of sales values under the transfer tax is also notional. The imposition of a capital gains tax may sound administratively difficult because the base-year value would need to be determined (estimated), and the value of the base would need to be adjusted for inflation and capital improvements.[9] Sales prices would need to be monitored or set at notional levels. But proper administration of the present sales tax version of the property transfer tax is equally difficult. Shortcuts to assess capital gains might be better than the shortcuts now used to assess sales.

There are some precedents for capital gains taxes on real estate transfers, but the practice to date does not offer a model that will work well in all low-income countries. Panama taxes real estate sales by either a transactions tax or a capital gains tax but still uses declared sales values as the basis for estimating sales (Bahl and Garzon 2010). The experience in Taiwan has been successful (Tsui 2008). The land value increment tax is a form of capital gains tax on transfers and is levied against cadastral values that are set annually by the Ministry of Finance. Arguably the major shortcoming of the tax in Taiwan is that the government-determined cadastral values do not closely approximate market values. Several African countries already impose a tax on income from capital gains (Egypt, Equatorial Guinea, The Gambia, Madagascar, Morocco, South Africa, Tunisia, and Zimbabwe).[10]

Big changes like the adoption of a capital gains tax on real property sales cannot happen quickly in low- and middle-income countries. Sales taxes on property transfers will most likely continue to be imposed. Can the present approach be improved? A moment's reflection will lead one to the conclusion that the problems with the property transfer tax are administrative, and the severity of the problem is dependent on the level of the nominal tax rate chosen. At very low legal rates, these problems with the property transfer tax may be less consequential since the gains from underdeclaration will be less, but when the tax rate is high, these problems are magnified. Nominal rates of property transfer taxes have been reduced in many countries, but they arguably still remain high enough to discourage accurate self-assessment.

Other Taxes and Charges on Real Property

Several other taxes or charges on the value of property or the income from property are part of the revenue structure of African countries. In a few cases, these constitute important sources of revenue, and in some cases, they have significant but untapped revenue potential. Included in this group are the tax on rental income (Democratic Republic of the Congo, Rwanda, and Zambia), the capital gains tax (The Gambia, South Africa, and Zimbabwe), estate, inheritance, and gift taxes (South Africa), land or ground rents (Ghana, Kenya, Mozambique, Sierra Leone, Tanzania, and Zambia), and various forms of value capture. In some cases, these levies might be important in strengthening the overall property tax practice in Africa.

The Tax on Rental Income from Real Property

In most African countries, income from renting out immovable property is taxable under the individual and corporate income tax. In some cases, rents are taxed under a separate schedule, and in some countries, they are devolved to local governments (Burundi and Rwanda). In Burundi, the tax on rental income from real property was ceded to communes in 1987 to finance services to meet the needs of the population, in particular, health and urban development. An urban development fund was created to which this tax and the recurrent property tax contribute. The tax is set annually on the net income of the previous year (Ntibatingeso 2015).

Many countries (Benin, Burundi, Cameroon, the Comoros, Congo, Democratic Republic of the Congo, Ethiopia, Mali, Rwanda, Uganda, and Zambia) levy a separate tax on rental income from real property. Some people may confuse the tax on income from rental properties with the property tax in countries that use rental value as the base for property taxation (Benin and Mali). There may even be a perception that this constitutes double taxation. In fact, the two taxes are quite different. One is a tax on rent as a source of income, while the other is a tax on the value of a property that is assessed according to its rental value. The property tax is assessed according to a notional rent, usually with a standard deduction for maintenance, and includes an imputed rent for owner-occupiers. The income tax on rents received by landlords is based on actual transactions and does not include imputed rents on owner-occupiers. The property and income tax bills facing a landlord in a given year will be assessed on quite different bases and will no more constitute double taxation than an income tax and a general consumption tax.

Value Capture and Special Assessments

Urbanization increases demand for land and for services to residential and nonresidential properties. Relaxation of government constraints on urban development (e.g., zoning changes that allow development on the urban fringe) and infrastructure investments that enhance the quality of public services drive up real estate values. These value increases are reflected to some extent in the property tax base, but this effect is diluted by revaluation lags and the low effective rates of the property tax in lower-income countries. Some governments have now turned to using other fiscal instruments to capture a portion of these land value increments to support the financing of public investments and public services (Smolka 2013; Youngman 2016).[11]

There is a strong case that the public sector should recoup the part of the increment in land values that is a result of government actions. First, this approach is equitable because it reclaims some of the benefits of government-sector actions for the general public. If an investment of USD 10 million in a new road will increase property values in affected areas by

USD 20 million, why not at least recover the cost of the project from the beneficiaries? Since these land value increments are unearned (the property owners did nothing to generate them), it might be fair and efficient to claim an even larger share than the cost of the project for the general public.

A second important advantage of value capture is the generation of revenues to support the public budget. Several inventive schemes have been developed to use expected land value increases to fund the cost of public investments, such as road improvements, large-scale capital projects, and general urban development. Under the right circumstances, these schemes can give the best of both worlds: the developer can move ahead with the project, and the government can avoid raising taxes to cover the cost of the infrastructure investment.

Ground Rent

Ground rent, also referred to in some countries as land rent, is not a tax payment for government services but a payment for the right to occupy and use land. However, it is often reported alongside property taxes. In countries where both property tax and ground rent are levied, taxpayers often view their coexistence as double taxation. Ground rent is levied in, for example, Eritrea, Ghana, Kenya, Lesotho, Mozambique, Sierra Leone, Swaziland, Tanzania, Uganda, and Zambia.

Ground rent or land rent is common in many African countries where land is owned by the state or held by the government (Tanzania), the king (Lesotho), or the president (Zambia) in trust on behalf of the citizenry. It is an amount (in many instances, a nominal amount) levied and collected for different types of rights (e.g., leasehold in Zambia) to occupy land for various purposes, such as constructing a house or engaging in agricultural activities. In some countries, the ground rent is collected by the ministry responsible for lands (Zambia), the land administration agency (Lesotho), or local-government authorities on behalf of the central government (Tanzania). In Zambia, the minister of lands determines the rate at which ground rent is payable.

The Tax Base

The property tax base can be determined in one of five ways: capital value of land and improvements, annual rental value of land and improvements, land value only, building value only, and the physical area of the property. Although countries in Africa may face similar economic constraints and land ownership issues, they have approached the taxation of property in very different ways. Some of the problems with the tax bases used in many

African countries result from retention of outdated laws or their replacement by inappropriate modern laws. The legal structure of the property tax often does not fit the implementation capacity of a country; therefore, property taxation in Africa is not easily administered or updated. Postcolonial changes, such as nationalization of all land, have also affected property taxation. This can be seen in the property tax systems in, for example, Mozambique and Tanzania, where the tax bases, perhaps unnecessarily, exclude land. In practice, African countries determine tax bases in various ways on different types of property.

There are many examples in Anglophone Africa. In Sierra Leone, the new Local Government Act that was implemented in 2004 provides for an annual rental value system. More than a decade later, there are still jurisdictions that use the old area-based system because of the absence of the necessary skills and capacity to undertake property valuations. In Lesotho, the 1980 property tax legislation has been inadequate to guide the implementation of the property tax, which is now levied only in the capital city, Maseru. Even there, coverage is extremely poor (Franzsen and Mc-Cluskey 2005). In Kenya, valuation of rural land is based on land area, while valuation of urban land ignores improvements on the land. Kenya is one of the few countries in the world that formally taxes only the land in urban areas. The approach to property taxation in Ghana and Tanzania could not be more different from that in Kenya in that they value only the buildings and exclude any element of land value. Even taxation of buildings is done in different ways in different countries. In the more developed urban areas of The Gambia, Ghana, and Tanzania, a value-based approach that uses depreciated construction costs is applied, but local authorities in Tanzania apply a flat rating, that is, a fixed amount per building according to use, building size, and location. Although the laws in Liberia, Namibia, and Swaziland allow for various options, local authorities use a split-rate system that requires separate valuation of land and improvements. Malawi and Zambia use capital values of land and buildings, whereas in Botswana, land and buildings are valued separately but are taxed collectively. In Nigeria, a federal country, the property tax is levied under the laws of the 36 individual states. In Lagos State, a capital value system is applied, whereas in many other states, property tax rates are based on annual rental values. In South Africa, the tax base is market value for urban and rural properties. However, before the new property tax law became operative in 2005, South African municipalities could choose their own tax base from three options: land value (site rating), land and buildings collectively (flat rating), or land and buildings separately (composite rating).

Francophone African countries generally use three different property taxes: on undeveloped urban land, on developed urban land, and on rural land. Furthermore, the central government generally levies and collects these taxes. In some countries, the tax on undeveloped urban land is determined with reference to capital values (Congo, Côte d'Ivoire, and Togo), whereas in others, it is based on annual values (the Central African Republic and Chad). The tax on developed land in urban areas is based on annual rental value (the Central African Republic, Chad, the Comoros, Congo, Côte d'Ivoire, Guinea, Madagascar, Mali, and Togo). The tax on rural land, where it exists, is generally based on fixed amounts per hectare (the Central African Republic, Chad, the Comoros, and Congo).

In Gabon, laws passed in 1996 and 2007 provide for three different property taxes based on value, but in practice, a 1963 law is still applied that provides for a rudimentary area-based system dating back to colonial times (Monkam 2011). The tax on rural land in Equatorial Guinea is based on size and potential income. However, because properties with an area below five hectares are exempted, it is unclear how large the remaining tax base is. In Côte d'Ivoire, an additional commune (local) tax on undeveloped land is levied on the same base as the central-government tax, but at a nominal rate. This effectively is a tax base–sharing arrangement. In 2012, Cameroon abolished its property tax base–sharing arrangement. All the revenue collected by the central government is now distributed to the local council where the property is situated. In the Central African Republic, the tax base for developed urban land is its annual rental value. However, in practice, although the procedure is not expressly mentioned in the General Tax Code, the market value of the property is determined as either the cost of the construction or the acquisition price of the property. The rental value is then expressed as a percentage of this so-called market value. The minimum rental value is taken to be 12 percent of the market value of the property. Benin introduced a new property tax in 1994, replacing the tax on developed property, the tax on undeveloped property, and the tax on rental income from property. It is levied only in communes that have an urban land register, while the other taxes remain applicable in the rest of the communes. The tax base is the actual rental value of the property as of January 1 of the year of imposition. The tax administration has established a scale of rental values according to location zones for each type of construction. This consolidation of taxes on property should reduce administration and compliance costs. Niger calibrates the property tax according to ownership of the property. If the property is owned by an individual, the tax base is annual rental value; if it is owned by a legal entity, the base is book value.

In Lusophone countries, the property tax is based on capital value in Cabo Verde, Mozambique, and São Tomé and Príncipe. In Cabo Verde, the taxable value is 25 percent of the total value of the property as declared annually by the owner. In Mozambique, this municipal property tax is lev-ied with reference to the book value (the value recorded in the cadastral records) of urban properties located within a municipality. In the absence of book values, self-declared values are used. In São Tomé and Príncipe, the values are annually adjusted for the age of buildings. In Angola and Guinea-Bissau, the tax base is annual rental value.

In North and Northeast Africa, annual rental value is the most common property tax base. Both Algeria and Djibouti treat developed and undevel-oped land differently, whereas Mauritania taxes only the rental value of buildings. The urban property tax levied by central and local governments in Morocco is also based on annual rental value. In Tunisia, the local prop-erty tax is area based, while the central-government tax is value based. In urban areas, Egypt taxes only buildings, again on the basis of annual rental value. However, Egypt also levies an agricultural land tax based on annual rental value, but with a minimum farm-size threshold. A rudimen-tary annual rental value system with adjustments for plot size applies in Ethiopian urban areas. Property taxes in Eritrea are based on area with ad-justments for location (e.g., in Asmara). An agricultural land tax based on area is also levied.

The coverage of the property tax is the percentage of properties that are identified, valued, and recorded in the valuation or tax roll (Kelly 2000). Because of capacity constraints, unwise policy choices, inappropriate laws, and, political pressures, property tax coverage is poor in most African countries. It is not uncommon in many African countries for 50 to 75 percent of properties to be off the valuation roll (Nairobi, Kenya), although there are jurisdictions where coverage has been improved significantly (Dar es Salaam, Tanzania). Poor coverage limits the revenue potential of the property tax and erodes public confidence in its fairness.

Some countries have attempted to manage this problem by limiting the property tax to urban areas (Botswana, Burundi, Chad, Lesotho, Tanza-nia, Uganda, and Zambia). This makes pragmatic sense because of the in-tensity of development and the location of high-value properties in urban areas. In contrast, rural areas are more likely to be composed of custom-ary land, small towns, and villages. But this approach to simplifying the property tax can be problematic. One issue is extending the coverage to include intense development activity in peri-urban areas that are typically on communal land and not in a designated rating area. A good example is the outskirts of Gaborone, Botswana, where modern high-value devel-opments such as shopping malls, gasoline (petrol) stations, and private hospitals have been constructed and are not paying any property tax.

In other instances, property taxation is restricted to those areas desig-nated by the minister as being taxable (Botswana, The Gambia, Kenya,

Lesotho, Uganda, and Zambia). In Rwanda, only property that has a free-hold title is liable for the property tax, a provision that applies to very few properties. Such policies have a damaging effect on revenues and taxpayer morale. A common approach in Francophone countries is differentiation in the treatment of developed land and undeveloped land in urban areas, as in Burundi, Chad, the Central African Republic, Congo, Cote d'Ivoire, Niger, and Togo. The problem with this broader approach to coverage is one of capacity to ensure that all properties are included in the valuation rolls. In Uganda, for example, the few qualified valuers are unable to provide services to all the many local-government authorities entitled to levy a recurrent tax on property (Franzsen 2010).

In some African countries, rural land is charged only a ground or land rent that is based on a right of occupancy. In other countries, however, rural properties are taxable in principle. In Mozambique, for example, the tax is called the land use charge. Even where the law also allows for a land or property tax on rural land, these taxes are not used in practice. In Uganda, there is simply no capacity to extend the system to rural areas. Scarce administrative resources are concentrated in the urban areas. This sometimes means that high-value properties, such as resort properties and private game parks in Rwanda and Botswana, are not taxed. In some Francophone countries, including the Central African Republic, the Comoros, Congo, Equatorial Guinea, and Gabon, a simple area-based approach is (in principle) applied to rural properties.

Centralized administrations in Francophone and Lusophone countries normally require that property owners provide information on ownership, leasing arrangements (if any), factual details, and values. Properly monitored, this is a cost-effective solution to what would otherwise be a difficult administrative task. Such processes are used in Benin, Burundi, Cabo Verde, Libya, and Rwanda. In tandem with self-declaration, the law normally provides for heavy penalties for nondeclaration, late declaration, or incorrect information. However, in practice, the system fails because of the lack of capacity within the centralized administration to ensure that self-declaration is comprehensive and reasonably accurate.

Exclusions, Exemptions, and Preferences

Exclusions (i.e., properties excluded by the legal definition of "property" in the relevant law[s]), exemptions, (i.e., not taxing property that is in principle taxable), and other forms of tax relief (i.e., through rebates, value reductions, and tax incentives) can erode the property tax base significantly, particularly when one level of government gives away the revenues of another level.[12] Exclusions from the tax base usually are permanent.

They may be constitutionally mandated and are very difficult to remove once they are in place. Typically, a property that is excluded from the property tax base is not valued, so it is difficult to estimate the revenue that is forgone. In South Africa, however, 30 percent of the value of taxable public service infrastructure (taxable public utilities) and property owned and used primarily for public worship by a religious community may not be taxed, but these properties must still be valued and recorded in the valuation roll. Many exemptions also do not have a sunset period.

Generous exemption regimes are a feature of the property tax systems in many African countries (Franzsen and McCluskey 2005). Properties that are exempt in other countries in the world, such as places used exclusively or primarily for public worship, public educational institutions, charitable institutions, cemeteries, public museums and libraries, foreign embassies and consulates, sports facilities, and public medical facilities, typically are exempt in most African countries as well. There may be a socioeconomic rationale for some of these exemptions because of the positive social externalities these properties generate (Kelly 2014). Most countries also provide for a list of statutory exemptions, which vary from country to country. Some of these are justified by the high cost of shelter, some are attempts at social engineering (stimulating what is thought to be merit consumption), some are cultural (tribal land), and some are just political pandering.

The third class of property tax relief is preferential treatments, such as rate reductions, special tax forgiveness programs, and property tax holidays. The laws in some countries (Lesotho, Tanzania) also grant ministers discretionary powers to give further property tax exemptions. This is dangerous because such discretionary power can be used for personal political gain and to the detriment of local-government budgets. Swaziland takes a more prudent approach. The minister may grant an additional exemption only if the property is used for a "public benefit." The Swaziland law also clearly states that if any property is exempt from another tax, that does not imply that it is also exempt from property tax, and a property tax exemption does not automatically entitle the property owner to exemption from payment of other fees and charges, such as those for refuse removal and sanitation.

Residential Property

In many developing countries in the world, residential properties benefit from preferential treatment under the property tax (Bahl 2009; Bird and Slack 2004; Blöchliger and Kim 2016; Kelly 2014). The international experience suggests that this can lead to serious tax base erosion. For example, a study of Punjab Province in Pakistan estimates that bringing owner-occupied property fully into the tax base would triple the level of property tax revenues (Bahl, Cyan, and Wallace 2015).

Many African countries have followed this tradition of giving property tax relief for residences (Benin, the Central African Republic, Egypt, Gabon, Guinea, Madagascar, Niger, Tunisia, and Uganda). In Uganda and Tunisia, exemption of owner-occupied residential properties significantly reduces the tax base and shifts the property tax burden to businesses, land-lords, and renters. There may be some perversity in this because renters include both wealthy expatriates and those who are too poor to buy residential property.

São Tomé and Príncipe exempts residential buildings constructed from poor materials (if the value is less than a specified amount) and taxpayers earning less than a specified amount per day, which makes perfect sense. These exemptions, available on application only, are difficult to verify and audit, but their redistributive intent is clear.

Tax rates are lower on primary residences in Côte d'Ivoire, the Democratic Republic of the Congo, and Eritrea. In Morocco, preferential treatment (a 75 percent rebate on the tax rate) is applied to primary residences but also is extended to secondary residences and holiday homes. Many countries in Africa and elsewhere have differential tax rates (classified rates), usually based on use. Not surprisingly, there is a tendency to have lower rates for residential property (South Africa, Swaziland, and Zambia).

The Central African Republic, Egypt, Equatorial Guinea, and South Africa all provide for value thresholds below which properties are not taxable. In South Africa, the threshold applies only to residential properties, and the threshold amount is determined locally. In Egypt, however, the threshold amount is determined by the central government and is high enough to exclude the vast majority of residential properties from the tax base.

Government-Owned Properties

Exemption of government-owned properties imposes a revenue cost because it deprives local governments of the right to charge for some of the land use within their boundaries. In Brazil, the constitution forbids the taxation of government-owned properties even if they are used for non-government purposes. In most low- and middle-income countries, the exemption is less strongly guaranteed but is still given by law or even in some cases by long-standing tradition.[13]

Taxation of government-owned property is always a difficult issue with few pragmatic, workable solutions. The problem tends to be acute where a local-government jurisdiction includes many properties owned by higher-level governments within its boundaries, which is typically the case in country and regional capital cities (Maseru, Lesotho). In some countries, some of the most valuable real estate is government owned and may constitute a significant part of the tax base (McCluskey and Franzsen 2013). These properties still require services, but if they are exempt, they do not pay for these services, and a higher tax rate is imposed on those who do pay (Bahl and Linn 1992). This raises equity issues, as well as tax neutrality issues where these buildings are used for commercial purposes and compete directly with the private sector. Some municipalities in South Africa have been taxing government property on the basis of use. There are certain government buildings, however, where an exemption is defensible. In South Africa, the property tax law was amended in 2015 to allow for municipalities to exempt, or grant a rebate to, property owned and used by "an organ of state" for public service purposes, including police stations, courts of law, public hospitals and clinics, and correctional facilities.

Government-owned property is exempt in many countries in Africa. In most Francophone countries (Burundi, the Central African Republic, Côte d'Ivoire, Democratic Republic of the Congo, Equatorial Guinea, and Gabon), the property tax is a central-government tax, and exemption answers the question, how can a government tax itself? But other issues remain, such as the use of government properties for commercial purposes, in which case the higher-level government should be taxed for its use of public services. In Benin and Madagascar, government properties are exempt only if they are not used commercially, but government-owned property is fully exempt in Egypt, Ghana, Sierra Leone, and Tanzania. In Liberia, where the property tax is also a national tax, the capital city, Monrovia, is mandated to perform various functions, such as waste-management services, for government-owned properties. The property tax exemption amounts to an unfunded mandate.

Although government property is exempt in Kenya, Lesotho, and Zambia, the law allows for payments or contributions in lieu of taxes. However, in Nairobi, the former city council (now the county government) rarely receives these payments. The same problem is reported in Zambia. Central governments' noncompliance may negatively affect compliance of other taxpayers.

In Ghana, Malawi, Namibia, South Africa, and Swaziland, most government-owned properties are assessed in the same manner as other property ownership categories and are taxable. In Malawi and Namibia, statutory rebates of 50 percent and 20 percent, respectively, apply, whereas in some jurisdictions in South Africa (e.g., Johannesburg and Pretoria) and Swaziland (Mbabane), government property may be taxed at higher tax rates than those applicable to other properties. In Pretoria (City of Tshwane), the tax rate for state-owned property in 2015 was three times higher than the rate for residential property. Unfortunately, even in countries where the property tax is payable on government-owned properties, the government often defaults. In Malawi, it seems to be politically and institutionally difficult for local authorities to enforce payment of taxes on the central government. In South Africa, where defaulters often face withholding of certain municipal services, cutting electricity and reducing water delivery to government buildings have been used successfully to collect arrears.

The Central African Republic, Côte d'Ivoire, Gabon, São Tomé and Príncipe, and South Africa grant specific exemptions or exclusions pertaining to infrastructure. In the Central African Republic, Côte d'Ivoire, and Gabon, electricity- and water-related infrastructure is explicitly exempted. However, in South Africa, infrastructure that has not been explicitly excluded is taxable (e.g., power stations, power lines, and gas and liquid fuel plants and pipelines). The rate may not exceed 25 percent of that determined for residential property, and the first 30 percent of the value is excluded from the tax base.

Vacant Urban Land

Especially in urban areas, vacant land parcels often command high prices, and excluding these properties from the tax base can have important revenue consequences. In Botswana, Lesotho, Uganda, and Zimbabwe, undeveloped land in peri-urban areas is communal land and is not liable for the property tax. With increasing rates of urbanization and urban development, vacant land is becoming increasingly valuable. It has location value and benefits from infrastructure financed by the public sector. The increments in land value that result from public infrastructure improvements should be subject to the property tax. Moreover, exemption of vacant properties shifts more of the tax burden to other property taxpayers. Finally, the taxation of vacant land, even at a differentially higher rate, might provide an incentive for development and discourage land speculation.

Vacant or undeveloped land within urban areas is taxed in several Anglophone countries (Botswana, Kenya, Namibia, South Africa, Swaziland, and Zimbabwe). A separate property tax on undeveloped urban land is more common in Francophone Africa (Benin, Burundi, the Central African Republic, Chad, Congo, Côte d'Ivoire, Gabon [under a new law but not yet implemented], Madagascar, and Togo).

Outside urban areas, much depends on whether the land is titled or held under traditional ownership rights. In some countries (Mozambique and Tanzania), all land is government owned and does not incur tax. Arguably, the land rent or ground rent charged in countries where land is government owned generates some revenue, although in Tanzania, for example, local governments collect the rent and then retain 30 percent. However, collection coverage is relatively poor. In principle, nothing prevents a property tax on government-owned land from coexisting with the ground rent, as is the case in Zambia for long-term leasehold interests.

In Botswana, Liberia, Namibia, and South Africa, vacant urban land is generally taxed at higher rates than those applied to other ownership or land use categories. In Pretoria, South Africa, the tax rate for a vacant parcel of land is more than six times the rate set for residential property owners. The argument is that expensive infrastructure and local services are in principle available to vacant lots, and that these properties should contribute revenue. This argument may be valid if the tax rate is on a par with the rate for developed lots. The higher rate is generally explained as an incentive to encourage the development of vacant lots. This is clearly the case in Namibia, where a penalty tax is levied if vacant plots in approved town-planning schemes are not developed within a specified period. The tax may be doubled if the plot remains vacant after two years and increased fourfold if it is not developed after five years.

Taxation of agricultural land is always a difficult issue because of subsistence levels of agriculture in many countries and the political clout of wealthy commercial landowners. In Kenya, the most valuable agricultural land is held freehold, is located outside urban areas, and is not taxable. Kelly (2014) points out that large commercial farms in Guinea, Tanzania, and Tunisia are not currently taxed, even though a rudimentary area-based tax could be considered for these types of property. In contrast, Egypt, Eritrea, Namibia, and South Africa tax agricultural land quite aggressively. In various Francophone countries, such as the Central African Republic, Chad, Congo, and the Comoros, agricultural and other rural land is in principle taxed a fixed amount per hectare. In the Central African Republic, agricultural buildings, such as sheds, are specifically exempted.

Kelly (2014) argues correctly that the taxation of commercial agricultural land could be based on simplified area-based assessments.[14] Complex income-based valuation approaches are unnecessary and unsustainable in African countries, with the possible exceptions of Namibia and South Africa. Namibia levies a land tax on commercial farms to generate revenue that is earmarked for the land reform program.

New Construction

African countries provide extensive relief for newly developed or renovated residential properties. The exemption periods vary in length: five to 10 years in Angola, five years in Benin (if the property is not used commercially), five years in Equatorial Guinea, Madagascar, and Morocco, three years in Gabon, and two years in Niger and São Tomé and Príncipe. Because residential property normally constitutes the largest sector of new construction, exempting it for lengthy periods could significantly narrow the tax base. Also, administering the exemption periods is difficult unless there is appropriate record keeping. Even during the holiday period, these exempt properties still use local public services. These tax holidays are prone to abuse. We can find no evidence that this relief stimulates residential housing starts or new construction of buildings used for business purposes. Indeed, given the low level of the property tax in most African countries, it is doubtful that it does.

New construction also receives favorable treatment in Francophone, Lusophone, and North African countries. Benin, Burundi, Chad, Equatorial Guinea, Madagascar, and Niger grant a temporary exemption to new buildings or refurbished buildings. In Cabo Verde, new buildings can receive an exemption for a period ranging from three to ten years. The exemption is for five years in Benin but ceases if the property is occupied for commercial purposes.

Tax Relief

Property tax relief concerns much more than the reduction of tax burdens. It should improve equity, correct egregious errors in the tax structure, stimulate certain consumption and production activities, and keep the public confident that the property tax is fair. All this needs to be balanced against erosion of the tax base, administrative complexity, and politics. Well-designed property tax relief can give the public confidence in the tax. Badly designed tax relief programs can benefit taxpayers who should not qualify and anger the public.

Tax relief programs in African countries, like those in most other countries, tend to be ad hoc collections of independent measures rather than a planned program. They seem to be answers to various specific questions: Will agricultural properties be included in the base (South Africa) or excluded (Niger)? Will residential properties be taxed at a lower rate than commercial properties? They also use a variety of instruments to get the job done—exemptions, exclusions, and tax rates—again with no apparent pattern. All these instruments involve lowering the effective tax rate.

The most obvious approach is to lower the statutory tax rate for targeted properties. As soon as different tax rates are determined for different property use or ownership categories, value or property size is no longer the only factor considered in distributing the tax burden. Those properties that pay tax at a lower rate are receiving preferential treatment. In the City of Perth, Western Australia, differential rates are justified and explained to all taxpayers in the city's annual property tax policy (Franzsen 2005). Determination of differential rates in African countries that use them is much less formal and sometimes seems to be based on anecdotal evidence regarding factors such as perceived affordability.

One approach used in Africa and elsewhere is to exempt all properties below a threshold value. Although this is a blanket approach, a well-designed value threshold with built-in features, such as some local adjustment, can achieve equity objectives, be administratively efficient, and not unduly compromise revenues. South Africa grants a very low minimum-value threshold for residential properties but allows municipalities to decide individually whether to increase the threshold. In Cape Town, for example, which has a large tax base with many low-value and high-value residential properties, the value threshold is presently more than thirteen times higher than the statutory minimum. Furthermore, rural municipalities with many low-value properties may request that the minister responsible for local governments reduce the minimum threshold, although this has not happened in practice. On the other hand, the residential property value threshold in Egypt seems excessive and applies uniformly throughout the country irrespective of regional differences in the value of housing. A value-based threshold works considerably better than an exemption based on the size of the dwelling, the system in Pakistan, where more than 50 percent of dwellings are exempt (Nabi and Shaikh 2011).

Another way of granting relief is through the valuation of properties. In the United States, individual states have adopted preferential current-use valuations for farming property, whereas "highest and best use" is generally the value base for other types of property. South Africa has explicitly opted to use market value for all property use categories and to grant relief through lower tax rates for certain property use categories, such as bona fide farms. Either way, the effective tax rates are lowered for certain properties.

South Africa and some other countries allow for the possibility of a rebate on the amount of the tax. These rebates are often associated with municipality-specific hardship relief programs aimed at providing, on application only, tax reductions based on disability or income levels. Contrary to the spirit (and arguably also the letter) of this law, the City of Tshwane (Pretoria) until 2015 granted a 30 percent rebate to all residential property owners. In Morocco, residential taxpayers receive a 75 percent rebate on their primary residences as well as second homes, in effect achieving the same outcome as they would under a differential tax rate regime.

Tax relief also may be given through tax deferral schemes. This is a practical way to address the "asset rich, cash poor" dilemma. However, a tax deferral scheme where payment is made at the time of transfer or the death of the taxpayer requires administrative machinery to manage it properly. Also, if too many taxpayers qualify for the scheme, it may negatively affect the local authority's cash flow. South Africa's law vaguely allows for deferral "under exceptional circumstances" without specifying what these are. We have not encountered other African countries where deferral is an option.

In some countries, such as Kenya and South Africa, the property tax is a recurrent business expense that qualifies as an income tax deduction in the case of nonresidential properties. The cost of obtaining a formal valuation from an architect for property tax purposes is explicitly allowed as an income tax deduction in Liberia.

Rate capping and phase-in provisions are also used to provide tax relief. Rate capping (South Africa) is typically an oversight mechanism available to a higher level of government to ensure that a lower-level taxing authority acts responsibly, whereas phase-in provisions are usually encountered when new laws or reforms of existing laws are implemented and specified categories of owners or use need to be protected against their impact. Great Britain and Northern Ireland have used transitional relief schemes after revaluations.

The law in some countries (Botswana, Kenya, and Namibia) provides for discounts for early payment. As an administrative measure to improve cash flow, this is understandable, but as a policy measure to enhance voluntary compliance, it is suspect. It is unlikely that a discount of, say, 5 percent will entice noncompliant taxpayers to become compliant. It is more likely a form of tax relief to the extent that taxpayers make use of it.

When relief is granted through tax base exclusions and preferential valuations, it becomes difficult or even impossible to quantify forgone revenue. This reduces transparency and local accountability. Ideally, those who pay more because others are paying less are entitled to know why they are paying more, and how much. Tax relief should be granted only when the individual and collective relief can be quantified, that is, once the property is on the valuation or tax roll and is properly assessed. In this respect, the law in South Africa is a good model.

Last, tax relief can be granted through tax amnesties. As a general policy principle, tax amnesties should be avoided because they may weaken voluntary compliance unless they are coupled with a credible threat of harsh enforcement against future defaulters (Mikesell and Birskyte 2007).

There is an important administrative dimension in the provision of tax relief. The provisions of the law must be clear. For example, granting an exemption or rebate to "the elderly" or "pensioners" is simply too broad. Hardship relief should ideally be means tested. Taxpayers should prove their age and income. This generally happens under the hardship schemes in South Africa. In the Democratic Republic of the Congo, there is a rather intricate and detailed system of tax relief for the property tax on developed land. Individuals with a net annual taxable income below a prescribed amount are exempted from the property tax, as are widows and widowers over 55 years old for a building used as a main residence, on condition that they occupy their main residence either alone, with a dependent or dependents (as defined by law), or with any other person of similar age and in a similar situation, and that their net annual taxable income is below the prescribed amount determined with reference to the income tax dispensation. These conditions suggest that monitoring eligibility requires significant administrative effort.

In both Egypt and Madagascar, the law provides for tax relief for property damaged by specified natural disasters, such as flooding or drought, and, in Egypt, also for land no longer suitable for agriculture as a result of war. In Libya, relief is determined with reference to the size of buildings and the number of occupants (Amin 2010b).

Property Tax Administration

Most policy analysts look to revenue performance as the key to identifying a good property tax practice. It is correct that revenue yield is the most important consideration, but there is much more to the story, including equity and fairness, collection of a target revenue at reasonable cost, effects on the allocation of land use, rates of compliance, and coverage of the tax base. Reform of any of these dimensions of property tax performance requires an analysis of both structural and administrative components, and analysis of the administrative efficiency of the property tax can be complicated.

Adequacy of Resources

The resources available to local authorities are often inadequate to enable efficient performance of their statutory functions and responsibilities. Partly, the problem is that there is no pool of trained personnel to administer a property tax effectively, or if there is one, the government cannot afford the salaries. This problem is compounded by limited or poorly administered funding, which leads to understaffing, poorly qualified staff, outmoded equipment, and the lack of physical resources necessary to carry out the tasks of property tax administration.

Most Anglophone countries lack appropriate educational or vocational training programs for valuers. The absence of valuation skills is a major problem. As a result, statutory valuation cycles are often not adhered to, and general revaluations are frequently postponed. The outcome is valuation rolls that are outdated (Kenya, Sierra Leone, and Uganda have valuation rolls that are over 20 years old). This severely compromises the revenue buoyancy of the tax base and leads to increased horizontal and vertical inequity.

In countries where the property tax is a local-government responsibility, the local officials responsible for tax collection are often inadequately skilled to perform this important task. Furthermore, local-government officials are sometimes unfamiliar with the detailed provisions of the laws they are supposed to administer, especially where these provisions are contained in different laws (South Africa and Tanzania). Poorly trained and unmotivated municipal staff and underdeveloped monitoring systems diminish the effectiveness of base expansion and collections and also open the door to corruption. Although national revenue agencies may have the necessary skills and may provide training opportunities, local officials may have limited resources and few opportunities to attend training courses.

Efficiency of Property Tax Administration

A method has been developed to link the important policy and administrative dimensions of the property tax to revenue outcomes (Bahl and Linn 1992; Bahl and Martinez-Vazquez 2008; Kelly 2000, 2014). This method links five crucial factors:

- The *coverage ratio* of the tax base, which has two components: the percentage of properties that are on the roll and are valued, and the percentage of assessed value that is taxable.

- The *valuation ratio*, which is the percentage of the legal property tax base of taxable properties that is assessed.

- The *collection ratio*, which is the percentage of the tax liability that is actually collected.

- The legal or statutory rate.

- The size of the legal tax base before statutory exemptions and preferential treatments.

The definition and coverage of the tax base and the determination of the tax rate are policy decisions. However, the coverage, valuation, and collection ratios are measures of administrative efficiency and can be influenced significantly by the effort and skill of the tax administration.[15] The example in box 2.1 demonstrates the application of the relevant ratios.

Identification and Ownership: Fiscal Cadastres

The fiscal cadastre is far from complete in most low- and middle-income countries. For example, it is reported that one of every four properties in Peru is not listed in the real estate cadastre, and, surprisingly, fewer than 40 percent of the excluded properties are slums. In Delhi, only 38 percent of all properties in the largest urban areas are on the tax register (Mathur, Thakur, and Rajadhyasksha 2009). In Chile, half of recent new building is not included.

Ideally, all properties should be recorded in the valuation roll, even if not all properties are valued. In essence, this is what the law requires in South Africa. Most countries in Africa fall far short of this standard, and coverage is often meager. For example, in Nairobi, Kenya, only about

---

Box 2.1 ADMINISTRATIVE EFFICIENCY

Consider the following scenario: For a variety of reasons, only 75 percent of the taxable land parcels in a jurisdiction have been identified and are included on the tax rolls. Moreover, the valuations are several years old, so properties are valued at only 60 percent of their current market value. The tax administration is collecting only 45 percent of the tax liabilities due. The calculation of the current administrative efficiency is as follows: administrative efficiency (AE) = coverage ratio (=0.75) × valuation ratio (=0.6) × collection ratio (=0.45). The index of administrative efficiency is 0.20.

If the administration is improved slightly, as shown in scenario 1 in the table below, the administrative efficiency increases to 0.33. If further improvements in administration occur, as shown in scenario 2, the level of administrative efficiency shows an increase of 259 percent.

Administrative Ratios	Current Performance	Scenario 1	Scenario 2
Coverage ratio	0.75	0.85	0.95
Valuation ratio	0.60	0.70	0.90
Collection ratio	0.45	0.55	0.85
Efficiency level	0.20	0.33	0.73
Increase in efficiency level		0.62	2.59

125,000 properties out of an estimated 400,000 are presently on the valuation roll, which was last updated in 1982. Only about 7 percent of properties are registered in Maputo, Mozambique; and in Addis Ababa, Ethiopia, 45 percent of all structures are not on the roll. Only 6 percent of identified plots are titled in Cameroon.

The objective of any property valuation roll should be that all property parcels are identified and given a unique reference number, the full inventory of properties is known, and the taxpayer is determined. An existing property tax roll will have much of this information, but current accuracy may be a problem. Identifying each parcel and its boundaries is the starting point in extending the coverage of the property tax.

The lifeblood of the ad valorem property tax is an active, formal, and transparent property market (Dale, Mahoney, and McLaren 2010). Information about rental or sales transactions is fundamental in determining assessments and in defending assessed values before tribunals and courts. The property market is the vehicle through which arm's-length transactions are usually negotiated. What are transacted are interests in land, whether they be licenses, leases, or freehold interests. Once the weight of the law recognizes and supports private rights, this security of tenure provides a key component of an effective land market. Even in a mature and efficient market, other factors, such as excessively high transfer taxes, can affect the quality and reliability of the data. Therefore, value-based property taxes require an active, transparent, secure, reliable market within which property interests can be traded and financed through the banking sector (Adair et al. 2006). Part of this process involves establishing a legal environment to ensure the proper recording of transfers, rentals, and sales.

Registration of titles or deeds and the availability of fiscal and legal cadastres support the effective administration of a mature property tax system. Further development of these will instill confidence in the ownership, occupation, and other limited rights pertaining to land and buildings and thus provide increased tenure security. More secure tenure rights and the recording and publicizing of transactional data should result in improved levels of transparency in property markets. This can increase access to and reduce costs of mortgage finance and have an overall positive impact on market values.

The lack of comprehensive registration of property interests or the absence of a fiscal cadastre is a constraint on the administration of property taxation in Kenya, Liberia, Tanzania, and Uganda, among other countries. Property registration exists in each of these countries, but the systems require major technological improvements. In Kenya, for example, only properties that are registered are liable to the property tax. This leads to situations where owners seek to avoid payment by not registering property. Clearly, registration of all property is the ultimate goal for many countries, but for the officials who administer the property tax, it should not matter whether the property is registered. If the property exists, it can be valued and taxed. The deficiencies in ensuring that all transactions are recorded with appropriate title issuances affect the potential coverage of the property tax. Both Mauritius and Zambia are presently implementing programs for modernization of their property registers.

In most countries, large numbers of properties are not included in the current valuation rolls. This is a huge problem in cities such as Monrovia (Liberia), Nairobi (Kenya), and, until about 2011–2012, also in the three municipalities in Dar es Salaam (Tanzania). The major problems are unclear ownership details (Liberia and Sierra Leone) and unclear demarcation of property boundaries (Liberia and Malawi). These factors negatively affect the coverage of the tax base and ultimately limit the revenue from the tax.

Another major constraint on coverage is that the property tax is normally levied only or mostly on freehold private land (Botswana, Mauritius, Namibia, and Rwanda) or state land that has been leased (Lesotho and Zambia). State-owned land and customary land are typically not taxed, although a land rent or ground rent is levied and collected in some countries (Botswana, Ghana, Lesotho, Mozambique, Sierra Leone, Tanzania, Zambia, and Zimbabwe). But in some cases, state-owned land may have significant development potential. A good example is the peri-urban areas in Botswana, Lesotho, and Sierra Leone, where the land is communal, but extensive development has taken place. In these cases, there does not appear to be any significant difference between taxable urban areas and nontaxable peri-urban areas; both exhibit similar levels of development and similar access to public services and utilities. South Africa is the only country that requires comprehensive coverage for property tax purposes, although extension of the property tax into communal areas continues to be a major challenge.

Land and property administration issues have taken on more importance in Lusophone Africa. Reforms of the land registration process are under way in Cabo Verde to provide a more efficient system that can respond to the requirements of international investors (Ramos, Varela, and Schofield 2016). In Mozambique, all land is owned by the state but may be held under 50-year leasehold interests.

In most countries of North and Northeast Africa, transparency of ownership rights is an issue. In Egypt, a parcel-based deeds registry project was begun in 2008 in an attempt to increase the number of registered properties. In 2008, only 5 percent of Cairo's three million properties was registered (Amin 2010a). In Eritrea, Ethiopia, and Sudan, traditionally held land and state land predominate, and private land is rented from the state. Land titling or registration programs are planned or under way in various countries in the region, including Djibouti, Somalia, South Sudan, and Sudan.

The use of self-declaration to broaden the tax base is widespread in Francophone countries. Self-declaration primarily focuses on requiring taxpayers to submit information on the properties they own or occupy. Declaration is mandatory and must be completed within prescribed time limits. Failure to do so will result, at least in theory, in a fine. In some countries, such as Madagascar and Rwanda, declarations are due annually. In Rwanda, weak local-government monitoring of self-declarations led to the transfer of administration to the national revenue authority.

Valuation

Most countries in Africa have value-based property tax systems that call for individual valuation of each property. In most instances, only valuers who are appropriately qualified and registered may perform these valuations.[16] When a country has a large number of properties to be valued but an inadequate number of valuers to do the job, the efficiency and revenue yield of the property tax are impaired. Some countries make the problem even worse by legislating a complicated property tax, as in Botswana and Namibia, where land and buildings must be valued separately. Almost inevitably the result is outdated valuation rolls and inequitable treatment of taxpayers. In such cases, it is easy for taxpayers to lose confidence in the system.

The following discussion highlights six issues that shape the valuation environment in African countries:

- The mismatch between the number of qualified valuers available and the number needed to keep the valuation roll up to date.

- The level of government that should be institutionally responsible for the valuation task.

- The frequency with which revaluations should be performed.

- Establishment of a credible objection and appeal system.

- Quality control and oversight.

- Education, training, and certification of valuers.

The Shortage of Qualified Valuers

In most Anglophone countries, only appropriately qualified and registered valuers may perform valuations for property tax purposes.[17] Although the principle of allowing only qualified valuers to undertake this task is sound, conforming to the law in practice poses great difficulties in some countries. There simply are not enough qualified valuers to perform this task in most countries where the law requires these high professional standards (Franzsen and McCluskey 2005; Mutema 2016). The data in table 2.4 underline the severity of the problem in both the public and private sectors. The shortage of valuers greatly limits the success of value-based property tax systems. In Uganda, the lack of qualified valuers means that for some

Table 2.4 Registered Valuers in Anglophone African Countries

Country	Date	Population in Millions (2016 Estimate)	Total Number of In-Country Valuers
Botswana	2005	2.2	<70
The Gambia	2014	2.0	Very few[1]
Ghana	2014	26.9	325[2]
Kenya	2005	46.8	<500
Lesotho	2005	2.0	<10
Liberia	2008	4.3	84
Malawi	2005	18.6	<25
Namibia	2005	2.4	<15
Nigeria	2005	186.0	<1,500
Sierra Leone	2016	6.0	Very few[3]
South Africa	2016	54.3	<1,400[4]
Swaziland	2005	1.5	<10
Tanzania	2016	52.5	<300[5]
Uganda	2016	38.3	<70
Zambia	2005	15.5	<50
Zimbabwe	2016	14.6	<150

Sources: CIA (2016); Franzsen and McCluskey (2005); Jibao (chapter 14); Mutema (2016); Viruly and Hopkins (2014).

Note: Mauritius is omitted from this table because no data are available on valuers there.

[1] There are three experienced but not yet qualified valuers within the relevant ministry and a few private firms operating in The Gambia.

[2] See the discussion of Ghana in chapter 14.

[3] There are very few qualified valuers, with one in each smaller town and only valuation technicians in Freetown, Sierra Leone.

[4] Only valuers allowed to undertake municipal property tax valuations were considered; candidate valuers were excluded.

[5] There are 74 fellows and 217 associated members in Tanzania (Mutema 2016).

local authorities, valuation rolls have not been completed and the property tax cannot be used; for other local authorities, valuation rolls are 50 years out of date. Ghana, Kenya, Tanzania, and Zambia also suffer from outdated valuation rolls.

Some countries try to get around this constraint by not explicitly specifying the qualifications. The relevant laws in Namibia state that a suitable person may be appointed as a valuer "by reason of his or her expertise in the field of real estate valuation." Lawyers, accountants, engineers, and quantity surveyors undertake valuations of real estate, although for property and land tax purposes, the practice is to appoint only qualified valuers. In Liberia, a member of the Liberia Chamber of Architects must undertake property tax valuations for commercial properties.

Although there appear to be enough qualified valuers in Kenya (more than 400), Tanzania (a country with a larger area) has fewer than 150 qualified valuers. Uganda, with a population over 38 million, has fewer than 70 valuers in the whole country and therefore simply cannot maintain the annual rental value system currently in place (Franzsen 2010). Government valuers also have other tasks apart from valuations for tax purposes, and many valuers in private practice are not involved or interested in doing valuations for property tax purposes. Technologies such as geographic information systems (GISs) can improve the administration of the property tax, but the capacity to develop and use these technologies may not exist in some countries.

The problem can be further illustrated by the data in table 2.5, which show, for four local-government authorities in Tanzania (including the three municipalities in Dar es Salaam), the number of in-house valuers and the number of taxable properties. It is no wonder that revaluations have been a problem for local-government authorities in Tanzania. The result is that valuation is normally contracted out to the private sector at a significant cost. This raises the question that we will frequently ask: What

Table 2.5 In-House Valuers and Tax Base Coverage

Local-Government Authorities	Number of In-House Valuers	Properties on Valuation Roll	Potential Number of Properties	Current Coverage (%)
Arusha City Council	7	7,000	>70,000	10
Kinondoni Municipality	6	154,000	300,000	53
Ilala Municipality	5	158,000	200,000	79
Temeke Municipality	9	160,000	200,000	80

can be done about the property tax in the absence of suitably qualified and affordable valuers or other professional assessors?

Responsibility for Valuation

Valuations need not be done by local governments alone. There are several options:

- A national-government ministry, such as the ministry responsible for lands (Kenya, Zambia) or the ministry of local government (Botswana).

- An autonomous government agency or corporation, such as BC Assessment (British Columbia, Canada), the Municipal Property Assessment Corporation (Ontario, Canada), Quotable Value New Zealand (New Zealand), or the Codazzi Institute (Colombia).

- Local authorities (Kenya, Namibia, South Africa, and Tanzania).

- A valuation committee (Egypt, Madagascar, and Sierra Leone).

- The private sector (Botswana, South Africa, and Swaziland).

- A combination of national or local government and the private sector (South Africa and Uganda).

- Self-assessment (Liberia and Rwanda).

In theory, each of these options has significant advantages and disadvantages. In practice, different countries have had different experiences with centralization or decentralization of the valuation authority. Centralizing the valuation responsibility within a national-government ministry or a semiautonomous government agency may result in economies of scale and a uniform approach across different taxing jurisdictions. This is the case in Ghana and probably would have been a more practical approach in Sierra Leone than the decentralized system that was implemented in 2004. However, centralized valuation approaches have caused problems in Kenya and Lesotho because of the inability of the central government to provide timely revaluations. Maseru, the capital city of Lesotho, appointed an in-house valuer in 2001 because the central-government ministry did not view municipal valuation as a priority (Franzsen 2003). Nairobi, Kenya, had the same complaints and also appointed its own in-house valuers. In Namibia, the Directorate of Valuation in the Ministry of Land Reform undertakes valuations for the land tax on commercial farms, although the law also allows for the appointment of a private-sector valuer. For the land tax, with a relatively small tax base of about 12,500 properties, the centralized approach has been working well.

Table 2.6 Valuation Responsibility in Selected Countries

Valuation Responsibility	Countries
Commissions or committees	Cabo Verde, Côte d'Ivoire, Egypt, São Tomé and Príncipe, Sierra Leone
Central-government valuers	Kenya, Lesotho, Malawi, Mauritius, Namibia, Uganda, Zambia
Municipal valuers	Kenya, Lesotho, Namibia, South Africa, Tanzania, Uganda, Zambia
Private sector	Botswana, The Gambia, Ghana, Malawi, Swaziland, South Africa, Tanzania
Self-assessment	Cabo Verde, Liberia, Rwanda
Central administrative office (such as a tax office)	Benin, Burundi, Equatorial Guinea, Ghana
Municipal assessment	Mozambique

The responsibility for performing the valuation task in selected African countries is summarized in table 2.6. In Botswana, Malawi, Namibia, and Swaziland, the responsibility for managing valuation rests with local governments, although central-government valuers have been used in Botswana in the past. In Zambia, the central government's valuation department generally undertakes valuations. However, in some cities, such as Lusaka and Kitwe, in-house valuers who operate under the guidance or supervision of the central-government valuers are also used. The Central Valuation Department within the Ministry of Finance and Economic Development undertakes valuations for both the national residential property tax and the general rates in Mauritius. In Ghana, the Land Valuation Board is responsible for the valuation of properties throughout the country. However, as in Zambia, the law allows for the participation of private-sector valuers who operate under the supervision of public-sector valuers. Private valuers appointed by local authorities also operate under the supervision of government valuers in Malawi, and local authorities in Swaziland appoint a private-sector valuer from a panel of eligible candidates determined by the responsible minister.

The valuation rolls in many African countries are outdated, and base coverage is poor, even in some of the capital cities (Maseru, Lesotho; Lilongwe, Malawi). However, coverage is reportedly good in Windhoek (Namibia) and Mbabane (Swaziland). In Mozambique, municipalities undertake the assessment function, but coverage is a problem because many of the leasehold properties are not registered and therefore are not included on the valuation rolls. Despite the shortage of valuers, the laws in several countries (Botswana, Lesotho, Malawi, Namibia, Swaziland, and Zimba-bwe) still dictate that values for land and improvements must be recorded separately. This is time consuming for valuers, implies at least two values that could be contested under the objection and appeal process, and fur-ther strains scarce resources. Clearly, this methodology is unsustainable in most or all these countries.

In some cities or countries, there are pressures to move toward priva-tizing property assessments (Botswana, South Africa, and Swaziland), whereas others are moving toward appointing in-house municipal valuers (Nairobi, Kenya; Maseru, Lesotho). Some of the larger municipal councils in Namibia (Windhoek) and South Africa (all eight metropolitan munici-palities) also have in-house departments responsible for valuations, whereas smaller councils make use of private-sector valuers (Franzsen 2003). One of the advantages of in-house valuation departments is the assess-ment expertise that these departments build up over time. However, it can be argued that municipalities should preferably not be seen to be too in-volved in the valuation and assessment process. Valuation and taxation should ideally be kept separate. Furthermore, valuations should not be manipulated or corrupted to attain equity. Equity is best attained through proper property categorization, adjustments to tax rates, or the use of tax rebates.

The central-government tax authority or directorate is responsible for the valuation of property in Francophone countries, for example, in Equatorial Guinea. Often this assessment of taxable value is undertaken with significant input from taxpayers who are required to provide annual data on changes to property. In Rwanda, property owners are now ex-pected to also declare the value of their properties.

In a few countries, such as Egypt and Sierra Leone, the law stipulates that a committee must determine values. If such a committee is made up of persons with knowledge of the local land market, this could give cred-ible results and also enhance taxpayer acceptance. In the highly centralized environment in Egypt, the committees in each governorate are chaired by an official from the Real Estate Tax Authority and include four mem-bers from the Ministry of Finance and the Ministry of Housing and two representatives of real estate owners nominated by the local popular coun-cil and selected by the governor.

Frequency of Valuations

Key to a value-based system is that all properties are valued with refer-ence to the same date of valuation, referred to as *tone of the valuation* in Anglophone countries, such as Kenya and Zambia. This promotes equity and a fair distribution of the tax burden. However, property values change over time and in different ways in different locations and for different property use categories. Although a fixed date of valuation seems a good strategy for equity, it leaves open the question of how often a blanket revaluation should take place.

Internationally, there are jurisdictions that revalue large numbers of properties annually, such as British Columbia (Canada), Hong Kong, Queensland (Australia), and Singapore. In these jurisdictions, valuation capacity and skills are not issues. In New South Wales (Australia), where the tax base is unimproved land value, a three-year valuation cycle applies, whereas Ontario (Canada) operates on a four-year cycle. At the other end of the spectrum for developed countries, properties in Germany were last revalued more than 60 years ago.

In various African Anglophone countries (Ghana, Liberia, Malawi, Swaziland, Tanzania, Uganda, and Zambia) the valuation roll for urban property is valid for five years, while Kenya's law provides for a ten-year cycle. Especially in fast-growing, dynamic cities, such as Mombasa and Nairobi, this period is probably too long. A ten-year revaluation cycle will almost certainly invite an assessment shock, and possibly even outrage, when the new valuation roll is announced. But undertaking a revaluation poses major challenges for Nairobi City County. Four valuers cannot value some 400,000 parcels in-house. The options are to use the valuation services of the private sector or the Ministry of Lands and Physical Planning. A further possibility is self-assessment. The 2014 amendments to South Africa's property tax legislation (which applies to urban and rural property) provides for a five-year cycle for local municipalities that may be extended for a further two years, a maximum of seven years. For metropolitan municipalities, the maximum period of any cycle is five years. The Zimbabwean law states a minimum period of three years and a maximum of ten years; in Lesotho, the law states that a three-year period may be extended for a further three years.

In Kenya, Lesotho, South Africa, and Zambia, the life of the general valuation roll may be extended. This is an important feature to ensure that the valuation roll does not lapse at the end of the statutory period, and that further reliance on it does not become unlawful. The legal status of the roll can be a problem when the revaluation frequency is included in the law. Arguments can be made that if the valuation roll is not updated in accordance with the law, the current roll may be unlawful.

In many Francophone and Lusophone countries, valuations supposedly occur annually. The law in essence dictates that property owners must annually declare their property holdings and the values of these properties, and then the tax authorities must audit these declarations and levy the relevant property taxes on undeveloped or developed land accordingly. This does not necessarily happen in practice (Monkam 2010). The process usually amounts to an annual declaration of property holdings, in most instances only when any change has occurred. Whether the central-government agency follows up on any changes or nondeclaration is unclear.

INTERIM OR SUPPLEMENTARY VALUATIONS

Even when general revaluations are conducted regularly, it is important that interim or supplementary valuations be undertaken so that changes to properties on the main valuation roll are recorded and values are adjusted accordingly. Typically, these valuations aim to capture properties that

- have been incorrectly omitted from the main valuation roll;

- have been included in the taxing jurisdiction since the last general valuation (e.g., when municipal boundaries have been extended);

- have been consolidated or subdivided since the last general valuation;

- have substantially increased or decreased in value; or

- were incorrectly valued in the last general valuation.

In jurisdictions with limited capacity, this is a very useful way to capture at least high-value new construction, such as shopping malls and office buildings. The City of Kitwe in Zambia has been using interim valuation quite effectively to increase the value of properties on the valuation roll. The impact on the city's property tax revenue has been noticeable.

DEALING WITH PRESSURES TO REVALUE MORE FREQUENTLY

Revaluations are often postponed beyond their legal lives, as has happened in Mombasa and Nairobi (Kenya), Maseru (Lesotho), and Mbarara (Uganda). Sometimes the solution is simply not to have a revaluation (The Gambia). However, three other solutions are possible and have been used to some extent by one or more African countries:

- Self-declaration and assessment of values.

- Private-sector valuation services.

- Indexing of values between general revaluations.

Some countries opt for self-declaration of property values (see box 2.2). Each taxpayer must periodically declare the value of the property to the tax administration (Burundi, Cabo Verde, Cameroon, Liberia, and Rwanda). This approach reduces objections and appeals by taxpayers

Box 2.2 Self-Declaration

There are three forms of self-declaration: a declaration of property ownership along with some basic data about the property; a declaration of the value of the property; or a combination of the first two. To the property tax purist, self-declaration may at first sight be unpalatable. Certainly, valuers would not be comfortable in an environment where the owner declares the valuation. Mostly, self-declaration attempts to address the scarcity of valuers. Data also are easily and cost-effectively gathered under a self-declaration system. Tax base coverage can be increased provided the law carries weight by ensuring that those who own property make a declaration.

Where the property tax is not based on value, a system of self-declaration makes perfect sense. Owners declare the properties they own along with specified parameters, such as location, use, size (of parcel and buildings), age, and condition. The tax administration can then base the assessment on these declarations. However, one could go one step further and allow taxpayers to determine their own assessment, as is done in several cities across India (Mathur, Thakur, and Rajadhyasksha 2009; M. G. Rao 2013; U. A. V. Rao 2008). Generally, legislation specifies when the declaration should be made and the penalties for late submissions. Such systems are used in Francophone (Rwanda) and Lusophone (Cabo Verde) countries.

Matters become more difficult when self-declaration is used in a value-based system, where the practice is less common. Self-declaration of property data is widely used in countries with mature value-based property tax systems and is not unheard of in low-income countries. Examples involve the request for updated information from owners at times of general revaluations, as happens in Kenya, Namibia, and South Africa. This option should not be discarded if the owners of commercial property can be required to have their declared values prepared by professional valuers or other recognized professional bodies, such as accountants. Book values are used in Niger for legal entities. Many high-value central business district properties are regularly valued for accounting purposes. The owner can treat the costs of valuation as a business expense for income tax purposes, as is the case in Liberia.

There are two ways in which the major problem, underdeclarations, can be addressed. First, the tax administration can audit the declared values and take action against any it feels are below the value standard (normally market value). Second, if a property is sold within a short time after declaration at a value, say, 20 percent higher than the self-assessment, back taxes must be paid before a clearance certificate can be issued to allow the sale to proceed (Franzsen and McCluskey 2016). If professional bodies are required to perform the valuations, they are obligated to prepare their valuations in an ethical manner and are normally governed by codes of ethics. However, the

> question remains whether the country has enough valuation capacity to make an audit of self-declaration a credible threat.
>
> In conclusion, self-declaration of value by owners has merit and should be considered by those countries or jurisdictions where revaluations have not been undertaken for several years, especially if they have relatively active property markets and an established property profession.

(Franzsen and McCluskey 2016), which can incur significant costs, especially in those countries where valuation tribunals deal with objections (Namibia and Uganda). Cabo Verde has developed self-declaration of value as the basis of the property tax. Because land registration is becoming more comprehensive, the authorities have good information on properties and are therefore better able to perform an audit. The disadvantage of self-declaration is the potential for underdeclaration (or sometimes overdeclaration) of property values. Also, in practice, good information about the market value of real estate is lacking. Liberia uses a somewhat refined version of this approach: taxpayers for all commercial properties are required to provide a valuation performed by a professional assessor (a member of the Chamber of Architects). In Rwanda, self-declaration of value is typically provided by a valuer acting on behalf of the taxpayer. However, self-declaration in Rwanda is not adequately policed, largely because of the lack of valuation skills within the local authorities. The valuations follow an overly detailed cost-based approach that comes with a high valuation fee.

Another strategy for dealing with revaluation is to outsource it to the private sector, as is done in Botswana, Kenya, Malawi, Namibia, South Africa, Tanzania, and Uganda. The advantage is that the valuation list can be prepared within a realistic time frame. The major disadvantage is the high cost of these expert services (The Gambia and Tanzania). Furthermore, this approach is possible only in countries where the private sector has sufficient capacity and skills to undertake the revaluation. Some African countries do not meet this test.

An additional problem with outsourcing is ensuring the quality of the end product. Countries that employ the private sector typically do not have any oversight or quality-assurance systems (South Africa and Tanzania). But it is essential that some form of government oversight be provided to ensure value for money (from the local government's perspective) and quality of valuations (from the taxpayers' perspective). Again, where will the country get the valuers with the skill to carry out the oversight responsibilities?

In Tanzania, private valuers were contracted to assist with the preparation of valuation rolls in Dar es Salaam and eight regional towns in 2000 and 2001. In many instances, the average cost per property of the valuation exercise was greater than the amount that could be raised from many of the low-value residential properties over the statutory five-year valuation cycle (McCluskey and Franzsen 2005). This was also the case when the new property tax system was implemented in some of the local municipalities in rural parts of South Africa between 2006 and 2011 (Franzsen and Welgemoed 2011).

A third possibility is indexing the values between general revaluations, as happens in Madagascar. The question is whether indexation of capital values, rather than regular revaluations, will alleviate the valuation problem. Under this option, the existing valuation list is indexed by an uplift factor. The rate of inflation or the retail price index might be used for the index, although neither of these is entirely suitable.

Although indexing will increase values of properties on the roll without physical inspections, these values will not accurately reflect physical improvements on properties, nor will they reflect changes in the relative value of properties since the last revaluation. This will lead to inequities and possibly to increasing dissatisfaction with the distribution of the burden. Indexation is not a technique to replace or even to assist with revaluation.

Objection and Appeal Processes

The property tax legislation should establish a formal objection and appeal process to allow property owners to challenge their valuations. International best practice (IAAO 2014) argues for a process that is quick, cheap, simple, stress free, rigorous, authoritative, and final. The following elements are important: (1) independence from those whose decisions are being reviewed; (2) timeliness and proportionality; (3) informal hearings to resolve the matter(s) in dispute; (4) comprehensive nontechnical information about the process; (5) nonadversarial hearings that are not too daunting or legalistic; (6) consistent and comprehensible decisions; and (7) good value to the taxpayer.

An objection and appeal process is an integral part of a value-based property tax system, but jurisdictions differ significantly in their approaches. Although there is some merit to the argument that the valuer who provided the original value should be compelled to deal with the objection, this is problematic because the valuer is essentially the judge in a dispute to which he is a party. This practice invites corruption and gives the appearance of being unfair. Still, it is less costly and may give the taxpayer an opportunity to provide more accurate data to the valuer. Some jurisdictions allow an informal query phase where the property owner and the valuer discuss the valuation, but in others, such as Malawi and South Africa, the valuer formally deals with all objections. An informal query phase can be quite helpful if the taxpayer has an issue with the tax rate rather than the property value or simply requires more information on the valuation process and methodology. Such a system leads to fewer formal objections and lower administration and compliance costs. If the taxpayer is dissatisfied with the valuer's explanation, he needs to lodge a formal objection. Another option is to allow for adjustments in the valuation roll, but to provide that if values are adjusted up or down by more than a specified percentage, these cases will automatically be reviewed by a valuation tribunal. In South Africa, any adjustment of more than 10 percent by the municipal valuer requires written reasons and is automatically reviewed by the Valuation Appeal Board. This process enhances the equity, transparency, and accountability of the system.

In many jurisdictions, objections are handled in a formal judicial process administered by a specified official or entity, often an appointed special tribunal. In Namibia, for example, a valuation court hears all objections for both the urban property tax and the land tax.[18] For the land tax levied on commercial famers, objections constituted 2.8 percent and 1.7 percent in 2002 and 2007, respectively. Out of a total of 342 objections lodged in 2002, 77 were withdrawn or canceled and corrections or verifications ordered for 24 properties. In 203 cases values were upheld by the valuation court. Values were changed in only 38 cases (29 reductions and 9 increases). In Cape Town, South Africa, objections and appeals have been reduced significantly because property owners have begun to accept and trust the computer-assisted mass appraisal (CAMA) approach the city embarked on in 2001. The regular, three-yearly revaluations also instill confidence in the system. Objections were reduced by 46 percent from 2006 to 2012, and appeals were reduced by 33 percent from 2009 to 2012 (Davies 2016). A valuation court or tribunal also deals with objections in Botswana, Kenya, Swaziland, Tanzania, Uganda, and Zambia, while a committee handles them in Ghana. The number of members varies from three (Swaziland and Uganda) and at least three (Kenya) to three to five (South Africa), four (Namibia), and even six to eight (Tanzania and Zambia). It is important, however, that at least one member be a qualified valuer, as is mandated in Kenya. In Uganda, a country with a shortage of valuers, the law pragmatically states that the additional members of the valuation court may be engineers or architects. This provision should be reviewed once there are enough qualified valuers to serve as members of this tribunal. In both South Africa and Uganda, the law also explicitly mentions gender representation on valuation tribunals. In Namibia, the land tax law allows for the appointment of two assessors on the basis of their expertise in agricultural matters.

A formal valuation tribunal that deals with all objections is costly, especially in countries where the tribunal may have as many as six or more members. Some countries (Namibia and Zambia) include ministry representatives. Given the judicial and technical tasks to be performed, this practice is questionable and should be reconsidered. Where the interests of ministries may be an issue, a better route may be for officials from these ministries to assist the tribunal as expert witnesses.

The law is often silent on the number of valuation tribunals that should be constituted. This can be important after a general revaluation that has resulted in many objections and appeals. If there is only one tribunal to deal with these matters, members could be sitting for several weeks, which would be unrealistic. In a geographically large jurisdiction, there could also be significant compliance costs for property owners who might need to travel long distances to attend hearings of the tribunal. This is an issue for the valuation court for the land tax in Namibia. To avoid constituting more than one court, the court could simply arrange to hold its sittings in different regions.

In countries where the property tax is a local tax, and even where an employee of the relevant council has undertaken the valuation, the council should also have the right to object to the value of any property or appeal it. This is the case in Kenya, Namibia, South Africa, Swaziland, Tanzania, and Zimbabwe. In Johannesburg, South Africa, the city council has objected to a significant number of property values as determined by the city's in-house valuation department.

In some Francophone countries, such as Cameroon, the Central African Republic, and Côte d'Ivoire, it is possible to appeal the tax rather than the value (as is the case in Anglophone countries) as assessed by the relevant central-government tax authority. The appeal is generally made to the tax department and thereafter to the minister.

To ensure that councils are not held for ransom by unscrupulous or opportunistic property owners, the laws of countries generally state that the property tax must be paid despite a pending objection or appeal (Namibia, South Africa, and Uganda). At least in South Africa, objections are dealt with expeditiously. Once the value is finalized in the objection or appeal process, the taxpayer is entitled to a refund if the value is reduced or is obligated to pay the additional tax if the value is increased. In Liberia and in Lagos, Nigeria, property owners are required to pay 50 percent of the tax before an appeal is heard.

In most countries, an objector can appeal the decision reached in the objection phase. Appeals may be adjudicated by a specially constituted valuation tribunal (South Africa) or the land tribunal (Lesotho). In those countries where a tribunal hears objections, appeals (usually only on a point of law) will be to the high court (Botswana, Ghana, Kenya, Namibia, Swaziland, Tanzania, Uganda, and Zambia).

Quality Control and Oversight

Few African countries presently control or even measure the quality of assessments. The South African law provides for some political oversight at the national level and since 2015 has provided limited political oversight at the provincial level. Ideally, this type of oversight, which can allow for studies of sales ratios and other statistical measures to determine the accuracy and consistency of valuations, should be done by an impartial entity with the required technical expertise. For example, an independent analysis might examine the rolls and apply some tests for equity to provide some measures of disparity in assessments within neighborhoods. Where market values of real estate sales are not accurately reported, as is usually the case in low-income countries, oversight becomes very difficult. This type of oversight exists in developed and mature property tax systems, such as those in Australia, Canada, New Zealand, and the United States (Franzsen and McCluskey 2000). We could not find evidence of comprehensive oversight being practiced in any African country, but Cape Town, South Africa, on its own accord, has its three-year valuation rolls audited by an impartial international expert team.

Valuation and Technology

Administration of the property tax lends itself to the application of modern information technology systems. The basic unit of analysis is parcels of land, which commonly number in the hundreds of thousands in a country. Several characteristics must be observed for each parcel, changes in these observed characteristics must be recorded annually, and a tax assessment and collection system must be part of this database. Storage and retrieval of data in real time, as well as reporting, are integral to the effective functioning of the administration. Geographic databases within geographic information systems (GISs) are becoming the norm in property tax administrations. Textual data displayed within a mapping environment are a powerful tool and are increasingly becoming the industry standard.

But there are transition costs, especially in African countries, where many systems are still manual. Information systems need to be designed, the quality of the raw data needs to be studied, staff must be trained to use the new system, maintenance arrangements need to be made, and the hardware and software need to be purchased. Some countries are ready for automation and can handle these transition costs, but others are not. Once these setup costs are borne, information technology can greatly simplify property tax administration. The number of properties typically involved and the amount of data required for each property render manual inventory collection and recording difficult. This is particularly true for valuation, billing, and collection.

Today, it is commonplace in most mature property tax assessment jurisdictions to use fully automated processes and procedures across the whole spectrum of property tax administration. Given the scale of the valuation task and the frequency of revaluations, automated approaches are essential. According to Kauko and d'Amato (2008), multiple regression analysis (MRA) is the orthodox approach to mass appraisal valuation. From an industry perspective, the CAMA model is required to meet the dual objectives of attaining acceptable industry-driven standards of predictive accuracy and facilitating explainability and defensibility of the assessed values. In box 2.3, we provide an example of a simple mass appraisal model.

In Africa, use of such automated valuation approaches is rare. The best examples are found in the valuation departments of the large metropolitan municipalities in South Africa, such as Cape Town and Durban. There has been some experimentation with mass appraisal in other countries (Cameroon, Egypt, Kenya, and Tanzania), but this has largely been restricted to academic research (Geho 2003; Mulaku and Kamau 2010). It is noteworthy that the property tax laws in South Africa and Uganda explicitly mention "mass valuation."

Educating and Training Valuers

Formal university education in real estate valuation is offered in only a few African countries (Kenya, Namibia, Nigeria, South Africa, Tanzania, and Zambia). This partly explains the shortage of skilled valuers. Research predominantly in Anglophone countries confirms this (Cloete 2009; Franzsen 2011). Mutema (2016) states that apart from South Africa and Nigeria, professional institutions are still in their infancy.[19] Even in those countries with active university programs, few of the graduates find employment in the public sector because of relatively low remuneration packages.

Clearly, for those countries with relatively robust valuer professions, there is an argument for having a value-based property tax. But for most countries where such training is not available, alternatives to value-based property taxation need to be sought. Because most countries lack proper academic and appropriate practical training programs for valuers generally and for those responsible for property tax valuations more specifically, statutory valuation cycles are often not adhered to, and general revaluations are frequently postponed. The outcome is valuation rolls that are often outdated (Ghana, Kenya, Uganda, and Zambia). The retention of properly

---

BOX 2.3 A MASS APPRAISAL APPROACH TO ESTIMATION OF MARKET VALUES

In this example, market value is estimated using a mass appraisal technique, multiple regression analysis (MRA). This technique assumes that average or typical market pricing patterns and relationships can be estimated from samples of recently sold properties. These price patterns and relationships can then be used to estimate the market value of all other properties in the same property class or location that have not been sold. The technique consists of the following steps:

1. Gather market sales data for parcels that have recently sold (say, over the previous two years). Include sales price, date of sale, and parcel attributes, such as size, shape, slope, and road frontage. Verify that the sales are not between connected parties.

2. In the sample of recently sold parcels, estimate the relationship between parcel attributes and sales price using MRA.

3. Collect parcel attributes for all unsold land parcels.

4. Apply the specified MRA equation and estimated coefficients to unsold parcels to derive their estimated market value.

5. Review the market value estimates to address any spurious results provided by the regression model.

The typical equation might look like the following, where the coefficients are estimated by MRA for each of the parcel characteristics:

$$\text{Market value} = 575{,}027 \text{ (constant)} + 6{,}724 \text{ (parcel size)} + 123{,}472 \text{ (tar road frontage)} + 201{,}428 \text{ (regular shape)} - 186{,}235 \text{ (irregular shape)} - 98{,}255 \text{ (unsurfaced road frontage)}.$$

Thus, the estimated market value of a parcel with lot size 500m², a tar road frontage, and an irregular shape is given by the following equation:

$$\text{Market value} = 575{,}027 + 6{,}724(500) + 123{,}472(1) - 186{,}235(1) = 575{,}027 + 3{,}362{,}000 + 123{,}472 - 186{,}235 = 3{,}874{,}264, \text{ say, } 3{,}800{,}000.$$

---

qualified valuers within the civil service is a serious problem in Botswana (Monagen 2000), Kenya, Tanzania, and Zambia (Chirwa 2000).

Tax Rates

The determination of the property tax rate in a decentralized system depends on budgetary needs. Ideally, legislators decide the statutory rate every year at budget time. In practice, however, the tax rate involves not only the legal rate but also decisions about tax relief and assessment policy. What really matters is the effective tax rate, the tax paid as a percentage of the market value of the property, and politicians can influence this in many ways.

African countries decide their legal rates in many different ways, as can be illustrated by how they address the following five issues:

1. Which level of government should be responsible for determining tax rates?

2. How often should tax rates be determined?

3. Should there be only one tax rate for all properties, irrespective of use or location?

4. Should there be a progressive rate structure?

5. What should the tax rate be?

Responsibility for Determining Tax Rates

In many Francophone countries and some Lusophone and North African countries, the central government levies the property tax. This is the case in, for example, the Central African Republic, Côte d'Ivoire, Mali, Niger, and Egypt. Tax rates are therefore determined nationally.

In those countries where the property tax is a local tax (the revenue from this tax is local revenue), there are various permutations. In some countries, the tax rate is determined locally, but within nationally set limits. In The Gambia, the maximum rate set in the law is 5 percent of the assessed value, which is based on depreciated replacement cost, not market value, and therefore, the effective tax rate is much lower. The law in Uganda provides for a minimum amount of tax per property for all properties on the valuation roll and also for a maximum countrywide rate of 12 percent of the "rateable value." However, it is stated in the property tax statute rather than in a regulation, which implies a tedious process if the maximum rate needs to be amended. In Namibia, the urban property tax law provides for a maximum tax rate, but councils can exceed this maximum with prior written approval from the relevant minister. In some countries, such as Botswana and Zambia, the local authorities can determine their own annual tax rates, but the relevant minister must approve them before they become effective. South African municipalities annually determine their own tax rates without any formal approval requirement, as do those in Kenya, Namibia, Swaziland, and Zambia. However, the minister of finance in South Africa may cap the annual increase in the tax rate or the annual increase in revenue from the property tax. In other words, oversight is much less direct.

Frequency of Determining Tax Rates

A problem across Africa is the static nature of the property tax rate in many countries, especially where these rates are determined by the central government, which adversely affects revenue buoyancy.[20] This problem is further exacerbated where revaluation of properties does not occur regularly. Static property values and static tax rates in an inflationary environment with rising expenditures and needs create serious budgetary problems for local authorities. The problem is compounded when local governments have no flexibility to determine tax rates. In such a situation, local governments probably also do not face hard budget constraints, and the goals of a fiscal decentralization strategy will be compromised.

In Tanzania, tax rates can be set locally but are included in bylaws that can take years to be amended. Tax rates in The Gambia and Mozambique are contained in regulations that can take even longer than bylaws to be revised. In several Francophone countries, tax rates are set in the national tax codes. In all these cases, the tax rate cannot be decided at budget time. Ideally, local authorities need to be able to respond quickly, preferably annually, to budgetary needs by appropriately increasing or decreasing tax rates.

Uniform Versus Differential Rates

If the value of all properties is accurately determined, all other features, such as location and land use (and, indirectly, ability to pay), should be accounted for in the tax base. There is no need for differential rates. However, a single, uniform tax rate is seldom encountered. In keeping with a worldwide pattern, the laws in many countries in Africa allow for the use of differential or classified tax rates. The differentiation may be based on ownership (Niger), location (Democratic Republic of the Congo and Zimbabwe), tenure status (Botswana), land use (Namibia, South Africa, and Zambia), or a combination of two or more of these features. Tax rate structures in Africa are complicated.

In Niger, a primary distinction is ownership. Different rates and bases are applied to properties owned by individuals (annual values) and those owned by legal entities (book values). A secondary distinction in the tax on individuals is that between residential use and nonresidential use, with a higher tax rate on nonresidential use. In Johannesburg, South Africa, a hybrid system imposes different tax rates for different property use categories (including residential, commercial, or agricultural), different property ownership categories, and different status (vacant or developed). A specific tax rate is determined for vacant plots irrespective of their zoned use category, whereas another tax rate is set for state-owned properties irrespective of actual use. In Cape Town, on the other hand, use is the only criterion, and state-owned property is taxed on the basis of actual use, such as residential, commercial, or institutional.

Many jurisdictions, especially in Francophone countries, differentiate developed from undeveloped property. In most cases, this differentiation goes beyond the tax rate and manifests itself in separate taxes. Some countries differentiate land and buildings, usually imposing a lower tax rate on buildings (Liberia, Malawi, and Namibia).

The vast majority of jurisdictions differentiate on the basis of use and then between residential and nonresidential property. Often, there are further distinctions within the category of nonresidential use, most commonly among commercial, industrial, and agricultural use. In some countries (Rwanda) or jurisdictions (Livingstone, Zambia), hotels have a separate higher tax rate. In contrast, hotels in Egypt are exempted.

Lower tax rates for residential use than for nonresidential use are common (Botswana, The Gambia, Guinea, Namibia, Niger, South Africa, Swaziland, Tanzania, and Zambia). In South Africa, the tax rate for residential properties is a base rate, and the tax rates for other use categories are determined as a ratio of this rate. The law also allows the national government to prescribe ratios for certain use categories. For example, municipalities may not tax properties used for agricultural purposes (bona fide farms), public benefit organizations, and taxable infrastructure at rates that exceed 25 percent of the rate determined for residential properties. Last, in South Africa, a municipality may apply only a single tax rate to residential property; it may not have different residential tax rates in different parts of the municipality.

Interestingly, Nairobi City County has a uniform tax rate for all taxable properties irrespective of ownership, location, or use. In many countries with annual rental value systems, there is a single statutory tax rate (Egypt). However, the effective tax rate for different property use categories may differ because of the way in which "net rental value" is determined. In Egypt, the tax is imposed on the net rental value of the real estate, which is determined by deducting 30 percent of the gross rental value of residential property and 32 percent of the gross rental value of other property types to cover maintenance costs.

In area-based and unit-value systems, the tax rate is expressed as a specific amount per square meter or hectare (Burundi, the Comoros, Democratic Republic of the Congo, Eritrea, and Sudan). Differentiation, often in an attempt to approximate value, is achieved by introducing location and size factors, as is done in Asmara, Eritrea, and Khartoum, Sudan.

Proportional Versus Progressive Tax Rates

Equity is generally the justification for progressive rates. The idea is that those who own more expensive properties have a greater ability to pay. There are three problems with progressive rate structures. First, they are difficult to administer (Rosengard 1998). Second, they may induce tax avoidance. Regarding the council tax and the progressive stamp duty in Great Britain, Mirrlees et al. (2011, 485) argue that "its 'slab' structure—with big cliff-edges in tax payable at certain thresholds—creates perverse incentives. Replacing these two taxes on a revenue neutral basis with a simple tax proportional to up-to-date consumption values of properties" would constitute a much-needed step forward. Third, they are not necessary. Accurate and up-to-date values should reflect the quality and accessibility of infrastructure and local services, and a proportional tax rate should then produce a fair distribution of the tax burden. A progressive tax rate structure of a value-based tax at the local level adds a redistributional component to the tax that may or may not be appropriate. Often, redistribution is best achieved at the national or state level through progressive income taxation.

Only a few countries in Africa or elsewhere levy a property tax with a progressive tax rate structure. Morocco uses progressive rates for the residence tax, and Mauritius uses progressive rates for the general rate in Port Louis. Namibia's national land tax on commercial farms contains elements of progressivity because second farms and farms owned by foreigners are taxed at higher rates, but this tax was introduced specifically to aid land reform and land redistribution. Other attempts at inserting progressivity into the property tax structure are less obvious, such as classified valuation rates and thresholds.

Determination of the Tax Rate

Taxpayers and politicians often err in thinking about the important relationship between the tax base and tax rates. They tend to focus on the rate and more specifically on whether tax rates are too high or too low. In fact, however, the statutory property tax rate gives us very little information about the tax burden when it is taken out of context. We cannot learn anything from comparative legal tax rates, for example, whether Djibouti's 25 percent property tax rate is higher than that in Nairobi (17 percent), Cape Town (0.6931 percent), or Monrovia (0.08 percent). In Djibouti, the tax base is annual rental value; in Nairobi, it is land value; in Cape Town, it is market value; and in Monrovia, it is the value of buildings only. Moreover, in Djibouti, this tax rate applies to undeveloped land; in Nairobi, it applies to all taxable properties irrespective of status or use; and in Cape Town and Monrovia, it applies only to residential property. What is important is the effective rate, that is, the tax paid as a percentage of the market value of the property. Effective tax rates account for factors such as preferential or assessed values that are lower than actual (market) values, value thresholds, partial exemptions, rebates, and discounts.

On the question of the "right" tax rate, there are three considerations. The first is that the rate must be such that the cost of administration is covered. In some instances, rates are set so low that the cost of assessment and collection can, at best, barely be recouped, as was the case in Blouberg and Mutale local municipalities in South Africa (Franzsen and Welgemoed 2011) and Tabora, Tanzania (McCluskey and Franzsen 2005). The second is whether taxpayers get good value for what they pay, that is, whether the quality of public services justifies the tax rate charged. In theory, this should get sorted out in a decentralized system by voters, who decide how satisfied they are with the political leadership. In practice, it is often decided by local property taxpayers' rate of compliance. The third is affordability, which is rarely properly addressed. Property values can be increased at the time of revaluation, and tax rates can be adjusted, but usually, little is done to measure the real effect on individual taxpayers. Significant increases due to a general revaluation and the application of national (or local) tax rates need to be ameliorated through phase-in provisions (South Africa).

Sometimes, rate increases are the only option to deal with budgetary shortfalls, but this can be politically dangerous. In 2014, an attempt in Nairobi to double the tax rate from 17 percent to 34 percent led to an outcry from taxpayers and a successful challenge in the High Court. In Namibia, a general revaluation of commercial farms was undertaken in 2012 for purposes of the land tax, and value increases since 2007 ranged between 120 and 980 percent. There was no indication that the tax rates, static since the 2004/2005 fiscal year, were going to be reduced, and the rate of objections increased from 1.7 percent in 2007 to 21.1 percent. Even more telling were the grounds for objection, which were not limited to valuation matters, as dictated by law, but included "socioeconomic" and "legal" issues, such as the tax rate, affordability, and even the constitutionality of the tax.

The property tax laws in the Central African Republic, Madagascar, Malawi, and Uganda provide for a minimum tax. Whether this is enforced in practice in any of these countries is unclear. The idea of a minimum tax, so that all property owners make at least some contribution to the funding of local services, is appealing. In Tanzania, where flat rating is often used, the local authority normally prescribes a minimum payment in the range of TZS 10,000 to TZS 15,000. But putting this into effect may be difficult because (1) the administrative and compliance costs may be high; (2) the amount levied needs to cover at least the cost of billing and collection; and (3) the amount charged will have to be administered in parallel with a means-tested tax relief scheme to ensure that those who cannot afford the tax are excluded.

Billing, Collection, and Payment

Billing

Some African countries still use manual billing systems, such as door-to-door delivery of tax bills. For example, tax bills are delivered manually in Khartoum, Sudan; The Gambia; Cameroon; and to some extent in Dar es Salaam, Tanzania. However, is delivery of a tax bill necessary? In some countries, such as Rwanda, the onus is shifted to the taxpayer to find out what his tax liability is. The names of taxpayers and their annual tax liability are typically published in a list that is displayed at the local-authority office (and possibly ward offices), as well as other places where taxpayers regularly congregate, such as cinemas and sports stadiums. Another option is to require taxpayers to declare ownership and location of their properties and the size and value of their taxable properties and to calculate the tax they must pay on their properties. This shifts the role of the tax authorities to auditing but requires that they are prepared and staffed to perform this function.

In South Africa, many municipalities bill taxpayers monthly, either electronically or through the postal system. Some municipalities publish advertisements on the back of the tax bill; the advertisers pay for the billing process. Other municipalities use billing as an opportunity to communicate much more than tax liability. Brief newsletters may inform taxpayers about municipal projects and the annual budget, in short, how their tax monies are being spent.

National revenue authorities can play a meaningful role in developing capacity and can provide training to local authorities to improve communication with taxpayers, but this does not seem to happen very often in those countries where the property tax is a local tax and its administration is a local responsibility. In Tanzania, the Tanzania Revenue Authority's training institute has apparently provided some training for local tax officials. In Kampala, Uganda, officials from the Uganda Revenue Authority have been seconded to the Kampala Capital City Authority to assist with collection, a strategy that seems to have been quite successful.

Collection

In some Francophone and Lusophone countries, the property tax is a central-government tax, levied and collected by the national revenue collection agency (or the national tax office). However, the revenue collected is in some instances remitted to the subnational governments for local purposes.

In Uganda, the relevant law dictates that division councils (in urban areas) and subcounty councils (in rural areas) are responsible for collecting property taxes and remitting a statutory percentage to the higher-tier city or municipal councils (in urban areas) and district councils (in rural areas). However, the law does not provide for proper oversight and control at the higher tier of government.

In 2008, the minister of finance in Tanzania announced that the collection of property tax in Ilala, Kinondoni, and Temeke, the three municipalities of Dar es Salaam, was to be transferred to the national revenue collection agency, the Tanzania Revenue Authority (TRA). He apparently acted without prior consultation with the relevant authorities (Fjeldstad 2014). Despite expectations that this would result in significantly improved collection levels, there is no clear evidence that the TRA performed better than the municipalities. As Fjeldstad (2014) points out, "Technical constraints, reflected in poor preparation, outdated property registers and valuation rolls, and inadequate incentives created a large degree of distrust amongst officials and impeded inter-organisational cooperation." There were no positive incentives for the TRA to perform this function, and there was clearly resistance from some local officials who were unwilling to cooperate with the TRA and were keen to see it fail. The TRA collected the tax for six years (2008–2014), after which collection reverted to the three municipalities, again without prior consultation. This experiment seems to have been a failure, not because centralizing collection is always a bad idea, but because, as Fjeldstad (2014) states, the "top-down driven process, lack of consultations, different modes of operation and patterns of accountability acted as barriers to sound working relationships between the municipalities and the TRA." In July 2016, it was again decreed that the TRA would forthwith collect property tax on behalf of all local authorities throughout Tanzania. There are important lessons here for other countries, notably The Gambia and Rwanda, where property tax collection has also been transferred to their respective national revenue authorities. Some of the new county governments in Kenya are also considering outsourcing property tax collection to the Kenya Revenue Authority.

There are obstacles to consider when the national revenue authority is saddled with the responsibility for collecting the property tax on behalf of local governments. First, the property tax is very different in structure from most central-government taxes, and its administrative burden can be significant. The revenue authority needs to realize this and act accordingly. Second, the important national taxes (the personal income tax, the corporate tax, and the value-added tax) are likely to remain the central government's priority, especially if administrative resources are scarce. Unless the national agency is properly motivated (possibly through a specific collection fee or a percentage of the amount collected), it is unlikely that collection of the property tax will receive sufficient attention (the fee charged by the Gambian Revenue Authority is 2 percent of collections). Third, the national agency can perform only the tasks and use only the enforcement mechanisms allowed under the property tax laws, and these may be quite different from the mechanisms they are accustomed to. Fourth, national taxes are taxpayer focused, but the property tax is very much property focused and requires very different maintenance of property and taxpayer databases. Last, the national agency will need to cooperate closely with all relevant local authorities on data gathering and maintenance, as well as with other agencies or ministries responsible for property-related data. All these factors will be crucial to the success of the process (Fjeldstad 2014). An alternative solution could be for national revenue authorities to assist with the proper training and skills development of local tax administrators and tax collectors concerning processes such as data management, billing, enforcement, and auditing.

Some countries, such as Tanzania, Uganda, and Zambia, have also attempted outsourcing property tax collection to the private sector. In 2001, the Lusaka City Council experimented with outsourcing rates collection to a private contractor. The exercise was deemed a failure, and the council took back the responsibility for collection, but apparently valuable lessons were learned (Franzsen and McCluskey 2005). In Moshi, Tanzania, the council has outsourced the collection of various municipal taxes and fees, and high collection fees (up to 20 percent) are payable. In South Africa, some municipalities experimented with outsourcing collection of the regional services council levies (which were abolished in 2006). The former Kampala City Council outsourced property tax collection at a fee of 10 percent. However, the Kampala Capital City Authority established in 2011 set up a new Directorate for Revenue Collection that has been extremely successful, more than doubling collection of the property tax in only four years. Although collection costs have gone up ninefold, the additional costs were recovered in one financial year, a good investment (Kopanyi 2015).

The perception that somehow the private sector will be better at performing what is surely a core municipal responsibility is somewhat perverse. Why would a private collector be more successful at collecting tax if the data provided to that collector are suspect? If the data are comprehensive, why would you want to outsource? In many instances, it seems an abdication of responsibility. Not surprisingly, none of these privatization experiments seem to have been successful. In the absence of proper control and oversight, the risks of corrupt practices and extortion of taxpayers by private collectors are high. Outsourcing should at most be considered to collect long-outstanding arrears (Doherty 2016).

Collection rates (the amount collected as a percentage of the amount billed) in African countries are generally low, although rates for local authorities may differ widely. In Zambia, the collection rates in 2011 for Lusaka and Ndola were 49.8 percent and 63.5 percent, respectively, but for Kitwe and Chigola, they were 78.7 percent and 74.2 percent, respectively. In South Africa's metropolitan municipalities, collection levels exceed 90 percent. However, for all municipalities, on average, arrears are increasing at an alarming rate. Before recent reforms in Kampala, collection rates below 50 percent were reported. In Niger, collection rates for residential properties are reported to be between 15 and 20 percent.

Payment

Many African countries still require property taxpayers to make payments in cash at regional or local-government offices (Mozambique, Tanzania). In other countries, such as Liberia, taxpayers are expected to make payments at a specified commercial bank and then show the proof of payment to the local authority. The compliance cost of such procedures is unnecessarily high and may discourage payment.

To curb corrupt practices and minimize security risks, cash payments should be minimized or avoided altogether. In South Africa, there are various payment options: payment at municipal offices; payment at certain banks, the post office, or retail stores; electronic payment; or payment by debit order. In Namibia, payment can be made in cash or by credit or debit card at the offices of the local authority or at any post office, by clients of a commercial bank at automated teller machines of that bank, and over the counter or on the Internet at all commercial banks. In Cameroon, Kenya, and Tanzania, it is possible to use mobile phones to pay local taxes. This reduces compliance costs significantly and, according to local authorities in Kenya and Tanzania, has had a positive effect on compliance.

Enforcement

Strict enforcement of compliance is essential for a successful property tax. Although the laws in African countries generally provide for numerous enforcement mechanisms, sometimes contained in more than one law, as in South Africa and Tanzania, many of these are infrequently used.

Many countries require proof of property tax payment as a condition for transferring land, but this is a reactive measure that does not encourage tax collection. Tougher and more politically dangerous measures are used much less often.[21] Significant and increasing arrears are problems in, for example, Lesotho, Malawi, South Africa, and Zambia and in many of the county governments in Kenya. Few, if any, countries in Africa have been able to reduce the year-to-year level of arrears. Table 2.7 illustrates the property tax collection performance of the three Dar es Salaam municipal councils. Revenue collections are increasing, but the key concern is the level of accumulated arrears, which is significant in each council.

Selective enforcement is also an issue.[22] Although these practices may in some instances be understandable because of ease of administration, they are inequitable. In Niger, for example, collection rates for residential properties are significantly lower than for properties belonging to legal entities, partly because the tax authority focuses on high-value commercial properties rather than residential properties.

Administrative Enforcement Measures

Administrative enforcement measures include (1) interest on arrears; (2) penalties; (3) withholding municipal services, such as issuance of business licenses and building permits, planning permission, electricity, and water; (4) clearance certificates, which must be issued by the council before any transfer of property can be registered; and (5) publishing the names of defaulters.

Most countries provide for payment of interest on arrears (Botswana, Kenya, Namibia, and South Africa) and fines or penalties on arrears (Kenya, Liberia, Madagascar, and Namibia). Madagascar has a severe penalty regime, but whether it is strictly enforced in practice is unclear. The former city council in Nairobi, in an attempt to enhance compliance, waived the interest on an annual basis if payment of the tax was received

Table 2.7 Property Tax Revenue Statistics for Dar es Salaam's Three Municipal Councils, 2015–2016

Municipal Council	Estimated Revenue in TZS (Billions)	Collected TZS (Billions)	Arrears TZS (Billions)	Percentage Collected
Kinondoni	7.95	9.0	1.1	113
Ilala	12.0	8.1	3.9	68
Temeke	4.5	3.1	1.4	69

Source: Dar es Salaam municipalities.

by a specified date (six months after the due date for payment). This may act as a disincentive to pay promptly.

In some countries, withholding specific municipal services can be quite effective in forcing compliance. In South Africa, for example, where water and electricity are generally bought in bulk from national or regional service providers and then sold to consumers as a municipal service, cutting the electricity supply or reducing water pressure is an effective measure to enforce the payment of overdue property taxes. In most African countries where water and especially electricity are not municipal services, there are other services, such as the issuance of business licenses and building permits, that can be withheld until property tax arrears are settled. These measures, however, presuppose the necessary control mechanisms and interdepartmental cooperation, which are lacking in many African countries. Withholding some municipal services, such as water, may have constitutional ramifications in some countries and political consequences in most countries.

Clearance certificates are mentioned in the laws of a number of African countries (Botswana, Eritrea, Kenya, Lesotho, Namibia, South Africa, and Uganda; see the example in box 2.4). If they are properly administered, they can be a very useful mechanism to recover arrears. However, as case law in South Africa since 2010 indicates, a variety of legal challenges regarding debt recovery, prescription (statute of limitation), and constitutionality can undermine their unfettered use. In Kenya, where certificates have almost become the default way of recovering arrears, officials cite corrupt practices in obtaining clearance certificates.

Box 2.4 RESTRAINT ON TRANSFER OF PROPERTY IN SOUTH AFRICA

A registrar of deeds or other registration officer of immovable property may not register the transfer of property except on production to that registration officer of a prescribed certificate—

(a) issued by the municipality in which that property is situated; and

(b) which certifies that all amounts due in connection with that property for municipal service fees, surcharges on fees, property tax and other municipal taxes, levies and duties during the two years preceding the date of application for the certificate have been fully paid.

An amount due for municipal service fees, surcharges on fees, property tax and other municipal taxes, levies and duties is a charge upon the property in connection with which the amount is against the property.

Source: Local Government: Municipal Systems Act 32 of 2000.

Legal Enforcement Measures

Legal measures include (1) civil action (debt collection though the courts); (2) attachment of wages; (3) attachment of bank accounts; (4) attachment of rent; (5) taking action against occupiers, notably in cases where the whereabouts of the owner are not known; (6) a tax lien (also referred to as a "first charge" or "preferential claim") against the relevant property; (7) seizure and public sale of personal property (movable property); and (8) forfeiture of the defaulting property through seizure and eventual public sale.

Debt collection through the courts is costly, cumbersome, and adversarial, but it seems to be the most common enforcement mechanism despite the costs and risks, such as losing the case because of poor or inaccurate data. It is used in Liberia, Kenya, and Tanzania. In Kenya, high filing fees rule out action against taxpayers with relatively minor arrears.

Enforcing against employers and banks can be used very effectively to collect arrears. This is practicable only if administrative processes are sufficiently sophisticated, which is not currently the case in most African countries. However, as information and communication technology systems are improved over time, this could be a useful mechanism to claim arrears. Enforcing against tenants (Botswana, South Africa, Tanzania, and Uganda) or other occupiers (Tanzania and Uganda) is a further option for properties that are not owner occupied. Although this measure is included in the Tanzanian law, it is not presently used in Arusha. It is used in South Africa, but a tenant cannot be expected to pay more than an amount equal to outstanding rent.

In some countries (South Africa, Tanzania, and Uganda), arrears constitute an automatic first charge on property (a tax lien). Because this mechanism may involve other creditors, such as mortgagees, of the taxpayer, it is useful where the administrative capacity exists to enforce it.

Seizure of movable property for possible sale in execution is a measure included in the laws of Tanzania, Uganda, and many other countries. However, it requires a warrant and the services of the bailiff or sheriff (with concomitant costs) and also presupposes a storage facility where such goods can be kept safely and securely. In practice, this option is not used.

Sales in execution of immovable property are seldom used in practice, although the laws in many countries (Botswana, Congo, Kenya, Lesotho, Liberia, Malawi, Namibia, Sierra Leone, South Africa, Tanzania, Uganda, and Zambia) provide for this mechanism. Because it entails the loss of the taxpayer's property, strict rules and procedures must be followed, and there are actual costs involved apart from the political costs. The process can take several years. In many jurisdictions, it is viewed as politically and socioeconomically too risky. Political and senior managerial support is generally lacking, especially where politicians are often high-profile defaulters. In Liberia, the law states that the officer of the court must give notice to all persons concerned of the intention to sell the property at public auction and convey title to the purchaser. The proceeds from the sale are applied in the following manner: first, to the payment of taxes, penalties, and interest due; second, to the costs of the court; and last, the balance if any, to the owner of the real property. The delinquent owner of the real property may bid at the auction.

Concluding Comments

Revenue from the property tax in African countries is an insignificant percentage of GDP. There is considerable potential for improvement, but inappropriate policy choices, weak administration, and lax enforcement have hampered advancement of the property tax in most countries. To be sure, better property tax performance is a challenge in Africa. The countries are poor, many political systems are unstable, and human capital to administer modern tax systems is inadequate.

The specific constraints differ from country to country. The problems in Accra (limited tax base), Cairo (political will and valuation), Dar es Salaam (valuation and enforcement), Freetown (valuation), Johannesburg (billing system), Kampala (valuation), and Nairobi (valuation and collection) illustrate this point. Policy adjustments could be made in many, if not most, African countries, but the main reason for the lackluster performance of recurrent property taxation appears to be the poor quality of the tax administration—an alarming confirmation of the general views of Dillinger (1991) and Kelly (2000). Why has there seemingly been so little improvement over the past 20 to 30 years? What is clear is that solving the problems besetting the property tax goes well beyond narrow public finance policy advice. Politics, governance, culture, and the general economic setting are also involved. The economist Carl Shoup said nearly 40 years ago that "a recent tour of some twenty less developed countries over a three-year period as an advisor on tax policy with the United Nations made it clear to him that sociology and political science and perhaps some anthropology must be called on to explain why this great reservoir of finance for urban progress is, with few exceptions, being tapped at a rate far below what to most of the outside observes seems quite practicable and desirable" (1979, 272–273).

The following are some of the specific challenges that African countries face:

- Property data are deficient and unreliable because of the absence of an efficient land information system. The inability to maintain up-to-date maps and records makes revaluation very difficult.

- Base coverage is poor; many properties are not captured in the tax net. The resource shortfalls are commonly linked to the very poor coverage of the property tax base in urban areas, with large variations in coverage among these areas and, therefore, incomplete and inadequate valuation rolls.

- Maintaining valuation rolls is problematic, especially in secondary cities and towns. Although valuation rolls in Kampala and in Dar es Salaam's three municipalities have been significantly updated with World Bank support, the valuation rolls in Nairobi and Mombasa are more than 30 and 20 years old, respectively, and thus are hopelessly out of date (Franzsen 2013).

- The property tax rate is a determinant of the level of revenue to be raised and is thus a political decision. The valuation of taxable property is a technical decision that defines the base to be taxed (in value-based systems). The two decisions, rate setting and valuation, should be independent. In practice, they usually are not. Tax rates are often too low to generate meaningful revenues and need to be revised more regularly.

- Taxpayer morale seems to be low in many countries because most taxpayers lack trust in their local councils. A common concern of taxpayers is what they perceive to be nonexistent or poor-quality local services in return for property tax payments. This may be a vicious circle because the resources available to local-government authorities are generally inadequate to finance their statutory functions and responsibilities.

- Poor administration (billing, collection, enforcement, and auditing practices) is endemic across the continent. Enforcement mechanisms other than costly and cumbersome debt collection through the civil court system (Kenya and Tanzania) are virtually nonexistent.

- Property tax is a central-government tax collected by national revenue authorities in many African countries, and it often is not a priority. This is even the case in some countries where it is a local tax.

- Although lack of political will is often used as a blanket excuse for poor performance and a cover-up for poor administrative processes and practices, it remains a real problem. Moreover, there is political interference when local politicians avoid taxing themselves and their constituents, especially if alternative sources of funding, such as intergovernmental grants or donor funding, are readily available to fund infrastructure and local services.

Addressing these challenges and enhancing the revenue performance of the property tax require political commitment and adequate resources. These challenges and future prospects for the property tax in Africa are discussed in the final chapter (chapter 36).

Notes

1. For some early discussions of these problems, see Hicks and Hicks (1955), Bahl (1979), and Dillinger (1991).

2. These data are not strictly comparable with the IMF tables but should not be too far off the mark. This data set has the advantage of including many countries that are not in the IMF comparison.

3. Of the 34 member states of the OECD, 31 are high-income countries, where the per capita annual income exceeds USD 12,735 (World Bank 2016).

4. The World Bank grouping was used for this approach (World Bank 2016).

5. One might think of the property tax in these cases as an intergovernmental transfer rather than a local tax because the central government is solely responsible for determining the amount of revenue received. For a discussion of the rationale, see Bahl and Linn (1992).

6. Focusing on some of the constraints and challenges for successful fiscal decentralization, Smoke (2015, 97) concludes that "this type of reform is more diverse and complex than has conventionally been acknowledged and . . . more careful analysis and strategic action tailored to a specific country are needed to help to realize more effective and sustainable decentralization."

7. To the extent that the tax on land is capitalized into land values, it likely is borne by all owners of land. Since land ownership is concentrated in the higher-income brackets, the distribution of the tax burden will be progressive (Alm, Annez, and Modi 2004; Bahl 2004).

8. For a discussion of this issue in Pakistan, see Bahl, Cyan, and Wallace (2015).

9. Alternatively, only properties purchased after a fixed date would be subject to the new gains tax.

10. The exact scope of capital gains taxes and their application to real estate acquisitions were not included as part of the research brief for the research fellows.

11. Land value recapture instruments are most advanced in Latin America, where practitioners and policy analysts have developed several workable approaches. Some of the intellectual leadership for this work has come from the Lincoln Institute of Land Policy, and in particular, from Martim Smolka. For a thoughtful review of the practice, see Smolka (2013).

12. For example, Jordan gives up 40 percent of revenues through a standard deduction (Bahl 2012). About 10 percent of all urban properties in large urban areas in India are exempt (Mathur, Thakur, and Rajadhyaksha 2009). In Chile, more than two-thirds of properties registered in the fiscal cadastre are exempt (Irarrazaval 2004), and in São Paulo, Brazil, 40 percent of all properties are exempt (De Cesare, 2012).

13. This issue is contentious. In India, the government established a working group in 1996 to study the exemption of government properties and make recommendations. The state governments, which proposed taxation of government properties, and the central government, which opposed this, could not come to an agreement (Mathur, Thakur, and Rajadhyaksha 2009).

14. For a discussion of how such a system might work, see the proposal for Pakistan in Bahl, Cyan, and Wallace (2015).

15. For a demonstration of the revenue consequences of improved administrative efficiency, see the discussion of the Kampala Capital City Authority in chapter 29.

16. These qualifications are the same as those in industrialized countries.

17. In this regard, subsection 39(1)(a) of South Africa's Local Government: Municipal Property Rates Act 6 of 2004 states: "A municipal valuer . . . must be a person registered as a professional valuer or professional associated valuer in terms of the Property Valuers Profession Act, 2000 (Act No. 47 of 2000)."

18. In Namibia, all settlements and withdrawals of objections before the valuation court sits will still be reviewed by the court.

19. The professional institutions in Kenya and Tanzania are active in setting and enforcing professional standards.

20. Revenue buoyancy is the percentage increase in revenues generated by a 1 percent increase in GDP and all discretionary changes that have taken place.

21. In some countries, especially in Anglophone Africa, the property tax is commonly levied under the terms of a law specific to the property tax (Botswana, The Gambia, Kenya, Lesotho, South Africa, Swaziland, Tanzania, and Uganda) or a more general local-government law (Namibia and Sierra Leone). This implies that only the enforcement mechanisms contained in these acts can be used unless other mechanisms in other laws have been incorporated by reference.

22. In 1998, the South African Constitutional Court found a selective enforcement practice under which only wealthy residential taxpayers in Pretoria were targeted to be unconstitutional because it infringed the right to equality before the law.

References

Adair, A., S. Allen, J. Berry, and S. McGreal. 2006. "Central and Eastern European Property Investment Markets: Issues of Data and Transparency." *Journal of Property Investment and Finance* 24(3): 211–220.

Alm, J., P. Annez, and A. Modi. 2004. "Stamp Duties in Indian States: A Case for Reform." World Bank Policy Research working paper 3413. Washington, DC: World Bank.

Amin, K. 2010a. "Property Tax System in Egypt." Paper presented at the Fellowship Workshop of the African Tax Institute/Lincoln Institute of Land Policy Project on Property Taxation in Africa, Stellenbosch, South Africa (December 4–5).

———. 2010b. "Property Tax System in Libya." Paper presented at the Fellowship Workshop of the African Tax Institute/Lincoln Institute of Land Policy Project on Property Taxation in Africa, Stellenbosch, South Africa (December 4–5).

Bahl, R. W., ed. 1979. *The Taxation of Urban Property in Less Developed Countries.* Madison: University of Wisconsin Press.

———. 2004. "Property Transfer Tax and Stamp Duty." ISP working paper 04-27. Atlanta: Andrew Young School of Policy Studies, Georgia State University.

———. 2008. "Opportunities and Risks of Fiscal Decentralization: A Developing Country Perspective." In *Fiscal Decentralization and Land Policies*, ed. G. K. Ingram and Y.-H. Hong, 19–37. Cambridge, MA: Lincoln Institute of Land Policy.

———. 2009. "Property Tax Reform in Developing and Transition Countries." Working paper. Washington, DC: USAID.

———. 2012. "Jordan: The Taxation of Real Property." Report submitted to USAID/ Jordan Fiscal Reform Project II (September 22, 2010).

———. 2014. "A Retrospective on Taxation in Developing Countries: Will the Weakest Link Be Strengthened?" In *Taxation and Economic Development: The Weakest Link? Essays in Honor of Roy Bahl*, ed. R. M. Bird and J. Martinez-Vazquez, 405–433. Cheltenham, UK: Edward Elgar.

Bahl, R. W., and R. M. Bird. Forthcoming. *Fiscal Decentralization in Developing Countries*. Cheltenham, UK: Edward Elgar.

Bahl, R. W., M. Cyan, and S. Wallace, S. 2015. "The Potential of Provincial Taxation." In *The Role of Taxation in Pakistan's Economic Revival*, ed. J. Martinez-Vazquez and M. Cyan, chapter 8. Oxford: Oxford University Press.

Bahl, R. W., and H. Garzon. 2010. "Panama Property Tax Report." Report prepared for the World Bank Latin America Department (June 2010).

Bahl, R. W., and J. F. Linn. 1992. *Urban Public Finance in Developing Countries*. New York: Oxford University Press.

Bahl, R. W., and J. Martinez-Vazquez. 2008. "The Property Tax in Developing Countries: Current Practice and Prospects." In *Making the Property Tax Work: Experiences in Developing and Transitional Countries*, ed. R. W. Bahl, J. Martinez-Vazquez, and J. M. Youngman, 35–57. Cambridge, MA: Lincoln Institute of Land Policy.

Bahl, R. W., and S. Wallace. 2005. "Public Financing in Developing and Transition countries." *Public Budgeting and Finance*, silver anniversary issue, 3–98.

———. 2010. "A New Paradigm for Property Taxation in Developing Countries." In *Challenging the Conventional Wisdom on the Property Tax*, ed. R. Bahl, J. Martinez-Vazquez, and J. Youngman, 165–201. Cambridge, MA: Lincoln Institute of Land Policy.

Bird, R. M., and E. Slack, eds. 2004. *International Handbook of Land and Property Taxation*. Cheltenham, UK: Edward Elgar.

Blöchliger, H., and J. Kim, eds. 2016. "Fiscal Federalism 2016: Making Decentralization Work." Organisation for European Co-operation and Development and Korea Institute of Public Finance. Paris: OECD Publishing.

Casanegra de Jantscher, M., and R. M. Bird. 1992. "The Reform of Tax Administration." In *Improving Tax Administration in Developing Countries*, ed. M. Casanegra de Jantscher and R. M. Bird, 1–15. Washington, DC: IMF.

Chirwa, B. B. 2000. "Property Taxation in Zambia." Paper presented at the African Property Tax Renaissance Conference hosted by the International Property Tax Institute, Cape Town, South Africa (June 21–23).

CIA (Central Intelligence Agency). 2016. *The World Factbook*. https://www.cia.gov/library/publications/the-world-factbook/geos/bn.html.

Cloete, C. E. 2009. "Training Valuers in South Africa—The Future." Paper presented at the Fourth Mass Appraisal Valuation Symposium of the International Property Tax Institute, Pretoria (March 25–26).

Dale, P., R. Mahoney, and R. McLaren. 2010. *Land Markets and the Modern Economy*. London: RICS Research.

Davies, T. 2016. "Exploring the Benefits of Technology." Report for KPMG (January).

De Cesare, C. 2012. "Improving the Performance of the Property Tax in Latin America." Policy Focus Report. Cambridge, MA: Lincoln Institute of Land Policy.

Dickovick, J. T., and R. B. Riedl. 2010. "Comparative Assessment of Decentralization in Africa: Final Report and Summary of Findings." Report prepared for the U.S. Agency for International Development (September).

Dillinger, W. 1991. *Urban Property Tax Reform: Guidelines and Recommendations*. Washington, DC: World Bank.

Doherty, P. K. 2016. "Principles and Practices of Effective Billing and Collection." Paper presented at the CARTAC Seminar on Property Taxation in the Caribbean Region, Saint Lucia (February 15–18).

Fjeldstad, O.-H. 2014. "Policy Implementation Without Institutional Cooperation: Central-Local Government Relations in Property Tax Collection in Tanzania." Paper presented at the annual conference of the International Center for Tax and Development, Arusha, Tanzania (December 7–9).

Fossat, P., G. Montagnat-Rentier, P. Petit, G. Parent, G. Chambas, and J. Russell. 2013. "Continued Modernization of the Malian Tax System and Administration, August." International Monetary Fund Technical Report. Washington, DC: IMF. *https:// www.imf.org/external/pubs/ft/scr/2013/cr13355.pdf.*

Franzsen, R. C. D. 2003. "Property Taxation Within the Southern African Development Community (SADC): Current Status and Future Prospects of Land Value Taxation, Botswana, Lesotho, Namibia, South Africa and Swaziland." Working paper WP03RF1. Cambridge, MA: Lincoln Institute of Land Policy.

———. 2005. "Land Value Taxation in Western Australia." In *Land Value Taxation: An Applied Approach,* ed. W. J. McCluskey and R. C. D. Franzsen, 191–226. Aldershot: Ashgate.

———. 2010. "Commentary." In *Challenging the Conventional Wisdom on the Property Tax,* ed. R. Bahl, J. Martinez-Vazquez, and J. Youngman, 108–117. Cambridge, MA: Lincoln Institute of Land Policy.

———. 2011. "Education of Valuers in South Africa." Paper presented at the Sixth Mass Appraisal Valuation Symposium, International Property Tax Institute, University of British Columbia, Vancouver, Canada (October 7–8).

———. 2013. "Policy Issues and Options—Taxation Laws for Kenya's County Governments." Report for the World Bank.

———. 2016. "Property Transfer Taxes." Paper presented at the CARTAC Seminar on Property Taxation in the Caribbean Region, Saint Lucia (February 15–18).

Franzsen, R. C. D., and W. J. McCluskey. 2000. "Some Policy Issues Regarding the Local Government: Property Rates Bill." *SA Mercantile Law Journal* 12(1): 209–223.

———. 2005. "An Exploratory Overview of Property Taxation in the Commonwealth of Nations." Lincoln Institute of Land Policy working paper. *www.lincolninst.edu /pubs/pub-detail.asp?id=1069.*

———. 2016. "Alternative Approaches to Value-Based Property Tax in Africa: An Exploratory View of Options." Paper presented at the second annual conference of the African Tax Research Network, Mahé Island, Seychelles (September 5–7).

Franzsen, R. C. D., and W. Welgemoed. 2011. "Submission on Proposed Amendments to the Municipal Property Rates Act (MPRA)." Report for the South African Local Government Association (SALGA).

Geho, M. L. 2003. "Prospects of Applying Computer Aided Mass Valuation in Tanzania." Paper presented at the FIG Working Week, Paris, France (April 13–17).

Hassane, B. 2009. "Property Taxation in Francophone Africa 4: Case Study of Niger." Working paper WP09FAD1. Cambridge, MA: Lincoln Institute of Land Policy.

Hicks, J. R., and U. K. Hicks. 1955. *Report on Finance and Taxation in Jamaica.* London: Crown Agents for Oversea Governments and Administrations.

IAAO (International Association of Assessment Officers). 2014. "Standard on Assessment Appeals." Kansas City, MO.

IMF (International Monetary Fund). 2014. *Government Finance Statistics Manual.* Washington, DC.

———. 2015. *2014 IMF Government Finance Statistics Yearbook.* Washington, DC.

———. 2016. "IMF World Longitudinal Data (WoRLD)." IMF e-Library Data. *http:// data.imf.org/?sk=77413F1D-1525-450A-A23A-47AEED40FE78&sId=1390030 109571.*

Irarrazaval, I. 2004. "Property Tax in Chile." In *International Handbook of Land and Property Taxation,* ed. R. M. Bird and E. Slack, 286–291. Cheltenham, UK: Edward Elgar.

Kauko, T., and M. d'Amato, eds. 2008. *Mass Appraisal Methods—An International Perspective for Valuers.* West Sussex: Wiley-Blackwell.

Kelly, R. 2000. "Designing a Property Tax Reform Strategy for Sub-Saharan Africa: An Analytical Framework Applied to Kenya." *Public Budgeting and Finance* 20(4): 36–51.

———. 2014. "Implementing Sustainable Property Tax Reform in Developing Countries." In *Taxation and Development: The Weakest Link? Essays in Honor of Roy Bahl,* ed. R. M. Bird and J. Martinez-Vazquez, 326–363. Cheltenham, UK: Edward Elgar.

Kopanyi, M. 2015. "Local Revenue Reform of Kampala Capital City Authority." International Growth Center working paper.

Mathur, O. P., D. Thakur, and N. Rajadhyasksha. 2009. *Urban Property Tax Potential in India.* New Delhi: National Institute of Public Finance and Policy.

Mbabane. 2013. *Municipal Council of Mbabane Annual Report 2012/2013. www.mbabane .org.sz/pdf/Annual%20Report%202013.pdf.*

McCluskey, W. J., and R. C. D. Franzsen. 2005. "An Evaluation of the Property Tax in Tanzania: An Untapped Fiscal Resource or Administrative Headache?" *Property Management* 23: 45–69.

———. 2013. "Property Taxes in Metropolitan Cities." In *Metropolitan Government Finance in Developing Countries,* ed. R. Bahl, J. Linn, and D. Wetzel, 159–181. Cambridge, MA: Lincoln Institute of Land Policy.

———. 2016. "Property Tax Reform in Africa: Challenges and Potential." Paper for the 17th Annual World Bank Conference on Land Policy and Poverty, Washington, DC (March 14–17).

Mikesell, J. L., and L. Birskyte. 2007. "The Tax Compliance Puzzle: Evidence from Theory and Practice." *International Journal of Public Finance* 30: 1045–1081.

Mirrlees, J., S. Adam, T. Besley, R. Blundell, S. Bond, R. Chote, M. Gammie, P. Johnson, G. Myles, and J. Poterba. 2011. *Tax by Design. www.ifs.org.uk/uploads/mirrleesreview /design/ch16.pdf.*

Monagen, N. 2000. "Property Tax in Botswana." Paper presented at the African Property Tax Renaissance Conference hosted by the International Property Tax Institute, Cape Town, South Africa (June 21–23).

Monkam, N. 2010. "Mobilising Tax Revenue to Finance Development: The Case for Property Taxation in Francophone Africa." Working paper no. 195. Pretoria: University of Pretoria, Economic Research Southern Africa (ERSA).

———. 2011. "Property Tax as Legislated and Practiced in Gabon." *Journal of Property Tax Assessment and Administration* 8(2): 53–69.

Mulaku, G. C., and J. Kamau. 2010. "Computer-Assisted Analysis of the Impact of Location on Residential Property Value: A Case Study of Nairobi, Kenya." *Appraisal Journal*, Summer, 270–282.

Mutema, M. 2016. "Property Valuation Challenges in Africa: The Case of Selected African Countries." Paper for the 17th Annual World Bank Conference on Land Policy and Poverty, Washington, DC (March 14–17).

Nabi, I., and H. Shaikh, H. 2011. *Reforming the Urban Property Tax in Pakistan's Punjab.* Lahore, Pakistan: Development Policy Research Centre.

Nhabinde, V. C. 2009. "An Overview of Property Taxation in Lusophone Africa." Working paper WP09LA1. Cambridge, MA: Lincoln Institute of Land Policy.

Norregaard, J. 2013. "Taxing Immovable Property—Revenue Potential and Implementation Challenges." IMF working paper. Washington, DC: IMF.

Ntibatingeso, D. 2015. "Property Taxes in Burundi." Draft background paper prepared for the World Bank's Land Governance Assessment Framework (LGAF).

Oates, W., and R. Schwab, R. 2009. "The Simple Analytics of Land Value Taxation." In *Land Value Taxation: Theory, Evidence, and Practice*, ed. R. F. Dye and R. W. England, 51–72. Cambridge, MA: Lincoln Institute of Land Policy.

Ramos, M., C. Varela, and S. Schofield. 2016. "Cabo Verde—The Challenges of Legal Security in Land Transactions." Paper for the 17th Annual World Bank Conference on Land Policy and Poverty, Washington, DC (March 14–17).

Rao, M. G. 2013. "Property Tax System in India: Problems and Prospects of Reform." Working paper no. 2013-114. New Delhi: National Institute of Public Finance and Policy.

Rao, U. A. V. 2008. "Is Area-Based Assessment an Alternative, an Intermediate Step, or an Impediment to Value-Based Taxation in India?" In *Making the Property Tax Work*, ed. R. W. Bahl, J. Martinez-Vazquez, and J. M. Youngman, 241–267. Cambridge, MA: Lincoln Institute of Land Policy.

Rosengard, J. K. 1998. *Property Tax Reform in Developing Countries.* Boston: Kluwer Academic Publishers.

Shoup, C. 1979. "The Taxation of Urban Property in Less Developed Countries: A Concluding Discussion." In *The Taxation of Urban Property in Less Developed Countries*, ed. R. W. Bahl, 271–284. Madison: University of Wisconsin Press.

Smoke, P. 2003. "Decentralisation in Africa: Goals, Dimensions, Myths and Challenges." *Public Administration and Development* 23: 7–16.

———. 2015. "Rethinking Decentralization: Assessing Challenges to a Popular Public Sector Reform." *Public Administration and Development* 35: 97–112.

Smolka, M. 2013. "Implementing Value Capture in Latin America: Policies and Tools for Urban Development." Policy Focus Report. Cambridge, MA: Lincoln Institute of Land Policy.

Soressa, A. N., and B. T. Gebreslus. 2009. "Property Taxation in North-East Africa: Case Study of Ethiopia." Working paper WP09NEA1. Cambridge, MA: Lincoln Institute of Land Policy.

Steffensen, J., and S. Trollegaard. 2000. "Fiscal Decentralisation and Sub-national Government Finance in Relation to Infrastructure and Service Provision: Synthesis

Report on 6 Sub-Saharan African Country Studies." Synthesis report directed by the World Bank.

Tommy, A., R. C. D. Franzsen, and S. Jibao. 2015. "Property Taxation in Sierra Leone: Current Practices, Performance and Options for Reform." Paper presented at the International Institute of Public Finance conference, Dublin, Ireland (August).

Tsui, S. 2008. "Alternative Value Capture Instruments: The Case of Taiwan." In *Making the Property Tax Work: Experiences in Developing and Transitional Countries*, ed. R. W. Bahl, J. Martinez-Vazquez, and J. M. Youngman, 127–161. Cambridge, MA: Lincoln Institute of Land Policy.

UN-Habitat. 2011. *Land and Property Tax—A Policy Guide*. Nairobi: United Nations Human Settlement Programme. (Principal author: Lawrence Walters.)

Viruly, F., and N. Hopkins. 2014. *Unleashing Sub-Saharan Africa Property Markets*. Report prepared for the Royal Institute of Chartered Surveyors. London: rics.org /research.

Wallace, S. 2008. "Property Taxation in a Global Economy: Is a Capital Gains Tax on Real Property a Good idea?" In *Toward a Vision of Land in 2015: An International Perspective*, ed. G. C. Cornia and J. Riddell, 47–64. Cambridge, MA: Lincoln Institute of Land Policy.

World Bank. 2015. "Registering Property." *www.doingbusiness.org/data/exploretopics /registering-property/reforms*.

———. 2016. "Income Levels." *http://data.worldbank.org/about/country-and-lending -groups*.

Youngman, J. 2016. *A Good Tax: Legal and Political Issues for the Property Tax in the United States*. Cambridge, MA: Lincoln Institute of Land Policy.

Legislation

Local Government: Municipal Property Rates Act 6 of 2004 (South Africa).

Local Government: Municipal Systems Act 32 of 2000 (South Africa).

PART II

Country Reviews

3

Benin

BERNARD TAYOH AND WILLIAM McCLUSKEY

Benin (previously Dahomey) is a small West African country with a narrow 100-kilometer (62-mile) coastline along the Bight of Benin on the Atlantic Ocean. The country is bordered on the west by Nigeria, on the north by Niger and Burkina Faso, and on the east by Togo. Benin has a land area of 112,622 km². The capital city is Porto-Novo, and Cotonou, with an estimated population of 682,000, is the largest city and the seat of government (CIA 2016).

Benin has a population of about 10.9 million (United Nations 2015; World Bank 2014) and an urbanization level of about 44 percent (United Nations 2014). The economy of Benin is underdeveloped and is dependent on subsistence agriculture and cotton production. Benin is classified as a low-income country (World Bank 2016a), and in 2015 the per capita GDP was estimated to be USD 762 (World Bank 2016b).

Political and Administrative Systems

Dahomey, a former French colony, gained independence on August 1, 1960. In 1975, the country was renamed the People's Republic of Benin through the initiative of a military and revolutionary government.[1] Facing mass protests and international pressure, the military regime stepped down in December 1989 after 17 years in power, paving the way for wide-ranging reforms. In response to a decision of an assembly of all the political forces and other stakeholders in the country, under the banner of the "Nation's Living Forces," a new constitution was drawn up, and a transitional government was established. Since then, regular elections have been held every five years.

The constitution of December 11, 1990, is the fundamental law of the country. The constitution provides for a presidential system with three separate and independent arms of government: the executive; the legislature, a unicameral parliament; and the judiciary. There is a dual legal system: a civil law system, modeled on the French system, and customary law.

Decentralization and Local-Government Finances

Benin is divided into twelve administrative units (*départéments*), each headed by a *préfet*. The départéments constitute the only level of decentralized structures of the state. Their roles and their relationship with local governments are defined in the decentralization laws and related decrees. The National Conference in 1990 opted for decentralized local government, and the resulting new constitution clearly provides for local self-government. The National Assembly finally approved the legal and political framework, including the decentralization laws, in 1999. Effective implementation of decentralization began in December 2002 when elections were held, and communal councils were subsequently established in February 2003.

The legal framework for decentralization and local governance consists of five laws (Law No. 97-028 on the organization of the territorial administration; Law No. 97-029 on the organization of the communes; Law No. 98-005 on the organization of communes with a particular statute; Law No. 98-006 on the electoral, communal, and municipal regime; and Law No. 98-007 on the financial regime of the communes), six decrees, and about 30 bylaws and regulations. These laws, which were all promulgated in 1999, paved the way for the first local council elections in late 2002 and the subsequent establishment of local government structures a year later.

After the decentralization reforms were implemented, the country was divided into 77 communes, the only level of decentralized local government. Three cities (Cotonou, Parakou, and Porto-Novo) were granted special status (*communes à statut particuliers*) because of their population size. This single level of decentralization replaces the former subprefectures. Chapter III of Law No. 97-029 of January 15, 1999, on the organization of the communes transferred the following mandates from the central government to the communes: communal planning, construction of infrastructure (building and maintenance of roads and street lighting), the environment, hygiene and sanitation (drinking water, waste management, and rainwater management), literacy, early childhood and primary education (construction, equipment, and maintenance of schools), health and social education (construction, equipment, and maintenance of public health centers), and economic services and investments (construction, equipment, and maintenance of markets and abattoirs).

Sources of Local Government Revenue

The communes' own sources of revenue are defined by Law No. 98-007 and comprise both fiscal resources (direct and indirect taxes, including taxes reverted by the state) and nonfiscal resources (payment for services, revenue from communes' estates, grants, state subventions, and loans). The creation of all local taxes is the prerogative of the national government's legislative machinery. Communes are allowed to set tax rates only within limits imposed by legislation, specifically, the annual Finance Law. The administration, control, and recovery of the taxes, as well as appeals, are handled by decentralized services of the central administration. There is an exception, however, for real property taxes in some communes, notably those with special status, that is, those that have an urban land register or land information systems (*registre foncière urbain*). The various registers serve as databases of information and statistics regarding land ownership, taxes, and urban allotments, thus allowing the communes to better administer and control these taxes at the local level.

Communes' fiscal resources include both the taxes that are collected within the boundaries of the commune by its agents and those collected by the state on behalf of communes, as well as those collected by the state and shared with the communes. They comprise the following: the real property tax, the tax on developed properties, the tax on undeveloped properties, business permits and licenses, the corporate tax, the local development tax, the tax on firearms, the garbage-collection tax, the parking tax, the tax on motorized boats, the tax on entertainment establishments and games, the tax on sale of local (artisanal) liquor, the publicity tax, the tax on water and electricity consumption, the income tax, the tax on occupation or trade (*taxe professionnelle unique*), and the value-added tax (VAT).

The property tax is applied in départements that have an urban land register in place. In those that do not, there are separate taxes on developed land and on undeveloped land. The property tax, the taxes on developed and undeveloped properties, the local development tax, the road and waterway tax, and business permits and licenses are considered the most important because of the revenue they generate. They represent over 90 percent of all local tax revenue. Communes' own resources are generally weak. In 2010, the communes' own resources on aggregate amounted to approximately 1.3 percent of the country's GDP.[2] The communes' total tax revenue represented about 3.8 percent of total tax revenue in that year. Nonetheless, table 3.1 demonstrates that local resources constitute a considerable proportion of communes' total resources (about 70 percent in 2007). Although the proportion has been declining since 2008 because of rising levels of transfers from the state, the actual figure has been rising.

Resources transferred by the state to local councils also include proceeds of central-government taxes paid to all communes and together made up about 47 percent of communes' total resources in 2010, up from about 31 percent in 2007. These transfers are mostly a share of the VAT and the public (road) and waterway tax. Ministerial Decree No. 2004-1146 of September 14, 2004, fixes the shares of the road tax as follows: 80 percent goes to the communes with special status (of this share, 60 percent goes to Cotonou, 24 percent to Porto-Novo, and 16 percent to Parakou), while the remaining 20 percent is shared with the other communes according to population (table 3.2). The sharing of the VAT is done annually through joint decisions between the minister of finance and the minister in charge of decentralization. In 2012, total taxes constituted 15.5 percent of GDP (IMF 2015), and property taxes (broadly defined to include property transfer taxes) constituted 0.24 percent of GDP (IMF 2016).

Table 3.1 Own Revenue Sources of Communes as a Percentage of Total Revenue

Fiscal Year	2003	2004	2005	2006	2007	2008	2009	2010
Tax revenue	50	47	47	48	48	39	35.3	36.8
Nontax revenue[1]	14	18	24	20	21	14.2	16.4	12.8
Communes' own sources	64	65	71	69	69	54.2	52.3	50
Total transfers from the state[2]	36	35	29.2	31.1	31	40.5	43.3	46.7
Other donor subventions for investment	No data	~	~	~	~	5.3	4.4	3.6

Source: Direction Générale du Trésor et de la Comptabilité Publique (2011).

[1] Includes revenue from disposal of commune property and from reserves.

[2] As of 2008, all funds transferred from the state, no matter their nature, were channeled through FADeC under two broad headings: functioning subvention and investment subvention.

Table 3.2 Central Government Revenues Versus Communes' Revenues

	2008		2009		2010	
	XOF	**%**	**XOF**	**%**	**XOF**	**%**
Communes' total resources in XOF millions and as a % of GDP	42.8	1.44	54.2	1.75	53.9	1.66
State tax revenue in XOF millions	512.2		500.5		526.0	
Communes' tax revenue in XOF millions and as a % of total tax revenue	17.0	3.3	19.4	3.9	19.8	3.8

Source: Direction Générale du Trésor et de la Comptabilité Publique (2011).

Land Tenure

Since Benin's independence, the country has had no comprehensive land policy. As a result, land management has been carried out by many different institutions that often have conflicting interests, and has been underpinned by a dual legal structure consisting of a customary regime along with a modern legal framework, under which some land is governed by customary rules and some by the modern regime. Before the arrival of the French in what was then Dahomey, the indigenous peoples lived under a sociopolitical order organized into kingdoms, clans, hamlets, and other settlements. The king, the land chief, the religious chief, or the clan administered lands in compliance with the existing traditional rules. The French introduced various technical and legal mechanisms aimed, for the most part, at ensuring their control of land management. Therefore, throughout the colonial period, they adopted various laws to reorganize traditional land rights throughout the country. This policy was most successful in areas where the colonial administration was based. It was in this context of customary law that the modern land regime was introduced in Dahomey. However, the colonial administration faced resistance and the survival of traditional customs and practices in parts of the country and was therefore forced to accept the coexistence of these two contradictory land regimes, the modern and the customary. This was the beginning of the dualistic system that is in force in Benin today, which is the source of many land-related conflicts.

Laws passed by the colonial administration introduced *immatriculation* in the name of the state as the principal means by which to establish ownership of land.[3] Vacant land without an owner, including land that had not been occupied or exploited for more than 10 years, came within the domain of the state. A portion of this domain was then fragmented and granted to some private individuals, who were given habitation or occupancy permits.[4] These permits allowed beneficiaries to occupy state-owned land in urban areas and granted insecure and revocable personal rights, implying that the land was already registered in the name of the state. Unlike land titles, housing permits entail permanent occupation, and the administration can withdraw without compensation plots that are unoccupied for six months. In urban areas, the primary land management tool is subdivision (*lotissement*), which is especially critical during the initial inventory assessment phase of each area. The lotissement provides the first factual and graphic documents for the subdivision of lands immatriculated in the name of the state. The issued habitation permits have effectively become pseudo-ownership titles, and although they are supposed to be nontransferable, they are bought and sold, and the administration recognizes and gives effect to their marketing.

Two modern land tenure laws were introduced alongside the customary land tenure regime: Law No. 60-20 (of July 13, 1960) on the habitation permit regime in Dahomey; and Law No. 65-25 (of August 14, 1965) on the organization of the land ownership regime in Dahomey (establishing the immatriculation regime). Law No. 60-20 represents a serious hindrance to the management of land, but Law No. 65-25 offers more security to landholders by granting a land title that cannot be challenged. Unfortunately, the complex procedures and the high cost of titles granted under Law No. 65-25 resulted in another major impediment to secure property rights for most citizens. Under these conditions, citizens prefer more precarious titles, such as the habitation permit, the administrative permit, the resettlement (*recasement*) certificate, or sales conventions. Nevertheless, land immatriculation and subsequent acquisition of a land title (*titre foncière*) remain the only way by which definite ownership of land can be obtained in Benin.

Customary Land Tenure

Most land in Benin is still governed by the customary land tenure system, especially in rural areas. In these areas, land is generally under the control of customary leaders, called land chiefs, who determine and enforce the traditional rules. A key aspect of these rules that is quite contentious is that women do not have the right to own land. These unwritten rules are mostly traditions inherited from people's ancestors, who were the first occupants. The multiple modes of access to land, the absence of formalized transfer deeds, the latent conflicts, and the multiple restrictions on access of women and youths to land are among the reasons justifying government intervention to introduce some minimal form of land reform. Thus, the government in 2003 commenced with steps to implement some security measures in these areas.

Despite minor differences among different cultural groups, the most common modes of access to land in rural areas in Benin are primitive occupancy, collective ownership, succession, donation, land purchase, rental, pledge, loan, and sharecropping.[5] Benin's Civil Code lays down the rules governing acquisition of property through sale.

Land Immatriculation and Titling

Collective Registration

Collective registration (*immatriculation collectif*) is an initiative to facilitate the transformation of occupancy permits in urban towns into definite land titles. This initiative, which started with a pilot phase that covered the three councils with special status (Cotonou, Parakou, and Porto-Novo), was extended to cover 30 of the 77 communes in the country in 2003. The goal of the commission charged with this the registration exercise was to register 65,650 parcels of land in all 77 communes by 2009.[6] However, only 6,370 new titles have been delivered.

The Urban Land Register

In the process of implementing the framework of assistance to local collectivities in urban management, the state established an urban land register (Registre Foncier Urbain, RFU) at the level of each urban and semiurban town. The goal of the RFU is to help boost local fiscal resources so as to enable the financing of urban development projects through the gathering of information on all parcels of land within the municipality, including details on titling, tax, and data relevant to the improvement of urban infrastructure.[7]

The Rural Land Plan

The Rural Land Plan (Plan Foncier Rural, PFR) is like a simplified land register aimed at securing customary land rights. The PFR assigns a site plan and number to every defined parcel of rural land. It attributes a rural land certificate (*certificat foncier rural*, CFR)[8] to the landowner, which must be converted to a land title within two years at no cost.[9]

Property Taxation

The annual property tax (*taxe foncière unique*, TFU) was instituted by Ordinance No. 94-05 (of September 16, 1994), amending the Finance Law of 1994. This tax replaced the previous tax on developed property, the tax on undeveloped property, the tax on rents, and the general tax on income from property. However, the TFU is applicable only in communes that have an urban land register, while the other taxes remain applicable in the rest of the communes.[10]

The Taxe Foncière Unique

The TFU is essentially an urban property tax. Although the modalities for the recovery and collection of the tax were not established until a 2005 law, the tax rate was fixed by the 2000 Finance Law.

Coverage

The TFU applies to developed and undeveloped properties in Benin. Developed properties include installations permanently attached to the ground, such as houses, foundations, factories, and, in general, all buildings constructed with concrete, metal, wood, or other permanent materials.

Liability for the TFU

The owner of the property during the year of imposition is liable for the TFU. If the owner cannot be identified, the possessor of the property, the agent of the taxpayer, his heir, his assign, the tenant, or any other beneficiary has to pay the tax in the name and on behalf of the property owner. However, if there is a usufruct, the person enjoying the right of use of the property has to pay the tax in the owner's name. Similarly, if there is a long-term lease, the tax is due from the lessee.

Exemptions

The following properties or persons are exempt:

- Property belonging to the state and local collectivities provided it is used for public purposes and not for any income-generating activity.

- Buildings used as schools or universities.

- Buildings and premises used for worship.

- Property for which the amount to be paid as tax is below the threshold fixed by decision of the minister of finance.

There is also a five-year exemption for new buildings or improvements provided they are not used for commercial purposes. However, if the exempted building or part is put into any other use than for habitation, the exemption ceases as of the year of the change of use, although the property will still benefit from the initial exemption. If the building is leased, it is liable for the property tax at the rate of 6 percent from the date of commencement of the lease. Additionally, for a building to benefit from exemption, the owner must, at the start of the construction or improvement, send an application to the director of taxes and lands. Company buildings and structures constructed in Benin's industrial free-trade zone enjoy a 10-year tax holiday from the tax on developed property and the TFU.

The Tax Base

The tax base is the assessed rental value of the property as of January 1 of the year of imposition. The tax administration has established a scale of rental values according to location zones for each type of construction.

Valuation

The tax administration carries out valuation on the basis of established zones.

Tax Rates

The central government sets the tax rate, usually in the Finance Law. For undeveloped property set aside for private use and not rented, the rate is 5 percent. A commune can reduce this rate to as low as 3 percent or increase it up to 7 percent. The tax rate is 6 percent for developed property that is privately used and not rented. This rate can be reduced to as low as 4 percent or increased up to 8 percent.

Collection

The tax administration sends out a notice to the taxpayer, who is required to respond within 20 days of receiving the notice by providing information regarding the property. If the taxpayer fails to report within this time, a penalty of 20 percent of the tax amount will be imposed. Therefore, the taxpayer is under no obligation to file a tax declaration. The tax is due by the last day of the month after the one during which the notice was sent.

Payment in cash or by certified check of an amount equal to 35 percent of the preceding year's tax is due by January 31, and a further 35 percent of the same amount is due by March 31. The balance becomes due only after the taxpayer receives a notice from the tax administration. All payments are made to the tax collector at the taxation office.

For leased property with rents of up to XOF 50,000, the tax is deducted from the rent and paid by the tenant to the tax collector. If there are two or more tenants, they share the tax amount proportionately. If the tenant is the state, the tax is paid by the state treasury.[11]

The Tax on Developed Property

The tax on developed property is applicable in communes or localities that do not have an urban land register.

Coverage

Coverage includes developed properties, uncultivated lands being used for commercial or industrial purposes, and industrial equipment that is permanently attached to the ground.

Liability for the Tax on Developed Property

The owner of the building is the taxpayer.

Exemptions

Public buildings, installations, and premises, as well as buildings necessary for the functioning of public services, are exempt. There is also a temporary exemption of ten years for new buildings and improvements when such buildings are used as residential dwellings and are constructed on lands with land titles, but the exemption period is reduced to five years if a building is constructed on land without a definite title. In both cases, the property owner is required to notify the General Directorate of Taxes through the taxation office at the département within four months of the commencement of construction.

The Tax Base

The tax base is the rental value as of January 1 of the year in which the tax is imposed, less expenses amounting to 40 percent for dwelling houses and a 50 percent abatement for factories and industrial buildings. Depreciation is also taken into account.

Tax Rates

Tax rates vary from one département to another, as well as among different municipalities within the same département, as shown in table 3.3.[12] The rate for each locality is fixed each year by the municipal council and must be between 15 and 30 percent except for the Atlantique Département, which is allowed an upper limit of 32 percent.

Collection

The taxpayer is required to declare and pay the tax at the taxation office. Payment is normally done in installments, and the amount paid in each installment is provisionally calculated on the basis of the total tax amount

Table 3.3 Tax Rates for Developed Properties in Communes with No Urban Land Register

Departément	Urban Locality (%)	Other Localities (%)
Atlantique	25–32	20
Atacora	30	24
Borgou	30	30
Mono	20	20
Ouémé	24	15
Zou	28	25

of the preceding year: 35 percent by the end of January and a further 35 percent by the end of March. Where the amount due is equal to XOF 5,000 or less, a single payment is due by January 31. The balance is due only after notice is sent to the taxpayer.

The Tax on Undeveloped Property

The property tax on undeveloped property is applicable both in localities that do not have an urban land register and those that do.

Coverage

In principle, all undeveloped properties in Benin are covered. The owner is liable for the tax, and if the owner cannot be found, the occupier.

Exemptions

Properties belonging to the state and local collectivities, as well as agricultural farms used for scientific research, are exempt. There is also a temporary exemption of 30 years for lands that have undergone reforestation, beginning on the date the reforestation started. Additionally, enterprises that have parcels of land within an industrial free-trade zone receive a 10-year exemption.

The Tax Base

Properties subject to the tax on undeveloped property are taxable on the basis of an administrative valuation as of January 1 of the tax year. The tax administration carries out the valuation in the relevant department in collaboration with the local municipal authorities. The assessment is based on the market value of the property. The property value is reassessed every five years, but this is problematic given the lack of a real property market.

Tax Rates

The applicable tax rates vary among localities, ranging from 4 to 6 percent. The relevant municipal or communal council sets the tax rate for each locality each year, with a fixed ceiling of 6 percent.

Collection

The tax amount is provisionally based on the total tax for the preceding year and is paid as follows: 35 percent by the end of January and 35 percent by the end of March. The balance is due only after notice is sent to the taxpayer. However, if the amount due is XOF 5,000 or less, a single payment is due by January 31.

The Revenue Impact of Property Taxes on Communes' Resources

Revenue sharing between the state and the communes is shown in table 3.4.[13] Proceeds from property taxes are not dedicated to any specific type of local project. All local taxes are pooled in a common fund from which local development programs are (in principle) funded. These include housing and urban planning, environmental management, hygiene and sanitation, nursery and primary education, civil status administration, public health, and other social programs. However, these services are hardly provided as required.

The tax on rental income is paid on all rental income of individuals and legal entities earned from the leasing of real property, whether developed or undeveloped, and located in localities where there is no urban land register. The tax rate is 10 percent for rental income up to XOF 50,000 and 20 percent for rental income above XOF 50,000. The tenant withholds the tax from the rent due and pays it directly at the taxation office.[14] It is paid quarterly in arrears, in January, April, July, and October of each year. Delayed payments incur a penalty of 10 percent of the tax due.

Table 3.4 Sharing of Revenue from Property Taxes Between the State and Communes

Tax	Share of the State (%)	Share of Communes (%)
Property tax (TFU)	10	90
Tax on developed property	10	90
Tax on undeveloped property	0	100

Source: Direction Générale du Trésor et de la Comptabilité Publique (2011).

Notes

1. Colonel Mathieu Kerekou, a senior army officer, seized power in 1972 and established a military revolutionary government in the country.

2. This is a significant increase from 2006, when communes' own resources were about 0.6 percent of GDP.

3. Immatriculation is the act, state, or process of being enrolled, as in an official register; immatriculated lands are those that have native or customary title.

4. This is still regulated by two laws: Law No. 20 (of July 13, 1960), along with decree No. 64-276 (of December 2, 1964), on the habitation permit regime in Dahomey; and Law No. 65-25 (of August 14, 1965) on the organization of the land ownership regime in Dahomey.

5. These modes are also highlighted in a land policy white paper approved in 2010, which discusses approaches for securing land rights and also the use of state land, land information systems, efficient (decentralized) land administration, and women's access to land (MHTPLRFCE 2011).

6. Before 2003, there were 15,000 land titles in Benin, 7,187 of which were in Cotonou.

7. By December 2010, the city of Cotonou had 55,000 parcels of land with 42,000 known owners.

8. A CFR holder is considered to be in the same position as the holder of an occupancy permit.

9. Conversion of CFRs to land titles has been quite slow because holders are concerned that titling entails the requirement to pay the property tax.

10. By 2011, only four communes were involved (Cotonou, Djougou, Parakou, and Porto-Novo). Further, no such distinction is observed when entries are being made in the national or local fiscal records; all are grouped under "property taxes."

11. In Benin, regular payment of the property tax creates a presumption of ownership of the property, while nonpayment is considered nonownership of the property.

12. The Ministry of Finance sets rate ceilings.

13. Complete and up-to-date figures of revenue collected could not be obtained. Available information reveals that by June 30, 2014, XOF 2,219.3 million had been collected out of an estimated 4,132 million, while XOF 1,737.7 million out of an estimated XOF 3,453 million had been collected by the same date in the 2013 finance year (Ministry of the Economy and Finance 2014).

14. The landlord, however, is responsible for ensuring that the tax is paid. The usual practice is for the rents to be paid to the landlord, who then pays the tax on behalf of the tenants.

References

CIA (Central Intelligence Agency). 2016. "Benin." In *The World Factbook*. https://www.cia.gov/library/publications/the-world-factbook/geos/bn.html.

Direction Générale du Trésor et de la Comptabilité Publique. 2011.

IMF (International Monetary Fund). 2015. *2014 IMF Government Finance Statistics Yearbook*. Washington, DC.

———. 2016. "IMF World Longitudinal Data (WoRLD)." IMF e-Library Data. http://data.imf.org/?sk=77413F1D-1525-450A-A23A-47AEED40FE78&sId=1390030109571.

MHTPLRFCE (Ministry of Housing, Town Planning, Land Reform and the Fight Against Coastal Erosion). 2011. "Livre blanc de politique foncière et dominale." Cotonou: Government of Benin.

Ministry of the Economy and Finance. 2014. "Projet de Loi de Finance pour la Gestion." Cotonou: Government of Benin.

United Nations. 2014. *World Urbanization Prospects*. Washington, DC: Department of Economics and Social Affairs, Population Division.

United Nations, Department of Economic and Social Affairs, Population Division. 2015. World Population Prospects: The 2015 Revision. *https://esa.un.org/unpd/Publi cations/Files/World_Population_2015_Wallchart.pdf.*

World Bank. 2014. *World Development Indicators*. Washington, DC.

———. 2016a. "Country and Lending Groups." *http://data.worldbank.org/about/country -and-lending-groups.*

———. 2016b. "GDP per Capita (Current US%)." *http://data.worldbank.org/indicator/NY .GDP.PCAP.CD.*

Legislation

Law No. 60-20 (of July 13, 1960) on the habitation permit regime in Dahomey.

Law No. 65-25 (of August 14, 1965) on the organization of the land ownership regime in Dahomey.

Law No. 97-028 on the organization of the territorial administration.

Law No. 97-029 on the organization of the communes.

Law No. 98-005 on the organization of communes with a particular statute.

Law No. 98-006 on the electoral, communal, and municipal regime.

Law No. 98-007 on the financial regime of the communes.

4

Botswana

WILLIAM McCLUSKEY, RIËL FRANZSEN,
AND MUNDIA KABINGA

Botswana is a semiarid, landlocked country in southern Africa. It shares borders with Zambia to the north, Zimbabwe to the east, South Africa to the east and south, and Namibia to the west. The land area is 582,000 km². Botswana gained self-governance in 1965 after 80 years as a British protectorate and became independent on September 30, 1966 (CIA 2016). It is classified as an upper-middle-income country and in 2015 had an estimated GDP per capita of USD 6,360 (World Bank 2016a, 2016b). The population of Botswana is estimated at 2.3 million (United Nations 2015), of which about 57 percent is urbanized (United Nations 2014). Gaborone, the capital city, has an estimated population of about 247,000 (CIA 2016).

Government

Botswana is a multiparty democracy. Administratively, the country is divided into ten districts, twenty-eight subdistricts, two cities (Gaborone and Francistown), three town councils, and a township authority. The other categories include major villages, villages, and settlements and are generally clustered into tribal administrations.

Land Tenure

There are three main categories of land ownership in Botswana: customary, state, and freehold (Republic of Botswana 1995). Customary land constitutes over 70 percent of the total land area; 17 percent of this land is designated as wildlife management areas (White 2009). Customary land is held and managed in trust for the citizens by a land board established in each tribal area under the authority of the Tribal Land Act. It is occupied on a customary basis for a variety of purposes, exclusively or in common, or by common-law lease for commercial or industrial use where formal security of tenure is desired. Other forms of formal land tenure are lease-hold, tenancy, license, and certificates of rights, any of which may be entered into on tribal, state, or freehold land.

Freehold land constitutes about 5 percent of the total land area in Botswana and entitles the landholder to perpetual and exclusive rights to the land. Freehold land is administered by the Department of Lands, which is responsible for registering all land transactions. State land is all land in Botswana that falls outside the described tribal areas. All state land is held in trust by the president under the State Land Act and is administered by the Ministry of Lands. It makes up about 25 percent of the land area and comprises national parks and wildlife management areas, forest reserves, and all urban land that is not freehold land.

Before Botswana gained political independence, title to state land was granted on a freehold basis. After independence, the government of Botswana no longer provided freehold title, but rather a form of tenure described as a fixed period state grant (FPSG). An FPSG is valid for 99 years for residential land and 50 years for industrial and commercial land. In urban areas FPSGs are generally limited to land that has been serviced (roads and utilities) and surveyed.

There is considerable pressure to change land use from residential to commercial and industrial, especially in and on the outskirts of the larger urban cities, such as Gaborone and Francistown. The government has identified acceleration of servicing and allocating land for residential, commercial, and industrial uses as a priority.

The Land Administration, Procedures, Capacity, and Systems (LAPCAS) project began in 2009 and focused on creating processes and systems for the efficient management of real property information in Botswana. Digitization of paper records and maps has been a central component of the project. Before the project, land registration was manual and paper based. Many parcels were not registered because of lengthy registration times, information was not updated, and property conflicts and corruption were common. The project instituted a unique numbering system for all land in the country, and some 254,401 deeds have been digitally scanned.

Property-Related Taxes

The central-government Botswana Unified Revenue Service (BURS) currently assesses and collects two property-related taxes, the capital gains tax (CGT) and the capital transfer tax (CTT), whereas the Deeds Registry assesses and collects the transfer duty. In contrast, urban councils collect property rates. In an effort to improve BURS's enforcement of the CGT and the CTT, the authorities have prepared draft legislation whereby the administration of transfer duties will be shifted to the BURS. This welcome administrative initiative will enable the BURS to improve its information platform and systems to capture transaction values from realization events, disposals, gifts, and inheritances cost-effectively. Investing in in-house capacity to verify market value would therefore be fully justified, although a centralized valuation department could be developed to support this function. Given the poor collection record of local authorities, the transfer of parts of the collection function for property rates from urban councils to the BURS could improve existing synergies and reduce the current level of noncompliance for property rates. Whereas total taxes in 2012 constituted 26.9 percent of GDP (IMF 2015), property taxes (as broadly defined by the International Monetary Fund) constituted only 0.06 percent of GDP in 2011 (IMF 2016).

The Transfer Duty

The transfer duty is levied under the Transfer Duty Act. Citizens are exempted from transfer duty when they acquire agricultural land. For both citizens and noncitizens, the first BWP 20,000 of the property value of nonagricultural land is not taxed; thereafter, a flat rate of 5 percent applies. For agricultural properties, the rate is 30 percent (KPMG 2014).

The Capital Gains Tax

The capital gains tax (the income tax on disposal of property) is levied in accordance with Section 35 of the Income Tax Act, Chapter 52:01 (Kabinga 2010). The proceeds of a disposal of both movable and immovable properties incur the tax. For immovable properties, the tax is levied on an indexed or market value of the capital gain. The individual or entity liable for payment of this tax is the seller. Valuation for the CGT is based on self-declaration but is subject to assessment by the commissioner general of the BURS. Individuals are exempt from the CGT if the property they are selling is their first principal residence.

The Capital Transfer Tax

Where income tax is not collected on property disposal, the capital transfer tax (CTT) is levied. The CTT is more or less an estate transfer duty and is levied in accordance with the Capital Transfer Tax Act of 1985 (KPMG 2014). The CTT is charged on the aggregate tax value of all chargeable disposals made by a donor to a donee in any tax year. For valuation, the CTT relies primarily on self-declaration. The act also provides for the commissioner general of the BURS to consult a qualified valuer to ascertain the value of any property.

Property Rates

Revenue Importance .

Revenue from rates plays a rather insignificant role in Botswana because almost all recurrent and development expenditures tend to be covered by a combination of revenue support grants (RSGs) from the central government and other own municipal revenues in the form of levies, fees, and charges. At the municipal-government level, actual incomes from rates vary but generally amount to less than 13 percent of municipal revenues. In the case of the Gaborone City Council, which is least dependent on central-government funding, rates contributed 27 percent to total revenue in 2006/2007 but declined to 13 percent by 2008/2009 (Kabinga 2010). The RSG from the central government is significant—more than 70 percent in 2008/2009. Other municipal revenue consists mainly of interest on investments and rate arrears, rentals from council housing, trade licenses, and sanitation fees (table 4.1).

The Tax Base

The tax base is the capital improved value of ratable property. Property rates are applied to both land and improvements, which are assessed sepa-

Table 4.1 Gaborone City Council Revenues (Percentages)

Revenue Source	2006/2007	2007/2008	2008/2009
Rates	27	21	13
Revenue support grant	60	70	71
Other revenues	13	9	16
Total revenue	100	100	100

Source: Kabinga (2010).

rately; therefore, two values need to be determined for all developed properties. The tax is determined with reference to the aggregate value of the land and improvements (Franzsen 2003).

Property owners pay rates in the cities (Francistown and Gaborone), towns (Jwaneng, Lobatse, and Selibe Phikwe), and townships (Sowa Township). Approximately 95 percent of the land in Botswana, mainly in rural and peri-urban areas, is not rated. Currently, as noted earlier, rates are levied by six urban councils, but with the promulgation of the Local Government Act, 2012, the levying of rates on property will be extended to rural and peri-urban areas. It is envisaged that rates will apply only in village or urban areas and not in areas supporting agricultural activities, such as communal grazing or subsistence farming, or to a residence located on agricultural land.

The law governing valuation and rating is contained in the Sectional Titles Act of 2003 and the Township Act of 1955. The Sectional Titles Act, Chapter 33:04, suggests that local authorities are mandated to conduct rate valuations. Further, the Township Act, Chapter 40:02, grants township authorities and town and city councils the power to make regulations and bylaws relating to the following: fixing and levying of rates on land for municipal purposes; fixing and levying of different rates for different classes of land; prescription of procedures for enforcement of payment of rates and service levies; and prescription of the process by which a ratepayer may object to the assessment of his property. All these regulations and bylaws are subject to the approval of the minister responsible for local government.

The contribution of rates to the actual recurrent revenue of all rating authorities has averaged not more than 10 percent for the past five fiscal years, indicating a marked vertical imbalance as far as own revenues are concerned. The most significant financing source is RSGs (cash transfers) from the central government, which make up more than 75 percent of councils' finance resources. This adversely affects their fiscal autonomy, creates funding uncertainty, and causes some inflexibility in the use of funds. The government of Botswana has therefore made a deliberate decision to use property rates as an important revenue source of urban councils and to extend them to district councils in rural and peri-urban jurisdictions. These authorities did not have powers to levy property rates before the promulgation of the Local Government Act of 2012, which came into effect in February 2013.

Exemptions

Although the rating laws are silent on property rate exemptions, the City of Gaborone provides exemptions to public libraries and museums, public hospitals and mental asylums, registered schools, places of worship, public cemeteries and crematoriums, residences of the clergy, public sporting and recreational facilities, agricultural show areas, orphanages, and charities. The Local Government Act of 2012 also provides for an exemption of subsistence farming areas. Further, if a parcel is used partly for these purposes and partly for some other purpose, the council may collect rates on the ratable part on a pro rata basis. The minister may also, on recommendation from a rating authority, exempt other property from rates.

Although land vested in the government is exempt from rates, in practice, a discretionary and equivalent contribution in lieu of rates is paid to the council for land occupied and used for government purposes (Republic of Botswana 1995). The payment in lieu of rates and the central government's annual contribution to municipal-government deficit financing make up the RSGs.

Valuation

In practice, the central government exclusively conducts the process of valuation, as well as fixing and levying tax rates. Before 2009, the Directorate of Lands in the Ministry of Lands carried out valuation, fixing tax rates, and billing. Currently, the Ministry of Local Government and Housing is responsible for preparing the valuation rolls and fixing rates for each city, town, and township in Botswana. Valuation is based on an appraisal of the market value the property is expected to realize if it is offered for sale.

The *Department of Lands: Operations Manual* (Republic of Botswana 1995) generally requires that councils conduct at least one general property valuation every five years. It also demands that councils undertake interim or supplementary valuations of land as circumstances and changes dictate. Revaluations for the six urban councils were undertaken in 2007 and 2009, but because supplementary rolls have not been undertaken, there has been no growth in the tax base since 2009.

General valuations are currently contracted out to private property valuers, largely because both municipal- and central-government departments lack adequate resources to conduct general valuations. Until 2009, interim valuation rolls were prepared on a quarterly basis by valuation officers in the Ministry of Lands and later by the Ministry of Local Government. The interim valuation rolls are limited to valuing newly titled land and developments on land previously classified as undeveloped in the last general valuation.

Objections and Appeals

The law prescribes that councils appoint a valuation court to review the valuation roll and interim valuations. The valuation court consists of three members: a chair, appointed by the minister, and two assessors nominated by the council and approved by the minister (Republic of Botswana 1995).

Once the valuation roll is produced, it is made public by notice in the official gazette. Objections to the roll may then be made within 21 days of publication. These objections are considered by the valuation court, and its decisions are subsequently published in the gazette. Parties dissatisfied with the findings of the valuation court may appeal within 30 days to the High Court, whose decision on the matter is final.

Although the law provides for valuation courts, government valuers tend to review and provide an independent assessment of objections. The Township Act allows local authorities to delegate the fixing and levying of rates to the Ministry of Lands, but the law is silent on the authority's powers to prescribe the regulations under which valuation for purposes of rates is to be conducted.

Tax Rates

Tax rates are determined locally and are set annually, but ministerial approval is required. Differential rates are applied to different property categories. All six rating authorities apply a significantly higher tax rate to undeveloped properties as an incentive to develop these properties (Franzsen and McCluskey 2005). The tax rates for the six rating authorities for 2001, 2009, and 2014 are set out in table 4.2. The tax rate for undeveloped parcels is generally four times higher than the tax rate for developed property within the same zoning (residential or nonresidential). The tax rates for Gaborone were significantly reduced after the general revaluation in 2009, but the tax rates in Lobatse, Selibe Phikwe, and Sowa were static from at least 2009 to 2014.

Billing, Collection, and Enforcement

Billing is done annually. An abatement applies for early payment (Franzsen 2003). In 2010, it was announced that First National Bank of Botswana (FNB) and the Gaborone City Council (GCC) had signed a revenue collection agreement to simplify and increase the available options for payment of GCC property rates and service charges by city residents and businesses. GCC rates can now be paid directly into the GCC's account at FNB branches and automatic teller machines. FNB customers can pay

Table 4.2 Tax Rates for the Six Rating Authorities

Jurisdiction	Residential Developed			Nonresidential Developed			Residential Undeveloped			Nonresidential Undeveloped		
	2001	2009	2014	2001	2009	2014	2001	2009	2014	2001	2009	2014
Francistown	0.88	1.10	1.14	1.10	1.40	1.43	3.52	4.60	4.58	4.40	5.70	5.72
Gaborone	0.43	0.50	0.15	0.52	0.60	0.22	1.71	1.9	0.88	2.08	2.30	1.20
Jwaneng	0.82	0.90	0.94	0.99	1.40	1.39	3.26	3.80	3.75	3.97	4.60	4.57
Lobatse	0.62	0.74	0.74	0.77	0.90	0.92	2.46	3.00	2.95	3.08	3.70	3.70
Selibe Phikwe	0.65	0.78	0.78	0.75	0.90	0.90	2.60	3.12	3.12	3.00	3.60	3.60
Sowa	0.33	0.43	0.43	0.40	0.52	0.52	1.32	1.72	1.72	1.60	2.08	2.08

Sources: Franzsen (2003); Ministry of Local Government (2015).

by mobile phone and online banking. However, collection is problematic, and arrears are significant.

Various enforcement mechanisms are provided in the law, including interest on arrears. Clearance certificates are used to ensure that transfers of property are not registered in the deeds office unless all outstanding rates are paid. The transferor remains liable until the town clerk is notified in writing of a transfer of ownership. A tenant or occupier can be held liable for tax arrears in certain cases. Last, a council may take possession of unoccupied ratable land after a period of five years (Franzsen 2003).

References

CIA (Central Intelligence Agency). 2016. "Botswana." In *The World Factbook*. *https://www.cia.gov/library/publications/the-world-factbook/geos/bc.html*.

Franzsen, R. C. D. 2003. "Property Taxation Within the Southern African Development Community (SADC): Current Status and Future Prospects of Land Value Taxation in Botswana, Lesotho, Namibia, South Africa, and Swaziland." Working paper WP03RF1. Cambridge, MA: Lincoln Institute of Land Policy.

Franzsen, R. C. D., and W. J. McCluskey. 2005. "An Exploratory Overview of Property Taxation in the Commonwealth of Nations." Working paper. Cambridge, MA: Lincoln Institute of Land Policy. *www.lincolninst.edu/pubs/pub-detail.asp?id=1069*.

IMF (International Monetary Fund). 2015. *2014 IMF Government Finance Statistics Yearbook*. Washington, DC.

———. 2016. "IMF World Longitudinal Data (WoRLD)." IMF e-Library Data. *http://data.imf.org/?sk=77413F1D-1525-450A-A23A-47AEED40FE78&sId=13900 30109571*.

Kabinga, M. 2010. "Property Taxation in Botswana and Zambia." Presentation at the Fellowship Workshop of the African Tax Institute/Lincoln Institute of Land Policy Project on Property Taxation in Africa, Stellenbosch, South Africa (December 4–5).

KPMG. 2014. *Botswana Tax and Budget Summary, 2014/2015*. *https://www.kpmg.com/BW/en/IssuesAndInsights/ArticlesPublications/Documents/Tax-and-Budget-Summary-2014-2015.pdf*.

Ministry of Local Government. 2015. Personal communication.

Republic of Botswana. 1995. *Department of Lands: Operations Manual*. Gaborone: Ministry of Local Government, Lands and Housing.

United Nations. 2014. *World Urbanization Prospects*. Washington, DC: Department of Economic and Social Affairs, Population Division.

United Nations, Department of Economic and Social Affairs, Population Division. 2015. World Population Prospects: The 2015 Revision. *https://esa.un.org/unpd/Publications/Files/World_Population_2015_Wallchart.pdf*.

White, R. 2009. "Tribal Land Administration in Botswana." Policy Brief 31. Cape Town: University of Western Cape, Institute of Poverty, Land and Agrarian Studies.

World Bank. 2016a. "Country and Lending Groups." *http://data.worldbank.org/about/country-and-lending-groups*.

————. 2016b. "GDP per Capita (Current US%)." *http://data.worldbank.org/indicator /NY.GDP.PCAP.CD.*

Legislation

Capital Transfer Tax Act of 1985.

Income Tax Act of 1995.

Local Government Act of 2012.

Sectional Titles Act of 2003.

State Land Act of 1980.

Township Act of 1955.

Transfer Duty Act of 1973.

Tribal Land Act of 1968.

5

Cabo Verde

RIËL FRANZSEN, WILLIAM McCLUSKEY,
AND VASCO NHABINDE

Cabo Verde is an archipelago scattered over ten larger islands and five islets in the Atlantic Ocean approximately 500 kilometers due west of Senegal. Portugal began abandoning its colonial empire after the 1974 coup in that country, and Cabo Verde became independent in 1975. The area is 4,033 km², and the estimated population is approximately 520,000 (United Nations 2015). The level of urbanization is around 66 percent (United Nations 2014). The capital city, Praia, is located on Santiago, the largest of the islands. Sal and Boa Vista are among the more important islands in Cabo Verde because of their tourism potential (Nhabinde 2009) and have experienced considerable real estate development. These developments have triggered a demand for land and have resulted in a booming property market. The 2015 GDP per capita was estimated at USD 3,080 (World Bank 2016b), and Cabo Verde is classified as a lower-middle-income country (World Bank 2016a).

Government

Local government in Cabo Verde consists of 22 municipalities. Further local-government entities may be established under the law as either a higher-tier or lower-tier category of local administration in relation to municipalities.

Land Tenure

Cabo Verde was largely uninhabited when the colony was founded by Portugal. After its founding, wealthy families were encouraged to settle by grants of large tracts of land, which were used to establish large farms and plantations farmed by sharecroppers. This system largely still exists, and most people do not own the land they work but lease land from large landholders. Despite independence from Portugal, land tenure has not been a key concern of the government for the past 40 years and is still largely governed by preindependence legislation. However, the country passed the Agrarian Reform Act in 1981, which sought to redistribute unproductive landholdings over a certain size.

Land is held freehold under a system of conveyancing. This implies that property transfers are finalized only after proper legal searches pertaining to the relevant property. Land registration reform began in 2010 with the objective of moving the records from a paper-based system to an electronic system. Until then two systems to record property details existed in Cabo Verde: a judicial system, located in the Ministry of Justice, and a municipal system. Each system contained only limited information on a small sample of the country's total land parcels. In addition, there was no source that contained up-to-date map-based information indicating parcel location. The judicial system is largely managed by the land registry and notaries and records the legal status of parcels and buildings. There is no legal requirement to register a parcel in the registry until the area has been properly surveyed. The municipal system was created to administer taxes on land and property. It is an alphanumeric registry linked to a tax system and is managed by the local authorities. To facilitate transparency and confidence in transferring land and in establishing ownership rights, the Land Management Information and Transaction System (LMITS) was developed (Maximiano and Martins 2016). The first component of LMITS was digitization of all paper records and formation of a historical archive of data on parcels and legal rights held at the Ministry of Justice's registry (*registo predial*), at the municipal tax offices (*matriz, registo matricial*), and by public notaries. The project has been designed to enhance the legal, procedural, and institutional environment of land administration within national and municipal governments (Maximiano and Martins 2016). The land registry data in Praia and Sal are now fully electronic, and certificates of registration are completed within three days (World Bank 2015). Ownership records and subsequent transfers are registered in a land registry, and any changes are also communicated to the tax office.

Taxation and Decentralization

The important taxes in Cabo Verde are the income tax; the value-added tax (VAT), with a standard rate of 15 percent and a reduced rate of 6 percent for lodgings and restaurants; excise taxes; and customs duties. A comprehensive property tax, the *imposto unico sobre o património* (IUP), is also levied.

Municipalities in Cabo Verde are primarily funded by the Municipal Financing Fund (Fundo de Financiamento dos Municípios, FFM). Using the revenue collected from the IUP, the VAT, excise taxes, stamp duties, and customs duties collected nationally during the previous year, the national government contributes 10 percent from the general government budget to the FFM. The FFM is then distributed according to the following formula: 75 percent to the Common Municipal Fund (Fundo Municipal Comum, FMC) and 25 percent to the Fund of Municipal Solidarity (Fundo de Solidariedade Municipal, FSM). The FMC is then distributed according to the following formula:

- 20 percent is distributed equally among the 22 municipalities.

- 50 percent is distributed on the basis of the population in each municipality.

- 15 percent is distributed on the basis of the child population (persons younger than 18 years of age) in each municipality.

- 15 percent is distributed according to the geographic size of the municipality.

The law also establishes the conditions under which municipalities and the national government will cooperate in the process of strengthening and developing the capacity of municipalities in Cabo Verde. These aspects are fundamental to the decentralization process, which involves returning powers to local government.

Another important element of the reform was the implementation of Law No. 79/VI/2005 of September 5, 2005, on local finances, which empowers municipalities to prepare, approve, change, and execute plans of action and to prepare their own budgets. In addition, they are entitled to collect revenue within their jurisdictions, apply for credit, determine their own budgeted expenditures and act accordingly, provide for public investment, and manage municipal properties. The law also empowers municipalities to determine tax rates, tariffs, and prices under the new powers and functions assigned to them. This law furthermore allows municipal assemblies to determine property tax exemptions or reductions for entities providing significant investment projects that contribute to the development of the municipality.

Previous Property Taxes

Property taxes in Cabo Verde were first introduced in 1933. These taxes were similar to those in other former Portuguese colonies (Nhabinde 2009). The relevant legislation has been amended several times since independence in 1975. For example, Decree-Law No. 56/80 of July 26, 1980, provided for temporary exemptions for new urban buildings and prescribed the methodology for calculating taxable income derived from urban buildings. Also, for new construction and existing buildings being refurbished, the building only has to be occupied (not necessarily completed) to determine taxability or the tax-exempt period.

Decree-Law No. 56/80 provided for a number of exemptions, including an exemption for a minimum of three years and a maximum of ten years for new buildings or buildings that have been restored or refurbished, and an exemption for building plots within urban areas that expires after two years from the date of acquisition if the construction is not completed. Requests for exemption are directed to the secretary of finance within 60 days of building completion and must be accompanied by documentation demonstrating that the building has been completed. Information required to compile valuation rolls for urban and rural buildings must be completed by December 31 of each year. The secretary of finance must determine the number of buildings in the roll and the total amount of registered income. The declaration for establishing the taxable income from urban buildings must be completed by July 31 of each year.

For the first valuation, commissions determined the taxable value of urban buildings. This practice was superseded by self-declarations of values by taxpayers, which were audited by finance secretaries. Municipalities were required to prepare municipal valuation rolls of all urban and rural buildings, as well as land zoned for constructing buildings (so-called construction land), based on declarations submitted to municipalities.

Decree-Law No. 56/80 also introduced changes regarding the contribution of urban buildings, while Decree-Law No. 55/80 of July 26, 1980, introduced changes regulating the taxes on succession and donation, as well as the transfer tax (the so-called sisa)[1] on property acquisitions or exchanges for consideration. These changes included exemption from taxation for an urban building if it was being used as the permanent residence of the owner. The duration of exemptions was fixed at ten years from the date the building was considered completed, or from the date of occupation, where the value of the building was less than CVE 2.5 million, and at five years if the value was greater than CVE 2.5 million but less than CVE 5 million. The exemption terminated if a building was no longer used as the permanent residence of the owner.

The Reformed Property Tax

Fundamental reform of the property tax commenced in 1998. Decree-Law No. 79/V/98 (of December 7, 1998), revoked the previous laws and transferred the power to collect property tax to municipalities. The main objective of this reform was to provide revenue and to transfer competencies to municipalities. This reform included rationalization of the various laws dealing with property-related taxes. The *imposto unico sobre o património* (IUP), or unique tax on property, which was introduced in 1998, replaced four taxes, namely the previous recurrent property tax, the tax on the transfer of property for consideration, the donations tax, and the succession tax in relation to real property. The IUP became operative in 2000 through the enactment of Decree-Law No. 22/2000. It is indeed a unique, comprehensive tax on property because it taxes the ownership of property, as well as the transfer of ownership (Nhabinde 2009).

The IUP is charged annually on a property owner at a tax rate of 3 percent of the taxable value as of December 31 of the previous year. The taxable value is 25 percent of the total value of the property as declared by the owner, and therefore the effective tax rate is 0.75 percent of total value. The municipal tax administration where the property is located levies and collects the tax. When the tax exceeds CVE 5,000 per year, it may be paid in two installments in April and September. If it is less than CVE 5,000, it must be paid as a lump sum in April. The interest rate on late payments is 1 percent, and the penalty rate is 3 percent. Payment is made at the municipal office of the municipality where the property is located. In some municipalities, such as Camara Municipality on Sal Island, online payment is possible.

The IUP is also charged on the transfer of property by donation, succession, or any other transfer for consideration, such as a sale. When property is transferred the transferee is liable for the tax. The tax rate on property transfers is 3 percent of the taxable value, and the tax is payable within 30 days of the signing of the public deed of sale. IUP is also payable by a transferor on the capital gain from the sale of construction land if the sales price exceeds the purchase price by more than 100 percent, or the sale of buildings and other real estate where the sales price exceeds the purchase price by more than 30 percent. However, the IUP is not charged on capital gains realized by real estate investment companies.

According to Decree-Law No. 18/99 (of April 26, 1999), taxpayers have the right to contest the assessment of taxable value as stated in the valuation rolls at any time and to obtain all documents relevant to the valuation. Taxpayers must submit their declarations of property on an appropriate form to the fiscal administration of the municipality where the building is located by July. If a taxpayer does not declare within the stipulated time, penalties specified in the General Tax Code can be levied.

A stated objective of unifying the various property taxes in one new law was to extend the tax base by reducing rates and rationalizing all taxes on properties and to reduce administration and compliance costs by decentralizing these taxes, which would, in principle, allow for better control of evasion and fraud. The decentralization of administration and revenues to the municipalities was also supposed to enhance revenue collections because there would be a closer link between tax payments and service delivery at the municipal level. Despite the significant rationalization achieved through the IUP, a separate stamp duty of 1 percent is still payable on deeds of sale of real estate (PWC 2013).

The law grants various exemptions from the IUP (PWC 2014). These include the following:

- State- and municipal-owned buildings classified as part of the national heritage or deemed to be of public interest.

- Properties of pensioners.

- Acquisition of properties with "tourist utility status" for the construction of tourist-related improvements.

- Acquisition of property to be used exclusively for industrial purposes.

- Property used exclusively for industrial purposes for ten years.

An issue to be addressed, especially in less developed municipalities, is that many properties are not yet included in the tax registers of municipalities. Furthermore, the tax rates on properties are relatively static, although the power to change these rates has been assigned to municipal assemblies. These rates are determined infrequently and in accordance with the needs of the municipal budgets. This results in the potential to either overtax or undertax one property relative to another.

Without proper oversight, the system of self-declaration of property values is open to abuse. The use of declared values pertaining to the date of acquisition is also problematic in an environment where property values are increasing rapidly, as has been the case in Cabo Verde. Effective tax rates (the tax as a percentage of actual market values as opposed to declared values) are likely to be very low.

As the property market develops further, there seems to be significant potential to enhance revenues from the IUP. Cabo Verde still has a long way to go in reforming all the key aspects of its property tax. On the positive side, Cabo Verde has developed a computerized map-based land information system (LMITS) that integrates the legal interests in land, ownership data, geospatial information on parcels, and the tax value of the land and buildings. Although this system does not directly address some of the current administrative problems of the property tax, it does provide the necessary baseline data to support future property tax reforms.

Note

1. A similar transfer tax, also called sisa, is still levied in Portugal.

References

CIA (Central Intelligence Agency). 2016. "Cabo Verde." In *The World Factbook*. *https://www.cia.gov/library/publications/the-world-factbook/geos/cv.html*.

Maximiano, L. P., and H. Martins. 2016. "Towards an Effective Land Information System—The Land Management Information and Transaction System (LMITS) in Cabo Verde." Paper presented at the World Bank Conference on Land and Poverty, World Bank, Washington, DC (March 14–18).

Nhabinde, V. C. 2009. "An Overview of Property Taxation in Lusophone Africa." Working paper WP09LA1. Cambridge, MA: Lincoln Institute of Land Policy.

PWC (Price Waterhouse Coopers). 2013. "Worldwide Tax Summaries—Corporate Taxes 2013/2014." *www.pwc.com/taxsummaries*.

———. 2014. "Worldwide Tax Summaries—Territories." *http://taxsummaries.pwc.com/uk/taxsummaries*.

United Nations. 2014. *World Urbanization Prospects*. Washington, DC: Department of Economic and Social Affairs, Population Division.

United Nations, Department of Economic and Social Affairs, Population Division. 2015. World Population Prospects: The 2015 Revision. *https://esa.un.org/unpd/wpp/Publications/Files/World_Population_2015_Wallchart.pdf*.

World Bank. 2015. "Registering Property." *www.doingbusiness.org/data/exploretopics/registering-property/reforms*.

———. 2016a. "Country and Lending Groups." *http://data.worldbank.org/about/country-and-lending-groups*.

———. 2016b. "GDP per Capita (Current US%)." *http://data.worldbank.org/indicator/NY.GDP.PCAP.CD*.

Legislation

Agrarian Reform Act, 1981.

Decree-Law No. 55/1980.

Decree-Law No. 56/1980.

Decree-Law No. 79/v/1998.

Decree-Law No. 18/1999.

Decree-Law No. 22/2000.

Law No. 79/VI/2005.

6

Cameroon

BERNARD TAYOH

Cameroon is situated in west central Africa, bordering Nigeria in the west, Lake Chad on the north, the Central African Republic and Chad on the east, and the Atlantic Ocean, Equatorial Guinea, Gabon, and Congo on the south. It has a surface area of 475,440 km² and a population of 23.3 million (United Nations 2015) that is growing at an annual rate of 2.6 percent, with approximately 54 percent of the people living in urban centers (United Nations 2014). The GDP per capita in Cameroon in 2015 is estimated to be about USD 1,217 (World Bank 2016b). Yaoundé is the capital.

Political and Administrative Organization

Cameroon is divided into 10 regions.[1] These regions are split into 58 divisions (*départements*), 360 subdivisions (*arrondissements*), and 374 local councils (communes). The regions, divisions, and subdivisions are administrative units that are managed by governors, senior divisional officers, and divisional officers, respectively, appointed by the president, while the communes are autonomous local-government entities managed by elected mayors.

The 1996 constitution empowers the president to appoint and recall the prime minister and all other ministers of his cabinet, court judges, and senior government officials. A minister is assigned to each of the 10 regions with responsibility for implementing the policy of the state in the region within the framework of the tasks assigned to him by the respective ministerial departments. Legislative power rests with the Parliament, which consists of the National Assembly and the Senate.

Land Tenure

Land tenure in Cameroon is characterized by the coexistence of a traditional or customary land tenure system and a modern land tenure system, which aims to promote and protect individual land ownership rights through the allocation of land titles. Cameroon was subjected to British and French colonial rule after World War II. After independence in 1960, the country had three different land tenure systems, one introduced by each colonial power and the historic customary tenure. Although these three land tenure systems administered land differently, each provided for the registration of customary land (*livrets fonciers*) in French Cameroon and certificates of occupancy in British Cameroon pre- and post-independence. The 1996 constitution provides that citizens have the right to own property individually or in association with others, and ownership includes the right to use, enjoy, and transfer property (USAID 2011).

The present regulatory framework for cadastral survey and land governance in Cameroon is defined by Ordinances Nos. 74-1 and 74-2 of July 6, 1974, which established rules governing land tenure of private (freehold) and state land. These laws unified the land tenure regimes of the two former territories and maintained land titling at the center of the national tenure regime. They are now complemented by many decrees and executive decisions or orders. The first of the two laws classifies land into private, public, or national. Private land can be owned by individuals, groups, corporate entities, or the state (*domaine privé de l'État*).[2] To qualify as private land, the land must be titled and registered in the national land registry.[3] Public land (roads, parks, waterways, and other lands for public use) is held by the state. All remaining land is classified as national land, which includes most unoccupied land, unregistered land, communal land held under customary tenure, informal settlements, and grazing land. The government can allocate parcels of national land to individuals, public entities, and communes under concession arrangements, but the beneficiary must register the land and obtain a certificate of title before he can acquire full ownership. The Ministry of State Property and Land Tenure (MINDAF) has overall responsibility for land allocations, land development, land surveys, and registration.[4]

The national land registry is based in MINDAF, and each regional and division office of the ministry has a land registry linked to the central land registry.[5] Each land registry is managed by a land register officer who is responsible for recording real property rights and issuing certificates of titles to property owners.

There are other types of land tenure, such as customary tenure and land leases, that are claimed and recognized by the occupiers and holders of these leases. Land titles and land leases, including concessions by the state,[6] are the only legal means of holding land property rights.[7] Although customary rights conditionally afford the possibility of registering land, they are not recognized by any deed that would offer protection to the holders of these rights prior to registration.

Property-Related Taxes

Land registration and titling processes in Cameroon include the requirement that the property must also be registered with the taxation department. After registration, the property owner is subject to one or several property-related taxes depending on whether he retains ownership of, develops, transfers, or leases the property. The most important of these taxes are the property tax, the stamp duty, the capital gains tax, and the tax on rental income. They are all embodied in the country's main tax legislation, the General Tax Code (GTC).[8]

Although a transfer tax is levied on some business transactions, real property transfers in Cameroon are not subject to a transfer tax per se. A stamp duty is charged on all instruments transferring real estate ownership or the right of usufruct. The stamp duty rate varies as follows:

- 15 percent for instruments and transfers of developed parcels in urban areas.

- 10 percent for instruments and transfers of urban undeveloped and rural developed estates.

- 5 percent for instruments and transfers of rural undeveloped estates.

The tax is calculated on the value of the property as declared on the contract or deed of transfer.

A tax on rental income is also levied on real estate income, based on the difference between the amount of gross income earned and the total amount of charges attached to the property that are deductible. A capital gains tax is levied at a flat rate of 10 percent on gains made by natural persons from the disposal of developed or undeveloped property alienated for consideration or granted as a gift. It must be paid to the taxation department before the property registration is finalized.

A real property tax is levied annually on all developed and undeveloped property situated in urban and semi-urban areas. Like most other taxes, the property tax is the prerogative of the central government and is administered at the local level by officials of the General Directorate of Taxation (the central government tax administration).

The Property Tax

Liability for the Property Tax

The property tax is levied on natural and legal persons who own developed or undeveloped properties, as well as de facto owners. If property is under an *emphyteutic* or renovation lease, or is the subject of a temporary occupation of the public domain, the lessee or the authorization holder is liable for the property tax.[9]

The property tax is levied annually and is collected by regional and divisional units of the taxation administration. However, the total proceeds from this tax are paid into and used by the treasury of the commune where the property is located.[10] Before October 2010, proceeds from the property tax were shared between the state and the local council of the area where the property was located. However, the 2010 joint ministerial circular took effect only in 2012, and the importance of the property tax as a source of local revenue is not yet fully established.

The Tax Base

Developed and undeveloped properties in the major towns of administrative units are subject to the property tax.[11] The tax is levied on such properties when they are located in urban or semi-urban areas that have such amenities as tarred or earth roads, water supply, electricity, and a telephone network. Properties in small towns and most rural areas are not included.

The tax is based on the value of the land and buildings as declared annually by the owner or any person required by law to file the tax return. Determination of the tax base is the prerogative of the General Directorate of Taxation, and its officials are the only recognized valuers for tax purposes. In addition to the system of declaration, and where a return is not filed, or where insufficiencies in the declaration are discernible, the law empowers the taxation authorities to conduct an administrative tax assessment of the property. Accordingly, the administrative tax assessment determines the property value by taking into account the land and improvements, its geographic location, and the types of amenities in the area. The approach is based on the following:

- Classification of towns, built-up areas, and localities.

- Classification of neighborhoods of a town into zones.

- Classification of lands into sectors in a town.

- Definition of value scales per square meter built or per square meter unbuilt by zone or sector, indexed by reference to construction and rental markets.

- The use of weighting coefficients according to the presence of urban factors, such as roads, water supply, and electricity and telephone services.

The gross taxable value of the property is determined by applying a price per square meter to both the size of the land and any constructed buildings, guided by the above attributes. The valuation exercise is undertaken annually. Although properties are grouped into the above categories for the purpose of determining the tax base, the tax rate is the same for all property categories.

Exemptions

Properties that are exempt from the property tax include properties belonging to

- state and local councils;

- religious, cultural, and charity organizations;

- hospitals and school establishments; and

- international organizations and diplomatic missions.[12]

Land used exclusively for farming, stockbreeding, or fishing is also exempt. Domestic and foreign companies investing in the productive sectors of the economy are, from April 2013, exempt from the property tax, provided the properties are designated solely for production purposes. Buildings used for industrial purposes or as warehouses or storehouses are exempt.[13]

Appeals Procedure

The procedure for raising objections or making appeals related to tax assessment is embodied in the GTC. It comprises a prior administrative phase and, where necessary, claims before the judiciary. All claims connected with taxes and penalties determined by the taxation authorities are first brought before the taxation department. Any taxpayer who feels wrongly taxed or who contends that his property has been overassessed is entitled to make a written claim to the head of the principal taxation center of the place of assessment. If the claim is deemed justified, the head of the taxation center grants tax relief as appropriate. If the aggrieved taxpayer is not satisfied with the outcome at the level of the local tax administration, he can forward the claim to the director general of taxes and thereafter to the minister of finance. If the taxation administration does not provide the desired relief, the claimant is entitled to refer the matter to the administrative bench of the Supreme Court.

The Tax Rate

The tax rate is set by central-government legislation and is embodied in the GTC. The code is supplemented by the 2009 Finance Law of the Republic of Cameroon.[14] The annual tax rate is 0.1 percent of the assessed property value.[15]

Tax Administration

Billing and collection of the property tax are also the prerogatives of the divisional and regional units of the Directorate of Taxation, which notify taxpayers of the assessed tax amounts. The tax is paid to the tax revenue collector in the taxation service of the place where the property is located.

The Tax Directorate of the Ministry of Finance in Douala has been hand-delivering property tax filing forms to taxpayers. The door-to-door effort lasts some two months and has the objective of raising at least CFA 3.5 billion in property taxes per annum instead of the usual CFA 2 billion. In addition, the Tax Directorate has signed agreements with mobile-phone companies to facilitate property tax payments via cellular phones. The total revenue from the property tax is transferred periodically to the local council of the area where the tax is collected and where the property is located.

Land Registration Obstacles

Some 40 years after the enactment of the present land governance framework and the requirement that titles be registered, the number of registered lands in Cameroon is still minimal. According to the Department of State Property in MINDAF, the number of land certificates was estimated to be 165,000 in 2012 out of a total of around 2,900,000 plots of land, including 1,550,000 in urban areas. In addition, both the government and individuals have contested many certificates of title on the grounds of irregularities, and the government has annulled several, most notably in Yaoundé and Douala.

Many land-related laws and decrees are not yet backed by implementing instruments, and many officials in the administration are not familiar with changes to the regulatory framework. In addition, there are provisions that have spawned jurisdictional conflict between various governmental structures, such as the Department of Surveys and the General Directorate of Taxation. Furthermore, the legal framework does not provide for the transfer of land management to local councils, which remain passive although they are the primary beneficiaries of the property tax. Despite the existence of the legal framework presented in this chapter, the customary management method is still prevalent. Most people still use the customary or traditional system to acquire land, particularly in rural areas, and this is unlikely to change significantly anytime soon. Cadastral information is still incomplete, and the same piece of land can be registered more than once, especially in urban centers. These factors, in large part, account for the dismal levels of revenue from property taxes throughout the country and undermine their importance as a source of revenue for local governments (World Bank 2011). Further, there is no effective mechanism within the tax administration to track changes on both registered and unregistered properties that could affect their tax base. Taxation officials still rely on declarations made by property owners when filing their returns, with the likelihood of significant and deliberate insufficiencies in most declarations.

Notes

1. Presidential Decree No. 2008/376 (of November 12, 2008) created regions to replace provinces. Many legislative texts and laws, however, still refer to provinces.

2. Ordinance No. 74-1, Article 2.

3. The process of registering land and acquiring a land certificate was outlined in Decree No. 76/165 (of April 27, 1976). This decree stipulates essentially that those seeking to register land they occupied before 1974 can apply directly for a land certificate; those seeking access to land they have not previously occupied must apply indirectly for a certificate. The indirect process for registering land requires supplementary documentation and usually takes more time.

4. Decentralized land consultation boards were introduced in all divisions in 2005 and are responsible for making recommendations on the use of national lands, supervising the demarcation of land, evaluating rights to land, and resolving land disputes.

5. Decree No. 2005/178 (of May 25, 2005) to organize the Ministry of State Property and Land Tenure.

6. These concessions are temporary titles held on land occupied after the coming into force of the 1974 land ordinances. Holders of these concessions are, in principle, required to take steps to obtain titles within 10 years.

7. Decree No. 76/165 (of April 27, 1976) to lay down conditions for obtaining land certificates.

8. All references to the tax code are to the General Tax Code of Cameroon (2010).

9. An *emphyteutic* lease is a long-term lease, varying between 18 and 99 years, that gives the lessee ownership rights over the property. A building or renovation lease is an agreement whereby the lessor allows the lessee to build structures on undeveloped land or renovate a building in exchange for remuneration. Such structures revert to the lessor at the end of the contract (Government of Cameroon 2009).

10. Article 48 of Law No. 2009/019 (of December 15, 2009) on local taxation.

11. Article 577 of the General Tax Code.

12. Article 587 of the General Tax Code.

13. Article 15 of Law No. 2013/004 (of April 18, 2013) outlining incentives for private investments in Cameroon.

14. Law No. 2008/012 (of December 29, 2008) bearing the Finance Law of the Republic of Cameroon for the year 2009.

15. Before January 2012, an additional local council tax of 0.01 percent of the property tax was charged annually. The taxpayer had to pay the tax directly to the council of the area where the property was located. Since 2012, local councils have also been entitled to the entire proceeds from the registration of land transfers conducted within their council areas (Government of Cameroon 2010).

References

CIA (Central Intelligence Agency. 2016. "Cameroon." In *The World Factbook*. *https://www.cia.gov/library/publications/the-world-factbook/geos/cm.html*.

Government of Cameroon. 2009. "Circular Defining the Modalities for Implementing the Fiscal Provisions of the 2009 Finance Law." Yaoundé: Ministry of Finance.

———. 2010. "MINADT/MINFI Circular." (Ministry of Territorial Administration and Decentralization/Ministry of Finance). Yaoundé: Ministry of Finance.

United Nations. 2014. *World Urbanization Prospects*. Washington, DC: Department of Economics and Social Affairs, Population Division.

United Nations, Department of Economic and Social Affairs, Population Division. 2015. World Population Prospects. The 2015 Revision. *https://esa.un.org/unpd/wpp/Publications/Files/World_Population_2015_Wallchart.pdf*.

USAID (U.S. Agency for International Development). 2011. *Country Profile—Cameroon*. Washington, DC: U.S. Agency for International Development.

World Bank. 2011. "Cameroon: The Path to Fiscal Decentralization Opportunities and Challenges." Report no. 63369. Washington, DC.

———. 2016a. "Country and Lending Groups." *http://data.worldbank.org/about/country-and-lending-groups*.

———. 2016b. "GDP per Capita (Current US%)." *http://data.worldbank.org/indicator/NY.GDP.PCAP.CD*.

Legislation

Decree No. 76/165 (of April 27, 1976).

Decree No. 2005/178 (of May 25, 2005).

General Tax Code of Cameroon (2010).

Law No. 76/165 (of April 27, 1976).

Law No. 2008/012 (of December 29, 2008).

Law No. 2009/019 (of December 15, 2009).

Law No. 2013/004 (of April 18, 2013).

Ordinances No. 74-1 and 74-2 (of July 6, 1974).

Presidential Decree No. 2008/376 (of November 12, 2008).

7

Central African Republic

BERNARD TAYOH AND RIËL FRANZSEN

The Central African Republic is a landlocked country in central Africa bordered by Chad to the north, Sudan to the northeast, Southern Sudan to the east, the Democratic Republic of the Congo and the Republic of Congo to the south, and Cameroon to the west. The country has a land area of 622,984 km² and a population of 4.9 million (United Nations 2015). The capital city is Bangui, with a population of about 794,000 (CIA 2016). The country has an urbanization level of 40 percent (United Nations 2014). With a per capita GDP estimated at USD 323 in 2015, the second lowest in Africa (World Bank 2016b), it is a low-income country (World Bank 2016a).

Government

The Central African Republic has a history of violent coups d'état and civil war. With the passage of its seventh constitution on December 5, 2004, a multiparty system was adopted. The country is divided into fourteen prefectures and one commune, the capital city of Bangui. In 2009, only four of the fourteen prefectures were effectively operational.

Land Tenure

Up to 1958, French colonial laws and decrees regulated most major issues in the territory. Land tenure regulations were based on a 1924 colonial decree that instituted the system of land registration and taxation. The General Tax Code passed in June 2008 governs all property taxes and other related taxes. Because of the growing importance of property taxes as a source of fiscal revenue, land and property issues have been placed directly under the Directorate General of Taxes and Land Tenure within the Ministry of Finance.

Property-Related Taxes

Property transfers are heavily taxed. In 2011, a 15 percent transfer tax and a fixed stamp duty of XAF 10,000, as well as a 1 percent tax on the registration of the new owner's name and a fixed stamp duty of XAF 5,000, were levied (World Bank 2010). However, the transfer tax was reduced to 7.5 percent in 2012. The other taxes remain at the same levels (World Bank 2015).

Recurrent Property and Land Taxes

For administrative purposes, property is classified as either developed or undeveloped. Different taxes are levied on developed and undeveloped properties.

The Tax on Developed Property

All properties built on solid foundations, such as houses, hangars, or factories, are liable for the tax unless they are expressly exempted.

Exemptions

The main exemptions from the tax on developed property include the following:

- Properties belonging to the state and local councils.

- Properties belonging to chambers of commerce, agriculture, industry, or arts and crafts that are not used for business purposes.

- Facilities located around ports and other internal travel infrastructure for public use by the state, chambers of commerce, or municipalities.

- Local-council facilities used for distribution of water and electricity.

- Houses or places of public worship.

- Buildings belonging to religious and public benefit organizations and used for educational, social, sporting, and humanitarian activities.

- Buildings located in rural areas and used for agricultural activities, such as barns, stables, and storage facilities.

- Buildings costing less than XAF 5 million.

- Buildings belonging to diplomatic missions and used to house their staff.

- Dwelling houses located in rural areas and belonging to nonprofit organizations.

- The principal residence of an individual.

This extensive list leaves only a very narrow tax base.

The Tax Base

The tax base is the annual rental value of the building, less 40 percent for maintenance and other expenses. The tax administration determines the rental value of each property on January 1 every year after it analyzes authenticated rents for different types and classes of property. The value can also be determined from declarations made by the property owner or by comparison with similar properties for which rental values are known. However, where it proves impossible to determine the value through any of these means, the tax administration has the discretion to make a direct assessment.

The practice that has been adopted, although it is not expressly mentioned in the General Tax Code, is first to determine the capital (market) value of the property and then to calculate the rental value. The market value is the cost of construction or the acquisition price of the property. The rental value is then expressed as a percentage of the market value. The minimum rental value is taken to be 12 percent of the market value of the property. The General Tax Code provides that the tax rate for developed property is 15 percent for individuals and 30 percent for legal entities liable for the corporate income tax. The minimum amount of the tax on developed property is XAF 30,000, irrespective of the taxable value.

The owner of developed property is liable for the tax on January 1 of the year of imposition. For a usufruct, the usufructuary (the person who benefits from the use of the property) pays the tax, and for an extended lease (usually 99 years), the lessee pays the tax. If a building is constructed on land belonging to another person, the owner or occupant of the building pays the tax. However, the owner of the land is still liable to pay the tax on the land.

The General Tax Code provides that the tax must be declared and paid at the tax office where the property is located. However, the current practice is that local tax offices are not deemed competent to perform this function; therefore, all declarations and taxes must be made and paid in Bangui.

All owners liable to pay the tax on developed property are obliged annually to file a tax declaration at the taxation office in Bangui by January 31. An owner of more than one property must declare each property individually. Late declaration or failure to declare incurs an automatic penalty of 25 percent of the tax due. Every tenant or occupant is required to file a special declaration with the General Directorate of Taxes concerning the building he is occupying before January 15 of each year. The information must indicate what the building is being used for, the address of the owner, and the total rents paid for the preceding year. Any violation of these requirements generates a fine of XAF 20,000 for each omission or wrongful declaration. Delayed declaration incurs a 50 percent increase in the fine. If the delay is more than two months, the fine is doubled; if it is more than three months, the fine is tripled.

The Tax on Undeveloped Property

The tax on undeveloped property is paid on all undeveloped properties except those expressly exempted by law. The tax is a national tax paid annually into the state treasury.

Exemptions

The main exemptions include the following:

- All public roads and fluvial navigation ways.

- Land belonging to chambers of agriculture, commerce, industry, and arts and crafts.

- Land belonging to the state and local councils.

- Land beneath any building, as well as an area of land surrounding a building up to five times the surface area of the building.

- Land set aside for sporting, cultural, social, and educational activities.

- Land belonging to registered religious bodies, provided they do not generate any income from the land.

- Land with a surface area of less than five hectares used for growing crops and situated within 25 kilometers of the nearest town.

- Land used for mining and quarrying activities.

Again, as with the tax on developed land, the exemptions are wide ranging and ultimately result in a narrow, eroded tax base.

The Tax Base

The tax base is the rental value of the property on January 1 of the year of imposition. The rental income to be considered and the applicable tax rate depend on whether the property is within or outside an urban area. The rental value of undeveloped property in an urban area is obtained by applying a coefficient of 12 percent to the market value of the property, taking into consideration maintenance and other related expenses of 40 percent. The tax rate for undeveloped property within an urban area is 27.5 percent. For undeveloped property outside urban areas, a flat rate per hectare of land is applied, as set out in table 7.1. The land tax is levied on the owner or de facto owner, the agent, or the person who has control of the land on January 1 of the relevant tax year.

The Valuation Cycle

The market value is determined for a period of two years by reference to transfer deeds for similar properties within that period or by comparison with known market values of similar properties. Whether a revaluation is undertaken after two years is left to the discretion of the tax administration. It is doubtful that transfer deeds provide accurate data on market values, given the high taxes and costs pertaining to property transfers.

Objections and Appeals

Any taxpayer who believes that he has been treated unjustly by the tax administration is entitled to bring a challenge before the General Directorate of Taxes and Lands. No time limit is set for lodging a complaint or challenge. If the taxpayer is not satisfied with the outcome at this stage, he can refer the case to the Ministry of Finance. An aggrieved taxpayer who does not obtain redress by administrative means is entitled to lodge a complaint with the Administrative Court.

Table 7.1 Taxes Levied on Undeveloped Land Outside Urban Areas

Type of Land Use	Amount per Hectare
Cultivated land for coffee, rubber, or palm-nut trees	XAF 2,000
Other crops	XAF 750
Unused land or grazing land	XAF 500

Source: General Tax Code of 2008.

Property Tax Revenue

The revenue from property taxes is earmarked for the state treasury no matter where the tax is collected. It is important to note that the only autonomous council in the country is the capital, Bangui. Even revenue from property taxes on properties in the Bangui municipality is allocated to the state treasury. Compliance costs are high because property taxpayers from all over the country are required to travel to Bangui for their tax declarations and payments. It is extremely difficult to tell how important property taxes are as a source of revenue to the government because revenue amounts from all taxes, as well as from other sources, are not made public. However, according to the International Monetary Fund, total taxes constituted only 9.9 percent of GDP in 2012 (IMF 2015), and property taxes (predominantly the high taxes on property transfers) constituted 0.1 percent of GDP in the same year (IMF 2016).

References

CIA (Central Intelligence Agency). 2016. "Central African Republic." In *The World Factbook*. *https://www.cia.gov/library/publications/the-world-factbook/geos/ct.html*.

IMF (International Monetary Fund). 2015. *2014 IMF Government Finance Statistics Yearbook*. Washington, DC.

———. 2016. "IMF World Longitudinal Data (WoRLD)." IMF e-Library Data. *http:// data.imf.org/?sk=77413F1D-1525-450A-A23A-47AEED40FE78&sId=1390030109571*.

Tayoh, B. 2009. "Property Taxation in Francophone Central Africa: Case Study of Central African Republic." Working paper WP09FAC3. Cambridge, MA: Lincoln Institute of Land Policy.

United Nations. 2014. *World Urbanization Prospects*. Washington, DC: Department of Economics and Social Affairs, Population Division.

United Nations, Department of Economic and Social Affairs, Population Division. 2015. World Population Prospects: The 2015 Revision. *https://esa.un.org/unpd/wpp /Publications/Files/World_Population_2015_Wallchart.pdf*.

World Bank. 2010. "*Doing Business 2011: Central African Republic—Making a Difference for Entrepreneurs*." Washington, DC: World Bank and International Finance Corporation. *https://www.ihk-krefeld.de/de/media/pdf/international/doing-business /zentralafrikanische-republik-doing-business-in-central-african-republic-2011.pdf*.

———. 2015. "Central African Republic—Registering Property." *www.doingbusiness .org/data/exploreeconomies/central-african-republic/registering-property/*.

———. 2016a. "Country and Lending Groups." *http://data.worldbank.org/about/country -and-lending-groups*.

———. 2016b. "GDP per Capita (Current US%)." *http://data.worldbank.org/indicator/NY .GDP.PCAP.CD*.

Legislation

General Tax Code of 2008.

8

Côte d'Ivoire

BERNARD TAYOH

Côte d'Ivoire gained its independence from France in August 1960. The country is located on the coast of West Africa and borders Liberia and Guinea to the west, Mali and Burkina Faso to the north, Ghana to the east, and the Gulf of Guinea to the south. It covers an area of 320,763 km². The population is approximately 22.7 million (United Nations 2015), and approximately 54 percent is urbanized (United Nations 2014). The official capital is Yamoussoukro (with a population of about 260,000), whereas Abidjan acts as the seat of government and the commercial capital. The population of Abidjan is estimated at 4.86 million (CIA 2016). In 2015, the country had an estimated per capita GDP of USD 1,399 (World Bank 2016b). Côte d'Ivoire is classified as a lower-middle-income country (World Bank 2016a).

Government

Côte d'Ivoire is a unitary state with a multiparty presidential regime. Under the present administration, Côte d'Ivoire is divided into 19 *régions*, which are further subdivided into 58 *départements*. Under the départements are 231 districts or subdepartments, as well as 197 communes. In accordance with the law on decentralization, the communes are permitted to perform a wide range of specified functions, such as the provision of educational buildings and equipment and cultural and social facilities, public health, and the maintenance of roads, markets, and bus stations. All government ministries have regional offices and in some cases also have offices within départements. This has the potential to foster intergovernmental cooperation and mentorship, but it also raises substantial questions about the true independence of the decentralized administrations.

Land Tenure

There are two systems of land tenure in the country, customary and statutory. The customary system continues to dominate, operating in more than 98 percent of the rural land of Côte d'Ivoire. Land ownership and land tenure issues have contributed a great deal to the recurrent social and political tension in the country. To address this situation, legislation was passed in 1998 instituting wide-ranging land tenure reforms for lands in rural areas. The 1998 Rural Land Law aimed to enhance land tenure security by transforming customary rights into private property rights, although still regulated by the state (USAID 2013). This law explicitly recognized customary landholdings and provided for an initial 10-year phase after promulgation (until January 2009) during which all persons claiming customary land tenure rights had to apply to have their rights officially recognized and to obtain a land certificate (*certificat foncier*). Land not claimed by January 2009 under this process would become the property of the state. In February 2009, given the lack of progress made with the implementation of this law, the government extended the time limit for issuing land certificates to January 2019 (USAID 2013). The statutory system comes into play only when land is registered, but registration has thus far been accomplished for less than 2 percent of rural land. The 1998 Rural Land Law envisioned that by 2019 Ivoirians with customary rights to land would register their land and obtain an individual land title. In theory, the customary land tenure system will disappear after 2019 (Zalo 2002).

Perhaps the most important point in this legislation was that it recognized and gave force to customary rights in land for native Ivoirians. The alienation of such lands is prohibited, although leasing and requisition for public purposes by the state are allowed. More than 75 percent of land in the country is held under customary land tenure where ownership is determined according to ancestral lineage. However, the 2002 coup that led to the division of the country into two distinct zones has had a severe impact on land administration (Tayoh 2009). The law also expressly denies nonnative Ivoirians (about 30 percent of the population) permanent ownership rights of real property or the transfer of such rights to their descendants. Nonnatives are allowed only long-term lease rights, that is, emphyteutic leases for a maximum of 99 years.

The other 25 percent of land in Côte d'Ivoire is either state-owned land or freehold land. State land is administered by the government through a specialized department of the Ministry of Agriculture. Digitization of the land registry has reduced compliance and administration costs for property transfers (World Bank 2016c).

Taxation

Law No. 2003-489 (of December 26, 2003) stipulates that all fiscal operations, including the levying and collection of taxes, must be expressly prescribed by law or authorized by the minister of the economy and finance. In 2012, total taxes constituted 16 percent of GDP (IMF 2015), and in 2013 property taxes (as defined by the International Monetary Fund) constituted only 0.07 percent of GDP (IMF 2016).

The central-government General Directorate of Taxes, which is a specialized agency in the Ministry of Economy and Finance, administers all taxes. The main legislative provisions governing the establishment and collection of taxes, including the property tax, are embodied in the General Tax Code (Code Général des Impôts, CGI) and are supplemented by an annual finance law.

Property Transfer Taxes and Fees

The property transfer tax was reduced in 2014 and again in 2016 and the registration fee was reduced in 2015 (World Bank 2016b). A registration tax of 4 percent of the property value is payable, as well as transfer fees of XOF 15,000 (for a new property certificate) and a further tax of 1.2 percent consisting of a 0.8 percent general service tax and a 0.4 percent tax for the registrar's salary. Where applicable, a 3 percent capital gains tax is payable by the vendor. This tax is not included for the purpose of determining the value for the other taxes and fees (World Bank 2016c).

Property and Land Taxes

The Tax on Developed Property

An annual property tax is levied on all developed properties, such as houses, installations, factories, and, in general, all buildings constructed of brick, iron, or wood and permanently attached to the ground. The tax base is the rental value of the land and buildings for the previous year. The tax on developed property is payable by the property owner.

The valuation process is undertaken annually by the tax administration of the area where the property is located. The rental value is considered to be the rental income that the property owner could obtain from leasing the property and is determined from written or verbal lease contracts; in the absence of such information, the value is established by comparison with similar properties in the same area for which information is available. If the value cannot be determined by any of these means, the tax administration performs a direct assessment. In this situation, the tax administration determines not only the rental value but also the market value for each category of property in the area. For a property used for industrial or commercial activities, the rental value is determined according to the use for which it is allocated.

Exemptions

The most important exemptions include the following:

- Buildings and other structures belonging to the state, and public establishments and decentralized collectivities used for the general benefit of the public and not for any profit-making purpose.

- Installations belonging to the state or decentralized collectivities and used for the distribution of water and electricity.

- Buildings and other places used for public worship or by charitable foundations.

- School buildings not used for profit.

- Buildings used for the provision of medical and social assistance; buildings used by agricultural establishments to protect animals and store harvests; installations belonging to the state railway corporation; state-owned buildings and structures situated in and around ports and airports and allocated to port and airport authorities for the realization of their objectives; and buildings used as sporting facilities and offices belonging to or allocated to formally recognized sporting associations and not used for any profit-making activity.

- Sporting grounds, dispensaries, markets, bridges, and roads that are put at the disposal of employees of agricultural and mining corporations at their exploitation sites and do not generate any property-related revenue.

The Tax Rate

Residential property incurs a tax rate of 4 percent on the rental value if the house is owner occupied and is not used for any commercial or industrial purpose.[1] This rate applies both to a single house occupied by the owner as his main dwelling and to a single secondary residence used personally by the owner and not used to generate any income. However, for a secondary residence, the owner must obtain a certificate of secondary residence from the General Directorate of Taxes; otherwise, the dwelling will be taxed at 11 percent.[2] A tax rate of 15 percent is applied to the rental value for buildings belonging to legal entities and used for business purposes.[3] This 15 percent rate also applies to properties owned by individuals that are used for commercial purposes.[4]

The Tax on Undeveloped Property

The tax on undeveloped property is levied on the market value of undeveloped land in urban areas. It includes land or plots that are inside towns and have been zoned for development by the local administration. The tax is also levied on undeveloped properties that are not within the boundaries of towns but are scheduled for residential or commercial development. However, properties in rural areas are exempt. The tax on undeveloped property is payable by the property owner or by the person who has right of control over the property on January 1 of the year of imposition.

The tax base is the market value of the property as of January 1 of the year of imposition. For properties within the periphery of towns and cities, special council commissions appointed by the minister of finance carry out the valuation in each commune. The determination of the market value is completed annually during the last two months of the preceding year. For other taxable properties that are not within towns, the valuation is done either by comparison with similar properties within the same area or by the tax administration.

Exemptions

The following properties are exempted from the tax on undeveloped properties:

- Land on which the administration has temporarily or permanently forbidden buildings or construction.

- Land on which the owner has been temporarily deprived of or cannot enjoy his property rights because of a situation beyond his control.

- State-owned land or land belonging to territorial collectivities that is used by the public but does not generate any income.

- Nurseries and experimental gardens aimed at carrying out research on improved seed and plant selection.

- Land used for schools, religious worship, or social or medical assistance or by associations known for and authorized to carry out physical education training and military preparations.

- Land, such as training fields, that belongs to or is used by formally recognized sporting associations and does not generate any income.

- Land around developed properties and used for commercial or industrial purposes, the value of which is normally considered in calculating income from the developed properties.

- Large industrial enterprises involved in the manufacture of building, construction, and other materials. This exemption covers the period of installation and exploration.

The last two exemptions especially erode the tax base quite significantly and thus negatively affect revenue potential.

The Tax Rate

The tax rate is fixed at 1.5 percent of the market value. This rate applies only from the end of the second year after the year during which the land was acquired; that is, a new landowner will enjoy at least a one-year tax holiday upon acquisition. The practice is that the property owner has to declare the tax. Collection is the responsibility of the state treasury or the regional tax office of the area where the property is situated.

The Communal Tax on Undeveloped Property

The communal tax on undeveloped property is imposed and collected in addition to the property tax on undeveloped property. The tax base is 0.5 percent of the market value on January 1 of the year of imposition and is calculated in the same manner as the tax on undeveloped property. The communal tax is declared on the same form and collected at the same time as the tax on undeveloped property. It amounts to tax sharing between the national government and communes.

General Provisions Regarding Property Taxes

For purposes of determining the rental value and the market value, which serve as the tax base, for the tax on income from property and the property tax, the property owner or, where a sublease exists, the principal tenant is required to make a tax declaration in person at the taxation office of the place where the property is located each year between January 1 and February 15. This requirement is the same for all other property-related taxes. Enterprises must declare by January 31.

Tax Collection

Valuation rolls are established annually and kept by the regional tax administration for the whole region. The rolls are based on market values and rental values and are used to determine taxpayer liability. The real property tax can be paid to the state treasury in two installments, with the first installment due by February 15 and the second no later than two months afterward. If the owner, as the principal taxpayer, cannot be identified, occupants or tenants of the property can be required to deduct the tax from their rents and pay it directly to the treasury. If the tax is not paid by the due date, a penalty of 25 percent of the tax amount is imposed.

Revenue Sharing of Property Taxes

The arrangements for revenue sharing between the state and local collectives are laid down in Law No. 2004-271 (of April 15, 2004). According to the law, all the revenue from the tax on income from property goes to the state, while all proceeds from real property taxes are allocated to the local collectives. The revenue is shared among the different levels of local collectives as follows: regions, 17 percent; départements, 28 percent; districts, 6 percent; towns, 6 percent; and communes, 43 percent.

Appeals

An aggrieved taxpayer is entitled to bring a challenge before the head of the regional tax administration service of the region concerned. If the taxpayer is not satisfied with the outcome at this stage, the matter can be referred to the Ministry of Finance. If the matter remains unresolved, the taxpayer is entitled to lodge a complaint with the court and ultimately with the Administrative Bench of the Supreme Court.

Property Tax Problems

Property taxation in Côte d'Ivoire has extremely limited coverage. The situation is made even worse by the prevalence of traditional and customary land tenure systems. However, it is envisaged that with ongoing reforms and the increasing rate of urbanization, coverage will increase. With respect to collection and enforcement, officials of the tax administration report that the average, the collection rate is about 65 percent. There is also evidence of widespread evasion and avoidance of the tax, which are likely due to inefficiencies in the administration. Last, the intricate revenue-sharing formula results in only nominal amounts going to local governments' budgets.

Notes

1. The 2016 Finance Law of the country effects a reduction of the tax rate to 3 percent (Fiscal Annex to Law No. 2015-840 [of December 18, 2015], on the 2016 state budget). It is uncertain whether this and other changes are already being implemented.

2. Reduced to 9 percent in the 2016 Finance Law.

3. The 2016 Finance Law reduces this to 12 percent for new enterprises in the first two years of establishment only.

4. Reduced to 12 percent in the 2016 Finance Law.

References

CIA (Central Intelligence Agency). 2016. "Cote d'Ivoire." In *The World Factbook. https:// www.cia.gov/library/publications/the-world-factbook/geos/iv.html*.

IMF. 2015. *2014 IMF Government Finance Statistics Yearbook*. Washington, DC.

———. 2016. "IMF World Longitudinal Data (WoRLD)." IMF e-Library Data. *http:// data.imf.org/?sk=77413F1D-1525-450A-A23A-47AEED40FE78&sId=1390030109571*.

Tayoh, B. 2009. "Property Taxation in Francophone West Africa: Case Study of Côte d'Ivoire." Working paper WP09FAC4. Cambridge, MA: Lincoln Institute of Land Policy.

United Nations. 2014. *World Urbanization Prospects*. Washington, DC: Department of Economics and Social Affairs, Population Division.

United Nations, Department of Economic and Social Affairs, Population Division. 2015. World Population Prospects: The 2015 Revision. *https://esa.un.org/unpd/wpp /Publications/Files/World_Population_2015_Wallchart.pdf*.

USAID (U.S. Agency for International Development). 2013. "Property Rights and Resource Governance—Cote D'Ivoire." Washington, DC. *www.land-links.org/wp -content/uploads/2016/09/USAID_Land_Tenure_Cote_dIvoire_Profile.pdf*.

World Bank. 2016a. "Country and Lending Groups." *http://data.worldbank.org/about /country-and-lending-groups*.

———. 2016b. "GDP per Capita (Current US%)." *http://data.worldbank.org/indicator /NY.GDP.PCAP.CD*.

———. 2016c. "Registering Property." *www.doingbusiness.org/data/exploretopics /registering-property/reforms*.

Zalo, L. D. 2002. "Country Case Study: Ivory Coast." Paper presented at the World Bank Regional Workshop on Land Issues in Africa and the Middle East, Kampala, Uganda (April 29–May 2).

Legislation

Law No. 2003-489 (of December 26, 2003).

Law No. 2004-271 (of April 15, 2004).

Law No. 2015-840 (of December 18, 2015).

Rural Land Law No. 98-750 (of December 23, 1998).

9

Democratic Republic of the Congo

JEAN-JACQUES NZEWANGA AND RIËL FRANZSEN

The Democratic Republic of the Congo (DRC) is the second-largest country in Africa, with a surface area of 2,344,858 km.[2] It is situated on the equator in central Africa and borders nine other countries: the Central African Republic and Southern Sudan to the north; Uganda, Rwanda, Burundi, and Tanzania to the east; Zambia and Angola to the south; and the Congo to the west. It also borders the Atlantic Ocean for only 37 kilometers. The population, consisting of more than 200 ethnic groups, is estimated at 77 million of which around 42 percent lives in urban areas (United Nations 2014, 2015). The capital city, Kinshasa, has a population of almost 11.5 million (CIA 2016). The DRC attained its independence in 1960 after having been a Belgian colony since 1908. Despite an abundance of natural resources (USAID 2007), the DRC is classified as a low-income country with an estimated GDP per capita of only USD 456 in 2015 (World Bank 2016a, 2016b).

Government and Decentralization

After its independence in 1960, the DRC was politically unstable until November 24, 1965, when General Joseph-Désiré Mobutu came to power after a military coup. From the beginning of the 1990s, the Mobutu regime governed the country with a mere semblance of democracy until the arrival of Laurent Kabila, who seized control with the assistance of

Rwanda, Burundi, and Uganda in 1997. The Kabila regime in turn was attacked by the coalition of countries that had originally helped him come to power. After his assassination in 2001 and an internationally brokered peace agreement in 2003, a government of national unity was established. However, there is ongoing civil war in the eastern part of the country.

A new constitution was adopted in 2005 and promulgated in February 2006. With the aim of consolidating national unity, damaged by successive civil wars, on the one hand, and the need to stimulate economic growth, on the other, the constitution submitted for referendum in 2005 proposed that the DRC should be restructured administratively into 25 provinces plus the city of Kinshasa as legal entities, exercising the decentralized competencies enumerated in the constitution. These provinces should also exercise other powers and functions jointly with the central government and share the national revenue with the central government: 40 percent for the provinces and 60 percent for the national government. Presently, there are 26 provinces (CIA 2016).

Under the previous 1998 legislation,[1] the DRC was divided into 11 provinces, each consisting of municipalities (in urban areas) and territories (in rural areas). The municipalities comprise towns, communes, or groups and areas, whereas the territories comprise districts, cities, areas, groups, and villages. Provinces are governed by governors, communes and towns by mayors, territories by territorial administrators, and districts by district commissioners. The City of Kinshasa is a city-province. Therefore, it is not divided into towns and districts and does not have a mayor.

The central government has exclusive authority over public finances; taxes on income, taxes on companies, and personal taxes, as well as customs and import and export duties; the national public debt; external loans for the needs of the republic or the provinces; and internal loans for the republic's needs. The central and provincial governments share concurrent responsibility for the establishment of other taxes, including consumption taxes and property and mining duties; environmental planning; and water and forestry administration. The provinces have exclusive responsibilities for the following:

- Provincial public finances and public debt.

- Internal loans for the needs of the provinces.

- Issuance of real estate titles in conformity with national legislation.

- Taxes and local and provincial duties, in particular, the property tax, local income tax (the tax on rental income), and the tax on motor vehicles.

Three central-government directorates have tax-collection responsibilities: the General Tax Office, which is responsible for collecting direct taxes, including the income tax and property taxes; the General Office for Administrative and Federal Revenue, which is responsible for collecting administrative, judicial, and federal fees; and the Customs and Excise Office, which is responsible for collecting customs and excise taxes.

Land Tenure and Law

The legal system in the DRC is based on the Belgian version of the French Civil Code. Customary laws and authority are recognized as long as they are not contrary to the constitution, the common law, public order, and good morals. Because of the ongoing conflict in the country, land tenure reform is currently not a priority (USAID 2007).

The land tenure system in the DRC is based on legislation from 1973 that regulates the ownership, possession, acquisition, and transfer of land and real estate.[2] The Land Code of 1983 (Law No. 52/83) provides that land is the exclusive, inalienable property of the state and consists of public domain land and popular domain land (USAID 2007). The public domain land of the state consists of all land that is earmarked for public usage or a public service. Unless it is not in use, public domain land cannot be given out in concessions.[3] Land that forms part of the state's public domain is governed by measures specific to assets used for public purposes.

All other land constitutes the state's popular domain and is governed by the so-called land system and its implementation measures. Land that is part of the state's popular domain can be urban or rural and can be earmarked for residential, commercial, industrial, or agricultural use or for animal rearing. According to the land law, in a general sense, the state's private domain can be a perpetual concession, an ordinary concession (e.g., *emphyteusis*,[4] usufruct, usage, or rental), or a land servitude. These are all real rights pertaining to the land. Concessions are granted either free of charge or for a fee. A perpetual concession is defined as the right, recognized by the state, of a natural person of Congolese nationality to use his assets indefinitely as long as the conditions pertaining to the real estate and the procedures prescribed by the law are fulfilled. For areas established in urban constituencies, the president of the republic or his representative has a map drawn up of plots to be granted. In rural regions, traditional chiefs, in practice, distribute and allocate land. Despite the formal land law, many Congolese, especially in rural areas, believe that the land belongs to them in an intimate and inalienable way, having been handed down to them by their ancestors. Therefore, it is difficult for them to understand why they are required to pay land rent for the occupation and use of land.

Because all land belongs to the state, there is no official land market. However, customary systems still informally govern land transactions even though the law does not acknowledge customary tenure (USAID 2007).

Taxation

In 2012, total taxes constituted only 10.2 percent of GDP in the DRC (IMF 2015). No data are available on property taxes, as defined by the International Monetary Fund, as a percentage of GDP. Taxes levied include personal and corporate income taxes, the value-added tax (with a 16 percent standard rate), mining royalties, the vehicle tax, and registration duties (KPMG 2014).

Property-Related Taxes

There are various property-related taxes in the DRC. A registration fee is levied at 1 percent of the price of the property. The transfer of assets is subject to registration duty at rates ranging from 5 percent to 10 percent of the price, depending on the type (developed or undeveloped), use (business premises or dwellings), and location of a property (KPMG 2014). A tax is also levied on rental income from buildings at a rate of 22 percent, 20 percent levied as a withholding tax on the lessee and the remaining 2 percent on the landlord (lessor) (KPMG 2014). There are no stamp duties, donation taxes, or death duties in the DRC (KPMG 2014).

Property Taxes

Section 13 of the Tax Code[5] stipulates that the land tax is an annual flat-rate tax on developed and undeveloped properties where the amount varies according to the nature of the buildings and the ranking of the locality where they are situated. In essence ranking implies an area zoning with reference to value. However, residential property situated in the first, second, third, or fourth zoned areas incurs property tax according to the surface area that has been covered by construction. The surface area of the parts of a building or construction, including cellars, the ground floor, and upper floors or attics, must also be taken into account in determining the total taxable surface area. Additional measures introduced in 1981 empower the minister of finance to amend the rates for the property tax when the economic and budgetary situation requires it. However, this requires clarification because the 2005 constitution clearly states that the property tax is exclusively a provincial competency.

Exemptions

Properties belonging to the following entities or individuals are exempt from the property tax:

- The state, provinces, towns, territories, communes, administrative constituencies, and offices and other public government institutions financed by budget grants.

- Religious, scientific, or charitable institutions.

- Nonprofit associations involved in religious, social, scientific, or philanthropic work that have received legal personality by special decrees.

- Foreign governments if the property is used exclusively as offices for embassies or consulates or for the accommodation of diplomatic or consular agents on a reciprocal basis.

- Individuals with a net annual taxable income below a prescribed amount determined with reference to the income tax dispensation (on condition of proof of payment of the professional tax on remuneration or of the minimum personal tax).

Persons who on January 1 of the tax year are over 55 years old and are widowed are also exempt from the tax on developed property for a building that is used as a main residence if they occupy their main residence either alone, with a dependent or dependents (as defined by law), or with any other person of the same age and in a similar situation, and their net annual taxable income is below the prescribed amount determined with reference to the income tax dispensation (on condition of proof of payment of professional tax on remuneration or of the minimum personal tax).

Further exemptions from property tax are granted for the following buildings or parts of buildings:

- Buildings used by the owner exclusively for agriculture or animal-breeding purposes, including buildings or parts of buildings that are used for preparing agricultural or breeding products, where these agricultural activities constitute at least 80 percent of the overall business conducted on the premises.

- Buildings that an owner uses for nonprofit purposes.

- Buildings used for public religious ceremonies; teaching or scientific research; or hospitals, hospices, clinics, dispensaries, or other similar welfare institutions.

- Buildings used for activities of chambers of commerce with legal personality.

- Buildings used for social activities of mutual companies and professional unions with legal status, except premises used for accommodation, alcohol outlets, or any kind of commercial activity.

The surface area of land whose owner is not engaged in any kind of profit-making activity for one of the objectives is also exempt.

Liability for the Property Tax

Property tax is paid by the owner (holder of the property deed) and other holders of limited real rights (e.g., possession, emphyteusis, concession, or usufruct) of taxable property, as well as by persons occupying immovable property that is part of the private domain of the state, provinces, towns, or communes under terms of a lease. The property tax is due from the owner even if a lease agreement contractually obliges the tenant to pay it, and even if the administration has been advised of this. The administration does not intervene in the distribution of taxes between owners and tenants.

If a property is transferred by sale or for any other reason, the new owner is required to declare it to the tax administration within one month from the date of transfer. Otherwise, the new owner will become jointly liable with the former owner for all property taxes that are still due on the property.

Tax Rates

Table 9.1 shows the tax rates for developed property based on the surface area of parcels as of 2002.[6] The annual tax on buildings is determined as indicated in table 9.2. The annual tax on undeveloped property is determined as indicated in table 9.3.

Table 9.1 Tax Rates for Developed Land by Locality

Locality	Rate
First ranked	CDF 1.50/m^2
Second ranked	CDF 1.00/m^2
Third ranked	CDF 0.50/m^2
Fourth ranked	CDF 0.30/m^2

Source: Nzewanga (2009).

Table 9.2 Tax Rates for Buildings According to Use and Locality

Locality	Rate
First ranked	CDF 75.00 per floor for buildings belonging to legal entities; CDF 37.50 per floor for buildings belonging to individuals and situated in Kinshasa; CDF 30.00 per floor for buildings belonging to individuals and situated in the interior of the country; CDF 75.00 for flats; CDF 11.00 for other buildings.
Second ranked	CDF 37.50 per floor for buildings belonging to legal entities; CDF 22.50 per floor for buildings belonging to individuals and situated in Kinshasa; CDF 19.00 per floor for buildings belonging to individuals and situated in the interior of the country; CDF 37.50 for flats; CDF 7.50 for other buildings.
Third ranked	CDF 30.00 per floor for buildings belonging to legal entities; CDF 11.00 per floor for buildings belonging to individuals and situated in Kinshasa; CDF 7.50 per floor for buildings belonging to individuals and situated in the interior of the country; CDF 18.75 for flats; CDF 7.50 for other buildings.
Fourth ranked	CDF 22.50 per floor for buildings belonging to legal entities; CDF 7.50 per floor for buildings belonging to individuals and situated in Kinshasa; CDF 4.00 per floor for buildings belonging to individuals and situated in the interior of the country; CDF 11.00 for flats; CDF 1.50 for other buildings.

Source: Nzewanga (2009).

Table 9.3 Tax Rates for Vacant Land by Locality

Locality	Rate
First ranked	CDF 30.00/m^2 for land in any first-ranked locality.
Second ranked	CDF 7.50/m^2 for land in Kinshasa; CDF 4.50/m^2 for land in the interior of the country.
Third ranked	CDF 3.00/m^2 for land in Kinshasa; CDF 2.00/m^2 for land in the interior of the country.
Fourth ranked	CDF 1.50/m^2 for land in any fourth-ranked locality.

Source: Nzewanga (2009).

Tax Collection

In the DRC, the fiscal year coincides with the calendar year, and the property tax is due for the entire year according to the taxable surface area in existence on January 1 of the relevant year. Newly constructed buildings or buildings that have been considerably modified are taxed on their new surface area from January 1 of the year after their occupation or modification. The owner is required to declare to the tax authorities the date of occupation or modification of newly constructed buildings or buildings that have been reconstructed or considerably modified within one month from the date of occupation or modification. A plan of the building must be attached to the tax declaration. Considerable modifications are defined as those that are likely to result in an increase or decrease of the taxable surface area by at least 20 percent.

Every individual and a representative of every legal entity must sign and submit a statement annually detailing all taxable and exempt properties. Owners of exempted properties are exempted from signing the statement but must still submit it. Once the declaration has been completed, dated, and signed, it must be handed over to the person who verifies taxes and is responsible for taxable items before April 1 of the fiscal year for those items that the taxpayer owned on January 1.

Finally, taxpayers liable for the tax are required to submit a declaration by locality for verification. This declaration must stipulate all buildings, whether they are taxable or not, situated on the same plot, as well as the surface area of each plot. Declaration forms are distributed to taxpayers; however, a taxpayer who does not receive the forms is not exempted from submitting the required declarations by prescribed deadline. Taxpayers who do not receive the necessary forms must request them from the tax administration.

Enforcement

All delayed payments of all or part of taxes, duties, liabilities, or any amounts whatsoever that are required to be paid to the General Tax Office incur interest at 8 percent per month, including penalties incurred. Any taxpayer can be prosecuted for not paying taxes on time. Before prosecution, however, the receiver of revenue sends the taxpayer a final warning, requesting payment within two weeks. When this period has expired, if the receiver of revenue considers it necessary under the circumstances, a summons is sent to the taxpayer demanding payment within eight days on penalty of seizure of his movable and immovable assets. After that period expires, the receiver of revenue can proceed with the seizure of any movable or immovable assets that are deemed sufficient to pay all amounts due. The assets seized are sold up to the limit of the amount due, including costs, at least eight days after the taxpayer has been notified of the judgment. The gross proceeds of the sale are paid to the receiver of revenue, who, after having deducted all amounts due, holds the surplus at the disposal of the relevant person for a period of two years, after which unclaimed amounts revert to the treasury.

Revenue Potential of the Property Tax

Given the visibility of land and buildings in the DRC, it could be argued that the property tax has huge potential in this country. The tax yield should be significant, but because of the informality of the property market, a rather narrow tax base, widespread tax evasion, and the lack of a properly skilled and motivated administration, it is not. The property tax accounts for less than 1 percent of total tax revenues collected by the General Tax Administration.

As has been previously mentioned, Congolese people in general believe that the land belongs to them and that they should not have to pay tax on it. This concept is extended to all other taxes in the Congolese fiscal system. The property tax is politically sensitive because it affects citizens in an area they consider the most fundamental in their lives. Therefore, governments that were committed from the beginning of the 1990s to the transition process leading to elections did not make an effort to collect this tax for fear of frightening off voters. For this and many other reasons, members of the Congolese political class are among those who have never paid property tax. The law provides for wide-ranging exemptions that have made the property tax insignificant. Various religious institutions, schools, private hospitals, nongovernmental organizations, public companies, chambers of commerce, and others are claiming entitlement to exemption from the property tax (and other taxes) on the grounds that they are not profit-making organizations.

Since independence in 1960, there has never been proper town planning of cities, nor have land use policies been initiated and implemented (USAID 2007). Consequently, the property tax base is not properly developed. In addition, the low level of purchasing power of the general population inhibits collection of this tax.

Notes

1. Decree-Law No. 081 (of July 8, 1998).
2. Law No. 021/73 (of July 20, 1973).
3. A concession is a contract by which the state recognizes that a group, an individual, or a juristic person acknowledged as such by private or public law has the right to

use real estate according to the conditions and methods prescribed by the law and its implementation procedures.

4. *Emphyteusis* is the right to full usage of uncultivated land belonging to the state, subject to the improvement and maintenance of the land and payment to the state of a fee in cash or in kind.

5. As amended by Law No. 075/87 (of October 4, 1987) and Law No. 111/2000 (of July 19, 2000).

6. Ministerial Decree No. 081 (February 26, 2002).

References

CIA (Central Intelligence Agency). 2016. "Democratic Republic of the Congo." In *The World Factbook*. *https://www.cia.gov/library/publications/the-world-factbook/geos/cg.html*.

IMF (International Monetary Fund). 2015. *2014 IMF Government Finance Statistics Yearbook*. Washington, DC.

KPMG. 2014. *Democratic Republic of Congo Fiscal Guide, 2013/14*. *www.kpmg.com/Africa /en/KPMG-in-Africa/Documents/2014%20Fiscal%20Guides/Fiscal%20Guide%20 DRC.pdf*.

Nzewanga, J. J. 2009. "Property Taxation in the Democratic Republic of the Congo." Working paper WP09FAB3. Cambridge, MA: Lincoln Institute of Land Policy.

United Nations. 2014. *World Urbanization Prospects*. Washington, DC: Department of Economics and Social Affairs, Population Division.

United Nations, Department of Economic and Social Affairs, Population Division. 2015. World Population Prospects: The 2015 Revision. https://esa.un.org/unpd /wpp/Publications/Files/World_Population_2015_Wallchart.pdf.

USAID (U.S. Agency for International Development). 2007. *Land Tenure and Property Rights Regional Report*. Vol. 2.1, *East and Central Africa*. Burlington, VT: ARD.

World Bank. 2016a. "Country and Lending Groups." *http://data.worldbank.org/about /country-and-lending-groups*.

———. 2016b. "GDP per Capita (Current US%)." *http://data.worldbank.org/indicator /NY.GDP.PCAP.CD*.

Legislation

Constitution of the Democratic Republic of the Congo, 2005.

Decree-Law No. 081 (of July 8, 1998).

Law No. 021/73 (of July 20, 1973).

Law No. 52/83 (the Land Code of 1983).

Law No. 075/87 (of October 4, 1987).

Law No. 111/00 (of July 19, 2000).

Ministerial Decree No. 081/02 (of February 26, 2002).

10

Egypt

KHALED AMIN, WILLIAM MCCLUSKEY,
AND RIËL FRANZSEN

Egypt is a North African country bordered by the Mediterranean Sea to the north, Palestine and Israel to the northeast, the Red Sea to the east, Sudan to the south, and Libya to the west. It is a large country with a surface area of 1,001,450 km² and a population estimated at 91.5 million (CAPMS 2016; United Nations 2015). Egypt is classified as a lower-middle-income country (World Bank 2016a) with an estimated GDP per capita of USD 3,615 in 2015 (World Bank 2016b). Cairo is the capital, with an estimated population of 18.7 million in the Cairo metropolitan area (CIA 2016). Approximately 43 percent of the population is urbanized (United Nations 2014).

Government Structures

Under the 2014 constitution, the Republic of Egypt has a unicameral parliament, the Council of Representatives. Since 2011, the country has faced severe political and economic challenges, and it has been rebuilding its constitutional institutions and reestablishing its economic and financial foundations since July 2013. Egypt is a unitary country and does not have elected regional or local governments below the central government. The role of elected local councils is to monitor the actions of the local governments and to approve their budgets and investment plans. Instead, Egypt is divided for administrative purposes into 27 governorates, which are further subdivided into 209 cities, 166 districts (*markaz*), 300 districts (*hai*), and 4,623 villages (*qariya*), each of which has its own legal identity (Egypt 2014). Governorates are established by presidential decree and can include one or more cities. The local entities have some administrative freedom and very limited financial discretion but are politically managed by the central government. In addition to the subnational administrative structure, the national budget structure further reflects the centralized nature of Egypt's public sector. The national budget is divided among the central administration, local administrations, and service authorities.

Land Tenure

Egypt's reforms to its land registration system have helped clarify land rights and have facilitated land market development for many Egyptians; before these reforms (as recently as 2006), only about 10 percent of real property in Egypt was registered (Rae 2002). The legal framework for agricultural land rights distribution in Egypt began with Law 178 of 1952, which limited the total amount of landholding per household to 200 feddans (84 hectares) and redistributed excess holdings to poor rural households. The law also established a rent ceiling at seven times the land tax value (amounting to approximately 15 to 20 percent of the gross crop value). Further laws in 1961 and 1969 consolidated reforms by reducing the ceiling on landownership to 100 feddans (42 hectares) and 50 feddans (21 hectares), respectively, although these laws retained higher ceilings for families with children (King 2009; Metz 1990). Law 96 of 1992 reversed Egypt's long-standing land reform (originally implemented by the 1952 land reform law), which granted permanent tenure rights to agricultural tenants (USAID 2011). The 1992 law sought to create a market in land by making land titling a key driver of the country's land administration.

Attempts to introduce markets in land and minimize state intervention have become prominent. Formal titling and land and property registration are major reform objectives of the government (Elrouby, Harju, and Corker 2005). In 2008, a parcel-based deeds registration project was launched; at that time, only 5 percent of Cairo's three million properties had a registered title. There are clear and growing signs of liberalization as a result of Law 96, which legitimizes the exchange of land. Nevertheless, the central government, governorates, and local governments strictly control urban land. Strict rules govern the sale and use of land. Egypt's administrative system is the product of the country's long and complex history. Accordingly, legislation regarding ownership and control of land reflects diverse influences, including ancient customs, Islamic law (*sharia*), and aspects of the French and British legal systems. Land in Egypt customarily belongs to the state, and only urban land and houses are privately owned. This tight state control over land was made necessary by the country's dependence on irrigation and the resulting need to regulate strictly all forms of land use.

In Egypt, five main types of land tenure can be identified:

- Leased land: land owned by the state and leased on a long-term basis; land that is permanently leased and cannot be sold; and other leased land that can be converted from public ownership to private after the end of the lease period.

- Trust land: land set aside for charitable or religious purposes and usually administered by the Ministry of Endowment, Awqaf (the ministry responsible for religious endowments).

- Encroachment land: land of which the possessor or user can gain ownership under a provision of the civil code if it is occupied continuously for 15 years and if the owner does not assert his rights.

- Private land: freehold land that is registered with the land registration division (primarily in urban areas).

- Public land: land that is registered as state property.

Land and Property Taxes

Property Transfer Taxes

A transfer tax on the sale of built real estate is levied at 2.5 percent and is payable by the seller. The seller may also be liable for a tax on capital gains.

Recurrent Property Taxes

For a long time, recurrent property taxes in Egypt were divided into two main taxes: the real estate tax and the agricultural land tax.[1] The laws governing property taxes in Egypt had developed over more than a century as a response to socioeconomic and political conditions. The real estate tax was introduced during the era of Prince Mohamed Ali in 1842. The tax rate at that time was 1/12 of the building's rental value (Amin 2010). Between 1954 and the late 1980s, at least 13 laws were issued to organize the real estate tax. In 2008, Law 196 replaced the Law 56 of 1954 (the buildings tax law). The government issued Law 196 with the aim of enlarging the tax base, modernizing the law, and ensuring improved implementation and overall administration of the real estate tax.

The government began the implementation of the new law in 2010 by asking all real estate owners to report their properties at the offices of the Real Estate Tax Authority (RETA). The RETA was given the authority to develop initiatives concerning property identification and registration, efficient valuation and tax roll processing, billing, collection, arrears processing, compliance, and enforcement. The law was expected to go into effect in January 2012, but significant turmoil, especially among residential property owners, and the political and socioeconomic challenges of the 2011 revolution led the Supreme Council of the Armed Forces to postpone implementation to 2013. The law was eventually implemented in 2014.

Some 17 laws or presidential decrees have been issued on application of the agricultural land tax (Amin 2010). The first law, in 1935, stated that the rental value of agricultural land was to be the basis of this tax. To date, there have been no significant reforms of the current laws pertaining to this tax. However, Law 53 of 1935 was subjected to a number of amendments in 1939 and 1978.

Revenue Importance

Table 10.1 shows the amounts collected annually for the real estate tax and the agricultural land tax from 2005/2006 to 2009/2010. The revenues from both taxes fluctuated somewhat erratically but showed a marked increase in 2007/2008. Amin (2010) suggests that the finalization of settlements under the old dispensation in anticipation of the new law was the primary reason for this increase. Table 10.2 shows the development of property tax revenues from fiscal year 2012/2013 to 2016/2017. The values in this table include the proceeds from the real estate tax, the agricultural land tax, and the amusement centers tax.

Probably a more telling statistic of Egypt's property tax system is that recurrent property taxes in 2010 constituted only 0.04 percent of GDP and 0.3 percent of total general tax revenue (Norregaard 2013). Together, property transfer taxes and recurrent property taxes constituted 0.73

Table 10.1 Property Tax Revenues in EGP, 2005/2006–2009/2010

Fiscal Year	2005/2006	2006/2007	2007/2008	2008/2009	2009/2010
Real estate tax	166,233,172	187,723,714	231,197,600	201,977,839	188,741,966
Agricultural land tax	163,424,022	163,424,022	176,139,494	180,825,551	167,327,230

Source: Amin (2010).

Table 10.2 The Development of Property Tax Revenue (Millions of EGP)

2012/2013 Actual	2013/2014 Actual	2014/2015 Actual	2015/2016 Provisional	2016/2017 Budgeted
531.0	428.0	636.7	3,472.8	2,649.0

Source: Financial Statement of Egypt's Ministry of Finance (2016).

Note: These amounts include the revenues of the real estate tax, agricultural land tax, and the amusement tax.

percent of GDP and 5.14 percent of total general tax revenue in 2010 (Norregaard 2013). In 2012, property taxes (broadly defined) constituted 0.83 percent of GDP (IMF 2016), which is above the average for developing countries (Bahl and Martinez-Vazquez 2008) but likely much lower than the potential level.

The Real Estate Tax

THE TAX BASE

Law 196 of 2008 and its amendments define the tax base as any constructed building and commercially used land. The definition of *building* is broad and includes

- any used land that generates revenue, whether it is attached to a building or not;

- any installation, such as a billboard, attached to a building that generates revenue;

- real property designed for managing and using public utilities;

- used vacant lands whether they are annexed to buildings or separate from buildings; and

- construction on the roofs or facades of properties if they are leased.

EXEMPTIONS

The following properties are exempted or not taxable (RETA 2016):

- Buildings owned by nongovernmental organizations (NGOs) that are used either in administration of the NGO or in carrying out its activities.

- Buildings belonging to academic and educational institutions.

- Hospitals, orphanages, and cemeteries.

- Residential buildings with an annual rental value less than EGP 24,000.

- Additional owned residential buildings with an annual rental value less than EGP 1,800.

- Residential buildings with a market value less than EGP 2 million.

- Commercial units with an annual net rental value less than EGP 1,200.

- Youth and sports centers.

- Buildings owned by foreign governments that through reciprocity exempt buildings owned by Egypt in their countries.

- Not-for-profit social facilities.

- Military facilities.

- Buildings owned by charities and workers' unions; educational and health facilities; not-for-profit organizations; professional syndicates; political parties and unions; and real estate specified as being for the benefit of surrounding agricultural land.

The law gives total or partial tax relief in the following cases:

- If the real estate is demolished or cannot be used in whole or in part.

- If the land on which a building is located becomes unusable.

- If the taxpayer's social situation is such that he is unable to pay the tax.

- To residents of a building unit if the rental value per room is less than EGP 8 per month.

Assessment

The RETA is responsible for calculating and collecting the real estate tax on buildings, agricultural land, and amusement centers. The tax is imposed on the net rental value of the real estate, which is determined by taking the gross rental value and deducting 30 percent of that value for residential property and 32 percent for other property types to cover maintenance costs. The gross rental value is estimated from three criteria: geographic location, construction status, and relevant utilities.

Every governorate must establish an assessment committee, which is responsible for assessing the rental value. These committees are formed by a ministerial decree in agreement with the minister of housing under the chairmanship of the RETA and include four members, one representative each from the Ministries of Finance and Housing and two representatives from the cadre of real estate owners nominated by the local popular council and selected by the governor.

A nationwide self-declaration of ownership and reassessment of rental values are to be conducted every five years. Increases in rental values are artificially fixed in the law at a maximum of 30 percent for residential property and a maximum of 45 percent for nonresidential property. Data on registered properties are to be updated each year to capture the following:

- New buildings.

- Additions to existing buildings.

- Property that has ceased to be exempt.

- Newly used lands that generate revenue.

- Any changes to registered buildings that affect their rental value.

- Property previously rented under old legislation that sets a fixed rental value per year.

Liability for the Tax

Although the tax base is annual rental value, the tax is imposed on the owner of the property. Owners are responsible for informing the RETA of any change in ownership, the name of the new owner, and the date of the contract (Ayyad 2014).

The Tax Rate

The tax rate is 10 percent of a property's net rental value. The tax is calculated by the RETA in the following steps:

- The basis for calculating the annual rental value is 60 percent of the market value assessment.

- The annual rental value is determined by applying 3 percent.

- An allowable deduction of 30 percent is given for residential property and 32 percent for nonresidential property to determine net rental value.

- After the net annual rent is determined, there is a deduction of EGP 24,000 for residential property.

- The tax due is 10 percent of the net annual rental value.

Tables 10.3 and 10.4 provide the calculations of the tax liability assessment for residential property (RETA 2015).

Table 10.3 Property Tax on an Owned Unit of Residence in EGP with an EGP 24,000 Exemption Limit

Market Value	Capital Value	Annual Rental Value	Net Rental Value	Tax Base	Tax Liability
2,000,000	1,200,000	36,000	25,200	1,200	120
2,500,000	1,500,000	45,000	31,500	7,500	750
3,000,000	1,800,000	54,000	37,800	13,800	1,380
3,500,000	2,100,000	63,000	44,100	20,100	2,010
4,000,000	2,400,000	72,000	50,400	26,400	2,640

Source: RETA (2015).

Table 10.4 Property Tax on an Additional Owned Unit of Residence in EGP

Market Value	Capital Value	Annual Rental Value	Net Rental Value	Tax Base	Tax Liability
100,000	60,000	1,800	1,260	1,260	126
150,000	90,000	2,700	1,890	1,890	189
200,000	120,000	3,600	2,520	2,520	252
250,000	150,000	4,500	3,150	3,150	315
300,000	180,000	5,400	3,680	3,680	378

Source: RETA (2015).

APPEALS

A taxpayer has the right to file an appeal (a so-called challenge) of the assessment of the rental value of a piece of real estate, or a part thereof, within 60 days after the date of notification. A prescribed application form must be completed and delivered to the RETA directorate responsible for the area in which the property is located.

Appeal committees consisting of three members examine appeals. A person may not serve as a member of both the assessment and appeal committees. Each committee is chaired by an expert who is not and has not been employed by the tax authority in order to ensure impartiality (Ayyad 2014). One of the remaining two members must be a representative of the RETA, and the other must be either an engineer selected by the Engineers Syndicate or a real estate valuation expert selected by the Central Bank of Egypt or the Egyptian Financial Supervisory Authority (Ayyad 2014). The challenger must pay a deposit of EGP 50. This amount, which is probably aimed at curbing frivolous appeals, will be refunded if the challenge is successful.

COLLECTION AND ENFORCEMENT

In 2014, it was reported that tax collection was commencing from 1.5 million property owners (Ayyad 2014). The RETA offices located within the governorates and districts are responsible for collection. The taxpayer has the option to pay the amount due as a lump sum or to make payment in two installments at the end of June and December.

To ensure compliance, the law provides for certain enforcement measures. Seizure of property, as provided for in the civil law (Law 308 of 1955), can be used to collect the property tax, penalties, and interest. This enforcement mechanism applies over and above the normal judicial processes for civil debt collection. Furthermore, the Public Treasury can impose a tax lien to recover the tax, penalties, and interest due by virtue of the law on the constructed real estate subject to the tax, as well as any rent payable, and on movable property located on the real estate that is owned by the taxpayer (the owner). Interest can be charged on arrears, based on the discount rate announced by the Central Bank of Egypt, normally the prime rate plus 2 percent. If the delay in payment continues, the law provides legal measures. Fines ranging between EGP 1,000 and EGP 5,000 can be imposed. A penalty equal to double the tax is imposed for tax evasion.

The Agricultural Land Tax

The agricultural land tax is levied in accordance with the following laws: Law 53 of 1935, Law 113 of 1939, Law 370 of 1953, and Law 51 of 1973. These laws have not been amended since and no reforms are presently under consideration.

THE TAX BASE

The tax is levied on all land used for agricultural purposes and land that can be used for agricultural purposes on the basis of its estimated annual rental value. The definition includes all rural areas within the jurisdiction of governorates.

EXEMPTIONS AND TAX RELIEF

The main exemptions to the agriculture land tax are the following:

- Ownerships of three feddans or less (this implies that most rural landowners are exempted).

- Agricultural land owned by the government.

- Annexes to agricultural land.

- Endowment land.

- Agricultural land occupied by buildings for housing and utilities.

- Owners whose tax liability does not exceed EGP 4 per year.

The laws also provide for tax relief in the following cases:

- Land affected by natural subsidence.

- Land that has become unarable because of the presence of public utilities, poor drainage, floods, depletion of water resources, or drought.

- Land that has become unarable because of natural causes.

- Land occupied by buildings connected to public housing.

- Land that has never been cultivated and is deprived of a means of irrigation or drainage or is in need of serious reparation at significant cost.

- Land that is no longer suitable for agriculture because of natural disasters or wars.

- Owners whose agricultural land tax liability does not exceed EGP 20 per year.

VALUATION

The rental value of one feddan (0.42 ha or 4,200m^2, approximately one acre) per year is estimated on the basis of the land's fertility and quality as determined by the relevant division and valuation committee. This committee is headed by a representative of the Ministry of Finance and includes five members (a representative of the Ministry of Agriculture, a representative of the Mapping Department, the village mayor, and at least two farmers) (Amin 2010). The valuations must then be approved by the relevant governor. Approved valuations are published locally in a recognized newspaper. Revaluations are to be conducted every 10 years. However, until the most recent valuations were undertaken, valuations for the agricultural land tax dated back to 1989. A revaluation was conducted in 2009 but was not initially adopted by the government. It was expected that the 2009 valuation would result in an increase in the revenue of this tax from less than EGP 200 million (in 2009/2010) to more than EGP 1.5 billion (Amin 2010). However, new values have now been implemented because tax revenues from this tax were expected to increase in 2014 (Azim 2014). According to the Ministry of Finance, the new assessments could see tax liability increase from EGP 42 to EGP 300 per feddan (Azim 2014).

Owners may object to the value determined by the division and valuation committee. There is an appeal committee in each governorate, headed by the head of the property tax authority at the governorate level. The committee members are a judge, representatives of the Ministries of Finance and Housing, and three landowners (who may not be from the area in question).

The Tax Rate

The agricultural land tax rate is 14 percent of the feddan's annual rental value.

Collection and Enforcement

RETA offices located in the governorates and districts collect the taxes. Owners are expected to make one annual payment, although in practice, taxpayers often reach a compromise to pay in installments (Amin 2010). The collection and compliance measures and procedures are the same as those applied for the real estate tax.

Revenue Potential of Property Taxes

In comparison with other countries in North and Northeast Africa, Egypt's 2.5 percent property transfer tax does not seem excessive. Although the sellers of property incur statutory liability, some, if not all, of the effective burden may be shifted to buyers.

Given the minimal contribution of recurrent property taxes as a percentage of GDP and general taxes (Norregaard 2013), there seems to be significant room for generating more revenue from these taxes. However, the current political climate and administrative capacity in Egypt are such that it would be extremely difficult to increase revenues from either the real estate tax or the agricultural land tax significantly.

Before the enactment of Real Estate Tax Law 196 of 2008, there were a variety of laws dealing with real estate taxation in Egypt (Amin 2010). Although the new law was meant to rationalize and modernize the former system of real estate taxes, it has been beset by delays since its enactment. However, it has now been implemented, especially since the amendments provided by Law 117 of 2014, and has simplified the system to some extent by applying only one uniform tax rate. According to the law, the tax applies to all real estate in Egypt, subject to the various exemptions and forms of tax relief. However, exemptions are extensive, including residential property with a value of less than EGP 2 million,[2] although the exemption applies to the value of only one property owned by a taxpayer and not to the cumulative value of all property owned. In addition, the 2014 amendments also exempt hotels and presumably resort properties as well. The expectation was that the RETA would receive some 22 million property declarations from owners, but because only 1.5 million tax bills (Ayyad 2014) were sent out in 2014, it appears that only about 6.8 percent of property owners are presently within the tax net of the real estate tax.

The new law decreases the revaluation period to every five years instead of the previous ten years, which is more in line with international best practice. However, at the onset of a new valuation cycle, value increases may not exceed 30 percent for residential and 45 percent for nonresidential properties. Artificially manipulating assessed values by insisting on a value ceiling was seen as the appropriate answer in an environment where a universal and seemingly static 10 percent tax rate applies across the country. The universal problem of increasing values, especially when a general revaluation is undertaken, is most commonly addressed by an appropriate reduction in the tax rate to be applied to the new values. This prevents windfall revenue gains, but it implies that the tax rate is not fixed in the legislation.

The new law also decreases the period of appeal of the valuation committee's assessments to sixty days instead of six months. However, depending on the number of objections received, it will be a major task for the appeal committees to adhere to the new, rather strict time constraints. International best practice overwhelmingly provides for a formal objection (in a valuation tribunal) and, in most cases, a further appeal to a specialized court or a high court. The wording of the law implies that there is no further right of appeal. The right to go to court and request a review also seems problematic. Generally, a review entails that where a court agrees that due process was not followed, the case should be heard again de novo.

The law is not retrospective and thus aims at encouraging taxpayers to comply with their tax obligations. The RETA started implementation with a national campaign requiring all owners of real estate to self-declare their ownership. Failure to declare could result in fines of between EGP 200 and EGP 2,000. The RETA has adopted a policy of targeting primarily high-value properties, such as offices, business parks, service facilities, and shopping malls.

A final concern regarding the real estate tax is that, given the significant value threshold legislated to appease taxpayers, an estimated 75 to 80 percent of residential properties, as stated by the former minister of finance (Hany Dimian) in 2015, could be excluded from the tax base because their assessed values will be less than the threshold of EGP 2 million (Ministry of Finance 2015). Because this tax is levied at the national level and also considers multiple ownership, it is arguably a wealth tax rather than a benefit tax.

The current concern about the agricultural land tax is the implementation of the new valuations after more than 25 years, but without reducing the 14 percent tax rate. Landowners are unlikely merely to accept an increase in tax liability that in some instances may exceed 700 percent.

Notes

1. Egypt has a separate law that governs the taxes on amusement centers (Law 24 of 1999).
2. Approximately USD 225,225 in September 2016.

References

Amin, K. 2010. "Property Tax System in Egypt." Paper presented at the Fellowship Workshop of the African Tax Institute/Lincoln Institute of Land Policy Project on Property Taxation in Africa, Stellenbosch, South Africa (December 4–5).

Ayyad, M. 2014. "Egypt Begins Collecting Property Tax for 1.5m Residential and Non-residential Units: Finance Minister." *Daily News* (Egypt), September 20. *www .dailynewsegypt.com/2014/09/20/egypt-begins-collecting-property-tax-1-5m-residential -non-residential-units-finance-minister/*.

Azim, A. M. 2014. "Agricultural Tax Rates to Remain the Same, Actual Taxes Could Increase According to Land Value: Ministry of Finance." *Daily News* (Egypt), January 19. *www.dailynewsegypt.com/2014/01/19/agricultural-tax-rates-to-remain-the -same-actual-taxes-could-increase-according-to-land-value-ministry-of-finance/*.

Bahl, R., and J. Martinez-Vazquez. 2008. "The Property Tax in Developing Countries: Current Practice and Prospects." In *Making the Property Tax Work: Experiences in Developing and Transitional Countries*, ed. R. W. Bahl, J. Martinez-Vazquez, and J. M. Youngman, 35–57. Cambridge, MA: Lincoln Institute of Land Policy.

CIA (Central Intelligence Agency). 2016. "Egypt." In *The World Factbook*. *https://www .cia.gov/library/publications/the-world-factbook/geos/eg.html*.

Egypt. 2014. "Factsheet: Vertical Division of Power." *https://portal.cor.europa.eu/arlem /Documents/EGYPT%20-%20FACT%20SHEET%201%20EN_4%20June%20 2014.pdf*.

Elrouby, S., K. Harju, and I. Corker. 2005. "Developing an Automated Cadastral Information System in Egypt." *www.fig.net/pub/cairo/papers/ts_34/ts34_03_elrouby_etal.pdf*.

IMF (International Monetary Fund). 2016. "IMF World Longitudinal Data (WoRLD)." IMF e-Library Data. *http://data.imf.org/?sk=77413F1D-1525-450A-A23A-47AEED40 FE78&sId=1390030109571*.

King, S. J. 2009. *The New Authoritarianism in the Middle East and North Africa*. Bloomington: Indiana University Press.

Metz, H. C. 1990. "Egypt: A Country Study." United States Library of Congress. *http://countrystudies.us/egypt/85.htm*.

Ministry of Finance. 2015. "Hany Dimian's Statement on Real Estate Tax." *www.mof .gov.eg/Arabic/MOFNews/Media/Pages/releas-a-28-10-14.aspx*.

————. 2016. "Financial Statement of Fiscal Years between 2012–2013 and 2016–2017." *www.mof.gov.eg.*

Norregaard, J. 2013. "Taxing Immovable Property—Revenue Potential and Implementation Challenges." IMF working paper. Washington, DC: IMF.

Rae, J. 2002. "Egypt Profile. In Land Tenure Review of the Near East, Part II: Individual Country Profiles." Rome: Food and Agriculture Organization.

RETA (Real Estate Taxation Authority). 2015. "Tax Calculation." *http://www.rta.gov.eg/En/CalculateTax* .

————. 2016. "Real Estate tax." *http://www.rta.gov.eg/En/BuildingTaxType?Length=2#4.*

United Nations. 2014. *World Urbanization Prospects.* Washington, DC: Department of Economics and Social Affairs, Population Division.

United Nations, Department of Economic and Social Affairs, Population Division. 2015. World Population Prospects: The 2015 Revision. https://esa.un.org/unpd/wpp/Publications/Files/World_Population_2015_Wallchart.pdf.

USAID (U.S. Agency for International Development). 2011. "Egypt—Land Tenure and Property Rights Profile 19." *http://usaidlandtenure.net/sites/default/files/country-profiles/full-reports/USAID_Land_Tenure_Egypt_Profile.pdf.*

World Bank. 2016a. "Country and Lending Groups." *http://data.worldbank.org/about/country-and-lending-groups.*

————. 2016b. "GDP per Capita (Current US%)." *http://data.worldbank.org/indicator/NY.GDP.PCAP.CD.*

Legislation

Law 53 of 1935.

Law 113 of 1939.

Law 178 of 1952.

Law 370 of 1953.

Law 56 of 1954.

Law 308 of 1955.

Law 51 of 1973.

Law 96 of 1992.

Law 24 of 1999.

Law 196 of 2008.

Law 117 of 2014.

11

Equatorial Guinea

BERNARD TAYOH AND RIËL FRANZSEN

Equatorial Guinea, officially the Republic of Equatorial Guinea, is located in west central Africa on the Bight of Biafra between Cameroon and Gabon. The country has an area of only 28,051 km² (World Bank 2014). The landmass consists of two parts: a continental region (Rio Muni) and an insular region comprising Annobon Island and Bioko Island, where the capital, Malabo, is situated. The country was formerly the colony of Spanish Guinea and acquired its present name after gaining independence in 1968. The country's official language, as specified in the constitution, is Spanish. However, French is also an official language. The total population is about 850,000 (United Nations 2015), of which about 145,000 live in Malabo (CIA 2016). Approximately 40 percent of the population is urban (United Nations 2014), and more than 70 percent of the urban population lives in slums.

The estimated GDP per capita in 2015 was USD 14,440 (World Bank 2016b). This high per capita figure is largely attributable to vast offshore oil reserves discovered in the mid-1990s. The oil and gas industry is the engine of growth and accounts for approximately 86 percent of GDP. However, national poverty estimates suggest that three-fourths of the population is living below the national poverty line of USD 2.00 per day, which is rather ironic for an African country classified as a high-income country in 2015. In 2016 the country was classified as an upper-middle-income country (World Bank 2016a).

In 1959, the Spanish Territory of Gulf of Guinea (previously Spanish Guinea) was established, with status similar to that of the provinces of metropolitan Spain. As the Spanish Equatorial Region, it was ruled by a governor general who exercised both military and civilian powers. On August 11, 1968, Equatorial Guineans voted for independence in a popular referendum, ushering in a new constitution that provided for a government with a General Assembly and a Supreme Court with judges appointed by the president. The regime of Francisco Macias, the first president, was characterized by abandonment of all government functions except internal security, which was accomplished and maintained by terror that led to the death or exile of about one-third of the country's population. As a result, the country's infrastructure, including the electricity network, water, roads, transportation, and health, fell into ruin. Macias was ousted by a coup d'état on August 3, 1979, and with the assistance of the United Nations Commission on Human Rights, a new constitution was drafted and then ratified by a popular vote on August 15, 1982. The 1982 constitution was replaced by a new constitution approved by a national referendum on November 17, 1991. It was amended in January 1995 and again in November 2011. The present constitution is officially referred to as the "January 1995 Constitution."

Business Climate and Economy

Although business laws promote a liberalized economy, the business climate of the country remains difficult. The laws are applied in a highly selective manner. Corruption among officials is widespread, and many business transactions are concluded secretly. There is little diversified industry apart from the oil and gas in the country, and despite the government's move to expand the role of free enterprise and promote foreign investment, success in creating an atmosphere conducive to investor interest has been limited (Tayoh 2014).

The discovery and exploitation of large oil and gas reserves have contributed to dramatic economic growth over the past decade, and the present economy is heavily dominated by hydrocarbon production. Forestry and farming are minor components of GDP. Subsistence farming remains the dominant form of livelihood.

Government

Equatorial Guinea has a unitary semipresidential government in which the president is head of state and head of the executive. The country is divided into two regions, seven provinces (Annobon, Bioko Norte, Bioko Sur,

Centro Sur, Kie-Ntem, Litoral, and Wele-Nzas), and eighteen districts.[1] The country is further divided into thirty municipalities and around one thousand village councils and residents' associations.

The legal system is a mix of civil and customary law. Tribal laws and customs are applied in the courts if they do not conflict with national laws. However, the current judicial system mostly applies customary law and is a combination of traditional, civil, and military justice (Tayoh 2014).

The 1995 constitution provides for the existence of various levels of "local collectivities, which are autonomous legal entities." The constitution stipulates that local collectivities are charged with the direction and administration of regions, provinces, districts, and *communes*. The local collectivities are responsible for the economic and social development of their own areas in accordance with guidelines laid down by the law (Tayoh 2014).

Local-Government Finances

The property tax is the most important tax and source of revenue for municipalities. However, collection of this tax is problematic, particularly for smaller municipalities. The main challenges include lack of data and information on taxable properties, poor staff capacity, fraudulent declarations, and lack of enforcement mechanisms at the local level.

The central government collects property taxes for Malabo and Bata and distributes the tax revenue, plus government subventions to cover operating and capital costs, to the 30 municipalities via the state budget. Another important source of local-government revenue is the tax on individuals (poll tax), but again there are serious enforcement challenges arising from lack of necessary data on population dynamics and lack of capacity, among other issues.

Land Tenure

In principle, all land in Equatorial Guinea belongs to the state, which can decide to allocate parcels to individuals as it deems appropriate. However, the state recognizes land ownership rights held by individuals provided the land is put to productive use, whether for agriculture or otherwise (Tayoh 2014).

Customary Tenure

In rural areas, land generally belongs to families and is handed down from generation to generation. Rights belong to the family as a whole, and no individual has property rights over such land. Property rights to land being used for agricultural purposes in rural areas are specifically guaranteed and protected by Article 29 of the 1995 constitution.

Private Ownership

Under Equatorial Guinea law, an individual or entity can obtain ownership rights to land through registration of his or its interest as private property. Decree-Law 05 of 1987 guarantees private ownership of rural land to property grantees. This decree-law provides that a buyer may become the owner of abandoned land by registering his interest and paying 10 percent of the land price to the government of Equatorial Guinea. This is done through the principle of *mise en valeur*, which accords ownership rights to those who intensively develop a parcel of land. The buyer is required to carry out a five-year plan for cultivation or construction and may not sell the land to a third person within this period. If these conditions are not fulfilled, the land is returned to the state, which then distributes the land to villages. In addition, individuals may apply for and obtain land from the government through a *gré à gré* agreement.[2] The land must be developed within a period of five years, or the state will confiscate it. Besides these, there are no other available data on land legislation. The closest land-related legislation is the short forest Decree-Law No. 14/1981 (of September 29, 1981), which recognizes and guarantees ownership rights over land obtained before 1975. The main objective of this decree is to establish and guarantee customary land rights.

Land Registration

Land held as freehold must be registered in the national land register in order to establish irrevocable ownership. Registration in the land registry is the final stage of a process that also involves assessment by inspectors and engineers of the Cadastral Department. Land registration is a complex, lengthy, and costly process. Government regulations require the landowner to pay a registration charge of 1.5 percent of the property value. In practice, however, the actual rate is usually between 18 and 25 percent. Each province of the country is supposed to have a land registry, but in practice, only the registries in Malabo and Bata are functional. No precise information on the number or percentage of registered lands is available, but the Directorate of Taxes estimates the level at less than 1 percent. Most registered properties are in Malabo and Bata (Tayoh 2014).

Tax Administration

All tax-related matters, including assessment, exemptions, mode of collection, and enforcement, are embodied in the General Tax Code 2005, promulgated by Law No. 04/2004 (of October 28, 2004) as revised in 2012 (hereinafter "Tax Code"), which sets out the main principles and regulations of the overall tax system.[3] The Tax Code vests authority for carrying out all tax-related operations in the Directorate of Taxes and Collections of the Ministry of Finance and Budget (MFB), which has offices stationed in each province of the country. Overall, the revenue administration is under the MFB, and its officials are charged with the assessment, collection, and enforcement of all taxes contained in the tax code. It is clearly observable, however, that the tax administration lacks capacity and is fragmented administratively, and that many of its officials lack adequate knowledge of the provisions of the Tax Code.

Taxes are a relatively minor component of government revenue, which is heavily dominated by royalties, profit sharing, and bonuses from the oil and gas sector (93 percent in 2010). In 2010, the value-added tax (with a standard rate of 15 percent) generated only about 0.6 percent of GDP. Although no disaggregated statistics were available for contributions from property-related taxes in 2010, they are thought to be insignificant compared with the large role for hydrocarbons but may make a significant contribution to local revenues. In 2012, total taxes constituted only 11.9 percent of GDP (IMF 2016), and property taxes collected by the central government constituted 0.03 percent of GDP (IMF 2016).

Property-Related Taxes

The Property Transfer Tax

There is no formal property market in Equatorial Guinea, and most property transfers are informal. Administrative formalities arise only when a buyer tries to transfer or ascertain ownership title. A property transfer tax is levied on the value of property transferred inter vivos; on capital gains in urban and rural property; and on the sale, lease exchange, or mortgage of real estate, among other transactions.

The state and autonomous bodies of the government are specifically exempt from the tax. Also exempt are nonprofit, educational, and religious institutions; local governments; transfers of real estate made in favor of foreign governments for diplomatic use; and transfers exempt under international agreements.

The tax is ad valorem and depends on whether the transfer involves nonresidents. The tax on real property transfers between residents is usually 5 percent but can range from 1 percent to 9 percent depending on the nature of the transfer and the amount involved (Article 454 of the Tax Code). The rate varies from 10 percent to 25 percent on real estate transfers between residents and nonresidents and between nonresidents.

The Capital Gains Tax

Capital gains derived from the sale of real estate assets are subject to the capital gains tax. The standard income tax rate (ranging from 0 to 35 percent) applies, except for nonresidents, who are subject to a 25 percent withholding tax.

The Stamp Duty

Legal instruments and transaction documents, including accounting and banking documents, rental and other contracts, and the registration of real property, incur a stamp duty that is assessed on the value declared at the time a juridical act is concluded. There is no exemption from this requirement. The rate varies from 1 percent to 10 percent, depending on the value of the instrument.[4]

The Property Tax

In principle, real property must be assessed and registered before any land tax is determined and collected. In practice, however, these taxes are assessed and collected, most often arbitrarily, by officials of the tax directorate after periodic field visits to unregistered properties, particularly where such land is being developed. The tax is levied on both urban and rural land, irrespective of whether the property is developed, if the area is accessible by a paved road created by the state or a local collectivity.

The Rural Property Tax

The rural property tax is levied on all rural properties and is based on size and potential income as determined by the tax administration. This is an annual tax payable in two installments, one every six months. The tax rate based on the size of the land is XAF 200 per hectare. The tax rates based on income are those of the corporate and personal income taxes and range from 0 to 35 percent depending on the amount.

Exempt properties include the following:

- Properties smaller than five hectares.

- Properties owned by the government.

- Properties owned by nonprofit organizations.

- Properties owned by religious institutions.

- Properties owned by representatives of foreign governments on a reciprocal basis.

A 50 percent deduction from the fixed rate is allowed for property used for husbandry and for cultivation of cocoa, coffee, coconuts, foodstuffs, and palm oil.

The Urban Property Tax

Owners of urban properties are subject to an urban property tax. The Tax Code defines urban property as "any land with or without buildings and the buildings built thereon, whenever located in urban areas." The tax is levied on actual or potential income from urban property, which is based on the value of the land and buildings as determined by the tax administration. The tax is an annual tax payable in two installments, one every six months. The tax base is 40 percent of the value of the land and any buildings on it, assessed together. The tax rate is 1 percent of the taxable base.

Exemptions

A taxable value threshold exempts property with a taxable base below XAF 1 million, provided that it is the only property of the owner or that the combined taxable base of all properties of an owner does not exceed that value. New construction and renovated properties are also exempt for the first five years. However, the taxpayer is required to file a declaration annually during the exemption period.

Liability for the Urban Property Tax

According to the Tax Code (Article 366), the owner of the property is liable for declaring and paying the tax, and if the property is in the possession of another person, the possessor also becomes liable for making the declaration. The term *possessor* as used in this context does not include a tenant but is limited to a person who, by occupying the property, acquires some form of real right (including a usufruct) over the property. According to the Tax Code (Article 379), the owner or possessor is obligated to carry out a preliminary declaration that will be used as a basis for annual taxation. As changes occur on the property over time, the taxpayer must inform the tax authorities within 30 days about such changes in the taxable base.

Valuation

Officials of the tax directorate carry out assessment and valuation on the basis of technical specifications furnished by the cadastral department and the declaration made by the property owner. In practice, the tax is collected each subsequent year without taking new developments into account, except where the property owner formally discloses such changes and the value thereof to the taxation officials.

Collection

The tax is paid directly at the state treasury of the district or province where the property is located. There is no specially designated or dedicated land tax or property tax revenue collector.

Enforcement

There is no documented information on overall tax compliance or compliance with property tax payments. However, local government officials in Malabo noted that payment and collection rates for the property tax are extremely low, partly because of the low level of land registration and the lack of capacity in the departments dealing with land registration and taxation (Jayoh 2014).

Penalties for late payments of the property tax are imposed at a rate of 25 percent of the tax owed. However, in cases other than late payment, such as incorrect declarations, the penalty is 50 percent of the tax due if no bad faith is established and 100 percent if the taxpayer made a fraudulent declaration. Given the low level of compliance, it is doubtful that these severe penalties are enforced in practice. Interest is payable on arrears at a rate of 10 percent per month.

Appeals

The Tax Code defines taxpayers' legal rights and, in principle, protects taxpayers from unreasonable treatment by the tax administration or its officials. Disputes and complaints from aggrieved taxpayers are to be settled by duly constituted tax boards on factual matters and abuses that arise in the application of tax standards. A taxpayer who is not satisfied at this level is entitled to seek redress from a higher-level body, the Central Economic-Administrative Tribunal, which has the ultimate power to rule on issues arising from the exercise of regulatory authority and also has jurisdiction in the area of taxation.

Prospects for the Property Tax in Equatorial Guinea

Despite Equatorial Guinea's status as an upper-middle-income country, the distribution of income is extremely unequal, and the majority of the population lives below the poverty line. Because of low oil prices, the government may refocus its attention on taxation in general as a source of revenue.

However, given the challenges with land rights and registration and poor taxpayer compliance, it is unlikely that the property tax will play a meaningful role in the short to medium term.

Notes

1. Decree-Law No. 2/1980 (of March 1980) regarding the administrative and territorial reorganization of Equatorial Guinea.

2. A *gré à gré* agreement is a contract where consensus is reached willingly, that is, without one party dictating the terms.

3. However, although the tax law clearly sets out the rules and regulations for operating in Equatorial Guinea, the oil and gas sector is excluded from its reach because there is a separate directorate in the MFB that caters to all oil-related revenues. The government signs individual production-sharing contracts with the oil and gas companies that contain specific tax and royalty arrangements for each deal. The contents of these arrangements are not made public, and the tax administration is not involved in them.

4. Article 454 of the Tax Code.

References

CIA (Central Intelligence Agency). 2016. "Equatorial Guinea." In *The World Factbook*. *https://www.cia.gov/library/publications/the-world-factbook/geos/ek.html*.

IMF (International Monetary Fund). 2016. "IMF World Longitudinal Data (WoRLD)." IMF e-Library Data. *http://data.imf.org/?sk=77413F1D-1525-450A-A23A-47AEED40FE78&sId=1390030109571*.

Tayoh, B. 2014. "Property Taxation in Equatorial Guinea." Unpublished working paper. Cambridge, MA: Lincoln Institute of Land Policy.

United Nations. 2014. *World Urbanization Prospects*. Washington, DC: Department of Economics and Social Affairs, Population Division.

United Nations, Department of Economic and Social Affairs, Population Division. 2015. World Population Prospects: The 2015 Revision. https://esa.un.org/unpd/wpp/Publications/Files/World_Population_2015_Wallchart.pdf.

World Bank. 2014. *World Development Indicators*. Washington, DC.

———. 2016a. "Country and Lending Groups." *http://data.worldbank.org/about/country-and-lending-groups*.

———. 2016b. "GDP per Capita (Current US%)." *http://data.worldbank.org/indicator/NY.GDP.PCAP.CD*.

Legislation

Decree-Law No. 2/1980 (of March 1980).

Decree-Law No. 14/1981 (of September 29, 1981).

Decree-Law No. 05 of 1987.

General Tax Code 2005, promulgated by Law No. 04/2004 (of October 28, 2004).

12

Gabon

NARA MONKAM

Gabon is located on the west coast of Africa, with Equatorial Guinea and Cameroon on the north, the Republic of Congo (Congo-Brazzaville) on the east and south, and the Atlantic Ocean on the west. It proclaimed its independence from France on August 17, 1960. Gabon has an area of about 267,667 km^2 and a population of approximately 1.7 million (United Nations 2015; World Bank 2014). The capital and largest city is Libreville. Approximately 87 percent of the population lives in urban areas (United Nations 2014). The two main cities, Libreville (with an estimated 707,000 inhabitants) and Port Gentil, constitute 85 percent of the urban population and 60 percent of the total population. Gabon is classified as an upper-middle-income country (World Bank 2016a). The 2015 GDP per capita was estimated to be USD 8,266 (World Bank 2016b). Because of Gabon's offshore oil revenue, this figure is exceptionally high compared with the average GDP per capita in Africa.

Government

Gabon is divided into four levels of administrative units: nine provinces, 47 *départements* (divisions), 15 subdivisions or districts, and 50 communes or municipalities. According to the decentralization process regulated by the Decentralization Law 15/96 (of June 6, 1996), there are two levels of local government, defined as "public entities distinct from the central

government and endowed with legal status and financial autonomy":
départements and municipalities, whether urban or rural. Urban municipalities can be subdivided into several *arrondissements* depending on the
size of the territory and the population density. Rural municipalities are
subdivided into one or more villages, and, in general, a village has a population of at least 100 people.

Both département and municipal councils have the authority to approve
local taxes and user fees within the limits of the central government's
mandate. The decentralization law also regulates the assignment of expenditure responsibilities, the assignment of revenue, and intergovernmental transfers among local governments. Beyond the general provisions
contained in the decentralization law, départements and municipalities are
not yet responsible for providing public services other than civil administration, a police force, and solid-waste collection. Furthermore, they remain
heavily financially dependent on the central government and lack sufficient
own-source revenues to ensure autonomy, accountability, and efficient provision of public services. Allocation of financial resources from the central government in the form of income tax refunds, which represent about
half of local governments' total revenues, is significantly biased toward rural municipalities even though 87 percent of the population lives in urban
areas, where public services should be focused. The tax revenue allocation
formula is fixed by Ordinance No. 005/81/PR (of March 3, 1981), which
largely favors rural areas (73 percent) to the detriment of urban areas
(27 percent) (World Bank 2006).

Land Tenure

Three government agencies administer land management and land development in Gabon: the Service des Domaines within the Ministry of
Finance; the Service du Cadastre within the Urban Planning Ministry;
and the Services de la Conservation Foncière (or land conservation).
Gabon has a dual land tenure system: a statutory system and a customary
system. All land without a title that has not been registered as individual
private property belongs to the national domain (Law No. 15/63, Article
2; Akomezogho 2006; Monkam 2010). Therefore, it is only through the
state that people can have access to land. All land held under customary
land tenure systems is legally state owned. In other words, the current
land legislation encourages individual private tenure through a formal land
registration procedure and does not recognize communally based land
tenure. However, most land remains in the hands of the indigenous communities in rural areas (local land chiefs, family heads, and village nota-

bles) and is managed through customary land tenure systems (Wily 2012). Because the population is relatively sparse and mostly urbanized, land legislation is not a priority of the central government.

The procedures for land registration prescribed in Law No. 15/63 (of May 8, 1963) are particularly lengthy and cumbersome. According to the Department of Taxation, there is no strict enforcement of land registration procedures, and as a result, there is significant illegal occupation of land. For example, in 2006, between 40,000 and 45,000 parcels of land were identified in the cadastre, but only about 15,000 land titles were distributed. The Department of Taxation has proposed reforms that would eliminate the provisional attribution phase and create an administrative structure that would consolidate all government services currently involved in the land registration process (Akomezogho 2006; Bruce 1998; Comby 1995; World Bank 2006).

State-owned land is divided into public and private domains. The state public domain is composed of the country's rivers, lakes, roads, railroads, ports, and bridges. The state private domain includes all land that is not registered as private property and does not have a title. However, the state can lease any land in its private domain for a term of 50 years, and the lease can be renewed for up to 49 years (Bruce 1998).

In Gabon, the property market remains imperfect (Monkam 2010). Because private individual titles to state land can be granted only through the land registration process, no legal property market exists for unimproved land in Gabon. Additionally, only a small portion of the population in Gabon goes beyond the first administrative phase in the land registration process because of the considerable fees and time involved in the various land registration procedures. This situation frustrates the development of the property market in Gabon.

Taxation

In 2012, total taxes constituted 15.1 percent of GDP (IMF 2015). At the national level, the largest part of Gabon's tax revenues (over 50 percent) comes from the tax on oil companies and the tax on oil-sector subcontractors. Other important taxes at the national level include (1) the corporate income tax on nonoil companies imposed on income and profit at a regular tax rate of 35 percent and a rate of 20 percent for public institutions, associations, nonprofit community-based organizations, and property development companies licensed for that purpose; (2) the personal income tax, which has 11 tax brackets with rates ranging from 0 to 50 percent; and (3) the value-added tax (Monkam 2009).

Property Transfer Taxes

The tax on property in mortmain (*taxe sur les biens de main morte*) is an annual tax representing the right of conveyance inter vivos or upon death and is levied on real property belonging to companies and collectivities. The tax base is the declared gross value of the real property on January 1 of the tax year, and the tax rate is 0.25 percent of the tax base. Exempt from the tax on property in mortmain are general or limited partnerships; public limited companies with the exclusive purpose of buying and selling real property, excluding their registered fixed assets; property belonging to public service companies providing social or medical assistance; and property permanently exempt from the property tax on improved and unimproved property (GDITC 2007, Articles 334–340). The Finance Act of 2015 reduced the rates on the sale of immovable property from 15 percent to 6 percent.

Property Taxes

The property tax legislation currently in place in Gabon is based on Law No. 15/63 (of May 8, 1963), which perpetuated the property tax established by the colonial system at the end of the 19th century (Comby 1995). In accordance with the Decentralization Law No. 15/96 (of June 6, 1996) and the General Direct and Indirect Tax Code (GDITC 2007), local governments are entitled to levy property taxes and other direct local taxes as part of their own revenue sources. However, the legislation stipulates that the tax rate and the tax base of each direct local tax and the administration of the tax collection are fixed by national law, and local governments are given no discretion. In particular, the legislation requires the central government to collect direct local taxes and distribute them in their entirety to local governments. Direct local taxes include the property tax on improved property, the property tax on unimproved property (vacant land), business taxes and fees, license fees, and the highway tax. The property tax on improved property, the property tax on unimproved property, and the land tax are the three types of property taxes levied in Gabon.

The land tax is a national tax levied and collected by the central government. Therefore, under the legislation, there is a dual property tax system: a value-based system, in which assessment is based on the net annual rental value, and an area-based system, in which assessment is based on property size.

The Property Tax on Developed Property

The property tax on improved property or developed land (*contribution foncière des propriétés bâties*) is based on the taxable income, which is equal to the annual rental value of the improved property on January 1, less 25 percent for maintenance and repairs (GDITC 2007). The tax is levied on improvements, whether registered or not, such as houses, factories, shops, and warehouses located in a département or municipality. The property tax on improved property is also levied on the plant and machinery within industrial plants that are an integral part of the building. The owner is responsible for paying the tax.

Valuation and Assessment

The property tax agent assesses the rental value of improved property annually and communicates the assessment by letter to the taxpayer. The rental value of improved property is determined by means of a bona fide lease, a declaration of rental value made by the taxpayer, a comparison with other premises for which rental values are known, or, in the absence of these instruments, a direct assessment by the property tax agent.

Objections and Appeals

The GDITC provides that an aggrieved taxpayer can challenge the assessment by writing to the Minister of Economy and Finance before December 31 of the following year. The minister assigns the matter to the general director of taxation, who follows the matter up with the property tax agent. If the tax agent totally or partially rejects the claim, the matter is referred to the Tax Commission. All claimants who have not received a ruling from the minister within six months of the date of submission of the claim can bring the case to the Administrative Court.

Tax Rates

The tax rate on improved property is fixed in legislation and is uniform across all categories of buildings. The property tax on improved property is levied and collected by the central government, and all collected revenues are remitted to local governments. The tax rate on improved property is set at 25 percent of 75 percent of the rental value.

Exemptions, Rebates, and Deductions

A rebate or reduction may be granted if a house is vacant or a commercial or industrial establishment becomes inoperative for reasons beyond the taxpayer's control and the premises remain idle for at least six consecutive months. The GDITC also allows for permanent and temporary exemptions. Permanent exemptions include the following:

- Buildings belonging to the state, international organizations, municipalities, chambers of commerce, and, provided that there is reciprocity, embassies and consulates.

- Facilities in seaports and infrastructure related to internal navigation routes.

- Water or electrical power supply infrastructure belonging to municipalities.

- Buildings used for worship, educational, and sporting purposes.

- Buildings belonging to missions or to duly authorized public benefit organizations and used for humanitarian or social purposes.

- Buildings serving rural farms or used for agriculture by farming cooperatives.

- Residential housing and outbuildings built by taxpayers on state land if it has been assigned to them under a permit authorizing occupation at no cost and the buildings are not used in whole or in part for rental to third parties or to operate businesses subject to the business tax or license fees.

Temporary exemptions from the tax are granted for new construction, refurbishment, and additions for three years, starting on January 1 of the year after completion. The exemption period is five years for industrial facilities and for buildings used for housing unless the buildings are offered for lease or are used as vacation homes.

Billing, Collection, and Enforcement

Pursuant to the GDITC, the general director of taxation, on the first of each month, issues a list of all taxpayers in a certain area (a taxpayer roll) and transfers the property tax bill notifications to the tax officials in charge of revenue collection. The tax officials make the necessary arrangements to notify taxpayers of their tax liability. The GDITC stipulates that no taxpayer may use the excuse of not receiving the tax bill at the appropriate time to defer payment or claim a reduction or waiver of fines and penalties. The legislation also allows for a one-time payment during the year of the property tax liability, regardless of its amount. The legislation allows the following enforcement measures against potential tax evaders:

- Interest on arrears equal to 10 percent of the tax liability can be charged when a tax payment has not been received by the last day of the second month following the month when the taxpayer roll and the corresponding property tax bill notifications were emitted. Subsequently, a 1 percent increase will be applied each month the tax liability is not paid;

- Property can be seized and sold at a public auction.

The Property Tax on Undeveloped Property

The Tax Base

The tax on unimproved property or undeveloped land *(contribution fonci-ère des propriétés non bâties)* is levied annually on all types of unimproved property. The owner is responsible for payment of the tax. Individuals or businesses holding a property deed or a temporary or permanent occupancy title and occupying the property in their own right are considered owners of the relevant property (GDITC 2007).

Valuation and Assessment

In urban areas, the value of unimproved property is the market value on January 1 of the tax year and is determined by means of comparable sales or comparison with similar properties in the area whose market values have been recorded. In rural areas, the market value of unimproved property is fixed per hectare on an annual basis pursuant to Decree No. 57/460 (of April 4, 1957) according to the type of agricultural activity, as described in table 12.1. In both urban and rural areas, the property tax agent assesses the market value of unimproved property every year. The administration of the property tax on undeveloped property and the objection and appeal process are similar to those enacted for the property tax on improved property.

Tax Rates

The tax rate on unimproved property is set in the legislation at 25 percent of 80 percent of the rental value. The central government levies and collects the property tax on unimproved property, and local authorities are entitled to 100 percent of the revenues.

Table 12.1 Fixed Market Value of Unimproved Property in Rural Areas

Type of Agricultural Activity	Fixed Market Value per Hectare (in XAF)[1]
Cultivated land producing coffee, palm oil, and rubber	600
Other agricultural activities	250
Second-category land with adjoining factories to process agricultural products	150
Idle land	150
Land used for livestock farming	150

Source: GDITC (2007).

[1] On January 21, 2014, USD 1.00 = XAF 460.00.

Exemptions, Rebates, and Deductions

The tax on unimproved property is subject to a variety of exemptions. Permanently exempted properties include streets, public places, roads, and rivers; property belonging to the state, international organizations, municipalities, chambers of commerce, and, provided there is reciprocity, embassies and consulates; land on which buildings have been erected and a certain portion of the land surrounding these buildings; land belonging to missions or duly authorized groups and used for educational, sporting, humanitarian, or social purposes; land with a surface area of less than five hectares within a radius of twenty-five kilometers of urban developments that is used exclusively for market gardening; and quarry and mine sites. Temporarily exempted properties include land outside urban centers that is used for livestock farming or land that has been cleared, ploughed, and sowed. Depending on the use of this land, the exemption period ranges from three to five years.

The Land Tax

The Tax Base

The land tax (*taxe sur les terrains*) is levied on building lots, building grounds, and unused land. The assessment of the tax is based on the size of the property, that is, square meters or hectares of land (an area-based system). The land tax on undeveloped building lots includes all land within the boundaries of urban centers. Building grounds include all land within the boundaries of urban centers that surrounds buildings subject to the tax on improved property. The tax code defines unused land as any land outside the boundaries of urban centers that has not been developed or improved during the five years preceding January 1 of the taxable year. Persons or businesses holding a property deed or a temporary or permanent occupancy title, license holders, and individuals with a usufruct right to land are liable for the land tax (GDITC 2007).

Valuation and Assessment

In urban areas, the land tax is based on the surface area in square meters of the property. In rural areas, the taxable base is assessed according to the size of the land in hectares. The legislation requires that before March 1 of each year, owners of land in rural areas must send tax officials a statement including the date when the individual land title was issued and the surface area of unused land.

Table 12.2 Land Tax Rates

First-class urban land	XAF 200 per m^2
Second-class urban land	XAF 40 per m^2
Rural land	XAF 1,000 per hectare

Source: GDITC (2007), Chapter 2, Annex.

Tax Rates

Differential tax rates are applied to urban and rural land. Land in urban areas is further subject to differential tax rates for different property categories. Tax rates for the various land categories are shown in table 12.2.

Exemptions, Rebates, and Deductions

The tax legislation provides for a variety of exemptions from the land tax. Permanently exempted properties include the following:

- Land subject to provisional grants.

- Land exempt from the property tax on unimproved property.

- Land used for commercial and industrial purposes, such as project sites, warehouses, and similar facilities.

- Land in urban areas with a surface area of no more than 4,000 m^2.

Temporary exemptions are available for the following property categories:

- Land temporarily exempt from the property tax on unimproved property.

- Urban land on which construction is prohibited.

- Acquired urban land for two years after acquisition on condition that the purchaser has expressly communicated the intention to build on the land to the tax administration before December 31 of the acquisition year.

The requirements of the tax legislation regarding objections and appeals and all aspects of property tax administration, including billing, collection, and enforcement, are similar across all national and local taxes.

The Property Tax System as Practiced in Gabon

Although comprehensive property tax legislation has been enacted, implementation of the provisions of the law remains a major problem. In accordance with the Decentralization Law No. 15/96, local governments can impose only two types of property taxes: the tax on improved property and the tax on unimproved property. Furthermore, property tax rates and bases are set by law, and local governments have no discretion. In addition, property tax revenues are collected by the national government and then passed on to local authorities.

Critical shortcomings persist in the fiscal decentralization process. Despite the general provisions in the decentralization law, municipalities are heavily dependent on central-government transfers. Although fiscal decentralization is demonstrated through guaranteed revenue transfers from the national government, the devolution of taxing authority would undoubtedly confer greater autonomy and accountability on local governments.

Despite rather detailed laws, property taxes as stipulated by the law have not yet been implemented. In practice, there is an area-based system. Specifically, two variants of property taxes called *redevances domaniales* or land taxes are being used. The first type of redevance domaniale is based on the assessed rate per square meter multiplied by the size of the unimproved land parcel. The second type of redevance domaniale is based on the assessed rate per square meter multiplied by the size of the improved land parcel. Both taxes are collected by the national government and distributed to local governments (Akomezogho 2006). The revenue from these two taxes is negligible. Various factors have contributed not only to the low level of tax revenues but also to the delay in the implementation of the property tax legislation as set forth in the Decentralization Law No. 15/96.

First, there is a lack of political will and bureaucratic support for such a change. This can be explained by a strong desire to maintain centralized power in order to prevent opposition groups from using decentralization to strengthen their power base. Additionally, because of the amount of discretion granted to government officials, tax evasion is rampant among government officials and influential taxpayers who own a large share of improved and unimproved property. Another factor is the central government's hesitation to impose additional taxes on an already heavily burdened and impoverished population.

Second, in 2008, Gabon's offshore oil production accounted for approximately 43 percent of GDP, 65 percent of the national budget, and 81 percent of exports (IMF 2008). Because the oil sector represents such a large share of total government revenues and has remained the main driving force of the economy, the central government has tended to overlook the negligible receipts from property taxes and therefore has put less emphasis on implementation of the decentralization law. Third, coverage of the land tax is poor because of problems with property discovery due to the lack of strict enforcement of land registration procedures. As a result, there is significant illegal occupation of land. Finally, resources allocated to the development of a broader and comprehensive fiscal cadastre are inadequate. The cadastre administration is characterized by insufficiently qualified staff, the inefficiency of manual systems used to systematically identify properties, and the lack of proper tax maps, aerial photography, vehicles for field surveys, and computers for data management.

The current local finance system can be characterized as follows:

- The local-government tax revenue structure is composed of locally levied taxes and shared taxes. Locally levied taxes include those on hotel accommodation, nightclubs, taxis, pleasure boats, car-wash facilities, movie theaters, and special events.

- The shared tax revenues are those collected by the central government and distributed to local governments. They include the property tax on improved property and the property tax on unimproved property, the taxes based on land area, business taxes, license fees, the highway tax, and the municipal tax on fuels.

The Importance of Property Taxes as a Revenue Source

The largest portion of local-government revenue is transfers from the state budget. There are two primary sources of these transfers: income tax refunds, constituting approximately 95 percent of transfers and about 43 percent of local-government total revenues; and annual subsidies, which represent about 33 percent of municipalities' annual revenues. As a result, local taxes that are collected entirely by the central government on behalf of the local governments do not constitute an important own source of revenue. Business taxes, in particular, are the largest source of local tax revenues. Property tax revenues are a negligible portion of local tax revenues because of the small number of registered titles. In general, revenues from local fees and licenses are lower than those from local taxes, although the number of fees and licenses imposed by city councils in the largest municipalities has been increasing.

Table 12.3 shows the total revenues for Libreville, Gabon's largest city. Unfortunately, the figures reported do not distinguish the different types of local tax revenues collected by the central government and refunded to local governments. As can be seen in table 12.3, total tax revenues decreased between 2003 and 2005. This decline can be attributed primarily to a decrease in local tax revenues collected entirely by the state on behalf of local governments, which represented, on average, 53 percent of Libreville's total tax revenue and 34 percent of total revenue between 2001 and 2005. Since business taxes are the largest source of local tax revenues in Gabon, they obviously drive these numbers and thereby confirm that only

Table 12.3 Total Revenues in the Commune of Libreville, 2001–2005

Local Taxes and Fees	2001 (XAF Millions)	2002 (XAF Millions)	2003 (XAF Millions)	2004 (XAF Millions)	2005 (XAF Millions)
Taxes collected by the communes[1]	2,258.4	2,178.8	2,095.3	2,255.9	2,197.5
Taxes collected by the state on behalf of the communes[2]	4,315.6	5,260.1	3,780.6	3,232.5	3,558.9
Local fees and licenses	1,331.5	1,011.9	1,349.6	1,811.9	1,308.1
Total tax revenues (A)	7,905.4	8,450.9	7,225.5	7,300.3	7,064.6
Subsidies	4,100.8	3,600.0	3,607.2	4,099.6	3,619.3
Provision of services	220.7	173.6	177.3	186.3	269.3
Sundry revenues	78.5	77.7	138.9	44.4	42.6
Past revenues	158.0	116.8	120.5	88.8	87.8
Total revenues (B)	12,463.5	12,418.9	11,269.4	11,719.4	11,083.6
% of local taxes collected by the state in (A)	55	62	52	44	50
% of local taxes collected by the state in (B)	35	42	34	28	32
% of local taxes in total revenues	63	68	64	62	64

Source: Yebe (2007).

[1] Local taxes collected by the communes include taxes applied to various activities, such as hotel accommodations, nightclubs, taxis, pleasure boats, car washing, movie theaters, and special events.

[2] Local taxes recovered entirely by the state on behalf of the Commune of Libreville include business taxes (*contributions des patentes*), license fees (*contribution des licences*), the highway tax (*taxe vicinale*), the municipal tax on fuels, and property taxes (*redevances domaniales*).

a small portion of local tax revenues is derived from property taxes. Additionally, local taxes collected by Libreville constituted, on average, approximately 19 percent of its total revenues during this period. In other words, refunds from the central government (taxes collected by the state on behalf of the commune and then returned to the commune) accounted for nearly two-thirds of total revenues in Libreville. In this context, the restrictions and limitations imposed on Libreville and all local governments are twofold. First, their especially weak taxing authority restricts their ability to collect their own revenue. As stated previously, the rates and bases of property taxes and other direct local taxes (shared taxes) that local governments are entitled to use as part of their own revenue sources are dictated and fixed by law. In addition, these local taxes are collected entirely at the national level and then are distributed to local governments. Second, transfers from the state and poor tax administration deter local governments in their efforts to efficiently improve the mobilization of the few locally levied taxes, licenses, and fees they have the power to collect.

For the most part, Gabon's heavy dependence on oil production and the nonapplication of the decentralization law because of a lack of political will account for the fact that the property tax is not used optimally as an important own source of revenue for local governments. Development of the property tax system in urban areas is in an embryonic stage, but taxation of rural properties as provided for in the law is still quite impractical. In short, the property tax is not an important own source of revenue in Gabon. Transfers from the central government in the form of income tax refunds and subsidies remain the most important source of revenue for départements and municipalities.

References

Akomezogho, F. A. 2006. "La question du droit du sol et la propriété foncière." Paper presented at the 35th Conférence Internationale du Réseau Habitat et Francophonie, Libreville, Gabon (November 18–22).

Bruce, J. W. 1998. "Country Profiles of Land Tenure: Africa." Research paper no. 130. Madison: University of Wisconsin–Madison, Land Tenure Center.

CIA (Central Intelligence Agency). 2016. "Gabon." In *The World Factbook*. *https://www .cia.gov/library/publications/the-world-factbook/geos/gb.html*.

Comby, Joseph. 1995. "Quel cadastre pour quoi faire? L'exemple du Gabon." Extract. *www.comby-foncier.com/cadastre_Gabon.pdf.*

GDITC (General Direct and Indirect Tax Code). 2007. *General Direct and Indirect Tax Code*. Ministry of Economy, Finance, Budget, and Privatization. Libreville, Republic of Gabon.

IMF (International Monetary Fund). 2008. *World Economic Outlook Database*. Washington, DC.

———. 2015. *2014 IMF Government Finance Statistics Yearbook*. Washington, DC.

Monkam, N. 2009. "Property Taxation in Two Francophone Countries in Central Africa: Case Study of Gabon." Working paper WP09FAA2. Cambridge, MA: Lincoln Institute of Land Policy.

———. 2010. "Mobilising Tax Revenue to Finance Development: The Case for Property Taxation in Francophone Africa." Working paper no. 195. Pretoria: University of Pretoria, Economic Research Southern Africa (ERSA).

———. 2011. "Property Tax as Legislated and Practiced in Gabon." *Journal of Property Tax Assessment and Administration* 8(2): 53–69.

United Nations. 2014. *World Urbanization Prospects*. Washington, DC: Department of Economics and Social Affairs, Population Division.

United Nations, Department of Economic and Social Affairs, Population Division. 2015. World Population Prospects: The 2015 Revision. https://esa.un.org/unpd /wpp/Publications/Files/World_Population_2015_Wallchart.pdf.

Wily, L. A. 2012. *Land Rights in Gabon: Facing up to the Past and Present*. Brussels, Belgium: FERN.

World Bank. 2006. Gabonese Republic, local infrastructure development project. Washington, DC.

———. 2014. *World Development Indicators*. Washington, DC.

———. 2016a. "Country and Lending Groups." *http://data.worldbank.org/about/country -and-lending-groups*.

———. 2016b. "GDP per Capita (Current US%)." *http://data.worldbank.org/indicator /NY.GDP.PCAP.CD*.

Yebe, R. A. 2007. "Fiscalité locale et décentralisation au Gabon: Cas de la Commune de Libreville ; Ministère des Finances et du Budget." Libreville: Secrétariat Général, Ecole Nationale des Régies Financières.

Legislation

Decentralization Law No. 15/96 (of June 6, 1996).

Decree No. 57-460 (of April 4, 1957).

Finance Act of 2015.

General Direct and Indirect Tax Code of 2007.

Law No. 15/63 (of May 8, 1963).

Ordinance No. 005/81/PR (of March 3, 1981).

13

The Gambia

WILLIAM MCCLUSKEY AND SAMUEL JIBAO

The Gambia is a very small country, with a total area of only 11,295 km². It is surrounded by Senegal to the south, east, and north and has a coastline of only 80 kilometers on the Atlantic Ocean to the west. The Gambia is relatively densely populated, with a population of around 2 million (United Nations 2015; World Bank 2014), of which 60 percent is urbanized (United Nations 2014). The estimated population of the capital city, Banjul, is 504,000 (CIA 2016). The Gambia is classified as a low-income country; its per capita GDP was estimated at USD 472 in 2015 (World Bank 2016a, 2016b). After over two centuries of colonial rule under the British, The Gambia gained internal self-government in 1963 and full independence in 1965. The Gambia and neighboring Senegal entered into a loose confederation called Senegambia in 1982, but it was terminated in 1989 when The Gambia refused to move closer to a more formal union.

Government

The Republic of The Gambia is a multiparty democracy; the 1997 constitution provides for a unicameral legislature. For administrative purposes, The Gambia is divided into eight local-government areas: Banjul City Council, Basse Area Council, Brikama Area Council, Janjanbureh Area Council, Kanifing Municipal Council, Kerewan Area Council, Kuntaur Area Council, and Mansakonko Area Council. The local-government areas are subdivided into 35 districts administered by local chiefs, and the districts are further subdivided into wards. Municipal statutory functions and responsibilities include solid-waste management, sanitation and cleaning services, street maintenance, water supply, municipal investment for new infrastructure, and operation and maintenance of public infrastructure and services. The Local Government Finance and Audit Act of 2004 states that the revenue and funds of a council consist of the following:

- Rates (which include the property tax) imposed by the council.

- Licenses, permits, dues, charges, fees, and royalties.

- Receipts derived from any public utility concern or any service or undertaking belonging to or maintained by a council.

- Rents derived from leasing any building or land belonging to a council.

- Project funds, donations, and grants other than those from general revenue.

This act further states that with presidential approval, each council is entitled to a general grant that shall not exceed 10 percent of the capital budget.

The three main revenue sources available to councils are property rates (including flat rates), licenses, and market fees. Table 13.1 shows the revenue sources of the three largest councils for the financial year 2014. In The Gambia, councils cover almost 100 percent of the cost of their services from their own-source revenues. The central government rarely gives grants and subventions to councils.

Table 13.1 Main Revenue Sources of Councils, 2014

	Banjul	Brikama	Kanifing
Administration	1,790,758	124,289	2,389,607
Licenses	22,014,100	17,092,525	33,729,383
Market fees	9,986,172	23,322,878	32,311,655
Rates	10,901,850	15,423,617	45,442,814
Miscellaneous	1,168,150	0	2,897,091
Total	45,861,030	55,963,309	116,770,550
Rates as a percentage of total revenue	23.8	27.6	38.9

Source: Annual reports of the councils (2014).

Land Tenure

The key land-related laws are the State Lands Act 1991, the Mortgages Act 1992, and the Land (Registration of Deeds) Act 1991. The State Lands Act, passed in May 1991, provides for the administration of land under a unitary title system in designated areas. Section 4 of the act states that all land in Banjul and Kombo Saint Mary shall be vested in the state and regarded as state land except land held in fee simple (freehold land or land that was acquired during the colonial era). The State Lands Act specifies the conditions under which a lease may be granted for an initial term of 99 years, with a provision for renewal subject to the payment of land rent and/or premium and depending on the purpose for which the land is to be used. Land rent is minimal and is paid yearly.

Section 5(1) of the State Lands Act empowers the secretary of state for local government and lands to declare any land in the provinces as state land. This is a gray area of the law because some provincial lands are customary lands. The owners of customary lands, locally known as *kabilos*, have acquired these lands over the years by farming, or certain families in the local communities have traditionally used these lands for generations. The Gambia is far from having a comprehensive land and property registration system that includes all real property. A major problem is the fragmentation of information on the transfer of property between the eight councils and the Department of Lands and Surveys (DL&S), which prevents a holistic view of ownership and property use patterns across the country. At present, the DL&S is responsible for the registration of leasehold parcels and the determination of the leasehold land rent. Each council is responsible for registering transfers of freehold property. This in effect creates nine separate property registration systems.

Taxation

Since 2004, the tax system and its administration in The Gambia have undergone fundamental reform aimed at strengthening revenue mobilization and tax administration because of the inefficiencies of the previous system. The Gambia Revenue Authority (GRA) became operational in 2004 with the primary objective of administering, assessing, and collecting revenue. It administers the following national taxes and duties: the personal income tax; the environment tax on individuals; the corporate income tax; the capital gains tax; the payroll tax; the domestic sales tax; the entertainment tax; the national education tax; pools betting, casino, gaming, and machine licenses; business registrations; stamp duties; rents of state land; and survey fees. The personal and corporate income taxes and the domestic sales tax account for the vast majority of the total tax revenue. In 2012, total tax revenue accounted for 14.5 percent of GDP (IMF 2015), whereas in 2008, property taxes (as defined by the International Monetary Fund) accounted for 0.53 percent of GDP (IMF 2016).

Property-Related Taxes

Property-related taxes include the capital gains tax (CGT) and stamp duties. In 2006, these accounted for 2.3 percent and 1.5 percent of total tax revenue, respectively (Estimates of Revenue and Expenditure 2007). The CGT is assessed on either 5 percent of the declared sale price or 15 percent of the capital gain, whichever is higher. The GRA is responsible for policing the CGT, but there appears to be general acceptance of declared figures and little quality control. In March 2015, the GRA was also given the responsibility to collect all local taxes, fees, and charges, including property rates (the recurrent property tax).

The Property Tax

The primary laws relating to property taxation in The Gambia are four acts of Parliament: the General Rate Act (Act No. 9 of 1992); the Local Government Act 2002; the Local Government Finance and Audit Act 2004; and the Local Government (Amendment) Act 2004. A recurrent property tax, called "rates," is levied at the local-government level and is collected annually. Property rates are governed by the Rating Valuation Act (Act No. 6 of 1987) and the General Rate Act of 1992. Property rates are payable by property owners, who are defined as including joint owners, lessees, tenants for life, any other persons entitled to receive rents, and agents. The General Rate Act of 1992 provides for the rating authorities, defined as the Banjul City Council, the Kanifing Municipal Council, and the respective area councils, to make and levy general rates.

The Tax Base

Property rates are based on the assessable value of the land as determined by the DL&S. The assessable value is the capital value of the owner's interest in the property, which is either the freehold interest or a leasehold interest for 60 years (Article 2 of the Rating Valuation Act 1987). The capital value is either the market value of the property or, if there is insufficient evidence to determine the market value, the replacement cost of the improvements.

The assessable value takes into account the value of the land plus the value of the buildings according to type, location, and use. Each local council decides the percentage of this value to be charged as the local rates. Property rates or the so-called compound rates are levied on premises that include

- any building together with all lands occupied therewith that is a distinct or separate holding or tenancy;

- any land, whether developed or underdeveloped; and

- any wharf, pier, or ramp.

The General Rate Act of 1992 further defines "building" to include any house, hut, shed, or roofed enclosure, whether it is used for human habitation or otherwise. Currently, only structures and buildings are assessed for rates. Land has been excluded largely because most land is state owned, and only leasehold interests are created in the land. There are, however, privately owned freehold interests in land that originated in colonial times and persist today. Even though most land is held under leaseholds with renewable rights, it is still possible to include land within the tax base. A more fundamental question is whether urban land should be included, and whether there are sufficient resources to value this component.

Exemptions

The General Rate Act provides for exemption of certain categories of premises from the payment of compound rates, including the following:

- Any mosque, church, chapel, meeting house, or other premises or any part thereof used exclusively for public religious worship.

- Premises certified by the chief education officer as being used exclusively as educational institutions.

- Premises that are used for recreational, sporting, and cultural activities.

- Premises certified by the director of health services as being used exclusively as hospitals, dispensaries, or clinics and not used for purposes of gain.

- Burial grounds and crematoriums.

- Premises declared by a resolution of the rating authority with the approval of the minister to be exempted from payment of the rate.

In addition, Section 21 of the General Rate Act states that "the rating authority may, with the approval of the Minister, if satisfied by any applicant by evidence on oath that on the ground of poverty it is desirable so to do, exempt from payment of rate any premises liable for such payment, or may reduce the amount for which the premises are liable for such rates."

Liability for the Property Tax

The liability to pay rates rests with the owner of the property. Under the General Rate Act, government buildings are also liable for this tax. Section 22 states that "subject to section 12, all premises which are the property of, or are held or let on lease by, the Government shall be liable for and subject to the payment of rate in the same manner and degree as premises and property of or held or let on lease by, private persons, and the rate due on such premises shall be paid by the Government out of the general revenue of The Gambia."

Valuation

The responsibility for the valuation of property for general assessments and supplementary assessments primarily rests with the DL&S, although the private sector can be involved. The DL&S is responsible for overall land administration in The Gambia, including the registration of leasehold interests in state land. In addition, the DL&S provides advice to the government on land-related matters and undertakes the valuation of government property.

The valuation unit within the DL&S has only three valuers, all of whom have extensive valuation experience but are not yet professionally qualified, and two valuation technicians. This staff is clearly insufficient to deliver a general assessment and would be barely adequate to compile supplementary assessments for the eight councils. The DL&S should be adequately resourced to enable it to fulfill its valuation obligations. There are private-sector companies that have historically been involved in compiling general assessments, but this resource has not been used since 2003. There are no university programs in The Gambia that could support the provision of graduate valuers, so persons with an interest in property valuation are sponsored to obtain qualifications overseas, such as in the United Kingdom.

The valuation methodology applied in the 2003 general assessment and the subsequent 2005 supplementary assessment is depreciated cost. This is considered appropriate given the lack of transactions to support any value-based system at that time. As previously noted, only structures and buildings have been assessed; land has been excluded. The decision to exclude land was premised on the fact that when the first general assessment was undertaken in 1986, there was confusion over actual boundaries of parcels. Land was also excluded in the 1994 and 2003 general assessments. Currently, there is more certainty about parcel boundaries, particularly in urban areas. The systematic registration of leasehold interests by the DL&S has created more confidence in parcel configurations. In addition, the aerial photography project undertaken in 2003 has provided a map-based resource that shows parcel delineations (at 1:1,250), but largely for the main urban areas. There is an urgent need to update these maps.

The law requires that general assessments be undertaken every five years, and that supplementary assessments be conducted annually. However, neither general nor supplementary assessments have been undertaken in accordance with the legislation. A "modern" property rates system was introduced in the mid-1980s, and the first general assessment was undertaken in 1986,[1] followed by a further general assessment in 1994, both compiled by the DL&S or its predecessor. In 2002–2003, with the assistance of the World Bank, two private firms conducted a general assessment,[2] which was implemented in 2003. This project involved the valuation of approximately 20,308 high-value properties within the eight councils.[3] For example, Banjul City Council has approximately 2,500 properties, Brikama Area Council 974, and Kanifing Area Council 1,857. In 2005, the DL&S undertook a supplementary assessment that valued some 864 properties in Basse, Brikama, and Kanifing Area Councils. However, because no further supplementary assessments have been undertaken, significant numbers of properties are effectively excluded from the valuation rolls. Unfortunately, data on valuation roll coverage in councils are not available, but evidence suggests that the number of unvalued properties could well exceed 100,000, and a significant number of these properties could potentially be liable for property rates.

Appeals

The General Rate Act grants property owners the right to appeal the value or the rates levied by the authorities. The act states that "any person who is aggrieved by any rate; or has any material objection to the inclusion or exclusion of any person in or from, or to the amount charged to any person in any rate; or is aggrieved by any neglect, act, or thing done or omitted by the rating authority, may appeal to the court having jurisdiction in any rating concerned."

Assessment

Section 4(2a) of the General Rate Act states that "subject to the provisions of this Act, the general rate for any rating area shall be a rate at a uniform amount on the rateable value of each premise in that area." The councils charge properties not included on the valuation roll (those that have not been included in earlier revaluations or have been constructed recently) a flat rate. A flat rate is effectively a prescribed tax amount that the taxpayer has to pay. It is not related directly to the value of the property, although there can be some differentiation for buildings of different quality. Flat-rate tariffs vary significantly among councils. For example, the Banjul council applies a standard tariff of GMD 500 for each property irrespective of type, use, or quality, but Brikama uses a variable-tariff structure to capture the "value" of properties. For low-quality housing structures, the rate is GMD 100; for high-quality residences and commercial buildings, it is GMD 2,000.

One problem with the property rating system in The Gambia is that there is no comprehensive database of real properties outside the existing paper-based valuation rolls. The digitization of all parcels throughout the country would provide an invaluable resource for administration of the property tax. Information on the location and size of each parcel of land provides the basic framework to develop a property tax system. The DL&S began a project in 2015 to develop capacity in digital mapping and training in geographic information systems. This important project could support the future development of property rates.

Tax Rates

The General Rate Act states that "every rating authority shall have the power to make and levy general rates," which implies that each council can set its own rates. It further states that "the authority has the power to make such rates as will be sufficient to provide for such part of the total estimated expenditure to be incurred by the authority during the period in respect of which the rate is made." This shows that in principle, rates are set annually as determined by the budgetary requirements of the council. Property tax rates in The Gambia are determined by each council subject to a maximum threshold rate set by the Ministry of Lands and Regional Government. The minister may, by order published in the *Gazette*, authorize these authorities to demand payment of rates in their rating area in installments at specified times.

The Gambia has set a maximum rate of 5 percent of assessed value, but in practice, tax rates are much lower. Table 13.2 illustrates the tax rates on

Table 13.2 Tax Rates for 2015

Council	Residential (%)	Commercial (%)
Banjul	0.4	0.7
Brikama	0.4	1.0
Kanifing	0.3	1.5

Source: Data supplied by the councils (2015).

residential and commercial property for 2015. Tax rates are relatively low, around 0.4 percent for residential property. In addition, tax rates are changed only after revaluations, which are infrequent.

Collection

Councils have a valuation list of fixed addresses to which to deliver each rates notice. As of March 2015, the GRA assumed responsibility for the collection of property rates. This decision was made largely because of the relative inability of councils to collect rates. According to Section 8 of the General Rates Act, when a rating authority makes and levies rates on any premises, it shall demand payment of such rates by issuing demand notes that specify the location of the premises for which the demand notes are issued and the ratable value of the premises. The act also allows payment of the property rates in installments at specified times.

Enforcement

The General Rates Act provides rating authorities with various mechanisms and procedures to enforce the collection of rates. For example, if the amount of the rate or any installment is not paid within 30 days of the due date, the rating authority is supposed to give notice to the owner stating the amount due and declaring that if payment is not made within 21 days, proceedings will be instituted. The act further states that failure to pay after 21 days will result in imposition of a penalty. It also mandates that in the event of default, a court may order

- that the goods and chattels of the taxpayer be seized;
- that the taxpayer's premises be sold by public auction;
- that the taxpayer be imprisoned for a period not exceeding three months; and
- that the taxpayer pay costs related to the enforcement to the rating authority.

The councils and municipal courts are trying to be proactive in enforcing compliance; each council has a debt-collection unit. The Gambia is traditionally strict on the enforcement of the collection of both subnational and national taxes because the country is not naturally endowed with minerals and thus has to rely heavily on taxation for its budgetary support. There is a relatively high level of public support for this action. This is to an extent due to a perception that the government is seen to be fulfilling its social responsibility as manifested by large-scale infrastructure projects, electricity projects, garbage collection, schools, and other facilities provided for the population.

The legislation should be changed to address the current low level of compliance and the cumulative level of arrears. Elements of the legislation, such as the enforcement of payment by delinquent ratepayers, are rarely applied in practice. The primary enforcement measure is to pursue the debt through the courts to seize goods and chattels, sell the ratepayer's property, and ultimately imprison the defaulter. This approach is both time consuming and expensive and is infrequently used. The legislation should be revised in two main ways: First, it should allow the authorities, and in particular the GRA, to apply alternative enforcement measures, such as (1) attaching liens to property belonging to the ratepayer; (2) linking payment of property rates to trade licenses, vehicle licensing taxes, planning permission, and building permits; and (3) requiring businesses that are applying for tax holidays and tax incentives to include a tax clearance certificate demonstrating that property rates have been paid. Second, interest should be levied on outstanding arrears. It is important that taxpayers be sensitized to the fact that their rate arrears do not disappear but remain as a debt to the council. Therefore, the debt should incur penalties and interest.

Property Tax Issues in The Gambia

The recurrent property tax in The Gambia effectively has no revenue buoyancy because of low property tax rates and almost no growth in the tax base due to the lack of capacity to undertake supplementary assessments. Greater buoyancy could be achieved if the administration would focus on expanding the number of properties on the valuation rolls and review the low tax rates. Own-source revenue administration in The Gambia is beset with collection and enforcement problems. As a result, the GRA was given the responsibility to collect all local revenue sources in 2014. Time will tell how effective and efficient this administrative change will be.

Property rates are levied on valued properties that are assessed in terms of their depreciated replacement cost. Properties that are not valued, which are typically the majority of properties within a local-government jurisdiction, should be charged a flat rate. However, many properties escape flat rates because of the lack of resources.

Revaluations and supplementary valuations are not undertaken regularly, largely because of the lack of capacity in the central government, which is responsible for preparing new valuation rolls. Properties liable to flat rating have slightly greater coverage, and this system is more easily administered at the local level. Given the complexities of valuation and the lack of valuers in the country, a jurisdiction-wide system of flat rating should be considered.

Property tax rates are generally low and remain fixed for several years. There is little incentive to increase tax rates because of the low levels of compliance. Enforcement of delinquent accounts is rare, and as a consequence, noncompliance and concomitant arrears are widespread. One of the objectives of the GRA is to address the amount of unpaid property rates.

Notes

1. Rating Valuation Act (Act No. 6 of 1987), Chapter 34:01.
2. Bayo Associates and Cityscape Associates (Gambia).
3. Data supplied by the DL&S. Properties that had an estimated value of less than GMD 300,000 (approximately USD 3,000) were excluded from the general assessment and were liable to flat rates.

References

CIA (Central Intelligence Agency). 2016. "The Gambia." In *The World Factbook*. *https:// www.cia.gov/library/publications/the-world-factbook/geos/ga.html*.

Estimates of Revenue and Expenditure. 2007. Department of State for Finance and Economic Affairs, Banjul.

IMF (International Monetary Fund). 2015. *2014 IMF Government Finance Statistics Yearbook*. Washington, DC.

———. 2016. "IMF World Longitudinal Data (WoRLD)." IMF e-Library Data. *http:// data.imf.org/?sk=77413F1D-1525-450A-A23A-47AEED40FE78&sId=1390030109571*.

United Nations. 2014. *World Urbanization Prospects*. Washington, DC: Department of Economic and Social Affairs, Population Division.

United Nations, Department of Economic and Social Affairs, Population Division. 2015. World Population Prospects: The 2015 Revision. *https://esa.un.org/unpd/wpp /Publications/Files/World_Population_2015_Wallchart.pdf*.

World Bank. 2014. *World Development Indicators*. Washington, DC.

———. 2016a. "Country and Lending Groups." *http://data.worldbank.org/about/country -and-lending-groups*.

———. 2016b. "GDP per Capita (Current US%)." *http://data.worldbank.org/indicator /NY.GDP.PCAP.CD*.

Legislation

General Rate Act 1992.

Land (Registration of Deeds) Act 1991.

Local Government Act 2002.

Local Government (Amendment) Act 2004.

Local Government Finance and Audit Act 2004.

Mortgages Act 1992.

Rating Valuation Act 1987.

State Lands Act 1991.

14

Ghana

SAMUEL JIBAO

Ghana is located on the west coast of Africa and is bordered by three French-speaking countries: Côte d'Ivoire to the west, Togo to the east, and Burkina Faso (formerly Upper Volta) to the north. To the south are the Gulf of Guinea and the Atlantic Ocean. The area is approximately 239,460 km², and the estimated population is about 27.4 million (United Nations 2015; World Bank 2014). Accra is the capital; other major cities include Cape Coast, Kumasi, Sekondi, Tema, and Temale. The country gained independence from the British on March 6, 1957. About 54 percent of the country's population lives in urban areas (United Nations 2014). The country's GDP per capita was estimated at USD 1,370 in 2015 (World Bank 2016b). Of the GDP in 2008, 28.3 percent was from the agricultural sector, while 21 percent and 50.7 percent were from the industrial and services sectors, respectively. Although Ghana is classified as a lower-middle-income country (World Bank 2016a), about 28.5 percent of Ghanaian population lives below the income poverty line of USD 1.00 per day.

Government

Ghana is a constitutional presidential republic with two tiers of government, central and local. It is divided into 10 regions. As of 2011, the Greater Accra Region comprised six districts (Dangme West, Ga West, Dangme East, Ga East, Ledzokuku, and Ga South), two metropolitan areas (Accra and Tema), and two municipal areas (Ashaiman and Adental). Each district and municipal or metropolitan area is administered by a chief executive who represents the central government but derives authority from an assembly headed by a presiding member elected from among the members. The Local Government Act of 1993 (Act 462) retained the 110 councils, consisting of 3 metropolitan, 4 municipal, and 103 district assemblies.

Land Tenure

The 1992 Constitution of the Republic of Ghana provides for three categories of land ownership: public land (state land vested in the president in trust for the people of Ghana); stool or skin lands (community lands vested in traditional or other community leaders on behalf of the community); and private and family lands (owned by families, individuals, and clans in the community). The laws of Ghana do not allow for freehold land. Non-Ghanaians can have access to residential, commercial, industrial, or agricultural land from any of the three categories of ownership on a leasehold basis for up to 50 years, subject to renewal. Ghanaians can legally have leaseholds from any of the three land ownership categories for a period of 99 years, subject to renewal.

The Land Registry Act 1962 (Act 122) has several deficiencies. Chief among them is prolific litigation, the common sources of which are the absence of documentary proof that a person in occupation of land has certain rights in respect of it; the absence of accurate maps and plans to enable identification of parcels and ascertainment of boundaries; and the lack of prescribed forms to be followed in dealings involving land or interests in land. Consequently, the government decided to introduce a system of compulsory land title registration throughout the country through the Land Title Registration Law 1986. The purpose of land title registration was twofold: first, to give certainty and facilitate proof of title; and second, to ensure dealings in land that are safe, simple, and inexpensive to prevent fraudulent actions against purchasers and mortgagees.

Property-Related Taxes

The Gift Tax and the Estate Duty

A gift is taxed at a rate of 5 percent of a value in excess of GHS 50.[1] The gift tax is payable by the donee on the total value of taxable gifts received by that person as gifts within a year of assessment. It is imposed on the following assets if they are given as a gift: permanent or temporary buildings; land; shares, bonds, and other securities; money, including foreign currency; and businesses and business assets.

The estate duty was imposed in Ghana by the Estate Duty Act 1965, which is almost entirely composed of selected sections from the estate duty legislation of England. The act imposes a charge on property that passes on death or is deemed so to pass in certain defined situations.

The Stamp Duty

The stamp duty is intended to pass on to the government a part of the consideration for any transaction involving land. The Internal Revenue Service (IRS) is responsible for enforcing the duty, although it can appoint other persons or institutions to collect the duty on its behalf. For land transactions, the Land Valuation Board (LVB) is responsible for assessing and collecting the duty on behalf of the IRS. The stamp duty is based on the ad valorem value of the transaction or, in the case of conveyance or transfer on sale of property, "the amount or consideration for the sale." In practice, the LVB, in assessing the stamp duty, has interpreted the ad valorem value to mean the open market value of the transaction. The stamp duty previously was 2 percent of the value of the transaction, but the Stamp Duty Act of 2005 reduced the duty from 2 percent to 0.5 percent. However, the stamp duty on the conveyance or transfer on the sale of a property is 0.25 percent where the property value is less than GHS 10,000. For properties valued between GHS 10,000 and GHS 50,000, the stamp duty is 0.5 percent, and for properties valued above GHS 50,000, it is 1 percent.

The Property Tax

Under Articles 245 and 252 of the 1992 Constitution of the Republic of Ghana and Sections 34(7)–(10) of the Local Government Act of 1993, all district authorities (DAs) are authorized to receive revenue from three sources: the District Assemblies Common Fund (DACF), ceded revenue, and own-source revenue raised through local taxation. District authorities thus enjoy some financial independence, but it is limited. The DACF is the main source of revenue and provides a constitutionally guaranteed minimum share of government revenue (no less than 5 percent of national revenue, increased to 7.5 percent effective January 1, 2008).[2] Payment of all staff working in the district currently under the responsibility of ministries is drawn from those ministries' budgets. Ceded revenue is revenue from several lesser taxes that the central government has ceded to DAs. It is collected by the Ghanaian IRS and is transferred to DAs as part of the IRS's decentralization program. The six main sources of own-source revenue are property rates, land rentals, fees, licenses, trading services, and miscellaneous income. Transfers from the government account for about

67 percent of the revenue income of DAs, and 4 percent is from internally generated revenue (MLGRD 2010).

During the colonial era up to 1953 and then to 1971, property rating was confined to only four municipalities: Accra, Cape Coast, Kumasi, and Sekondi/Takorandi. In 1971, the Local Administration Act (Act 359) extended valuation for rating purposes throughout the entire country. Since then, all local-authority areas in Ghana have become valuation areas, but local revenue generation continues to be a challenge for DAs nationwide (see table 14.1). The distress is even more profound in the Northern, Volta, Brong Ahafo, Upper East, and Upper West Regions, as well as the southern rural areas, where poverty levels are exceptionally high, and where many of the DAs have a limited own-source revenue base (table 14.2). The weak capacity of local DAs to assess, bill, and collect taxes and the lack of political will to enforce revenue collection explain the low level of internally generated revenue.

Despite the low revenue yield, the property tax is increasingly becoming an important source of internal revenue for major DAs, such as the Accra Metropolitan Assembly (27 percent in 2011), the Kumasi Metropolitan Assembly (17.0 percent in 2011), the Tema Metropolitan Assembly (20 percent in 2011), the Bibiani-Anwiaso Bekwai District Assembly (24.0 percent in 2011) in the Western Region, and the Sekyere East District Assembly (35.0 percent in 2011) in the Ashanti Region. In each of the DAs, there has been some effort to automate, albeit partially, the processes of property identification, assessment, collection, accounting, monitoring and auditing, and enforcement.

Table 14.1 Property Taxes and Total Internally Generated Revenue, 2006–2011

Year	Total Property Tax in Cedis	Total Internally Generated Revenue	Property Tax Percentage of Total Internally Generated Revenue
2006	68,607,636,859	319,844,449,435	21.5
2007	79,602,360,439	424,406,169,624	18.8
2008	11,073,348	39,167,729	28.3
2009	15,616,551	62,520,118	25.0
2010	15,972,989	83,525,949	19.1
2011	19,493,994	114,972,832	17.0

Source: Author's compilation using Local Government Finance Data.

Table 14.2 Property Tax Percentage of Total Internally Generated Revenue by Region, 2006–2011

Local Authority	2006	2007	2008	2009	2010	2011
Ashanti Region	25.4	22.4	22.4	16.0	21.2	20.2
Brong Ahafo Region	15.9	14.7	14.7	16.7	16.2	18.3
Central Region	19.6	23.5	32.3	24.5	51.0	17.3
Eastern Region	18.0	22.8	18.8	19.8	19.4	16.7
Greater Accra Region	23.9	18.0	19.4	41.3	14.9	15.9
Northern Region	13.7	13.2	24.2	10.9	27.7	18.7
Upper East Region	5.0	3.8	13.1	11.0	22.7	15.8
Upper West Region	10.4	8.4	8.4	9.4	30.7	5.7
Volta Region	12.3	17.3	17.8	16.9	13.5	8.9
Western Region	23.6	18.2	21.6	19.2	19.7	17.0

Source: Author's computation using the LGFD project database.

Table 14.1 shows that property tax revenue as a share of internally generated revenue declined from 21.5 percent in 2006 to 18.8 percent in 2007. It increased to 28.3 percent and 25.0 percent in 2008 and 2009, respectively, before declining again to 19.1 percent and 17.0 percent in 2010 and 2011, respectively. The increased revenue performance of the property tax in 2008 and 2009 can be attributed to the improvement in record keeping and the enhanced collection resulting from the introduction of information and communication technology.[3] However, challenges to delivery of demand notices and effective enforcement continue to undermine optimal property tax revenue generation in the 10 regions.

The Tax Base

In Ghana, the property tax is levied on premises comprising buildings or structures or similar development. It covers all buildings within a locality (including buildings owned or occupied by the government and the local council) except buildings used for charitable purposes, public religious worship, public hospitals and clinics, public educational purposes, and cemeteries and crematoriums, as well as buildings used for diplomatic missions, subject to approval by the ministry responsible for foreign affairs. Legislation further permits the rating authority to reduce the amount of any rate because of the poverty of a person liable. Vacant lands do not incur the property tax. However, from January 2008, different rates (flat rates) were assigned to undeveloped plots within the Accra Metropolitan Area.

Assessment and Valuation

Before independence in 1957, the system of valuation for rating purposes was based on the number of rooms in a house. It was assumed that each room had one window; therefore, the municipal council officials would simply count the number of windows in a house to determine the ratable value. A house with more windows would have a higher ratable value and higher rates. Prior to independence, the Municipal Councils' Ordinance (Ordinance No. 9 of 1951) was enacted, which altered the basis of valuation to annual rental value. The basis of valuation was changed again (Local Government Ordinance 1954) from annual rental value to adjusted replacement cost, which was retained in the Local Government Act of 1993 (Ayitey, Kuusaana, and Kidido 2013). The ratable value of premises is defined as "the replacement cost of the buildings, structures and other developments comprising the premises after deducting the amount which it would cost at the time of valuation to restore the premises to a condition that would be serviceable as new." The act provides that the ratable value should be no more than 50 percent of the replacement cost for owner-occupied premises and no less than 75 percent of the replacement cost in other cases. Thus, ratable value in Ghana is simply a percentage of the replacement cost of premises less depreciation.

Section 43 of the Provisional National Defense Council (PNDC) Law 42 of 1982 mandates the formation of a land valuation board that is responsible for the valuation of properties throughout the country for rating purposes. This act, however, allows for the participation of private-sector valuers under the supervision of public-sector valuers. The Accra Metropolitan Assembly (AMA) employs the traditional land use zones in determining the rates. It is assumed that owners of properties in areas of higher value, for instance, in first-class residential areas, are high-income earners and thus have a greater ability to pay. The tax liability for any property is the product of the ratable value and the corresponding tax rate.

During 1986–1987, the government, with assistance from the World Bank, initiated a revaluation aimed at supporting and strengthening the developmental capacities of local governments. A component of this Local Government Development Project was the revaluation of all ratable properties within a selected local authority in order to update the valuation roll. Accra was selected for the project, and the Land Valuation Board was designated as the implementing agency. Some 71,258 properties were revalued, with a total ratable value of GHS 4,116 billion, an average value of 57,769 million. In 2007, 120,339 properties were revalued in the AMA, with a total ratable value of GHS 38,679 billion, an average ratable value of GHS 321,419 million (AMA 2007). On average, the ratable value of properties in the AMA increased by about 456 percent.

The ideal frequency of revaluations for ad valorem assessments is considered to be every five years; however, because of the high cost (some GHS 30 billion for the last revaluation in the AMA), revaluations are conducted infrequently. Indexation has been adopted as an interim measure in the AMA. In 2008, pilot projects using computer-assisted mass appraisal (CAMA), which is believed to bring a degree of fairness and equity to the valuation process (Moore 2005), were initiated in the Bibiani-Anwiaso Bekwai District Assembly, the Sekyere East District Assembly, and the Kumasi Metropolitan Assembly.

The Local Government Act of 1993 provides that a person aggrieved by a valuation or rate imposed on his premises by a rating authority may apply to the Rate Assessment Committee for a review. A taxpayer who is not satisfied with the decision of the Rate Assessment Committee can appeal to the High Court.

The Ghana Institute of Surveyors licenses professionally qualified valuers and valuation firms in the country. In 2014, the institute had a membership of 323 professionally qualified valuers and 39 technicians. The Department of Land Economy of the Kwane Nkrumah University of Science and Technology produces on average some 70 graduates in land economy annually, but not all of these graduates specialize in valuation. The number of valuers in the public sector is not available. In 2008, there were about 55 professional valuers in the LVB, a number well below what is required. This has adversely affected the ability of the LVB to perform its statutory function. The more proactive DAs have tended to rely on private valuers to carry out valuation activities. The AMA, for instance, hired seven firms in 2008 to undertake valuation projects.

Tax Rates

The Local Government Act of 1993 states in Section 94(1) that "the District Assembly shall be the sole authority for the district and subject to any special provision in the Act or any other enactment; no other authority other than the Assembly shall, notwithstanding any customary law to the contrary, have power to make or levy rates in the district." Section 95 of the act mandates that each district assembly levy sufficient rates to meet its estimated expenditures. According to Section 96 of the Local Government Act, rates are classified as general or specific. Specific rates are rates levied on specified areas for the purpose of specified projects approved by the district assemblies, while general rates are rates made and levied on the whole district for the purpose of developing the district. Although the assemblies are mandated by law to make and levy rates, Section 100 of the Local Government Act of 1993 states that "the Minister may issue guidelines for the making and levying of rates." Interviews conducted with senior officials of the Local Government Ministry and the Accra Municipal Assembly in 2008 indicate that the minister has never given such guidelines to the assemblies. The property tax is paid by the owner of the property. Property owners in the AMA paid a yearly rate in 2008 ranging between GHS 8.00 (80,000 old cedis) and GHS 50.00 (500,000 old cedis).

Billing, Collection, and Payment

Section 98 of the Local Government Act of 1993 states that when a rating authority has given notice of a rate, it shall be the duty of every person liable to pay the rate to pay the amount to a rate collector or other person duly appointed or authorized by the district assembly to collect and receive the rate at the time and place specified by the rating authority. Property owners are notified of their liabilities through bills delivered by the assembly.[4] At the launch of new property rate bills in Accra in August 2007, the mayor of Accra revealed that private companies had been contracted to collect the property rates on behalf of the AMA. It was argued that this action was in line with the policy of private-sector participation and would give time for the assembly to restructure its revenue-collection machinery to improve revenue mobilization. In 2008, 13 revenue offices were opened to give ratepayers additional payment points in the AMA. However, the AMA required companies, firms, and large property owners to settle their bills only at the Finance Office of the AMA (Darison 2011).

Enforcement

Section 106(1) of the Local Government Act mandates that if the amount of the general or specific rate due on any premises is not paid within 42 days, the district assembly may apply to a court for an order for the sale of the premises. In principle, enforcement would appear to be straightforward because the government frequently knows the location of the property owner and has direct access to the property in case of noncompliance. In reality, enforcement of this tax is weak in Ghana. This in part reflects poor record keeping and weak human resource capacity in most DAs, but it is widely felt that the primary barriers to enforcement are social and political factors.

Property Tax Issues in Ghana

One major problem affecting DAs in Ghana, especially the AMA, is ineffective governance. The root causes range from the lack of political will on the part of the assembly to poor institutional networks and collaboration, inadequate databases and logistics, poorly motivated staff, and political interference. The results are inadequate revenue mobilization and low institutional and financial capacity of the assemblies. Inadequate revenue mobilization, insufficient financial resources, and the low institutional capacity of DAs, including the AMA, have led to inadequate public health facilities, poor road infrastructure, poor service delivery, nonenforcement of bylaws and regulations, and poor development control, which add to negative public attitudes toward the environment and development.

In most DAs, the valuation of property has been adversely affected by inadequate data, lack of knowledge of the property market, and a property market that is not well developed. The way forward would be for the Land Valuation Board and the DAs to minimize valuation complexity by improving data quality and accessibility and to create a sound property data system to provide uniformity and clarity of open market value for all properties. Some DAs, however, are making efforts to introduce information technology and CAMA approaches within their property tax administration. The gains made so far should be consolidated, and lessons learned should be extended to other assemblies.

Notes

1. Ghana rebased its currency in July 2007. One new GHS is equivalent to 10,000 old cedis.

2. Apart from the DACF, there are other transfers known as recurrent expenditure transfers, such as payment of salaries and remunerations of staff of DAs and payments for the operational and administrative expenses of the administrative structure of the civil service at the district level.

3. From 2000 to 2009, the AMA implemented a pilot project called the Urban Management Land Information System in collaboration with the Ministry of Local Government and Rural Development, supported by the Swede Survey AB and Geo-Tech Systems. The system recorded in digital form information on buildings, parcels, use, value, ownership, and rates.

4. Timely delivery of bills remains a challenge, and lack of it is undermining property tax revenues.

References

AMA (Accra Metropolitan Assembly). 2007. "Repository of Districts in Ghana." Accra. *www.ghanadistricts.com.*

Ayitey, J. Z., E. D. Kuusaana, J. K. and Kidido. 2013. "Potentials and Hurdles in Property Rating in Ghana: Evidence from the Wa Municipality." *The Ghana Surveyor* 5(1): 1–13.

CIA (Central Intelligence Agency). 2016. "Ghana." In *The World Factbook. https://www .cia.gov/library/publications/the-world-factbook/geos/gh.html.*

Darison, A. B. 2011. "Enhancing Local Government Revenue Mobilization Through the Use of Information Communication Technology: A Case Study of Accra Metropolitan Assembly." M.S. thesis in development and policy, Kwame Nkrumah University of Science and Technology.

MLGRD (Ministry of Local Government and Rural Development). 2010.

Moore, J. W. 2005. "Performance Comparison of Automated Valuation Models." Paper presented at the 71st International Association of Assessing Officers Annual International Conference on Assessment Administration, September 19–23, Anchorage, AK.

United Nations. 2014. *World Urbanization Prospects.* Washington, DC: Department of Economics and Social Affairs, Population Division.

United Nations, Department of Economic and Social Affairs, Population Division. 2015. World Population Prospects: The 2015 Revision. *https://esa.un.org/unpd/wpp /Publications/Files/World_Population_2015_Wallchart.pdf.*

World Bank. 2014. *World Development Indicators.* Washington, DC.

———. 2016a. "Country and Lending Groups." *http://data.worldbank.org/about/country -and-lending-groups.*

———. 2016b. "GDP per Capita (Current US%)." *http://data.worldbank.org/indicator /NY.GDP.PCAP.CD.*

Legislation

Constitution of the Republic of Ghana, 1992.

Estate Duty Act 1965.

Land Registry Act 1962 (Act 122).

Land Title Registration Law 1986.

Local Administration Act of 1971 (Act 359).

Local Government Act of 1993 (Act 462).

Municipal Councils' Ordinance (Ordinance No. 9 of 1953).

Provisional National Defense Council (PNDC) Law 42 of 1982.

Stamp Duty Act of 2005.

15

Kenya

WILLIAM McCLUSKEY, RIËL FRANZSEN,
AND WASHINGTON OLIMA

The Republic of Kenya is bordered by Tanzania on the south, Uganda on the west, Southern Sudan and Ethiopia on the north, Somalia on the east, and the Indian Ocean on the southeast. It gained its independence from the United Kingdom in December 1963. The country covers an area of approximately 582,646 km² and has a population of approximately 46 million (United Nations 2015). Only about 26 percent of the population is urbanized (United Nations 2014). The capital city, Nairobi, has an estimated population of 3.9 million, and the second-largest city, Mombasa, has an estimated population of 1.1 million (CIA 2016). The estimated per capita GDP was USD 1,377 in 2015 (World Bank 2016b).

Government

Kenya is a constitutional republic. There are two levels of government: the national government and 47 county governments. In 2010, the new Constitution of the Republic of Kenya (hereinafter "the constitution" or "the 2010 constitution") was passed and promulgated. The 2010 constitution paved the way for a new local-government structure, which became a reality after the first county-government elections held in March 2013. In this structure, the 47 county governments cover all of Kenya as a single subnational level of government.

Before the new county governments came into existence, local authorities were constituted under the Local Government Act of 1963 (Chapter 265). There were 175 local authorities: 1 city council, 45 municipal councils, 62 town councils, and 67 county councils. The Local Government Act allocated local authorities several public service responsibilities, including provision of primary education, public health, cultural and social facilities, and public markets (World Bank 2012). This act was repealed by the announcement of the election results in March 2013, and the various administrative structures were absorbed into the new county governments. This reform has placed new responsibilities on new, larger, and potentially more efficient jurisdictions. County governments are the primary providers of basic infrastructure, including water, early childhood development, waste-management facilities, and local roads. It is important to consider whether they have adequate fiscal powers and the capacity to deploy them.

Land Tenure

When Kenya was founded as a settler colony, large tracts of the most fertile agricultural land were set aside for the exclusive occupation of white settlers under freehold or leasehold tenure. At independence in 1963, the newly established government inherited three types of landholding: urban land, which is government owned and is acquired by individuals under leases for up to 99 years; farm land held by individuals and companies through freehold tenure; and trust land, which is not registered under any individual or group but rather is occupied by the community and governed by customary land law. In December 2009, the government of Kenya adopted a National Land Policy with the purpose of resolving the many land tenure problems in the country.

Several new laws pertaining to the administration of land were passed in 2012, including the National Land Commission Act, the Land Registration Act, and the Land Act. Under the new laws, land has been reclassified into (1) public land; (2) private land; and (3) community land. Public land is mainly land that is occupied by the state, including land that has been transferred to the state, unalienated land, and land for which no heir can be identified. In addition, the following are regarded as public land: land containing minerals; forests; reserves; national parks; water catchment areas; seas, lakes, and rivers; land between the high-water mark and the low-water mark; and any land that has not been classified as private land. Community land is typically land that has been registered in the name of a community, any land transferred to a community, and land declared to be community land by an act of Parliament. Private land includes land that has been registered and held under freehold tenure, registered leasehold land, and other land declared private land by an act of Parliament.

Before passage of the Land Registration Act No. 3 of 2012, land registration was governed by various acts. These included the Land Titles Act 1908 (Chapter 282); the Government Lands Act 1915 (Chapter 280); the Registration of Titles Act 1920 (Chapter 281); and the Registered Land Act 1963 (Chapter 300). The primary objective of the Land Registration Act of 2012 is to consolidate and rationalize the registration of land titles in Kenya. The coverage of the cadastre can be described as piecemeal because no comprehensive national cadastre has yet been developed. At present, the cadastre is parcel based and contains mainly privately owned (freehold and leasehold) land parcels because there has been no systematic attempt to register and map publicly owned lands. In addition, no buildings or physical improvements are included in the cadastre. As a result, the cadastre has limited capacity to support a property tax.

Taxation

In 2012, total taxes amounted to 15.6 percent of GDP (IMF 2015), while property taxes, broadly defined to include transfer taxes, amounted to only 0.01 percent of GDP (IMF 2016). According to the 2010 constitution, read with the County Governments Act of 2012, the 47 county governments enjoy significant autonomy from control by the national government. However, at first glance, they have rather limited own-revenue powers. Section 209 of the constitution states the following:

209. (1) Only the national government may impose—
    (*a*) income tax;
    (*b*) value-added tax;
    (*c*) customs duties and other duties on import and export goods; and
    (*d*) excise tax.
(2) An Act of Parliament may authorise the national government to impose any other tax or duty, except a tax specified in clause (3) (*a*) or (*b*).
(3) A county may impose—
    (*a*) property rates;
    (*b*) entertainment taxes; and
    (*c*) any other tax that it is authorised to impose by an Act of Parliament.
(4) The national and county governments may impose charges for the services they provide.
(5) The taxation and other revenue-raising powers of a county shall not be exercised in a way that prejudices national economic policies, economic activities across county boundaries or the national mobility of goods, services, capital or labour.

Although the constitution guarantees "property rates" as a source of county revenue, the scope of "may impose" is unclear (Franzsen 2013). Some counties seem to think that it implies that they have control over all aspects of the property tax, including determining the tax base.

The Kenya Revenue Authority (KRA) in the Ministry of Finance is primarily responsible for tax administration in Kenya. The KRA collects income taxes, the value-added tax, and all other national taxes. Property-related taxes and fees collected by the KRA include the stamp duty payable on the transfer of real estate and the annual land rent on leasehold properties. Although the KRA is charged with the collection of the stamp duty and the land rent, the Valuation Division within the Ministry of Lands and Physical Planning (MLPP) conducts the assessment of the amount payable. County-level taxes in Kenya include land rates (the property tax) and the entertainment tax plus various development approval charges, business fees (called the "single business permit"), and various user charges.

Property-Related Taxes

Land Rent

Land rent, or ground rent, is chargeable on all property leased from the government or county authorities. Properly speaking, it is not a tax but a rent payable for the right to occupy government-owned land. The MLPP administers land rent. The leaseholder is responsible for paying the tax. Billing is done annually, and the KRA currently undertakes collection. No transfer of rights is permitted before payment of the tax and issuance of a land rent clearance certificate.

The Stamp Duty

The stamp duty or property transfer tax is governed by the Stamp Duty Act, 2012, Chapter 480. It is payable on transfers, leases, partitions, exchanges, and acquisition of immovable property. The person who acquires the property pays the tax. The tax is based on the purchase price, self-declaration, or the market value of the property as determined by the government valuer (the chief valuer in the MLPP). There is no centralized database of transactions that could inform whether the declared price is the full market value. The current tax rates are 4 percent of market value for urban properties and 2 percent of market value for rural properties.

The Capital Gains Tax

Capital gains arising or deemed to arise in Kenya are subject to tax. Previously suspended provisions dealing with capital gains were brought back into operation, and the capital gains tax (CGT) took effect on January 1, 2015. Capital gains are taxed separately from other income at a rate of 5 percent. The CGT is imposed on securities and land transactions. Disposals of less than 100 acres of agricultural land outside municipal boundaries are exempt from the CGT.

Immovable property can potentially incur three separate taxes: the recurrent property rates, the stamp duty, and the CGT. The last two are transaction driven and are collected irregularly. A person who acquires immovable property by transfer of ownership can register the new title deed only if outstanding property rates have been paid. When a property is transferred, the MLPP assesses the value of the unimproved site, which incurs the stamp duty and possibly the 5 percent CGT. The taxpayer must pay all outstanding taxes and fees owed to the county and, after payment of the stamp duty, receives the ownership title.

The Property Tax

The most important property-related tax in Kenya is the recurrent property tax, commonly called "rates" or "land rates," which the counties levy. Under Article 209 of the constitution, county governments are explicitly assigned the power to impose "property rates." Land value taxation as presently practiced in Kenya is a result of British colonial administration in East Africa dating back to the beginning of the 20th century. The property tax in Kenya was first introduced in 1900 in Mombasa. The basis was annual rental value. In 1901, the annual rental value basis was introduced in Nairobi. However, because few properties had been developed, unimproved site value rating was introduced in 1928 (Gachuru and Olima 1998; Olima 2005).

Historically, the property tax has been an important source of revenue for Kenyan local authorities. For example, before independence in 1963, the city of Nairobi generated 45 percent of its revenue from rates. Revenue from rates increased slowly between 2008–2009 and 2012–2013 but decreased significantly in 2013–2014 and again in 2014–2015, as shown in table 15.1.

The Tax Base

Until counties came into existence in March 2013, property rates were the primary own-source revenue for municipalities (cities and larger towns), town councils (small towns), and county councils (rural authorities) (Franzsen and Olima 2003). The property tax (rates) is still being levied under the Rating Act 1986 (Chapter 267) read with the Valuation for Rating Act 1984 (Chapter 266). This legislation provides that a rating authority can

Table 15.1 Nairobi City County Own-Source Revenue

Own Revenues	2008-2009 KES Millions	%	2009-2010 KES Millions	%	2010-2011 KES Millions	%	2011-2012 KES Millions	%	2012-2013 KES Millions	%	2013-2014 KES Millions	%	2014-2015 KES Millions	%
Property rates	1,774	29	1,825	29	1,800	28	2,222	31	2,470	33	2,661	27	2,666	23
Contributions in lieu of rates	112	2	100	2	–	–	–	–	–	–	–	–	–	–
Single business permit (SBP)	988	16	886	14	942	15	1,121	16	1,029	13	1,544	15	1,814	16
Cess	163	3	197	3	206	3	258	4	190	3	215	2	243	2
Rents	351	6	560	9	643	10	559	8	647	8	674	7	679	6
Lease income	240	4	140	2	57	1	1,176	16	88	1	197	2	202	2
Other revenue	2,420	40	2,637	41	2,735	43	1,752	25	3,251	42	4,740	47	5,979	51
Total	6,048	100	6,345	100	6,383	100	7,087	100	7,675	100	10,031	100	11,583	100

Source: Nairobi City County (2015).

Table 15.2 Property Rating in Kenya Before Local-Government Reorganization

Type of Local Authority	Number of Rating Authorities	Number Using Valuation Rating	Number Using Area and Valuation Rating
Municipalities	36	36	8
Councils	27	24	9
Counties	39	15	10
Total	102	75	27

Source: Franzsen (2013).

use any of the following assessment bases: area rating; agricultural rental value rating; unimproved land value rating (unimproved site value rating); or unimproved land value rating plus improvement rating (separate tax rates for the land and the building components of a property).

Despite the range of tax base options allowed, most cities and towns opted for unimproved site value as the tax base (Kelly 2000; World Bank 2012). Of the previous 175 local authorities, 102 used some form of property rates; 75 used a valuation-based approach and 27 used a combination of both area and valuation rating. Most municipalities and town councils relied on valuation rating, while counties opted for a combination of area and valuation rating. In other words, rates for rural and agricultural properties were generally based on area rating, while urban property was primarily rated according to parcel market values. Table 15.2 provides a breakdown of the property ratings used by the previous local authorities.

Assessment

In Kenya, land is valued for property rates on the basis of its market value as provided in the Valuation for Rating Act (although the act does give other valuation options, such as area rating). The basis of valuation of any land is "the sum which the freehold in possession free from encumbrances therein might be expected to realize at the time of valuation if offered for sale on such reasonable terms and conditions as a *bona fide* seller might be expected to impose" (Section 8). Section 8(2) defines the value of unimproved land as follows: "The value of unimproved land shall . . . be the sum which the freehold in possession free from encumbrances . . . might be expected to realize at the time of valuation if offered for sale on such reasonable terms and conditions as a *bona fide* seller might be expected to impose, and if the improvements, if any, thereon, therein or thereunder had not been made."

A major legislative issue is that county governments are continuing to levy rates in accordance with the existing rating legislation. Kenya's constitution assigns lawmaking powers to both national and county governments. The implication of this is that each county can draft its own rating legislation to permit it to levy property rates. In 2015, the Nairobi City County prepared a draft valuation and rating bill that was awaiting consideration by the county assembly. Other counties, including Kiambu and Mombasa, are preparing draft valuation and rating bills. It is clearly not in the best interests of property rating in Kenya to have 47 separate rating and valuation laws (Franzsen 2013). Ideally, national framework legislation should be enacted that would deal with matters of uniformity, such as definitions of *ratable owner* and *ratable property*, objections, appeals, enforcement, and the national treatment of properties such as those entitled to exemptions.

Under the Rating Act, the ratable owner is the person liable to pay the property rates. This person is defined as (1) the owner of the registered freehold interest or the tenant for life of a ratable property; (2) the lessee of a property holding under a registered lease for a definite term of not less than 25 years, a registered lease that is renewable from time to time at the will of the lessee, or a registered lease that is for an indefinite term or is renewable indefinitely; or (3) a lessee of public land held under a registered lease.

Exemptions

Exempt properties include the following: places for public religious worship; cemeteries, crematoriums, and burial or burning grounds; hospitals or other institutions for the treatment of the sick; educational institutions, including the residences of students provided directly by educational institutions or forming part of, or ancillary to, educational institutions; charitable institutions and libraries; outdoor sports facilities; and national parks. These properties are exempt from rating only as long as they are not used for profit-making purposes.

Valuation

In Kenya, land is valued on the basis of market value, and assessment of the property tax is the responsibility of the county government. The county government then submits the valuation roll to the county assembly, informs the public that the list is available for inspection purposes, and handles objections. The valuation roll becomes final when the county certifies it.

Before 1991, valuation rolls were prepared every five years (Syagga 1994). Since 1991, the legislation has provided for a 10-year cycle. The law also provides for the preparation of annual supplementary valuation rolls. In practice, valuation rolls are not maintained; several of the current rolls date back to the early 1980s. Supplementary rolls tend to be undertaken in an ad hoc manner. This inability to prepare revaluations regularly cannot be attributed to the lack of valuers, because Kenya has a long tradition of educating and training valuers (Franzsen and Olima 2003). Nevertheless, counties do not have the resources to maintain and update valuation rolls. Historically, the previous municipal and city governments were responsible for preparing valuation rolls, but the responsibility for undertaking valuation for property rates now rests primarily with the counties. County governments have options for valuation provision. First, if a county has a valuation department, valuation can be undertaken in-house. Currently, Nairobi City County, Mombasa, and Nakuru have valuation departments, although the number of valuers employed is insufficient to undertake a general revaluation. Second, counties can subcontract valuation to the private sector, which appears to have sufficient capacity to undertake county revaluations. Third, the MLPP has a valuation department that county governments can request to prepare valuation rolls for their areas (Akello 2008; Olima 1999). The MLPP charges a fee of 0.25 percent of the total value, discounted to 50 percent of that value, to prepare the valuation roll. A fourth option that could be considered is a partnership between the MLPP and the private sector. It is difficult to estimate accurately the number of properties that should be on county valuation rolls, but it is clear that many parcels are not included. Although comprehensive data on the current status of valuation rolls across the country are not available, existing evidence suggests that valuation rolls are significantly out of date. For example, Nairobi City County is using a valuation roll last revalued in 1982; Machakos, in 1983; and Mombasa, in 1991. The following counties have more recently valued rolls: Kisumu (2008), Nyeri (2009), and Kiambu (2014). Overall, though, the legislative requirement that general revaluations be undertaken every 10 years has never been achieved.

Tax Rates

The Rating Act authorized the former local authorities to set the tax rate within a given range. The tax rate could be a per-unit rate under area rating or a value rate under valuation rating. Either tax rate could be determined uniformly or differentially. Differential rates could be proportional or based on value, size, or land use. Local authorities could set a value-based rate of up to 4 percent without obtaining central-government approval, which was required for tax rates exceeding 4 percent.

Currently, the new counties largely apply uniform area tax rates or uniform value-based tax rates. Counties that have higher tax rates are primarily those that have outdated valuation rolls. Given the static valuations, the Nairobi County Council can increase revenues only by increasing the tax rate. Although there had been some differentiation between different property use categories in the past, from 1997, a uniform tax rate was imposed on all property categories. Table 15.3 provides a history of tax rates from 1982 to 2015 (since the 1982 valuation roll became operative). The tax rate that was suggested for 2015 in the 2014–2015 Draft County Finance Bill was 25 percent.

Billing and Collection

County governments can rely on in-house staff, other government departments, or the private sector for collection. Several of the previous large municipal councils experimented with contracting out revenue collection to firms of lawyers, but the results were somewhat disappointing. In addition, Nairobi City County contracted with the KRA to collect property rates, but contractual issues led to abandonment of the arrangement.

Counties send payment notices annually that show the assessed value and the amount of tax that must be paid. In general, collection rates are disappointingly low, ranging from 5 to 60 percent of the in-year billed amount. The reasons for the low collection rates are (1) lack of taxpayer confidence; (2) poor understanding by taxpayers of how the tax is levied, collected, and enforced and how the revenues are spent; (3) the absence of enforcement mechanisms; and (4) perhaps most important, the lack of political will. There are also problems in actually delivering the bills. Where notices are mailed, it is not uncommon that 50 percent are returned as undeliverable. Hand delivery is also widely used.

Bills are normally prepared in December and sent out in early January. Taxpayers have until March 31 to make payment. After that date, any unpaid amount incurs a penalty and interest. Normally, payment is made in one lump sum. Counties have the power to make special arrangements with large taxpayers for installment payments. In addition to cash payments made at county offices, payments can be made by electronic transfers through banks and M-Pesa[1] and other similar electronic payment systems. Counties have been struggling to collect property rates and in particular to force delinquent ratepayers to comply. For example, Nairobi City County collects, on average, 45 percent of the billed amount; Kiambu County's collection performance is poor, only 10 percent; and Machakos County is only marginally better at around 20 percent. Counties generally have amassed significant arrears over the years. In order to attempt to persuade ratepayers to deal with their arrears, counties typically give waivers of interest on arrears, but with limited success.

Table 15.3 Nairobi County Council Property Tax Rates Since 1982 (Percentage)

Category	1982–1987	1988–1990	1991–1992	1993	1994–1995	1996	1997	1998–2000	2001–2006	2007–2013	2014	2015
Residential	2.25	4.00	5.00	7.00	9.00	12.00	13.00	14.00	15.00	17.00	34.00	25.00
Commercial	8.00	9.00	10.00	10.00	10.00	13.00	13.00	14.00	15.00	17.00	34.00	25.00
Industrial	6.00–7.00	9.00	9.00	10.00	10.00	13.00	13.00	14.00	15.00	17.00	34.00	25.00

Source: Nairobi City County (2015).

Note: To show the overall trends, agricultural properties and their unique treatment are omitted.

Enforcement

The Rating Act deals with procedures for enforcing payment of rates against defaulters. When a ratable owner fails to pay within the stipulated period, there are various legal instruments for encouraging and ensuring compliance, including charging interest on arrears, giving discounts for prompt payment of the rates, fines, tax liens, foreclosures, and recovery from tenants. However, these mechanisms are either not employed or are ineffective in achieving compliance. Instead of taking aggressive enforcement action, county governments tend to rely on ensuring that rate clearance certificates will not be issued. The clearance certificate can be a very useful enforcement mechanism because it requires the taxpayer to settle in advance any property tax that is owed before the property can be transferred. In addition, a clearance certificate must be obtained if a taxpayer requests a business license or other permit from the county.

Property Tax Issues in Kenya

A critical property tax issue in Kenya is the legislative vacuum, which means that counties are relying on existing legislation or are in the process of drafting their own valuation and rating laws. The government of Kenya should provide national framework legislation that counties can customize. Also, there is a severe lack of valuation resources within the counties, which means that valuation services must be supplied by either the private sector or the MLPP. Valuation service provision tends to be targeted at general revaluations. However, there is a need to contract valuation service providers to undertake annual supplementary valuations to ensure buoyancy within the property rating system. This resource gap has led to shortcomings in the following important valuation tasks: (1) the identification of subdivisions; (2) the ability to undertake parcel inspections; and (3) the ability to prepare supplementary valuations.

The problems that county governments face in the administration of property taxation include incomplete title registration and cadastral coverage, which make the actual identification of parcels a difficult task; lack of capacity; ineffective and poorly applied enforcement mechanisms; and a lack of willingness to pay the tax. County governments do not have the capacity to systematically maintain and coordinate the updating of their valuation rolls. This seriously inhibits adherence to a regular revaluation cycle. In addition, the existence of an informal property market and the requirement to use market values in property assessment make the process difficult because of the lack of reliable and fully representative sales data.

National and county governments in Kenya must coordinate efforts to strengthen the capacity and capability of county governments to administer the property tax to achieve realistic collection and compliance rates. Revenue collection from the property tax is exceptionally low, primarily because of noncompliance and ineffective enforcement. The key issues to be addressed are weak administration and an associated lack of political support. The current legislation demonstrates the lack of modern thinking on improving property tax collection and needs to be updated and revised. Clearly, a legal framework that supports rather than hinders progress in property tax administration is also required. There have been developments that have shown some promise, for example, linking administrative components such as property identification, valuation, billing, collection, and enforcement with other revenue sources, such as the user charges and single business permits.

A major impediment to improving the property tax is lackluster administration and the lack of political support for collection and enforcement. In this regard, the KRA is engaging in discussions with several counties to take over their collection of property rates and single business permits.

Mobilizing political will and support requires a paradigm shift in how politicians view the property tax. In addition, taxpayers must be convinced of the benefits of paying the tax through obtaining better local services and amenities. The perception that the taxes and fees are being administered efficiently and fairly is paramount. Certainty that penalties for noncompliance will be enforced reduces the sense of unfairness among those who pay their taxes promptly but feel that others enjoy all the benefits of public services without contributing to their delivery.

Note

1. M-Pesa (M stands for "mobile"; *pesa* is Swahili for "money") is a mobile-phone-based money transfer and microfinancing service, launched in 2007 by Vodafone for Safaricom and Vodacom.

References

Akello, E. O. 2008. "Challenges to Urban Authorities Land Tax Revenue in Kenya: The Case of City Council of Nairobi." M.S. thesis, Royal Institute of Technology, Stockholm, Sweden.

CIA (Central Intelligence Agency). 2016. "Kenya." In *The World Factbook*. https://www.cia.gov/library/publications/the-world-factbook/geos/ke.html.

Franzsen, R. C. D. 2013. "Policy Issues and Options: Taxation Laws for Kenya's County Governments." Washington, DC: World Bank.

Franzsen, R. C. D., and W. H. A. Olima. 2003. "Property Tax Issues in Southern and East Africa: Lessons from South Africa and Kenya." *Journal of Property Tax Assessment and Administration* 8(1): 1–18.

Gachuru, M. W., and W. H. A. Olima. 1998. "Real Property Taxation—A Dwindling Revenue Source for Local Authorities in Kenya." *Journal of Property Tax Assessment and Administration* 3(2): 5–23.

IMF (International Monetary Fund). 2015. *2014 IMF Government Finance Statistics Yearbook*. Washington, DC.

———. 2016. "IMF World Longitudinal Data (WoRLD)." IMF e-Library Data. *http:// data.imf.org/?sk=77413F1D-1525-450A-A23A-47AEED40FE78&sId=1390030109571*.

Kelly, R. 2000. "Designing a Property Tax Reform Strategy for Sub-Saharan Africa: An Analytical Framework Applied to Kenya." *Public Budgeting and Finance* 20(4): 36–51.

Nairobi City County. 2015.

Olima, W. H. 1999. "Real Property Taxation in Kenya." In *Property Tax: An International Comparative Review*, ed. W. J. McCluskey, 358–374. Aldershot: Ashgate.

———. 2005. "Land Value Taxation in Kenya." In *Land Value Taxation: An Applied Approach*, ed. W. J. McCluskey and R. C. D. Franzsen, 91–114. Aldershot: Ashgate.

Syagga, P. M. 1994. *Real Estate Valuation Handbook: With Special Reference to Kenya*. Nairobi: Nairobi University Press.

United Nations. 2014. *World Urbanization Prospects*. Washington, DC: Department of Economic and Social Affairs, Population Division.

United Nations, Department of Economic and Social Affairs, Population Division. 2015. World Population Prospects: The 2015 Revision. *https://esa.un.org/unpd/wpp /Publications/Files/World_Population_2015_Wallchart.pdf*.

World Bank. 2012. *Devolution Without Disruption: Pathways to a Successful New Kenya*. Report prepared for the World Bank and Australian Aid. Nairobi.

———. 2016a. "Country and Lending Groups." *http://data.worldbank.org/about/country -and-lending-groups*.

———. 2016b. "GDP per Capita (Current US%)." *http://data.worldbank.org/indicator /NY.GDP.PCAP.CD*.

Legislation

County Governments Act 2012.

Government Lands Act 1915.

Land Act 2012.

Land Registration Act 2012.

Land Titles Act 1908.

Local Government Act 1963.

National Land Commission Act 2012.

Rating Act 1986.

Registration of Titles Act 1920.

Registered Land Act 1963.

Stamp Duty Act 2012.

Valuation for Rating Act 1984.

16

Liberia

RIËL FRANZSEN AND SAMUEL JIBAO

Liberia, with an area of 111,369 km², is bordered by Sierra Leone to the west, Guinea to the north, Côte d'Ivoire to the east, and the Atlantic Ocean to the south. It gained its independence from the United States in 1847. The population is approximately 4.5 million (United Nations 2015), of which about 50 percent is urbanized (United Nations 2014). The capital is Monrovia, with an estimated population of 1.3 million (CIA 2016). Other secondary cities and towns include Buchanan, Ganta, Gbanga, Harbel, and Kakata. Classified as a low-income country (World Bank 2016a), Liberia had an estimated per capita GDP of USD 456 in 2015 (World Bank 2016b), the lowest in Anglophone West Africa (World Bank 2014).

Government

Liberia is a unitary sovereign state. The legislative power is vested in two separate houses, the Senate and the House of Representatives, both of which must pass all legislation. Administratively, Liberia is divided into 15 counties (CIA 2016), which are subdivided into districts, which are further subdivided into clans. A district commissioner appointed by the president governs each district within a county. Below the districts are chiefdoms, which are governed by paramount chiefs. The chiefdoms constitute Liberia's

---

This chapter is in large part an updated version of Jibao 2009a.

tribal authority and are accountable to the district commissioner. At present, there are 215 chiefdoms with 476 clans spread across the 15 counties (Jibao 2009a).

The ravages of a protracted civil war, especially damaged infrastructure, are still evident throughout Liberia and continue to affect governance. However, the peace accord reached in 2003 is still intact, and institutions and infrastructure are being rebuilt with significant international assistance. Successful elections in 2005 ushered in a new era for the country (UNCDF 2006). In 2006, the new government formulated the Interim Poverty Reduction Strategy Program. Although essential services such as electricity and piped water are available only in a few urban areas, some progress has been made toward restoring and even extending these services (Jibao 2009a). The 2014–2015 Ebola epidemic in the region, however, was a setback for Liberia.

Liberia is also embarking on decentralization, but given the current institutional environment and level of development, this is rightly viewed as a long-term process. However, counties must be able to generate a significant proportion of their revenues to perform the functions that have been devolved to them and to be accountable and autonomous (Olabisi 2013).

Land Tenure

In 1984, most land belonged to the state. A limited amount of land was held in freehold, almost entirely in urban areas, although some plantation and other commercial farm operations were also privately owned. The 1984 constitution, which became effective in 1986, excluded private property rights in any mineral resources on or beneath the land and in the land beneath the sea and any waterways. Moreover, only Liberian citizens could own land, although noncitizen educational, missionary, and benevolent institutions were allowed ownership as long as the relevant holdings were used for the purposes for which they were acquired. Property that was no longer so used reverted to the state. Many foreign businesses have entered into long-term leases on concessions of agricultural and forestry land (Jibao 2009b).

Given the history of the country, it is not surprising that security of land tenure is basically nonexistent in Liberia. The operations of the land and property markets are largely informal, unregulated, and nontransparent; most transactions take place outside a formal registration process. Various factors account for the weak protection of property rights, including the legacy of the civil wars that led to the destruction of property records in the deeds registry; the acknowledgment of both statutory and customary tenure rights and informal arrangements under the law; an unclear legal distinction between public and tribal lands; the absence of an institutional framework for land administration and management; numerous corrupt and fraudulent land transactions; and frequent land disputes and the institutional inability and lack of political will to solve these disputes. The illegal sale and resale of land, multiple ownership claims to the same piece of land, and the absence of many landowners from Liberia for more than a decade characterize the current unstable land tenure system (Richards 2006).

In 2009, the government established the Liberia Land Commission. This commission focuses on four areas: development of an appropriate land rights policy, land administration, land use, and land disputes. In November 2012, the Land Commission released a draft Land Rights Policy Statement for public information, the first comprehensive land policy in the country's history. It proposes four primary land tenure categories: government land, public land, customary land, and private land. According to the Land Commission, the primary goal is the creation of a credible legal cadastre. This, however, is a long-term project. Secure titles and clear rights are especially important to formalize the property market and underpin a buoyant tax base for the property tax. The current lack of secure tenure undermines the tax base of the property tax, market values. The promulgation of the Land Rights Bill, which was still pending in September 2016, will be a significant step toward the creation of secure tenure and a formal property market.

Property-Related Taxation

In 2012, total tax revenue amounted to 21.1 percent of GDP (IMF 2015), and property taxes amounted to 0.12 percent of GDP (IMF 2016). Liberia does not levy property transfer taxes, a stamp duty, an estate or death tax, or a gift tax. A capital gains tax that generates an insignificant amount of revenue is levied, as is a sales tax at a standard rate of 7 percent. As in many other African countries, there is also a withholding tax on rental income that, in Liberia, raised slightly more revenue than the recurrent property tax in 2012 and 2013. The Center for National Documents and Records/ Archives levies a fixed fee of approximately USD 15 for the registration of deeds.

The only property-related tax is the so-called real estate tax, also known as the real property tax, a recurrent property tax that, in principle, is imposed on real estate (immovable property) such as land, buildings, and other improvements. It is an annual tax levied under Chapter 20 (Real Property Tax) of the Liberia Revenue Code of 2000 (the Revenue Code). Unlike analogous taxes in other Anglophone countries in West Africa, this

Table 16.1 Real Estate Tax Collection in Liberia, 2006–2011

Year	USD	% of Tax Revenue	% of GDP
2006	392,434	0.37	0.06
2007	790,394	0.46	0.11
2008	1,386,274	0.66	0.16
2009	1,279,330	0.49	0.11
2010	1,840,207	0.53	0.14
2011	2,590,155	0.63	0.17

Source: Revenue Department, Ministry of Finance, in Olabisi (2013).

tax is levied and collected by the central government. A special division, headed by a director, and charged with the responsibility of administering the real estate tax exists in the Ministry for Finance. In 1980, it was decreed that 30 percent of revenue collected centrally from the real estate tax and other traditional sources of revenue for local councils (fees and licenses) should be allocated to local government. Currently, revenues such as fees, licenses, and the real estate tax are still collected by the central government and are paid into the consolidated fund, although these revenues should be earmarked for the counties.

The Property Tax

The Revenue Importance of the Property Tax

The real estate tax, administered by the Real Estate Tax Division within the Ministry of Finance, is an insignificant source of revenue (table 16.1). The property tax is clearly underperforming its revenue potential. Commercial properties in Monrovia, Buchanan, Paynesville, Margibi, and a few other urban areas are contributing a significant portion of the total property tax collected. It is noteworthy, however, that there seems to be a steady increase in the property tax as a percentage of total tax revenue and of GDP.

The Tax Base

The Revenue Code provides for the property tax to be imposed on almost all properties in Liberia; in other words, in principle, the base coverage is extensive. In practice, however, the property tax is levied and collected only in Monrovia and a few other major urban jurisdictions. This is partly due to the lack of accurate and credible property data. As previously indicated, tenure security is problematic throughout the country because of the problems and capacity constraints with the surveying, mapping, and registration of deeded land (Bruce and Kanneh 2011). In addition, there is limited capacity within the Real Estate Tax Division to administer the property tax. This understaffed division is responsible for the identification and assessment of properties, the review of certified appraisals, and maintenance of the property register, as well as the billing and collection of the tax.

There is no comprehensive register of residential and nonresidential properties in Liberia. A further problem is that illegally constructed buildings are not recorded and are therefore not taxed. In 2012, there were only 5,000 properties on the property register for Montserrado County (Monrovia). According to government estimates, this is only about 30 percent of the actual number of properties. For a population of about 1.3 million (CIA 2016), a figure of fewer than 20,000 properties still seems unrealistically low. In short, the tax base coverage is very poor.

The property tax is imposed on each parcel of land not specifically exempted from taxation in the Revenue Code. It consists of (1) a tax on each parcel of unimproved land, including underimproved land (as defined), at rates prescribed in the code and dependent on geographic classification; and (2) a tax on each parcel of improved land at a stated percentage of its assessed value. The tax is based on market value, which Section 2000 of the Revenue Code defines as follows: "The term 'market value' is the capital sum which land, buildings or improvements might be expected to realize as at the date of assessment if offered for sale on such reasonable terms and conditions as a bona fide seller would require."

Assessment

Before the enactment of the Revenue Code in 2000, properties were valued on the basis of their cost of construction. Although the Revenue Code still recognizes this method if property has not yet been reassessed, the current basis of assessment is market value. Section 2001(b) states: "Each parcel of land so subject to assessment and taxation shall be inspected and its assessed value determined on the basis of its market value as at the date of inspection. Such assessed value shall be carried on the real property assessment record books kept by the Minister for the period of 5 years from the date such valuation becomes operative."

Exemptions

Exemptions from the property tax include the following:

- All public lands, buildings, and improvements owned by the central government.

- Property owned by churches and religious societies.

- Foreign and domestic missions.

- Educational, charitable, and fraternal organizations, provided that the property is used for religious, educational, charitable, or fraternal purposes and is not used for profit or that these properties are not rented or leased except to similar public benefit organizations.

- Properties held by the University of Liberia.

- All properties of foreign governments on lands leased from or deeded by Liberia.

- All property that is exempt from the real property tax under the terms of statutes, treaties, or agreements passed or entered into by the government, provided that the land is used in accordance with the conditions of such agreements.

- Real property used under a renewable resource contract or property used within a mineral exploration license area, a mining license area, or a petroleum area and used for mining or petroleum exploitation purposes.

The rationale for the last exemption is unclear. Why should these properties not be viewed as commercial property and taxed accordingly?

Valuation

Section 2001 of the Revenue Code provides that valuations of taxable properties must be undertaken at least every five years. However, given the lack of valuation capacity and skills within the Real Estate Tax Division (and elsewhere in the government), these general revaluations are not undertaken as required. Before the civil war in 1989, there were about 84 valuers, but by 2008 available statistics showed that there were only 34 government valuers and 17 registered private valuation firms involved in valuation (Jibao 2009b). This seriously inhibited adherence to the statutory five-year valuation cycle. Some properties have not been valued for the past 25 years, despite an environment where property values have been increasing rapidly since the end of the civil war, in many instances by more than 600 percent between 1998 and 2008 (Jibao 2009a).

Assessment and valuation are the legal mandate of the minister of finance. Section 2006 of the Revenue Code states: "All land, whether improved or unimproved, subject to assessment and taxation on the basis of its assessed value, shall be assessed or reassessed as the case may be by officials appointed and authorized by the Minister to act as real estate assessors." In practice, however, the government relies on self-declaration of residential property values. To regularize self-declaration, an administrative regulation was passed in 2009 to allow for self-declaration of values. Administrative Regulation No. 7.2006-1/MOF/R/28 August 2009 sets out the revised responsibilities of property owners, tax assessors, and enforcers, as well as all private and public appraisers, in regard to the assessment of property. The Ministry of Finance determined and published so-called technical appraisal rates (values per square foot of buildings based on quality and use) and land values that taxpayers must use. From the 2009 fiscal year, property owners must file a schedule of their properties with the Real Estate Tax Division.

The administrative regulation provides that residential property owners have the option of making a self-declaration of the value of their properties or acquiring a certified appraisal from a member of the Liberia Chamber of Architects. The practice within the government is to readily accept self-declared values and to challenge only values deemed unreasonably low. However, self-declaration applies only to properties used exclusively as owner-occupied residences. Residential properties that are rented out are deemed commercial, and their owners must submit a certified appraisal, as is required for all commercial and industrial (income-generating) properties.

Owners of commercial or industrial properties must submit certified appraisals for every property to the Real Estate Tax Division. These appraisals must be conducted and certified by a recognized architectural firm affiliated with the Liberia Chamber of Architects, which prescribes the format of appraisals. Every certified appraisal must be supplemented by

- all legal claims to the property;
- the full contact details and address of the taxpayer;
- the location and a description of the property;
- full-view photos of the property; and
- the amount of annual rent paid (and copies of leases notarized or registered and probated), if applicable.

Because of the costs involved in obtaining certified appraisals, residential property owners generally opt for self-declaration, and certified appraisals are submitted mostly for nonresidential properties. The owners of nonresidential properties can deduct the cost of appraisals as an expense for the purposes of income taxation. If the Real Estate Tax Division accepts the certified appraisal, the value remains valid for five years. As a result, there is no general revaluation cycle, but rather an ad hoc five-year assessment period for each individual property. Straight-line depreciation is applied to buildings over a period of 15 years at 2 percent per year. Thus, the maximum allowable depreciation is 30 percent. Given the current system of self-declaration of values computer-assisted mass appraisal (CAMA) is not presently contemplated. If it were to be considered in the medium to long term, CAMA will present challenges in an environment where there is no homogeneity in any neighborhood or zoning laws to regulate property use. The absence of building permits and proper town planning will also need to be addressed for a CAMA system to become a viable option.

Tax Rates

Different tax rates apply to land and buildings (and other improvements). The tax rates that had been in place since 2000 were amended, effective January 1, 2011, as indicated in table 16.2.

For the land component, the tax is determined as follows:

- Unimproved land within the corporate limits of a city or municipal or commonwealth district (a city or town lot) is taxed at 2 percent of the land's assessed value.

- Urban land (of one acre or more) is taxed at 3 percent of the land's assessed value.

- Unimproved urban land used as farmland is taxed at 4 percent of the land's assessed value.

- Unimproved rural land (outside a city, town, or municipal or commonwealth district) is taxed at LRD 5.00 per acre. However, a minimum tax of LRD 200.00 per parcel is payable.

Table 16.2 Former and Current Tax Rates

Property Category	Tax Rates (2000–2010)	Tax Rates (from 2011)
Residential buildings (used exclusively for residential purposes)	0.25	0.08
Commercial buildings	1	1.5
Industrial buildings	0.5	1.5
Undeveloped city or town lots	7	2
Urban land (one acre or more)	5	3
Urban farmland (land and buildings)	10	4
All undeveloped land (located outside city or town limits)		LRD 5.00 per acre

Source: Liberia Revenue Code of 2000 as amended in 2010.

If a building or improvement is wholly or partly used for commercial or industrial purposes, the tax rate is 1.5 percent of the assessed value (table 16.2). This also applies to residential properties used partly for commercial purposes (mixed use). A building used exclusively for residential purposes is taxed at 0.08 percent of its assessed market value.

Urban properties (land and improvements) used for farming is taxed at 4 percent of the assessed market value. Buildings and other improvements on public land are taxed at one-seventh of 1 percent of assessed value for residential use (0.14 percent) and at 1.0 percent of assessed value for commercial purposes.

What is noteworthy from table 16.2 is that in the new tax rate regime, the tax rate for residential properties was reduced significantly, whereas the tax rates on nonresidential properties were increased significantly—for commercial properties by 50 percent and for industrial properties by 200 percent. In 2011, commercial properties on aggregate accounted for 30 percent of the total real property tax bills but contributed 79 percent of the total revenue. Residential properties accounted for 50 percent of bills but contributed only 5.9 percent of revenue. Industrial properties and

---

Box 16.1 EXAMPLES OF TAX LIABILITY IN MONROVIA

Property assessed value = [(Total square area × technical appraisal rate) − age depreciation] + land value.

Two residential apartments of 3,000 ft² each and both 10 years old.

Property 1: Class A lot, located in Mamba Point, and building of above-average quality.

$$[(3,000 \text{ ft}^2 \times USD \ 35.00) - 20\%] + USD \ 50,000.00 = USD \ 134,000.00$$

Real property tax = USD 134,000.00 × 0.08% = USD 107.20 per year.

Property 2: Class C lot, located in Congo Town, Old Road, and building of below-average quality.

$$[(3,000 \text{ ft}^2 \times USD \ 20.00) - 20\%] + USD \ 2,000.00 = USD \ 50,000.00.$$

Real property tax = USD 50,000.00 × 0.08% = USD 40.00 per year.

The Ministry of Finance determines and publishes the "technical appraisal rates" (values per square foot of buildings based on quality and use) and land values to be used by taxpayers.

unimproved land (constituting the remaining 20 percent of the tax bills) accounted for only 8.2 percent of the revenue. Given that the tax rate for commercial properties is almost 19 times higher than the rate for residential properties, this is not surprising. Despite a reduction in the tax rates on land in 2011, these rates are still significantly higher than the tax rates on buildings. However, the revenue contribution from the land component is insignificant. The examples in box 16.1 explain how the property value and tax are determined for residential properties of different quality in two neighborhoods of Monrovia.

Billing and Collection

The property tax covers a period of twelve months from January 1 of each year and is due on July 1 of the year in which it is levied. Every person who has acquired title to real property subject to taxation under the law must within 30 days after the effective date or within 30 days after acquisition, whichever is appropriate, file a schedule of all such property acquired at the office of the minister nearest to the property. This schedule must contain a complete description of the property, including its location, area, lot number, use classification, and the actual consideration paid on its acquisition.

When the tax is due, a bill stating the assessed value and the tax due is prepared. The Real Estate Tax Division presently undertakes billing annually, and in practice, tax bills are delivered manually. One major constraint on billing, which results in significant losses of revenue, is the poor numbering of property in the country. Some houses have no numbers and cannot be identified to be served with demand notices. There is also a lack of information on owners. Taxpayers are expected to make payments by obtaining a "bank payment slip" from a branch office of the Ministry of Finance located closest to the relevant property and then to make payment at a branch of the Central Bank of Liberia. The compliance cost of this procedure is significant (Olabisi 2013), especially where taxpayers are not close to any of these branch offices. A taxpayer who finds it difficult to pay the lump-sum amount stated in the tax bill may negotiate to pay in installments.

Interest at market rates may be charged if the tax is not paid during July of the year in which it is levied. The minister may add an administrative penalty to the amount due, or to any underpayment, of 5 percent per month for each month or part of a month after July 31 that it remains unpaid, but this penalty is not to exceed 25 percent.

Enforcement

According to Section 2007 of the Revenue Code, taxes on real property, interest, penalties, and other charges that may be levied on any property in Liberia continue to be outstanding until they are paid. Such unpaid taxes take precedence over all other charges on the real property involved. Delinquencies are reported to the Minister of Justice for collection through the Tax Court. This adversarial process is costly, cumbersome, and largely ineffective. Presently, enforcement efforts primarily target commercial properties. In the long term, this practice may entrench the impression that residential property owners need not pay their taxes (Olabisi 2013).

Upon receipt of a report of nonpayment of property taxes, the minister of justice may bring a suit to the Tax Court in the county in which the property is located to recover the delinquent property tax and all penalties and interest. The ministerial officer of the court gives notice to all persons concerned of the intention to sell the property at public auction and convey title to the purchaser. The proceeds from the sale are applied in the following manner: first, to the payment of taxes, penalties, and interest due; second, to the costs of the court; and last, the balance, if any, to the owner of the real property. Nothing in the act, however, prevents the owner of the real property from bidding at the public auction.

Proper enforcement remains a serious problem because application of the provisions of the law could create social unrest. In reality, this law has yet to be fully implemented, although tax officials and taxpayers recognize its existence. The main argument put forward by a senior government official against its use is that most property owners currently lack the funds to pay these taxes because life has yet to return to normal after years of civil war. The code, however, makes provision for persons aggrieved by a decision of the minister about any tax imposed under the Revenue Code to appeal to the Board of Tax Appeals. Interviews with senior officials of the Real Estate Tax Department in 2008 indicated that there were no cases of tax appeals or objections to assessment or valuation. These officials noted that one of the factors that limit objections by taxpayers is that they are required to pay 50 percent of the assessed tax before the appeal is heard. Furthermore, the Board of Appeal was not yet functional, so all objections were directed to the department for review.

Property Tax Issues in Liberia

Years of conflicts have left the social fabric of Liberia devastated. The necessary physical, economic, and social infrastructure was destroyed during the intermittent civil wars (UNCDF 2006). One of the major aspects of the peace agreement signed in 2003 was to request the National Transition Government to adopt solutions to the critical issues that had caused the internal conflicts. These included important reforms to prevent misappropriation of state revenues, improvement of budgetary management and procedures and procurement procedures and oversight, anticorruption measures, support for key financial and management institutions, and improvement of the governance aspects of wide-scale capacity building (Jibao 2009b).

The political will to decentralize has been acknowledged, and the government's willingness to work toward decentralization is publicly evident (UNCDF 2006). However, local-government administration is unlikely to be effective for many years. Furthermore, the existing legal framework is obsolete and requires extensive amendments. It is unlikely that comprehensive fiscal decentralization can be accomplished soon because of the low capacity of the local councils and the past high levels of centralization of revenue administration in the country.

Monrovia, the capital city, is mandated to provide various services, such as waste management, but it has minimal control over raising and collecting property taxes and an array of other taxes, which the city spends in partnership with the central government. Although the city, in principle, has the capacity to generate additional revenues from its property base, it has no right to levy the property tax, nor does it have direct access to its share of revenues raised by the central government. This has resulted in inadequate sanitation facilities, poor institutional capacity to promote public health, and poor road infrastructure (Jibao 2009a).

The Revenue Code defines the property tax base broadly, but coverage across the country is extremely limited. Even within the few jurisdictions where there is a property tax roll, coverage is generally poor. In addition, it is difficult to establish the open market value on which the property tax is assessed under the new regime in Liberia because of inadequate data, a paucity of relevant skills, and a dearth of knowledge of a property market that is not yet well developed. Although the current system contains elements of an area-based system, it is in essence a simplified value-based system that relies heavily on ad hoc self-declaration and self-assessment or certified appraisals by members of the Liberia Chamber of Architects. Through regulation, the Real Estate Tax Division has effectively freed itself from the insurmountable task of determining discrete values for all taxable properties by shifting the burden to property owners and taking on the role of auditing the assessed values that owners produce. Reliance on self-declaration of values by residential property owners is a pragmatic solution that could be quite successful if there is sufficient administrative capacity within the Real Estate Tax Division to exercise sufficient oversight to ensure that it functions properly. Probably a bigger challenge is to ensure that those residential properties that are not currently on the tax roll get recorded. The system in place regarding commercial properties is a pragmatic solution to the lack of capacity within the government. Again, if enough audits are undertaken of the certified values provided by the property owners, such a system should be able to function quite well.

The differentiation of tax rates may also present problems and cause distortions. The significant reduction in the tax rate for residential property may benefit rich households as well as poor ones. A higher tax rate, coupled with appropriate hardship relief measures, would be a better approach but presupposes administrative capacity within the Real Estate Tax Division.

Property tax collection is also a challenge. Automating billing should be a priority (Olabisi 2013). Compliance is low because of the low level of income of many property owners throughout the country. Enforcement continues to be a problem because Liberia still lacks the legal environment required to assure dispute settlement based on proper evidence (Jibao 2009a).

References

Bruce, J. W., and B. N. Kanneh. 2011. *Reform of Liberia's Civil Law Concerning Land—A Proposed Strategy*. Report to the Land Commission. Monrovia.

CIA (Central Intelligence Agency). 2016. "Liberia." In *The World Factbook*. https://www.cia.gov/library/publications/the-world-factbook/geos/li.html.

IMF (International Monetary Fund). 2015. *2014 IMF Government Finance Statistics Yearbook*. Washington, DC.

———. 2016. "IMF World Longitudinal Data (WoRLD)." IMF e-Library Data. http://data.imf.org/?sk=77413F1D-1525-450A-A23A-47AEED40FE78&sId=1390030109571.

Jibao, S. 2009a. "Property Taxation in Anglophone West Africa Appendix 3: Liberia." Working paper WP09AWA9. Cambridge, MA: Lincoln Institute of Land Policy.

———. 2009b. "Property Taxation in Anglophone West Africa: Regional Overview." Working paper WP09AWA8. Cambridge, MA: Lincoln Institute of Land Policy.

Olabisi, O. 2013. "Optimising Real Estate Tax in Liberia: Implications for Revenue Performance and Economic Growth." Working paper. London: International Growth Centre.

Richards, P. 2006. *Community Cohesion in Liberia: A Post-war Rapid Social Assessment*. Washington, DC: UNDP and World Bank.

UNCDF (United Nations Capital Development Fund). 2006. *The Liberian National Decentralization and Local Development Program*. Government of Liberia, and United Nations Development Programme. www.uncdf.org/sites/default/files//Documents/ldld_58379_prodoc_0.pdf.

United Nations. 2014. *World Urbanization Prospects*. Washington, DC: Department of Economic and Social Affairs, Population Division.

United Nations, Department of Economic and Social Affairs, Population Division. 2015. *World Population Prospects: The 2015 Revision.* *https://esa.un.org/unpd/wpp /Publications/Files/World_Population_2015_Wallchart.pdf.*

World Bank. 2014. *World Development Indicators.* Washington, DC.

———. 2016a. "Country and Lending Groups." *http://data.worldbank.org/about/country -and-lending-groups.*

———. 2016b. "GDP per Capita (Current US%)." *http://data.worldbank.org/indicator /NY.GDP.PCAP.CD.*

Legislation

Constitution of the Republic of Liberia, 1984.

Land Rights Bill, 2014.

Liberia Revenue Code, 2000 (as revised in 2009 and 2010).

17

Madagascar

JEAN-JACQUES NZEWANGA, RIËL FRANZSEN,
AND WILLIAM McCLUSKEY

Madagascar is a large island state in the Indian Ocean approximately 650 kilometers off the coast of East Africa, from which it is separated by the Mozambique Channel. It was a colony of France from 1896 to 1960. Its surface area is 587,041 km², and the population is estimated at 24.2 million (United Nations 2015). Tananarive, also known as Antananarivo in Malagasy, is the capital city and has a population of about 2.6 million (CIA 2016). Malagasy and French are the two official languages. Approximately 35 percent of the population is urbanized (United Nations 2014). With a per capita GDP estimated at USD 402 in 2015 (World Bank 2016b), Madagascar is one of the poorest countries in the world and is classified as a low-income country (World Bank 2016a).

Government

Since independence in 1960, Madagascar has been beset by political crises, including a period of military government at the beginning of the 1970s. There are six provinces. The devolved local authorities, regions and *communes*, are incorporated bodies with administrative and financial autonomy granted under Article 134 of the constitution. The local authorities have access to the following fiscal resources (Article 150 of the constitution):

- Income from duties and taxes approved by the local councils and paid directly into the treasuries of the local authorities.

- The proportion of duties and taxes paid into the state treasury that the councils receive by law.

- Income from subsidies, whether conditional or not, that are agreed by the state budget for all the local authorities and reflect their particular situation or are compensation to these authorities for expenditures on programs or projects that are decided by the state but implemented by the local authorities.

- Income from local authorities' own assets.

- Charges and fees levied for the use of local services.

Land Tenure

Both freehold and community-based tenure systems operate in Madagascar (USAID 2007). Act No. 2005-019 (of October 17, 2005) defined the principles governing the status of land in Madagascar and established the right to property, including the right to nontitled land, allowing the applicant to choose to secure his right to property either by a procedure based on registration or by one of certification under Act No. 2006-031 (of October 18, 2006). This act defines nontitled private property and how it is managed. It thus applies to all lands occupied under customary law and practice that have not yet been subjected to the properly constituted legal system, whether these lands constitute a family inheritance passed from generation to generation or traditional family grazing land that does not include the extensive grasslands that are the subject of specific legislation.

In accordance with the principle of decentralizing land management, basic local-authority units are responsible for establishing a land office within their administration to manage arrangements for these nontitled properties (USAID 2007). Each basic local-authority unit must set up a local occupancy plan that shows the locations of property within its territory, such as public and private property, titled property, and any boundaries of occupied lands existing on its territory. The land occupancy plan is a helpful geographic information tool for sound land management by the local authority and, in principle, for property tax purposes. A document recognizing ownership, known as a "property certificate," is issued to the occupier after a well-established, straightforward local-authority procedure has been completed. The certificate of recognition of a property right issued at the end of the procedure constitutes proof of ownership rights over property, just as the property title in the land tenure system recognizes rights over titled properties. Mechanisms have been put in place to settle disputes that might persist after the various measures advocated in the law have been applied.

In Madagascar, the time gap between the needs of individuals for security of land tenure and the ability of the central government to issue property titles severely inhibits development. In March 2004, the Madagascan Ministry of Agriculture, Animal Husbandry, and Fisheries initiated the National Land Program. The principal objective of this program was to respond to the huge demand for security of land tenure within the shortest possible time by formalizing unwritten property rights and by safeguarding existing, written property rights and correcting anomalies in them. The purpose of this new land policy was to manage land in a way that favored private investment, agricultural production, the management, protection, and renewal of natural resources, and the development of local authorities by making the tools for local management and taxation available to them.

Taxation

The Finance Law (Code of Taxes) of 2007 provides for all taxes levied by the central government. The following property-related taxes are levied under this act:

- The value-added tax (VAT).

- The capital gains tax.

- The tax on transactions.

- The stamp duty, which was abolished for property-related documents in 2009 (World Bank 2015).

The most important local taxes in 2014 were the following:

- The land tax.

- The land tax on developed property.

- The supplementary tax on developed property.

- The tax on registration rights.

Tax reforms were introduced in 2008 and 2009. The reasons for reform included increasing the level of competition among businesses, accelerating regional growth, combating corruption, attracting direct foreign investors, and responding to demands for transparency by the people and for increased professionalism by the government role players involved.

The aim of the tax reform introduced in 2008 by Act No. 2007-033 (of December 14, 2007) is threefold:

- To make the system simple, attractive, and consistent for businesses.

- To increase people's purchasing power while at the same time eliminating harmful taxes.

- To strengthen the resources of district authorities through a genuine process of decentralization.

For example, the capital gains tax on property has been merged into the income tax at a single rate of 25 percent. Registration fees have been significantly reduced and simplified. The rate of the VAT has been increased to 20 percent to compensate for the loss of net resources through transfer to the regions. The land tax and the tax on built-up property have been simplified, and more detail has been introduced on how these taxes must be calculated and collected, with the aim of making more resources available for the communes. Moreover, the supplementary land tax on developed property has been abolished (World Bank 2015).

In 2012, total taxes amounted to only 9.1 percent of GDP (IMF 2015). In 2010, property taxes as defined by the International Monetary Fund constituted 0.04 percent of GDP (IMF 2016). The percentage has been in steady decline since 2004, when it was 0.232 percent of GDP (IMF 2016).

Property-Related Taxes

The Capital Gains Tax on Property

A capital gains tax on property exists (as part of the income tax system) and is paid into the state treasury. Gains accrued by individuals when they transfer fixed property for payment are subject to this tax. The tax is 25 percent of the taxable gain. It is due from the person disposing of fixed property who realizes a profit and is paid to the collector of taxes responsible for registering deeds and declarations of property changes at the same time as the registration fees.

Registration Fees for Deeds and Transfers

Registration fees are allocated to the general budget. They are flat rate or proportionate, depending on the deeds and transfers to which they are applied. Proportionate fees are applied to the transfer of property, beneficial rights, or the enjoyment of immovable property either inter vivos or as the result of death. These fees are based on the cost of the property in addition to any charges that may be added. Exchanges of property are subject to a 4 percent duty. Property of whatever kind is assessed on its actual market value at the time of transfer, based on a self-declared valuation made by the parties.

Recurrent Property Taxes

The Land Tax

The land tax is an annual tax based on the landholding existing on January 1 of the tax year. The revenue from this tax is allocated to the budget of village settlements. The tax on land is payable at the principal town of the commune where the land is located. Unless exempted, lands irrespective of their legal status and the use to which they are put are taxable in the name of the owners or actual occupiers from January 1 of the tax year.

Exemptions

The following properties are permanently exempt from the land tax:

- All land belonging to the state, local authorities, or other public bodies that provide a public service or a service recognized as being of public benefit and produce no revenue.

- Land that is used free of charge and is exclusively used for charitable purposes that are free of charge, or for the teaching or practice of religion.

- Land that forms a necessary and immediate part of buildings such as courtyards, passages, or gardens not exceeding 20 acres.

Land recently put under cultivation and constituting an extension of farmed land is liable for the tax only from the sixth year after the year it was developed. This exemption is granted for lands where coffee trees have been planted and where the coffee beans have yet to be harvested, and lands where trees are to be grown and are newly planted. For reforested land where the tree density is at least 1,500 live trees per hectare, the exemption period is extended until the end of the year in which the first crop is actually harvested. To take advantage of the exemptions described, the owner or the occupant must annually send a declaration to the offices of the commune where the property is located before October 15, indicating the location and area of the land, the type of crop, and the date that work was begun on developing or refarming the land.

Tax Rates

For purposes of determining land tax liability, land is categorized into six classes according to use (see table 17.1). The taxable amount is derived by

Table 17.1 Categories of Agricultural Use

Category	Agricultural Use
1	Cocoa, coffee, sugarcane, coconut trees, cotton, cloves, oil palms, aromatic plants, pepper, sisal, vanilla
2	Woods, forests, lakes, swamps
3	Market gardening, fish rearing, and rice and other plants not listed elsewhere in this article
4	Natural and artificial pasture land, unproductive land, fallow land
5	Unworked land that could be productive
6	Non-agricultural use

Source: Article 10.01.07 of the Tax Code of 2011.

applying a tariff approved for four years by the town council and expressed in ariary (MAG) per hectare for land in categories 1 to 5 and a percentage of the market value for land in category 6. Category 6 applies to all land use other than agriculture, such as

- undeveloped land within the built-up area of a commune, recognized by order of the mayor and in keeping with the town-planning scheme if one exists;

- land containing disused buildings; and

- land containing traditionally constructed buildings that are not in keeping with the site or location, excluding those lands used for rice growing, market gardening, fish rearing or orchards, which remain subject to the fixed rate for their category.

For category 6 land, the tax rate is 1 percent of the market value of the land. This market value is determined from the most recent land transfers or, in the absence of these, by comparison with standard prices established by the municipal board (described later) set up under the Tax Code.

The owners or actual occupiers of land subject to the tax must send to the office in the commune where the property is located, before October 15 of each year, a written declaration stating the location of the land or lands; the area under each type of cultivation or other uses; the names of the tenants, if any; and the amount of rent payable. However, in rural areas, these declarations may be replaced by a straightforward verbal declaration that is recorded in a register kept in duplicate by the mayor or his/her representative, who must send the copy to the relevant local tax office before October 31. If there are any changes to the rental conditions between October 15 and January 1 of the tax year, the owners are obliged to send corrections to the relevant tax office before the beginning of the tax year. Commune officials or their representatives from the area where the property is located may make an on-site inventory of, or carry out checks on, lands that are liable to tax.

Enforcement

Delays in filing the declaration described in the 2008 Tax Regulations are liable to a penalty of 5 percent per month of delay, up to a maximum of 100 percent. The penalty for evasion is 50 percent of the tax evaded. The penalty for repeated offenses is increased to 100 percent.

Tax Relief

In the event of partial or total loss of crops or harvest due to circumstances beyond the control of the taxpayer, such as storm damage, floods, locust invasions, fires, or landslides, the taxpayer may ask for tax relief or a reduction in the land tax on the lands affected. Claims must be made in the prescribed manner to the department responsible for the tax administration within three months of the incident leading to the application. The relief granted is proportionate to the loss of gross income for the tax year in question.

If a disaster strikes all or the majority of lands in a commune, the mayor of the commune affected may apply for collective relief or tax reduction on behalf of all the taxpayers within the area. A decision on blanket relief from all or part of the tax burden may then be made according to the procedure described in the 2008 Tax Regulations.

The Property Tax on Developed Land

The property tax on developed land is an annual tax based on the rental value of buildings as of January 1 of the tax year and is collected by the local communes. The person liable for the tax is the owner or the holder of a beneficial right whose name appears on the register under that of the bare owner in the case of a beneficial right, or, failing this, of an apparent owner. Subject to specified exemptions, the following properties are taxable:

- Any construction, regardless of the nature of the materials used. If different parts of a property are completed over a period of time, each part is taxable independently from the time of its completion.

- Land under industrial or commercial use, such as work yards and depots for merchandise, materials, or goods, whether they are occupied by the owners or by others in return for payment or free of charge.

- Industrial equipment that is fixed and permanent or rests on special foundations that form an integral part of the building, and all commercial installations comparable to these structures.

Exemptions

The following properties are permanently exempt from the tax on developed land:

- All property belonging to the state, local authorities, or other public establishments that is used for a public service or general public benefit and does not generate income.

- Property or sections of property given over exclusively and free of charge to charitable, educational, or religious entities.

- New buildings and renovations and extensions to buildings, which are exempt for five years from the year of their completion.

The exemption applies to the person and lapses when there is a change in ownership, but heirs continue to benefit from an exemption granted to a deceased person for five years from the date of the property's construction. To benefit from the exemption pertaining to new buildings or renovations, the owner must send the residency or occupancy permit, or a duplicate, for the property or part of the property for which he is requesting exemption to the commune office where the property is located. In built-up areas where this occupancy procedure is not required, the owner must produce a certificate from the mayor of the commune where the property is located, certifying that the building in question has been completed.

Rental Value

As previously stated, the tax is based on the rental value of the property. This rental value is equal to:

- the rent due for the year, which must not be lower than that obtained by applying the assessment criteria in the report of the municipal board described in the Tax Code; or

- 30 percent of the rental value obtained by applying the assessment criteria in the report of the board for owner-occupied property, if the building is the taxpayer's primary residence.

Administration

The commune makes the assessments on which the property tax on developed land is based on the advice of a municipal board that is composed as follows:

- Chairman: the mayor or his deputy.

- The leader of the district or his deputy.

- Two representatives of the people per fifty thousand inhabitants, half appointed by the mayor and half by the leader of the district.

- Two highway or public service engineers.

- A representative of the tax office, who serves as the secretary of the board.

The board's decisions are valid if they are taken with at least 50 percent of its members present. An owner must be informed in good time if the board wishes to make an on-site inspection visit. The board may also ask highway engineers, the public services department, or any other competent department for their advice when it is setting the rental value.

The board meeting must be held within 30 days of receiving the assessment proposal presented by the office responsible for setting the tax base. If the board does not approve the proposal, it shall return it with its comments to the tax office within 15 days of the meeting. The tax office responsible for setting taxes then has 30 days from receiving this file to present a new proposal or supply new evidence to support the initial proposal. The board then has 15 days from the date it receives the file to make its observations. After this period, the tax office can make its final assessment with or without the board's comments.

The assessments that form the basis of the property tax on developed land may be revised each year. If there is no revision, an annual increase of 5 percent in the taxable value will be applied for a further three years. However, if a revision is carried out during this period, the new assessment will be applied immediately.

Tax Rates

The tax is calculated by applying a proportionate rate to the determined rental value. The municipal board votes on the rate, which must be between a minimum of 5 percent and a maximum of 10 percent. However, the tax due must not be less than MAG 2,000 per property.

Taxpayers' Responsibilities

Before October 15 of each year, owners of taxable properties must submit a written declaration on a prescribed form that includes the following details:

- The names of tenants, if any, the nature of the premises let (for example, whether furnished or not), and the amount of the rent.

- The nature of the premises occupied by the person making the declaration.

- The name of any persons occupying the property free of charge and the nature of the premises they occupy.

- The nature of any vacant premises.

If there are changes in the conditions of the rental between October 15 and January 1 of the (new) tax year, the owner must submit a corrected declaration before the beginning of the new tax year.

Enforcement

A penalty of up to 50 percent of the tax evaded can be applied but may not be less than MAG 10,000. Refusal to comply is punishable by a fine of MAG 200,000.

Economic considerations (population purchasing power and financial resources for local or devolved authorities) and social considerations (fraud, corruption, growth in the informal sector) play an important role in determining tax revenues in Madagascar. Although mechanisms exist for gathering appropriate valuation information, there is little technical capacity to analyze or apply a valuation assessment in a uniform, robust fashion. Despite this, the main challenges appear to be lack of administrative capacity and willingness to enforce the existing arrangements.

References

CIA (Central Intelligence Agency). 2016. "Madagascar." In *The World Factbook. https://www.cia.gov/library/publications/the-world-factbook/geos/ma.html.*

IMF (International Monetary Fund). 2015. *2014 IMF Government Finance Statistics Yearbook*. Washington, DC.

———. 2016. "IMF World Longitudinal Data (WoRLD)." IMF e-Library Data. *http://data.imf.org/?sk=77413F1D-1525-450A-A23A-47AEED40FE78&sId=1390030109571.*

Nzewanga, J. J. 2009. "Property Taxation in Francophone Africa: Case Study of Democratic Madagascar." Working paper WP09FAB4. Cambridge, MA: Lincoln Institute of Land Policy.

United Nations. 2014. *World Urbanization Prospects*. Washington, DC: Department of Economic and Social Affairs, Population Division.

United Nations, Department of Economic and Social Affairs, Population Division. 2015. World Population Prospects: The 2015 Revision. *https://esa.un.org/unpd/wpp/Publications/Files/World_Population_2015_Wallchart.pdf.*

USAID. 2007. *Land Tenure and Property Rights Regional Report*. Vol. 2.1, *East and Central Africa*. Burlington, VT: ARD.

World Bank. 2015. "Registering Property." *http://www.doingbusiness.org/data/exploretopics /registering-property/reforms.*

———. 2016a. "Country and Lending Groups." *http://data.worldbank.org/about/country -and-lending-groups.*

———. 2016b. "GDP per Capita (Current US%)." *http://data.worldbank.org/indicator /NY.GDP.PCAP.CD.*

Legislation

Act No. 2005-019 (of October 17, 2005).

Act No. 2006-031 (of October 18, 2006).

Act No. 2007-033 (of December 14, 2007).

Finance Law (Code of Taxes) of 2007.

General Tax Code of the Republic of Madagascar (Code Général des Impôts de la République de Madagascar) of 2011.

18

Mauritius

RIËL FRANZSEN AND WILLIAM McCLUSKEY

Mauritius is an island nation in the Indian Ocean. It gained independence from the British on March 12, 1968, and became a republic on March 12, 1992. The Republic of Mauritius includes Mauritius Island, Rodrigues Island, and the small outer islands of Agaléga, Tromelin, Diego Garcia (Chagos Archipelago), and St. Brandon (Cargados Carajos Shoals). Mauritius Island has a land area of approximately 2,040 km² with some 177 kilometers of coastline (CIA 2016). The population is estimated at 1.27 million (United Nations 2015); about 135,000 live in the capital, Port Louis (CIA 2016). The urban population is about 40 percent (United Nations 2014). In 2015, the GDP per capita was USD 9,252 (World Bank 2016b), which classifies Mauritius as an upper-middle-income country (World Bank 2016a). English is the official language but is spoken by only about 1 percent of the population (CIA 2016).

Government

There are two tiers of government in Mauritius, the central government and local governments. The latter are composed of four types of local authorities: cities, towns, villages, and districts. The country is divided into nine districts. Two districts, Port Louis and Plaines Wilhems, are governed

We gratefully acknowledge the review of this chapter by Yodhun Bissessur, director of Valuation and Real Estate Consultancy Services, Port Louis, Mauritius.

by municipal councils. The other seven districts are governed by district councils. They are Black River, Flacq, Grand Port, Moka, Pamplemousses, Rivière du Rempart, and Savanne. There are also three dependencies, Agaléga Islands, Cargados Carajos Shoals (St. Brandon), and Rodrigues (CIA 2016). There is only one city, Port Louis. There are four towns (Beau Bassin-Rose Hill, Curepipe, Quatre Bornes, and Vacoas-Phoenix) and some one hundred and thirty villages.

According to the Local Government Act of 2011, the purpose of a local authority is to

- promote the social, economic, environmental, and cultural well-being of the local community;

- improve the overall quality of life of people in the local community;

- ensure that services and facilities provided by the council are accessible and equitably distributed and that resources are used efficiently and effectively to best meet the needs of the local community;

- ensure transparency and accountability in decision making; and

- provide for the prudent use and stewardship of local community resources.

The municipal city council, the municipal town councils, and the district councils perform such functions as are necessary and in particular

- develop, implement, and monitor strategic plans and budgets;

- plan for and provide services and facilities to the local community;

- raise revenue to enable the council to perform its functions;

- develop, implement, and monitor corporate and financial management control techniques;

- establish norms and standards in the conduct of affairs;

- perform and discharge the functions and exercise the powers under any law relating to local authorities; and

- implement actions that are incidental or conducive to the performance of any of a council's functions under the Local Government Act.

Land Tenure

In Mauritius, there are two types of land tenure systems, freehold land and leasehold land. These classifications apply to land held by the government and to private land (Olima 2010). Government land, which comprises *pas géométriques* (a stretch of coastal land above the high-water mark) and state lands, may be leased upon application to the Ministry of Housing and Lands that specifies the intended use. Upon approval, the ministry issues a letter of intent, and the Government Valuation Department undertakes a valuation to determine the rent payable. The Registry of Mortgages within the Ministry of Finance and Economic Development collects the rent. Leases of land by the government are granted for periods of 60 or 99 years depending on the use and purpose. The operation of the property market is fairly formal and well developed, and transfers of property rights or interests are generally effected within a formal registration process. Since 2009 there has been significant progress in land management (Deane, Pattison, and Luchoo 2016).

The Ministry of Housing and Lands (MHL) in Mauritius is responsible for keeping a record of all state lands, whether allocated or otherwise, and thus helps the decision makers in state land allocation and management. Land recording and management are critical issues in a country where land is a scarce resource. Although the ministry has been successful in recording ownership rights and providing a description of land boundaries, it has been unable to keep pace with development and especially with recording changes in ownership and boundaries. The Land Administration, Valuation, and Information Management System (LAVIMS) that is presently being implemented is expected to address these difficulties (Vaibhav 2016). The LAVIMS project is an initiative by the government of Mauritius designed to modernize land administration by improving different departments' access to information and creating a complete and up-to-date national valuation roll. The responsibility for LAVIMS is shared between the MHL and the Ministry of Finance and Economic Development. LAVIMS is really four projects in one: development of the cadastre; implementation of a digital deeds management system; valuation of properties; and information management.

LAVIMS has collated vast amounts of information and uses a dedicated information management system (IMS) to store and provide access to these data. Central to the IMS is the cadastre, which identifies every land parcel in Mauritius (Deane, Pattison, and Luchoo 2016). The LAVIMS Real Property Inventory has surveyed over 450,000 properties, including all residential and commercial properties in the country. Building on the success of LAVIMS, the government of Mauritius is now contemplating an even broader-based spatially enabled infrastructure, the National Spatial Data Infrastructure (NSDI). An operational NSDI would contain up-to-date and accurate spatial data on land, infrastructure, utilities, and the environment (Deane, Pattison, and Luchoo 2016).

The Registrar General's Department is in the process of shifting from paper-based to paperless operations. One of the major goals is to become more responsive to the digitization of documents and to enable esubmission, epayment, and edelivery using modern information and communication technologies. The Registrar General's Department initiated the Mauritius eRegistry Project to ensure a modern working environment and to improve customer service. The first phase, the automation of services within the department, was implemented in 2014. The second phase of this project was implemented in April 2015, with online submission of documents commencing on June 30, 2015 (Republic of Mauritius 2015b).

Taxation

The main taxes levied are the personal income tax, the corporate tax, the value-added tax (VAT), customs and excise duties, a transfer tax on land, and taxes on financial transactions. In 2012, total taxes constituted about 18.9 percent of GDP (IMF 2015). Table 18.1 shows the relative importance of taxes collected by various revenue departments in 2002/2003 and 2003/2004.

In 2012 and 2013, property taxes broadly defined, including property transfer taxes and the tax on financial transactions (mostly transfer taxes) collected by the national government, exceeded 5 percent of total taxes. Property taxes also constitute a significant percentage of GDP (table 18.2). There was an appreciable and steady increase from 2003 to 2008 and then

Table 18.1 National Revenue Collection, 2002/2003 and 2003/2004

	2002/2003		2003/2004	
	MUR (Millions)	%	MUR (Millions)	%
Customs and Excise Department	8,854.8	35.6	9,793.2	35.0
VAT Department	8,769.9	35.2	9,739.8	34.8
Large Taxpayer Department	1,889.8[1]	7.6	2,294.0[1]	8.2
Indirect taxes	19,514.5	78.4	21,827.0	78.1
Income Tax Department	1,975.5	7.9	2,636.0	9.4
Registrar General's Department	1,376.9	5.5	1,468.9	5.3
Large Taxpayer Department	2,038.0	8.2	2,032.6	7.3
Direct taxes	5,390.4	21.6	6,137.5	21.9
Total	24,904.9	100	27,964.5	100

Source: Republic of Mauritius (2005).

[1] The amount of VAT collected from large taxpayers is included in the figures for the VAT Department.

Table 18.2 Property Taxes as a Percentage of GDP, 2003–2012

Year	2003	2004	2005	2006	2007	2008	2009	2010	2011	2012
Percentage	0.989	0.947	1.003	1.024	1.265	1.571	1.515	1.442	1.347	1.393

Source: IMF (2016).

a slight decline from 2009 to 2011, most likely the result of the worldwide economic crisis. In 2012, the percentage increased slightly. In comparison with most other African countries (see table 2.2 in chapter 2) and developing countries generally, this is significant.

Property-Related Taxes and Charges

As is evident from table 18.2, property-related taxes and charges are quite important in Mauritius. Apart from general rates (soon to be replaced by the local rate) that are collected by local authorities, a number of taxes are levied and collected at the national level:

- The registration duty.
- The land transfer tax.
- The capital gains tax (the *morcellement* tax).[1]
- The *campement* site tax.
- The campement tax.
- The tax on the transfer of leasehold rights in state land.
- The stamp duty.

There is also a land conversion tax levied under the Sugar Industry Efficiency Act of 2001 (Republic of Mauritius 2015b).

The Registration Duty

Section 3 of the Land (Duties and Taxes) Act of 1984 provides that a duty shall be levied on the registration of any deed witnessing a transfer of property (irrespective of the date on which the transfer takes place) and on the creation of a mortgage or a fixed charge (*sûreté fixe*). The registration of deeds and documents presented to the department incurs either a fixed registration duty of MUR 50, a proportional duty ranging from 0.1 percent to 12 percent, or a donation duty ranging from 10 percent to 45 percent, together with a 10 percent surcharge (Republic of Mauritius 2015b). This duty is payable on the value of the property at the time of registration and at the rate in force at the time of registration, in accordance with the Registration Duty Act of 1804 (as amended). The buyer pays the registration duty.

The Land Transfer Tax

The land transfer tax is levied under Section 4 of the Land (Duties and Taxes) Act of 1984 and is payable upon transfer and acquisition of immovable property. The transferor (usually the seller) must pay the land transfer tax. Currently, the transfer tax rate is 5 percent.

The Capital Gains (Morcellement) Tax

The capital gains (morcellement) tax was introduced in the Finance Act of 2010. It replaced the national residential property tax (NRPT),[2] which was governed by the Income Tax Act of 1995 but was repealed by the Finance Act of 2010 (PKF 2012). The capital gains tax or the land transfer tax, whichever is higher, is payable by the transferor on the transfer of immovable property (Republic of Mauritius 2015b). It is levied on the transfer of any lot in a morcellement and applies to the excess of the sale price of the lot over the purchase price together with the costs of infrastructure works and notarial costs at the rate of

- 30 percent when any lot is transferred less than five years from the date of acquisition of the property;

- 25 percent when any lot is transferred more than five years but less than ten years from the date of acquisition of the property; or

- 20 percent when any lot is transferred more than ten years but less than fifteen years from the date of acquisition of the property.

If the transfer takes place within five years from the date of acquisition, the land transfer tax rate is 10 percent of the sales price. The tax is only 5 percent of the sales price if the transfer takes place after five years from the date of acquisition (Republic of Mauritius 2015b).

The Campement Site Tax

The campement site tax is levied on any campement, that is, land that is situated wholly or partly within 81.21 meters from the high-water mark and has access to the sea but does not include freehold land (Republic of Mauritius 2015b). The coastal region in Mauritius is divided into five zones specified in the Land (Duties and Taxes) Act, depending on the quality of the beach and the sea. The campement site tax varies from MUR 2 per

Table 18.3 Land Value Zones for the Campement Site Tax

Zoning	Rate per Square Meter
Zone A	MUR 6
Zone B	MUR 5
Zone C	MUR 4
Zone D	MUR 3
Zone E	MUR 2

Source: Republic of Mauritius (2015b).

square meter to MUR 6 per square meter depending on the zoning of the campement site (table 18.3). It is payable by either the lessee, the proxy of the owner, or the occupier and must be paid on or before July 31 every year. If the taxpayer fails to pay, a surcharge is payable as follows:

- 10 percent of the tax for the first month or part of the month during which the tax remains unpaid.

- 2 percent of the tax excluding the surcharge for each subsequent month or part of the month during which the tax remains unpaid.

The maximum surcharge is 50 percent of the total tax payable. The overall revenue from this tax is insignificant.

The Campement Tax

The campement tax was introduced on July 1, 2002, and applies to a campement site together with any building, structure, flat, or apartment used at any time as a residence. The tax is levied on the owner of a campement at the rate of 0.5 percent of the market value of the campement after deducting the campement site tax and the local rate, if any (Republic of Mauritius 2015b). In relation to a campement, the term *owner* means the following:

- In the case of a bungalow or a group of bungalows or apartments located on a leasehold campement site located on *pas géométriques*, the holder of the title deed of each bungalow or apartment, as the case may be.

- In the case of a bungalow or a group of bungalows or apartments located on a campement site owned or leased by a *société* or partnership where the associate or partner does not hold the title deed of the bungalow or apartment, the associate or partner in proportion to his share in the société or partnership.

If an owner uses the campement as his sole residence and the market value is less than the amount specified in the law (presently MUR 5 million), the owner is exempt from the campement tax.

The Tax on the Transfer of Leasehold Rights in State Land

A tax of 20 percent payable by the transferor and the transferee in equal proportion is levied on the registration of a deed of transfer of

- leasehold rights in state land;

- shares in a civil society, partnership, association, or company that reckons among its assets any leasehold rights in state land; or

- shares in a company that is an associate in a partnership that reckons among its assets any leasehold rights in state land (Republic of Mauritius 2015b).

Table 18.4 shows the revenue collected from the registration duty, the land transfer tax, the stamp duty, the campement site tax, the campement tax, and the land conversion tax from 2011 to 2014 (Republic of Mauritius 2015b). The importance of the two transfer taxes, the registration duty and land transfer tax, is clear. Collectively, these two taxes accounted for 88 percent of the property-related taxes collected nationally in 2011 and 61 percent in 2014.

Table 18.4 Revenue Collected for the Financial Years 2011–2014 (MUR Millions)

Taxes	2011	2012	2013	2014
Registration duty	2,242.2	2,147.9	1,376.6	1,240.3
Land transfer tax	1,183.6	1,267.3	1,613.6	1,484.7
Stamp duty	78.5	80.4	80.8	74.1
Campement site tax	2.9	3.6	1.3	4.3
Campement Tax	2.8	2.7	2.5	1.8
Land conversion tax	41.5	185.0	44.9	96.3
Other taxes and charges[1]	339.6	316.6	1,408.2	1,558.3
Total	3,891.1	4,003.5	4,527.5	4,459.8

Source: Republic of Mauritius (2015b).

[1] "Other taxes" include the tax on the transfer of leasehold rights in state land and mortgage fees.

Local Grants and Taxes

In every financial year, there shall be paid to the local authorities (excluding village councils) a grant from the Consolidated Fund calculated according to a prescribed formula that gives due consideration to the financial and development needs of a particular council. To ensure a fair allocation of the grants, account must be taken of

- the human resource needs of a council;

- the special needs of the area falling under the jurisdiction of a council in regard to accelerated development;

- the possibility that a council can increase its revenue through local rates, fees, or charges, and the opportunities for the development of business, industry, and commerce within the area of the council; and

- the state of public finance and of the economy of Mauritius in general.

Local authorities also generate revenue to provide local services, including street lighting and waste management, among others. Own-source revenues include the local rate, licenses and permits, and the sale of goods and services.

The Local Rate

The recurrent property tax, commonly referred to as the *local rate*, is governed by Sub-part C of Part IX of the Local Government Act of 2011. This tax will replace the almost identical general rate (Olima 2010) still levied and collected under the repealed Local Government Act of 1989. As soon as the first, country-wide valuation roll is implemented the local rate will become payable. Therefore, the remainder of this discussion will deal with the local rate as though it were already collectable.

The local rate is levied annually by the City Council of Port Louis and the four municipal town councils on the owners of immovable property situated in the rating area of the relevant council. It is defined to include any surcharge or interest on the rate and any costs incurred in the recovery of the rate. A *rating area* of a city or town means the administrative area for which it is responsible. Should a new municipal town council be proclaimed, it is prohibited from levying a local rate in the first three years of its existence.

The Tax Base

The tax is levied on the "cadastral value" of "immovable property." The cadastral value of any property is its market value. Immovable property includes (1) land, other than agricultural land, or a flat or an apartment, whether owned individually or jointly or in which a person has any interest; and (2) a building or part of it that is occupied, whether or not its construction has been completed.

Market value means the price a property will fetch in a free, unforced sale in an open, competitive market if it is vacant. *Cadastral database* means a database of immovable properties that a council must keep and maintain electronically. The data that must be captured include the full name and address of the owner; a brief description of the property (e.g., the area of the land and buildings and the street name); use (residential, commercial, or industrial); net annual value; cadastral value; and any other particulars the council may require. Owners are obligated under the law to notify in writing the council of the city, town, or district where the property is located of any improvement, alteration, or additions made to the property.

Exemptions

The following properties are exempted:

- Immovable property owned and occupied by the government of Mauritius or a statutory corporation exclusively owned by the government of Mauritius.

- Immovable property owned and occupied by any foreign state or any organization or body accorded diplomatic immunity under any enactment.

- Immovable property owned and occupied by a local authority and situated within its rating area.

- Agricultural buildings or agricultural land.

- Immovable property belonging to the Curepipe War Memorial Board or the Austin Wilson Home.

- Any church, chapel, mosque, temple, or similar building used solely as a place of public worship.

The following properties may be exempted in any specified financial year if the minister responsible for local government so decides:

- Immovable property owned and exclusively occupied by any religious institution.

- Preprimary, primary, and secondary schools, as well as tertiary institutions receiving grants from the government.

- Immovable property exclusively used as an orphanage, infirmary, or crèche.

- Immovable property belonging to a charitable institution.

- Immovable property or any part thereof belonging to an association registered under the Registration of Associations Act and exclusively used for the purposes of training its members for sporting competitions.

- Unoccupied immovable property owned by a statutory corporation exclusively owned by the government or agencies of the government.

- Any other property for which exemption is considered expedient.

Liability for the Tax

The owner of the property is liable for the tax. Under the law, the term *owner*, in relation to any property, includes (1) the lessee of immovable property situated on state land; (2) the person who receives or, if such property were to be let, would be entitled to receive the rent, whether for his own benefit or that of any other person; and (3) if the owner cannot be found or ascertained, the occupier.

Valuation

The central government is responsible for valuation. The chief executive of a council must ensure that the values of all the immovable property in the rating area of the local authority, as determined by the government valuer, are retrieved from the digital cadastral database kept and maintained under Section 4 of the Cadastral Survey Act of 2011.

A ratepayer who is aggrieved by a notification that specifies the value of his property may lodge a written notice of appeal with the secretary of the Valuation Tribunal. The notice must state the grounds of the appeal. The Valuation Tribunal consists of a chairperson (who must be a barrister who holds or has held judicial office) and two other persons, all appointed by the president for three-year terms. An appeal on a point of law may be lodged with the Supreme Court.

Tax Rates

The law empowers the city and municipal town councils to determine their own tax rates. Councils are entitled to levy different rates based on different cadastral values and different rates based on use, whether residential, business, commercial, or industrial.

Table 18.5 Tax Rates for the General Rate in Port Louis, 2010

NAV Bands	Tax Rate (%)	Number of Properties	Percentage of Properties
0–480	0.00	1,282	3.4
481–1,050	0.00	3,572	9.6
1,051–1,575	0.00	3,714	10.0
1,576–1,750	0.00	974	2.6
1,751–2,100	0.00	1,244	3.3
2,101–2,450	0.00	1,190	3.2
2,451–3,875	5.50	6,112	16.4
3,876–6,375	6.90	7,257	19.5
6,376–8,500	9.00	3,394	9.1
8,501–10,625	9.60	2,060	5.5
10,626–12,750	9.90	1,343	3.6
12,751–17,000	10.50	1,707	4.6
17,001–23,125	15.30	1,134	3.0
23,126–30,000	18.00	574	1.5
30,001–35,000	19.20	250	0.7
35,001–44,000	20.40	290	0.8
44,001–54,000	21.60	191	0.5
54,001–75,000	24.80	236	0.6
75,001–100,000	26.50	151	0.4
Greater than 100,001	28.00	555	1.5
		37,230	100.0

Source: Olima (2010).

The City Council of Port Louis groups properties into value bands. Each band incurs a different rate. Table 18.5 presents the general rates levied by the City Council of Port Louis for the year 2010. Approximately 32 percent of the properties have a net annual value (NAV) of MUR 2,450 or less and are therefore exempt from this tax; 13,369 properties out of 37,230, or 35.9 percent, have an NAV between MUR 2,451 and MUR 6,375.

Tax Relief

Subject to ministerial approval, a council may remit in whole or in part the local rate payable on account of poverty. The council must be able to provide the names of those who received relief, as well as the amount remitted and the reason for remission.

Billing and Collection

The municipal councils carry out billing and collection. When the tax is due, demand notices are sent to taxpayers. The law is very explicit on collection procedures and provides that any local rate levied for any year is due on January 1 of that year and is payable in two equal installments, due by January 31 and July 31. Nonreceipt of a tax bill is not an excuse for nonpayment. A payment notice must specify the location of the property and provide a description sufficient for identification. It must also state the value of the property, the percentage rate of the tax, the amount payable, and the period for which it is payable. If a surcharge or interest is payable, this must also be stated.

In general, collections are low, and delinquent taxpayers and untraceable property owners contribute to the accumulation of arrears. Because debts older than five years are written off, taxpayers have little incentive to pay.

Enforcement

The Local Government Act specifies procedures for enforcing and ensuring local rate payments. For any local rate not paid within the prescribed period, Section 99(1) provides for a surcharge of 10 percent of the rate due and payable. Section 100 states that if the sum due for a local rate or surcharge is not paid in the financial year in which it is due and payable, it shall incur interest at a rate of 15 percent.

A council, through the financial controller, must take action for recovery of the rate by summary process under the Recovery of State Debts Act within one year of the date on which the rate becomes due. Financial controllers are held personally responsible for any failure, without reasonable excuse, to start proceedings for recovery of the tax. A council may also request in writing that the director general of the Mauritius Revenue Authority collect and enforce the local rate on its behalf. In collecting and enforcing the local rate, the director general exercises the powers conferred on him by the Mauritius Revenue Authority Act and the Income Tax Act, with necessary adaptations and modifications as required by circumstances. Any amount collected by the director general must be remitted to the relevant council within 10 days after the month in which it was collected. The director general may retain an administration fee prescribed by the minister of finance.

The Revenue Importance of Property Taxes

In both 2010 and 2011, the general rate (the predecessor of the local rate) constituted 14.4 percent of the revenue of Port Louis. As is clear from table 18.6, grants from the central government are the major source of revenue, although the general rate's contribution has been increasing slightly

Table 18.6 Revenue in Port Louis, 2013 and 2014

Revenue Source	2013 MUR	2013 %	2014 MUR	2014 %
Grant-in-aid	505,871,271	64.8	494,114,603	64.7
General rate	116,766,499	15.0	121,983,475	16.0
Investment Income	2,847,654	0.4	3,487,456	0.5
Rentals	38,383,391	4.9	37,383,720	4.9
Trade fees	72,763,720	9.3	76,858,548	10.1
Permits	23,678,284	3.0	15,504,489	2.0
Other income	2,742,657	0.4	9,768,104	1.3
Transfer from the Theatre Fund	225,283	0.0	9,033	0.0
Transfer from the General Fund	17,583,434	2.3	4,039,034	0.5
Total	780,862,193	100.0	763,148,462	100.0

Source: City Council of Port Louis (2015).

Table 18.7 Tax Revenue, 2012 and 2013

Revenue	2012 (MUR Millions)	2013 (MUR Millions)
Taxes on property		
Recurrent property taxes (the general rate)	4	6
Tax on capital transactions	4,503	4,380
Nonrecurrent property tax	49	96
Total taxes on property	4,556	4,482
Total tax revenue	75,047	79,753
Property taxes as a percentage of total tax revenue	6.1	5.6
Recurrent property taxes as a percentage of total tax revenue	0.005	0.008

Source: Republic of Mauritius (2015a).

since 2010. Property taxation plays an important role as a source of revenue for both the central government and local governments in Mauritius. Revenue from all property taxes, broadly defined, represented 6.1 percent and 5.6 percent of total tax revenue in 2012 and 2013 in Mauritius (table 18.7). However, the general rate as a percentage of total tax revenue is insignificant, constituting only 0.008 percent of tax revenue in 2013.

Notes

1. *Morcellement* is the division of a plot of land into two or more lots.

2. The NRPT was charged on all residential properties across the country and was payable by an owner of residential property with an annual income exceeding MUR 400,000 and all companies, societies, and nonresident individuals irrespective of their income. The tax was based on the surface area of the land, residential buildings, and apartments.

References

CIA (Central Intelligence Agency). 2016. "Mauritius." In *The World Factbook*. https://www.cia.gov/library/publications/the-world-factbook/geos/mp.html.

City Council of Port Louis. 2015. *Annual Report Financial Year 2014*. http://www.mccpl.mu/downloads/annualreport2014.pdf.

Deane, G., T. Pattison, and N. Luchoo. 2016. "Land Administration and Valuation Information System (LAVIMS)—Five Years of Operations in Mauritius." Paper presented at the 17th Annual World Bank Conference on Land and Poverty, Washington, DC (March 14–17).

IMF (International Monetary Fund). 2015. *2014 IMF Government Finance Statistics Yearbook*. Washington, DC.

———. 2016. "IMF World Longitudinal Data (WoRLD)." IMF e-Library Data. http://data.imf.org/?sk=77413F1D-1525-450A-A23A-47AEED40FE78&sId=1390030109571.

Olima, W. H. A. 2010. "Property Taxation in Mauritius." Presentation at the Fellowship Workshop of the African Tax Institute/Lincoln Institute of Land Policy Project on Property Taxation in Africa, Stellenbosch, South Africa (December 4–5).

PKF. 2012. *PKF Mauritius Tax Guide 2012*. www.pkf.com/media/387149/mauritius_2012.pdf.

Republic of Mauritius. 2005. *Report of the Revenue Authority for the year ended 30 June 2004* (No.8 of 2005). www.mra.mu/download/repra04.pdf.

———. 2015a. *Digest of Public Finance Statistics 2014*. Statistics Mauritius, Ministry of Finance and Economic Development. http://statsmauritius.govmu.org/English/Documents/digest/Digest_PublicFinance_2014.pdf.

———. 2015b. *Registrar General's Department Annual Report—Financial Year 2015*. http://registrar.mof.govmu.org/English/Documents/Annual%20Report%202015.pdf.

United Nations. 2014. World Urbanization Prospects. https://esa.un.org/unpd/wup/Publications/Files/WUP2014-Report.pdf.

United Nations, Department of Economic and Social Affairs, Population Division. 2015. World Population Prospects: The 2015 Revision. https://esa.un.org/unpd/wpp/Publications/Files/World_Population_2015_Wallchart.pdf.

Vaibhav, A. 2016. "Cadastre in Africa: A Leap Towards Modernization." *http://geos patialworld.net/Regions/ArticleView.aspx?aid=2514.*

World Bank. 2016a. "Country and Lending Groups." *http://data.worldbank.org/about /country-and-lending-groups.*

———. 2016b. "GDP per Capita (Current US%)." *http://data.worldbank.org/indicator /NY.GDP.PCAP.CD.*

Legislation

Cadastral Survey Act of 2011.

Finance Act of 2010.

Income Tax Act of 1995.

Land (Duties and Taxes) Act of 1984.

Local Government Act of 1989.

Local Government Act of 2011.

Mauritius Revenue Authority Act of 2004.

Recovery of State Debts Act of 1876 (as amended).

Registration Duty Act of 1804 (as amended).

Sugar Industry Efficiency Act of 2001.

19

Morocco

RIËL FRANZSEN AND MARIA ELKHDARI

Morocco, located in northwestern Africa, is bordered by the Atlantic Ocean to the west and north, Western Sahara (which it occupies) to the south, and Algeria to the east. A former French protectorate, it became independent in 1957. Morocco covers an area of 446,550 km², and its population is estimated at 34.4 million (United Nations 2015), of which about 2 million live in the capital, Rabat. The largest city is Casablanca, with an estimated population of 3.5 million (CIA 2016). Other important cities are Fes, Marrakech, and Tangier. About 60 percent of the population is urbanized (United Nations 2014). The GDP per capita was estimated at USD 2,878 (World Bank 2016c). Although Morocco is classified as a lower-middle-income country (World Bank 2016a), about 15 percent of the population lives below the poverty line (CIA 2016).

Government

Morocco is a parliamentary constitutional monarchy. The most recent constitution was approved by popular referendum in 2011. In 2015, the number of regions was reduced from 16 to 12. Morocco also occupies and claims about 80 percent of the territory of Western Sahara (also known as the Sahrawi Arab Democratic Republic), a vast territory covering 266,000 km² (CIA 2016).

King Mohammed VI came to the throne in 1999. He presides over a stable economy marked by steady growth, low inflation, and gradually falling unemployment, although poor harvests and the post-2008 economic difficulties in Europe contributed to an economic slowdown. In response to the deteriorating economic climate and fiscal trends, Morocco has embarked on a major fiscal consolidation effort since 2013. On average, real GDP grew by 3.8 percent from 2013 to 2015, underperforming its trend of 4.6 percent per year during 2003–2012 (World Bank 2016d).

Morocco has been effecting wide-ranging reforms that have formed the basis of a more open and democratic society, a more modern state of law and institutions, greater separation of powers, and increased decentralization (World Bank 2016d). The law is a hybrid civil law system based on French and Islamic law. The country held regional and local elections in September 2015 whose results should deepen the decentralization agenda and local governance. Even before 2011, the institutional evolution of local government in Morocco went through several reforms. Various laws and decrees were passed to expand the jurisdiction and resource system of subnational governments (Burn, Jaida, and Zirari 2005).[1]

Subnational governments in Morocco are structured as follows: 12 regions, 62 provinces, 13 prefectures, 221 urban *communes*, and 1,282 rural communes. Regions are primarily responsible for economic development and environmental protection. The provinces and prefectures are in charge of rural investment and oversight of the activities of the communes but provide no local services (Burn, Jaida, and Zirari 2005). Since the Communal Charter of 1976, the communes have been the most important component of decentralized government. Communes are managed by communal councils, elected for a period of six years, that handle the routine business of the communes and decide measures necessary to ensure the full economic, social, and cultural development within their jurisdictions.

Land Tenure

Morocco's land tenure regime is characterized by legal and administrative plurality and the lack of comprehensive land legislation (Balgley 2015; USAID 2011). The current legal framework governing land is a mix of customary law, Islamic law, French civil law, and a series of decrees. About 42 percent of Morocco's land is held collectively by tribes under the trusteeship of the state. Land is also commonly held in joint ownership by multiple and often multigenerational family members. In both cases, the land tenure systems constrain the development of formal land markets (USAID 2011) and result in social strife (Balgley 2015). There are five distinct categories of land, which are administered in completely different ways:

(1) privatized, titled land (called *melk*), which accounts for about 28 percent; (2) religious land endowments (called *habous*) that can be leased but not sold; (3) land granted to members of the military by the monarchy (called *guich*); (4) collective tribal land (called *soulaliya*); and (5) state-owned land, which accounts for about 30 percent (Balgley 2015; USAID 2011). *Guich* and *habous* land accounts for only about 310,000 hectares (USAID 2011).

Land administration in Morocco is complicated by parallel systems of registration, the formal cadastral system (instituted by the French in 1913) and a traditional system. Within the formal system, land rights must be registered with the Land Registry (Conservation Foncière), situated in the Ministry of Justice (USAID 2011). Traditional systems recognize informal documentation of land rights. These rights are typically evidenced by Islamic title deeds or by witnesses, and landholders and traditional leaders maintain records. This informality poses major challenges to formalizing land tenure in the country. However, a formal and quite sophisticated land market exists in Morocco's urban areas (USAID 2011).

Morocco ranks 76th of 189 economies in the ease of registering property (World Bank 2016b). In 2013, Morocco increased property registration fees, but in 2014, transferring property was simplified by reducing the time required to register a deed of transfer at the tax authority. In 2016, electronic communication links among different tax authorities were established to further simplify and speed up registration processes (World Bank 2016b).

Taxation

The National Tax Structure

The General Tax Administration (Direction Générale des Impôts) in the Ministry of Economy and Finance administers the following taxes:

- All national taxes, including the corporate tax, the personal income tax, the value-added tax (VAT), customs duties, and registration and stamp duties.[2]

- Certain local taxes managed for the benefit of local authorities (the residence tax, the tax on communal services, and the business tax).

The General Tax Administration functions through a regional tax directorate in each of the administrative regions. Its regional structure also assists with the collection of the local-government taxes administered on behalf of local authorities. At the territorial level, the General Tax Administration is organized by type and size of taxpayer rather than by tax types. Each taxpayer thus has a single point of contact that deals with all taxpayer issues relating to the various taxes. The taxation system is basically declarative; therefore, control and audits are critical functions. Tax audits follow strict procedures that uphold the rights of taxpayers (Tax Administration 2016).

Table 19.1 provides an overview of the distribution of taxes. What is notable is the importance of stamp duties and registration fees in the overall fiscal landscape of Morocco. In 2015, property transfer taxes (registration duties and stamp duties) constituted the most significant share of overall property taxes. Other tax revenues, which likely include the three local taxes collected on behalf of local authorities, constituted only 1.3 percent of overall tax revenue.

In 2012, total taxes constituted 24.5 percent of GDP (IMF 2015). As is evident from table 19.2, property taxes, as broadly defined by the International Monetary Fund, have amounted to more than 1 percent of GDP since 2007, significantly above the 0.6 percent average for developing countries (Bahl and Martinez-Vazquez 2008; Norregaard 2013). As is clear from table 19.1, recurrent taxes are not important in the overall fiscal landscape. Thus, the most significant part of the percentage of GDP reflected in table 19.2 is the revenue from the various property transfer taxes. A major spike in revenue in 2007 was followed by a noticeable decline in 2008, but thereafter, there was a steady annual increase.

Table 19.1 Distribution of Taxes, 2015 Fiscal Year

Tax Type	MAD (Billions)	Percentage
Income tax	36,540	19.6
Corporate tax	42,780	22.9
Value-added tax	56,197	30.1
Domestic consumption tax	26,646	14.3
Customs duties	7,250	3.9
Stamp duties and registration fees	14,876	8.0
Other tax revenues	2,430	1.3
Total	186,719	100.0

Source: Citizen Budget (2015).

Table 19.2 Property Taxes as a Percentage of GDP, 2005–2010

Year	2005	2006	2007	2008	2009	2010
% of GDP	0.74	0.75	1.60	1.33	1.48	1.53

Source: IMF (2016).

Subnational Taxes and Charges

An important reform of the subnational fiscal regime commenced in 2007 with the enactment of Law No. 47/06 (published in the *Official Gazette*, no. 5583, December 3, 2007), supplemented by Law 39/07 (published in the *Official Gazette*, no. 5591, December 31, 2007). These laws were introduced to simplify local taxation and to improve its administration; align local taxation with the decentralization program by strengthening fiscal autonomy; and harmonize state and local taxation and amalgamate duplicate taxes (Local Tax Guide 2008). According to Law No. 47/06, subnational authorities have the following taxing powers:

- Regions have the power to levy the tax on hunting licenses, the tax on mining, and the tax on port services.

- Provinces and prefectures may levy the tax on driving licenses, the tax on motor vehicles, and the tax on the sale of forest products.

- Urban and rural communes may levy the following taxes and fees: the residence tax, the tax on communal services, the business tax, the tax on vacant urban land, the tax on building operations, the tax on housing estate operations, beverage taxes (including the tax on mineral and table water), the tourist tax, the tax on public passenger transport, and the extraction tax on quarries.

In rural communes, the residence tax, the tax on communal services, and the tax on housing estate operations are due only in the delimited centers, peri-urban areas, and holiday resorts and spas. The tax on vacant urban land is due only in the delimited centers, as determined in a planning document.

Table 19.3 provides an overview of local taxes collected centrally and locally, as well as transfers received from the central government, from 2011 to 2014. Local taxes constituted more than 34 percent of total revenues for local authorities in each of these financial years. The revenues of local authorities collected in 2014 were MAD 31.9 billion, an increase of 0.4 percent over 2013, due to an increase of 6.4 percent in revenue transferred by the state in 2014, coupled with a decrease of 1.2 percent in revenue administered by local authorities and 17.1 percent in revenue managed by the state on their behalf. However, it is evident from table 19.3 that from 2011 to 2014, each component remained relatively stable. Table 19.4 shows the importance of taxes and transfers by type of local authority. Not surprisingly, urban communes generate more of their own tax revenue than their rural counterparts. Table 19.5 provides an overview of the

Table 19.3 Revenue of Local Authorities, 2011–2014

Resource	2011		2012		2013		2014	
	MAD (Billions)	%	MAD (Billions)	%	MAD (Billions)	%	MAD (Billions)	%
Local taxes collected centrally	4,226	14.7	4,690	16.3	5,929	18.6	4,918	15.4
Local taxes collected locally	5,819	20.2	6,284	21.9	6,987	22.0	6,901	21.6
Transfers	18,708	65.1	17,771	61.8	18,880	59.4	20,093	63.0
Total	28,753	100	28,745	100	31,796	100	31,912	100

Source: General Treasury (2012, 2014).

Table 19.4 Revenue Sources by Type of Local Authority, 2014

	Urban Communes	Rural Communes	Regions	Provinces/ Prefectures
Own sources	53.9	21.7	47	5.4
Transfers	46.1	78.3	53	94.6

Source: General Treasury (2014).

revenues collected or received by type of local authority. Table 19.6 states the relative importance of specific taxes for local authorities collectively. It is notable that the three local taxes administered by the General Tax Administration (the tax on communal services, the business tax, and the residence tax) were collectively quite significant in both 2013 (26.7 percent) and 2014 (18.1 percent). However, the residence tax (the recurrent property tax on residential property) is rather insignificant, only 1.4 percent (2013) and 0.9 percent (2014).

Property-Related Taxes and Charges

Various taxes may be imposed on the transfer of immovable property: a capital gains tax, the registration duty, and various stamp duties. There is no gift tax or estate tax in Morocco (IBFD 2016).

The Capital Gains Tax (*Taxe sur les Profits Immobiliers*)

The capital gain is determined by calculating the difference between the sale price (less concomitant costs) and the acquisition price (including fees pertaining to the acquisition, any duly justified investment expenses, and interest). The acquisition price, acquisition costs, capital expenditures, and interest are revalued by applying a coefficient corresponding to the year of acquisition, established annually by ministerial order. The purchase price of a property acquired by inheritance is

- the original purchase price paid by the deceased for the property inherited, plus investment spending, including expenses of restoration and equipment, or the building cost if built by the deceased; or

- the market value of the buildings at the time of transfer by inheritance or donation in favor of the deceased, which is declared by the ceding heir, subject to adjustments in land profits under the Tax Code.

Table 19.5 Revenue from Local Sources, 2014 (in MAD Millions)

Revenue Source	Prefectures	Provinces	Urban Communes	Rural Communes	Total	%
Revenues collected by the local authorities						
Local taxes and various fees	728	91	2,152	582	3,554	11.1
Products of services	24	227	1,447	279	1,977	6.2
Products goods	5	2	946	417	1,370	4.3
Subtotal	757	321	4,545	1,278	6,901	21.6
Revenues collected centrally on behalf of local authorities						
Tax on communal services	136	0	2,428	121	2,685	8.4
Business tax			1,811	173	1,984	6.2
Residence tax			231	17	248	0.8
Subtotal	136	0	4,470	312	4,918	15.4
Transfers						
Share of VAT revenue	270	4,956	7,121	5,453	17,800	55.8
Share in the revenues from corporate and personal income tax	714	43	0	0	757	2.4
Support funds and grants	24	663	575	274	1,536	4.8
Subtotal	1,009	5,662	7,696	5,727	20,093	63.0
Total	1,901	5,983	16,711	7,316	31,911	100

Source: General Treasury (2014).

Table 19.6 Tax Revenues of Local Authorities, 2013 and 2014

Tax Revenue	2013		2014	
	MAD Billions	%	MAD Billions	%
Direct taxes				
Tax on communal services	3,327	12.2	2,685	9.9
Business tax	2,227	8.2	1,984	7.3
Residence tax	375	1.4	248	0.9
Tax on undeveloped urban land	1,121	4.1	901	3.3
Share of the corporate tax	373	1.4	509	1.9
Share of the personal income tax	359	1.3	248	0.9
Subtotal: direct taxes	7,782	28.6	6,576	24.3
Indirect taxes				
Share of VAT revenues	16,902	62.0	17,800	65.9
Tax on construction operations	720	2.6	718	2.7
Tax on estate operations	260	1.0	265	1.0
Beverage taxes	161	0.6	156	0.6
Tax on quarry mining products	175	0.6	178	0.7
Tourist tax	178	0.7	191	0.7
Tax on port services	150	0.6	168	0.6
Other indirect taxes	929	3.4	976	3.6
Subtotal: indirect taxes	19,475	71.4	20,452	75.7
Total: local tax revenue	27,257	100	27,029	100

Source: General Treasury (2014).

Note: Law No. 47/06 on the taxation of local governments, promulgated by Decree 1-07-195 30/11/2007 (B.O. No. 5584 of December 6, 2007), as amended and supplemented by Law No. 05-10, enacted by Decree No. 1-10-22 of 11/2010 (B.O. No. 5822 of March 18, 2010), replaced the municipal administration tax (*taxe d'édilité*) with the tax on communal services (*taxe des services communaux*), the patent tax (*l'impôt de la patente*) with the business tax (*taxe professionelle*), and the city tax (*taxe urbaine*) with the residence tax (*taxe d'habitation*). The receipts from the municipal administration tax, the patent tax, and the city tax have been allocated to the receipts for the tax on communal services, the business tax, and the residence tax, respectively.

The following exemptions apply to capital gains:

- The sale of a residential building occupied as a principal residence for at least six years from the date of acquisition (this exemption also applies to the land on which the house is built if the land area is less than five times the area covered by the building).

- The first sale of social housing where the building area is between 50 and 80 m² and the sale price does not exceed MAD 250,000, excluding VAT, and the building was occupied by its owner as a principal residence for at least four years before the date of the sale.

- The gain realized by any person on the sale of buildings with a total value of less than MAD 140,000 in the relevant calendar year.

- The gratuitous (that is, for no consideration) transfer of immovable property or real rights between spouses, between parent and child, or between siblings.

For capital gains from the disposal of undeveloped urban land or of real property rights relating to such property, the rate of withholding tax is set according to the time between the date of acquisition and the alienation of such buildings as follows:

- 20 percent if the property was owned for less than four years.

- 25 percent if the duration is four or more years but less than six years.

- 30 percent if the duration is six years or more.

Any gain realized from the disposal of immovable property other than properties mentioned above, including buildings or agricultural land, is subject to a tax of 20 percent. However, the tax payable shall not be less than 3 percent of the sale price. Nonresident companies are liable for corporate tax on any capital gains arising from the sale of immovable property situated in Morocco at a standard rate of 30 percent (IBFD 2016).

The Registration Duty

A registration duty is payable when real property is transferred. The tax rate depends on the type of transfer or the transacting parties. The highest rate is 6 percent, and the lowest rate is 1.5 percent.

When a building is acquired for residential, commercial, business, or administrative purposes, a registration fee at a reduced rate of 4 percent is payable. The 4 percent rate also applies to the land on which these buildings are constructed if the land area is not more than five times the built area.

The first sale of any public housing or a unit in a low-value housing estate acquired from the developer by a natural or legal person who has concluded an agreement with the state as provided by the Tax Code is subject to a reduced tax rate of 3 percent. *Social housing* means any housing unit with a total covered area between 50 and 80 m² whose sale price does not exceed MAD 250,000. *Low-value housing* means any residential unit with a covered area between 50 and 60 m² whose first sale price does not exceed MAD 140,000.

The acquisition of vacant land is subject to a reduced rate of 4 percent, as is the acquisition of land with structures to be demolished or land for subdivision and earmarked for the construction of residential, commercial, business, or administrative buildings within a maximum of seven years from the date of acquisition of the land. To avoid penalties and surcharges, the required documentation must be filed with the tax inspector in charge of registration within 30 days from the date of acquisition.

As of 2007, taxes from several authorities must be cleared before a transfer takes place, and it is the responsibility of the notary to assure that the money for the transaction is sufficient to cover any unpaid taxes. The so-called *attestation fiscale* is required by law. The tax-collection authority enters the request for tax clearance in its automated system; this triggers requests for clearance from the Direction Régionale des Impôts to verify the payment of the house tax (*taxe d'habitation*) and the tax on communal services (*taxe des services communaux*) and from the Commune Urbaine de Casablanca (in Casablanca) to verify the payment of the urban tax. Once clearance is obtained from both agencies, the tax-collection authority delivers the tax clearance certificate showing that the seller has cleared all taxes (World Bank 2016b).

The Stamp Duty

The public notary certifies the signatures of the parties in the sales deed only if a notarial deed is established. Since January 2011, the stamp duty has been paid directly at the Land Registry. It is no longer necessary to purchase the stamps and stamp each page, as previously required. The parties, in some cases assisted by their lawyers, can prepare the deed. At this point, the parties usually pay all fees and taxes to the notary, who then pays all taxes and fees to the authorities on behalf of the parties (World Bank 2016b). Listing of the registered sales deed in the land registry is an additional formality that is separate from registration. The buyer applies for the listing of the registered deed on the land registers. According to Law 14-07, which entered into force on May 23, 2012, such listing must be completed within three months from the date the deed was drafted. The buyer must also apply for the inscription of the registered deed in the land registers (the Conservation Foncière, du Cadastre et de la Cartographie). A fixed fee of MAD 75 and a stamp duty of 1 percent of the property value, with a minimum of MAD 450, are payable (World Bank 2016b).

Recurrent Property Taxes

There are several recurrent property taxes at the local level. The General Tax Administration collects the residence tax (*taxe d'habitation*), the tax on communal services (*taxe des services communaux*), and the business tax (*taxe professionnelle*) on behalf of local authorities. The two relevant locally levied and collected taxes are the tax on vacant urban land (*taxe sur les terrains urbains non-bâtis*) and the tax on building operations (*taxe sur les operations de construction*).

The Residence Tax

In 2007, the residence tax replaced the urban property tax, also known as the city tax (*taxe urbaine*). The residence tax applies to buildings of any kind occupied in whole or in part by their owners as a principal residence or as a secondary residence, or occupied without consideration by the owner's spouse, ascendants, or descendants. The residence tax is applied within the jurisdiction of an urban commune and in its peri-urban areas, as well as to properties identified as summer and winter resorts or spas. The tax is payable by the owner or the usufructuary, but if the owner is unknown, it can be collected from the occupier. Where land and a building on that land are owned by different persons, the owner of the building is liable for the tax (Local Tax Guide 2008).

The Tax Base

The residence tax is based on the annual rental value (ARV) of buildings. However, a reduction of 75 percent is applied to the rental value of occupied buildings for the following persons:

- The owner or usufructuary, or the owner's spouse, ascendants, or descendants.

- The members of real estate companies.

- Moroccan citizens living abroad if the building is a primary residence and occupied for free by their spouse, ascendants, or descendants.

This reduction also applies to the value of a holiday (second) home.

Exemptions

The following properties are fully and permanently exempt:

- Royal residences.

- Buildings belonging to the state, local authorities, charities, or public benefit organizations.

- Buildings available free of charge at the disposal of some organizations specified by law.

- Buildings belonging to foreign states as offices or housing for diplomatic missions, subject to reciprocity.

- Buildings belonging to international organizations with diplomatic status and used as offices or housing for the mission chiefs.

- Buildings used exclusively for public worship or education or as historic monuments if they are not used commercially.

New buildings and additions to buildings constructed by individuals as principal residences are exempt for five years after the date of their completion. Buildings in the former province of Tangier enjoy a permanent reduction of 50 percent. The five-year tax holiday for the owners of newly completed construction materially erodes the tax base.

Valuation

In each municipality, the ARV of a building is determined by a commission that annually conducts an inventory of properties. Values are determined with reference to the average rents for similar homes in the same neighborhood. The rental values are revised every five years by a 2 percent increase. The governor of the prefecture or province appoints the commission's members for a term of six years. The commission must include an inspector of taxes proposed by the General Tax Administration and a representative of the local tax services of the municipality proposed by the president of the municipal council. The commission can be divided into as many subcommissions as are necessary to perform its work. Each subcommission must include an officer of the General Tax Administration and a representative of the tax services in the municipality. The census commences on a date that must be publicly advertised at least 30 days in advance through posters, newspapers, and other appropriate advertising modes used in the locality. Properties are listed by street in the order of their location. At the close of census operations, the commission must publish a grid of rental values on the basis of average rents of similar properties in the area.

Tax Rates

The graduated residence tax rates are set out in table 19.7.

Administration

The residence tax is collected centrally, and the revenue is apportioned, with 90 percent transferred to the relevant commune's budget and the

Table 19.7 Tax Rates for the Residence Tax

Annual Rental Value	Tax Rate (%)
Below 5,000 MAD	0
5,001–20,000 MAD	10 – MAD 500
20,001–40,000 MAD	20 – MAD 2,500
Above 40,000 MAD	30 – MAD 6,500

Source: Adapted from Deloitte (2015).

remaining 10 percent retained in the general budget of the state as a fee for the cost of management.

The Tax on Communal Services

The tax on communal services replaced the municipal administration tax, and the base has been broadened to cover households and business (Local Tax Guide 2008). The tax on communal services is a tax to pay for communal services in urban and rural communes and is charged annually in addition to the residence tax. The tax is levied on the owner or usufructuary. If the owner or usufructuary cannot be identified, the occupant is liable. However, if the building is the owner's principal residence, the 75 percent discount of the rental value used in the calculation of the residence tax applies. The tax is payable on existing buildings and constructions of any kind, regardless of their use, as well as equipment, tools, and any other means of production specifically covered.

For property subject to the residence tax or the business tax, including properties that benefit from permanent or temporary exemptions, the tax is based on the rental value used to calculate those two taxes. For property not subject to the business tax or the residence tax, it is based on the actual rents where such a property is leased, or on its presumptive rental value if the property were freely available to a third party. The applicable tax rates are

- 10.5 percent of the rental value for buildings located within the municipal boundaries of urban municipalities, as well as spas and summer and winter resorts; and

- 6.5 percent of the rental value of properties located in the peri-urban areas of urban municipalities.

Taxpayers are subject to the same obligations for the tax on communal services as they are for the residence tax in case of completion of construction or change of ownership of the property. However, the five-year exemption provided for the residence tax does not apply to the tax on communal services. The revenue from the tax on communal services is divided as follows: 95 percent to the communes and 5 percent to the region (Local Tax Guide 2008).

The Business Tax

The business tax replaced the patent tax in 2007 and is payable annually by natural or legal persons, whether Moroccan or foreign, engaged in business or professional activities for profit. Business and professional activities subject to the business tax are classified according to their nature in one of the classes of occupations as determined by law.

The business tax is based on the gross annual rental value of normal and current tangible assets that the taxpayer uses for business activities. For business and professional activities other than hotel establishments, the rental value is determined by reference to actual leases or rentals, by way of comparison, or by direct reporting without using the correction procedure under the law (Local Tax Guide 2008). However, the rental value may not be less than 3 percent of the overall cost of land, buildings, fixtures, equipment, and tools. For hotel establishments, the rental value is determined by applying fixed coefficients to the cost of buildings, equipment, tools, fixtures, and fittings of each establishment depending on the overall cost of tangible elements of hotel establishments, provided that the establishment is operated by the owner or the tenant. The coefficients are defined by law as follows:

- 2 percent if the cost is less than MAD 3 million.
- 1.50 percent if the cost is at least MAD 3 million but less than MAD 6 million.
- 1.25 percent if the cost is at least MAD 6 million but less than MAD 12 million.
- 1 percent if the overall cost is at least MAD 12 million through leases and rental actions.

The tax rates based on the rental value as determined by law are as follows:

- Class 3 (C3): 10 percent.
- Class 2 (C2): 20 percent.
- Class 1 (C1): 30 percent.

However, there are minimum amounts payable for each of the three classes and for urban and rural communes. A taxpayer who does not file a registration for business tax within 30 days after the date of commencement of business is liable to a surcharge of 15 percent of the amount due or that would have been due in the absence of an exemption or reduction, with a minimum of MAD 500.

The revenue from the business tax is divided as follows (Local Tax Guide 2008):

- 80 percent of the revenue is remitted to the council of the commune where the business is operated.

- 10 percent is remitted to chambers of commerce, industry, and services, craft rooms, and rooms of marine fisheries and their federations. The distribution of this portion among these chambers and federations is fixed by regulation.

- 10 percent of the tax revenue is retained for the benefit of the general budget as a management fee.

Other Taxes on Immovable Property

Local authorities levy a number of other taxes or charges relating to immovable property.

The Tax on Undeveloped Urban Land

The tax on undeveloped urban land is levied for the benefit of urban communes. It applies to undeveloped urban land within the boundaries of urban municipalities or delimited centers (with a town-planning document), but it excludes undeveloped land already allocated for use of any kind. It is payable by the owner. Joint owners can request to be charged in proportion to their shares of ownership. However, each joint owner remains liable to pay the entire tax (Local Tax Guide 2008).

The tax is an amount per square meter of the land area; any fraction of a square meter is rounded up to a whole square meter. The tax rates on vacant urban land are fixed as follows:

- Building area: MAD 4 to 20 per square meter.

- Villa area, individual housing area, or other areas: MAD 2 to MAD 12 per square meter.

The tax on undeveloped urban land is due for the entire year on the basis of the factual situation as of January 1 of the tax year. The municipal taxation service conducts an annual census of properties subject to the tax on undeveloped urban land.

The Tax on Building Operations

The tax on building operations is levied for the benefit of urban and rural communes. It is a one-time tax on any new construction, reconstruction, or expansion of any kind before a building permit is issued to the taxpayer. The tax is calculated on the basis of the total area in square meters to be covered by the construction. As is the case with the tax on undeveloped urban land, a fraction of a square meter is rounded up to one square meter. Should any part of the construction protrude on any public area, a 100 percent surcharge will be applied to the protruding area. The tax is due at the time building permit is issued, and proof of payment must be produced before any construction work may commence. The tax rates per square meter are set out in table 19.8.

Table 19.8 Tax Rates for the Tax on Building Operations

Type of Building Operations	Tax
• Collective residential buildings or housing developments	MAD 10 to MAD 20/m²
• Industrial, commercial, or administrative buildings	
• Single units	MAD 20 to MAD 30/m²

Source: Local Tax Guide (2008).

The Social Solidarity Contribution on the Construction of Housing Units

If a person constructs a housing unit for personal residential use and the built area does not exceed 300 m², the social solidarity contribution is not payable. However, if the constructed area is over 300 m², the owner is liable for this contribution on the entire area covered. The amount of this contribution is MAR 60 per square meter covered by the housing unit.

For buildings whose area exceeds 300 m², payment of the tax at the relevant tax office must be accompanied by a written statement specifying the area covered by the new construction and the amount of the contribution, as well as the building and occupancy permits. This declaration must be filed within 90 days after the date of issuance of the occupancy permit by the competent authority.

Property Tax Issues in Morocco

Subnational elections were held in 2015, and the decentralization program is well under way. However, the Moroccan tax system is still largely centralized, and the General Tax Administration still collects some of the local taxes, albeit through decentralized regional offices.

Although property taxes constitute a significant percentage of GDP (the highest on the African continent), recurrent taxes on property represent a relatively small proportion of these taxes. The residence tax has an extremely narrow base because of the significant 75 percent value reduction for primary residences and the five-year exemption for newly constructed property.

Raising recurrent property taxes (while protecting low-income property owners) would increase revenues and also overall fairness, since this move would mainly affect the better-off (Jewell et al. 2015). Because the overall tax percentage of GDP is already at 24.5 percent, however, there may not be much room to increase revenue from recurrent property taxes unless relief is given elsewhere in the tax system.

Notes

1. These include the first Communal Charter (Law of June 3, 1960, Decree of December 2, 1959); the second Communal Charter (Law of September 30, 1976); a new communal reapportionment adopted in 1992 (Decree of June 30, 1992) that doubled the number of communes; and a further new Communal Charter (Law No 78-00 of October 3, 2002).

2. The central government redistributes 1 percent of the corporate tax and the personal income tax to the regions.

References

Bahl, R. W., and J. Martinez-Vazquez. 2008. "The Determinants of Revenue Performance." In *Making the Property Tax Work*, ed. R. W. Bahl, J. Martinez-Vazquez, and J. M. Youngman, 35–57. Cambridge, MA: Lincoln Institute of Land Policy.

Balgley, D. 2015. "Morocco's Fragmented Land Regime: An Analysis of Negotiating and Implementing Land Tenure Policies." IPE Summer Research Grant Report, University of Puget Sound. *www.pugetsound.edu/files/resources/balgley.pdf*.

Burn, N., L. Jaida, and H. Zirari. 2005. "Local Budgets and Gender in Morocco." Report for UNIFEM and the European Union. Casablanca: Association Démocratique des Femmes du Maroc (ADFM).

CIA (Central Intelligence Agency). 2016. "Morocco." In *The World Factbook*. *https://www.cia.gov/library/publications/the-world-factbook/geos/mo.html*.

Citizen Budget. 2015. "Citizen Budget." Budget Office, Ministry of Economy and Finance. *www.finances.gov.ma/Docs/2015/DB/citizen_budget2015.pdf*.

Deloitte. 2015. *Guide to Fiscal Information: Key Economies in Africa, 2014/15*. *http://www2.deloitte.com/content/dam/Deloitte/et/Documents/tax/ZA_Fiscal_Guide_2015_29012015.pdf*.

General Treasury. 2012. *Bulletin Mensuel de Statistiques des Finances Locales— Décembre 2012*. Rabat: General Treasury of the Kingdom, Ministry of Economy and Finance.

———. 2014. *Bulletin Mensuel de Statistiques des Finances Locales—Décembre 2014*. Rabat: General Treasury of the Kingdom, Ministry of Economy and Finance.

IBFD (International Bureau for Fiscal Documentation). 2016. "Morocco—Key Features." Amsterdam: International Bureau for Fiscal Documentation.

IMF (International Monetary Fund). 2015. *2014 IMF Government Finance Statistics Yearbook*. Washington, DC.

———. 2016. "IMF World Longitudinal Data (WoRLD)." IMF e-Library Data. *http:// data.imf.org/?sk=77413F1D-1525-450A-A23A-47AEED40FE78&sId =1390030109571*.

Jewell, A., M. Mansour, P. Mitra, and C. Sdralevich. 2015. "Fair Taxation in the Middle East and North Africa." IMF Staff Discussion Note. Washington, DC: IMF.

Local Tax Guide. 2008. "Guide de la fiscalité locale." Direction des Finances Locales, Direction Générale des Collectivités Locales, Ministère de l'Intérieur. *www.befec.ma /documentation/fiscalite/Fiscalite_local/Guide_de_la_Fiscalite_Locale_Francais.pd*f.

Norregaard, J. 2013. "Taxing Immovable Property—Revenue Potential and Implementation Challenges." IMF working paper. Washington, DC: IMF.

Tax Administration. 2016. "The General Tax Administration." *http://portail.tax.gov.ma /wps/portal/DGI-Ang/Dgi-Internet-Ang/About-us*.

United Nations. 2014. *World Urbanization Prospects*. Washington, DC: Department of Economic and Social Affairs, Population Division.

United Nations, Department of Economic and Social Affairs, Population Division. 2015. World Population Prospects: The 2015 Revision. *https://esa.un.org/unpd/wpp /Publications/Files/World_Population_2015_Wallchart.pdf*.

USAID (U.S. Agency for International Development). 2011. "USAID Country Profile—Property Rights and Resource Governance: Morocco." Washington, DC.

World Bank. 2016a. "Country and Lending Groups." *http://data.worldbank.org/about /country-and-lending-groups*.

———. 2016b. "Doing Business: Morocco." *www.doingbusiness.org/Reports/Subnational -Reports/~/media/giawb/doing%20business/documents/profiles/country/MAR.pdf*.

———. 2016c. "GDP per Capita (Current US%)." *http://data.worldbank.org/indicator /NY.GDP.PCAP.CD*.

———. 2016d. "Morocco—Country Review." Washington, DC. *www.worldbank.org /en/country/morocco/overview*.

Legislation

Communal Charter of 1976.

Communal Charter (of October 3, 2002).

Law No. 47/06 (of November 30, 2007).

Law No. 39/07 (of December 31, 2007).

Law No. 14/07 (of May 23, 2012).

20

Mozambique

WILLIAM McCLUSKEY AND VASCO NHABINDE

Mozambique is a former Portuguese colony that gained independence in 1975. Located in southeastern Africa, it borders the Indian Ocean to the east, Swaziland and South Africa to the south and southwest, Zimbabwe to the west, Zambia and Malawi to the northwest, and Tanzania to the north. The land area is 799,380 km², and the population is estimated at 28 million (United Nations 2015). The level of urbanization is about 32 percent (United Nations 2014). The capital city, Maputo, has a population of about 1.2 million (CIA 2016). It is an important port city not only for Mozambique but also for neighboring landlocked Zimbabwe and the northern provinces of South Africa. In 2015, the estimated GDP per capita in Mozambique was USD 529 (World Bank 2016b). Mozambique is a low-income country (World Bank 2016a).

Government

There are 11 provinces, including the capital city of Maputo. There are 128 districts within the provinces that primarily cover rural areas (CIA 2016), and there are 51 municipalities covering urban areas. The 2004 Constitution of the Republic of Mozambique acknowledges two types of local authority, municipalities and settlements.

Immediately after independence in 1975, Mozambique reorganized its administrative structures and reestablished municipalities. The majority of municipalities were institutionalized by Law No. 7/78 and were referred to as executive councils. At this time, all sources of revenue were controlled by the central government, including property taxes. Most municipal services, such as sanitation, public health, and street cleaning, were provided free to citizens. Executive councils effectively functioned as agents of the central government, and direct central-government budget transfers financed almost all their expenditures. Because they had no control over the transfers and could not predict them, local budgeting was problematic. Revenues were often depleted long before the end of the fiscal year, and the delivery of municipal services was significantly weakened. However, the establishment of municipalities and the redefinition of their legal and financial status in 1997 significantly enhanced their leeway in determining their own revenues and expenditure priorities. Under the central government's new policy to reduce its role in local service delivery, it initiated plans allowing municipalities to levy some own sources of revenue, including property taxes.

Since 2004, imposition of the property tax has been a municipal competency for those municipalities with the administrative capacity to charge, collect, and enforce the tax. However, only Maputo Municipality and a few of the larger urban municipalities, such as Beira, Matola, and Nampula, have the necessary administrative capacity to take on this responsibility.

Land Tenure

Land tenure in Mozambique has had a major impact on the evolution, or lack of it, of land and property taxes in the country. When Mozambique became independent in 1975, the government assumed ownership of all land. Article 82 of the 2004 constitution explains that the state recognizes and guarantees the right of ownership of property. The constitution further provides in Article 109 that all land is owned by the state, and land may not be sold or otherwise alienated or disposed of, nor may it be mortgaged or subjected to any form of attachment (Land Law of 1979, Law No. 6/79) (GoM 1997; Kanji et al. 2005; Nhabinde 2009). The Land Law of 1979 had four principal objectives:

- To rationalize and regularize land allocation.

- To legitimize grants already made.

- To simplify the process somewhat through provision of criteria and standard procedures.

- To reaffirm the rights of peasant landholding communities.

This law also established a new property right in land, the so-called DUAT (*direito de uso e aproveitamento dos terras*), also referred to as the "land use and benefit right." There are three main ways in which a person or entity may obtain a DUAT:

- Through occupancy of land according to customary norms and practices.

- Through good-faith occupation of land for a period of ten years.

- By application to the state. In this case the state grants DUATs for renewable periods of 50 years.

DUATs obtained by occupancy are perpetual and do not require plans for exploitation of the land. Delimitation and registration are voluntary, and local communities are not obliged to delimit or register their land to prove their DUAT ownership. However, local communities can register their DUAT. This is important where communities want to transfer their DUAT to an investor. Members of local communities can also obtain DUATs for individual plots within the community land.

The Land Law established that land has no sale (or market) value or rental value. Because land is deemed to have no market value and cannot be included in an individual's patrimony, it cannot be used as collateral for credit, nor can revenue based on its value be raised. There are two important legal instruments that regulate the use of land in Mozambique. Decree No. 66/98 is more general and is applicable nationwide, while the subsidiary regulation, Decree No. 60/06, is applicable to cities, municipalities, and villages. These two legal instruments determine how individuals can have access to land as defined in the Land Law. As noted, access to land for economic activity is granted for a period of 50 years and is renewable for another 50 years. According to the Land Law, the right of land use (granted by the title) is transferable, but only the constructed improvements can be used as security for credit purposes.

Land is the basis of subsistence for most Mozambican families living in rural areas and is probably the most important asset people in rural areas have. In this regard, Law No. 19/97 introduced an important innovation in the right to land in this traditional (customary law) system of land tenure by giving communities the right to participate in the process of land allocation for investment projects. In urban areas, land can be publicly auctioned if the objective of the auction is to promote the construction of buildings for residential, commercial, or services use.

Although land in principle has no value, Law No. 19/97, Decree No. 66/98, and Decree No. 60/06 provide for the payment of an annual fee on the grant of titles for land use and charges for land acquisition. These annual fees are payable in two installments, the first by the end of March and the second before the end of June. One problem with these annual fees is that they are fixed, low amounts, so they are not buoyant, and the revenue is negligible and, in most cases, less than the cost of administration.

The law provides for penalties for those who try to evade the payment of fees on land titles to ensure that they use the land for the permitted purpose. However, in most cases, the penalties are not enforced. Perhaps a more serious problem is the lack of mapping and identification of properties subject to these annual land fees. As a consequence, Mozambique has taken a significant positive step regarding its system of land management by introducing the Land Information Management System (LIMS), which allows for the exact identification of a land parcel, its location, its owner, and its use at the provincial level.

Because land is deemed to have no market value and the land use fees are administratively determined, the actual value of land in the market is distorted; therefore, land revenue is lower than it could be. In addition to low tax rates, many properties are exempt because they are owned by the state or by associations of public utilities recognized by the Council of Ministers (Law No. 19/97). These exemptions exclude significant areas of land and also serve as an incentive for individuals to register their businesses as associations or cooperatives to gain the advantages of exemption.

Furthermore, the formula for redistribution of the revenue collected (40 percent to the national treasury, 12 percent to the districts, 24 percent to mapping services, and 24 percent to the National Directorate of Land) penalizes areas that are more efficient in tax collection. Moreover, the Treasury keeps the largest part of the revenue instead of returning it to the districts and provincial governments where it was collected, and where increased levels of expenditure are needed.

In general, most provinces have improved their levels of revenue collection from land titles, largely because of the implementation of a new system of land management that helps identify parcels subject to the land tax. The government believes that when the new system of land management is fully operational and the number of exemptions is reduced, tax revenue from land titles will be significantly higher. Mozambique also needs to consider the market value of land in calculating tax revenue from land titles. This will increase the level of revenue for the country and especially for districts and provinces, but it can happen only when the law recognizes that land has value.

Taxation

A corporate income tax is levied at a standard rate of 32 percent (a reduced rate of 10 percent applies to agricultural enterprises). A value-added tax is levied at 17 percent.

A DUAT must be registered in the LIMS, the land use charge must have been paid (for which a tax clearance certificate must be obtained), and the owner and the purchaser must be registered for tax purposes. A *sisa* (property transfer tax) receipt must be obtained from the tax authority and submitted with the sale and purchase agreement to the notary along with the name of the buyer. The sisa is based on the declared transaction price or whatever price the tax authority determines. Decree 46/2004 reduced the sisa from the previous level of 10 percent to 2 percent of the declared price (PWC 2016). Revenue from the sisa is allocated to municipalities. Currently, there are no formal processes whereby transaction details are recorded in Mozambique. All transactions are liable for the sisa, which must be paid before a notary can fully complete the legal processes. However, there is no recording of the agreed price in a central database or even in electronic format, such as a spreadsheet.

The transfer for monetary value of the right of ownership of real property or of other equivalent rights is subject to the sisa as provided for in Article 94(1) of the Civil Tax Act (CTA). Article 102 of the CTA establishes a rate of 2 percent that is charged on the value declared for the purposes of the sale and purchase or on the official taxable value of the property, whichever is higher. The sisa is payable by the person who acquires the right of ownership of the property and must be paid before the signing of the deed of sale and purchase or any other act equivalent to it or leading to an eventual sale and purchase transaction (Nhabinde 2009).

Property and Land Taxes

Before 2003, the central government collected the property tax and redistributed the revenue to municipalities according to a fixed formula that took into account the population of the municipality and revenue from other sources. However, in 2004, municipalities deemed to have sufficient administrative capacity were given the opportunity to levy and collect property taxes. Districts (rural areas), however, as administrative arms of the central government, have no taxing authority. Land is charged a land use fee, only part of which is reallocated to the district. Property tax revenue nationally is generally lower than the revenue from the taxes on real estate transfers and donations. This can be explained in part by the low assessed values, primarily on residential properties.

Table 20.1 illustrates the adjustment factors for land in districts. Some of the key adjustments relate to location (protection zones and development zones), size of parcels, use of land for charitable purposes, and ownership of the land.

Table 20.1 Adjustment Factors for Land in Districts

Location or Category	Index
Maputo Province	2
Other provinces	1
Partial protection zones	1.5
Development zones	0.5
Up to 100 ha	1
101–1,000 ha	1.5
>1,001 ha	2
Charity use	0.5
Nationals	0.8
Nonnationals	1

Source: Ministerial Diploma 144/2010.

Table 20.2 illustrates land use rates. The land use charge was introduced in 1999. In 2010, the rates were revised to reflect the revaluation of the Mozambican currency (effected in July 2006, whereby 1,000 old Mozambican meticals became equal to 1 new Mozambican metical). Rates are relatively low, particularly for protected types of farming, such as cattle and wildlife. In addition, land used for tourism, such as hotel land within

Table 20.2 Land Use Rates per Hectare for Districts

Parcel Use	Rate per Hectare, 1999	Rate per Hectare, 2010 (Current) (MZN)	Rate per Hectare, July 2010 (USD)	Rate Per Hectare, December 2015 (USD)
Nonagricultural land	30,000	75	2.16	1.47
Agricultural land	15,000	38	1.08	0.74
Cattle farming	2,000	5	0.14	0.10
Wildlife farming	2,000	5	0.14	0.10
Permanent crops	2,000	5	0.14	0.10
Land up to 1 ha within 3 km of coastline	200,000	500	14.39	9.80

Source: Authors' calculations; Land Law Regulations 77/1999; and Ministerial Diploma 144/2010.

three kilometers of the coast, is charged MZN 500 per hectare. Therefore, a hotel parcel of one hectare would have an annual land use charge of less than USD 10.

The Municipal Property Tax

The municipal property tax (*imposto predial autárquico*, IPRA) is levied annually on the value of buildings situated within a municipality (PWC 2016). The IPRA is part of the municipality tax base. According to Law 1/2008, this tax is based on the "book value" of urban properties located within a municipality, which is defined as the value recorded in the cadastral records. The tax is levied on the value of an urban building that is regarded as infrastructure. If the value is not recorded in the cadastral record, the tax is levied on the self-reported value. An urban property is defined as land on which a fixture has been attached. The methodology for estimating the market value of a building usually takes into consideration the following criteria:

- Basic construction value or cost per square meter.

- Gross construction area (building).

- The application coefficient (type of use, such as housing, commerce, services, warehouse, or industry).

- The location coefficient (e.g., rural, peri-urban, urban).

- The age coefficient.

The regulations require the taxpayer to register the building in the municipal tax register. A municipal building valuation committee is supposed to undertake assessment of the value of all buildings. The law stipulates an annual tax rate of 0.4 percent of the value of residential buildings and 0.7 percent of the value of buildings used for commerce, industry, storage, or services.

The IPRA must be paid annually in two installments, by June 30 and December 31. Properties exempt from the IPRA include buildings of the state; municipal buildings; diplomatic missions; officially recognized nonprofit entities of humanitarian, cultural, scientific, artistic, or charitable character; museums and educational institutions; and buildings constructed by the state Housing Fund (Fundo de Fomento de Habitação). New residential buildings are also exempt for five years from the date the housing permit is issued in the name of the owner. Idle municipal land is not subject to the IPRA. This exemption results in a considerable loss of potential revenue on vacant urban land and may encourage inefficient land use and speculation.

The main challenges municipal governments face in collecting the IPRA are (1) creation and maintenance of building registers and (2) determination of the value of each building included in the building register. Municipalities are responsible for maintaining the building register, but there are serious problems in determining the assessed value. Currently, the values recorded in the building register are extremely outdated and are considerably lower than current market values.

The finances of municipalities in Mozambique are regulated by Law No. 11/97 and by the Local Government Tax Code (Decree No. 52/00). In exercising the rights allowed by these two laws, Maputo collected on average 78 percent of its budgeted revenue, which financed 99 percent of its budget, during the period 2004 to 2006. During the same period, government transfers represented 51 percent of local revenue. Total revenue represented 0.28, 0.32, and 0.32 percent of Mozambican real GDP between 2004 and 2006 (Nhabinde 2009). Although the weight of this municipality in the country's GDP is increasing gradually, there is still significant potential to be exploited. For example, if properties were revalued and there was a serious attempt to incorporate more properties into the tax base, Maputo could significantly increase revenue from the property tax.

The Municipality of Maputo

Maputo, as the capital city and most important commercial center in Mozambique, has diverse economic activities and includes some of the most expensive residential and commercial property in the country. Although it is one of the most developed urban areas in the country, there are still many properties within the city limits that have not been identified and registered for property tax purposes. A study conducted with the support of the World Bank found that only 14,700 out of an estimated total of 225,000 properties were registered (less than 7 percent). In order to maximize the potential of the property tax, it is essential that the ownership of buildings be systematically identified and recorded. The cited study recommended a land survey of Maputo in order to identify, map, and register all property, including property entitled to an exemption. The survey could also be accompanied by a campaign to inform people of the importance of paying taxes.

In addition to the property registration problem, the majority of properties in Maputo that are on the valuation roll are not valued at a level close to their market prices. On average, the property taxes on buildings in Maputo represented only about 10 percent of total revenue for the period

2004 to 2006. If charges on land tenure are added to the property tax revenues during the same period, this figure increases to 36 percent of total revenue. Besides adding previously untaxed properties to the system, the municipality should consider valuing properties according to their market value. Valuation could be done either by the Maputo Municipal Commission or by a private entity.

Of the expected 2014 revenue from property taxes for the Municipality of Maputo, 27 percent was derived from commercial and business properties, and 73 percent was derived from residential properties. The mapping and identification of untaxed properties will increase the revenue potential of the property tax (see table 20.3). The current tax rate for residential buildings is 0.4 percent; for commercial buildings, it is 0.7 percent.

By law, all state-owned residential properties that are rented out to individuals are exempted from the property tax. Therefore, residents occupying such residences are not liable for payment of the property tax since the whole property is regarded as state owned. A possible solution would be for the state to sell these properties; thus, the buyer or user would become liable for property taxes. However, the state would then forgo the rental income. A more feasible option would be to deem these properties owner occupied by the tenants and to levy property tax on the tenants. One recommendation regarding such residential properties is that they should be mapped and identified for property tax purposes (in most cases, data are available from files constructed during the sales process), even at their low property value.

Table 20.3 Potential Growth in Taxable Properties in Maputo Municipality, 2007–2014

Year	Residential Properties	Other Properties	Registered Plots	Total Properties
2007	21,961	1,725	104	23,790
2008	30,248	2,123	133	32,504
2009	41,738	2,622	174	44,534
2010	57,721	3,247	229	61,197
2011	80,029	4,033	305	84,367
2012	111,300	5,028	412	116,740
2013	155,354	6,292	566	162,212
2014	217,781	7,902	785	226,468

Source: Department of Revenue, Maputo Municipal Area.

Prospects for the Property Tax in Mozambique

The end of the civil war in Mozambique in 1992, along with the introduction of the program of economic rehabilitation, sparked the drive for the land reform. At that point, most municipalities in Mozambique were still arms of the central government. The central government enacted many laws and resolutions to regulate the lives of citizens and the municipal services to be delivered to them.

Most local-government structures existed only as central-government agencies and had no clear responsibilities for local service delivery. It was only in 1998, with the first democratic elections at the local-government level, that the importance of local governments for service delivery became apparent. This was manifested in changes to the law, for example, the return of property taxes to municipalities.

The development of new municipal structures required a new balance of funding through central-government grants and transfers, on the one hand, and new local-government sources of revenue, on the other. Mozambique initiated significant fiscal reforms at the municipal level, including the (re)introduction of property taxes. Property taxes on improvements constituted 0.7 percent of GDP in 2011 (IMF 2015). These figures are low compared with international standards in developing countries (Bahl and Martinez-Vazquez 2008; Norregaard 2013) confirming that Mozambique still has a long way to go to fully exploit the recurrent property tax as a source of revenue. Especially in regard to specialized valuation and municipal tax administration, including transparency and accountability, much can be done to enhance locally collected revenues from the property tax.

References

Bahl, R. W., and J. Martinez-Vazquez. 2008. "The Determinants of Revenue Performance." In *Making the Property Tax Work*, ed. R. W. Bahl, J. Martinez-Vazquez, and J. M. Youngman, 35–57. Cambridge, MA: Lincoln Institute of Land Policy.

CIA (Central Intelligence Agency). 2016. "Mozambique." In *The World Factbook. https://www.cia.gov/library/publications/the-world-factbook/geos/mz.html*.

GoM. 1997. Constitution of Mozambique.

IMF (International Monetary Fund). 2015. *2014 IMF Government Finance Statistics Yearbook*. Washington, DC.

Kanji, N., L. Cotula, T. Hilhorst, C. Toulmin, and W. Witten. 2005. *Can Land Registration Serve Poor and Marginalised Groups?* DFID Research Report no. 1. Nottingham, UK: Russell Press.

Maputo Municipal Area. 2015. Department of Revenue.

Nhabinde, V. C. 2009. "An Overview of Property Taxation in Lusophone Africa." Working paper WP09LA1. Cambridge, MA: Lincoln Institute of Land Policy.

Norregaard, J. 2013. "Taxing Immovable Property—Revenue Potential and Implementation Challenges." IMF working paper. Washington, DC: International Monetary Fund.

PWC (Price Waterhouse Coopers). 2016. "Worldwide Tax Summaries—Mozambique." *http://taxsummaries.pwc.com/uk/taxsummaries.*

United Nations. 2014. *World Urbanization Prospects.* Washington, DC: Department of Economic and Social Affairs, Population Division.

United Nations, Department of Economic and Social Affairs, Population Division. 2015. World Population Prospects: The 2015 Revision. *https://esa.un.org/unpd/wpp /Publications/Files/World_Population_2015_Wallchart.pdf.*

World Bank. 2016a. "Country and Lending Groups." *http://data.worldbank.org/about /country-and-lending-groups.*

———. 2016b. "GDP per Capita (Current US%)." *http://data.worldbank.org/indicator /NY.GDP.PCAP.CD.*

Legislation

Civil Tax Act.

Constitution of the Republic of Mozambique of 2004.

Decree 46/2004.

Decree No. 66/98.

Decree No. 60/06.

Law No. 7/78.

Law No. 6/79 (the Land Law).

Law No. 11/97.

Law No. 19/97.

Law 1/2008.

Local Government Tax Code (Decree No. 52/00).

21

Namibia

RIËL FRANZSEN AND WILLIAM MCCLUSKEY

Namibia is located in the southwestern corner of Africa and covers an area of 834,295 km². Established as a German colony, it was administered by South Africa from 1917 to 1990. The country gained independence from South Africa on March 21, 1990. Namibia's population is estimated at 2.5 million (United Nations 2015), of which an estimated 370,000 live in the capital, Windhoek (CIA 2016). The urban population is estimated to be around 47 percent (United Nations 2014), but despite rapid urbanization, Namibia is still mainly a rural society. In 2015, the estimated per capita GDP was USD 4,677 (World Bank 2016b). According to the World Economic Forum, Namibia will be the most competitive economy in the Southern African Development Community by 2017. Namibia is classified as an upper-middle-income country (World Bank 2016a).

Government

Namibia's current constitution came into force on March 21, 1990, and provides for a three-tier system of governance: the central government, regional councils, and local authorities. Legislation governing subnational governments includes the Regional Councils Act No. 22 of 1992 and the Local Authorities Act No. 23 of 1992. Local authorities are established in urban areas; regional councils cover the rural areas. Under the Local Authorities Act, there are four types of local authorities: Part I municipalities, Part II municipalities, towns, and villages. There are 3 Part I municipalities, 15 Part II municipalities, 26 towns, and 18 villages (CLGF 2015; Local Government Act 1992). Municipal councils are the most autonomous local authorities. There are 14 regional councils and 57 unitary local authorities.

The central government provides subsidies to village councils, regional councils, and newly established town councils. Regional councils do not generally provide services directly, but local councils' responsibilities include water and sanitation, waste management, electricity, and local economic development (CLGF 2015; Kuusi 2009).

Local-Council Revenue Sources

The local authorities' own-source revenues consist of property tax (rates), charges and fees, and revenue from leasing or selling immovable property such as land. Because of their size, the Part I municipalities (Swakopmund, Walvis Bay, and Windhoek) generally have a solid financial basis and enjoy considerable autonomy in the determination of the property tax and in obtaining loans under the provisions of the Local Authorities Act. The significantly smaller Part II municipalities have a more fragile financial basis and are subject to control exercised by the Ministry of Regional and Local Government, Housing, and Rural Development in setting property rates and obtaining credit facilities (Fjeldstad et al. 2005; Jibao 2010; Kuusi 2009). Both regional councils and local authorities are empowered to levy local taxes. Each local authority must transfer 5 percent of its property tax (rates) income to its regional council (CLGF 2015).

Most of the smaller councils cannot balance their budgets without substantial transfers from the national government, as is evident from table 21.1,

Table 21.1 Aggregated Revenues for Local Authorities, 2014/2015

Estimated Revenue	NAD	%
Government transfers		
Restricted/conditional grants	524,068,364	13.4
Unconditional grants	288,428,420	7.3
Locally raised revenue		
Property rates	321,721,977	8.2
Licenses and fees	23,448,484	0.6
Other (e.g., electricity and water provision)	2,767,389,118	70.5
Total income	3,925,056,363	100

Source: CLGF (2015).

which provides an overview of the revenues of local authorities for the 2014/2015 fiscal year. The current trend under the Decentralization Enabling Act No. 33 of 2000 is that the local authorities are being pushed toward financial self-sufficiency to obtain a more autonomous status. The government of Namibia has started to develop a system of recurrent and development grants to local authorities aimed at improving service provision and capacity building (Kuusi 2009).

Property rates constitute less than 10 percent of the aggregate revenue of all local authorities. The most important own revenue sources are so-called trading services, that is, the sale of commodities, especially electricity and water, in bulk to end consumers (see table 21.1). Property taxes broadly defined, including the stamp duty and the transfer duty, constituted 0.17 percent of GDP in 2010 and 0.26 in 2011 (IMF 2016), whereas overall taxes as a percentage of GDP were 31.0 percent in 2012 (IMF 2015). Because Namibia is an upper-middle-income country (World Bank 2016), there is likely scope for generating more revenue from the recurrent property tax.

Land Tenure

Article 16 of the 1990 constitution protects the rights of Namibians to acquire, own, and dispose of all forms of immovable and movable property. Under the constitution, all communal land is vested in and formally controlled by the government. In addition, the constitution stipulates that all land that is not "otherwise lawfully owned" belongs to the state. Two important laws regulate land tenure of rural land, the Agricultural (Commercial) Land Reform Act No. 6 of 1995 and the Communal Land Reform Act No. 5 of 2002.

The Agricultural (Commercial) Land Reform Act provides for the acquisition of agricultural land by the state for the purposes of land reform and for the allocation of such land to citizens who do not own or otherwise have the use of any agricultural land or of adequate land, especially those citizens who have been socially, economically, or educationally disadvantaged by past discriminatory laws or practices. This law also vests a preferential right to purchase in the state, provides for the compulsory acquisition of certain agricultural land, and regulates the acquisition of agricultural land by foreign nationals.

The Communal Land Reform Act provides for the allocation of rights to communal land, establishes communal land boards, and provides for the powers of chiefs, traditional authorities, and the land boards in regard to communal land. The communal land boards exercise control over the allocation and cancellation of customary land rights by chiefs or traditional authorities, decide on applications for the right of leasehold, and establish and maintain a register and a system of registration for recording the allocation, transfer, or cancellation of customary land rights and rights of leasehold. In essence, all rural land in the communal areas is held and managed according to customary tenure systems. Generally, traditional leaders allocate land rights. An allocation of residential or arable land confers use rights, usually for life. Upon the death of the holder of a customary land grant, the rights either revert to the traditional leader for reallocation or are passed on according to terms of customary laws.

The form of tenure in urban areas known as "permission to occupy" that was introduced by the South African government has been converted to freehold. The Deeds Registry records legal rights in land, such as ownership, mortgages, and servitudes, under the Deeds Registries Act No. 47 of 1937. The Deeds Registry is based on the cadastral identification of the land parcels (a unique cadastral number).

The Valuation Profession

The valuation profession is not well developed and regulated in Namibia. In 2001, there were fewer than 15 registered valuers in Namibia (Franzsen 2003), and this is still the case (Mutema 2016). Farmers and other stakeholders apparently rarely receive professional advice, and many individuals who are not professional valuers, such as estate agents, attorneys, quantity surveyors, and engineers, provide valuation-related services. However, some of the current problems should be rectified when the regulations of the Property Valuers Profession Act No. 7 of 2012 are implemented, which will allow for the proper determination of qualifications and the categorization and registration of valuers as professional valuers, associate professional valuers, valuers in training, and student valuers in training. There is a valuer general in the Ministry of Land Reform. Valuation education has commenced at the Namibia University of Technology in 2015.

Property-Related Taxation

Capital gains are not taxable in Namibia, and there are no estate or inheritance and capital acquisition taxes. An estate duty and a donations tax were mooted in the 2003/2004 budget but have not been enacted to date (Deloitte 2015).

A stamp duty is imposed on various instruments, such as transfers of shares, transfer deeds, and partnership agreements, at scheduled rates. Effective June 1, 2013, the stamp duty on acquisitions of immovable property by individuals is 0 for property valued at NAD 0 to NAD 600,000 and NAD 10 for every NAD 1,000 or part thereof of the value of immovable

Table 21.2 Transfer Duty Payable by Natural Persons

Property Value	Tax Rate
NAD 0–NAD 600,000	0%
NAD 600,001–NAD 1 million	NAD 0 plus 1%
NAD 1 million–NAD 2 million	NAD 4,000 plus 5%
Over NAD 2 million	NAD 54,000 plus 8%
Agricultural land acquired by natural persons and financed by the Agricultural Bank of Namibia	
NAD 0–NAD 1.5 million	0%
NAD 1.5 million–NAD 2.5 million	NAD 0 plus 1%
Over NAD 2.5 million	NAD 10,000 plus 3%

Source: Transfer Duty Act 14 of 1993.

property valued at NAD 600,001 or more. For legal entities and trusts, the stamp duty is NAD 12 for every NAD 1,000 or part thereof of the value of the immovable property (Deloitte 2015).

The transfer duty (which is primarily based on the South African system of transfer duty) is levied on the acquisition of immovable property and is based on the value of the property. Table 21.2 shows the effective tax rates from June 1, 2013, for any property, including mineral rights, acquired by natural persons. Any property, including mineral rights, acquired by persons other than natural persons (e.g., a company), including trusts, is taxed at 12 percent of the value of the property. The Inland Revenue Department reviews cases where undervaluation by the contracting parties is suspected.

The Land Tax

Namibia historically had no tax on farmland. In 2004, as part of the postindependence efforts to achieve land reform, the government introduced the commercial farm agricultural land tax under the Agricultural (Commercial) Land Reform Second Amendment Act No. 2 of 2001 (amending the Agricultural (Commercial) Land Reform Act of 1995). A comprehensive set of regulations was published to enable the administration of all aspects of the land tax. The regulations currently in force are the Land Valuation and Taxation Regulations of 2007. The first valuation roll, with a 2002 valuation date, was completed and implemented in 2004.

The law states that every owner of commercial agricultural land must pay a land tax based on the unimproved site value (USV) of the land. The value of the land is recorded in the valuation roll, and the tax is calculated at a flat rate or a progressive rate, as provided for in the law. The revenue generated from the land tax is earmarked for the Land Acquisition and Development Fund, that is, primarily for land reform purposes (Franzsen and McCluskey 2008).

Valuation

The minister of land reform appoints a valuer from the public or private sector to prepare a provisional valuation roll for the land tax. To date, the appointed valuer has been an employee of the Directorate of Valuations and Estate Management (DVEM) within the Ministry of Land Reform (MLR). The appointed valuer may assign or delegate some of the functions but remains ultimately responsible and accountable. The provisional valuation roll must contain at least the following data:

- A description of the agricultural land in question.

- The name and address of the owner of the land.

- The area of the land in hectares and its carrying capacity.

- The unimproved site value of the land.

The law provides for very specific valuation criteria. In determining the value of any agricultural land, the valuer

- must consider the carrying capacity of such land (as supplied by the Ministry of Agriculture, Water, and Forestry at the date of valuation);

- may use a mass appraisal approach to value the land and may for this purpose (1) divide the Republic of Namibia cadastral map into value zones to create an isovalue map showing the values of agricultural land per hectare, and (2) create value zones, each of which may contain agricultural land with the same carrying-capacity classification;

- may conduct random inspections of any agricultural land but is not obliged to conduct physical inspections of all farms; and

- must disregard in respect of such agricultural land (1) the value of the improvements on such land; (2) any depreciation in the value of such land caused by excessive grazing, bush encroachment, and other bad farming practices on, or poor management of, such land; (3) any mortgage or other judicial encumbrance on such land; (4) any appreciation of the land value attributed to proximity to a town; (5) any appreciation of the land value attributed to tourism or mining potential; and (6) any depreciation or appreciation of the land value resulting from a public road or railway line crossing through the land.

The main valuation roll is valid for five years. The current law does not provide for an extension of this period. Since it is impractical to physically visit more than 12,000 farms, a mass appraisal approach has been adopted in practice for the valuation process. The DVEM is understaffed because its valuation-related responsibilities include not only valuations for land tax purposes but also, for example, valuations for expropriation purposes and support to and oversight of local-authority valuation rolls for the urban property tax.

The law allows for objections to the provisional valuation roll, which are adjudicated by a valuation court. The valuation court must also exercise overall quality control of the valuation roll. However, it is inappropriate and impractical for a court to deal with quality control of the roll in its entirety, and in practice, the valuation court merely deals with objections.

Table 21.3 provides an overview of the three valuation rolls to date. As indicated, the 2002 provisional valuation roll was the first for the land tax. Therefore, the 2.8 percent objection rate is surprisingly low. Out of a total of 342 objections to the 2002 roll, 74 were withdrawn, and 203 values were upheld by the valuation court. Only 38 values were changed, 29 reductions and 9 increases in values. The 1.7 percent objection rate in 2007 is also low. Especially noteworthy in 2007 is the large number of withdrawals of objections. This suggests that once the valuation methodologies were explained, many objectors were satisfied that their farms had been valued fairly. It should be noted, however, that some farmers were apparently reluctant to have their farm values reduced, fearing that lower values might result in less compensation should the Namibian government buy their farms for land resettlement purposes.

When the 2012 provisional roll was published, farm values had dramatically increased since 2007; increases ranged from 120 to 990 percent. Not surprisingly, the objection rate increased sharply, to 21.1 percent. A total of 2,584 objections were filed. The grounds for objections provided by

Table 21.3 Provisional Valuation Roll Objections, 2002, 2007, and 2012

	2002 Roll		2007 Roll		2012 Roll	
Description	Number	%	Number	%	Number	%
Agricultural properties	12,395	–	12,467	–	12,271	–
Objections	342	2.8	215	1.7	2,584	21.1
Withdrawals	74	0.6	147	1.2	–	–

Source: Ministry of Land Reform (2015).

objectors, many of whom based their objections on more than one ground, were noteworthy: 1,159 of the objection grounds were related to valuation; 1,245 were related to socioeconomic issues; and 3,811 were related to legal issues, 508 of which referred to the possible unconstitutionality of the land tax. The tax rate was raised by 614 objectors. Under the law, only valuation issues can be raised as valid grounds for objections. The key factor that resulted in the explosion of valid and invalid objections was that there was no indication that the tax rates were going to be adjusted when the provisional roll was implemented. The 2012 provisional roll, however, was never implemented because the constitution of the valuation court was found to be invalid. Given the public outcry, the ministry thought it prudent to review all aspects of the land tax, especially the criteria for the determination of USVs.

Tax Rates

The land tax rates are progressive. The rationales are, first, to persuade individuals to give up some of their land units because they cannot afford to pay the tax, and second, to raise much-needed revenue to buy more commercial agricultural land for the resettlement program. By implementing a commercial land tax, the government aims to influence the market by imposing higher tax rates on large or excessive landholdings or on farmland that is not being used. Environmentalists have criticized the introduction of the land tax for its potential to place additional strain on a sector already experiencing financial difficulties.

The current tax rates for the land tax on commercial farmland, which have not been amended since its introduction in 2004, are the following:

- For a single farm owned by a Namibian, the rate is 0.75 percent of USV per hectare.

- For a single farm owned by a foreigner, the rate is 1.75 percent of USV per hectare.

- For any additional farms owned by the same owner, the rate shall be increased by 0.25 percent of the USV per hectare for each farm progressively, according to the number of farms owned.

The tax on commercial agricultural land is levied in proportion to its size and USV. There are more than 30 value zones across Namibia that provide the NAD value per hectare of all commercial farmland. Box 21.1 provides an example of how the tax is calculated. Table 21.4 shows the collection levels of the land tax since its introduction.

Table 21.4 Revenues from the Land Tax Since Its Inception in 2004/2005

Land Tax Fiscal Year	Assessments Issued	Total Amount of Assessments Issued (NAD)	Actual Amount Collected (NAD)	Percentage Collected
2004/2005	–	–	3,689,351	–
2005/2006	7,715	33,564,305	24,791,783	73.9
2006/2007	8,571	34,017,004	28,921,226	85.0
2007/2008	8,505	33,506,418	27,154,590	81.0
2008/2009	8,612	47,523,580	38,162,866	80.3
2009/2010[1]	8,695	47,381,823	38,162,866	80.5
2010/2011	8,328	46,366,315	37,223,136	80.3
2011/2012	8,400	46,296,217	36,800,000	79.5
2012/2013[2]	8,292	46,052,314	22,307,003	48.4
2013/2014[3]	8,092	44,739,787	23,531,757	52.6
2014/2015[4]	8,131	44,512,943	38,954,777	87.5
Total	83,341	423,960,706	319,699,355	74.5

Source: Adapted from Ministry of Land Reform (2015).

[1] The identical amounts in column 4 for 2008/2009 and 2009/2010 seem unlikely.

[2] In 2012/2013, a general exemption applied because of a severe drought, which may explain the significantly lower collection rate.

[3] The amounts collected for 2013/2014 and 2014/2015 show a significant upward trajectory.

[4] The 87.5 percent collection rate (of amount paid as percentage of amount billed) in 2014/2015 is the highest since the tax was introduced.

Administration

Under the law, the commissioner of inland revenue must issue land tax assessments, and the Department of Inland Revenue (DIR) must administer the land tax. In practice, however, the DIR merely receives land tax payments. Compliance with the letter of the law may be confusing for taxpayers. It is also problematic for the MLR, a ministry with limited or no tax expertise, to administer the tax (issuing payment notices and clearance certificates), as is the practice at present. Furthermore, using qualified valuers to administer the tax is a perverse allocation of scarce skills. Tax collection involves much more than issuing a payment receipt, as is currently the case. The DIR was originally involved only in the design of invoices.

The introduction of the land tax in Namibia in 2004 can generally be described as a success. It was introduced only after significant consultation with and general agreement among all role players. Especially noteworthy was the willingness of the Namibia Agricultural Union, representing predominantly white farmers, to support the introduction of this tax. Despite the issues that resulted in the abandonment of the 2012 provisional valuation roll, all role players, including taxpayers, still seem willing to support this tax if the valuation criteria are revised and if tax rates become more responsive to assessed values.

Presently, the minister of land reform and the MLR are too involved in the administration of the land tax. The collection and enforcement of the land tax should be the sole responsibility of the commissioner of inland revenue and the DIR because the DIR is specifically set up to collect and enforce taxes. However, this does not happen in practice. The current lack of coordination and cooperation between the DVEM and the DIR, as well as noncompliance with the letter of the law regarding the administration of the tax, raises concern.

The Property Tax

The property tax system (called "rates") in Namibia is historically based on the system operative in the former Cape Province of South Africa (Franzsen 2003). The tax is levied only within urban local authorities. Generally, local authorities can decide on any of the following tax bases:

- A general rate on the value of the whole property.

- A site value rate on the value of the land only.

- An improvement rate on the value of the improvement.

- A site and improvement rate on the value of the land and the value of improvements, calculated separately.

- An area rate in settlement areas in rural areas.

Section 79 of the Local Authorities Act rather pragmatically provides that a town or village council may, with the prior approval of the responsible minister for such a financial year or years as the minister may specify, determine and collect a rate (property tax) on taxable property in its area on a basis other than valuation.

Exemptions

The following properties are exempt from the payment of property rates:

- Any land or building or any part of such land or building used exclusively for the principal activities of any church, mission, hospital, school, hostel, or amateur sporting organization and not used for profit or gain, whether directly or indirectly.

- Any land or building or any part of such land or building used exclusively for the principal activities of any state-aided institution or institution aided by any charitable institution.

- Any land or building used wholly and exclusively for the residence of any priest or minister employed full-time by any church or mission.

- Any land used for the boarding and lodging of persons employed full-time on the medical, nursing, and maintenance staff of any hospital.

- Any land used for the boarding and lodging of any pupils or persons employed full-time as teachers or other members of the staff of any school or hostel.

- Any land or building of which the ownership vests in, or that is occupied by, any nonpolitical youth organization that has as its aim the education of the youth or any particular group of youth and development among such youth of the qualities of citizenship.

Although state-owned properties are taxed, a 20 percent rebate applies (other than to dwellings). A rebate of between 60 and 75 percent applies to small holdings of agricultural land within municipal boundaries.

Valuation and Assessment

Municipalities are responsible for identifying and valuing real property for the purposes of taxation. The valuations are compiled into a valuation roll and are used to calculate the rates bill for each property owner in the municipal area. The Local Authorities Act requires that properties be valued every five years for rating purposes. The act stipulates that a valuer shall value any ratable property as follows:

- For the land portion of such ratable property, at a price that in his opinion a willing buyer will be prepared to pay and a willing seller will accept, both acting in good faith.

- For any improvements on such land, on the basis of the estimated costs of the construction or erection of such improvements with due regard to any structural depreciation, obsolescence, or any change of circumstances in the vicinity of such improvements.

In arriving at the land value, the valuer analyzes sales of vacant land and improved properties to determine the likely selling price in each locality. The City of Windhoek has an in-house valuation department. There are about 57,000 ratable properties in Windhoek, and the values for the valuation roll currently in use were last determined in 2010 (City of Windhoek 2016). Private-sector valuers are contracted in all other instances.

Objections and Appeals

The valuer submits the provisional valuation roll to the minister. Any interested person can then inspect the roll at a place and time made known by the minister in the *Government Gazette*. If owners (or the local authority) do not agree with the valuations, they can lodge an objection in writing within 21 days with the valuation court. The valuation court certifies the valuation roll once all objections have been adjudicated. If a taxpayer feels aggrieved by a decision of the valuation court, he can appeal to the High Court.

Tax Rates

Valuations are determined every five years, but the tax rate is determined by municipalities every financial year. Part I municipalities have considerable autonomy in setting their tax rates. They require ministerial approval only if the effective tax rate on the total value exceeds 2.5 percent (Franzsen 2003). Part II municipalities and town and village councils are subject to stricter controls by the Ministry of Regional and Local Government; thus, the tax rates set by these councils must be approved by the responsible minister.

Table 21.5 Tax Rates in the City of Windhoek, 2015/2016

Base	Rate Expressed as a Monthly Tariff	Rate Expressed as an Annual Tariff	Rate as a Percentage
Land ("ground value")	NAD 0.000914	NAD 0.010968	1.10968
Improvements	NAD 0.000471	NAD 0.0056521	0.56521

Source: City of Windhoek (2016).

The City of Windhoek taxes land and improvements separately and sets the tax rate on site value much higher than the rate on the value of improvements as a strategy to encourage property improvement in the municipality (Franzsen 2003). The 2015/2016 tax rates for the City of Windhoek are provided in table 21.5. It is noteworthy that the city expresses and markets the rate as a monthly tariff. A solid-waste-management charge is also levied monthly on every plot in Windhoek. It is based on the collective value of land and improvements, and the 2015/2016 monthly tariff is NAD 0.000186.

In addition to the normal rates, the Local Authorities Amendment Act of 2000 provides for the payment of penalty rates for land that remains unimproved after prescribed periods. It states that

> a local authority council shall levy, in addition to any rate for the financial year and with the prior approval of the minister, a penalty rate—
> - Not exceeding two times the rate levied under section 73(1), on rateable property which remained unimproved for a period of two years or more.
> - Not exceeding four times the rate levied under section 73 (1), on rateable property which has remained unimproved for a period of five years or more.

It is noteworthy that where councils use classified tax rates, the tax rates for the land component are significantly higher than the rate on improvements. This is in line with land taxation theory, which espouses the use of land taxes to encourage more intensive use of scarce land resources. This practice does, however, load a tax onto an unproductive asset that may not be able to be profitably developed because of prevailing market forces or the inability of the taxpayer to plan, fund, or deliver development.

Billing and Collection

The Local Authorities Act provides for monthly billing and collection of rates. The City of Windhoek used to have an early payment incentive discount of 10 percent, but this has been discontinued because of political pressure (Franzsen 2003). Payment of rates has been made simple in Windhoek. The following options are available (City of Windhoek 2016):

- Over-the-counter payments can be made at any First National Bank branch or at any post office countrywide, but a copy of the municipal account being settled is required for this payment option.

- Internet payments can be made through all commercial banks in Namibia.

- Payments of First National Bank clients can be made at automated teller machines.

- Credit and debit card payments can be made at customer care centers at the municipal office in Katutura Township or the city center.

- Payments can be made over the counter at other commercial banks but must reflect the banking details of the city.

Enforcement

To ensure compliance, tax clearance certificates are required before formal transfer of property is allowed. In addition, the Local Authorities Act provides that a local authority may charge interest on any rates not paid on or before the prescribed date at a rate not exceeding the rate prescribed under the provisions of the Prescribed Rate of Interest Act No. 55 of 1975. The law also allows for the seizure and public sale of properties that have been in arrears for at least three years. This measure is apparently not used (Franzsen 2003).

Despite the legal and technical issues with the 2012 provisional valuation roll, the introduction of the land tax on commercial farms was well planned and communicated and must be viewed as a success. In contrast, property rates, on aggregate, provide less than 10 percent of revenue for local authorities and seem underused. Because of the lack of valuation capacity in Namibia, valuation of property remains a challenge, especially for Part II municipalities and smaller councils. Therefore, the pragmatic provision in the Local Authorities Act for a tax base other than value is understandable for small towns and village councils, where an area-based approach is a more feasible and cost-effective option.

References

CIA (Central Intelligence Agency). 2016. "Namibia." In *The World Factbook*. *https://www.cia.gov/library/publications/the-world-factbook/geos/wa.html*.

City of Windhoek. 2016. "City of Windhoek." *www.windhoekcc.org.na*.

CLGF (Commonwealth Local Government Forum). 2015. "The Local Government System in Namibia." *www.clgf.org.uk/default/assets/File/Country_profiles/Namibia.pdf*.

Deloitte. 2015. *Guide to Fiscal Information—Key Economies in Africa, 2014/15. http://www2.deloitte.com/za/en/services/tax/tools-and-publications.html*.

Fjeldstad, O.-H., G. Geisler, S. Nangulah, K. Nygaard, A. Pomuti, A. Shifotoka, and G. Van Rooy. 2005. "Local Governance, Urban Poverty and Service Delivery in Namibia." Bergen: Chr. Michelsen Institute.

Franzsen, R. C. D. 2003. "Property Taxation Within the Southern African Development Community (SADC): Current Status and Future Prospects of Land Value Taxation, Botswana, Lesotho, Namibia, South Africa, and Swaziland." Working paper WP03RF1. Cambridge, MA: Lincoln Institute of Land Policy.

Franzsen, R. C. D., and W. J. McCluskey. 2008. "The Feasibility of Site Value Taxation." In *Making the Property Tax Work: Experiences in Developing and Transition Countries*, ed. R. W. Bahl, J. Martinez-Vazquez, and J. M. Youngman, 268–306. Cambridge, MA: Lincoln Institute of Land Policy.

IMF (International Monetary Fund). 2015. *2014 IMF Government Finance Statistics Yearbook*. Washington, DC.

———. 2016. "IMF World Longitudinal Data (WoRLD)." IMF e-Library Data. *http://data.imf.org/?sk=77413F1D-1525-450A-A23A-47AEED40FE78&sId=1390030109571*.

Jibao, S. 2010. "A Comprehensive Review of the Administration of Property-Related Taxes in Namibia." Draft working paper. African Tax Institute and Lincoln Institute of Land Policy.

Kuusi, S. 2009. "Aspects of Local Self-Government: Tanzania, Kenya, Namibia, South Africa, Swaziland and Ghana." Helsinki: Association of Finnish Local and Regional Authorities. *http://shop.kunnat.net/uploads/p091111111921D.pdf*.

Ministry of Land Reform. 2015. "Land Tax Revenues and Statistics." Internal document.

Mutema, M. 2016. "Property Valuation Challenges in Africa: The Case of Selected African Countries." Paper for the 17th Annual World Bank Conference on Land Policy and Poverty, Washington, DC (March 14–17).

United Nations. 2014. *World Urbanization Prospects*. Washington, DC: Department of Economic and Social Affairs, Population Division.

United Nations, Department of Economic and Social Affairs, Population Division. 2015. World Population Prospects: The 2015 Revision. *https://esa.un.org/unpd/wpp/Publications/Files/World_Population_2015_Wallchart.pdf*.

World Bank. 2016a. "Country and Lending Groups." *http://data.worldbank.org/about/country-and-lending-groups*.

———. 2016b. "GDP per Capita (Current US%)." *http://data.worldbank.org/indicator/NY.GDP.PCAP.CD*.

Legislation

Agricultural (Commercial) Land Reform Act No. 6 of 1995.

Agricultural (Commercial) Land Reform Second Amendment Act No. 2 of 2001.

Communal Land Reform Act No. 5 of 2002.

Constitution of the Republic of Namibia of 1990.

Decentralization Enabling Act No. 33 of 2000.

Deeds Registries Act No. 47 of 1937.

Land Valuation and Taxation Regulations of 2007.

Local Authorities Act No. 23 of 1992.

Local Authorities Amendment Act No. 24 of 2000.

Prescribed Rate of Interest Act No. 55 of 1975.

Property Valuers Profession Act No. 7 of 2012.

Regional Councils Act No. 22 of 1992.

Transfer Duty Act No. 14 of 1993.

22

Niger

BOUBACAR HASSANE, RIËL FRANZSEN,
AND WILLIAM McCLUSKEY

Niger is a Sahelian country in eastern West Africa, bordered by Algeria and Libya to the north, Chad to the east, Nigeria and Benin to the south, and Burkina Faso and Mali to the west. A former French colony and part of French West Africa, Niger gained its independence in 1960. Its area is approximately 1.267 million km², and the estimated population is 19.9 million (United Nations 2015). Niger is a low-income country and is also classified as one of the least developed countries (World Bank 2016a), with a GDP per capita estimated at USD 359 in 2015 (World Bank 2016b). Only 19 percent of the population is urbanized (United Nations 2014).

Government

Niger is a unitary state. Since the country acquired independence, several political regimes have followed one another, along with political upheavals. The 2010 Constitution (of November 25, 2010) replaced the 1999 Constitution. Because of its historic links with France, Niger has continued to maintain the French administrative tradition.

Early in the twenty-first century, Niger embarked on a decentralization process that led to the creation of new territorial units: *regions*, *départements*, and *communes*. Urban and rural communes were established after the first local elections, held in 2004. There are 266 communes in total. However, the traditional chiefdom system is also recognized in Niger, and its status is defined by law. As auxiliaries of the government, traditional chiefs are key players in local governance. They have a significant supporting role in administration, dispute settlement, and the collection of local taxes.

Land Tenure

The legal system is strongly influenced by the French system but coexists with customary law, which continues to prevail in certain areas. Property rights in the sense of the French Civil Code are recognized, as is customary tenure, which is formalized through the Rural Code (1993).

A major problem is the lack of thorough property identification to ensure greater coverage of the tax base. The existing land registry is incomplete and largely ineffective. Large tracts of land, especially in rural areas, are governed by customary law, with uncertainties about the nature of the underlying real property rights. This presents a problem with tenure security that adversely affects property values and the development of a formal property market. The Rural Code adopted in 1993 attempted to formalize and clarify customary land rights. Since that time, a simplified procedure in rural areas has allowed for the allocation of rural land deeds, which have the value of real property deeds. However, implementation of this new system has been slow and in many instances ineffectual. Taking into account the complexity and cost of drawing up land deeds, the government initiated a new system of simplified land deeds in 2006. It is hoped that these will improve tenure security.

Property and Land Taxes

Niger's current tax system is a legacy of colonization by the French, who introduced certain taxes, such as property taxes. This system was adopted when the country gained its independence. The most recent reform, enacted in 2007 and implemented in 2008, consisted of merging the tax on developed land levied on individuals and the property tax applied to legal entities. At the same time, the previous tax on land and property rights (*impôt forfaitaire sur le droit de propriété foncière et immobilière*) was abolished.

The land and property taxes currently imposed in Niger are the property tax and the special tax on capital gains from property transfers. Apart from these two taxes, other levies on property include the following: land registration duties, which cover all duties payable on property transfers and leases, concessions, changes, title deed establishments and mortgage registrations; stamp duties; and the land registrar's fees. The land registration fees were reduced in 2009 and again in 2014 (World Bank 2015). Property taxes as defined by the International Monetary Fund constituted

0.137 percent of GDP in 2005, 0.148 percent in 2006, and 0.144 percent in 2007 (IMF 2016) but only 0.06 percent in 2010 (IMF 2015).

The Property Tax

The property tax (*taxe immobilière*) was introduced by the Finance Law of 2008 and fuses the two preexisting property taxes, the property tax levied on individuals and the property tax applied to legal entities. The following properties are taxable:

- Developed land: houses, factories, workshops, shops, warehouses, garages. Included in this category are structures that are permanent, semipermanent, improved, or ordinary adobe and permanently attached to the ground.

- Uncultivated land and commercial, industrial, or small parcels of land. This category essentially refers to building sites and other similar properties and notably excludes cultivated land, fields, gardens, and orchards. This option appears to be dictated by the specific situation of the country, which is based on agriculture in small farming operations, especially in rural areas. It is believed that the taxation of such operations would hinder the development of agriculture, which already faces many difficulties, and would be a serious obstacle to the attainment of food self-sufficiency, a national priority in Niger. Of course, failure to raise local revenues in rural areas hinders the provision of infrastructure and public services in these areas, which are needed for rural development.

The Tax Base

Although some simplification occurred under the new law, taxable property belonging to individuals is still distinguished from that belonging to legal entities. For individuals, the tax is based on the rental value of buildings or land. Individuals subject to the property tax include the owners of buildings, usufructuaries in case of usufruct, and, in certain cases, lessees. The tax rate for properties owned by individuals is 10 percent for commercial, industrial, professional, and other rented premises and 5 percent for premises used for other purposes, such as residences. For legal entities, the tax is based on the fixed asset value. Property owned by legal entities incurs a tax of 1.5 percent of the value of the fixed asset.

Exemptions

There are several permanent or temporary exemptions. Permanent exemptions include the following:

- Buildings used for public worship, schools and universities, medical assistance or social welfare works, or agricultural operations to house animals or to store crops.

- Buildings belonging to foreign governments and official residences of diplomatic and consular missions accredited by the government of Niger, subject to reciprocity.

- Buildings used as principal residences.

- Ordinary or improved adobe buildings that are not used to generate income.[1]

- Buildings or structures that belong to the state, territorial units, or public administrative institutions and do not generate income.

- Facilities in river ports, airports, or domestic waterways that are subject to public utilities concessions granted by the government to chambers of commerce or municipalities.

- Facilities established to distribute drinking water or electricity belonging to the state or territorial units.

- Buildings belonging to nonprofit organizations and used in carrying out their activities.

- Cemeteries.

- Buildings belonging to property-development companies whose exclusive objective is the construction and sale of buildings.

Temporary exemptions include new structures for two years. In order to benefit from this exemption, the owner must make a formal declaration to the tax authority.

Valuation

The rules for the valuation of property differ depending on whether the property belongs to individuals or to legal entities. The taxable base of property belonging to legal entities is the value of the fixed asset, that is, the value of the building as it appears on the balance sheet in the accounts of the relevant entity. The system is defined by accounting law. The system for valuing the property of legal entities is based on comparing actual leases reflecting rents as of January 1 of the tax year with the rental value of similar properties and administrative estimates. This is an example of piggybacking the difficult valuation aspect of the property tax on an established process and is a pragmatic solution. In practice, however, estimation of the rental value of properties is difficult because the formal rental market is underdeveloped. Most leases are verbal agreements, and formal leases are infrequent. Administrative estimates made by the tax authority are subjective and potentially open to abuse.

Administration

The property tax is a national tax administered by the central government through decentralized offices of the General Tax Directorate. The central government sets the tax rates and controls the collection process. The territorial units, particularly the communes, have no jurisdiction in this regard. The Finance Law provides that the collected revenue is to be shared between the state and the territorial units, 80 percent for the state and 20 percent for the communities. This formula confirms the low level of decentralization in Niger. The notable consequences are the lack of visibility of property taxes at the local level and their low impact on local development and service delivery. Too little revenue trickles down to local government to support local service provision.

Property Tax Issues in Niger

The revenue from property taxes is nominal, constituting less than 2 percent of total revenue from taxes (table 22.1). Despite the low level, income from property taxes is a large proportion of the revenue of the territorial units, for whom mobilization of resources is a serious problem. For example, the revenue remitted to communes accounts for approximately 40 percent of the revenue of the Niamey I Commune, one of the five communes of the capital city, Niamey.

The land and property tax system could constitute a significant source of revenue, particularly for a developing country like Niger, and at the same time support the ongoing decentralization process. However, the recurrent property tax is not presently an important source of revenue. The property tax system in Niger is subject to several problems and constraints. Before 2007, the tax rates on property owned by individuals varied according to the use of the property. The 2008 Finance Law instituted the single property tax and reduced rates to 5 percent or 10 percent of the rental value of property belonging to individuals and 1.5 percent of the fixed asset value of property belonging to legal entities. The current tax rates, as well as the narrow tax base due to excessive exemptions, are areas of concern. Furthermore, taxpayer compliance is an issue. The administration has

Table 22.1 Revenue from Land and Property Taxes (XOF Millions)

Land and Property Taxes	2004	2005	2006	2007
Tax on property belonging to legal entities[1]	1,154.5	1,149.7	1,252.4	1,227.7
Tax on developed land belonging to individuals[2]	261.5	440.1	687.6	734.9
Special tax on capital gains related to property transfer	39.8	50.8	37.4	27.6
Fixed tax on land and property rights[3]	0.0	0.0	9.6	40.8
Total	1,455.8	1,640.6	1,987.0	2,031.0
Land and property tax as a percentage of revenue from taxes[4]	1.8 (79,146)	1.9 (84,554)	1.9 (104,630)	1.5 (130,433)
Land and property tax as a percentage of GDP[5]	0.1 (1,468,393)	0.1 (1,777,043)	0.1 (1,906,837)	0.1 (2,035,386)

Source: Hassane (2009), based on data from the National Institute of Statistics (Institut National de la Statistique) and the General Tax Directorate (Direction Générale des Impôts).

[1] This category refers to direct land and property taxes and excludes other levies related to real estate, such as registration fees and land registry duties.

[2] The Finance Law 2008 instituted a single property tax, which is a fusion of the property tax for legal entities and the tax on properties belonging to individuals.

[3] This tax was collected only in 2006 and 2007 and was abolished in 2008.

[4] The total revenue in XOF millions from taxes for each year is indicated in parentheses.

[5] The gross domestic product (GDP) in XOF millions for each year is indicated in parentheses.

targeted properties belonging to legal entities because they are easier to identify and generally of higher value than properties belonging to individuals. Collection and enforcement efforts are focused on properties located in urban areas, particularly in industrial areas where factories and businesses are located.

A serious problem in Niger is the low level of collection of property taxes. There are several reasons for this: first, identification of taxable properties is difficult because few title deeds are drawn up; second, tax administration is inadequate, and tax officers lack motivation to collect the taxes; and third, public engagement in paying the tax is lacking because of a low benefit correlation. These problems are exacerbated by the absence of effective enforcement measures.

The compliance rate of payment of property taxes is closely linked to the problems in identifying taxable properties and taxpayers. Collection rates for individuals are particularly low and are estimated to be between

15 and 20 percent. For properties belonging to legal entities, the collection rate is estimated at around 95 percent. A further problem is that the tax authority prefers to concentrate its efforts on more profitable taxes such as the single wage tax, the value-added tax, and the corporate income tax. Although the narrow collection focus is administratively defensible and is likely an example of proper allocation of limited resources, it is unfair and may result in taxpayer resentment and even noncompliance.

The tax administration is overstretched and beset by insufficient personnel, inadequate equipment, and logistical problems. The legislation has provided for enforcement processes, but they are rarely implemented. The lack of political commitment, the low level of the tax authority's capacity, the low-compliance culture of the citizens, and corruption among tax officers constitute a substantial obstacle to the collection of property taxes in Niger.

Note

1. Adobe mud blocks are one of the oldest and most widely used building materials. Adobe is a low-cost, readily available construction material, usually manufactured by local communities.

References

CIA (Central Intelligence Agency). 2016. "Niger." In *The World Factbook*. *https://www .cia.gov/library/publications/the-world-factbook/geos/ng.html*.

Hassane, B. 2009. "Property Taxation in Francophone Africa 4: Case Study of Niger." Working paper WP09FAD1. Cambridge, MA: Lincoln Institute of Land Policy.

IMF (International Monetary Fund). 2015. *2014 IMF Government Finance Statistics Yearbook*. Washington, DC.

———. 2016. "IMF World Longitudinal Data (WoRLD)." IMF e-Library Data. *http:// data.imf.org/?sk=77413F1D-1525-450A-A23A-47AEED40FE78&sId=1390030109571*.

United Nations. 2014. *World Urbanization Prospects*. Washington, DC: Department of Economic and Social Affairs, Population Division.

United Nations, Department of Economic and Social Affairs, Population Division. 2015. World Population Prospects: The 2015 Revision. *https://esa.un.org/unpd/wpp/Publi cations/Files/World_Population_2015_Wallchart.pdf*.

World Bank. 2016a. "Country and Lending Groups." *http://data.worldbank.org/about /country-and-lending-groups*.

———. 2016b. "GDP per Capita (Current US%)." *http://data.worldbank.org/indicator /NY.GDP.PCAP.CD*.

Legislation

Constitution of 1999.

Constitution of 2010.

Finance Law of 2008.

Rural Code of 1993.

23

Rwanda

WILLIAM MCCLUSKEY AND JEAN-JACQUES NZEWANGA

The Republic of Rwanda is located in central Africa and is bordered by Uganda to the north, Tanzania to the east, Burundi to the south, and the Democratic Republic of the Congo to the west. It has a land area of 26,338 km². It is one of the most densely populated countries in Africa, with an estimated population of 11.6 million (United Nations 2015), of which only about 29 percent is urbanized (United Nations 2014). The capital is Kigali and its population is 1.1 million (National Institute of Statistics of Rwanda, Fourth Population and Housing Census 2012). In 2015, Rwanda's estimated per capita GDP was USD 697 (World Bank 2016b), thus the country is classified as a low-income country (World Bank 2016a).

Government

Rwanda was part of German East Africa from 1890 until it was occupied by Belgium in 1916. Rwanda gained independence on July 1, 1962, when it was separated from Burundi. The first republic began immediately after independence. Political power changed with coups d'état and military take-overs. The assassination of the president in 1994 unleashed the Rwandan genocide, in which more than 800,000 people were killed. Parliamentary elections were held in 2003, and a new constitution was adopted.

Local government is provided for by the Organic Law of 29/2005 and is enshrined in Chapter 1 of the constitution. There are five provinces. The

Ministry of Local Government is responsible for local government, which comprises four levels: 30 districts, 416 sectors, 2,148 cells, and 14,837 villages. Sources of local revenues include the property tax, the trading license tax, the tax on rental income, and other local nontax revenues such as various user charges, fees, fines, and penalties (IPA 2011; Cyan, Karuranga, and Vaillancourt 2013). The local authorities have been given powers to administer, collect, and set rates or tariffs for both local taxes and nontax sources.[1]

Land Tenure

During the precolonial period, land tenure in Rwanda was characterized by collective ownership of land. During colonial times, land tenure was transformed into a dual system of written statutory law and customary arrangements. The Rwandan National Land Policy, adopted in February 2004, emphasizes an appropriate land administration system as a key to land tenure security through registering and transferring land. The land policy states that "clarification of land rights is required through the development of appropriate land administration systems, which can guarantee the security of land tenure and promote investments in land" (*National Land Policy* 2004). The Organic Law (Property Act) No. 08/2005 of July 14, 2005, Determining the Use and Management of Land in Rwanda specifically calls for registration of land rights. The land policy requires that land be governed by one legal framework, and that the dual legal system based on written law and customary arrangements be abolished.

Article 3 of the Organic Law (Property Act) No. 08/2005, which deals with the property system in Rwanda, states that land forms part of the common heritage of all citizens of Rwanda. Notwithstanding people's acknowledged rights, only the state has a preeminent right to administer all land situated within the national boundaries. Thus, the state alone has the power to grant rights of occupancy and use of the land. Rights to property are granted by the state in the form of a lease. The period of a land lease cannot be less than three or greater than ninety-nine years. The same organic law protects those who acquire land by custom, by a permit granted by the competent authorities, by purchase, or by a long-lease contract in line with the provisions of the organic law. The organic law therefore offers protection to land rights, whether these arise from custom and practice or from written law.

In Rwanda, a distinction is made between urban and rural land. Urban land is land within the jurisdiction of urban districts, as defined by the law. All other land is defined as rural. Private land belonging to individuals comprises land acquired by customary or written law and not included in public lands or in state, district, or town lands. State public property is made up of all land that is given over to public use or public service, together with public lands reserved for environmental protection for the nation's benefit.

The land tenure regularization process under the Rwanda Natural Resources Authority (RNRA), which began in 2008, has now been completed. It is estimated that some 10.3 million parcels have been digitized, demarcated, and adjudicated. Parcel data are contained in the Land Tenure Regularization Database, which has 8.4 million titles, 6.1 million of which have been physically collected. Approximately 90 percent of titles have been collected by owners within the three districts of Kigali: Gasabo, Kicukiro, and Nyarugenge.

The digitization of all parcels throughout the country represents an invaluable resource for the administration of the property tax. Information on the location and size of each parcel of land provides the basic framework for developing a property tax system. The land tenure system is a modification of the Torrens system that is used in Australia and New Zealand (McCluskey 2005). The Register of Titles records the certificates of registration that identify the object that is owned (the parcel), the owner, and the legal ownership rights.

The Lands and Mapping Department within the RNRA has primary responsibility for the registration of land titles. The objective is to establish a decentralized office of the department within each district linked to the Land Administration Information System. The department authorizes a unique property identifier that is allocated to each parcel using the following protocol: province, district, sector, cell, and parcel. It is mandatory that landowners register their land. An order from the minister responsible for land management defines the methods by which land is to be registered. The legal provisions governing the use and management of lands within urban areas, require that a land registry office responsible for land registration is established in each district (Nzewanga 2009).

The Property Tax

As in most African countries, the earliest tax legislation in Rwanda was a legacy from colonial days. For example, the Order of August 1912 set up a proportionate tax system and a property tax. Among the legislative instruments that were altered to adapt to changes in the economic environment was the Act on Property Tax of 1973. The Ministry of Finance and Economic Planning was responsible for administering taxes and customs duties until 1997, when the Rwandan government instituted the Rwandan Revenue Authority and gave it the responsibility for national tax collection.

The government of Rwanda developed the Fiscal and Financial Decentralizations Policy (2006, revised in 2012) and the Law on the Organization and Functioning of the District (2006), which empowers districts to determine rates and collect local taxes and fees, as well as other nontax revenues. The Law No. 17/2002 put in place two taxes and one fee: the property tax, the rental income tax, and business licenses. In order to establish the sources of revenue, strengthen management, and streamline implementation of fiscal decentralization, the following legal instruments were put in place:

- Law No. 51/2011 of December 31, 2011, Establishment of the Sources of Revenue and Property of Decentralized Entities.[2]

- Ministerial Order No. 005/12/10/TC of June 26, 2012, Determination of the Modalities for the Implementation of Law No. 59/2011 of 31/12/2011.

- Presidential Order No. 25/01 of July 9, 2012, which established the list of fees and other charges levied by decentralized entities and determination of their thresholds.

Table 23.1 illustrates the main revenue sources available to districts and their relative importance in RWF millions.

Table 23.1 Districts' Own-Source Revenues, 2011–2012

Revenue Source	Collection	Importance (%)
Land lease fee	4,200	19.5
Rental income tax	3,362	15.6
Trading tax	3,342	15.6
Market fees	3,051	14.2
Public cleaning fee	2,852	13.3
Official document fee	1,464	6.8
Quarry and forest fee	905	4.2
Fixed asset tax	891	4.1
Parking fees	555	2.6
Land and plot fee	310	1.4
Billboard fee	309	1.4
Burning fee	112	0.5
Communication tower fee	94	0.4
Number plate fee	44	0.2
Total	21,491	100.0

Source: Cyan, Karuranga, and Vaillancourt (2013).

A formal property tax in Rwanda was imposed under Law No. 17/2002, which essentially introduced an area-based tax. This tax remained in force until 2012, when Law No. 59/2011 provided for a value-based property tax called the fixed asset tax (FAT).

The Tax Base

The tax base of the FAT is

- the market value of land parcels;

- the market value of buildings and all improvements on the land that have been registered with the Land Registration Office and for which the owner has obtained a freehold title deed;

- the value of land used for quarry purposes; or

- the market value of a usufruct with a title deed.

The legislation defines market value as the "amount of money for which a property should be sold on the date of its valuation in the open market by a willing buyer"; improvements are defined as "immovable structures or amenities that are not buildings but increase the actual value of a parcel of land or a building"; and a building is defined as "an immovable and stable construction that protects humans properties, animals or machinery permanently, or in the long term, from disasters. Buildings also include houses."

Liability for the Fixed Asset Tax

The FAT is assessed on and paid by the owner or deemed owner. The law defines the following persons as deemed owners:

- The holder of a fixed asset where the title deed has not yet been registered in the name of the owner.

- A person who occupies or deals with an asset for at least two years as if he is the owner and as long as the identity of the legally recognized owner of such asset is not known.

- A proxy who represents an owner who lives abroad.

- A usufructuary.

Exemptions

The following assets are exempt from the FAT:

- Fixed assets used exclusively for medical purposes or caring for vulnerable groups, and those meant for educational and sporting activities, where no profit-making activity takes place.

- Fixed assets exclusively intended for nonprofit research activities.

- Fixed assets belonging to the government, provinces, or decentralized entities, as well as public institutions, except those used for profit-making activities.

- Fixed assets used primarily for religious activities, except those used for profit-making activities.

- Fixed assets used primarily for charitable activities.

- Fixed assets belonging to foreign diplomatic missions in Rwanda if their countries do not tax fixed assets of Rwanda's diplomatic missions.

- Land used for agriculture, livestock, or forestry if the area is not more than two hectares.

- Fixed assets and usufructs used primarily for residential purposes if the assessed value does not exceed RWF 3,000,000. If the assessed value exceeds this threshold, only the excess value is taxed.

The Tax Rate

The annual tax is 0.1 percent of the taxable value.

Valuation

If the fixed asset is a developed parcel, the market value is the land value plus the depreciated value of the buildings and other improvements. If a parcel of land, a building, an improvement, or a usufruct has been purchased, the purchase price is taken as the tax base unless it is patently clear that the purchase price is below the market value. The following methodologies for determining the value of the fixed asset have been suggested: (1) If the fixed asset was valued by a valuer certified by the Institute of Real Property Valuers in Rwanda within the past five years and no major changes to the building structures leading to an increase or decrease in value by more than 20 percent have occurred, this value should be recorded. (2) If the fixed asset was bought within the past five years in the open market and no major changes in the building structures leading to an increase or decrease in value by more than 20 percent have occurred, the purchase price should be recorded. (3) If the building was constructed within the past five years, the construction costs plus the value of the land should be recorded. (4) In all other cases, an estimation of the market value should be recorded, which should represent the price for which the owner would be willing to sell the fixed asset to a third party.

Assessment

Every taxpayer must file a tax declaration on the official form in the district where the asset is located not later than March 31 in the first tax year (effectively self-assessment). The district, in addition to collecting the amount of the tax due, shall levy a fine not exceeding 40 percent of the tax due if the declaration form is not submitted, is submitted late, is substantially incomplete, or contains incorrect or fraudulent information with an intent to evade the tax.

The district reviews the tax declaration within six months starting from April 1 of the year the tax declaration was filed. If the tax declaration was filed late, the six-month period starts on the date the district receives it. The review is based on the nature and general state of the fixed asset, its location, and its actual or zoned use. The tax assessment notice contains at least the following information:

- The tax base calculation.

- The calculation of the market value of the relevant fixed asset.

- The calculation of the tax.

- The name of the owner or his proxy.

- The address of the owner, the proxy, or the usufructuary.

- The due date for the tax payment.

- The mode of payment.

- The consequences of late payment or nonpayment.

- A statement of the taxpayer's right to object and appeal.

Market values are reassessed every four years. An owner must file a new fixed asset tax declaration not later than March 31 of the first year of each tax assessment cycle. The tax based on the new self-assessed value should be paid for four consecutive years without the need to file a new tax declaration.

If, because of changes to a fixed asset, the value of that asset increases or decreases by more than 20 percent within an assessment cycle, the taxpayer is required to file a new tax declaration with all details of the changes in the district where the asset is located within one month after the value has changed. Upon receipt of the tax declaration, the decentralized office reviews the new tax declaration and, where applicable, issues a new assessment. Reasons for an increase in value include the upgrading of a building or the addition of floors to a building, general renovation, or extension or improvement of a building. Reasons for a decrease in value include the demolition of a building, in whole or in part, after a natural disaster. A fluctuation of the market value between two general revisions is not a reason for a new assessment.

Objections and Appeals

A taxpayer, his proxy, or a usufructuary may file an objection disputing the calculated market value stated in the tax assessment notice in the decentralized office where the asset is located within one month after receipt. The objection must be in writing, justified, clear, and signed by the taxpayer, the proxy, or the usufructuary. Within two months after receiving the letter of objection, the district must notify the objector of its decision. If the district is satisfied that the objection was justified, it must reimburse the overpaid tax with interest within one month after notifying the taxpayer of the decision. If the district does not notify the objector of its decision within two months, the objection is deemed to be well founded. If a taxpayer remains dissatisfied with the decision of the district, he can lodge an appeal with the competent court. If the court finds that the taxpayer's appeal is justified and that the tax was unfairly imposed, the district must reimburse the overpaid tax and pay accrued interest within one month after the decision has been handed down.

Payment

The tax, as assessed by the taxpayer, must be paid to the district where the fixed asset is located not later than March 31 of the tax year. An objection or appeal against the assessed tax does not relieve the taxpayer of the obligation to pay the tax assessed. When taxpayers exercise their right to object or appeal, they must still pay the total amount of the assessed tax by the due date.

A taxpayer may request that the district authorize payment in installments. Payment in installments cannot exceed a period of 12 months. The taxpayer must submit to the decentralized entity a tax installment payment plan that indicates an immediate payment of at least 25 percent of the tax due. Failure by the taxpayer to make payments in accordance with the conditions of the tax installment payment plan results in the immediate obligation to pay the entire outstanding tax due.

A tax not paid when it is due incurs interest at the rate of 1.5 percent. Interest is calculated on a noncompounding monthly basis, starting from the day the tax should have been paid and including the day of payment. Every part of a month counts as a complete month. A surcharge equivalent to 10 percent of the tax due must also be paid. However, this surcharge shall not exceed RWF 100,000.

If a taxpayer is temporarily unable to pay the tax due because of special circumstances, the council of the district, upon a written request by the taxpayer or his proxy, may grant a deferral of payment for up to six months without any fine. In this case, interest shall be paid on the amount outstanding.

Enforcement

An unpaid FAT is a debt that can be claimed before competent courts. The district where the fixed asset is located has the right to

- attach rent owed by a tenant to the taxpayer up to the amount of tax outstanding;

- attach money owed to or held on behalf of the taxpayer by third parties;

- seize and sell movable assets belonging to the taxpayer; or

- seize and sell fixed assets belonging to the taxpayer.

The Land Lease Fee

The land lease fee (LLF) is an important source of revenue that is fully administered at the district level. It is charged on a parcel of land that is held under a lease and is payable to the district. The amount payable varies according to the land use (residential or commercial) and by district. LLF payers do not receive a written bill but rather are informed through various media that they should make payment within the prescribed time limits. This approach can confuse fee payers and hinder achieving good compliance.

Each district is required to determine the fees to be paid annually on land leases based on the infrastructure in the area where the land is located and according to the land's use. Every four years, the district must publish a document indicating annual fees to be paid on parcels held under land leases in each village within the district. A parcel located in an urban area generally has a levy of between RWF 30 and 80/m^2; rural parcels generally have a much lower levy of around RWF 5 to 10/m^2; parcels located in a trading center are levied at RWF 10 to 30/m^2; and parcels on which trading or industrial activities are carried out are levied at RWF 50 to 80/m^2.[3] These classifications give the district some flexibility in assessing the land fee. Most districts typically rely on the application of only a limited number of rates. This has the advantage of keeping administration simple.

If the area of a parcel is greater than two hectares and it is used for agricultural purposes, an LLF of RWF 4,000/hectare is applied. Parcels of land used for quarry exploitation are also subject to the LLF at a rate between RWF 10 and 30/m^2. The following types of land are exempt from the LLF: (1) land used for agricultural and livestock activities that is less than two hectares in area; (2) land reserved for the construction of houses in rural areas where no basic infrastructure has been installed; and (3) any other land determined exempt by the council of the district.

Tax Collection

In 2013, the government of Rwanda assigned the Rwanda Revenue Authority (RRA) the responsibility to collect decentralized taxes on behalf of districts (RRA 2012). Since 2002, districts had been responsible for collecting own-source revenue from trade licenses, the fixed asset tax, and the rental income tax. However, because of insufficient tax collectors and other challenges, revenues have been lost through an inefficient collection process. The RRA has gained extensive experience in tax collection and has developed efficiencies through the use of technology.

Apart from using the RRA's experience to collect decentralized taxes, the move also aims to establish a one-stop tax center where a taxpayer, a public institution, or any other organization can get information about any tax (Kagarama 2010). Because the law establishing the sources of revenue and property of districts and governing their management has not yet been updated, the Tax Administration and the Ministry of Local Government have signed a memorandum of understanding that gives the RRA the right to collect these taxes on behalf of the districts.

Taxes and fees collected are the primary source of income of districts and must be used in accordance with the districts' budget plan. Districts, for their part, have the responsibility to sensitize taxpayers within their jurisdiction and to develop and implement an education program in association with the Tax Administration.

Property Tax Issues in Rwanda

The relatively low revenue derived from the FAT in Rwanda is primarily related to the few properties that are liable for the tax. Those legally obligated to pay the FAT are those with freehold title to the land. People who develop their land are eligible to apply for a freehold title. However, few people actually claim one because they would then have to pay the FAT. There are clearly problematic issues involving those who pay the FAT and those who currently pay the LLF but should be paying the FAT. There is a strong argument that all owners within urban areas should pay the FAT irrespective of whether they have freehold or leasehold title (IMF 2014).

The FAT relies on owners' self-assessment and self-declaration. Such declarations are normally accompanied by certified appraisals undertaken by valuers approved by the Institute of Real Property Valuers of Rwanda. The valuation reports are comprehensive and in some cases much more detailed than they are required to be. The valuation is based on depreciated costs. Several firms of valuers are used, but they adopt a fairly consistent reporting style. It is difficult to measure the level of uniformity in valuations across similar buildings, largely because of the lack of standardized building costs within specific locations.

The districts and sectors have insufficient skills to effectively manage a value-based property tax system such as the FAT. Even given the small numbers of properties liable for the FAT, there are structural problems with administration: the lack of diligent recording of self-declarations received, inappropriate filing of declarations, failure to capture key information electronically, and the application of incorrect information in determining the amount of the tax. District and sector staffs are not sufficiently trained in valuation to be able to comprehensively understand technical valuation reports.

The FAT rate is 0.1 percent of market value, about a tenth of the commonly levied international rates. This tax rate is extremely low and, because the annual tax revenue is fixed for the four-year assessment cycle, significantly detracts from the importance of the tax. A gradual increase of this rate toward the 1 percent benchmark in the short term would increase local revenues substantially (Kopanyi 2014).

The World Bank (2011) estimates that 67 percent of land in Rwanda (17,647.8 km^2 out of a surface area of 24,340 km^2) is given over to subsistence agriculture; therefore, it will be difficult to raise significant tax revenue from property taxes, particularly in rural areas. The focus of the FAT should be on urban areas where significant high-value property development is occurring.

Owners of property held under freehold title are obliged to self-assess their property. This process can work efficiently but requires quality control to verify the submitted values. The government should establish valuation procedures and protocols with advice from the Institute of Real Property Valuers in Rwanda.

The decision to shift tax-collection responsibility from the districts to the RRA is a positive move. Districts have generally been struggling to administer the FAT. The RRA has capacity and experience in tax collection, as well as the data and resources to provide synergies between the property tax and other national taxes. This should improve tax collection and reduce arrears.

Notes

1. Law No. 17/2002, modified by Law No. 33/2003, and currently Law No. 59/2011, which establish the sources of revenue and the property of decentralized entities and govern their management.
2. These are essentially districts.
3. The actual amount of the fee can vary from district to district because of districts' authority to decide fee rates.

References

CIA (Central Intelligence Agency). 2016. "Rwanda." In *The World Factbook*. https://www .cia.gov/library/publications/the-world-factbook/geos/rw.html.

Cyan, M. R., C. Karuranga, and F. Vaillancourt. 2013. "Local Government Revenue Potential in Rwanda." Atlanta: Andrew Young School of Policy Studies, Georgia State University.

IMF (International Monetary Fund). 2014. "Rwanda: First Review Under the Policy Support Instrument Staff Report and Press Release." Country Report no. 14/185. Washington, DC.

IPA (Institute of Policy Analysis). 2011. "East Africa Taxation Project: Rwanda Country Case Study." Kigali: Institute of Policy Analysis and Rwanda Research.

Kagarama, B. 2010. "Reforms in Domestic Revenue Mobilisation: The Rwanda Revenue Authority Story." Paper presented at the EAD Conference, Nairobi, Kenya.

Kopanyi, M. 2014. "Financing Expansion and Delivery of Urban Services in Rwanda." London School of Economics and Political Science. London: International Growth Centre.

McCluskey, W. J. 2005. "Property Tax Systems and Rating in New Zealand." In *Land Value Taxation: An Applied Analysis*, ed. W. J. McCluskey and R. C. D. Franzsen, 115–146. Aldershot: Ashgate.

National Land Policy. 2004. Kigali: Government of Rwanda.

Nzewanga, J. J. 2009. "Property Taxation in Francophone Africa: Case Study of the Rwanda." Working paper WP09FAB5. Cambridge, MA: Lincoln Institute of Land Policy.

RRA (Rwanda Revenue Authority). 2012. *Annual Activity Report for 2012*. Kigali.

United Nations. 2014. *World Urbanization Prospects*. Washington, DC: Department of Economic and Social Affairs, Population Division.

United Nations, Department of Economic and Social Affairs, Population Division. 2015. World Population Prospects: The 2015 Revision. *https://esa.un.org/unpd/wpp /Publications/Files/World_Population_2015_Wallchart.pdf.*

World Bank. 2011. Rwanda Economic Update, Spring Edition. Washington, DC.

———. 2016a. "Country and Lending Groups." *http://data.worldbank.org/about/country-and-lending-groups.*

———. 2016b. "GDP per Capita (Current US%)." *http://data.worldbank.org/indicator/NY.GDP.PCAP.CD.*

Legislation

Law No. 17/2002 (modified by Law No. 33/2003).

Law No. 59/2011.

Organic Law (Property Act) No. 08/2005 (of July 14, 2005).

24

Senegal

NARA MONKAM

The Republic of Senegal is located in West Africa and has been an independent republic since 1960. It is bordered on the north by Mauritania, on the east by Mali, on the west by the Atlantic Ocean, and on the south by Guinea and Guinea-Bissau and surrounds The Gambia on three sides (The Gambia's fourth border is the Atlantic Ocean). The capital and largest city of Senegal is Dakar. Senegal has an area of 196,190 km² and a population of approximately 15.1 million (United Nations 2015). The urban population is approximately 44 percent (United Nations 2014). In 2015 the estimated per capita GDP was USD 900 (World Bank 2016b). Thus, Senegal is classified as a low-income country (World Bank 2016a).

Senegal's key industries include groundnuts, chemical production, tourism, fisheries, and services (IMF 2008). Most of the population is concentrated in regions of Dakar, Touba, Thiès, Rufisque, Kaolack, M'Bour, and Saint-Louis (United Nations 2008). The city of Dakar has an estimated population of 1 million while the Dakar metropolitan region has a population of about 2.5 million (World Atlas 2015). The other largest cities in Senegal by population are Pikine (about 874,000), Thiès Nones (about 530,000), Saint-Louis (about 176,000), Kaolack (about 172,3000),

---

This chapter is an edited version of Monkam 2009. In regard to property taxes, that paper has not been updated since January 2015.

Ziguinchor (about 160,000), and Tiebo (about 100,300) (World Atlas 2015).

Government Structures and Fiscal Decentralization

Senegal is divided into five levels of administrative units: 14 regions, 45 *départements*, 117 *arrondissements*, 150 *communes*, and 349 rural municipalities ("*communautés rurales*"). Regions are administered by an elected regional council and a state-appointed governor and, as such, remain under the control and authority of the central government. *Départements* and *arrondissements* are strictly administrative entities and wield no independent political power. Communes in urban areas and rural municipalities are administered by elected government officials (Dickovick 2005). According to the Decentralization Law 96-06 (of March 22, 1996) there are two (tiers) levels of sub-national governments in Senegal termed as *collectivités locales*, which are defined as "elected structures of government with some independence from the centre." Such *collectivités locales* encompass on the one hand, the 14 elected regional governments; and on the other hand, two forms of local governments: communes in urban areas and *communautés rurales* (rural municipalities) in rural areas.

Regions are administered by a regional council and by an executive office composed of a president, a first and second vice presidents and two secretaries, all elected within the council. All members of the regional council are elected by direct universal suffrage for a five-year term. Communes in urban areas are governed by a municipal council and an executive office composed of a mayor and one or several deputy mayors elected within the council. As with regions, all members of the municipal council are elected by direct universal suffrage for a five-year term. *Communautés rurales* in rural areas are ruled by a rural council and an executive office that consists of a president and two vice presidents elected within the council. Members of the rural council are also elected for a five-year term.

An area of legislative competence of the regions is to promote economic, educational, social, health, cultural, and scientific development at the regional level while respecting the autonomy and attributions of the communes and *communautés rurales*. In accordance with the 1996 Decentralization Law, the planning, programming, and management of local development strategies fall within the competence of communes; while areas such as land occupation planning, occupation authorization, allocation of national domain lands, investment projects in human capital, maintenance and improvements of public roads, parks and open spaces, come within the competences of rural communities. The 1996 Law also define the assignment of expenditure responsibilities, revenue assignment, and the intergovernmental transfers among local governments.

Land Tenure

Two laws regulate national land tenure and land management in Senegal: the National Domain Law of 1964 (Loi n° 64-46 du 17 juin 1964 relative au Domaine National, Law 64-46) and the Rural Council Law of 1972 (Loi n° 72-25 du 19 avril 1972 relative aux Communautés Rurales, Law 72-25). Under the National Domain Law of 1964, all land not in the public domain that was unregistered or not registered within a two-year grace period became the property of the state as part of the national domain (Law 64-46, Articles 1 and 14). Public domain land includes all land that is registered in the name of the state and that is nontransferable. National domain land consists of all state-controlled land for which a land title has not been issued (Durand-Lasserve and Ndiaye 2008). National domain land represents around 98 percent of the land in Senegal. Hence, since enactment of the 1964 national domain law, the law has not recognized customary land ownership or traditional tenure.

Under the Rural Council Law of 1972, rural councils are given the right to allocate land in rural areas according to customary practice provided the land is efficiently used (Law 72-25, Article 24). Since 1964, however, these lands have been held in the national domain and cannot be sold (Law 64-46). The government is reluctant to lose ownership of national domain land in rural areas because it can maintain control over agriculture, herding, and natural resource management. Hence, parties who receive land allocations have only right of use (Bruce 1998). For land in urban areas, Law 87-11 1987 and Decree 87-271 1987, both enacted in 1987, authorized the sale of national domain lands allocated for housing in urban areas with the aim of encouraging ownership and succession of land (Bruce 1998).

Overall, the current land legislation in Senegal encourages individual private tenure through a formal land regularization procedure in urban areas (Law 64-46, Article 3) but recognizes communally based management and use of the land in rural areas. De facto, however, a considerable portion of land in Senegal, both urban and rural, is still managed through customary land tenure systems. In urban areas, even though the law has not recognized customary rights since the National Domain Law of 1964, customary ownership of land is still widespread (Durand-Lasserve and Ndiaye 2008). Additionally, because the law does not clearly prescribe a framework for applying either national or customary land tenure laws, which are often contradictory, rural councils have unfettered discretion and often use whichever law will benefit wealthy or influential members of the community at the expense of poorer or less influential members (Bruce 1998).

Formal land tenure rights are granted primarily in three forms:

1. The land title (*titre foncier*) provides an individual with full ownership of the land.

2. The lease or *bail* permits occupancy of the state's private domain or national domain land. These leases typically are written for a 30-year term and are renewable.

3. Surface rights (*droit de superficie*) grant property rights for a period of 50 years and can be renewed one time.

Surface rights can be inherited, transferred, and mortgaged. At this time, however, a temporary restriction has been placed on the transfer of surface rights without prior government authorization during the first five years after tenure regularization. Additionally, surface rights fees must be paid in full at the time of delivery. Surface rights can be converted into a land title (*titre foncier*) after the land has been developed and the costs (fees and taxes) attached to the land have been paid in full (Durand-Lasserve and Ndiaye 2008). The procedures required to obtain land tenure rights in Senegal are regulated by Decree No. 91-748 of July 29, 1991, the Code du Domain de l'État (CDE) (1976), and the Commission de Contrôle des Opérations Domaniales (CCOD).

Land-Related Taxes

A property-related tax is any tax on the ownership, occupation, or transfer of property, whether immovable (real property) or movable or personal property (e.g., vehicles, books, and jewelry), and whether tangible (e.g., vehicles and land) or intangible property (shares and rights). In Senegal, the national government levies the following property-related taxes:

- The property transfer tax (*droits d'enregistrement*) is levied on company creation and company mergers; on capital increases, transfer of shares, and transfer of securities; on the sale, lease, exchange, or mortgage of real estate; on the sale or lease of movable property; and on selected transactions, such as transfer of goodwill, financial claims, and sales at auction. It is composed of a proportional rate and a fixed rate.

- The capital gains tax (*taxe de plus-valuer immobilière*) is levied on capital gains derived from the sale of improved or unimproved property and the sale of rights over such property (*droit réel immo-bilier*). Specifically, the tax is imposed on the portion of capital gains that is not the result of the owner's efforts. The seller or the owner of the property is subject to this tax. Capital gains are defined as the difference between the transfer price or market value of either the property in question or the right over the property and the acquisition price.

- Death and gift duties (*droits sur les successions, donations et legs*) are levied on the net value of property transferred by inheritance or inter vivos. The tax rates vary between 3 percent and 50 percent, depending on the relation of the beneficiary to the deceased or the donor.

Other property-related taxes include stamp duties (*droits de timbre*), the tax on vehicles (*taxe sur les véhicules à moteur*), and the special tax on company-owned vehicles (*taxe spéciale sur les véhicules de sociétés*). In 2012, total taxes constituted 19.3 percent of GDP (IMF 2015), but property taxes broadly defined, including transfer taxes, constituted only 0.1 percent of GDP (IMF 2016).

The Property Tax

The current property tax legislation in Senegal is quite comprehensive and is based on the 1996 Decentralization Law. In accordance with the 1996 Decentralization Law and the General Tax Code (GTC) local governments are entitled to levy property taxes and other direct local taxes as part of their own revenue sources. However, the legislation stipulates that the central government assesses, levies, and collects all but a few local taxes, and the proceeds are largely, if not totally, transferred to local governments. Only the following taxes and charges are collected at the local level, specifically at the commune level: the fiscal minimum tax, charges for the use of public places, and advertising charges (Sylla 2008b). Three types of property taxes are levied in Senegal: the tax on improved property (*contribution foncière des propriétés bâties*), the tax on unimproved property (*contribution foncière des propriétés non bâties*), and the surtax on unimproved or insufficiently improved land (*surtaxe sur les terrains non bâtis ou insuffisamment bâtis*). In general, property taxes in Senegal are levied under a value-based system in which assessment is based on the annual rental value or the capital value, depending on the property taxed.

De facto, the Cadastre, one of the eight directorates within the Office of Taxes and Domain (Direction Générale des Impôts et Domaines, DGID), is not yet involved in property identification and valuation and assessment of property. The DGID performs these functions. Currently, the DGID's valuers prepare and maintain the valuation roll with the assistance of local-government officials who are trained by DGID staff. Property identification is based on a manual system. First, the DGID's valuers survey the land, locate and identify taxable properties, and, if possible, collect basic information such as the nature of the property, the name of the property owner or tenant, the number of people living in the house, and the amount of rent. Second, the DGID's agents request from property owners and principal tenants a document providing relevant and detailed information about their property to aid in the identification process.

Finally, using the collected information, the DGID's agents construct a fiscal cadastre, that is, "a compilation of the basic property information necessary for valuation, assessment, billing, collection, and enforcement" (Kelly and Musunu 2000). However, the coverage ratio remains very low in Senegal. According to Sylla (2008b), approximately 40 major cities and 36 communes were entered in the fiscal cadastre in 2008, but coverage had not yet been extended to other smaller communes and rural properties. This poor coverage ratio can be attributed to the following factors: (1) insufficient physical, human, and financial resources; (2) political and religious leaders' use of their influence to exclude their properties from the fiscal cadastre; (3) lack of enforcement against taxpayers who fail to provide required property information forms; and (4) difficulty in identifying owners of unimproved property and insufficiently improved land.

In 2005, Senegal secured a project loan from the African Development Bank to modernize the cadastre and acquire topographic equipment such as total station surveying tools and global positioning systems. This project was called Projet d'Appui à la Modernisation du Cadaster and ended in 2009. A new project called the Urban Property Management Support Project (Projet de Modernisation de la Gestion du Foncier Urbain, PAGEF) is being financed by the European Union and focuses on the automation of land and government property procedures. The purpose of PAGEF is to ensure the availability, reliability, and accessibility of real estate information while ensuring the transparency of the land management framework.

In Senegal, as previously mentioned, communes and rural communities can generate part of their own funding from local taxes and other sources of revenues (AIIDS 2001; Law 96-06, Article 250). Property taxes are an example of local taxes. From the available data, it appears that revenues derived from local taxes, especially property taxes, are limited in general and are far below their potential. Senegal therefore is underusing its property tax capacity. Table 24.1 presents some of the local taxes levied in Senegal from 2008 to 2011. It appears that between 2008 and 2011, the total amount of property tax levied in Senegal represented, on average, approximately 22.7 percent of total local taxes.

Table 24.1 Local Taxes Levied in Senegal, 2008–2011 (in XOF)

Taxes	2008	2009	2010	2011
Tax on the removal of household refuse (TEOM)[1]	6,113,779,682	6,897,341,147	7,890,445,591	8,151,919,820
Property tax on improved property (foncier bâti)	8,946,480,072	10,196,349,370	11,411,364,055	10,829,189,752
Property tax on unimproved property (foncier non bâti)	1,561,119,168	1,776,819,462	1,150,480,562	1,147,341,912
Fiscal minimum tax (minimum fiscal)	7,560,200	6,952,600	6,090,600	14,481,200
License fees (licence)	7,890,000	5,711,000	5,087,000	5,935,000
Single general contribution (CGU)[2]	1,803,685,000	1,603,096,000	1,618,965,750	1,055,662,250
Business tax (patente)	30,568,646,414	31,676,468,021	34,373,449,452	34,510,586,725
Surtax on unimproved property (surtaxe foncière)	698,026,510	9,485,800	488,280,810	513,524,810
Total	49,707,187,046	52,172,223,400	56,944,163,820	56,228,641,469

Source: Senegal/MEF/DGID.

[1] TEOM = taxe d'enlèvement des ordures ménagères.

[2] CGU = contribution globale unique. The single general contribution is levied on enterprises whose annual revenues do not exceed XOF 50 million. Local governments receive 60 percent of the CGU payments, while 40 percent goes to the state.

The Tax Base

As noted previously, three types of property taxes are levied in Senegal: the tax on improved property, the tax on unimproved property, and the surtax on unimproved or insufficiently improved land.

The Property Tax on Improved Property

The assessment of the property tax on improved property, also known as the property tax on developed land or the tax on buildings (GTC, Articles 283–295), is based on the rental value of all developed land containing permanent structures, including factories, on January 1 of the taxable year. The rental value is defined as the value of both land and improvements in terms of the net annual rent that the owner could derive from them (GTC, Articles 290–291).

The GTC permits both permanent and temporary exemptions from the tax on improved property. Permanently exempted properties include buildings or constructions belonging to the state, to municipalities, or to public institutions provided that they are used for a public purpose or provide services of general utility and do not generate revenue; drinking water or electrical power supply infrastructure systems belonging to the state or municipalities; buildings used for worship; buildings used by the owner for educational, health, or social purposes; buildings used to house farm animals or to store agricultural harvests; and residential housing occupied by the owner if the rental value does not exceed XOF 1,500,000 (GTC, Article 285). Temporary exemptions are granted for new construction, remodeling, or additions for five years starting after the year of completion. This exemption does not apply to industrial plants and buildings used for commercial or industrial purposes. To benefit from a temporary exemption, the owner must send a statement to the head of the tax service for the area where the building is situated within four months of the start of construction, specifying the nature of the new building, its location, and its floor area.

The Property Tax on Unimproved Property

The assessment of the tax on unimproved property, also known as the property tax on undeveloped land (GTC, Articles 296–302), is based on the market value of the property on January 1 of the taxable year. The tax legislation in Senegal allows for the following exemptions from the property tax on unimproved property: buildings or constructions belonging to the state or to municipalities provided that they are used for a public purpose or provide services of general utility and do not generate revenue; gardens and tree nurseries created by the administration and agricultural collectives (*sociétés d'intérêt collectif agricole*); undeveloped land used by commercial and industrial companies for purposes related to their specific activities; land surrounding residential housing; land used for recreational activities; land used for worship; and land used by the owner for educational or health purposes.

The Surtax on Unimproved or Insufficiently Improved Land

The assessment of the surtax on unimproved or insufficiently improved land (GTC, Articles 303–307) is based on the market value of the land. The GTC allows exemptions from the surtax on unimproved or insufficiently improved land for land on which building is prohibited, and land whose owners are temporarily deprived of its use for reasons beyond their control.

Assessment and Valuation

The Property Tax on Improved Property

The annual rental value of improved property on January 1 of the taxable year is determined by the cadastral method. The "cadastral method," also called corrected area method (*"méthode de la surface corrigée"*), is conducted by cadastral technicians and experts. This method incorporates elements such as area, number of rooms, existing installations, material used, and age of the building, on which correction coefficients are applied to scientifically determine the rental value. Where the cadastral method fails, values are determined by comparison with other similar premises in the area for which rental values have been recently established. The rental value of the equipment in industrial plants is determined by means of direct appreciation (*voie d'appréciation directe*) as defined by the Ministry of Finance (Sylla 2008a). In accordance with the GTC, for most taxes imposed in Senegal, including property taxes, taxpayers who believe that they have been wrongfully taxed or overtaxed can submit a written claim to a conciliation commission created by the Ministry of Finance within 30 days after an appeal to the competent director has been unsuccessful.

The Property Tax on Unimproved Property

The market value of unimproved property is determined as of January 1 of the taxable year by the cadastral method. Failing that, the market value of unimproved property is assessed on the basis of conveyances (*actes translatifs*) of taxable properties within the past three years. If unimproved land has not been developed for three years, the market value is determined by comparison with other land that is similar in size, quality, and features within the same area and for which the market value was assessed on the basis of conveyances that were less than three years old.

The Surtax on Unimproved or Insufficiently Improved Land

In Senegal, the surtax on unimproved or insufficiently improved land is assessed on the basis of the market value of the land. As noted previously, the market value of the land may be determined by the cadastral method, on the basis of conveyances, or by comparison.

Tax Rates

The Property Tax on Improved Property

The tax rate on improved property is fixed in the legislation by the central government and varies depending on the category of buildings. The tax rate on improved property is 5 percent of the rental value for all properties except industrial plants and factories. For industrial plants and factories, the rate is 7.5 percent.

The Property Tax on Unimproved Property

The tax rate on unimproved property is also fixed in the legislation and is 5 percent of the market value of unimproved property.

The Surtax on Unimproved or Insufficiently Improved Land

In Senegal, differential surtax rates are applied to unimproved or insufficiently improved land according to market value tiers established by each local jurisdiction. Tax rates in communes of the Dakar region and in capital cities of communes in the remaining regions of Senegal vary between 1 and 3 percent according to the assessed market value of the land.

Tax Administration

Pursuant to the GTC and as mandated by the minister of finance, the general director of taxes and domains issues each month a list of all taxpayers in a certain area (a valuation roll or *établissement des rôles*) and transfers the corresponding property tax bill notifications (*avertissements, titres de perception*) to the Treasury's tax officials who are in charge of revenue collection (*receveurs de recettes*). The date on the tax bill notification determines the starting point of the time limit on property tax collection, prescription, and claims. The Treasury's tax officials responsible for revenue collection subsequently make the necessary arrangements to immediately notify taxpayers of their tax liability. The Treasury department in charge of collection of local taxes in Senegal is called Recettes des Perceptions Municipales (GTC 2012, Articles 620, 643–662; Sylla 2008b).

The tax legislation also requires payment of the property tax liability, regardless of its amount, at the latest on the last day of the first month after the month when the valuation roll and the corresponding property tax bill notifications were emitted. However, in the event of permanent departure from Senegal, personal bankruptcy, liquidation subject to supervision of a court, voluntary or mandatory company liquidation, job resignation, or a taxpayer's death, property tax payments are due immediately after issuance of tax bill notifications (GTC 2012, Articles 644–645). If property tax bills are not paid, the tax legislation permits the following enforcement measures against delinquent taxpayers: (1) Interest on arrears equal to 10 percent of the unpaid tax liability can be charged when a tax payment has not been received by the last day of the second month after the month when the valuation roll and the corresponding property tax bill notifications were emitted. Subsequently, an additional interest charge of 10 percent of the principal can be added to the taxpayer's liability if payment is not received within one year after the application of the first interest charge on arrears. (2) Seizure and auction can also be implemented through the following procedures:

- To start the process, the Treasury's tax collector issues a demand notice (*summation sans frais*) giving the taxpayer 12 days to settle the tax debt.

- If after 12 days the tax liability has not been paid, the Treasury's tax collector sends out a warning letter (*commandement*) that is delivered in person to the taxpayer.

- After the issuance of the warning letter, a property seizure order may be obtained. The seizure order directs the Treasury's agents to take possession of all or part of the property.

- Finally, a property sale order is entered.

The following are some of the penalties allowed at different stages of the prosecution of tax evaders in Senegal:

- Warning letter (*commandement*): 3 percent of the tax liability.

- Property seizure (*saisie*): 5 percent of the tax liability.

- Inventory of property under seizure (*recollement*): 2.5 percent of the tax liability.

- Notice of property sale order: 1.5 percent of the tax liability.

- Bill posting: 1 percent of the tax liability.

- Inventory before sale: 1 percent of the tax liability.

- Seized property sale report (*procès-verbal de vente*): 1 percent of the tax liability (GTC 2012, articles 654–662).

Property Tax Issues in Senegal

Low Coverage Ratio

As previously noted, the coverage ratio of property remains very low in Senegal. However, the government has established an adequate legal framework to ensure comprehensive coverage of the property tax, and the Taxation Department is reforming property tax administration to bring this about. These administrative reforms also will help increase the accuracy level of valuations, particularly in places where valuation currently is not being done annually as stipulated by law or as frequently as needed to reflect changes in absolute and relative property market values.

Objections and Appeals

In Senegal, the number of objections and appeals concerning property information, valuation, or tax assessment is very large. Although the large number of objections and appeals can affect local-government budget estimates because of tax abatements and refunds, they nevertheless help update the fiscal cadastre. For instance, when DGID agents are confronted by potential taxpayers who are reluctant to provide detailed information about their property or refuse to make their property accessible to valuers, they intentionally apply a high market or rental value, depending on the property tax type, which results in a high tax liability. By doing so, the agents are relying on the inevitable objections filed by these potential taxpayers to obtain the necessary property information for the fiscal cadastre.

Tax Rates

Even though some aspects of political and fiscal decentralization are currently in place in Senegal, as reflected in elections and intergovernmental transfers to subnational governments, certain shortcomings in the fiscal decentralization process persist. In particular, property tax policy and administrative authority are not devolved to local governments. The central government sets property tax rates, gives no discretion to communes and rural communities, and collects taxes and transfers them to local governments. So far, there has been no evidence that the central government is ready to devolve administration of property taxation to local governments.

Collection and Enforcement

Compliance is not properly enforced in Senegal, especially for the tax on unimproved property and the surtax on unimproved or insufficiently improved land. Furthermore, the Taxation Department has concentrated its administrative resources on collecting property taxes in communes of the Dakar region, where the largest portion of Senegal's economic activity takes place (Sylla 2008b). As a consequence, the potential tax revenue from other communes and rural communities is simply forgone. Adopting an approach that would not only promote voluntary taxpayer compliance but also systematically apply penalties and sanctions as stipulated by law in as many local areas as possible would go a long way toward increasing the collection ratio.

In conclusion, it is apparent that the property tax has yet to become an important own source of revenue in Senegal. Transfers from the central government remain a major source of revenue for communes and rural municipalities alike (Dickovick 2005).

Overall, although the property tax system is somewhat effective in the city of Dakar and the communes in the Dakar region, taxation of rural properties is still impractical in Senegal. According to Kelly (2000), the six major functions of a property tax system—tax base identification, tax base valuation, tax assessment, tax collection, tax enforcement, and dispute resolution and taxpayer service—are related to four fundamental ratios: coverage, valuation, tax rate, and collection. As the property tax system is currently practiced in Senegal, the coverage, valuation, and collection ratios have been low. Nevertheless, there is tremendous potential for improving basic property tax administration through an increase in these ratios. If the property tax in Senegal is properly administered, it clearly has the potential to become an important source of revenue.

For the most part, poor tax administration in terms of coverage, valuation, collection, and enforcement ratios account for the fact that property tax is not used optimally as an important own source of revenues for local governments in Senegal. However, the potential is enormous and can be tapped if the Taxation Department implements its tax administration reforms, and if these reforms are synchronized with a broader fiscal decentralization effort.

References

AIIDS (Amicale des Inspecteurs des Impôts et Domaines du Sénégal). 2001. *Les impôts locaux.* L'impôt 2e Trimestre, no. 9.

Bruce, J. W. 1998. "Country Profiles of Land Tenure: Africa, 1996." Research paper no. 130. Madison: University of Wisconsin–Madison, Land Tenure Center.

CIA (Central Intelligence Agency). 2016. "Senegal." In *The World Factbook. https://www.cia.gov/library/publications/the-world-factbook/geos/sn.html.*

Dickovick, J. T. 2005. "The Measure and Mismeasure of Decentralisation: Subnational Autonomy in Senegal and South Africa." *Journal of Modern African Studies* 43(2): 183–210.

Durand-Lasserve, A., and S. Ndiaye. 2008. "The Social and Economic Impact of Land Titling Programmes in Dakar, Senegal." In *Main Findings of the Socioeconomic Survey in Five Settlements in Dakar and Pikine.* Oslo: Ministry of Foreign Affairs, Government of Norway.

IMF (International Monetary Fund). 2008. "Senegal: Selected Issues." IMF Country Report No. 08/221. Washington, DC.

———. 2015. *2014 IMF Government Finance Statistics Yearbook.* Washington, DC.

———. 2016. "IMF World Longitudinal Data (WoRLD)." IMF e-Library Data. *http://data.imf.org/?sk=77413F1D-1525-450A-A23A-47AEED40FE78&sId=1390030109571.*

Kelly, R. 2000. "Designing a Property Tax Reform Strategy for Sub-Saharan Africa: An Analytical Framework Applied to Kenya." *Public Budgeting and Finance* 20(4): 36–51.

Kelly, R., and Z. Musunu. 2000. "Implementing Property Tax Reform in Tanzania." Working paper WP00RK1. Cambridge, MA: Lincoln Institute of Land Policy.

Monkam, N. 2009. "Property Taxation in West Africa: Case Study of Senegal." Working paper WP09FAA3. Cambridge, MA: Lincoln Institute of Land Policy

Sylla, M. 2008a. *Cours sur les impôts locaux.* Dakar: Direction Générale des Impôts et des Domaines, Centre des Grandes Entreprises.

———. 2008b. Personal interview with head of tax collection for the Large Taxpayer Unit, Office of Taxes and Domains (Recouvrement, Centre des Grandes Entreprises à la Direction Générale des Impôts et Domaines), Dakar, Senegal (November 27).

United Nations. 2014. *World Urbanization Prospects.* Washington, DC: Department of Economics and Social Affairs, Population Division.

United Nations, Department of Economic and Social Affairs, Population Division. 2015. World Population Prospects: The 2015 Revision. *https://esa.un.org/unpd/wpp/Publications/Files/World_Population_2015_Wallchart.pdf.*

World Atlas. 2015. "Senegal Facts." *www.worldatlas.com/webimage/countrys/africa/senegal/snfacts.htm.*

World Bank. 2016a. "Country and Lending Groups." *http://data.worldbank.org/about/country-and-lending-groups.*

———. 2016b. "GDP per Capita (Current US%)." *http://data.worldbank.org/indicator/NY.GDP.PCAP.CD.*

Legislation

Code du Domain de l' Etat (CDE). 1976. La loi n° 76-66 du 2 juillet 1976 portant Code du domaine de l'Etat. *Journal Officiel de la Republique du Sénégal*, no. 4056 (July 28).

Decree 87-271. 1987. Decree No. 87-271 of March 3, 1987, on the Implementation of the Law Authorizing the Sale of National Domain Land for Housing Located in Urban Areas. Le décret n° 87-271 du 3 mars 1987 portant application de la loi autorisant la vente des terrains domaniaux destinés à l'habitation situés en zones urbaines. *Journal Officiel de la Republique du Sénégal*, no. 5164 (March 14).

Decree 91-748. 1991. Décret n° 91-748 du 29 juillet 1991, projet de décret organisant la procédure d'exécution des opérations de restructuration foncière des quartiers non lotis des limites des zones déclarées de rénovation urbaine. Republic of Senegal, Ministry of Economy and Finance.

General Tax Code (GTC). 2012. Code général des Impôts (CGI), Loi n° 2012-31 du 31 décembre 2012 publiée au J.O. n° 6706 du 31-12-2012. Dakar: Direction Générale des Impôts et des Domaines du Sénégal. *http://www.gouv.sn/IMG/pdf/cgi2013.pdf*.

Law 64-46. 1964. National Domain Law of 1964 (Loi n° 64-46 du 17 juin 1964 relative au Domaine National). Republic of Senegal. *www.impotsetdomaines.gouv.sn//index.php?option=com_content&task=view&id=23&Itemid=45*.

Law 72-25. 1972. Rural Council Law of 1972 (Loi n° 72-25 of 19 avril 1972 relative aux Communautés Rurales). Republic of Senegal.

Law 87-11. 1987. Law no. 87-11 of February 24, 1987, Authorizing the Sale of National Domain Land for Housing Located in Urban Areas. La loi n° 87-11 du 24 février 1987 autorisant la vente des terrains domaniaux destinés à l'habitation situés en zones urbaines. *Journal Officiel de la Republique du Sénégal*, no. 5164 (March 14).

Law 96-06. 1996. Decentralization Law no. 96-06 of March 22, 1996 (Loi n° 96-06 du 22 mars 1996 portant Code des Collectivités Locales). Republic of Senegal. *www.gouv.sn/IMG/pdf/code-colleclocales- sen.pdf*.

Law 96-07. 1996. Decentralization Law no. 96-07 of March 22, 1996 (Loi n° 96-07 du 22 mars 1996 portant transfert de compétences aux régions, aux communes et aux communautés rurales). Republic of Senegal. *www.sendeveloppementlocal.com/LOI-N-96-07*.

25

Sierra Leone

SAMUEL JIBAO

Sierra Leone is located on the west coast of Africa and is bordered by Guinea to the north and northeast, Liberia to the south and southeast, and the Atlantic Ocean to the west. The country gained independence from the British on April 27, 1961. It has a land area of 71,740 km². Freetown is the capital city. Other major cities include Bo in the south, Kenema in the east, and Makeni in the north. It has an estimated population of 6.5 million people (United Nations 2015) with an annual average growth rate of 2.6 percent. Approximately 40 percent of the population is urbanized (United Nations 2014).

Sierra Leone, a low-income country (World Bank 2016a), recorded impressive GDP growth rates of 6 percent in 2011, 15.2 percent in 2012, and 20.1 percent in 2013 after the start of iron ore production in 2010. The country's growth rate in 2013 was higher than that of any other country in sub-Saharan Africa for that year. However, the country continues to be one of the poorest in the world and ranked 183rd out of 187 countries on the United Nations Human Development Index of 2013 (UNDP 2013). About 70 percent of Sierra Leone's population lives on less than USD 1.00 per day.[1] The country's GDP per capita was estimated at USD 653 in 2015 (World Bank 2016b). Agriculture, which includes forestry, fishing, and hunting, continued to account for more than half of GDP in 2014, but its relative weight has been declining (50.5 percent in 2014, down from 58.2 percent in 2009), indicating a structural shift toward mining and quarrying (20.2 percent in 2014, up from 3 percent in 2009). Manufacturing accounted for a mere 1.6 percent of GDP in 2014, largely unchanged since 2009. The Ebola epidemic, which lasted from mid-2014 to the end of 2015, has had a devastating effect on the country's economic growth and social development (World Bank 2014).

Government

Administratively, Sierra Leone has a two-tier system of government, the central government and 19 local councils (the 5 city councils, Bonthe Municipality, and 13 district councils). The 13 district councils comprise 149 chiefdom councils. Chiefdom councils are tiers of local governments underneath the local councils that should, by law, collect certain revenues and share them with the local councils (Tommy, Franzsen, and Jibao 2015). In principle, the chiefdom councils are not recognized as a level of government, but there are provisions in the Local Government Act of 2004 that mandate that the chiefdom councils administer some key revenue sources and share the revenue with the local councils.

Land Tenure

Sierra Leone has multiple land tenure systems. Customary land law and practices are largely based on imported legislation and some locally enacted legislation. There is also a range of categories of land ownership in Sierra Leone, including state land, private land, communal land, and family land (*National Land Policy* 2005). State or public lands are defined as lands ceded by the colonial government to the government of Sierra Leone after independence in 1961, unoccupied land, and land compulsorily or otherwise acquired by the government. Private land is land in which the owner has a freehold interest.[2] Communal land, sometimes referred to as chiefdom or community land, is land held in trust by the chief on behalf of the community. Family land is land of which the principal interest is vested in a family group with a common ancestry. In the provinces, communal and family lands predominate, although private freehold tenure is progressively creeping into the tenure system, particularly in the urban centers. Informal settlements constructed on urban and peri-urban land in and around the capital city, Freetown, are subject to both statutory and customary tenure systems.

The Ministry of Lands, Country Planning, and the Environment is charged with institutionalizing and facilitating access to land and developing a rational and relatively orderly system of land administration. Despite this recent intervention, the lands sector has continued to be beset by major problems, including general indiscipline in land transactions, evidenced by land encroachments, falsification of documents, multiple sales and registrations of the same land, and unauthorized or haphazard development;[3] and the absence of clearly defined political, administrative, government, and private property boundaries. These lapses in land administration have resulted in inadequate security of land tenure, land conflicts, and protracted litigation. Furthermore, there is inadequate institutional capacity in the governance of land use and land tenure issues. Because of the weak regulatory framework, limited oversight, and intense speculation in the Sierra Leone land market, landowners are highly vulnerable to pressure from investors (Tommy, Franzsen, and Jibao 2015).

Land-Related Taxes

Table 25.1 summarizes the taxable base, the tax rates, and the taxing authorities for each of the property-related taxes in Sierra Leone.

The Capital Gains Tax

Legally, administration of the capital gains tax is guided by the Income Tax Act of 2000 as amended. Section 57(1) of the Income Tax Act of 2000 provides that gains realized or losses incurred on the disposal of business or investment assets are taken into account in determining chargeable income. This provision in the Income Tax Act is rarely implemented owing, in part, to the weak administrative capacity of the Revenue Authority, but also because no organized property market exists in the country.[4] Because of the difficulties in the administration of the tax due to the huge informal market in property, the Finance Act of 2007 mandated that the "purchaser of real property shall withhold tax at the rate specified in Part IV of the First Schedule," which was amended to read 10 percent of the sales value.[5]

The Stamp Duty

The stamp duty is applied to documents, such as conveyance documents concerning land transfers, bonds, debentures, covenants, and warrants. The transfer of an interest in real property from one natural person to another by means of an instrument called a deed must be registered at the office of the registrar general. The registration process involves the payment of a stamp duty of 0.1 percent.

Estate Duty and Gift Taxes

No estate duty is levied in Sierra Leone, and no donation or gift tax is applied because they are not provided for in the law.

Table 25.1 Taxes Applied to Land and Improvements in Sierra Leone

Tax	Tax Base	Basis for Determining Ratable Value	Tax Rate	Taxing Authority	Payment Due
Capital gains tax	Real property when sold	Gains realized or losses incurred on the disposal of business or investment assets	Added to the chargeable income for income tax purposes, charged at 30% after deduction of a specified threshold amount	Central government	Once, as part of the income tax
Stamp duty	Any transfer of registered land or other property rights	Formula based	0.1%	Central government	At the time of transfer of rights
Lease rent	Lease value	Lease value	10% of value	Central government	Annually
Recurrent property tax (city rate or town rate)	Buildings, whether occupied or unoccupied	Area based plus adjustment factors	Multiple rates	Subnational governments	Two installments annually

The Property Tax

Section 45(1) of the Local Government Act of 2004 stipulates that local councils shall be financed from three sources: own revenue collections; central-government grants for devolved functions; and transfers for services delegated by central-government ministries. The primary sources of own revenue are defined as the local (poll) tax; property rates; licenses; fees and charges; a share of mining revenues; interests and dividends; and any other revenue due to the government but assigned to local councils by statutory instrument by the minister responsible for finance. At that time, qualified valuation staff were in short supply, existing records were poor, computers were not used, and the rate of tax defaults was very high. In addition, there were no internal instructions or manuals for valuers (Tommy, Franzsen, and Jibao 2015). Immediately after the decentralization reforms, city-council governments, which lacked significant tax administrative capacity, relied heavily on market duties, which were relatively easy to collect. The remaining revenue came from property taxes, business registration fees, licenses, miscellaneous fees and charges, and the local poll tax (Jibao and Prichard 2011; Prichard and Jibao 2010). The property tax as a percentage of GDP is extremely low (less than 0.1 percent) owing to inadequate capacity and the small coverage of the tax (table 25.2). In 2010, this tax was effectively administered in the major cities of Bo, Kenema, Makeni, and Freetown. Despite the low ratio of the tax to GDP, there has been significant improvement in the collection of this tax in the city councils, as shown by the upward trend in the ratio between 2008 and 2010.

Table 25.3 also shows that the property tax became an increasingly important source of local-government revenue from 2006 to 2010, increasing by a quite remarkable 300 to 500 percent in the city councils of Kenema, Bo, Makeni and Freetown, a striking achievement. However, these gains

Table 25.2 The Property Tax as a Percentage of GDP

Year	Total Property Tax Revenue (Millions of SLL)	GDP at Current Market Price (Millions of SLL)	Property Tax as Percentage of GDP
2005	1,017.35	4,307,570	0.024
2006	914.73	4,875,079	0.019
2007	969.17	5,825,084	0.017
2008	1,355.6	6,538,014	0.021
2009	3,635.83	7,340,925	0.050
2010	3,868.79	7,605,300	0.051

Table 25.3 The Property Tax as a Share of Own Revenue in Selected City Councils, 2005–2010

Council	2005	2006	2007	2008	2009	2010
Kenema City	17.0	9.9	13.7	17.1	20.7	21.1
Bo City	13.2	10.5	11.0	13.4	21.6	27.5
Makeni City	0.0	2.1	13.7	17.8	20.3	41.8
Freetown	45.1	38.9	49.8	51.2	28.3	55.9
Bonthe Municipality	0.0	8.3	45.0	12.9	12.9	23.8
Sembehun City	0.0	1.7	10.9	6.9	0.0	0.0

Source: Calculations using Local Government Finance Department data.

occurred from a very low base, and overall revenue yields remain far from sufficient to meet local expenditure requirements (Jibao and Prichard 2013). Sembehun City and Bonthe Municipality have yet to implement any major reform in their property tax administration because of the lack of political commitment (Jibao and Prichard 2011).

The success story in the city councils of Kenema, Bo, Makeni, and Freetown is due to the massive reform programs undertaken by the local councils with the help of the Local Government Finance Department and the financial and technical support provided by the World Bank and the United Nations Development Programme (UNDP).[6] Stakeholder reports indicate that the new software has limited the potential discretionary power exercised by tax collectors and the council, thus reducing corruption and increasing trust among taxpayers (Jibao and Prichard 2011). The reform programs have been very successful in generating more property tax revenue in the smaller city councils, but all indications are that there has been little or no systematic modernization of tax-collection methods in Freetown, and increased property tax collection and revenue gains by the Freetown City Council have come from a small group of large taxpayers rather than greater coverage, compliance, and transparency (Jibao and Prichard 2011).

As of 2010, the property tax was limited to the major city councils. District councils have no accurate database to support levying of property rates. In the councils where such data exist, the lists of properties are incomplete and out of date, the ownership or occupancy of many of these properties is unknown, and the valuations are very old. Another problem is that no valuation officers are available in these councils. Besides, officials in these councils believe that most of the buildings located within their jurisdiction are makeshift structures and that most of the good properties were burned down during the 10 years of civil war. Recognizing these problems, the Local Government Finance Department (LGFD) has initiated the development of a property cadastre and business license register in certain district councils with the support of donors such as the World Bank, the European Union, and the UNDP.

The Tax Base

Under Section 75(1) of the Local Government Act of 2004, the property tax (known as the city rate in Freetown and the town rate in other urban towns) is levied on buildings, whether occupied or unoccupied. It covers all buildings within a locality, including buildings owned or occupied by the government or the local council. However, buildings used for charitable purposes, public religious worship, public hospitals and clinics, public educational purposes, cemeteries and crematoriums, and diplomatic missions as may be approved by the ministry responsible for foreign affairs are exempt. Vacant land, whether in rural or urban areas, is not subject to the property tax. However, individuals who lease government-owned land pay lease rent.

Although the tax base includes government buildings, whether owned or occupied, the government has not been paying property tax for the buildings it owns. It seems that councils agree not to levy the tax on government-owned buildings in return for not having to pay whatever they may owe to the central government. Although this study could not ascertain who benefits more from this informal arrangement because of the paucity of tax liability data at both levels of government, it can be speculated that because the central government is much larger and owns much property, it is more likely to benefit from this arrangement.

Assessment and Valuation

Under the Local Government Act of 2004, councils are to appoint valuers and an assessment committee to compile the valuation list. The assessment committee consists of such members of the council as the council may decide. Unlike the smaller city councils that have been undertaking general revaluation exercises that involved updating assessments of properties,[7] the Freetown City Council has not revalued its properties for the past two decades even though the act provides that this exercise is to be carried out every five years.[8] The smaller city councils have a valuation department with at least one valuer trained by an expert valuer under a program supported by the UNDP and the LGFD. The Freetown City Council has a valuation department consisting of about 16 surveyors who are trained only in measuring the size of buildings. Valuation and assessment have been carried out entirely manually in the Freetown City Council.

The Local Government Act of 2004 requires that the property tax be levied on the assessed annual value of assessed buildings,[9] but the Freetown City Council still uses an adjusted area-based method in which the effective floor area is combined with the property category to determine the ratable value of a property. Each property category has an attached tariff that allows the council to differentiate between properties. To determine the property tax rate, the ratable value is multiplied by the so-called rate call, which is currently set at 10 for domestic properties and 20 for commercial properties. Although this method of valuation is relatively simple, it is highly inaccurate and generally regressive because it does not take location, which influences the value of property, into account. The smaller city councils include in their computation of the value of the property several additional characteristics, such as the dimensions of the structure; the type of materials used (timber, mud, corrugated iron sheets, or bricks); location and accessibility (access to roads, hospitals, water, and electricity); and the comfort of or facilities in the property. This approach ensures a more progressive and buoyant set of values but cannot entirely eliminate some degree of subjectivity.

There is currently no clearly defined mechanism for objections and appeals. Section 73(1) of the Local Government Act, however, states that objections to, and amendments of, any valuation list or roll shall be determined and made in accordance with such procedures as the minister responsible for local government may prescribe. This has not happened to date.

Tax Rates

In Sierra Leone, rate setting is guided by Section 69(1) of the Local Government Act of 2004. This act mandates that the property rates provided for in the estimates of a local council in any financial year shall be a uniform rate on the assessed annual value of assessed buildings and a single rate for each class of assessed buildings. The act is not clear about how "classes of buildings" should be interpreted but implies that each council can set its own rates on each class of assessed buildings.

However, Section 76 of the Local Government Act of 2004 mandates that such rates are subject to guidelines issued by the national government. Currently, two classes of assessed buildings exist in the city councils: domestic and commercial. Domestic property is defined as property that does not have financial profit as its primary aim, whereas commercial property is defined as property that has that aim. As previously noted, the current annual rate is 10 times the valuation for domestic properties and 20 times the valuation for commercial properties.[10] In principle, the budget profile of the council determines the rate call or mill rate, which should vary from council to council because budget profiles vary by council. In practice, however, all councils using the cadastral system have a uniform rate and similar classes of assessed buildings despite variations in characteristics of the councils in size, poverty level, and the capacity of the council to generate revenues. Clearly, the donor-driven cadastral system, coupled with weak capacity among councils, has eroded the level of local autonomy the Local Government Act of 2004 anticipated or mandated.

Billing, Collection, and Payment

In principle, collecting the property tax should be easier than collecting other local taxes because the taxable entity cannot be moved. In practice, however, property tax collection in Sierra Leone has been very difficult because of a lack of capacity, poor record keeping, and weak enforcement of tax laws. Because of the lack of automation in the Freetown City Council, demand notices are generated manually and handed over to staff of the unit to deliver by hand. The incentive package for staff members who distribute demand notices is USD 1.60 per week, which is grossly inadequate to motivate efficient delivery. In addition, the poor numbering of houses in Freetown hampers effective delivery of demand notices. Demand notices are distributed twice a year in line with the tax payment schedule stipulated in the Local Government Act, but there is no robust system at the Freetown City Council to determine the number of demand notices delivered and answered by taxpayers.

Unlike the Freetown City Council, the smaller cities are now able to generate demand notices electronically, which they distribute to taxpayers. Major administrative reforms in these cities since 2008 have led to the naming of streets and the numbering of properties and houses. In addition, the property tax is now to be paid through the banking system. This can be seen as an improvement, but it poses problems for those property owners who have to pay very small amounts of tax. The long waiting lines at the banks are a barrier to voluntary compliance. The Local Government Act allows payment of the property tax in two or more equal installments. Door-to-door collection of taxes has also been an effective means to enhance property tax revenues, especially in district councils (e.g., Bo District, Koinadugu, and Kono). Apparently, many people are normally more comfortable dealing with a person at the door than making a journey (Tommy, Franzsen, and Jibao 2015).

Enforcement

The Local Government Act mandates that in case of nonpayment of the property tax, the mayor of the city council may order the bailiff to seize the property and sell it by public auction to the highest bidder within 20 days. If the full amount of the property tax payable is not realized after this process, the law mandates that the mayor issue another warrant requiring the bailiff to demand payment of the unrecovered part of the property tax from the occupier (if any) of the building.

In principle, enforcement appears straightforward because the government frequently knows the location of the property owner and has direct access to the property in case of noncompliance. In reality, enforcement of the property tax is weak, reflecting poor record keeping and weak human resource capacity. However, it is widely believed that the primary barrier to enforcement is the politicization of the system. Although it is reported that the names of delinquent taxpayers are occasionally published in local newspapers, court actions against defaulters have been very rare because of lack of political will, since most property owners are wealthy and have strong connections with the political elite (Jibao and Prichard 2011). This unfortunate situation is consistent with experiences elsewhere, because strong ties between large landowners and political elites have been widely viewed as the primary explanation for weak property tax collection in developing countries (Bird 1974, 1991).

Property Tax Issues in Sierra Leone

Even though much progress has been made in the implementation of the property tax, especially in the major cities, the revenue from this tax remains suboptimal. One of the obstacles in its implementation is the lack of any open and transparent property market, which impedes recording of transaction prices.

Another issue is the effort by local governments and donors alike to expand the coverage of the property tax to district councils. Although this is commendable, there are many limitations to such expansion, including the following:

- Poor service delivery in these communities.

- High levels of poverty, with some 70 percent of the population (of which 80 percent live in rural areas and 20 percent in the capital city, Freetown) living on less than USD 1.00 per day (*PRSP* 2005).

- Weak capacity among council administrators.

- A weak political link between council administrations and chiefdom administrations, which severely undermines the successful implementation of this tax at district and chiefdom levels.

State actors need to focus resources on consolidating the gains already made in the implementation of this tax at the city-council level and to ensure that punitive measures are in place for cities that are slow to implement reforms, such as the Freetown City Council.

Finally, it is necessary to undertake a gradual expansion of the property tax to district and chiefdom levels. Priority must be placed on improving collection, valuation list coverage, and determination of proper property values. However, without a system of effective collection and enforcement, there is little to be gained from increasing base coverage and valuation.

Notes

1. The levels are 15 percent in Freetown and 79 percent in the rest of the country.
2. Private land is dominant in the western area and the major cities in Sierra Leone.
3. The indiscipline in land transactions is due to improper survey practices, the lack of reliable maps and plans, and the resulting use of unapproved, old, or inaccurate maps.
4. Organized entitles to support a property market, such as valuers (appraisers), estate agents, and advertising outlets to ensure the adequacy and accuracy of information for buyers and sellers, are nonexistent.
5. This act implicitly replaced the capital gains tax with a property transfer tax. There is some ambiguity in the implementation of this tax in Sierra Leone, to the extent that the terms *property transfer tax* and *capital gains tax* are used interchangeably.
6. The reforms involve identification and valuation of new and existing properties through geographic information systems; introduction of tax identification numbers; and software that applies preconfigured parameters in order to generate a tax assessment and a rate demand notice based on property details supplied by valuers.
7. This has occurred only once, though, as part of the ongoing reform process within the smaller councils.
8. However, when new properties are identified within the city, the valuation department values them.
9. The term *assessed annual value* is not defined in the act. It was defined in the repealed Freetown Municipality Act 1973 and similar acts for the other urban areas as "the amount at which the premises can reasonably be expected to be let in the open market in an average year."
10. In Freetown City, rates are referred to as "rate calls," while the other councils refer to rates as "mills." The difference is that most other councils have implemented the cadastral system that provides for mill rates, while Freetown has yet to implement the cadastral system.

References

Bird, R. 1974. *Taxing Agricultural Land in Developing Countries.* Cambridge, MA: Harvard University Press.

———. 1991. "Tax Administration and Tax Reform: Reflections on Experience." In *Tax Policy in Developing Countries*, ed. J. Khalizadeh-Shirazi and A. Shah, 38–56. Washington, DC: World Bank.

CIA (Central Intelligence Agency). 2016. "Sierra Leone." In *The World Factbook. https:// www.cia.gov/library/publications/the-world-factbook/geos/.sl.html.*

Jibao, S., and W. Prichard. 2011. "Rebuilding Local Government Finances After Conflict: The Political Economy of Property Tax Reform in Post-conflict Sierra Leone." Unpublished paper.

———. 2013. "Rebuilding Local Government Finances After Conflict: The Political Economy of Property Tax Reform in Post-conflict Sierra Leone." Working Paper no. 12. London: International Centre for Tax and Development.

National Land Policy. 2005. Freetown: Ministry of Lands and Country Planning, Government of Sierra Leone.

Prichard, W., and S. Jibao. 2010. "Building a Fair, Transparent and Inclusive Tax System in Sierra Leone." Country report. Sierra Leone: Christian Aid Sierra Leone.

PRSP (Poverty Reduction Strategy Paper). 2005. Freetown: Ministry of Economic Development and Planning, Government of Sierra Leone.

Tommy, A., R. C. D. Franzsen, and S. Jibao. 2015. "Property Taxation in Sierra Leone: Current Practices, Performance and Options for Reform." Paper presented at the International Institute of Public Finance Conference, Dublin, Ireland (August).

UNDP. 2013. Human Development Report. United Nations Development Programme. New York.

United Nations. 2014. *World Urbanization Prospects.* Washington, DC: Department of Economics and Social Affairs, Population Division.

United Nations, Department of Economic and Social Affairs, Population Division. 2015. World Population Prospects: The 2015 Revision. *https://esa.un.org/unpd/wpp /Publications/Files/World_Population_2015_Wallchart.pdf.*

World Bank. 2014. *World Development Indicators.* Washington, DC.

———. 2016a. "Country and Lending Groups." *http://data.worldbank.org/about/country -and-lending-groups.*

———. 2016b. "GDP per Capita (Current US%)." *http://data.worldbank.org/indicator /NY.GDP.PCAP.CD.*

Legislation

Finance Act of 2007.

Income Tax Act of 2000.

Local Government Act of 2004.

26

South Africa

RIËL FRANZSEN

South Africa is bordered by the Atlantic Ocean on the west and by the Indian Ocean on the south and east. Its neighbors are Namibia in the northwest, Zimbabwe and Botswana in the north, and Mozambique and Swaziland in the northeast. The kingdom of Lesotho forms an enclave within the southeastern part of South Africa. In 1910, four British colonies (the Cape of Good Hope, Natal, Orange Free State, and Transvaal) formed the Union of South Africa, and in 1961, the country gained its independence from Britain. Pretoria is the administrative capital, and Cape Town is the legislative capital. The country has an area of about 1.2 million km² and an estimated population of 54.5 million (United Nations 2015). About 64.8 percent of the population resides in urban areas (United Nations 2014). In 2015, the GDP per capita was estimated at USD 5,724 (World Bank 2016b); therefore, South Africa is classified as an upper-middle-income country (World Bank 2016a).

Government and Institutional Structures

South Africa is a constitutional democracy with three levels of government, referred to as the national, provincial, and local spheres of government. In April 1994, a new, nonracial constitutional democracy was established under the interim Constitution of the Republic of South Africa Act 200 of 1993.

At the local-government level, there has been significant institutional reform, which was set in motion by the Local Government Transition Act 209 of 1993 and gained momentum after the *White Paper on Local Government* was published in 1998 (Franzsen 1996; Franzsen and McCluskey 2000). Table 26.1 sets out the institutional reforms in the local sphere of government in South Africa.

Municipalities cover all of South Africa. Metropolitan municipalities (Category A municipalities) are single-tier municipalities. In nonmetropolitan areas, a two-tier system applies: there are district municipalities (Category C municipalities), and within each district municipality, there are two or more local municipalities (Category B municipalities). Across the nine provinces, there are 8 metropolitan municipalities, 44 district municipalities, and 205 local municipalities, a total of 257 municipalities. The local-government sphere is basically set up and governed under the following important statutes:

- Local Government: Municipal Demarcation Act 27 of 1998.

- Local Government: Municipal Structures Act 117 of 1998.

- Local Government: Municipal Systems Act 32 of 2000.

- Local Government: Municipal Finance Management Act 56 of 2003.

Table 26.1 Local Government Institutional Reform Since April 1994

Date	Status and Reforms Enacted
Before April 27, 1994	• Racially segregated municipalities • Limited local governance in rural areas
After April 27, 1994	Establishment of 843 transitional councils and a two-tier structure in both metropolitan and nonmetropolitan areas
From December 5, 2000	Rationalization and amalgamation: 283 municipalities • 6 metropolitan municipalities (Category A) • 231 local municipalities (Category B) • 46 district municipalities (Category C)
From August 3, 2016	Further rationalization and amalgamation: 257 municipalities • 8 metropolitan municipalities (Category A) • 205 local municipalities (Category B) • 44 district municipalities (Category C)

- Local Government: Municipal Property Rates Act 6 of 2004.
- Municipal Fiscal Powers and Functions Act 12 of 2007.

Land Tenure and Property Registration

Although the vast majority of property in South Africa is held as freehold, communal property and state-owned land are also significant. Some local municipalities in, for example, the KwaZulu-Natal and Limpopo Provinces consist primarily of communal land. Through the Communal Land Rights Act of 2004, the South African government intended to clarify land rights by transferring title from the state to local communities and establishing administrative structures to govern the process of issuing land tenure rights to individuals in communal areas and registering those rights. However, the Constitutional Court declared the Communal Land Rights Act unconstitutional. Any law that had been repealed by this law returned into force, and therefore, the Protection of Land Rights Act 31 of 1996 still applies. In short, land tenure reform in South Africa is aimed at guaranteeing legally enforceable rights to land and buildings under a unified, nonracial system of land rights. The land restitution process is also still under way. The impact of this process on property values in regard to disputed land claims is significant. Disputed land claims, together with the large percentage of communal land in many rural local municipalities, create significant challenges to the collection of local taxes, especially the property tax, in affected municipalities.

Both capital and rental markets are well developed and function efficiently, and the deeds office holds accurate and detailed property records for almost all property in the country. However, unresolved and potential land claims resulting from the protracted land restitution process affect land values of relevant properties.

Property-Related Taxes

The Value-Added Tax

South Africa's value-added tax (VAT) is modeled on the New Zealand general sales tax and can be classified as a modern VAT system. It has a broad base, and the sale of immovable property by property developers who are registered VAT vendors incurs VAT at the standard rate of 14 percent.

The Transfer Duty

The transfer duty was introduced in South Africa in 1686 and is the oldest tax still levied, now under the Transfer Duty Act 40 of 1949. It is payable by any person who acquires "property." As defined in the act, "property" in essence constitutes land and improvements to land (so-called fixtures), as well as limited real rights in property, such as usufruct, rights of way, and mining rights. Any transaction through which property is acquired, regardless of its form, constitutes acquisition. The transfer duty is also payable when the value of property is enhanced by the renunciation of a right pertaining to property (e.g., when a holder of a usufruct renounces the right of use, with the result that bare ownership becomes full ownership once more). Since 2011, tax rates have been the same for natural persons and persons "other than natural persons" (trusts and companies). Acquisitions by inheritance are exempt if the property acquired belonged to the deceased. Transactions that incur the VAT are also explicitly exempt from the transfer duty. However, the acquisition of shares in a private company or a contingent right to property in a trust owning primarily residential property is taxed as if the property itself is transferred (SARS 2013). Effective March 1, 2017, the tax is levied under the sliding scale in table 26.2.

Amendments to the rate structure (amounting to tax relief for low-value properties) have regularly been effected since March 1, 2002. Although the maximum rate of 13 percent is high compared with rates in many countries in the world, the 0 percent rate threshold has been increasing regularly as well, ensuring that especially low-value residential property can be purchased without any transfer duty or only a small amount.

The law provides that the transfer duty is payable on the consideration payable (in the case of a sale or exchange), the value declared by the parties (in the case of a donation), or the market value, whichever is highest. The transacting parties must declare the actual consideration or declared value

Table 26.2 Transfer Duty Tax Rates

Value	Rate and Amount
ZAR 0–ZAR 900,000	0%
ZAR 900,001–ZAR 1,250,000	3% of the value above ZAR 750,000
ZAR 1,250,001–ZAR 1,750,000	ZAR 10,500 plus 6% of the value above ZAR 1,250,000
ZAR 1,750,001–ZAR 2,250,000	ZAR 40,500 plus 8% of the value above ZAR 1,750,000
ZAR 2,250,001–ZAR 10,000,000	ZAR 80,000 plus 11% of the value above ZAR 2,250,000
Above ZAR 10,000,000	ZAR 933,000 plus 13% of the value above ZAR 10,000,000

Source: Transfer Duty Act 40 of 1949.

to the revenue authority. The revenue authority in practice reviews these carefully, especially for transactions between connected persons, such as family members. Buyers who may be liable for the capital gains tax (CGT) should the property be alienated in the future tend to declare the market value for transfer duty accurately to ensure that the base cost for CGT purposes is not adversely affected.

The Estate Duty and the Donations Tax

The estate duty or a donations tax may be payable when property is transferred by succession or donation. The estate is the principal taxpayer of the estate duty, which is levied under the Estate Duty Act 45 of 1955. The donations tax is levied under the Income Tax Act 58 of 1962, and the principal taxpayer is the donor. When immovable property is donated, the donations tax (donor), the CGT (donor), and the transfer duty (donee) may all be payable.

The Capital Gains Tax

The capital gains tax was introduced in October 2001 as part of the income tax system and is based on capital gains realized on the disposal of assets, including immovable property. The CGT is levied as part of the income tax. The basic principle of total receipts minus base costs applies. If the asset is the taxpayer's primary residence and the receipts are less than ZAR 2 million, there is no CGT. If the receipts exceed ZAR 2 million, there is a ZAR 2 million exemption from the capital gains (income minus base cost).

For example, A, who bought her primary residence for ZAR 1 million in 2002, donates this residence to her brother, B, in December 2016. At this date, the market value of the property is ZAR 3.5 million. The capital gain will be ZAR 500,000 (ZAR 3.5 million minus the ZAR 1 million base cost and the ZAR 2 million exemption). After the annual exclusion of ZAR 40,000 is deducted, the remaining ZAR 460,000 is multiplied by the 40 percent multiplier, and the remaining amount, ZAR 184,000, is then included in A's taxable income. Apart from the CGT, A, the donor, will also be liable for the donations tax at 20 percent of the market value of the donation, ZAR 3.5 million. B, the donee, must pay the transfer duty on the acquisition of this property on the market value at the date of acquisition, ZAR 3.5 million. Under the sliding scale, the transfer duty will be ZAR 222,500, an effective tax rate of 6.36 percent.

The Property Tax

The recurrent property tax (known as "rates on property") is levied by local governments. South Africa has a long history of recurrent property taxes. A property tax was first introduced in the Cape of Good Hope colony in 1836 (Franzsen 1996). For almost a century, property taxes were levied and collected under the terms of four provincial ordinances from the previous constitutional framework. Under these ordinances, municipalities generally could select one of three possible tax bases: a land value tax (called "site rating"), a tax on land and buildings collectively (called "flat rating"), or a tax on land and buildings separately (called "composite rating") (Franzsen 1996). The new constitutional and institutional framework necessitated an overhaul of the various former provincial property tax systems (Franzsen 1996; Franzsen and McCluskey 2000).

Presently, municipalities derive their power to levy the property tax from Section 229 of the Constitution of the Republic of South Africa, 1996. In 2004, the previous provincial laws were repealed by a national law that provides for a single, uniform system of property tax for the whole country. The new law is founded on the principles of certainty, uniformity, equity, and simplicity. The Local Government: Municipal Property Rates Act 6 of 2004 (MPRA) was promulgated on July 2, 2005, but it could become operative in a municipality only when that municipality had adopted its municipal property tax policy and had prepared its first valuation roll under the act. Municipalities were required to bring their valuation records and administration up to date within a transitional period of four years (2006 to 2009), which was later extended to six years. Only 27 municipalities (fewer than 10 percent) had implemented their first valuation under the MPRA by July 1, 2007. The vast majority implemented the MPRA in 2008 or 2009, and only a few local municipalities implemented the MPRA in 2010 or 2011. District municipalities are explicitly prohibited from levying the property tax; only metropolitan and local municipalities may do so. Table 26.3 provides a summary of key aspects of the previous and the new property tax laws.

The Importance of Property Tax Revenue

Unlike many other countries in Africa and elsewhere in the developing world, revenue from the recurrent property tax in South Africa exceeds 1 percent of GDP. In 2013, it constituted 1.3 percent of GDP. If other property taxes (the transfer duty, the estate duty, and the donations tax) are included, the revenue amounted to 1.6 percent of GDP (IMF 2014). Table 26.4 provides an overview of the importance of property taxes as a percentage of total tax revenue. As is evident from table 26.4, the property tax is an important source of revenue for municipalities. There was a marked increase in the contribution from the recurrent property tax in

Table 26.3 Old (Pre-2004) and Current Property Tax Laws

	Previous Provincial Laws	MPRA
Tax base	• Multiple bases • Utilities mostly excluded • Mostly urban properties • Exemptions stated in law	• Uniform base (market value) • Some public utilities included • Urban and rural properties • Exemptions to be determined locally under national guidelines
Valuation	• Municipal responsibility • Physical inspection required • Discrete, individual valuations • No external monitoring of and quality control over valuation roll	• Municipal responsibility • Physical inspection optional • Mass valuation allowed • Limited external monitoring of the quality of valuation rolls
Tax rate	• Determined locally • Determined annually • Differentiation allowed indirectly • Nontransparent rebates and other tax relief	• Determined locally • Determined annually • Differentiation possible • Transparency of rebates and tax relief
Administration	• Annual or more frequent billing allowed	• Annual or more frequent billing allowed
Property tax policy	• No community participation • No property tax policy required	• Community participation compulsory • Annual property tax policy required

Table 26.4 Property Taxes as a Percentage of Total Tax Revenue, 2011–2013

	2011		2012		2013	
Tax Category	ZAR Billions	%	ZAR Billions	%	ZAR Billions	%
Total tax revenue	803		879		975	
Transfer duty, estate duty, and donations tax	8	1.00	9	1.02	10	1.02
Recurrent property tax	33	4.11	36	4.10	44	4.51
All property taxes	41	5.11	45	5.12	54	5.54

Source: IMF (2014).

Table 26.5 Revenue Sources as a Percentage of Municipal Operating Revenue, 2008/2009–2012/2013

Revenue Source	2008/2009 %	2009/2010 %	2010/2011 %	2011/2012 (estimated) %	2012/2013 (estimated) %
Property tax	14.9	14.9	16.9	16.8	16.0
Service charges	39.0	41.0	50.3	52.8	55.0
Interest	3.0	1.6	1.1	1.0	0.9
Transfers	33.1	32.6	21.8	20.5	19.5
Other sources	9.9	9.9	9.9	9.0	8.5
Total	100	100	100	100	100

Source: National Treasury (2011).

2013. Table 26.5 shows the importance of the property tax as an own source of revenue for the local-government sphere.

Since the 2006/2007 fiscal year, the aggregate annual growth of property tax revenue has been more than 10 percent (National Treasury 2011). Service charges (electricity, water, sanitation, and refuse removal) are the largest source of municipal revenue, especially electricity and water. However, a very large percentage of this revenue flows through municipal coffers back to Eskom (the national electricity supplier) and the relevant water boards. It is estimated that, depending on the municipality, between 65 and 85 percent of municipal electricity revenue is used to buy bulk electricity from Eskom. As pointed out by the National Treasury (2011), municipalities traditionally used the surplus from their trading services (especially electricity) to cross-subsidize other services. However, rapid increases in bulk tariffs have decreased these surpluses because municipalities have sought to (and, in some instances, have been forced to) absorb some of these increases, and because the higher prices are leading to an increasing number of defaulting taxpayers and inducing customers to consume less. This generally implies that the revenue from the property tax is becoming more important, although this is not clear from table 26.5.

The Tax Base

Under the previous law, municipalities could select one of three tax bases, as indicated earlier. An important policy decision was to do away with tax base options and to legislate only one uniform tax base for the whole country. Under the MPRA, the property tax is levied on owners of immovable property based on the "market value," comprising land and buildings as one composite value. The rating of property is no longer confined to property in urban areas. In principle, all properties that are not excluded from the tax base must be valued so that municipalities can compute the revenue forgone should property be exempted. In short, the law now extends property taxation to properties in formerly untaxed rural areas that now form part of local municipalities. This means that commercial farms and, in principle, also subsistence farms and residential properties in informal settlements in rural areas are taxable. The base was also extended to include certain types of "public service infrastructure," that is, public utilities. Amendments in 2009 and 2015 have provided more clarity on which types of infrastructure are taxable, and which (e.g., roads and railway lines) are not.

Exclusions

The MPRA excludes various properties from the tax base, including the following:

- At least the first ZAR 15,000 of the market value of a property used for residential purposes.

- 100 percent of the following public service infrastructure: roads, waterways, railway lines, airports, and harbors (to be phased in over five years from July 1, 2015).

- 30 percent of the value of taxable public service infrastructure.

- The coastline and offshore islands.

- Mineral rights.

- Property used primarily as a place of public worship.

- Property owned by land reform beneficiaries, but for only 10 years from acquisition.

- Parts of national parks, nature reserves, and botanical gardens.

Exemptions, Value Reductions, and Rebates

The MPRA, especially when read with the Local Government: Municipal Systems Act of 2000, makes specific reference to the effect of the property tax on the poor. Municipalities must annually adopt a municipal property tax policy that allows them to promote local social and economic development. Relief is granted on the basis of age or physical or mental disability coupled with the taxpayer's income. All exemptions, rebates, and reductions projected for a financial year must be reflected in the municipality's annual budget for that year.

Municipalities decide on any exemptions, value reductions, or rebates. These may be granted to a specific category of owners of properties or to the owners of a specific category of property. However, exemptions, reductions, and rebates must be properly quantified and justified because they must be reflected in the annual budget. The metropolitan municipalities operate well-designed tax relief programs to assist poor and indigent taxpayers.

Valuation

The MPRA requires that the general basis of valuation of all properties in the valuation roll be "market value," which it defines as "the amount the property would have realized if sold on the date of valuation in the open market by a willing seller to a willing buyer."

Municipal Valuers

Only a person who is appropriately qualified and registered as a "professional valuer" or a "professional associated valuer" with the South African Council for the Property Valuers' Profession (under the Property Valuers Profession Act 47 of 2000) may be appointed as a municipal valuer. In the metropolitan municipalities and a few large local municipalities, in-house valuers are used. However, most local municipalities must outsource valuation services to the private sector through an open, competitive, and transparent bidding process as provided for under the Local Government: Municipal Finance Management Act. The procurement of valuation services is one of the most challenging property tax issues in South Africa (Franzsen 2014; Franzsen and Welgemoed 2011). Especially in many small local municipalities, councils simply do not know what to ask for in their tender specifications when they advertise for the appointment of a municipal valuer, how to evaluate the tenders received, and how to evaluate the work done by the appointed municipal valuer.

Valuation Criteria

The MPRA provides detailed criteria for valuation. It states that physical inspection of the property to be valued is optional, and that "comparative, analytical and other systems or techniques may be used, including aerial photography and computer-assisted mass appraisal (CAMA) systems or techniques, taking into account changes in technology and valuation systems and techniques" (Section 45(2)(b)). If the available market-based data of any category of ratable property are insufficient, the MPRA mandates the application of a mass valuation technique, which may include a technique based on predetermined bands of property values as approved by the municipality concerned.

Valuation Cycles

Until the law was amended with effect from July 1, 2015, a valuation cycle was four years, with a possible extension of one further year under unspecified "exceptional circumstances." Under the amended law, for metropolitan municipalities, the valuation cycle remains a maximum of four years with a maximum one-year extension should exceptional circumstances warrant it; for local municipalities, the maximum is five years with a maximum two-year extension.

The City of Cape Town operates on a three-year cycle. It also successfully makes extensive use of CAMA of residential property. Cape Town also voluntarily has the overall quality and accuracy of its valuation audited by an impartial international organization.

Valuation Practices in the Metropolitan and Larger Local Municipalities

Some metropolitan municipalities use sophisticated CAMA models founded on credible numbers of comparable sales. In other metropolitan municipalities and some large local municipalities, a simpler mass valuation approach is used in which points are awarded for various subjectively determined value-adding variables or attributes. The total number of points for a property is then compared with the purchase price of the property to calculate a value per point, which is then extrapolated and applied to the total points of other property that is the subject of valuation. Although comparable sales are used, a method of comparison is lacking. Use is also made of expert judgment, but the number of comparative variables is very limited, which significantly affects accuracy. Cape Town uses reasonable levels of regression analysis based on a substantive number of variables and sales data. As one of the pioneers of CAMA in South Africa, Cape Town presently seems to achieve the highest levels of accuracy in the country, but even there, the estimated coefficient of dispersion (COD) is about 0.7 for residential property (Boshoff and Franzsen 2015).[1]

The number of valuers in the eight metropolitan municipalities ranges between five and twenty, depending on the relationship between in-house valuers (full-time employees of the municipality) and private valuers appointed on short-term contracts. A positive feature of the South African system is the extensive use of data collectors, which reduces the workload of the qualified valuers.

Valuation Rolls

The valuation roll must list all properties (even properties not valued) in the municipality and must include the following information for every property if it can be reasonably determined:

- A description of the property.
- The relevant property category within which the property falls.
- The physical address of the property.
- The extent (size) of the property.
- The market value of the property if it has been valued.
- The name of the owner.
- Any other prescribed particulars.

The municipal valuer must submit the certified roll to the municipal manager. Within 21 days of receipt, the manager must publish a notice in the provincial gazette and a further notice once a week for two consecutive weeks in the media, stating that the roll is open for public inspection for at least 30 days from a date specified in the notice. A similar notice must be delivered to every property owner, as well as an extract from the valuation roll pertaining to the property of that owner. A municipality with an official website must publish these notices and the valuation roll on its website.

Objections and Appeals

The MPRA provides for a detailed objection and appeal process. An objection can be lodged only in regard to an individual property and not against the valuation roll itself. Any person (not only the owner) may lodge an objection to a matter included in or omitted from the valuation roll. The municipal manager must assist illiterate objectors who want to lodge objections.

The municipal valuer must promptly consider all objections, make a determination based on all the facts, including the submissions by the objector (and the owner, if the owner is not the objector), adjust or add to the valuation roll in accordance with the decision, and inform every objector and owner of a property subject to an objection of the relevant decision. Within 30 days, an objector may request the reasons for the decision, and the reasons must be provided within 30 days of receipt of the application. An aggrieved objector or owner or the municipal council may lodge an appeal in the prescribed manner with the relevant valuation appeal board. The lodging of an appeal does not defer a person's liability to pay the property tax. If the value is adjusted upward or downward by more than 10 percent, reasons must be provided to the municipal manager. These adjustments are automatically reviewed by the relevant valuation appeal board.

The member of the executive council responsible for local government in a province must establish as many valuation appeal boards (VABs) as necessary in the relevant province, but at least one in each metropolitan municipality. A VAB consists of a chairperson (who must have a legal qualification and sufficient experience) and between two and four additional members with sufficient knowledge of or experience in property valuation. At least one of the additional members must be a professional valuer or professional associate valuer as defined by the Property Valuers Profession Act.

Supplementary Valuations

For various reasons, it may become necessary to undertake a new valuation during a valuation cycle. In such circumstances, a supplementary valuation roll must be compiled at least once a year. The MPRA provides for supplementary valuations to be done by the municipal valuer in any instance where

- a property was incorrectly omitted from the valuation roll;

- a property was included in a municipality after the last general valuation (e.g., because of a change in municipal boundaries);

- a property was subdivided or consolidated;

- a property's improved value substantially increased or decreased for any reason after the last general valuation;

- a property was substantially incorrectly valued during the last general valuation;

- a property needs to be revalued for any other exceptional reason;

- there was a change in the use category of a property; or

- there was a clerical or typing error.

Supplementary valuations must reflect the value of the property at the date of valuation determined for the last general valuation. Generally, the property tax becomes payable on the valuation as stated in the supplementary valuation roll on the first day of the month after the posting of a notice to the owner regarding the new value. If there was a clerical error or the value is reduced, the property tax becomes payable from the date the error was made or the date of the incorrect valuation; and if a property has been rezoned, from the date the change in use category occurred.

Quality Control and Oversight

Presently, the law stipulates that the minister responsible for local government may monitor and issue reports on the effectiveness, consistency, uniformity, and application of municipal valuations for property tax purposes. This stipulation is inadequate. Monitoring is an important function that must be performed regularly and should not be left to a politician who may have very little knowledge of the administration of property taxation (Franzsen and McCluskey 2000).

Amendments enacted in 2015 provide for more oversight at the provincial level. The member of the executive (MEC) responsible for local government is tasked to monitor the determination of a date of valuation for a general valuation, the appointment of municipal valuers, and whether the municipal manager has submitted a project plan regarding the municipal general valuation. Although an MEC may perform such a task admirably, technical oversight rather than political oversight would have been more appropriate.

Valuation Capacity, Education, and Training

The valuation profession in South Africa is well-established, for example, the South African Institute of Valuers, a professional association of valuers, was established in 1909. Despite a long history, the state of the profession remains an area of some concern (Cloete 2009; Franzsen 2011). Table 26.6 provides the numbers of valuers in South Africa. It is immediately apparent that the numbers of professional valuers and associate professional valuers collectively declined steadily between 1985 and 2010 and increased only between 2010 and 2015. There were fewer valuers at the end of 2015 who could do property tax valuations than there had been in 1985. Although the increase in the number of professional valuers between 2010 and 2015 is heartening, it may to some extent explain the decrease in the number of associate professional valuers over the same period. However, the constantly decreasing number of associate professional valuers over the last 30 years is alarming, as is the 40 percent decrease in the number of candidate valuers between 2010 and 2015. Age and gender are also issues. In 2010, more than 60 percent of the professional valuers were more than 50 years old, and only 11 percent were female (Franzsen 2011). In 2015, 16 percent of professional valuers and associate professional valuers, in other words, valuers who may, under the law, do municipal property tax valuations, were white males 65 or older. However, by 2015, almost 20 percent of the professional valuers and associate professional valuers were female. It must also be noted that apparently, only about 20 to 25 percent of these valuers actually do municipal valuations (Zybrands

Table 26.6 Valuers in South Africa, 1985–2015

Category	1985	1990	2000	2010	2015
Professional valuers	549	549	385	575	756
Associate professional valuers	1,114	1,097	970	713	625
Subtotal	1,663	1,646	1,355	1,288	1,381
Candidate valuers	360	439	628	1,068	626
Total	2,023	2,085	1,983	2,356	2,007

Source: SACPVP (2010, 2016).

2003). Degree programs with a specialization in valuation are limited, as is continued professional training in, for example, CAMA (Boshoff and Franzsen 2015).

Tax Rates

Tax rates are set locally by municipalities and must be expressed annually as a "cent in the Rand amount." The MPRA allows municipalities to levy different tax rates on different categories of property, which must be defined in the property tax policies of the municipality. However, the same tax rate must apply to all residential properties within a municipality.

Although tax rates are determined locally, the law provides that the national government minister responsible for local government may, with the concurrence of the minister of finance and by notice in the *Gazette*, set an upper limit on the percentage by which the revenue from property tax on properties or a tax rate on a specific category of properties may be increased. These ministers may also determine maximum ratios between the tax rate for residential properties (which constitutes the "base rate") and other property use or ownership categories. To date, such ratios have been fixed for public service infrastructure, properties used for agriculture, and properties used by public benefit organizations. The tax rate for these three categories may not exceed 25 percent of the tax rate for residential property. Table 26.7 states the 2015/2016 tax rates in four of the large metropolitan municipalities.

It is noteworthy that in Cape Town and eThekwini, "state-owned property" is not a use category. Quite correctly, these two metropolitan municipalities view state-owned property as an ownership rather than a use category, and these properties are therefore taxed on the basis of their zoned or actual use. Tshwane (which includes the capital city, Pretoria) and

Table 26.7 Tax Rates in Four Metropolitan Municipalities, 2015/2016

Category	Cape Town		eThekwini		Johannesburg		Tshwane	
	c/ZAR[1]	Ratio	c/ZAR	Ratio	c/ZAR	Ratio	c/ZAR	Ratio
Residential	0.6931	1.00	1.115	1.000	0.6531	1.00	1.013	1.00
Commercial and business	1.2508	1.80	2.528	2.267	1.8287	2.80	3.056	3.02
Industrial	1.2508	1.80	3.262	2.926	1.8287	2.80	3.056	3.02
Vacant land	1.2508	1.80	4.998	4.483	2.6124	4.00	6.573	6.49
Agricultural	0.1251	0.18	0.279	0.250	0.1632	0.25	0.253	0.25
State-owned	–	–	–	–	0.9796	1.50	3.056	3.02
PSI[2]	0.2234	0.18	0.279	0.250	0.1632	0.25	–	–

Source: Metropolitan municipality budgets for 2015/2016.

[1] "c/ZAR" refers to "cent in the Rand amount."

[2] "PSI" refers to public service infrastructure, that is, public utilities.

Johannesburg incorrectly tax state-owned property as though it constitutes a use category. It is also noteworthy that all four of these metropolitan municipalities tax vacant land at higher tax rates than developed property—in the case of Tshwane, almost 6.5 times higher.

Billing and Collection

The MPRA provides that a municipality must furnish each person liable for payment of the property tax with a written notice specifying, among other things,

- the amount of tax due;
- the date on or before which the amount is payable;
- how the amount was calculated; and
- the market value of the property as listed in the current valuation roll.

The law clearly states that a person is liable for payment of a rate whether or not that person has received a written notice. A person who has not received a written notice must make the necessary inquiries from the municipality. A person liable for the property tax also has a duty to furnish the municipality with an address to which official correspondence can be directed. In many municipalities, especially in rural areas, the lack of postal and physical addresses presents councils with challenges regarding the issuance of notices and tax bills.

The property tax may be paid monthly (or less often, as may be prescribed in the Municipal Finance Management Act) or annually, subject to agreement by owner of the property. Various payment options are available to taxpayers, such as payment in cash or bank-guaranteed check at the municipality, by direct debit order, by Internet banking, or at the post office or a number of commercial banks and large supermarket stores. A municipality may defer liability for payment, but only in "special circumstances," which the MPRA does not specify.

Collection levels (the amount collected as a percentage of the amount billed) are high, generally exceeding 90 percent, particularly in the metropolitan municipalities. However, across all municipalities, arrears are increasing at an alarming rate. In many instances, this increase is due to a perceived lack of service delivery, municipalities' failure to properly enforce the tax against defaulters because of political reasons or poor administration (inadequate credit and debt control processes), corruption, or a combination of these factors. However, property tax arrears are merely part of a much bigger problem. By mid-2014, municipalities' overall consumer debt amounted to a staggering ZAR 923.4 billion (Magubane 2014), of which almost ZAR 53 billion was owed to the eight metropolitan municipalities (Maswanganyi 2014). Furthermore, there is growing concern among some commercial consumers of municipal services that they may face increasing property taxes (because the law allows for tax rate differentiation) to subsidize noncompliant, mostly residential consumers (Magubane 2014).

Enforcement

The MPRA specifies that if a property owner has not paid the tax levied on the property by the due date, the municipality may recover the amount in whole or in part from a tenant or occupier of the property, regardless of any contractual obligation between the landlord and the tenant to the contrary. The amount that can be recovered is limited to the amount of outstanding rent. The municipality may also recover the tax from an agent of the owner.

Further enforcement measures contained in the Local Government: Municipal Systems Act of 2000 include the imposition of interest on arrears; termination of municipal services, such as electricity; restriction of services, such as water; refusal to issue the municipal clearance certificate required before any formal transfer of ownership can take place in the deeds office; and finally, seizure and public sale by the municipality of the relevant property. A public sale can take place only after at least three years of delinquency.

Property Tax Issues in South Africa

The MPRA introduced so-called rates policies to the South African property tax system. Every metropolitan and local municipality must adopt a rates policy (a property tax policy) consistent with the MPRA. It must explain to property owners and taxpayers, as well as the broader community, why differential tax rates are used, how the different tax rates were decided, what rebates and exemptions are granted, and on what basis these were decided. The property tax policy must be revised annually (if required) and must take the form of a bylaw so that it can be enforced. Community participation in the determination of a property tax policy is compulsory.

A municipality's property tax policy is required to treat all persons liable for the property tax equitably. The property tax policy must also determine the criteria to be applied by the municipality if it levies different tax rates for different property use categories, exempts a specific use or ownership category of property, grants rebates or rate reductions, or increases or decreases tax rates. Any exemption, rebate, or reduction provided for and adopted in a property tax policy must comply with and be implemented in accordance with a national framework. No relief may be granted to owners of properties on an individual basis.

The very broad base of the South African property tax is, in principle, a sound policy. There are, however, a few areas of concern. Although the law extends property taxation to formerly untaxed rural areas that now form part of metropolitan or local municipalities, there are various practical issues, especially regarding the valuation of communal property and the billing and collection of the tax on property owned communally. In addition, the tax base was also extended to include some public utilities (called public service infrastructure), but the definition of "public service infrastructure," read in conjunction with the definition of "property," is problematic. An amendment to the law, effective July 1, 2015, that excludes certain types of public service infrastructure as defined and explained has alleviated some of the concerns in this regard.

An issue that should be revisited is the single "market value" tax base. Especially in rural local municipalities with predominantly communal land, it is questionable whether this one-size-fits-all tax base is appropriate (Franzsen 2014).

In some instances, the cost of the first general valuation roll could not be recouped from the property tax over the first four- or five-year valuation cycle (Franzsen and Welgemoed 2011). The 2015 amendments extended valuation cycles to a maximum of five years (plus a possible two-year extension) for all local municipalities. This is a prudent step given the cost of a comprehensive general valuation and the paucity of capacity to undertake more regular valuations. Local municipalities still have the right to undertake general revaluations more often should the need arise. Metropolitan municipalities must still revalue every four years, with a possible one-year extension if the provincial MEC agrees.

As was previously noted, valuation education in South Africa is inadequate, and the valuation profession is in decline. Also, the MPRA provides that the minister in charge of local government is responsible for external quality control over the quality of valuation rolls. International practice suggests that this highly technical review task should be performed by a technical entity specifically established for this purpose (Daud et al. 2013; Franzsen and McCluskey 2000). A valuer general office was established in South Africa in 2015, but municipal valuations have been explicitly excluded from the responsibilities of this office.

Last, nonpayment of taxes (including the property tax) and municipal tariffs for electricity, water, sanitation, and other services is becoming problematic in many if not all municipalities. Politically, there seems to be little appetite for proper enforcement.

Note

1. The COD is a statistical concept that measures how closely the valuation model (based on a multiple regression analysis) predicts the estimated price of a property in comparison with the actual sale price. High CODs can be interpreted as showing wide variance between estimated and actual prices; therefore, low CODs are preferred.

References

Boshoff, D., and R. C. D. Franzsen. 2015. "Modernizing the Property Tax System in South Africa: How Hard Can It Be?" Paper presented at the 10th Mass Appraisal Valuation Symposium of the International Property Tax Institute, Amsterdam, The Netherlands (June 16–17).

CIA (Central Intelligence Agency). 2016. "South Africa." In *The World Factbook. https:// www.cia.gov/library/publications/the-world-factbook/geos/sf.html*.

Cloete, C. E. 2009. "Training Valuers in South Africa—The Future." Paper presented at the Fourth Mass Appraisal Valuation Symposium of the International Property Tax Institute, Pretoria (March 25–26).

Daud, D. Z., N. Kamarudin, R. C. D. Franzsen, and W. J. McCluskey. 2013. "Property Tax in Malaysia and South Africa: A Question of Assessment Capacity and Quality Assurance." *Journal of Property Tax Assessment and Administration* 10(4): 5–18.

Franzsen, R. C. D. 1996. "Property Tax: Alive and Well and Levied in South Africa?" *SA Mercantile Law Journal* 8(3): 348–365.

———. 2011. "Education of Valuers in South Africa." Paper presented at the Sixth Mass Appraisal Valuation Symposium of the International Property Tax Institute, University of British Columbia, Vancouver, Canada (October 7–8).

———. 2014. "Is Property Tax the Answer for All Municipalities in South Africa?" Paper presented at the International Property Tax Institute (IPTI) Conference on Opportunities and Challenges for Local Government Funding: The Way Forward, Sydney, Australia (November 13–14).

Franzsen, R. C. D., and W. J. McCluskey. 2000. "Some Policy Issues Regarding the Local Government: Property Rates Bill." *SA Mercantile Law Journal* 12(1): 209–223.

Franzsen, R. C. D., and W. Welgemoed. 2011. "Submission on Proposed Amendments to the Municipal Property Rates Act (MPRA)." Report for the South African Local Government Association (June).

IMF (International Monetary Fund). 2014. *Government Finance Statistics Yearbook.* Washington, DC.

Magubane, K. 2014. "Households Lead in Delinquent Municipal Debt." *Business Day Live,* July 21. *www.bdlive.co.za/national/2014/07/21/households-lead-in-delinquent -municipal-debt.*

Maswanganyi, N. 2014. "SA Metros Owed Almost R53bn in Outstanding Debt." *Business Day Live,* August 29. *www.bdlive.co.za/economy/2014/08/29/sa-metros-owed-almost -r53bn-in-outstanding-debt.*

National Treasury. 2011. *Local Government Budgets and Expenditure Review. www.treasury .gov.za/publications/igfr/2011/lg/default.aspx.*

SACPVP (South African Council for the Property Valuers' Profession). 2010. Personal communication from the registrar.

———. 2016. Personal communication from the registrar.

SARS (South African Revenue Service). 2013. *Transfer Duty Guide. www.sars.gov.za /AllDocs/OpsDocs/Guides/LAPD-TD-G01%20-%20Transfer%20Duty%20 Guide%20-%20External%20Guide.pdf.*

United Nations. 2014. *World Urbanization Prospects.* Washington, DC: Department of Economics and Social Affairs, Population Division.

United Nations, Department of Economic and Social Affairs, Population Division. 2015. World Population Prospects: The 2015 Revision. *https://esa.un.org/unpd/wpp /Publications/Files/World_Population_2015_Wallchart.pdf.*

World Bank. 2016a. "Country and Lending Groups." *http://data.worldbank.org/about /country-and-lending-groups.*

———. 2016b. "GDP per Capita (Current US%)." *http://data.worldbank.org/indicator /NY.GDP.PCAP.CD.*

Zybrands, A. 2003. "Commentary on the Municipal Property Rates Bill." Presentation to the Property Rates Bill Workshop, Benoni, South Africa (April 7–8).

Legislation

Constitution of the Republic of South Africa, 1996.

Constitution of the Republic of South Africa, Act 200 of 1993 (interim constitution).

Estate Duty Act 45 of 1955.

Income Tax Act 58 of 1962.

Local Government: Municipal Demarcation Act 27 of 1998.

Local Government: Municipal Finance Management Act 56 of 2003.

Local Government: Municipal Property Rates Act 6 of 2004 (MPRA).

Local Government: Municipal Structures Act 117 of 1998.

Local Government: Municipal Systems Act 32 of 2000.

Local Government Transition Act 209 of 1993.

Municipal Fiscal Powers and Functions Act 12 of 2007.

Property Valuers Profession Act 47 of 2000.

Protection of Land Rights Act 31 of 1996.

Transfer Duty Act 40 of 1949.

27

Sudan

SHAHENAZ HASSAN AND RIËL FRANZSEN

Until the secession of South Sudan on July 9, 2011, Sudan was the largest country in Africa, and with a land area of 1.86 million km², it is still one of the largest. The country has a population of about 40.2 million (United Nations 2015), and in 2015 the GDP per capita was estimated at USD 2,415 (World Bank 2016b). Almost 34 percent of the population in Sudan is urbanized (United Nations 2014). Khartoum, with an estimated population of 5 million, is the capital and largest city (CIA 2016; United Nations 2014). Sudan is classified as a lower-middle-income country (World Bank 2016a).

Government

Sudan is a presidential republic with a three-tier federal government system. Currently, there are 18 states and 134 localities.[1] The federal level is concerned with policy making, planning, supervision, and coordination. States are administered by elected governors. Each state has five to seven ministries. The state governments are responsible for policy making, planning, and implementation at the state level. Localities are administered by commissioners and are concerned mostly with implementation of state policies and service delivery. There are elected legislatures at each government level (Fjeldstad 2016).

Sudan's history of decentralization dates back to 1951, when the Local Governments Act was enacted. This law divided the country into urban and rural councils (Hamid 2002). Decentralization was introduced as a system of governance to deal with the multiethnic and multicultural society of Sudan. The Fourth Constitutional Decree of 1991, which finally adopted a federal system of governance, was followed by further constitutional decrees in 1993 and 1995 that further consolidated the federal system. The 1993 amendment subdivided the country into 26 states; the 1995 amendment devolved more powers and functions to the states. The 1998 constitution reaffirmed the federal system and included a map detailing the names, boundaries, and capitals of the states. However, the central government retained most of the important decisions affecting citizens, as well as financial powers and budgetary controls (Hamid 2002). Until the secession of South Sudan in July 2011, the government was bound by the North/South Comprehensive Peace Agreement (CPA). The CPA, concluded in 2005, provided both parts of the country the opportunity to address the devastation of infrastructure by years of civil war, which resulted in displacement and underdevelopment. Both the Interim National Constitution and the CPA of 2005 called for fiscal decentralization and the empowerment of subnational governments (Fjeldstad 2016). Fiscal decentralization was fueled by a decade-long oil boom.

The loss of oil revenues after the secession of South Sudan necessitated major fiscal adjustments, notably cuts in investment spending, which inevitably have affected the flow of federal transfers to state governments. However, transfers to states increased by about 8 percent in 2012 (IMF 2012). Although the total revenue in Sudan's states has increased substantially since 1995, so has their dependency on transfers to meet their responsibilities for basic service delivery. Large increases in transfers to states have contributed to rapid growth in state spending but have also weakened incentives for states to raise their own revenue (IMF 2012).

Since 2012, the states have been the main power base at the subnational level. In each state, its elected legislative assembly approves its laws and budgets and oversees the performance of the various ministries and departments. The state's governor appoints some of the assembly members in order to include underrepresented groups, such as women and educated elites (Hamid 2002).

Under Schedule C of the 2005 constitution the exclusive executive and legislative powers of states include "local government." Each state is composed of a number of urban and rural localities, which are important in Sudan's federal system. Localities have various responsibilities, including economic and financial matters, education, public works, and public health. These responsibilities must be coordinated with agencies at the provincial and state levels (Hamid 2002). Localities funding sources include various taxes, donations collected occasionally for specific purposes, and intermittent transfers from the state government to especially resource-poor localities (Hamid 2002). Localities also have powers to raise additional funds from their residents through specific charges, taxes, rents, or land sales. Not surprisingly, the available funding sources seldom cover all of a locality's expenditures because of weak tax bases and poor administration (Hamid 2002). As Fjeldstad (2016) points out, subnational levels of government need adequate revenue to fulfill service delivery responsibilities, conduct expenditure assignments, and address local needs. Own-revenue mobilization by both states and localities is low. Inadequate and unevenly distributed own revenues of both states and local governments levels and unpredictable levels of transfers from the federal government pose serious obstacles to the policy of decentralization (Fjeldstad 2016).

The Interim Constitution of 2005 provides the framework for the various types of taxes and other sources of revenue to which the various levels of government are entitled. Despite Sudan's federal structure, the federal government in 2010 still collected about 97 percent of total tax revenues and 86 percent of total tax and nontax revenues combined (Fjeldstad 2016). Thus, despite assigning more expenditure responsibilities to state governments, the federal government has effectively maintained control over revenue collection. Although the states' own-revenue mobilization has increased in recent years, they are heavily dependent on federal transfers. Referring to a 2012 International Monetary Fund report (IMF 2012), Fjeldstad (2016) states that, on average, less than one-third of the states' expenditures are funded by their own revenue sources. As is to be expected in any federal system, there are large differences in states' dependency on federal transfers. In 2010, Khartoum relied on the central government for about 38 percent of its needs, whereas in Blue Nile State, the figure was 86 percent; conversely, own revenues contributed the highest percentage of total revenues in Khartoum, 62 percent, but the lowest in Blue Nile, only 14 percent (Fjeldstad 2016). The revenue sources of states are listed in table 27.1.

Under the current law, subnational governments in Sudan have a high degree of autonomy in proposing new tax legislation and amending existing tax laws. Relevant laws and fiscal resolutions issued by the states specify sources of revenue and procedures for imposing and collecting taxes (Fjeldstad 2016).

Localities have some own revenues and other revenues they share with the states. Each state assigns taxing powers for own revenues to localities through local-government legislation. Although the main categories of local revenue sources are prescribed by law, localities decide what revenue sources they want to use and set the relevant tax rates or tariffs for fees (Fjeldstad 2016). Local-government own revenues include property taxes, 40 percent of locally generated income taxes, taxes on locally manufactured

Table 27.1 Own Revenue Sources Assigned to States

State personal income tax
Service charges for state services
Licenses
State land and property tax
Royalties
Levies on tourism
Stamp duties
Agricultural taxes
State government projects and national parks
Excise duties
Border trade charges or levies in accordance with national legislation
Any other tax determined by law

Source: The 2005 Interim National Constitution as stated in Fjeldstad (2016).

products, the tax on agricultural land, the advertising board levy, the tax on entertainment facilities and amusement parks, the livestock tax or tax on herds, and the tax on fruit-producing trees. Apart from these taxes, there are also fees for trade and business licenses and a plethora of other fees, charges, and duties levied on local economic activities, as well as income from investments, land sales, and rents. Own revenues collected by the localities are mostly for their own use, although the livestock tax is shared with the state.

Localities also receive transfers of shares of various taxes from their states. The 2003 Local Development Act identifies which taxes accruing to states should be shared with localities (Fjeldstad 2016; table 27.2). The Sudan Chamber of Tax collects these taxes.

These are still major constraints on fiscal decentralization in Sudan. In addition, the weak own-revenue mobilization efforts can be attributed to factors such as poor infrastructure, lack of trained staff, and poor quality of data on economic activities and revenue bases (Fjeldstad 2016).

Land Tenure

Land is a central issue for both rural and urban communities in Sudan. It is not just a means for livelihood and basic survival but also has profound cultural and sociopolitical dimensions. However, there is no unified legal framework of land tenure across Sudan (Pantuliano 2007). According to the 2005 constitution, all levels of government shall institute a process to progressively develop and amend the relevant laws to incorporate customary laws, practices, local heritage, and international trends and practices

Table 27.2 Localities' Share of State Taxes, Fees, and Duties

Revenue Sources	Percentage to Locality
Fees on vehicle licenses and driving licenses	60
Real estate tax	60
State stamp duty	40
State personal income tax	40
Land and river transportation fees	40
Fees on the registration of clubs, societies, and associations	40
Sale proceeds of investment lands	40
Agricultural and animal production tax	60
Service fees	60
Fees on veterinary examinations and on slaughtering and slaughterhouses	60
Fees on residential plans and designation and allocation of lands for residential, commercial, agricultural, industrial, and investment purposes	40
Fees on the state's forestry products	60
Value-added taxes	60

Source: Local government laws from various states as reported by Fjeldstad (2016).

pertaining to land. The country has an old system of land registration through which an individual, an enterprise, or the government could establish title to a piece of land. Formal registration was extensive in northern Sudan, especially in Khartoum and in central and northern states. Before 1970, all unregistered land belonged to the state, which held ownership in trust for the people, who had customary rights to it. In 1970, the Unregistered Land Act declared that all wastelands, forest lands, and unregistered lands were government land (USAID 2007). Although this act was repealed by the Civil Transactions Act of 1984, the state retained ownership of all unregistered land (USAID 2007). Despite the fact that official land law has been transformed under successive governments, legislation is essentially founded on colonial land laws (Pantuliano 2007).

Under the 1970 Unregistered Land Act, urban planning was the responsibility of the central government. Under this law, the government would identify a piece of land for specific purposes, such as housing, commercial areas, industrial areas, or infrastructure. The land would then be gazetted, surveyed, and demarcated into blocks and subsequently into individual plots. At this stage, applications would be invited, and plots would be awarded upon payment to successful individuals or entities under either freehold or leasehold tenure.

One of the key obstacles to the efficient operation of land markets is dysfunctional land administration in both the central government and local governments. Survey departments are inefficient, and there is no reliable information on which to base new land allocations and transfers or secure tenure rights. Customary land management still exists in some localities, but customary rights have been eroded over time (USAID 2007). Land tenure issues are not limited to rural areas but are also a concern in and around cities in the north, including Khartoum (Pantuliano 2007). Reform of Sudan's land administration should be a priority (USAID 2007).

Taxation

Sudan relies heavily on oil revenues. In 2012, total taxation constituted only 5.4 percent of GDP (IMF 2015). The primary direct tax is the income tax. The income tax structure is unusual in containing four distinct elements:

- The business profits tax, which applies to both incorporated and unincorporated businesses.

- The land rent tax, introduced in 1964, which is more correctly a tax on building rent.

- The individual income tax, introduced in 1964.

- The capital gains tax.

Fjeldstad (2016) points out that the ministries of finance in the various states do not collect taxes. The responsibility for the collection of state tax revenues is allocated to field offices of the federal Sudan Chamber of Tax. The Chamber of Tax has offices in all states and in many localities. For instance, the Chamber of Tax collects the property tax, the state income tax, and stamp duties. Depending on the nature of the taxes, the Chamber of Tax transfers the collections to the states' ministries of finance either in whole or in shares. The high cost of revenue collection is a major challenge in many localities.

Property-Related Taxes and Fees

Land Rent

The Ministry of Urban Development is responsible for administering land rent, which is applied to all holders of government leaseholds. The person who acquires and uses the property, that is, the leaseholder or tenant, is liable for the tax. Assessment is value based, and the Ministry of Urban Development is responsible for valuations.

The Registration Fee

The property's buyer pays a registration fee. If the transfer is concluded within six months of the date of sale, the registration fee is 2.5 percent of the selling price of the property. If the transfer is finalized between six months and one year after the date of acquisition, the rate is 5 percent, and if the transfer is made after one year from the date of acquisition, the rate is 6 percent (World Bank 2016c). The increase in the rate is clearly a mechanism to encourage formalizing and finalizing the transfer. The Ministry of Finance's Chamber of Tax collects the tax.

Stamp Duties

Stamp duties are imposed on property transfers and financial transactions and are levied by state governments but are also collected by the Chamber of Tax. Some are fixed; others are ad valorem. Although the revenue is relatively minor, the effects of stamp duties on individuals and businesses are significant (Fjeldstad 2016).

The Property Tax

The property tax, locally referred to as *awayed*, is levied by local-government councils in accordance with the Decentralization Decree of 1991 to raise revenue for providing services to local residents. It was introduced by the colonial system at the end of the 19th century and was called *atyan* (agricultural land) because originally only agricultural land was taxed. In 1964, a new law was introduced to include all properties. The tax rate and tax base of each local tax and the administration of the tax collection are devolved to local governments. The tax is levied on the owners of any property included in the local government's jurisdiction.

The Tax Base and Assessment

The awayed is levied on the basis of a property's location and use (such as residential, industrial, and commercial). For commercial and industrial property the size of the building is also considered. The owner of the property is liable for the tax. In addition, persons or businesses who hold a property deed or a temporary or permanent occupancy title and are using the property are deemed to be owners.

Exemptions

The law exempts the following properties:

- Buildings belonging to the central government, local governments, or any independent governmental authority.
- Buildings used for social or cultural purposes.
- Buildings belonging to charitable, religious, or educational bodies.

A locality council may grant discretionary relief on the grounds of poverty.

Tax Rates or Tariffs

Councils determine differentiated tariffs depending on the zone where the property is located, physical attributes of the property, and whether the properties are being used for residential, commercial, or industrial purposes. In Khartoum Locality, for example, properties are grouped into four "levels" (tables 27.3 and 27.4). Within each level further differentiation occurs. For residential properties building materials (that is, building quality) is a factor and also whether the property is occupied by the owner or a tenant. It is evident from table 27.3 that the tax burden on owner-occupied residential buildings is significantly less than that on tenant-occupied buildings. Although the owner is liable for the tax, much,

Table 27.3 Awayed on Residential Properties in Khartoum

Structure	Rented Property (SDG)				Owner-Occupied Property (SDG)			
	Level A	Level B	Level C	Level D	Level A	Level B	Level C	Level D
Mud building	250	200	100	100	20			
Improved mud	500	400	300	200	35			
Brick	650	500	400	300	60			
Concrete, one floor	1,500	1,000	750	500	120			
First floor	1,000	750	500	300	60			
Second floor	1,000	750	500	300	60			
Additional floor	1,000	750	500	300	60			
Flats and apartments	According to the commercial buildings code				60			

Source: Khartoum Locality (2012).

Table 27.4 Awayed on Commercial and Industrial Properties in Khartoum

Item	Level A	Level B	Level C	Level D
Shops with floor area less than 16 m² in large shopping centers	SDG 600	SDG 400	SDG 300	
Shops with floor area between 16 and 40 m² in large shopping centers	SDG 1,000	SDG 750	SDG 600	
Shops with floor area greater than 40 m² in large shopping centers	SDG 2,000	SDG 1,500	SDG 1,000	
Shops in suburb shopping centers		SDG 25 per m²		
Shops in suburb shopping centers in neighborhoods and new industrial zones		SDG 20 per m²		
Bank headquarters		SDG 25 per m²		
Bank branch offices		SDG 20 per m²		
Factories' production areas		SDG 15 per m²		
Factories' storage and administration areas		SDG 10 per m²		
Companies' headquarters		SDG 50 per m²		
Companies' branch offices		SDG 35 per m²		
Gasoline (that is, petrol) stations		SDG 5 per m²		
Private universities		SDG 5 per m²		
Private schools		SDG 5 per m²		
Private hospitals		SDG 15 per m²		
Private kindergartens	SDG 5 per m²	SDG 4 per m²	SDG 3 per m²	

Source: Khartoum Locality (2012).

if not all, of the burden will likely be shifted to the tenant. It seems that the differential rates are based on occupancy rather than actual use. Letting out residential property is effectively perceived as commercial use. Table 27.4 provides the tariffs for commercial and industrial properties in Khartoum. For these properties size (square meters) and specific use (for example, shops, banks, or private hospitals) are differentiating factors irrespective of the level within which they are located. However, for shops located in shopping centers in levels A, B, and C, special tariffs apply.

Billing, Collection, and Enforcement

The awayed office in each locality carries out billing and collection activities. Tax notices are delivered to taxpayers by the middle of the year, and payment is due before the end of the year. Tax notifications are normally distributed door-to-door by an agent company. The tax may be paid in installments by agreement with the council.

Enforcement mechanisms against noncompliant taxpayers include the following:

- A warning letter is delivered in person to the taxpayer giving him one week to settle his debt.

- Interest of 5 percent is added on the amount of the tax due.

- Property seizure is authorized by a court. The seizure order directs the tax collector to take possession of all or part of the property of the taxpayer necessary to settle the debt.

- A property sale order is authorized by a court.

An administrative problem faced by states and localities is the widespread failure of many government institutions to pay the taxes and charges they owe to states and localities. Local-government officials cannot easily enforce the tax against these entities (Fjeldstad 2016).

As Fjeldstad (2016) points out, there is a need to significantly enhance the financial capacity of Sudan's subnational governments to raise their own revenues and meet their expenditure responsibilities. One revenue source that requires serious attention is the recurrent property tax. Federal and state policies that relate to the transfer system and revenue sharing also need to be reviewed. According to Fjeldstad (2016), the fundamental issues to be addressed in reforming the subnational revenue system in Sudan are

- redesigning the current revenue structure;

- building institutional capacity; and

- enhancing tax compliance through improved service delivery.

Note

1. Before South Sudan's secession, there were twenty-six states. Ten of these now constitute South Sudan. In 2012, two additional states were created.

References

CIA (Central Intelligence Agency). 2016. "Sudan." In *The World Factbook.* https://www .cia.gov/library/publications/the-world-factbook/geos/.su.html.

Fjeldstad, O.-H. 2016. "Revenue Mobilization at Sub-national Levels in Sudan." Report SR 2016:1. Bergen: CMI and University of Bergen.

Hamid, G. M. 2002. "Localizing the Local: Reflections on the Experience of Local Authorities in Sudan." Riyadh: Arab Urban Development Institute. *www.passia.org /goodgov/resources/Localizing.pdf.*

IMF (International Monetary Fund). 2012. "Sudan: Selected Issues." International Monetary Fund Country Report no. 12/299. Washington, DC.

———. 2015. *2014 IMF Government Finance Statistics Yearbook.* Washington, DC.

Khartoum Locality. 2012. Personal Communication by Officials from the Awayed Office.

Pantuliano, S. 2007. "The Land Question: Sudan's Peace Nemesis." Working paper. London: Humanitarian Policy Group and Overseas Development Institute.

United Nations. 2014. *World Urbanization Prospects.* Washington, DC: Department of Economic and Social Affairs, Population Division.

United Nations, Department of Economic and Social Affairs, Population Division. 2015. World Population Prospects: The 2015 Revision. *https://esa.un.org/unpd/wpp /Publications/Files/World_Population_2015_Wallchart.pdf.*

USAID (U.S. Agency for International Development). 2007. *Land Tenure and Property Rights Regional Report.* Vol. 2.1, *East and Central Africa.* Burlington, VT: ARD.

World Bank. 2016a. "Country and Lending Groups." *http://data.worldbank.org/about /country-and-lending-groups.*

———. 2016b. "GDP per Capita (Current US%)." *http://data.worldbank.org/indicator /NY.GDP.PCAP.CD.*

———. 2016c. "Registering Property in Sudan." *www.doingbusiness.org/data/explore economies/sudan/registering-property/.*

Legislation

Civil Transactions Act of 1984.

Decentralization Decree of 1991.

Fourth Constitutional Decree of 1991.

Interim Constitution of 2005.

Local Development Act of 2003.

Local Governments Act of 1951.

Unregistered Land Act of 1970.

28

Tanzania

WILLIAM McCLUSKEY AND RIËL FRANZSEN

The United Republic of Tanzania consists of two formerly separate states in East Africa: Tanganyika and Zanzibar. Tanganyika was granted independence in December 1961; Zanzibar achieved independence in December 1963. The two united to form the United Republic of Tanzania in April 1964. On the mainland, Tanzania is bounded on the north by Uganda and Kenya, on the east by the Indian Ocean, on the south by Mozambique, Malawi, and Zambia, and on the west by the Democratic Republic of the Congo, Burundi, and Rwanda. Zanzibar comprises the islands of Unguja and Pemba, located off the coast northwest of Dar es Salaam, the commercial capital and largest city. Tanzania covers a total area of 945,087 km². The administrative capital is Dodoma. The population of Dar es Salaam is more than 5 million (CIA 2016) and is expected to exceed 10 million by 2030 (Viruly and Hopkins 2014). The country has a population of 53.5 million (United Nations 2015). The urban population is around 32 percent (United Nations 2014). The per capita GDP was estimated at USD 879 in 2015 (World Bank 2016b), and Tanzania is therefore classified as a low-income country (World Bank 2016a).

Government

Tanzania is a constitutional republic with a two-tier system of government administration consisting of the central government and local governments. There are 30 regions and 106 administrative districts. The local governments are urban authorities and rural authorities as established under the Local Government (Urban Authorities) Act of 1982 and the Local Government (District Authorities) Act of 1982. The local-government system was established in the colonial period and continued after independence until 1972, when local-government authorities were abolished. They were reinstated in 1978 (Kayuza 2006).

Land Tenure

The origins of the present land tenure system in Tanzania lie in its colonial past, during which land in Tanzania, as in many other African countries, was held under customary tenure, whereby powers to control and allocate land were vested in a tribe, a clan, a family, or chiefs. The Germans, the first colonial administrators, followed by the British, made significant changes to the land tenure system. The British passed the 1923 Land Ordinance, under which all lands, whether occupied or unoccupied, were declared public lands, and all interests over the lands were placed under the control of the governor (UN-Habitat 2013). The Land Ordinance remained operational until 2001, when, in accordance with the 1995 National Land Policy, the Land Act and the Village Land Act were enacted to govern landholdings under a right of occupancy in urban and rural areas (USAID 2007). Like the 1923 Land Ordinance, the Land Act treats land as public property that is vested in the president as trustee, acting on behalf of all Tanzanian citizens (USAID 2007).

The land title registration system is a hybrid based on a Torrens titling and a deeds registration system and is used for both urban and rural lands (Mukandala 2009; UN-Habitat 2013). This system of titling authenticates and guarantees ownership of a parcel of land or a legal interest in land. For land administration purposes, there are three classifications of land: reserved land (about 28 percent), village land (about 70 percent), and general land (only about 2 percent), which is all land that is not reserved land or village land (Olima 2010) and is mainly urban land and other land already granted title (USAID 2007). Reserved land is all land set aside for special purposes (such as preserved forests, game parks, and reserves). Village land is land that belongs to registered villages, where the village councils do not own the land but only manage it (Wily 2003 as reported in Olima 2010). Village councils play an important role in allocation of these lands (USAID 2007). The commissioner of lands is responsible for land administration and delegates functions and authority to land officers and municipalities (USAID 2007).

At present, there exists a dual land tenure system consisting of both statutory and customary rights of occupancy, with public land vested in the president as trustee. The customary tenure system applies only in rural areas or registered villages within urban areas. Under the dual land tenure system, landholders with a certificate of occupancy generally have explicit security of tenure (Olima 2010; UN-Habitat 2013). However, security of tenure for landholders within informal settlements without formal certificates of occupancy remains unclear. The legislation is silent on conferring security of tenure on landholdings in unplanned areas. In addition, land occupiers in unplanned urban areas do not qualify for security of tenure under the customary tenure system (Olima 2010).

The land tenure system has significantly influenced the operation of the real estate market. According to the Land Act of 1999, the interests in or rights over land of an occupier with a right of occupancy are limited to unexhausted improvements on the land, since land is the property of the state. Therefore, transactions of vacant land are restricted under the law. However, under amendments to the law (Land Amendment Act No. 2 of 2004), the sale of vacant land is now permitted but is subject to the approval of the commissioner for lands (UN-Habitat 2013). Land markets are fairly active in the urban and peri-urban areas but are not sufficiently formalized because many transactions are still not recorded. In rural areas, transfers are generally governed by customary practices (USAID 2007).

Taxation

Tax administration in Tanzania is the responsibility of the Tanzania Revenue Authority (TRA) within the Ministry of Finance. National taxes include the corporate and personal income taxes, the value-added tax, excise duties, customs duties, the stamp duty, and the capital gains tax. Local-authority taxes include the property tax, business licenses, building permit fees, development levies, hotel levies, and bus terminal fees.

Property-Related Taxes and Fees

The property-related taxes and fees administered in Tanzania include land (ground) rent, the stamp duty, the capital gains tax, and the property tax (called "rates"). With the exception of rates and land rent, the taxes have been collected by the TRA. However, effective July 1, 2016, the TRA has also been given responsibility for administration of the property tax, including valuation and collection.

Land Rent

Land rent is an annual payment for the right to use and occupy any parcel of land. It is charged on the holders of granted rights of occupancy throughout Tanzania. District councils are responsible for enforcing and collecting land rent on behalf of the Ministry of Lands, Housing, and Human Settlement Development (MLHHSD). Six months after payment is due, land rent incurs interest at a rate of 1 percent. The amount of land rent payable is determined by the commissioner at the MLHHSD with regard to

- the area of the land that is the subject of the right of occupancy;

- the use of land permitted by the right of occupancy that has been granted;

- the value of the land as evidenced by sales, leases, and other dispositions of land in the market in the area where the right of occupancy has been granted; and

- the amount of any premium required to be paid on the grant of a right of occupancy (UN-Habitat 2013).

Land rent varies from one local authority to another (Olima 2010). Table 28.1 shows the land rent schedule for Kinondoni Municipality, which is located in Dar es Salaam.

Land rent in Tanzania is shared revenue; local governments are allocated 20 percent of the annual collections (Olima 2010; UN-Habitat 2013). The contribution of annual land rent is substantial. In 2008, the target collection was TZS 18 billion, and the actual collection was TZS 13 billion (Olima 2010).

Table 28.1 Land Rent Schedule for Kinondoni Municipality

Zone	Subject Area	Uses	Rates (TZS)
Outside CBD	Usino Estate	Residential	40/m²
		Commercial/residential	60/m²
		Commercial/service trades	120/m²
	Oyster Bay	Residential	50/m²
		Commercial/residential	75/m²
		Commercial/service trades	150/m²

Source: Handbook on Land Rent Rates for Tanzania Mainland as reported in UN-Habitat (2013).

The Stamp Duty

The stamp duty or property transfer tax is governed by the Stamp Duty Act of 1972. It is levied and payable on the acquisition and transfer of real property rights and is based on the fair market value of the property. The tax is computed at the rate of 1 percent of the fair market value of the property, but never on a value lower than the sale price (Olima 2010). The central government does billing, and the TRA collects the duty.

The Capital Gains Tax

The capital gains tax is paid on the profit from the sale or disposal of an investment in land or a building. It is governed by the Income Tax Act of 2006. The TRA is responsible for assessment of this tax. The tax rates on disposal of property are 10 percent of the gain for a resident person and 20 percent of the gain in an up-front payment for a nonresident person (UN-Habitat 2013).

The Property Tax

The property tax, called "rates" in Tanzania, is levied by local-government authorities and is governed by the Urban Authorities (Rating) Act of 1983 and the Local Government Finance Act of 1982. The tax is based on the market value of improvements and is levied on all taxable properties in both urban and rural areas. The property owner has the responsibility to pay property rates. In the absence of the owner, the rating authority is empowered to demand the amount due from a tenant or occupier (McCluskey et al. 2003).

The legislation provides that buildings and improvements on the land constitute taxable objects in Tanzania. In practice, land value is excluded from the ratable value of property since the Land Act of 1999 provides that all land in Tanzania is the property of the state, and the rights of an individual are limited to the unexhausted improvements to the land. However, a property owner pays land rent for the use and occupation of land to the government (McCluskey and Franzsen 2005; Olima 2010).

Tanzania provides for the application of either a simple flat rating system or an ad valorem property tax. All local authorities in Tanzania may impose the flat rating system through the provision of local bylaws under the Local Government Act of 1982. This system has been refined from an original flat amount per building to one that reflects adjustments for location, size, and building use (Franzsen and Semboja 2004).

If a property is not valued and included on a valuation roll, it is liable to flat rates. In this context, flat rates are a rather simplified property-based tax used by some local government authorities (LGAs) and implemented through a bylaw. Flat rates are applied through a fairly nontechnical approach. Properties liable to flat rates are not valued as such but are assessed a tax amount based on such factors as property use, location, and size.

Given the large number of properties and the lack of valuers within some LGAs, flat rates are seen as a viable alternative to value-based rating. It is generally accepted that a property liable to flat rates will have a tax bill approximately 50 percent lower than the amount that could be charged if the property were to be valued. Therefore, there is a real financial benefit to valuing properties. Table 28.2 shows the basis of property rates across four LGAs. All four LGAs use value-based rating. Because of the potential of increased revenue from value-based rates, there is a growing trend to increase the number of properties liable to value-based rating. Kinondoni and Ilala no longer use flat rates, which is a positive move.

Under the Urban Authorities (Rating) Act of 1983, authorities are permitted to levy an ad valorem property tax. Although assessments of properties under this tax should be based on market values, all valuations are in fact based on replacement cost, largely because of the lack of market value information. Table 28.3 illustrates the relatively low coverage of properties on the valuation rolls. The three Dar es Salaam municipalities have by far the greatest number of properties on their valuation rolls. Each of them is taking steps to ensure greater coverage. For example, Kinondoni has been using about 60 graduate students (in real property valuation) to undertake fieldwork on unvalued properties; the information they gather is then passed to valuers for valuation purposes. Ilala has been aggressively undertaking annual supplementary valuations since the revaluation in 2012 that saw an 11 percent increase in the number of properties on the valuation roll. Arusha has been using groups of students to undertake field inspections for properties captured on the flat rating system. Tables 28.4 and 28.5 show the revenue-collection performance of Kinondoni Municipality over the five-year period from 2009/2010 to 2013/2014 and for 2013/2014.

Table 28.2 Property-Rating Methodologies

LGA	Value Based	Flat Rates
Arusha	Yes	Yes
Ilala	Yes	No
Kinondoni	Yes	No
Temeke	Yes	Yes

Table 28.3 Properties Currently on Valuation Rolls and Valuation Roll Coverage

LGA	Current Number of Properties on Valuation Rolls	Potential Number	Coverage of Valued Properties (%)	Coverage of All Properties Liable for Value-Based Rates and Flat Rates (%)	Comments
Arusha	7,000	>70,000	10	26	In 2002, through a World Bank project, some 3,271 properties were valued. A further World Bank project in 2014 resulted in a total of 7,000 properties being valued. Some 11,000 properties liable to flat rates are included on the valuation roll.
Kinondoni	154,000	250,000–300,000	53	53	Properties were valued under a 2010–2012 World Bank project.
Ilala	158,000	200,000	79	79	Consultants completed the revaluation of 143,000 properties in 2012. The LGA prepares supplementary valuations annually.
Temeke	160,000	>200,000	80	80	Properties liable to flat rates are being progressively valued.

Table 28.4 Budgeted and Actual Revenue for Kinondoni Municipality, 2009/2010–2013/2014 (TZS)

Source	Budgeted	Actual
Property tax	15,284,000,000	9,754,301,156
City service levy	36,450,000,000	40,764,803,834
Licenses	11,101,675,718	2,714,135,008
Hotel levy	3,769,340,000	3,361,410,467
Billboards	3,000,000,000	9,020,450,639
Land rent	828,000,000	354,828,637
Miscellaneous	34,904,157,409	33,251,687,617
Total own-source revenue	105,337,173,127	99,221,617,358

Source: Kinondoni Municipal Council (2015).

Table 28.5 Revenue Collection in Kinondoni Municipality, 2013/2014 (TZS)

Source	Budgeted	Actual
City service levy	10,000,000,000	13,300,340,189
Mfuko wa barabara (road fund)	5,254,407,200	7,882,602,095
Plot sale compensation fees	7,000,000,000	3,552,696,013
Cost sharing	2,450,000,000	3,090,693,116
Property tax	4,500,000,000	2,857,710,201
Trade licenses	2,600,323,017	2,749,264,594
Mfuko wa Afya (basket fund)	2,460,747,000	2,460,747,000
Advertisement fees	2,000,000,000	2,235,475,672
Garbage collection fees	1,200,000,000	2,014,747,858
Community contributions	1,150,000,000	1,532,370,905

Source: Kinondoni Municipal Council (2015).

Exemptions

Certain property can be exempted from property tax liability in accordance with the provisions of the Local Government Finance Act of 1982 the Urban Authorities (Rating) Act of 1983 and Urban Authorities (Rating) Exemption from Liability of Rates Order 1997. Legislation provides that the following buildings are exempt from the property tax:

• Property personally occupied by the president.

• Property used for public utility undertakings.

- Premises used primarily for public worship, with the exclusion of property used for residential or social purposes in connection with places of public worship.

- Public libraries and public museums.

- Cemeteries and crematoriums.

- Civil and military airports.

- Property used for sporting purposes or solely for educational purposes.

- Railway infrastructure.

- Other property as may be prescribed by the particular urban local authority.

Property that, in the opinion of the minister, is being used for public purposes is exempt from liability of rates payable under the provisions of the Urban Authorities (Finance) Act. The following properties and improvements are specified:

- Property owned by the government and its departments and used exclusively as office accommodation, laboratories, or warehouses.

- Government residential property used exclusively by government officers and employees.

- Property used by or reserved for use by a local authority.

- Property used exclusively for educational institutions.

- Property owned by a religious institution and not used in any way for commercial purposes.

In addition, government buildings are exempt from property rates even though this exclusion is not stated in the law. The responsible minister is required to pay service charges in lieu of property rates, but the central government has not been remitting these payments to local authorities. Because government buildings are numerous and occupy prime locations in urban areas, this has significantly affected the actual revenue of local authorities.

Valuation

The Urban Authorities (Rating) Act of 1983 requires that property valuation be based on the capital market value or, where the market value cannot be ascertained, the replacement cost of the buildings, structures, and other improvements, adjusted for depreciation. The law provides for a maximum allowable depreciation rate of 25 percent. According to the act, properties should be revalued every five years unless the responsible minister approves less frequent revaluations. The act also provides for supplementary valuations where physical changes to properties have occurred during a valuation cycle.

Objections and Appeals

When the valuation roll is published, taxpayers may visit the offices of a local authority to inspect the roll. The local authority must set a date for the filing of objections, which should be at least 23 days after the date of publication of the notice in the gazette. An owner may submit a written complaint against the valuation to the rating authority on or before the date specified by the authority and must identify the concerned property, the value of the property as entered in the roll, the grounds for the objection, and the value the individual considers appropriate. The rating authority may also object to a property or its value entered in the roll or the omission of a property that should have been included in it. The objection is presented to both the valuer responsible for the roll and the owner or occupant of the property or any appointed representative. Objections properly made are lodged with the Rating Valuation Tribunal. The law provides for an appeal to the High Court against a decision of the Rating Valuation Tribunal on a point of law.

Tax Rates

There are no uniform, nationally determined tax rates. Rates are determined locally but irregularly. In Ilala Municipality, different rates are applied to various categories of properties—residential, commercial, and industrial—with a maximum and minimum rate per square meter. For example, the rate is 0.15 percent for residential property, whereas a rate of 0.2 percent applies to nonresidential properties (2016).

The value-based rating approach is predicated on determining the value of the property based on its depreciated replacement cost. The amount of property tax payable is then the product of the assessed value and the tax rate. Tax rates are determined by the LGA. As can be seen in table 28.6, these rates have not been changed for a long time. In addition, the tax rates are quite modest, ranging from a low of 0.12 percent to a high of 0.40 percent. Relatively low tax rates that have not kept pace with inflation lead to the lack of revenue buoyancy from property rates. In practice, the real value of the revenue collection diminishes over time because of inflation. The Arusha City Council completed a revaluation in 2016 and

Table 28.6 LGA Tax Rates

LGA	Residential (%)	Commercial (%)	Res/Com (%)	Comments
Arusha	0.2	0.4	0.3	Rates set in 2002
Ilala	0.15	0.2	–	Minimum flat rate set at 10,000 TZS
Kinondoni	0.15	0.2	–	Rates set in 2004
Temeke	0.15	0.15	0.15	Minimum flat rate set at 15,000 TZS

will have to consider its tax rates in the light of property value increases. Ilala is proposing to amend its tax rates to 0.175 percent for residential property and 0.25 percent for industrial property.

Collection and Enforcement

Revenue-collection activities are administered through the local-authority treasurer's office. Currently, most local authorities have computerized the preparation of bills, but delivery is largely done manually through coordination by ward executive officers.

The Urban Authorities (Rating) Act is silent on the dates on which tax payments are due and the number of installments allowed. Under the by-laws issued by Dar es Salaam councils, for example, the tax deadline is defined as 30 days "after receipt of the property tax bill." Also, tax payments in municipalities in Dar es Salaam are mainly made as a lump sum, although large taxpayers are allowed more than one installment.

Despite the various legal provisions to enforce payment, collection rates appear to be quite low (e.g., less than 50 percent in Dar es Salaam). There are several possible explanations for this low collection rate, including lack of taxpayer education and understanding, inadequate local service levels, and taxpayer resistance. Some attribute the low collection rates largely to a lack of political will and to administrative inefficiency (Kayuza 2006).

The Local Government Revenue Collection Information System

The Local Government Revenue Collection Information System (LGR-CIS) is a holistic system and database, underpinned by a multipurpose geographic information system (GIS), that is designed to incorporate all LGA functions to ensure that LGAs have a single view of customers, taxpayers, land, and property and the means to manage all revenue sources efficiently and reliably. The LGRCIS is a web-based application accessed through a web browser. Development of a local-government revenue administration system began in 2005 and led to the release of the Municipal Revenue Collection Manager (MRECOM). This system was rolled out in a number of LGAs, for example, Kinondoni in 2006 and Ilala and Temeke in 2007. Other LGAs (such as Moshi and Morogoro) also implemented MRECOM. Currently, some 12 LGAs use MRECOM.

The use of LGRCIS is seen as a key tool in improving collections within LGAs. Improvements tend to be correlated with accurate taxpayer record keeping, efficient bill preparation, and taxpayer confidence that their payments are properly recorded, with electronic receipts. From a technical perspective, the integration of GIS will positively contribute to the management of the collection process through the application of visualization tools and other reporting analytics. The objective of the President's Office—Regional Authority for Local Government is for a national roll from LGRCIS to all LGAs. All 186 LGAs by March 2016 have had the necessary software installed on servers and terminals.

Enforcement

Procedures for enforcement of property tax compliance are provided in the Urban Authorities (Rating) Act of 1983 and the Local Government Finance Act of 1982. The legal provisions that are available to councils to enforce rates compliance include the following:

- A penalty imposed at a rate not exceeding 1 percent per month on the amount of the tax that remains unpaid.

- A distraint on the personal goods and chattels of the rates defaulter.

- Institution of proceedings for the sale of the premises of those taxpayers whose rates are in arrears.

- Recovery of unpaid rates through deductions from the defaulter's salary.

- A penalty of 25 percent per year of the amount of tax in arrears or imprisonment for a term not exceeding 12 months, or both.

- A fine not exceeding TZS 50,000 or imprisonment for a term not exceeding three months for a person who fails or refuses to pay rates.

Although legislation provides for various enforcement mechanisms, local authorities still find it a challenge to implement them in enforcing property tax compliance. Legal procedures are generally very time consuming and expensive. Because of the lack of resources, local authorities tend not to apply enforcement legislation.

Table 28.7 Own Sources of Urban Local-Government Revenue
in Tanzania

1. Business licenses	10. City buildings rent
2. Property tax	11. Transport of quarry products fees
3. Advertising fees (billboards)	12. Abattoir slaughter fees
4. Industrial cess/city service levy	13. Medical services fees
5. Liquor licenses	14. Building permit fees
6. Human resource licenses	15. Hotel levy
7. Transport of mineral products fees	16. Fence building fees
8. Health inspection and food handling fees	17. Meat inspection fees
9. Billboards tax	

Local-Government Revenue Sources

Local-government authorities in Tanzania are authorized to raise own-source revenue from a range of sources provided for in the Local Government Finance Act of 1982. However, the power of local governments to raise their own revenues is subject to the approval of the minister responsible for local government. This provision is designed to limit the number of available sources and prevent proliferation of nuisance sources.

Own-source revenues of local governments can be categorized as internal or external. Internal sources of revenue include all local taxes and miscellaneous fees, charges, and other payments, while external sources typically are central-government grants and borrowing. Previously, the Local Government Finance Act of 1982 provided for 56 revenue sources from which a local authority could choose. At present, local authorities have fewer revenue sources at their disposal, since sources perceived as nuisance taxes have been abolished. Table 28.7 illustrates some of the revenue sources still available to urban local-government authorities.

The Role of the Tanzania Revenue Authority

In the 2016/2017 budget speech on June 8, 2016, the minister for finance and planning announced that responsibility for collection of the property tax would be delegated to the TRA, effective July 1, 2016. The minister explained that the reason for the transfer was to ensure maximum collection of the property rates revenue.

It is clear that annual property tax collection rates by the LGAs, mostly between 30 and 50 percent, are low by international standards, but the property tax has significant potential to raise much-needed revenue for LGAs in Tanzania if administration of collection and enforcement procedures is improved and if the number of properties subject to the property tax is increased. Clearly, the government of Tanzania believes that transferring the administration of the property tax to the TRA can enhance revenue collection because of the TRA's considerable experience in the collection of income taxes, corporate taxes, and the value-added tax.

Low collection rates have clearly been a concern for some time, and in an attempt to improve collection rates, the government transferred the responsibility for collecting the property tax to the TRA, effective in the financial year 2008/2009. The Dar es Salaam municipal councils (Ilala, Kinondoni, and Temeke) were selected to pilot the new approach. The TRA collected the property tax for five years, 2008/2009 to 2012/2013, with the aim of increasing revenue and building capacity for the Dar es Salaam LGAs.

During the financial years 2005/2006 to 2007/2008, the average annual revenue collection by the three municipal councils was 68 percent of the estimated collection. The TRA collected 68.14 percent of the target during the period 2008/2009 to 2010/2011, but the collection level declined to 16.5 percent of the collection estimate in the fifth year of the revenue-collection piloting. Collection of the property tax reverted to the Dar es Salaam municipal councils in January 2014. It is apparent from the figures that the TRA's attempts to improve collection rates were unsuccessful.

Anticipated Benefits and Advantages of Collection by the TRA

Several perceived benefits of this administrative change are anticipated:

- Synchronizing all taxes of large taxpayers will improve efficiency.

- The TRA can use stringent enforcement powers that are not available to LGAs.

- The decentralized structure of the TRA will enable the development of a regional property tax administrative framework.

- A customized version of LGRCIS will permit the continued use of this system for administration.

- The TRA has an embedded culture of professionalism in dealing with taxpayers.

- Current databases developed by the TRA will support the property tax through increased information.

Anticipated Challenges

A number of significant challenges with respect to this new decree can be identified, including the following:

- In the short term, the total revenue collected from the property tax is anticipated to drop drastically because the TRA has yet to put in place the collection system and build up the necessary capacity.

- A critical transition period was not built in to facilitate the move, so major administrative disruption and other issues are likely to be encountered. Data transfer from LGAs to the TRA will be incomplete, and data will be unharmonized and nonstandardized. LGAs have largely withdrawn from collection and have stopped sending demand notices, but the TRA does not have a billing system in place. The lack of trust between the TRA and LGAs could adversely affect relationships between them.

- The TRA will need to develop a valuation administration strategy and build up capacity, skills, and experience in property valuation (including increasing coverage and updating and maintaining property database of LGAs) and billing and collection of property taxes.

- The impact on LGAs needs to be assessed and addressed with the aim of formulating the system and mechanisms for remittance of collected property tax revenue to LGAs and considering the significant immediate effect on LGAs' cash flows from the property tax, which affect their operational budgets. Transparency, reliability, and timeliness of transfers will be key.

- Communication with LGAs will have to be increased to align objectives, manage the transition, and coordinate and manage required activities.

The Property Tax in Zanzibar

In Zanzibar, the central government is primarily responsible for some key public services, such as health, education, and housing. The Zanzibar Municipal Council (ZMC) was established under the Zanzibar Municipal Council Act (No. 3 of 1995) and serves a population of some 300,000. The council has a number of statutory functions, including acquisition of and dealing with land, street cleaning, control of open spaces, control of roads, naming and numbering of streets, management of public markets, sewerage, solid-waste management, and flood-mitigating drainage. However, the ZMC has been allocated own sources that produce relatively low revenues. The central government contributes some 45 percent of ZMC revenue in the form of a block grant to the ZMC to meet its revenue shortfall.[1] Clearly, given the fiscal pressures on the central government, it is likely that this grant will decrease over time. This will place greater responsibility on the ZMC for efficiently administering its own-source revenues and argues for the property tax to become a local source of additional revenue.

ZMC own-source revenues largely consist of income generated from public markets, business licenses, car parking fees, advertising fees, the property tax (rates), building permits, sanitation charges, the hiring of grounds for celebrations, health fees, court charges, public transport operator badges, and liquor licenses (ZUSP 2014). The main revenue sources assigned to the ZMC are typically those that can be attached to the use of land and buildings. The one notable exception is that the ZMC has only a very restricted right to levy a property tax. This prevents the city from benefiting from increased property values associated with economic growth and investment and a buoyant tax base that grows dynamically with new construction.

Responsibility for Levying the Property Tax

The responsibility for levying property rates lies with the Zanzibar Revenue Board (ZRB) under the provisions of the Property Tax Act of 2008 (PTA), but because of various political and administrative difficulties, this responsibility has not yet been implemented. At the same time, the ZMC is levying rates (the property tax) on some 1,370 properties under the provisions of Section 11 of the Towns Decree, Chapter 100. R.L.Z. 1934 (as amended).[2] It is anticipated that the PTA will be amended to provide that the property tax will be a revenue source for local councils. In 2014, presidential assent was given to the Zanzibar Local Government Authority Act (Act 7 of 2014). Under Section 70(a) of this act, a local government may generate revenue from a "council property tax." The right of a local government to levy a property tax is discretionary, however, and details of the tax have yet to be formulated through regulations. Also, it seems that the ZRB is looking to implement the property tax under the provisions of the Property Tax Act of 2008.

The Current Property Rates System

The levying of property rates in Zanzibar is restricted to the Stonetown area of the ZMC. Therefore, no property located outside this area is being assessed for property rates. Within the ZMC, the Rates and Rent Department is responsible for administering rates.

As previously noted, the PTA gives the sole mandate for the levying of a property tax in Zanzibar to the ZRB, but this act has not been implemented. The ZMC has no authority to levy property rates under the PTA and therefore has continued to levy rates under much earlier colonial legislation, the Towns Decree, Chapter 100, 1934 (as amended).[3] This legislation established the valuation basis for property rates as the gross annual value of a property, which is the "estimated annual rent at which such premises might be expected to let from year to year to a tenant." The tax rate was set at 10 percent of the gross annual value. The legislation has been amended to change the basis of valuation to either (1) the declared purchased price when the property is sold or (2) the estimated cost of construction of a new property. In effect, the current property tax is based on taxpayer self-declaration. The current tax rate is 0.5 percent of the declared price or construction cost.

The PTA provides that the basis of valuation of a property is the market value. Where the market value cannot be ascertained, the replacement cost of the building or structure is applied.[4] In addition, the tax rate has been amended to 0.1 percent of the assessed value of the property.[5] The PTA broadens the property tax base through a provision that gives the minister the power to declare any area within Zanzibar a taxable area.[6] All properties within a taxable area, subject to specific exemptions, are deemed taxable.[7] A taxable area means the whole area of a district, council, or part comprising ratable properties.[8]

Property Tax Revenues

The ZMC undertook responsibility for administering property taxes in 2008 and levies two taxes: (1) the rent tax, levied on commercial or residential properties at 25 percent of the rental value; and (2) the rates tax, levied on buildings at 0.5 percent of the building cost or the purchase price. Values are supposed to be updated every 10 years but have not been updated since 2003 except in cases where properties have changed ownership.

The collection of rents and rates is inadequate. No enforcement of the property taxes is undertaken, and no court action has been instituted against delinquent taxpayers since 2008. The tax is effectively voluntary—if a taxpayer chooses not to pay, no enforcement action will be taken against him. Of the 1,370 properties on the valuation roll, only 855 are actually making any payment, while 515 properties are valued and billed but have consistently not made payments.

Property Tax Issues in Tanzania

The primary function of the property tax as a local source of revenue is to generate sufficient revenue for local-government expenditures. However, local authorities in Tanzania and Zanzibar are failing to exploit the property tax as a source of revenue. It is evident that property tax collection rates have remained very low, and that property tax revenue is unlikely to increase to acceptable levels unless deliberate measures are taken to change the situation.

Although records of property tax revenue collection depict a gradual annual increase, collection levels in comparison with potential levels should be an issue of concern but are not. More important, there is a problem when increasing the number of taxable properties does not bring about a corresponding increase in collected revenue. This can be due to low compliance, as manifested by significant property tax arrears, particularly in the municipal councils in Dar es Salaam (Kayuza 2006; Olima 2010).

Tax coverage is haphazard in both rural and urban areas. For instance, in Ilala Municipality, property tax coverage is less than 50 percent. Enforcement mechanisms are weak. Most local authorities are grappling with the challenges associated with collection and enforcement that have resulted in widespread noncompliance by taxpayers. In addition, exemptions can be granted at the discretion of the minister with no consultation and with no regard as to the potential loss of revenue. The grant of exemptions by the central government is not accompanied by an obligation to repay local authorities for the resulting loss of revenue.

The present legislation provides for an extremely liberal approach to the granting of exemptions, which are resulting in a significant loss of potential revenue to urban local authorities. For example, information supplied by the Iringa council indicates that there are 333 government and educational properties and 49 buildings used for public religious worship, approximately 3.7 percent of the total tax base of 10,412 properties. Widespread exemptions often create difficulties for municipalities, particularly if there are large numbers of exempt properties within the municipal area. The range of exemptions needs to be more tightly controlled.

Better application of the legal provisions available for increasing collection rates would improve revenue, equity, and efficiency. Consequently, the government must ensure that all buildings are on the tax rolls, that these buildings are valued close to market value, that the tax is correctly assessed, and that the revenue is collected.

Lack of political will among leaders has negatively affected the efficiency and effectiveness of the property tax. Local authorities are unwilling to invest in expansion of the tax base through improved information management systems. Limited human and technical capacity to undertake tax assessment, valuation, tax collection, and enforcement is a major problem in both local authorities and the central government. Local authorities are unable to recruit and retain qualified valuers to improve the valuation and assessment of property. Clearly the level of salaries is a key issue where if LGAs could provide competitive salaries then retention and recruitment could improve.

Notes

1. ZUSP (2014), ZMC 5-Year Revenue Enhancement Plan, Zanzibar Urban Strategic Project—Change Management Programme.
2. Data supplied by Rates and Rent Department, ZMC.
3. Zanzibar Township (Assessment and Rating) Rules, 1934.
4. PTA, Sections 3 and 8.
5. PTA, Section 6.
6. PTA, Section 27(1)(a).
7. PTA, Section 28.
8. PTA, Section 3.

References

CIA (Central Intelligence Agency). 2016. "Tanzania." In *The World Factbook*. https://www.cia.gov/library/publications/the-world-factbook/geos/tz.html.

Franzsen, R. C. D., and J. Semboja. 2004. "Analytical Report: The Enhancement of Local Revenues in the City of Dar es Salaam." Washington, DC: World Bank.

Kayuza, H. M. 2006. "Real Property Taxation in Tanzania: An Investigation on Implementation and Taxpayer Perceptions." Doctoral thesis, Royal Institute of Technology, Stockholm, Sweden.

Kinondoni Municipal Council 2015.

McCluskey, W. J., and R. C. D. Franzsen. 2005. "An Evaluation of the Property Tax in Tanzania: An Untapped Fiscal Resource or Administrative Headache?" *Property Management* 23(1): 43–69.

McCluskey, W., R. Franzsen, T. Johnstone, and D. Johnstone. 2003. "Property Tax Reform: The Experience of Tanzania." In *Our Common Estate*. London: RICS Foundation.

Mukandala, I. M. 2009. "An Evaluation of the Effectiveness of Rural Land Title Certification Programme in Tanzania: The Case of Mbozi District—Mbeya Region." M.S. thesis, Ardhi University, Tanzania.

Olima, W. H. A. 2010. "Property Taxation in Anglophone East Africa: Case Study of Tanzania." Working paper WP10NEA7. Cambridge, MA: Lincoln Institute of Land Policy.

UN-Habitat. 2013. *Property Tax Regimes in East Africa*. Global Urban Economic Dialogue Series. Nairobi: UN Human Settlements Program.

United Nations. 2014. *World Urbanization Prospects*. Washington, DC: Department of Economic and Social Affairs, Population Division.

United Nations, Department of Economic and Social Affairs, Population Division. 2015. World Population Prospects: The 2015 Revision. *https://esa.un.org/unpd/wpp /Publications/Files/World_Population_2015_Wallchart.pdf.*

USAID (U.S. Agency for International Development). 2007. *Land Tenure and Property Rights Regional Report.* Vol. 2.1, *East and Central Africa.* Burlington, VT: ARD.

Viruly, F., and N. Hopkins. 2014. *Unleashing Sub-Saharan Africa Property Markets.* Report prepared for the Royal Institute of Chartered Surveyors. London: rics.org /research.

Wily, L. A. 2003. "Community-Based Land Tenure Management: Questions and Answers About Tanzania's New Village Land Act, 1999." Issue Paper no. 120. London: International Institute for Environment and Development.

World Bank. 2016a. "Country and Lending Groups." *http://data.worldbank.org/about /country-and-lending-groups.*

———. 2016b. "GDP per Capita (Current US%)." *http://data.worldbank.org/indicator /NY.GDP.PCAP.CD.*

ZUSP (Zanzibar Urban Strategic Project). 2014. Zanzibar Urban Strategic Project— Change Management Programme Report. Zanzibar.

Legislation

Mainland Tanzania

Income Tax Act of 2006.

Land Act 4 of 1999.

Land Amendment Act No. 2 of 2004.

Land Ordinance of 1923.

Local Government (District Authorities) Act of 1982.

Local Government Finance Act of 1982.

Local Government (Urban Authorities) Act of 1982.

Stamp Duty Act of 1972.

Urban Authorities (Rating) Act of 1983.

Urban Authorities (Rating) Exemption from Liability of Rates Order 1997.

Village Land Act 5 of 1999.

Zanzibar

Property Tax Act of 2008.

Towns Decree [Chapter 100] of 1934 (as amended).

Zanzibar Local Government Authority Act (Act 7 of 2014).

Zanzibar Municipal Council Act (No. 3 of 1995).

Zanzibar Township (Assessment and Rating) Rules, 1934.

29

Uganda

RIËL FRANZSEN AND WILLIAM MCCLUSKEY

The Republic of Uganda is a landlocked country in East Africa that is bordered on the east by Kenya, on the north by South Sudan, on the west by the Democratic Republic of the Congo, on the southwest by Rwanda, and on the south by Lake Victoria and Tanzania. Uganda gained its independence from the United Kingdom on October 9, 1962. Its area is approximately 241,038 km^2, and the estimated population is around 39 million (United Nations 2015), of which only about 16 percent lives in urban areas (United Nations 2014). The capital city, Kampala, has an estimated population of 1.9 million (CIA 2016). Uganda is a low-income country with an estimated per capita GDP of USD 705 in 2016 (World Bank 2016a, 2016b).

Government

Uganda is a constitutional republic with two levels of government, the central government and a rather intricate system of local government. In May 2016, President Yoweri Museveni, who took office in 1986, commenced his fifth term as president.

Article 176 of the 1995 constitution provides that the system of local government in Uganda is based on the district as a unit "under which there shall be such lower governments and administrative units as Parliament may by law provide." Among various broad principles, the constitution also states that "there shall be established for each local government a sound financial base with reliable sources of revenue." There are five types of local councils: city, municipality, town, district, and division. In 2010, the Kampala City Council became the Kampala Capital City Authority under the Kampala Capital City Authority Act of 2010.

The country is divided into the Kampala Capital City Authority and 111 districts spread across four administrative regions (CIA 2016). Under the Local Government Act of 1997, the districts are further subdivided into subdistricts, counties, subcounties, parishes, and villages. Primarily because of rampant population growth and rapid urbanization, the local-government institutional landscape has changed dramatically over the past 20 years. The number of districts increased from 39 in 1999 to 111 in 2013. Town councils increased from 60 in 2004/2005 to 174 in 2013, and municipalities from 13 to 22 in 2010/2011 (Oxfam 2013). However, each time a new district is carved out of an old one, at least two self-accountable urban councils are established. It is in these urban centers that most of the property taxes, business licenses and permits, and market revenues are collected as own revenue sources. As a result, there is a significant revenue shift from rural to urban areas (Oxfam 2013).

In the 2008/2009 financial year, districts contributed 78 percent of all local revenues. Town councils and municipalities contributed 11 percent each. In 2009/2010, the contribution from districts drastically fell to 54 percent, while the contributions from town councils and municipalities rose to 21 percent and 25 percent, respectively. It is expected that urbanization will further reduce the revenue bases for the rural areas (Oxfam 2013).

Land Tenure

There are four types of landholding in Uganda: customary, leasehold, freehold, and *mailo* (UN-Habitat 2013). In 1975, legislation introduced new land tenure arrangements in Uganda by vesting title of all land in the state and converting all freehold and *mailo* tenure into leaseholds (USAID 2007). However, this law was not effectively implemented because freehold land and *mailo* land were not converted to leasehold in practice. Uganda's Land Act of 1997 formally recognizes the present four types of land tenure (USAID 2007).

Mailo tenure was introduced as a result of the 1900 Buganda Agreement. Under this agreement, land was divided among the kabaka (king) of Buganda, other notables, and the protectorate government. The basic unit of subdivision was a square mile (hence the name *mailo*). The Office of the Commissioner in the Ministry of Land, Housing, and Urban Development is responsible for land registration through a deeds system (Olima 2010; UN-Habitat 2013).

Customary tenure constitutes the bulk of land tenure in Uganda (USAID 2007). The 1995 constitution provided the impetus for streamlining land administration and management that resulted in the enactment of the Land Act of 1997 in 1998. The first important step was the development of the Land Sector Strategic Plan (LSSP) I (2002–2012). LSSP I provides the operational, institutional, and financial framework for the implementation of sector-wide reforms and land management, including the implementation of the Land Act (Oput and Orlova 2016). A main objective of LSSP I was to increase the availability, accessibility, affordability, and use of land information for planning purposes. However, it also provided for the introduction of a unified and accessible Land Information System (LIS). As part of the development and implementation of the LIS, the government put in place 21 ministry zonal offices, which also effectively enabled definition of the 21 cadastral zones for the country. The National Land Information Centre (NLIC), based in Kampala, was established to provide technical support for the design, development, and implementation of the LIS. It also serves as the repository for all land-related information. This was a significant improvement because previously members of the public had had to travel across the country to obtain services, first at their local district land office, then at the Surveys and Mapping Department in Entebbe, and finally at the Ministry Headquarters in Kampala (Oput and Orlova 2016). The rationalization and streamlining of processes resulted in the reduction in the number of days to register property from 227 in 2006 to 52 in 2012 (Oput and Orlova 2016; World Bank 2016c).

In 2009, only about 20 percent of land in Kampala (a city with an area of approximately 200 km^2) was categorized as planned land with leasehold land titles, while the remaining 80 percent consisted of unplanned, informal land. Within both formal and informal categories, mailo land is the predominant system of tenure. Only about 3 percent of land in Kampala is held under freehold land titles. Slum areas occupy about 22 percent, mostly on mailo land (Olima 2010). About 46 percent of city land was indicated as agricultural or simply undeveloped. Under the mailo system, absentee landlords have created a state of total neglect, which has led to conflict, fraud, and even forgery of ownership documents (UN-Habitat 2013).

One of the consequences is haphazard land development, which spawns congestion, depreciation of property values, and degeneration of the urban property fabric. The property market is not well developed, and customary practices, rather than formal processes, govern land transactions (USAID 2007). All these factors undermine the potential of a mature value-based property tax. However, in Kampala and other major urban centers, the property market is apparently quite well organized. High demand for land for urban development results in high prices (UN-Habitat 2013).

Taxation

Tax administration in Uganda is centralized in the Uganda Revenue Authority (URA). The URA is responsible for the collection of revenues to be deposited in the National Consolidated Account. National taxes include the personal and corporate income taxes, licenses and fees, customs duties, excise duties, the value-added tax (at a standard rate of 18 percent), the rental income tax, stamp duties, and the capital gains tax (Olima 2010).

Under the 1995 constitution and the Local Government Act of 1997, local governments are permitted to collect local taxes and fees within their jurisdictions. Article 191 of the constitution allows local governments to levy, charge, collect, and appropriate fees and taxes in accordance with any laws enacted by Parliament. Revenue collected by local governments includes property rates (the property tax), urban authority permits, the local hotel tax, taxi charges, market fees, trading license charges, parking fees, and the local services tax (Bendana and Mayanja 2012; Kopanyi 2015). For the Kampala Capital City Authority, the local services tax is important. It is levied on the wealth and income of all persons in gainful employment, self-employed persons, and practicing professionals, including commercial farmers.

The Local Government Act states that in urban areas (cities and municipal councils), the division councils collect revenue. A division council retains 50 percent of the revenue it collects in its area of jurisdiction and remits 50 percent to the city or municipal council. In rural areas, the subcounty councils collect revenue. A subcounty council retains 65 percent of the revenue it collects, or any higher percentage the district council may approve, and remits the remaining 35 percent to the district council.

Property-Related Taxes and Fees

Besides property rates, owners of property in Uganda may be liable for other property-related taxes, including the property transfer tax, the rental income tax on immovable property, and the capital gains tax. The rental income tax is levied under the Income Tax Act of 1997 and is administered by the URA.

The Stamp Duty

The stamp duty is regulated by the Income Tax Act. It is payable on transfers and acquisition of immovable property, and its revenue goes to the central government. The person who acquires the property is liable for the tax. The tax is based on the purchase price, which should reflect market value or a value determined by the Office of the Chief Government Valuer (Ministry of Lands, Housing, and Urban Development), which is responsible for valuations (Olima 2010; UN-Habitat 2013). The responsibility for setting rates lies with the Ministry of Finance. Currently, the tax rate is 1 percent of the market value of the property. Because the Office of the Chief Government Valuer employs only four valuers, it is unlikely that it has the capacity to follow up all cases where underdeclaration is suspected.

Ground Rent

The Uganda Land Commission charges ground rent on leaseholds and on all land being converted from customary tenure to freehold tenure, as well as on land without a title that is directly transferred to freehold (UN-Habitat 2013). Ground rent on leaseholds is based on unimproved site value and is charged at 1 percent of the market value of the land (Olima 2010). However, revaluations are not conducted, and amounts tend to be nominal. According to Oxfam (2013, 19), challenges for the ground rent include the following:

- Developers are slow to take up leasehold plots made available by councils, which narrows the base in most councils.

- The absence of a land board for municipalities hinders revenue collection.

- Collection of the revenue by the district administration hampers the revenue performance of the urban local governments.

The ground rent database is reportedly seriously out of date and more than 90 percent incorrect (Kopanyi 2015).

The Property Tax

The property tax (called "rates") in Uganda dates back to 1948, when the first valuation list was prepared for Kampala, later followed by other major towns, such as Entebbe, Jinja, Masaka, and Mbarara (Olima 2010). Until the Local Governments (Rating) Act of 2005 was enacted, the property tax was levied under the Local Government (Rating) Decree of 1979. The previous system could never be effectively implemented. As indicated by a report of the Ministry of Water, Lands, and the Environment in 2002, this had a dramatic impact on local revenues throughout the country, but especially in Kampala, because the former Kampala City Council at the time accounted for more than 50 percent of the total urban property in Uganda (MoWLE 2002). Rates were levied only in Kampala, the municipal councils, some town councils, and a few trading centers. However, in 2001, the chief government valuer reported that most towns and trading centers had last been valued in 1960, and that many towns and trading centers had never been rated, that is, had never introduced a property tax (Nsamba-Gayiiya 2001).

The current rating system is governed by the Local Governments (Rating) Act (LGRA) of 2005, which provides for the valuation, assessment, billing, and collection of rates and applies to the Kampala Capital City Authority (KCCA), municipal councils, town councils, and districts. The act is supplemented by the Local Governments (Rating) Regulations of 2005. The Fifth Schedule of the Local Governments Act of 1997, read with the LGRA, provides that the property tax shall be levied by urban councils as well as district councils, but coverage is weak. Although the law compels district councils to levy rates, no district has thus far introduced rates in rural areas. Even within jurisdictions that do levy rates (e.g., the KCCA and the municipal councils of Jinja, Masaka, Mbale, and Mbarara), it is estimated that many properties are not included in the valuation lists. According to the LGRA, all local governments in Uganda are permitted to impose tax rates (within prescribed limits) on the basis of the ratable value of any property within their areas of jurisdiction.

The Revenue Importance of Property Rates

Property rates generated about 2 percent of total tax revenue but less than 0.5 percent of GDP in 2008/2009 (Olima 2010). However, it is clear from table 29.1 that as a local tax and as a percentage of total own-source revenue, property rates are important. It also seems that since the enactment and implementation of the LGRA, there has been a significant, albeit somewhat erratic, growth in revenue from the property tax. The abolition of the graduated personal tax (a poll tax) in 2006 necessitated a renewed focus on the property tax. It is also noteworthy that the introduction of the local services tax and the local-government hotel tax did not impede the growth of the property tax.

The Tax Base

The tax is based on annual rental value, and the owner of the property is liable for payment. The tax base extends to all properties in urban areas and on commercial and industrial buildings outside urban areas, but residential properties are only taxed if they are rented. For vacant properties, the tax is based on the rental market potential of the property.

Table 29.1 Own-Source Revenue Performance, 2003/2004-2010/2011 (UGX Millions)

Source	2003/2004	2004/2005	2005/2006	2006/2007	2007/2008	2008/2009	2009/2010	2010/2011
Local services tax	–	–	–	–	–	3,838	9,195	6,542
Hotel tax	–	–	–	–	–	985	1,496	5,752
Graduated tax	36,526	60,389	10,866	4,429	–	–	0	0
Property tax (PT)	6,788	3,526	26,716	37,817	28,487	24,936	45,598	52,438
User fees	13,100	10,504	23,096	20,946	64,854	33,153	39,924	12,294
Licenses	5,805	4,091	12,206	11,779	13,479	9,171	13,369	21,080
Others	17,888	12,201	27,781	23,684	9,065	46,626	33,222	66,117
Total	80,107	90,361	100,665	98,655	115,065	118,710	142,802	164,223
PT as percentage of total	8.5	3.9	26.5	38.3	24.8	21.0	31.9	31.9

Source: Local Government Finance Commission database as reported in Oxfam (2013).

Note: These are aggregated figures for Kampala, the districts (with their subcounties), municipalities (with their divisions), and town councils.

Exemptions

Properties in rural areas are exempt. Exemptions in urban areas are generally based on one of four conditions: ownership, the way in which the property is used, the incidence of the tax burden on the taxpayer, and the importance of the property. The general principle of exemption is that property should be exclusively used for the purposes for which the exemption is given. The list of exempted properties in the LGRA includes the following:

- Owner-occupied residential houses in urban areas.

- Official residences of the president, as well as official residences of traditional and cultural leaders.

- Places of public worship and residences of religious leaders.

- Public outdoor sports or recreation facilities or properties designated as public open schemes.

- Cemeteries, burial grounds, and crematoriums.

- Public charitable and educational institutions supported by endowments or voluntary contributions.

- Properties of institutions with which the government has contractual obligations not to levy taxes.

- Properties of organizations that Uganda is obliged to exempt from taxes under international treaties and diplomatic privileges.

- Properties owned by local councils.

The exemption of owner-occupied residential property not only significantly erodes the potential tax base (Kopanyi 2015; Oxfam 2013) but also is inequitable and violates the benefit principle. Only second homes are taxed. Shifting the burden from landlords to tenants significantly advantages ownership over rental. Exempting the residences of religious leaders and traditional leaders also violates the benefit principle. Exempting owner-occupied residential properties forgoes an estimated 45 percent of the tax revenue (Oxfam 2013).

Apart from exemptions, there are other relief measures. These include rebates for expenditures on renovations and repairs of property, as well as relief based on old age, sickness, or loss of employment of the ratepayer.

Valuation

Valuation and assessment are based on the annual rental income of the property as determined by a registered valuer (a person who holds a practicing certificate under the Surveyors' Registration Act of 1974) appointed by their local government. The LGRA eliminated the valuation monopoly of the chief government valuer and allowed local authorities to appoint their own registered valuers. In 2010, however, the country had only 32 registered valuers (Olima 2010; UN-Habitat 2013); thus, it is extremely difficult, if not impossible, for local authorities to prepare and regularly update valuation rolls (Franzsen 2010; Franzsen and McCluskey 2005a). Not surprisingly, the preferred five-year valuation cycle is rarely adhered to. The law stipulates "five years, or such longer period as a local government may determine," pragmatically acknowledging the shortage of valuers in the country.

In 2009, the Kampala City Council had three in-house valuers, the Ministry of Lands, Housing, and Urban Development employed four valuers, and the remaining twenty-five valuers were in private practice (UN-Habitat 2013). With assistance from the World Bank, the Kampala City Council undertook a revaluation of all its properties over the period 2003 to 2005. Approximately 110,500 properties were revalued (UN-Habitat 2013).

A valuation court must be appointed by a district, city, or municipal council to adjudicate all objections to the draft valuation list. It consists of three persons. The chairperson must be a magistrate or an advocate with at least five years' experience, whereas the other two members may be architects, engineers, "or such other persons as the local government may think fit to appoint." Given the paucity of valuers in the country, this seems a pragmatic response. Once the valuation court has heard all objections and has adjusted the draft valuation list as it deems fit and proper, the chairperson certifies the list so that it becomes the (new) valuation list at the commencement of the next financial year. A person aggrieved by the finding of the valuation court may appeal "the principle upon which any valuation has been made" to the High Court.

The law stipulates that a local authority may of its own accord, on application by an owner, or at the request of the responsible minister make a supplementary valuation list. Given the scarcity of resources, this does not happen in practice. For example, the KCCA is still using the 2005 valuation list, complemented by a supplementary list from 2009 (Kopanyi 2015).

There are currently only two entities that provide training for valuers or valuation technicians in Uganda. Previously, the last professional valuers were trained in the 1980s, and valuation technicians were last trained at an institution in Entebbe in 1992 (Nsamba-Gayiiya 2001).

Tax Rates

A local government may not impose a tax rate that exceeds 12 percent of the ratable value of a property or is less than 1/10th of a currency point. A currency point is currently UGX 20,000, which implies a minimum of UGX 2,000 per ratable property (UN-Habitat 2013). Because the regulations are silent on how the rates are set, there is no systematic approach to rate setting.

Local governments may also take into consideration other factors in setting the rate, such as

- the desire to have a uniform rate for all subcounties or divisions within the jurisdiction of a local government;

- the ratepayer's ability to pay;

- the likely reaction from the public to an increase in rates; and

- trends in the general economic performance within the area.

The law mandates that property rates be used to provide specific services, such as road construction and maintenance, street lighting, antimalaria drains, garbage collection, physical planning, and other services required by the taxpayers within their areas. In addition, the law requires that a minimum of 75 percent of the revenue be used for these services. This limitation is hugely problematic.

The Entebbe Municipal Council has been setting differential rates for commercial and industrial properties and for residential properties. In 2009, the Kampala City Council persisted with a 10 percent rate on commercial and industrial properties and a 6 percent rate on residential properties, which had already been used in 2002 (Franzsen and McCluskey 2005b).

Billing and Collection

Tax billing is done annually by local authorities, who are also required under the act to publish the chargeable rates in the official gazette and local newspapers. In the early years of the 21st century, it was rumored that about 30 percent of tax bills in Kampala were not delivered to taxpayers (Olima 2010). Local authorities are required to prepare and send demand notes indicating the amounts due for payment only to all property ratepayers who have failed to pay by the due date.

Revenue collection is generally administered by the local authority's own staff. However, the former Kampala City Council had contracted private collectors to undertake revenue collection. The private debt collectors were paid a commission of 10 percent of the amount collected (Kopanyi 2015; Olima 2010). Despite the engagement of private debt collectors, the collection rate was still low, approximately 50 percent of the projected figures (Olima 2010). The Masaka Municipal Council also experimented with the privatization of collection, apparently without success (Nsamba-Gayiiya 2001). Although outsourcing may address the lack of capacity to collect the tax, it is unlikely to decrease unwillingness to pay it.

Enforcement

Local governments can enforce the payment of property rates by several mechanisms, including sending demand notices, charging penalties and interest, recovering property rates from tenants and occupiers, prohibiting transfer of a property, and imposing a first charge on a property. These mechanisms are underused, and enforcement efforts are generally low (Olima 2010). Impracticable enforcement provisions abound, and enforcement against absentee property owners is lengthy and costly (Oxfam 2013). Taking defaulters to civil court seems to be the most common method, but it is costly, and settling a case may take years (Bendana and Mayanja 2012). Nsamba-Gayiiya (2001) states that although the enforcement measures provided for in the law seem adequate, some of them are politically unacceptable and therefore are not used in practice. If political will to enforce payment is absent and taxpayers are aware that these measures are not invoked, an adverse impact on voluntary compliance is inevitable, especially if service delivery is poor. Furthermore, proper enforcement is possible only if the underlying data are reliable.

The Kampala Capital City Authority

Revenue Enhancement Since 2011

As indicated earlier, the KCCA replaced the former Kampala City Council (Kopanyi 2015). Since its establishment in 2011, the KCCA has implemented various policy and administrative reforms regarding its own-source revenues. The first important step was the creation of the Directorate of Revenue Collection. Since its inception, revenue enhancement from own sources has been quite remarkable. This unit has selectively and gradually invested in upgrading revenue databases and improving procedures, as well as overall administration and especially revenue collection (Logan 2016). As a direct result of this investment, the overall amount of own-source revenues increased more than 100 percent, from UGX 41 billion in the 2011/2012 fiscal year to UGX 85 billion in the 2014/2015 fiscal year. Own-source revenue increased significantly as a percentage in comparison with central-government grants, and even when donor revenues were included (Kopanyi 2015). If these figures are compared with the figures for 2007/2008, they are even more impressive. Table 29.2 provides the details of own-source revenues for the Kampala City Council for 2007/2008.

At 30.6 percent, property rates constituted a major component of own-source revenue for the Kampala City Council in 2007/2008. It should also be noted that a significant amount was budgeted for rates arrears, but only 8.2 percent of the arrears were collected. As a percentage of total local revenue, including central-government grants, rates constituted only 10.7 percent (UN-Habitat 2013). It must be kept in mind that the local services tax and the local-government hotel tax were both introduced in 2008/2009. From table 29.3, it is clear that the property tax is well established as the principal source of own revenue despite the lack of base expansion and revaluation. From table 29.4, it is evident that grants from the central government still play an important role.

The Directorate for Revenue Collection

What is especially noteworthy is that the KCCA's Directorate for Revenue Collection (DRC) achieved the revenue gains in the absence of a general revaluation and any supplementary valuation. In other words, there was basically a collection-led strategy, implemented by skilled and motivated staff (Kopanyi 2015). Some of the key staff members of the DRC were recruited from the Ministry of Finance and the URA. The DRC also focused on the five most important revenue sources, which are responsible for 80 percent of the total own-source revenue: property rates, road user fees, business license fees, the local services tax, and

Table 29.2 Own-Source Revenues for the Former Kampala City Council, 2007/2008

Revenue Source	Actual Collection (UGX Millions)	Revenue Sources as a Percentage of Own-Source Revenue
Rates (current)	7,178	30.6
Business licenses	4,980	21.2
Taxi-park (general)	3,989	17.0
Markets	1,552	6.6
Ground rent	2,308	9.8
Other revenues	2,277	9.7
Rates arrears	334	1.4
Other arrears	851	3.6
Subtotal of own-source revenue	23,468	100

Source: Adapted from Kampala City Council Financial Report (2009) as reported in Olima (2010).

Table 29.3 Own-Source Revenues for the KCCA, 2011/2012–2013/2014

	2011/2012		2012/2013		2013/2014	
Revenue Source	UGX Millions	%	UGX Millions	%	UGX Millions	%
Property rates	11,325.0	28.7	14,516.4	26.1	24,146.2	33.4
Parking fees	5,390.3	13.6	12,530.4	22.6	15,917.1	22.0
Business licenses	8,766.3	22.2	13,268.4	23.9	12,926.4	17.9
Local services tax	9,076.7	23.0	8,697.4	15.7	11,401.5	15.8
Other	4,964.7	12.6	6,529.2	11.8	7,830.9	10.8
Total own-source revenue	39,523.0	100	55,541.8	100	72,222.1	100

Source: http://www.kcca.go.ug/uDocs/KCCA%20credit%20rating%20report.pdf.

Table 29.4 Revenues for the KCCA, 2011/2012–2013/2014

	2011/2012		2012/2013		2013/2014	
Revenue Source	UGX Millions	%	UGX Millions	%	UGX Millions	%
Total own-source revenue	39,523.0	34.8	55,541.8	33.6	72,222.1	31.9
Grants	71,895.6	63.3	88,160.3	53.4	154,112.9	68.0
Other	2,170.7	1.9	21,485.6	13.0	159.3	0.1
Total income	113,589.3	100	165,187.7	100	226,494.3	100

Source: http://www.kcca.go.ug/uDocs/KCCA%20credit%20rating%20report.pdf.

ground rent. Another important aspect of the reform was improved tax-payer communication (Logan 2016).

The DRC also monitored its cost of collection, which increased nine-fold from 2011 to 2014. As Kopanyi (2015, 9) indicates, however, there are important factors to consider:

- The baseline reflects an administration with limited in-house capacity, extensive outsourcing of collections to private collectors, and lack of fundamental investments. In short, it was a low-cost but unsustainable collection.

- The DRC needed (and still needs) more basic investments to establish systems and capacities, and these investments must be compared with the collection impacts. Whereas experience suggests that investments in revenue collection should be recovered in three to five years, the DRC's investments were largely recovered in one year.

- Some operating costs can also be considered one-time, start-up investments.

As Logan (2016) indicates, the DRC's reform efforts are ongoing. The DRC has adopted a comprehensive property registry and valuation program that combines the development of a city address module that will map the location and basic characteristics of all buildings with a computer-assisted mass appraisal (CAMA) program that will record current property values on a regular basis. Also, the KCCA envisions an urban and a fiscal cadastre because the current cadastral map of land in Kampala does not include buildings and infrastructure (Kopanyi 2015). The urban cadastre would link the land and fiscal cadastres and also provide the basis for urban planning, land use planning, zoning, construction permitting, and planning and developing infrastructure services. The fiscal cadastre would consist of a property tax register (Logan 2016). Although these efforts will require a significant financial investment, the KCCA is confident that the start-up costs will be recouped through improved tax base coverage and prudent revenue collection.

Kopanyi (2015) alludes to a 2013 report suggesting that median monthly rentals across the five divisions in Kampala had increased by 300 percent since the 2005 general valuation. Furthermore, if the KCCA can persuade the government to abolish the exemption of owner-occupied residential properties, significantly more property tax could be collected from high-value residential properties (Bendana and Mayanja 2012).

Property Tax Issues in Uganda

The current property tax system in Uganda is under severe strain. The 2005 law, as amended in 2006, does not provide for effective mobilization of the property tax because it exempts owner-occupied residential buildings, with a devastating effect on revenue. There is also a clear gap between law and policy, on one hand, and the realities most local governments are facing, on the other hand. Members of the general public are largely unaware of their civic duty to pay the property tax, and political support is absent at the highest level of government. Taxpayers have limited awareness of property tax collection, to the extent that some think that they should not pay any tax on their properties. In addition, some property owners confuse the property tax with ground rent (Oxfam 2013).

Local governments simply do not have the capacity to effectively administer the property tax. The first issue is the lack of a comprehensive property information database. This complicates property identification, and as a result, many properties are not included on valuation lists and tax registers.

There is a severe shortage of technical officers and valuers, and therefore, many valuation lists are seriously out of date. For example, properties in the central business district of Kampala City were revalued only after fifteen years in 2005, despite the mandate of the law that revaluations be carried out every five years. Most, if not all, local governments other than the KCCA depend on the Ministry of Lands, Housing, and Urban Development to create, prepare, and update their valuation lists. The low capacity to systematically maintain and coordinate the fiscal cadastre information has seriously inhibited the possibility of adhering to the valuation cycle where valuation lists exist.

Local governments need to do general revaluations or at least update their valuation lists through supplementary valuation lists, but they have no funds to do so (Oxfam 2013). Therefore, many high-value buildings constructed and completed since 2005 are not yet included on valuation lists. Property valuations are undertaken through competitive contracts at costs many urban and especially rural local governments cannot afford. A modern CAMA system may be a goal in Uganda generally and the KCCA more specifically (Kopanyi 2015). In the short term, however, the goal should be to consider a more rudimentary and simplified system of property assessment that acknowledges short- to medium-term capacity constraints. In principle, the law already allows for mass valuation. Furthermore, there are positive developments in land management that will eventually lead to base expansion for the property tax.

However, the paucity of trained personnel is not limited to valuation. There are serious problems with collection, enforcement, and monitoring changes of users, particularly where exempt owner-occupied properties are traded in the market. Improvement of the property tax system in the short term will require a marked improvement of all the important aspects of a property tax system: tax base coverage, valuation and assessment, billing, collection, and enforcement. Collection and compliance are adversely affected by significant arrears in tax payments, as demonstrated by the 2007/2008 financial statements for Kampala. However, many councils fail to enforce the tax against delinquent taxpayers. Given the extent of the arrears, many municipalities have transferred collection of the property tax to private firms, with varying success. Many urban local governments also lack the political will to enforce payment of the property tax even though they have the enforcement mechanisms under the law to do so. However, recent developments in Kampala, where the focus has been improved tax administration, clearly indicate that well-targeted inputs can generate significant revenue enhancement.

In short, the weak performance of the property tax is due to inefficient tax administration, inaccurate public perceptions, and the broad absence of political support. Strict enforcement and improved taxpayer education could result in improved revenues. Networking with other stakeholders, such as the Surveys and Mapping Department, the National Water and Sewerage Corporation, and the Uganda Electricity Board, to improve information in property and taxpayer databases should also be considered. The failure to address the need for reforms in property taxation has made it very difficult for Uganda's cities and districts to deliver effective services.

Even if property tax policy changes and the relevant laws are amended to create a system that is better suited to Uganda's land and decentralization policies and acknowledges the limited short-term property data available, as well as capacity issues, the efforts and costs involved in achieving this goal will be wasted if the tax is not collected efficiently (Bahl 1998). In short, a collection-led approach to property tax reform could do much to enhance revenue from this underused source of local-government revenue. The significant enhancement of own-source revenue in the KCCA from 2011/2012 to 2014/2015, which was achieved primarily by focusing on revenue collection, is proof enough. It can and should be replicated in other local governments in Uganda.

References

Bahl, R. W. 1998. "Land Taxes Versus Property Taxes in Developing and Transition Countries." In *Land Value Taxation: Can It and Will It Work Today?*, ed. D. Netzer, 141–171. Cambridge, MA: Lincoln Institute of Land Policy.

Bendana, C., and B. Mayanja. 2012. "KCCA to Tax Big Residential Homes." New Vision, December 29. *www.newvision.co.ug/new_vision/news/1311995/kcca-tax-residential -homes#sthash.QHSZnRDa.dpuf.*

CIA (Central Intelligence Agency). 2016. "Uganda." In *The World Factbook. https://www .cia.gov/library/publications/the-world-factbook/geos/ug.html.*

Franzsen, R. C. D. 2010. "Commentary" [on A. Dornfest, "In Search of an Optimal Revaluation Policy: Benefits and Pitfalls"]. In *Challenging the Conventional Wisdom on the Property Tax*, ed. R. W. Bahl, J. Martinez-Vazquez, and J. M. Youngman, 108–117. Cambridge, MA: Lincoln Institute of Land Policy.

Franzsen, R. C. D., and W. J. McCluskey. 2005a. "Ad Valorem Property Taxation in Sub-Saharan Africa." *Journal of Property Tax Assessment and Administration* 2(2): 63–72.

———. 2005b. "An Exploratory Overview of Property Taxation in the Commonwealth of Nations." Working paper. Cambridge, MA: Lincoln Institute of Land Policy.

Kopanyi, M. 2015. "Local Revenue Reform of Kampala Capital City Authority." International Growth Center working paper. London: London School of Economics and University of Oxford.

Logan, S. 2016. "Local Revenue Reform with the Kampala Capital City Authority." *International Growth Center Blog. www.theigc.org/blog/local-revenue-reform-with-the -kampala-capital-city-authority/.*

MoWLE (Ministry of Water, Lands, and the Environment). 2002. *Land Sector Strategic Plan: Analysis of Economic Rationale and Investment Programme.* Final Report (January). Kampala.

Nsamba-Gayiiya, E. 2001. "Property Assessment and Taxation in Uganda." Paper presented at the IRRV/IPTI International Conference on Property Taxation, Cambridge, United Kingdom (May).

Olima, W. H. A. 2010. "Property Taxation in Anglophone East Africa: Case Study of Uganda." Working paper WP10NEA8. Cambridge, MA: Lincoln Institute of Land Policy.

Oput, R., and Orlova, N. 2016. "Strengthening of the Uganda Land Administration and Management System: Development and Implementation of the Land Information System Infrastructure." Paper presented at the 17th Annual World Bank Conference on Land and Poverty, Washington, DC (March 14–17).

Oxfam. 2013. "Revenue Mobilisation at Local Government Level for Sustained Service Delivery: Challenges, Opportunities and Proposals." Tax Policy Paper (December). *www.seatiniuganda.org/publications/research/60-tax-policy-paper/file.html.*

UN-Habitat. 2013. *Property Tax Regimes in East Africa.* Global Urban Economic Dialogue Series. Nairobi: UN Human Settlements Program.

United Nations. 2014. *World Urbanization Prospects.* Washington, DC: Department of Economic and Social Affairs, Population Division.

United Nations, Department of Economic and Social Affairs, Population Division. 2015. World Population Prospects: The 2015 Revision. *https://esa.un.org/unpd/wpp /Publications/Files/World_Population_2015_Wallchart.pdf.*

USAID (U.S. Agency for International Development). 2007. *Land Tenure and Property Rights Regional Report.* Vol. 2.1, *East and Central Africa.* Burlington, VT: ARD.

World Bank. 2016a. "Country and Lending Groups." *http://data.worldbank.org/about /country-and-lending-groups.*

———. 2016b. "GDP per Capita (Current US%)." *http://data.worldbank.org/indicator /NY.GDP.PCAP.CD.*

———. 2016c. "Registering Property in Uganda." *www.doingbusiness.org/data/explore economies/uganda/registering-property/.*

Legislation

Constitution of the Republic of Uganda of 1995.

Income Tax Act of 1997.

Kampala Capital City Authority Act of 2010.

Land Act of 1997.

Local Government Act of 1997.

Local Governments (Rating) Act of 2005.

Local Government (Rating) Decree of 1979.

Local Governments (Rating) Regulations of 2005.

Surveyors' Registration Act of 1974.

30

Zambia

RIËL FRANZSEN, MUNDIA KABINGA, AND CHABALA KASESE

Zambia is a landlocked country in southern Africa with a surface area of 752,618 km². It is bordered by the Democratic Republic of the Congo to the north, Tanzania to the northeast, Malawi to the east, Mozambique, Zimbabwe, Botswana, and Namibia to the south, and Angola to the west. Zambia has an estimated population of 16.2 million (United Nations 2015), of which 41 percent lives in urban areas (United Nations 2014). The GDP per capita is estimated at USD 1,305 (World Bank 2016b). About 2.2 million people live in Lusaka, Zambia's capital city (CIA 2016). Zambia is a lower-middle-income country (World Bank 2016a).

Government

Zambia attained political independence from Britain in 1964. The Republic of Zambia has a three-tier governance structure: the central government and provincial and local governments. There are 10 provinces. Local governments consist of city councils (Chipata, Kitwe, Livingstone, Lusaka, and Ndola), municipalities, and district councils.

Land Tenure

Zambia has two main types of land ownership, state land and customary land. Under the Lands Act of 1995, all land in Zambia is vested in the president. State land makes up slightly more than 6 percent of the country's land area and consists of former Crown lands (land used for colonial settlement and mining developments), land acquired after the Land Acquisition Act of 1971, and converted land (land converted from customary tenure through the issuance of title). The registrar of deeds issues and registers title deeds for state land, which is held under renewable 99-year leaseholds. Customary land is a combination of communal trust land and natural reserves and constitutes almost 94 percent of the country's land area. The administration of customary land relies on unwritten customary law and tribal customs and traditions (Mudenda 2006; Sichone 2008).

Property-Related Taxes

Property-related taxes collected in Zambia in 2008 constituted 0.6 percent of total revenues and a negligible 0.034 percent of GDP (IMF 2016). In 2010, total tax revenues were made up as follows: the personal income tax (34.1 percent), the corporate income tax (17.8 percent), the value-added tax (24.4 percent), excise taxes (8.6 percent), trade taxes (9.8 percent), and property taxes (0.3 percent) (IMF 2015). Thus, property taxes tend to be an unimportant source of central-government revenues. The central government collects a property transfer tax, ground rent, and various other property-related taxes and charges.

The Property Transfer Tax

The property transfer tax in Zambia is levied and collected under the Property Transfer Tax Act of 2005 (Chapter 340 of the Laws of Zambia). The property transfer tax is based on the realized (open-market) value of all land. Land is defined as "any building, structure or other improvement." The person transferring the property is liable for the tax. According to the act, the property transfer tax is payable to the commissioner general of the Zambia Revenue Authority (ZRA). The Minister of Finance and National Planning sets the property transfer tax rate in Zambia. The uniform tax rate has changed several times. In 2012, the tax rate was increased from 3 percent to 5 percent, and in 2014, it was doubled to 10 percent. However, it was reduced to 5 percent, effective January 2016.

To determine the realized value of land transactions, the Property Transfer Tax Act allows the commissioner general to use assessments conducted by the Government Valuation Department or any relevant organization he considers expedient. In practice, the ZRA relies largely on selected private valuation companies to provide independent assessments of land-related transactions. The basis of assessment for the property transfer tax is the market value at the time of application for state consent to assign or transfer property.[1] In practice, the ZRA keeps a record of transactions to establish trends. If any value declared by a taxpayer falls outside the basic zone, the ZRA will investigate and may impose its own value based on the established trend. The ZRA has established a unit responsible for the property transfer tax, but the ZRA officers who are in charge of property and value verifications are not qualified valuers.[2] The ZRA does use its powers to increase underdeclared values for the property transfer tax, following a schedule of established market prices for different areas that it compiles in liaison with the Government Valuation Department (GVD). At the beginning of 2016, the ZRA also started carrying out physical inspections, for example, to confirm whether a property is vacant land, as claimed by the taxpayer. Furthermore, transactions above ZMK 500,000 (the low-cost residential value threshold) must be accompanied by a professional valuation (Mukonde 2015).

The ZRA is solely responsible for billing and collecting the property transfer tax. The revenue performance of property transfer taxes has been good because it is an easy tax tool and the rate has been increased regularly. However, the revenue potential of the property transfer tax is rather low because it is limited to formal transactions. Informal exchanges that are not accompanied by a change of title at the deeds registry are excluded and may have been encouraged by the increases in the tax rate. Even at a rate of 5 percent, there are risks that taxpayers may underdeclare. However, there is no empirical evidence to support this argument.

Ground Rent

Ground rent is indeed a rent, rather than a tax. It is a regular payment made by the holder of a leasehold property to the owner (the government), as required under the lease. In Zambia, all land is vested and held in perpetuity for and on behalf of the people of Zambia by the president of the republic pursuant to the Lands Act of 1995 (Chande 2014; Kasese 2013). Therefore, the president is the freeholder. Ground rent is created when a freehold piece of land or a building is leased. In Zambia, ground rent starts accruing once a statutory 99-year lease is granted to any person for any parcel of land and is payable to the Ministry of Lands. Although ground rent and various land charges contribute considerably to the total income of the Ministry of Lands, the contribution of property-related taxes to central-government revenues is low.

The minister of lands sets the rates for ground rent and various land charges (consent, registration, consideration for plots allocated by the ministry, issuance of certificates of title, and survey fees). The rate for the ground rent is determined with reference to the relevant category of local authority (city council areas, municipal council areas, district councils, and small district councils) and zoning (Chande 2014). The rate structures for ground rent and the various land fees are summarized in table 30.1.

Table 30.1 Schedules of Ground Rent and Land Charges at the Ministry of Lands

Type of Land Fee	Fee Type	Tax Base	Fee Amount
Consent fee	Flat fee	All land transfers	ZMK 333.60
Consideration	Variable, dependent on zone	New plots allocated by lands commissioner	Variable
Ground rent	Variable, dependent on zone	Leaseholds in hectares	Variable
Registration fees/ change of title	Variable, dependent on value	Registration·of certificate of title	1% of property value (maximum of ZKM 15,000)
Leases	Variable, dependent on value		2% average of annual rent (maximum of ZKM 15,000)
Mortgages	Variable, dependent on value		1% of value (maximum of ZKM 4,000)

Source: Ministry of Lands (2016) and Statutory Instrument 44 of 2006.

The Ministry of Lands could greatly benefit from simplifying and streamlining the number of land charges (Kabinga 2010). Furthermore, the collection of ground rent should be centralized in the Ministry of Local Government and Housing. Kabinga (2010) argues that having one point of contact and increasing the frequency with which ground rent can be collected to twice a year would likely enhance the overall collection of ground rent.

The Withholding Tax on Rental Income

There is a withholding tax on rental income in Zambia. It is borne by landlords insofar as tenants are required to withhold 10 percent of the actual rent under the lease and to pay the relevant amount directly to the ZRA.

The Property Tax

The most important property-related tax is the recurrent property tax, called "rates" or "council rates." This tax is levied by local governments. The Rating Act No. 12 of 1997 also provides for "special rating." Section 21 states that "where, in the opinion of the rating authority, a capital works scheme executed by it under any statutory power has benefited owners of a rateable area, the rating authority may, with the prior consent of the minister, determine and levy a special rate on the rateable property in that area in order to defray the capital costs of the scheme." However, no rating authority in Zambia has so far levied a special rate to defray the capital costs of any works scheme (Kasese 2013).

The property tax is levied and collected under the Rating Act No. 12 of 1997, which was subsequently amended by the Rating (Amendment) Act No. 9 of 1999. Only "rating authorities" are entitled to levy the property tax. Some newly created district councils have not yet been declared rating authorities (Kasese 2013) even though some of these councils may have valuation rolls. In contrast, there are six rating authorities that do not yet have valuation rolls (Kasese 2013).

The Importance of Property Tax Revenue

On average, the property tax accounted for 30 percent of all municipal-government revenues from 2001 to 2006. However, the specific contribution of property rates to total municipal revenues varies widely from one municipality to another. In the Lusaka and Kitwe City Councils, property tax collections for 2008 accounted for 21.4 percent and 51.5 percent of total municipal income, respectively. These differences are partly due to variations in the rate of collection and the degree of diversity in revenue sources (Kabinga 2010).

In the Lusaka City Council, there was a persistent decline in property tax revenue collection from 2006 to 2008, whereas the Kitwe City Council saw a marked increase in property tax collection during the same period. However, the Lusaka City Council has a more diverse portfolio of revenue streams, which makes its total revenue more than double that of the Kitwe City Council but also makes revenue administration more challenging. Despite these differences, the property tax is by far the largest single contributor to municipal own revenue in Zambia and is therefore extremely important for local governments. Other significant contributors to municipal revenues include fees and charges from bus terminals, trade licenses, market levies, rentals (from peri-urban land parcels), and social grants (Kabinga 2010).

In Lusaka, property tax collections as a proportion of total municipal revenues declined from 50.1 percent in 2001 to 21.4 percent in 2008. During the same period, there was a steady increase in the percentage of other sources in total municipal revenue. Central government grants in lieu of the property tax are insufficient (less than 0.2 percent of total municipal revenues) and exceedingly erratic. Despite the property tax's decline in importance over this period, it remained the single largest contributor to Lusaka City Council revenues (Kabinga 2010). Intercity bus terminal fees increased their proportion of contributions to total municipal revenues from 0 percent in 2004 to 11 percent in 2008. Similarly, various trade taxes increased their proportion of contributions to total municipal revenues from 2.7 percent in 2007 to 7.4 percent in 2008 (Kabinga 2010). However, the Lusaka City Council has achieved a steady increase in property tax revenues since the implementation of its 2010 valuation roll.

The Tax Base

Municipal property rates are levied and collected under the legal provisions of the Rating Act of 1997 as amended in 1999 (Chande 2014). According to that act, all land and improvements on state land in 46 of the 108 districts of Zambia are taxable except the official residence of the president of the republic, land used for agricultural purposes, and land used for the operation of public utilities (transmission lines, dams, reservoirs, and water and sewage plants). The tax base was further broadened by bringing in common leasehold units, removing business properties in customary land tenure areas from the customary land exemption, and restricting exemptions to public use and agriculture. The act also provides for the Minister of Local Government and Housing to levy the property tax at a special rate and provide additional exemptions by statutory order.

In 1997, the tax base coverage was extended to include vacant land, and in 1999, a flat-rate tax was introduced to coexist with the capital value–based system, so that properties not yet recorded on the valuation roll could also be taxed. Although this created some complexity and inequity in the overall system, it was meant to broaden the tax net and increase revenues. However, the legality of the flat-rate tax was successfully challenged in the High Court in 2005. Because main and supplementary valuation rolls are rarely prepared as often as the Rating Act stipulates, the property tax tends not to be collected from new property developments. This is especially evident in Lusaka. The Lusaka City Council, while acting within certain provisions of the Rating Act, usually relies on adjustments of the property tax rate instead of preparing supplementary valuations. The Kitwe City Council, in contrast, relies more on the preparation of supplementary valuation rolls, thereby increasing the buoyancy of the tax base, and has experienced a systematic and marked increase in property tax revenues every three or so years.

Undeveloped land incurs the same tax rates as developed land. Furthermore, there is some ambiguity about what constitutes agricultural land that is located within city boundaries. In Lusaka, for instance, owners of newly titled lands in emerging prime areas (which were converted from customary land) refuse to pay the property tax on the ground that their estates are used for agricultural purposes and therefore are completely exempt from the tax. This is a perennial concern of land-based taxes.

Statutory Instrument 67 of 2006 provides exemptions from the property tax to a host of entities, such as Christian schools, hospitals, clinics, tertiary institutions of learning (colleges), community centers, and retirement homes. In practice, municipalities tend to extend additional exemptions to land occupied by diplomatic missions (embassies) and government departments. Many commercial buildings in Lusaka, for instance, are government owned and therefore are not taxable. In spite of provisions in the Rating Act that the central government pay grants in lieu of rates, these grants tend to be paid erratically. Therefore, there is a need to make the legislation on exemptions and the power to grant them more explicit. Furthermore, past ministerial exemptions to the state mining conglomerate, Zambia Consolidated Copper Mines (ZCCM), are still in effect despite amendments to the Rating Act in 1999 and the privatization of the mines. There is a need to revoke the ministerial order, harmonize legislation, and ensure that private mining companies start remitting property taxes to the appropriate rating authorities (local councils).

Liability for the Property Tax

The Rating Act states that the property owner is responsible for the payment of the property tax. If the occupant of a property does not own it, the act requires that the occupant provide the municipality with information on the property's owner or owners. In practice, the property tax is levied on and collected from occupants. The Rating Act stipulates that all property tax payments must be made to the relevant rating municipality.

Valuation

The Rating Act of 1997 prescribes that the Government Valuation Department (GVD) must prepare all main and supplementary valuation rolls. Only valuation surveyors certified or registered by the Valuation Surveyors Registration Board of Zambia may undertake the valuation of properties for property tax purposes (Chande 2014). However, in practice, valuers from in-house municipal valuation departments (e.g., in Lusaka) or private-sector valuers acting under the supervision of a registered valuer from the GVD usually prepare valuation rolls. Whenever valuation is outsourced to a private-sector valuer, the Public Procurement Act of 2008 must be followed (Kasese 2013).

The GVD is a government department under the Ministry of Local Government and Housing. In 2012, it employed a total of eight valuation surveyors tasked to advise the government on issues relating to real estate, but primarily valuation. One of its main mandates is to assist local authorities to fully use their respective capacities to levy the property tax as cost-effectively as possible through the management and implementation of the National Rating Programme. Apart from its head office, the GVD has two regional offices in Lusaka and Kitwe, covering the southern and northern regions of the country (Kasese 2013).

The valuation roll is expected to show the land or parcel number, the address of the property, the name(s) of the leaseholder(s), a description of the property, the land area, and the taxable value of the property (land and improvements). The Rating Act of 1997 stipulates that municipalities must prepare a new valuation roll every five years. However, it also allows the Minister of Local Government and Housing to lengthen the period between revaluations. In practice, valuation rolls are rarely prepared every five years (Chande 2014; Kabinga 2010), and there is a need to strengthen the capacity of valuers responsible for this important task. The Rating Act of 1997 also provides for supplementary valuation rolls to be prepared between main valuations. The only condition is that supplementary valuations cannot be conducted within three months of preparation of a main valuation roll. In practice, only the Kitwe City Council endeavors to prepare a supplementary valuation roll every three years. The Lusaka City Council, on the contrary, prefers to apply for periodic marginal increments to the tax rate instead of undertaking supplementary valuations (Kabinga 2010). Table 30.2 provides an overview of the currency of valuation rolls in many rating authorities across Zambia.

Digital data and maps for all titled properties are available at the offices of the Ministry of Lands, the Deeds Registry, and the surveyor general. However, there is no direct access to real-time data. In practice, appointed valuers must rely on printouts and cadastral maps that are already out of date at the time of the valuation exercise. This data gap widens over the five-year valuation cycle. Furthermore, supplementary revaluations tend to capture relatively few properties because they typically target mostly prominent new developments (Mukonde 2015). According to information from the GVD, rating authorities in Zambia normally use comparative sales to value residential properties. Heavy reliance is placed on information obtained from estate agents (Kasese 2013). For residential properties with so-called spot features, such as a swimming pool or a tennis court, further investigation is carried out on the construction cost of the spot feature, which is then added to the property value (Kasese 2013).

For commercial properties, the "investment method" (income capitalization) is used. This method involves the conversion of an income flow from a particular property into an appropriate capital sum by the use of a cap rate derived from the rate of interest that an investor would require or

Table 30.2 Currency of Valuation Rolls in 2013

Rating Authority	Type of Roll	Year When Previous Roll Was Prepared	Year When Current Roll Was Prepared	Time Between Previous and Current Rolls
Chililabombwe	Supplementary	2001		5 years
	Main		2006	
Chingola	Main	1999	2007	8 years
Chipata	Main	1993	2011	18 years
Choma	Main	1993	2005	12 years
Kabwe	Main	1993	2007	14 years
Kalulushi	Main	2004	2007	3 years
Kasama	Main	1995	2006	11 years
Kitwe	Main	2003	2008	5 years
Livingstone	Main	1995	2005	10 years
Luanshya	Main	1996	2007	11 years
Lusaka[1]	Main	1995	2007	7 years
	Supplementary	2000		
Mansa	Main	1993	2008	15 years
Mazabuka	Main	1993	2008	15 years
Mbala	Main	1993	2006	13 years
Mongu	Main	1994	2006	12 years
Mufulira	Main	2001	2007	6 years
Ndola	Main	1998	2006	8 years
Solwezi	Main	1992	2010	18 years

Source: Kasese (2013).

[1] The 2013 main valuation roll prepared for the Lusaka City Council was not implemented until January 1, 2016.

wish to obtain from the property. In essence, the GVD considers the monthly rental value for a particular property, that is, the maximum rent for which it could be let on the open market on a given set of letting terms, less expenses such as maintenance, insurance, and the value-added tax, and then capitalizes the net rental value (Kasese 2013).

Zambia's valuation system is predominantly manual. Kasese (2013) reports that in the Lusaka City Council, the calculations in the various valuation processes are computer aided because they can be quite complex. The final property value is then reduced to a value per square meter. According to the valuer responsible for the 2007 valuation exercise in Lusaka, most calculations were computer aided. However, for the Kitwe City Council's 2003 and 2008 valuation rolls, the relevant values per square meter were derived by sheer manual computation, using calculators. The valuation exercise in the Chingola Rating Authority, a medium-sized municipality, was also conducted manually for inspections and assessments. However, its report system is computer aided (Kasese 2013).

To date, neither the GVD nor any rating authority has established any partnership with utility companies, such as the Zambia Electricity Supply Corporation or water and sewerage companies, to capture new developments. The GVD relies on the completion certificates issued by local councils and physical identification of property developments under construction to identify newly constructed buildings (Kasese 2013).

Objections and Appeals

The Rating Act permits an occupier or leaseholder to object to the assessed property values. A rating valuation tribunal reviews the written objections. These tribunals are appointed by the Minister of Local Government and Housing and consist of seven persons: a chairperson (who must be a legal practitioner), a deputy chairperson (a representative of the Attorney General's Chambers), three registered valuation surveyors, and one representative each of the Ministry of Local Government and Housing and the GVD. This makes the formal objection process a costly exercise. The Rating Act further stipulates that a taxpayer who has lodged an objection shall not be liable to pay any property tax until the objection is heard and the value is approved by the valuation tribunal, and that any person who is aggrieved by a decision of the tribunal may appeal to the High Court within 30 days.

Tax Rates

Local authorities, in consultation with the minister responsible for local government and housing, set annual property rate levels. Municipalities in Zambia generally differentiate annual property rates for commercial and residential properties. Table 30.3 provides an overview of tax rates in various rating authorities in 2012. Table 30.4 states the tax rates for three of the four city councils in 2015.

With the implementation of the 2013 valuation roll in Lusaka in 2016, tax rates were decreased from 0.2 percent and 0.4 percent to 0.1 percent and 0.2 percent for residential and commercial or industrial properties, respectively. In Kitwe, a general revaluation was under way in 2016, and the proposed tax rates to be considered by the valuation tribunal are 0.25 percent and 0.8 percent for residential and commercial or industrial properties, respectively.

Table 30.3 2012 Tax Rates for Some Rating Authorities

Rating Authority	Tax Rate (Percentage)		
	Residential Property	Commercial Property	Heavy Industrial/ Mining Property
Chingola	0.5	2.0	–
Kalulushi	0.4	1.0	1.0; 1.5
Kitwe	0.3; 0.4; 0.5	1.125	–
Livingstone	0.3	0.5	–
Lufwanyama	1.0	2.0	2.0; 4.0
Lusaka	0.2	0.4	–
Mansa	0.5	1.0	2.0
Ndola	0.3	1.0	0.8; 1.55

Source: Kasese (2013).

Table 30.4 2015 Tax Rates for Three City Councils

City Council	2015 Tax Rates (Percentage)		
	Residential	Commercial/Industrial	Hotels
Kitwe	0.3	1.0	–
Livingstone	0.7	0.3	0.4
Lusaka	0.1	0.2	–

Source: Kitwe, Livingstone, and Lusaka City Councils (2015).

Billing and Collection

Property tax collection by councils has been relatively poor for several reasons, including lack of administrative capacity, poor property coverage, broad-ranging exemptions, and zoning constraints. Councils have not built sufficient capacity for undertaking valuations and administering property tax collection. Before 1995, councils were financially sound and sufficiently resourced to prepare supplementary valuation rolls. At that time, councils found property tax collection easier, mainly because property ownership was centralized in the hands of a few corporations, so there was a smaller taxpayer base. Councils also relied on rental income from their large stock of residential properties for their financial viability. Owing to a combination of privatization spin-offs and a presidential directive in 1995 instructing councils to sell their residential housing units to tenants, the demographics of ratepayers have changed considerably, and the size and complexity (because of subsequent transfers) of the tax base has increased without a proportionate increase in the staffing of the property tax collection department. Finance departments also have to administer an increasingly diverse stream of revenues with insufficient staff and physical and financial resources.

Municipalities are responsible for billing and collecting annual property rates. Finance departments conduct billing and collection of property rates. Once the annual property rates values have been determined, property occupants are billed in two equal installments. The first invoice is sent out between April and May and must be paid by June of the same financial year. The second invoice is sent between September and October, and payment is due by December of the same financial year. Operationally, this billing system makes it easier to identify defaulting taxpayers and allows for remedial action to be taken within a given financial year.

Table 30.5 provides information on property tax collections in four of the large rating authorities. Rating authorities have advanced different explanations for the undercollections. According to Kasese (2013, 64), the primary reasons for poor collection include the following:

- Lack of public confidence in local authorities due to the perpetually deplorable state of roads and other public infrastructure (e.g., bus stations and markets) and the poor quality of municipal services (e.g., garbage collection), which leads to apathy and noncompliance.

- Pronouncements by political candidates and sitting councilors, especially during campaign periods, that tend to affect taxpayer compliance.

- General political interference in local governments.

- The general economic decline due to the 2008 global economic meltdown.

Table 30.5 Property Tax Collection in Four Rating Authorities, 2011

Rating Authority	Expected Revenue (ZMK Thousands)	Total Revenue Collected (ZMK Thousands)	Underollection (ZMK Thousands)	Collection Rate (%)
Chingola	17,508,728	13,000,000	(4,058,728)	74.2
Kitwe	15,987,157	12,588,003	(3,399,154)	78.7
Lusaka	49,947,629	24,883,678	(25,063,950)	49.8
Ndola	25,303,971	16,060,465	(9,243,506)	63.5

Source: Kasese (2013).

- High unemployment rates, especially in cases where leaseholders received offers to buy institutional houses (as sitting tenants) but subsequently lost their jobs, mainly because of the retrenchments from the privatization of state-owned enterprises.

- Dishonest conduct and corrupt practices by some officials.

Despite having computerized billing systems, most rating authorities in Zambia have only a single place for payment of the property tax within the local authority's office premises, usually in the revenue hall of the civic center. In 2012, this was still the case for Lusaka and Ndola, the two largest rating authorities in the country. However, plans were under way to establish at least two additional points of payment in Lusaka (Kasese 2013). The Kitwe City Council, however, has several payment points around the city besides the one at the civic center. Kasese (2013) points out that unlike the ZRA, the Zambia Electricity Supply Corporation, and other service providers, like Multi-Choice Zambia, rating authorities seem to be slow to embrace electronic methods of payment.

Enforcement

If the tax is not paid within 30 days of written notification, the municipality is allowed to issue a warrant to the sheriff of Zambia to seize any goods found on the taxable property, or to recover the outstanding amount through civil action. In practice, municipalities tend to issue warrants to the sheriff of Zambia to seize the occupant's property proportionate to the outstanding property tax arrears when the arrears exceed ZMK 500 (about USD 100). Nevertheless, the overall collection rate in Zambia is below par (Kabinga 2010). The Rating Act of 1997 does not presently provide for the attachment of wages. This could be more effective, more proactive, cheaper, and less cumbersome than a warrant of distress pertaining to movable assets (Kasese 2013).

Property Tax Performance in Three City Councils

The Lusaka City Council

According to Akakandelwa (2012a), Lusaka's total housing stock in 2010 was about 300,000 units, measured against an estimated population of 2.2 million. Only 10 percent of this housing stock was formal housing; the remaining 90 percent consisted of squatter units. These informal units housed about 70 percent of the city's population on less than 20 percent of its residential land. The estimated housing shortage in Lusaka was about 200,000 housing units (Akakandelwa 2012a).

Akakandelwa (2012a, 89) states that the number of residential properties within his study area in Lusaka decreased by about 5 percent between 2002 and 2012, while during the same period, the number of commercial properties increased by about 8 percent. These percentage changes were calculated from the number of current operating residential properties and commercial properties that were initially residential but are now operating as commercial properties because of land use changes. It would be interesting to know whether these changes are reflected in the current valuation roll, and whether the property tax is being levied accordingly.

In 2001, the Lusaka City Council experimented with outsourcing property tax collection to a private contractor. Although the exercise was deemed a failure and the council took back responsibility for collection, valuable lessons were learned. In 2003, the council conducted a very visible taxpayer education program: large billboards all across the city to encourage taxpayers to pay their taxes to ensure improved levels of services from the council (Franzsen and McCluskey 2005). According to Kasese (2013), the particularly low collection rate in Lusaka in 2011 has been attributed to the following factors:

- Tax collection officers faced challenges in identifying the new properties listed in the new valuation roll despite a deliberate effort to provide some orientation for them in doing so.

- Bills were not properly sent to new properties (e.g., the newly constructed high-value Levy Park shopping mall).

- There were hardly any follow-ups even if bills had been issued.

However, when the 2007 valuation roll was eventually implemented in 2011, the result was a significant 33 percent increase in revenue from the property tax in 2012 (Chande 2014). Chande (2014) explains that the irregularity of revaluations in Lusaka is due to the high costs of valuations, the need to inspect every property physically, and the rapidly increasing number of properties because of urbanization. Furthermore, fieldwork by Chande suggests that assessed values for the 2007 Lusaka valuation roll were significantly lower than the actual market values that, according to the law, should be reflected in the valuation roll (Chande 2014). As indicated in table 30.2, the current valuation roll is the 2013 roll, which was implemented only in January 2016. The property tax accounted for 22.8 percent of total revenue for the Lusaka City Council in 2015, and the collection rate was about 66 percent, significantly better than the 49.8 percent in 2011 (see table 30.5).

The Kitwe City Council

The Kitwe City Council appointed the senior valuation officer of the GVD (Northern Region Office) to conduct the preparation of the Kitwe main valuation roll in 2008. The exercise commenced only toward the end of 2008 because of the cumbersome procedure of formally approving the valuation surveyor, financial constraints, and political interference, among other reasons. As allowed for by law, the GVD valuer was assisted by an in-house surveyor of the Kitwe City Council. During the revaluation, all residential, commercial, and industrial properties in Kitwe were inspected and valued. The local surveyor inspected public institutions, such as schools, hospitals, clinics, and many others. Property statistics captured in the Kitwe main valuation roll by early 2012 in compliance with the regulations and procedures of a rating valuation are indicated in table 30.6. The 2008 main valuation roll was implemented in January 2012 and expired at the end of 2015. However, the new 2014 valuation roll was not approved by the minister until March 2016 and has not yet been implemented. The last supplementary valuation roll was undertaken in 2012 and implemented in 2014.

In 2015, the Kitwe City Council levied the property tax at the tax rates indicated in table 30.7. It is noteworthy that the tax rate for mines is almost six times higher than the rate on residential properties, and the rate on commercial and industrial properties is more than three times the rate for residential property.

The revenue raised by the Kitwe City Council is indicated in table 30.8. In 2015, property rates constituted 49.6 percent of revenue raised by the council (ZMW 44,336,200) and 28.9 percent of total municipal revenue (including grants and the contribution to the local development fund). The council's target was to collect at least 75 percent of the budgeted amount (approximately the percentage collected in 2011; see table 30.5), rather than the 58 percent actually collected.

The Livingstone City Council

The date of valuation for the current valuation roll is May 5, 2014. This roll was approved on July 11, 2015, and was implemented on January 1, 2016. Because the 2015 valuation roll was approved only after the July 1 billing date had passed, midyear bills were not sent out until October 2015. This resulted in a very poor in-year collection rate.

The tax rates approved by the council for 2014 and 2015 are provided in table 30.9. Despite a new valuation roll with presumably higher values on average, the tax rate was increased for nonresidential properties (except

Table 30.6 The 2008 Kitwe Main Valuation Roll

Category	Properties		Land	Improvement	Total
	Number	Percentage		Values (ZMK)	
Residential	41,302	95.0	138,155,431,189	2,763,962,547,642	2,902,117,978,831
Commercial	1,548	3.6	119,291,517,605	1,286,235,107,444	1,405,526,625,049
Industrial	119	0.3	8,398,150,000	36,277,715,000	44,675,865,000
GRZ	92	0.2	19,992,924,001	255,363,197,000	275,356,121,001
Mining	02	0.0	13,000,000,000	393,000,000,000	406,000,000,000
Others	395	0.9	4,173,069,000	7,322,958,000	11,496,027,000
Total	43,458	100.0	303,011,091,795	4,742,161,525,086	5,045,172,616,881

Source: Adapted from Akakandelwa (2012b).

Table 30.7 2015 Tax Rates for the Kitwe City Council (%)

Residential	0.3
Commercial	1.0
Industrial	1.0
Mining property	1.7
Others	Variable

Source: Kitwe City Council.

Table 30.8 2015 Revenue for the Kitwe City Council

Revenue Source	Budgeted (ZMK)	Actual (ZMK)	Performance (%)
Property rates	38,136,309	22,012,690	58
Local taxes	570,000	297,482	52
Fees and charges	30,872,169	14,294,580	46
Licenses	256,000	32,284	13
Levies	7,397,634	879,759	12
Permits	1,779,200	859,386	48
Charges	15,157,500	5,849,884	39
Other income	15,000	110,135	734
Central-government grants	27,156,155	26,307,694	97
Local development fund	7,000,000	5,600,000	80
Total	128,339,967	76,243,894	

Source: Kitwe City Council.

Table 30.9 Tax Rates for the Livingstone City Council, 2014 and 2015

Property Use Category	2014 (%)	2015 (%)
Residential	0.3	0.3
Hospitality	0.5	0.4
Industrial, commercial, and institutional	0.5	0.7

Source: Livingstone City Council.

for hotels, where there was a 20 percent reduction of the tax rate), and the same tax rate (0.3%) was retained for residential properties.

The total property tax collectible (billed) in 2015 was ZMK 18,986,717, but the overall amount collected from January to October 2015 was only ZMK 5,363,339, that is 28.2 percent. In 2014, when the previous valuation roll was still in force, the total collectible property tax was ZMK 8,952,807, of which ZMK 7,340,584 (82.0 percent) was collected in-year. The substantial increase of 212 percent in projected revenues from the property tax in 2015 could be due to increased values, as well as improved coverage, with more properties on the new roll. However, apart from the late billing, the significant decrease in collections could also be explained by significant increases in individual tax bills.

Property Tax Issues in Zambia

The limited role of property-related taxes in the financing of central- and municipal-government incomes is, to a large extent, testimony to the inherent weaknesses in the current legislation and tax administration. The reduction of the property transfer tax rate to 5 percent is generally welcomed.

The government should consider abolishing the system of payment of grants in lieu of rates. These payments are at best infrequent and erratic. Government properties should rather be taxable on the basis of actual use.

Existing legislation, ministerial exemptions, and special agreements with newly privatized companies must be reviewed to address anomalies. All mining properties should in principle become taxable. The complete exemption of land used for agricultural purposes should be reviewed. Land used purely for subsistence farming could continue to be exempt. However, all nonsubsistence or commercial agricultural lands should be declared taxable.

The larger municipalities should employ qualified valuers and thus develop in-house capacity to undertake their own main and supplementary valuation rolls. The GVD can then provide more strategic oversight to these municipalities while giving additional support to smaller municipalities and new district councils.

In developing in-house capacity, rating authorities in Zambia should endeavor to address the frequency with which general and supplementary valuations are undertaken. Capacity could also be increased or realigned if councils would consider and implement simplified mass appraisal approaches in their valuation processes. More regular supplementary valuations will at least capture new property developments. In this regard, other authorities can learn from the Kitwe City Council, which undertook several supplementary valuations that increased not only its overall coverage of properties but also the value of existing properties on the roll. This translated into higher property tax revenues from these additional and revalued properties.

All rating authorities need to develop their in-house capacity to adequately administer revenues from all revenue sources, but especially the property tax. Their finance departments need to be adequately staffed and resourced to undertake the billing and collection of the property tax, and the necessary political and managerial support must be provided to enforce against defaulters. Implementation of alternative payment options should be a priority. This will reduce administration and compliance costs and should positively affect revenue collection.

Notes

1. There is no time limit per se regarding the declaration of value, which can even be made as long as three years after the sale, but it is up to the ZRA to adjust values because it goes by current market values. The state consent to assign property is valid for 12 months and is issued by the Ministry of Lands. If the consent expires before it is lodged at the Ministry of Lands, together with the other documents required for issuance of a title deed, the seller has to apply for a fresh consent.

2. They are revenue officers who are part of the Small and Medium Taxpayer Office, but they are based at the Ministry of Lands for property transfer tax purposes. They have general qualifications and may be rotated at any time. They do not carry out valuations but simply verify them. The GVD has qualified valuers and may be called on to assist.

References

Akakandelwa, S. 2012a. "An Analysis of Residential Commercial Land Use Changes in Lusaka City: What Are Its Effects on Formal Housing Stock?" B.S. thesis, Copperbelt University, Zambia.

———. 2012b. "Statutory Valuations in Zambia." Research paper, Copperbelt University, Zambia. *http://www.academia.edu/5783751/STATUTORY_VALUATIONS_IN_ZAMBIA_by_Sydney_Akakandelwa.*

Chande, C. E. 2014. "Conversion of Customary Land Tenure to Statutory Land Tenure as a Land Value Capture Tool to Finance Infrastructure Services: The Case of Lusaka." Master's dissertation, Erasmus University, The Netherlands.

CIA (Central Intelligence Agency). 2016. "Zambia." In *The World Factbook. https://www.cia.gov/library/publications/the-world-factbook/geos/za.html.*

Franzsen, R. C. D., and W. J. McCluskey. 2005. "An Exploratory Overview of Property Taxation in the Commonwealth of Nations." Working paper. Cambridge, MA: Lincoln Institute of Land Policy. *http://www.lincolninst.edu/pubs/pub-detail.asp?id=1069.*

IMF (International Monetary Fund). 2015. *2014 IMF Government Finance Statistics Yearbook*. Washington, DC.

———. 2016. "IMF World Longitudinal Data (WoRLD)." IMF e-Library Data. *http://data.imf.org/?sk=77413F1D-1525-450A-A23A-47AEED40FE78&sId=1390030109571.*

Kabinga, M. 2010. "Property Taxation in Botswana and Zambia." Presentation at the Fellowship Workshop of the African Tax Institute/Lincoln Institute of Land Policy Project on Property Taxation in Africa, Stellenbosch, South Africa (December 4–5).

Kasese, C. 2013. "Property Taxation in Zambia." M.Phil. dissertation, University of Pretoria.

Mudenda, M. M. 2006. "The Challenges of Customary Land Tenure in Zambia." Paper presented at "Shaping the Change," 23rd FIG Congress, Munich, Germany, October 8–13.

Mukonde, E. 2015. "Land Valuation and Taxation." Draft background paper prepared for the World Bank's Land Governance Assessment Framework (LGAF). Lusaka.

Sichone, F. 2008. "Land Administration in Zambia with Particular Reference to Customary Land." Paper presented at a seminar organized by the Zambia Land Alliance, University of Zambia, Zambia, June 28.

United Nations. 2014. *World Urbanization Prospects.* Washington, DC: Department of Economic and Social Affairs, Population Division.

United Nations, Department of Economic and Social Affairs, Population Division. 2015. World Population Prospects: The 2015 Revision. *https://esa.un.org/unpd/wpp /Publications/Files/World_Population_2015_Wallchart.pdf.*

World Bank. 2016a. "Country and Lending Groups." *http://data.worldbank.org/about /country-and-lending-groups.*

———. 2016b. "GDP per Capita (Current US%)." *http://data.worldbank.org/indicator /NY.GDP. PCAP. CD.*

Legislation

Land Acquisition Act of 1971.

Lands Act of 1995.

Property Transfer Tax Act of 2005 (Chapter 340 of the Laws of Zambia).

Public Procurement Act of 2008.

Rating Act No. 12 of 1997.

Rating (Amendment) Act No. 9 of 1999.

Statutory Instrument 44 of 2006.

Statutory Instrument 67 of 2006.

31

Zimbabwe

JOHN CHAKASIKWA, RIËL FRANZSEN,
AND WILLIAM McCLUSKEY

Zimbabwe, located in southern Africa, gained independence on April 18, 1980. It has an area of 390,757 km² and a population of some 15.6 million (United Nations 2015). The 2016 GDP per capita was estimated at USD 924 (World Bank 2016b). The capital city is Harare, and the secondary cities and towns are Bulawayo, Gweru, Masvingo, and Mutare. Urbanization is currently estimated to be 32 percent (United Nations 2014). Zimbabwe is a low-income country (World Bank 2016a).

Government

At independence, Zimbabwe embraced a republic system of government. At first, it had a one-party system, but it is now a multiparty democracy. There are three tiers of government: national, provincial, and local. The 91 local authorities in Zimbabwe consist of 60 rural district councils and 31 urban councils.[1] Zimbabwe's national taxes include the value-added tax (VAT), the corporate tax, the tax on domestic dividends and interest, the capital gains tax, the tobacco levy, the carbon tax, customs duties, excise duties, stamp duties, the withholding tax on tenders, the banking levy, the presumptive tax, road access fees, the ATM levy, and mining royalties. At the subnational level, in addition to charges and fees such as license fees and parking fees, property taxes or rates (value based and area based) are collected.

Land Tenure

The laws that govern land tenure and ownership of land and buildings in Zimbabwe include the following:

- The Agricultural Land Settlement Act (Chapter 20:01).

- The Communal Land Act (Chapter 20:04).

- The Constitution of Zimbabwe of 2013.

- The Deeds Registry Act (Chapter 20:05).

- The Gazetted Land (Consequential Provisions) Act (Chapter 20:28).

- The Land Acquisition Act (Chapter 20:10).

- The Land Occupation Conditions Act (Chapter 20:11).

- The Regional, Town and Country Planning Act (Chapter 29:12).

- The Rural District Councils Act (Chapter 29:13).

- The Rural Land Act (Chapter 20:18).

- The Titles Registration and Derelict Lands Act (Chapter 20:20).

- The Urban Councils Act (Chapter 29:15).

Section 71(2) of the 2013 constitution of Zimbabwe provides that "every person has the right, in any part of Zimbabwe, to acquire, hold, occupy, use, transfer, hypothecate, lease, or dispose of all forms of property."[2] Section 72 of the constitution provides for rights to agricultural land and empowers the state to identify and compulsorily acquire agricultural land to cater for agriculture, land reorganization, forestry, environmental conservation, or the use of wildlife or other natural resources or the relocation of persons dispossessed by the use of land for one of these purposes.

In urban areas, most land is under individual private tenure through title deeds for private developed property. Title deeds entitle the holder to own the land (including buildings on the land) indefinitely. Holders can pass land on as and when they wish, either while they live or through their estate at death. Agricultural and resettlement lands belong to the state under state tenure. Under the constitution's Section 72(2), the state can identify and acquire ownership of all land unless it is specifically demarcated and set aside for urban use under the terms of the Regional, Town and Country Planning Act (Chapter 29:12). Communal land is held under traditional chiefdoms and is recognized by the state as provided for in the Communal Land Act (Chapter 20:04).

According to the law, all land without a title that has not been registered as individual private property belongs to the state. An individual can sell his improved parcel of land if he has secured a title issued by the registrar of deeds under the Deeds Registry Act (Chapter 20:05). Individual registration of land is achieved through formal administrative structures. The Deeds Registry Act provides that in urban areas, "the ownership of land may be conveyed from one person to another only by means of a deed of transfer executed or attested by a registrar." The legislation also provides for "deeds registries at Harare and Bulawayo, each to serve its respective area as defined in the Schedule."

In rural areas, for both resettlement and agriculture, the land registration process goes through the local district land committee, the provincial land committee, and then the national chief lands officer. The land registration process in rural areas is more involved and bureaucratic than it is in urban areas, and it culminates in a permit or an offer letter, pending issue of a long-term lease. A permit is an authority to hold any portion of gazetted land as an A1 farm.[3] An offer letter offers an A2 farm to the bearer and is issued under specified terms by or on behalf of the minister who is responsible for land, pending the land settlement lease.[4]

Communal land that is not registered is customarily administered by local land chiefs and village headmen. Traditional governance structures comprise traditional leaders (chiefs and headmen) who are custodians of the national indigenous cultural, traditional, and normative heritage of Zimbabwe. The Communal Lands Act provides for the occupation, use, and administration of communal land for agricultural or residential purposes.

Property-Related Taxes

In Zimbabwe, the following property-related taxes are levied by the national government:

- The capital gains tax.

- The stamp duty and the transfer duty.

- The value-added tax.

- The property business income tax.

- The presumptive tax on informal traders' rent.

At local government level property tax (called "rates") are levied.

The Capital Gains Tax

A property owner is liable for the capital gains tax when he sells his land or property. The fair- or open-market value of the land or property is considered as gross income, and 20 percent is payable on the assessed capital gains realized by the owner of the property from the time he acquired it to the time he disposes of it. The Capital Gains Tax Act (Chapter 23:01) provides for this tax, which is collected by the central government.

The Stamp Duty and the Transfer Duty

Registration in the Deeds Registry upon the acquisition of immovable property is liable for the stamp duty at graduated rates ranging from 1 percent to 4 percent depending on the purchase price (see table 31.1). The Stamp Duties Act (Chapter 23:09) provides for this duty, which the central government collects. Any registration involving the transfer of mining locations by the mining commissioner is liable for the transfer duty. The Mines and Minerals Act (Chapter 21:05) provides for this duty, which the central government also collects. The purchaser in each of these cases is liable for these duties. Where an instrument is chargeable with ad valorem duty in respect of an amount stated in any foreign currency, the duty shall be calculated in Zimbabwean currency, according to the current rate of exchange on the date of the instrument.

The Value-Added Tax

The value-added tax (VAT) is imposed on the sale of certain property (under the Value Added Tax Act (Chapter 23:12). The sale of land only and of buildings for residential purposes is exempt from the VAT, but the sale of buildings for commercial purposes incurs a 15 percent VAT on the gross

Table 31.1 Stamp Duty Rates in Zimbabwe

Property Value/Purchase Price (USD)	Stamp Duty (%)
Up to 5,000 for every 100 or part of the value	1
More than 5,000 to 20,000 for every 100 or part of the value	2
More than 20,000 to 100,000 for every 100 or part of the value	3
Above 100,000 for every 100 or part of the value	4

Source: PKF International Limited, http://www.pkf.com/media/1959044/zimbabwe%20pkf%20tax%20guide%202013.pdf.

Note: A transfer duty of 1% is imposed on the transfer of mining rights (Deloitte 2015).

sale amount (consideration). The VAT is also charged and collected by property agents or managers on the commission they charge to property owners for whom they act. The VAT is then remitted to central government.

The Tax on the Business Income from Land

Income from the buying and selling of land (property) is taxed just like any other business income. The taxable (net) income, after allowable deductions from the gross income, is subjected to a 25 percent tax rate. Persons liable for this tax include property dealers, sellers, and estate agents. The Income Tax Act (Chapter 23:06) provides for this tax and the tax is collected at central government level.

The tax on rental income of property is levied separately. It is collected by the central government and is treated as a tax on business income (the rent collected). Informal traders, such as market stall owners, pay a presumptive tax of 10 percent of the rentals to the owner of the land or property on which they trade informally. This is also remitted to the central government by the land or property owners.

The Property Tax

The property tax, commonly known as "rates," has been in existence in Zimbabwe since the early 20th century, when the Rhodesian colonial government legislated for land occupation and ownership through the Land Apportionment Act of 1930 and later the Land Tenure Act of 1969. The property tax system inherited from the Rhodesian colonial era was largely based on the rating systems in South Africa (Brakspear 1999).

Zimbabwe's property tax is assigned to local authorities, consisting of municipal councils, town councils, rural district councils, and local boards, which are responsible for the valuation and assessment of the property, as well as the levying and collection of the tax within their jurisdictions. The legislation that provides for property taxes includes the Urban Councils Act, the Rural District Councils Act, the Communal Land Act, the Rural Land Act, and the Finance Act. Section 276(2)(b) of the new constitution of Zimbabwe provides for the "functions of local authorities": "An Act of Parliament may confer functions on local authorities including—a power to levy rates and taxes and generally to raise sufficient revenue for them to carry out their objects and responsibilities."

Revenue sources for local authorities are mainly water, sewer, and refuse charges and property rates. Determining revenue-collection figures of local authorities to estimate the total property tax as a percentage of GDP has been difficult because of bureaucratic obstacles. As a result, only one case study on the capital city, Harare, has been done. From 2008 to

2010, property rates contributed an average of 41 percent of the total revenue collected by the Harare City Council. Although the Harare City Council has diverse sources of revenue, smaller local authorities do not; thus, property rates are their main tax source. This means that property rates are a more significant revenue source for some 50 percent of small towns.

The property tax takes different forms in Zimbabwe, including land rentals, rates, the unit tax, development levies, and supplementary charges. Land rentals are collected by the Ministry of Lands, but the rest are collected throughout the country by the 91 local authorities. This entails coverage throughout the country, not just in major cities and towns. Rates are mainly levied on property in urban areas; land rentals and the unit tax are levied on rural land; and supplementary charges are levied on communal land. Development and special development levies are imposed by rural district councils on all owners of rural land within a council's area, including owners of mining locations, shop or liquor licensed dealers, holders of permits issued under the Communal Land Act, all heads of household within any communal or resettlement ward of the council, and those carrying out the following businesses: extracting sand, extracting gravel, extracting clay or making bricks or clay products, extracting or crushing stone, and operating a sawmill.

The Tax Base

The tax base for property taxes in Zimbabwe depends on the location of the property: urban, rural (commercial farms), or communal land. The laws provide that the property tax can be a flat tax or can be based on area or value.

The property tax system in Zimbabwe's urban areas is traditionally and mostly value based and takes into account the value of land and improvements for tax purposes (Bird and Slack 2003; Franzsen and McCluskey 2008). The Zimbabwean legislation provides for the following tax bases, which are all used extensively:

- Land value (site value).

- Land and improvements as separate taxable objects at different rates.

- Improved value.

The Urban Councils Act defines "property" as "land . . . includ[ing] improvements thereon." "Property" thus means "land and structures." The property base coverage in urban areas therefore includes all urban land and buildings. Improvements are defined to include the following:

- All buildings, movable or immovable.

- Incomplete buildings, occupied in whole or in part.

- All work done or material used on any land by or on behalf of any owner or occupier of, or any holder of an interest in, that land, but only insofar as the effect of that work or material is to increase the value of the land, and the benefit of that work or labor is unexhausted at the time of valuation.

The tax bases for the property tax in rural and communal areas are rural (farm) land and communal land within the council area. The taxes for both rural and communal lands are flat taxes and area-based taxes. Rural land used for farming incurs land rental and the unit tax, which is a flat tax but is also area based insofar as it depends on the natural farming region in which the farmland is located. The development levies and supplementary charges levied on communal land are also flat taxes based on the area of the land.

Exemptions

Although all property within a council area is ratable, the laws specify that the following properties in urban areas are exempt from the property tax:

- Property belonging to the state, local authorities, or international organizations.

- Buildings used for public religious worship and religious education.

- Buildings used for educational or sporting purposes.

The following properties in rural and communal areas are exempt from rates:

- Parks and wildlife land or forest land.

- Municipal areas, town areas, or local-government areas.

- A town ward of a rural district council or an area that has been declared a "specified" area.

- The area of any township.

- State land.

Assessment and Valuation

The current legislation that provides for open-market valuation of non-residential property and for the rating unit plus the zoning (site value) system for residential property was promulgated on December 22, 1995. It effectively changed the previous assessment of land and improvements on residential property, as provided for by the old, repealed legislation, to assessment based on the number of rating units and the zone where the property is located.

In urban areas, the property tax is levied on nonresidential and residential property, which is defined as "land . . . includ[ing] improvements thereon and any portion of such land or such improvements." The law requires councils to conduct the valuation of property in a manner that arrives at a fair and equitable valuation or assessment of the property. The basis of valuation differs between nonresidential (commercial) property and residential property. While a valuation is required on nonresidential property, assessment is undertaken for residential property. The difference is in the formula used to calculate the ratable or taxable value.

The basis of valuation for commercial property is "the estimated price which a buyer would be willing to give and a seller would be willing to accept if the property to be valued were brought to voluntary sale in the open market" at the date fixed by the council for either a general valuation or a supplementary valuation. The law provides that in determining the open-market value, the valuation officer must ignore any exceptional temporary circumstances. The valuation officer must also have "due regard . . . to other property in the vicinity."

The assessment of residential property for property tax purposes consists of calculating the number of rating units to be assigned to the property and determining the rating zone within which the property is situated. The rating unit for any residential property is an area equal to the minimum size of stands or plots permitted under any town-planning scheme applicable within the locality in which the residential property is situated, or an area a council may fix for all residential properties situated in localities where there is no town-planning scheme regulating the minimum size of stands or plots. The number of rating units to be assigned to any residential property is calculated by dividing the land area of the property by the rating unit applicable to the property. Every council divides the council area into one or more rating zones, using the following criteria:

- Each rating zone should contain residential properties of approximately the same size and value.

- Each rating zone should contain residential properties that are adjacent to one another.

- No rating zone should consist of a single residential property.

In rural and communal areas, every owner of a farm or lessee and holder of an offer letter or land settlement permit for a farm is required to pay the special unit tax, which is fixed for that location, to the relevant council. The unit tax depends primarily on the productive capacity of the farmland. This tax is progressive because the greater the capacity of the land for agricultural production, the greater the unit tax the owner will have to pay.

A valuation officer for each urban council carries out the valuation of property for tax (rating) purposes. The Urban Councils Act requires that each council conduct the following:

- A general valuation of all nonresidential property within its area. For that purpose, the council is required to fix a date falling within the period during which the valuation is being carried out.

- A general assessment of all residential property within its area.

- The preparation of a general valuation roll of all property within its area.

The general valuation roll prepared by the valuation officer is expected to contain the name of the owner of the property, a description of the property, and the area of the land. In addition, for nonresidential property, it should contain the valuation of the property or the valuation of the land and the valuation apportioned to the improvements. For residential property, it should contain the number of rating units assigned to the property, the rating zone in which the property is located, and any other particulars that a council may require.

The interval between revaluations is a minimum of three years and a maximum of ten years unless the minister of local government, through a statutory instrument, extends it to up to fifteen years. As of March 2016, the valuation rolls of most local authorities except Harare and Bulawayo, the two major cities, had expired for several reasons, but mainly because of the hyperinflationary environment that ended in 2009.

Besides the general valuation, there is provision for councils to carry out supplementary valuations of the following properties:

- Any property that does not appear on the current valuation roll.

- Any nonresidential property whose value has been materially affected by (1) alterations, additions, or demolitions; (2) a town-planning scheme or the construction of any public work or undertaking; (3) a flood or other disaster; or (4) any cause peculiar to that property.

- Any properties that have been consolidated or any property that has been subdivided into lots.

- Any property for which there are errors in the general valuation roll affecting the value or assessment of the property.

According to the law, the valuation or assessment of any property appearing on a supplementary valuation roll is for all purposes to form part of the general valuation roll on the basis of which the valuation or assessment is calculated.

In rural and communal areas where rural levies and the unit tax are collected, no valuation is undertaken. The levies and the unit tax are reviewed from time to time.

The Valuers Council ensures that valuers practice ethically and professionally, since the council's mandate is "ensuring that the competence and conduct of valuers practicing in Zimbabwe are of a standard sufficiently high for the protection of the public" (Valuers Act). The two main universities—the University of Zimbabwe and the National University of Science and Technology—produced some 415 graduates in property-related disciplines from 2000 to 2010. However, Zimbabwe had only 85 registered valuers in 2010. Many valuers have moved out of the country, particularly since the economic environment deteriorated in 2007. There are not enough valuers to meet the needs of urban councils that require valuation officers.

Objections and Appeals

After completing the valuation roll, the valuation officer signs it and submits it to the council for inspection. Owners and occupiers of property are informed by notice published in the *Government Gazette* and in two issues of a newspaper and are invited to lodge an objection with the clerk of the valuation board in writing within 21 days. The objections can be against the following:

- The valuation of any nonresidential property owned or occupied.

- Any apportionment of such valuation.

- The number of rating units assigned to any residential property owned or occupied.

- The rating zone within which a residential property has been placed.

- Any error, omission, or incorrect description in relation to any property.

Once the clerk of the valuation board receives the objections, he must within 21 days publish a notice in the *Government Gazette* and in a newspaper detailing the place at and date on which the valuation board will sit to consider the objections. At least 28 days before the valuation board sits, the clerk must mail a copy of the notice of the objections meeting to every objector and forward a copy of the notice to the valuation officer, together with copies of all objections that the valuation board is to consider. If the council objects to any valuation or assessment appearing in the valuation roll or to any proposed amendment, it must give notice in writing to the owner or occupier of the property concerned and to the clerk of the valuation board at least 28 days before the day on which the valuation board will sit to consider the valuation roll. Appeals against the decision of the valuation board can be referred to the Supreme Court by either party within 30 days of the valuation board's decision.

Tax Rates

In urban areas, the local authorities (municipal councils and town councils) are responsible for the valuation of property, as well as the levying and collection of the tax within their areas. Therefore, they are responsible for determining the tax rates. Most of the public services that the municipal and town councils provide to residents are funded by the budget, for which the property tax is a key revenue source. The tax rates are therefore determined annually through the annual budget process, and the property tax rates depend on the amount of revenue from other sources and the costs of the services that the municipal and town councils must deliver to residents.

The law provides that any local authority is empowered to choose the assessment method for the properties in its jurisdiction. Therefore, the structure of the tax rates depends on the assessment system adopted by the municipal or town council. For example, Harare Municipality uses an area-based system, and the tax rates range from a minimum of USD 4 per month for a high-density (low-income) property of 200 m² to a maximum of USD 32 per month for a low-density (high income) property of 4,500 m². For other urban areas, the tax rates range from USD 2 to USD 25 per month.

In rural (commercial farmland) areas, local authorities (rural district councils and local boards) determine the tax rate for property rates, development and special development levies, and supplementary charges, while land rental charges and the unit tax rates are determined by the minister of finance in the central government. The amounts charged for property rates, development and special development levies, and supplementary charges are supposed to be determined annually to supply revenues for the annual budget. However, some local authorities may have a longer review cycle because of reduced ability of residents and property owners to pay their taxes due to the difficult economic situation. In rural areas, amounts charged for land rentals and for the unit tax are uniform within each natural region of Zimbabwe but vary between A1 and A2 farms.[5] The current land rental charges and development levies are shown in table 31.2. The current unit tax rates are shown in table 31.3.

In communal areas, communal development and land development levies are imposed. These were previously set by the Minister of Local Government but are now set by the minister of finance. The current rates were set in 2009 and have not been reviewed since then. The rates for communal development and land development levies are progressive and depend on the area and use of the land and, for mining land, the type of mineral mined, such as gold, silver, platinum, or precious stones or base minerals.

Table 31.2 Land Rental Charges and Development Levies in Zimbabwe

	Natural Region	Land Rental Amount	Development Levy Amount
A1 Farm	1, 2, 2a, 2b, 3, 4, 5	USD 10 per year	USD 5 per year
A2 Farm	1, 2, 2a, 2b, 3, 4, 5	USD 3 per hectare per year	USD 2 per hectare per year

Source: Schedule to Chapter 10 of the Finance Act (Chapter 23:04).

Table 31.3 Unit Tax Rates in Zimbabwe

Natural Region	Tax Amount
1	USD 3 per hectare per year
2	USD 3 per hectare per year
2a	USD 3 per hectare per year
2b	USD 3 per hectare per year
3	USD 2 per hectare per year
4	USD 2 per hectare per year
5	USD 1 per hectare per year

Source: Third Schedule of the Rural District Councils Act (Chapter 29:13).

Billing and Collection

Administration of the property tax or rates is the responsibility of subnational governments. In most local authorities, bills are issued to taxpayers (property owners) at the end of every month and are hand-delivered to each property address by council collectors. The monthly bills carry the following information:

- The name of the property owner (the taxpayer).

- The address of the property (which must be the delivery or postal address).

- The period or month to which the tax applies.

- The rating unit(s) on the valuation roll.

- The tax rate applied.

- The tax payable.

The bills also include any amount in arrears, the rate of interest on these arrears, and the total outstanding debt. Councils have started to combine the bills for charges like water, the sewer network, refuse collection, and the property tax. This measure is designed to cut costs and synchronize the enforcement of revenue collection.

The tax is due in the middle of the month following the billing month. About 95 percent of the tax receivable is paid by taxpayers who make cash payments at revenue halls or offices. Only a few taxpayers have started using Internet banking to pay their tax bills. This is partly due to the low level of mobile and Internet banking in the market, the basic level of telecommunication infrastructure, and low public confidence in the banking system after Zimbabwe's world-record-breaking inflation of 2008 that was preceded by widespread bank failures and closures. Section 275(4) of the Urban Councils Act provides that "a council may accept payment of any rate by instalments in such equal or varying amounts as may be determined by the council." Due consideration is given to financial hardship of property owners.

In rural areas, no billing is done for those who are liable for the unit tax. Currently, no council appears to be collecting any taxes other than the unit tax, which councils indicate is paid only by mining companies. No billing is done in communal areas.

Enforcement

Most councils have debt-management sections that are required to make follow-up calls for any unpaid or outstanding tax payments. Outstanding arrears incur interest at 10 percent per year, which is the bank rate. This is meant to ensure that taxpayers have an incentive not to delay payment of their property tax.

In Zimbabwe's urban council areas, the councils provide water and network services to properties within their jurisdictions. The easiest and least costly enforcement mechanism is to withhold certain services, such as water supply. Electricity in Zimbabwe is supplied only by a government utility company, the Zimbabwe Electricity Supply Authority. Some councils have sought permission from the authority to unilaterally switch off electricity if property owners or residents fail to pay their rates.

To enforce payment of land rentals, the law states that any person who has a farm but "is in arrears in paying any rental or development levy or any portion thereof shall not receive any financial assistance that is payable directly or indirectly from public funds for any purpose connected with his or her farming operations." This measure penalizes landholders who do not pay their property taxes.

Property Tax Issues in Zimbabwe

In many countries, there are constitutional provisions for the implementation of property taxes by local or subnational government, but in Zimbabwe, acts of Parliament assign the property tax to local governments. Constitutional provisions for the powers, duties, and functions of local authorities, including that of administering the property tax, would curtail discretion, unilateral decisions, interference, and ad hoc decisions on political grounds that adversely affect residents (taxpayers).

The economic challenges that Zimbabwe faced between 2000 and 2008 left more than 85 percent of the population with extremely low incomes. The hardest hit were those in rural areas. Current legislation allows for rural land development levies, and collection has been centralized and administered by the Ministry of Lands on A1 and A2 farms, which are expected to be productive and stimulate economic growth while ensuring food security. These levies, however, are difficult to collect from the majority of the rural (peasant) population, which lives on subsistence farming. The only viable and feasible tax base currently is commercial agricultural land. The current tax base for farmland excludes farm buildings and improvements and is essentially based on area rather than value.

Because all taxpayers must make their payments on the same due date, there are long lines, and those receiving the payments are overwhelmed. The number of cash offices does not meet the demand during these peak periods. Some councils have been trying to establish payment offices in the zones or suburbs for taxpayers' convenience. However, there are problems with this manual system, including failure to update taxpayer accounts on payment, resulting in undeserved penalties and interest charges.

Notes

1. The current numbers have been provided by the Zimbabwe Local Government Association.

2. The New Constitution of Zimbabwe was enacted in 2013 to repeal the one that came into operation on April 18, 1980, Zimbabwe's Independence Day.

3. An A1 farm is one held under a permit allocated under the Model A1 Scheme (villagized, self-contained, and three-tier land use plans with plots of three hectares). "Gazetted land" (that is, agricultural land whose compulsory acquisition is specifically provided for in section 16B of the Constitution), which covers a broader spectrum of agricultural land than simply "agricultural land required for resettlement purposes" (see section 16B(2)(a)(iii) of the Constitution).

4. An A2 farm is one held under a 99-year lease allocated under the Model A2 Scheme (Commercial Farm Settlement Scheme). A land settlement lease is a 99-year lease of a Model A2 farm.

5. Persons liable to pay the development levy under the Schedule to Chapter 10 of the Finance Act (Chapter 23:04) are not liable to pay the development levy under the Third Schedule of the Rural District Councils Act (Chapter 29:13).

References

Bird, R. M., and E. Slack. 2003. "Land and Property Taxation Around the World: A Review." Research paper. Cambridge, MA: Lincoln Institute of Land Policy.

Brakspear, G. 1999. "Rating in Zimbabwe." In *Property Tax: An International Comparative Review*, ed. W. J. McCluskey, 216–232. Aldershot: Ashgate.

CIA (Central Intelligence Agency). 2016. "Zimbabwe." In *The World Factbook*. *https://www.cia.gov/library/publications/the-world-factbook/geos/zi.html*.

Deloitte. 2015. *Guide to Fiscal Information: Key Economies in Africa, 2014/15*. *http://www2 .deloitte.com/content/dam/Deloitte/et/Documents/tax/ZA_Fiscal_Guide_2015 _29012015.pdf*.

Franzsen, R. C. D., and W. J. McCluskey. 2008. "The Feasibility of Site Value Taxation." In *Making the Property Tax Work*, ed. R. W. Bahl, J. Martinez-Vazquez, and J. M. Youngman, 268–306. Cambridge, MA: Lincoln Institute of Land Policy.

United Nations. 2014. *World Urbanization Prospects*. Washington, DC: Department of Economics and Social Affairs, Population Division.

United Nations, Department of Economic and Social Affairs, Population Division. 2015. World Population Prospects: The 2015 Revision. *https://esa.un.org/unpd/wpp /Publications/Files/World_Population_2015_Wallchart.pdf*.

World Bank. 2016a. "Country and Lending Groups." *http://data.worldbank.org/about /country-and-lending-groups*.

———. 2016b. "GDP per Capita (Current US%)." *http://data.worldbank.org/indicator /NY.GDP.PCAP.CD*.

Legislation

Agricultural Land Settlement Act (Chapter 20:01).

Capital Gains Tax Act (Chapter 23:01).

Communal Land Act (Chapter 20:04).

Constitution of Zimbabwe of 2013.

Deeds Registry Act (Chapter 20:05).

Finance Act (Chapter 23:04).

Gazetted Land (Consequential Provisions) Act (Chapter 20:28).

Income Tax Act (Chapter 23:06).

Land Acquisition Act (Chapter 20:10).

Land (Consequential Provisions) Act (Chapter 20:28).

Land Occupation Conditions Act (Chapter 20:11).

Mines and Minerals Act (Chapter 21:05).

Regional, Town and Country Planning Act (Chapter 29:12).

Rural District Councils Act (Chapter 29:13).

Rural Land Act (Chapter 20:18).

Stamp Duties Act (Chapter 23:09).

Titles Registration and Derelict Lands Act (CAP 20:20).

Urban Councils Act (Chapter 29:15).

Value Added Tax (Chapter 23:12).

Valuers Act (Chapter 27:18).

PART III

African Countries by Region

32

Anglophone Africa

RIËL FRANZSEN AND WILLIAM McCLUSKEY

A ll Anglophone countries in Africa are former British colonies, are members of the Commonwealth of Nations, and have English as their official language. The five Anglophone countries in West Africa—The Gambia, Ghana, Liberia, Nigeria, and Sierra Leone—are all located on the northwest or west coast of Africa. In this chapter, only Lagos State in Nigeria is briefly reviewed. The Gambia, Ghana, Liberia, and Sierra Leone are covered more extensively in other chapters.

The three Anglophone countries in East Africa—Kenya, Tanzania, and Uganda—are discussed in other chapters. Because Seychelles, an offshore archipelago in the Indian Ocean, is a member of the African Union and also of the Common Market for Eastern and Southern Africa and the Southern African Development Community (SADC), it is grouped with the East African Anglophone countries. Although a recurrent property tax does not presently exist in Seychelles, the administration and taxation of the acquisition of immovable property by noncitizens are briefly discussed.

There are eight Anglophone countries in southern Africa: Botswana, Lesotho, Malawi, Namibia, South Africa, Swaziland, Zambia, and Zimbabwe. Because the island state of Mauritius (east of Madagascar) is a member of the African Union and the SADC, it is grouped with the southern African countries. In this chapter, the property tax systems of Lesotho, Malawi and Swaziland are summarized briefly. The property tax systems of Botswana, Namibia, South Africa, Zambia, and Zimbabwe are discussed in more detail in other chapters.

Nigeria

Nigeria borders Cameroon to the east, Chad to the northeast, Niger to the north, Benin to the west, and the Gulf of Guinea to the south.[1] It achieved independence in 1960 and has a land area of 923,768 km^2. Its population of approximately 182 million is the highest of any country in Africa (United Nations 2015; World Bank 2014b). In 1991, Abuja became the capital city. Previously, the capital had been Lagos, the largest city in the country and its commercial capital. The per capita GDP in 2015 was estimated at USD 2,640 (World Bank 2016b), and about 48 percent of the population is urbanized (United Nations 2014).

Government

Nigeria has a bicameral legislature and a three-tier system of government: federal, state, and local governments. It is divided administratively into the Federal Capital Territory (Abuja) and 36 states, which are further subdivided into 774 local-government areas.

Local councils in Nigeria receive revenue from both internal and external sources. The 1976 local-government reforms ensured that the internal revenue sources of local governments would include tenement rates (the property tax); education rates; street lighting taxes; the flat rate tax and the poll tax; fines and fees, which include court fines and fees, motor parking fees, forest fees, public advertisement fees, market fees, regulated premises fees, fees for registration of births and deaths, and licensing fees; and miscellaneous sources, such as rents from council estates, royalties, interests on investments, and proceeds from commercial activities. The country's 1999 constitution mandates that local governments receive a percentage of federal and state revenues. The revenue-allocation formula assigns 20 percent of federal revenue and 10 percent of internally generated state revenues to local governments. The property tax as a revenue source for local-government programs is generally overlooked in Nigeria because most local councils still rely on federal and state governments' revenue allocations rather than the sources specifically and constitutionally allocated to them.

Land Tenure

The Land Use Decree (1978) nationalized all land in the country and handed over its administration to committees constituted at the state- and local-government levels. One justification for the decree was the rationalization of customary land tenure systems, which were held to be a constraint on agricultural development.The decree envisaged that "rights of occupancy" would replace all previous forms of title and would form the basis on which all land was to be held. These rights were to be of two kinds: statutory and customary. Statutory rights of occupancy were to be granted by the governor and confined principally to land in urban areas. In contrast, a customary right of occupancy "means the right of a person or community lawfully using or occupying land in accordance with customary law and includes a customary right of occupancy granted by local government under this Decree."

The Property Tax

In Nigeria, the term *property tax* describes taxes that are imposed primarily on land and buildings. Real property refers to land and generally to whatever is erected on, grows on, or is attached to land. The 1999 constitution governs the property tax across local governments in Nigeria (Fatimilehin 2003). In some Nigerian states, the property tax is referred to as "tenement rates" and is charged by local-government authorities across these states under their respective tenement rate laws. Tenement rating can be traced back to the Assessment Act of 1915, which gave state governments jurisdiction over property taxation (Ipaye 2007). Since then, there has been a series of constitutional provisions that guide the administration of tenement rating or property taxation in Nigeria. Tenement rates are based on the ratable value of the property, which is calculated by establishing the gross rental value of the property and deducting expenses. In determining gross value, valuers are free to consider the actual rent payable on the tenement or the rent payable on comparable tenements within the vicinity. If the tenement cannot be valued by direct reference to a rent because of the special nature of the property or the paucity of rental evidence for similar tenements in the area, the valuer may use depreciated replacement cost or any other relevant method.

The government of Lagos State rationalized several property taxes into a single property charge, referred to as the land use charge (LUC), in 2001 to replace all other state- and local-government taxes on real property, including the tenement rates, ground rents, and neighborhood improvement charges. As a result, once the LUC is imposed on a property, the rates and charges that were payable under the previous legislation are no longer applicable.

The LUC in Lagos State is imposed on the owner of the property, but if the owner is not in occupation of the property, the collecting authority is authorized to collect it from the occupier, who is usually the tenant. The tenant, in turn, is authorized to deduct the amount of the payment from monies that he may owe the owner of the property. There is thus an indemnity in favor of the tenant or occupier against the owner, who retains the burden, if not the liability, for the LUC.

The LUC is assessed on capital value. The State Zonal Office is responsible for identifying, surveying, and valuing ratable properties in the state and compiling the valuation list. The law specifically stipulates that valuers must be qualified estate surveyors and valuers registered by the Estate Surveyors and Valuers Registration Board.

Exemptions

The LUC law exempts the following from property rates:

- Any church, chapel, mosque, meetinghouse, or other building exclusively used for public religious worship.

- Buildings used for public hospitals and clinics.

- Buildings used for charitable purposes.

- Buildings used for public educational purposes, including public universities, colleges, and schools.

- Buildings on burial grounds and crematoriums.

- Buildings owned by diplomatic missions as may be approved by the ministry responsible for foreign affairs.

Tax Rates

State governments are responsible for setting the tax rates in Nigeria. The 1999 constitution provides for state legislative authorities to determine the design and structure of property taxes, while local authorities perform the administrative functions. In Lagos State, for example, as a result of resistance to the LUC, the state government revised the rates payable downward. The current rates are as follows:

- Commercial property used for residential purposes: 0.5 percent of the assessed property value.

- Commercial property used for business purposes: 1.25 percent of the assessed property value.

- Industrial premises used for manufacturing purposes: 0.5 percent of the assessed property value.

- Owner-occupier residential property: 0.15 percent of the assessed property value.

The hiring of consultants to collect rates has been controversial. Before 1998, the law allowed each rating authority to appoint rate collectors. These rate collectors could include independent contractors, as well as employees of the council.

A ratepayer has the right to file an appeal against the rating assessment to the Assessment Appeal Tribunal on condition that 50 percent of the amount assessed is paid along with the fees that the Appeal Tribunal pre-scribes for filing an appeal. This condition has limited the number of appeal cases in Nigeria, and tax experts are challenging this clause on the grounds that it violates Section 36 of the 1999 constitution.

Enforcement

The Lagos State Land Use Charge Law provides for the state to impose the following penalties on defaulters.

- Payment increases of up to 25 percent, 50 percent, and 100 percent, respectively, where the taxpayer delays payment for up to 75, 105, or 135 days from the date of receipt of the assessment.

- The appointment of a receiver over the property until all outstand-ing taxes, penalties, and administrative charges are paid if payment is not received after 135 days from receipt of the assessment.

- Application to a superior court by the commissioner of finance to recover the sum assessed. Pending the determination of the case, the court can attach the earnings accruing from the property.

- Penalties of up to NGN 100,000 or three months' imprisonment for noncompliance with the LUC.

Seychelles

Seychelles is the smallest African country, with an area of only 455 km², and consists of some 115 small islands located approximately 1,600 km off the coast of East Africa in the Indian Ocean. After a long dispute be-tween the United Kingdom and France, it was finally ceded to the former in 1814. It was granted independence in 1976. Mahé is the largest island and is home to 90 percent of the total population of about 100,000; it is also home to the capital, Victoria (World Bank 2014b). Approximately 54 percent of the population lives in urban areas (United Nations 2014). In contrast to other African countries, the 2015 per capita GDP, estimated at USD 15,476, was high (World Bank 2016b). It is presently the only high-income country in Africa (World Bank 2016a).

Government

The 1993 constitution brought an end to socialism. Because of the small size and population of the country, there is no local government. However, the government is decentralized to 25 administrative districts. Seychelles has a hybrid legal system composed of English, French, and customary law.

Land Tenure

The predominant form of land tenure in Seychelles is freehold. However, there are stringent restrictions on the acquisition of immovable property by noncitizens. The acquisition of real property requires the formal approval of the minister responsible for land use and habitat. A person with a Seychelles passport may acquire property without permission. Holders of foreign passports may not purchase a freehold interest in any immovable property owned by the state. However, subject to approval and on terms of conditions that may be set, a noncitizen may acquire and hold state-owned property under a long-term lease. If immovable property is purchased for a holiday home or residential development outside of an area to which the so-called Villas Policy, a sanction duty (based on the market value of the property) is payable in addition to the applicable 5 percent stamp duty. This policy addresses the concept of construction and sale of villas and holiday accommodation by promoters in approved tourism resorts and ownership of such immovable property by non-Seychellois throughout Seychelles.

Property-Related Taxes

Taxes and other revenues constitute 40.7 percent of GDP (World Bank 2014b), significantly more than in other African countries. The most important taxes are the business tax (levied under the Business Tax Act of 2009, with relatively low rates) and the value-added tax (VAT), which replaced the goods and services tax in 2013. The VAT rate is 15 percent. There is no capital gains tax, inheritance tax, or recurrent property tax in Seychelles.

A stamp duty is payable on the acquisition of real estate and is set at 5 percent of the purchase price (or market value). However, noncitizens who acquire a legal interest in land and property pay an additional administrative fee of 1.5 percent and a sanction duty, as well as the stamp duty (MLUH 2016).

Lesotho

Lesotho, a former British colony, gained independence in 1966. It is a small country with a surface area of 30,355 km² and is completely encircled by

South Africa. The capital is Maseru. The population, of which only about 27 percent is urbanized, is approximately 2.14 million (United Nations 2014, 2015), of which about 270,000 live in Maseru. Although an income tax and value-added taxes are levied, Lesotho is heavily dependent on remittances from the Southern African Customs Union (SACU).[2] In 2015, the GDP per capita was estimated at USD 1,067 (World Bank 2016b). The Local Government Act 1997 (as amended) provides the legal and institutional framework for decentralized local government in Lesotho. The 1993 National Constitution of Lesotho provides for a decentralized local government. Currently, Lesotho has 10 district councils, 1 municipal council (Maseru), 11 urban councils, and 64 community councils.

Land Tenure

Lesotho had a dual land tenure system with customary and statutory land tenure systems existing side by side. However, land reform resulted in the passing of the Land Act 1979, which nationalized all land in Lesotho, with rights to be leased from the state. Subsequently, the Land Act 2010 provides for the grant of titles to land, the conversion of titles to land, the better securing of land titles, the administration of land, and the expropriation of land for public purposes. In 2010, the Land Administration Authority (LAA) was established as an autonomous government agency with the goal of improving land administration services (including surveying and mapping) and reducing land administration costs. However, the LAA is not responsible for the allocation of land, land valuation, or land use and physical planning. These are the responsibilities of district, urban, and municipal councils and the Ministry of Local Government and Chieftainship (LAA 2015).

Ground Rent

Ground rent is an annual levy for the occupation and use of a land parcel. It is payable by every leaseholder and is collected by the LAA. A leaseholder is exempt from ground rent for his primary residence. Ground rent is payable on second residential property, commercial property, industrial property, and commercial agricultural land. Ground rent can be paid at the LAA accounts office or by direct deposit into the LAA's bank account (LAA 2015).

The Property Transfer Tax

A transfer tax (called "transfer duty"), a stamp duty, and a registration fee are levied (Deloitte 2015; Franzsen and McCluskey 2005b). The registration fee is a fixed amount of LSL 50. The transfer duty is levied at 3 percent on the first LSL 10,000 and 4 percent on the remaining amount, whereas the stamp duty is 1 percent on the first LSL 7,000 and 3 percent on the remaining amount (World Bank 2014a). These taxes and the registration fee are collected by the registrar of deeds.

The Recurrent Property Tax

The recurrent property tax (called "rates") is levied, assessed, and collected under the terms of the Valuation and Rating Act, 1980. The tax base is "land and improvements," and the owner, broadly defined in the act to potentially include both the owner and the occupier, as liable for the tax (Franzsen and McCluskey 2005b). Coverage is poor because only properties in a "designated area" are taxable. In 2003, only Maseru was a designated area, and even there, many new properties were not yet on the valuation roll (Franzsen 2003).

The following properties are exempt:

- State-occupied property.

- Properties used for "public benefit," such as libraries, museums, schools, and churches.

- Properties below a value threshold set by the Minister of Finance.

Although government properties are exempt, the government must pay a grant in lieu of rates (Franzsen 2003).

Under the law, separate valuations must be obtained for both land and improvements, and the valuation roll must show both values, as well as the total value. Revaluations must take place every three years, although the currency of the valuation roll can be extended up to a maximum of six years. The minister responsible for local government must appoint a qualified valuer. In 2001, the Maseru Council appointed an in-house valuer (Franzsen and McCluskey 2005b). Before an appeal, the parties may agree on a value to be recorded in the valuation roll. The Land Tribunal hears appeals.

Municipal councils set tax rates annually, but ministerial approval of these locally set rates is required. The law allows for differential rates for different property use categories. Rates are payable in two semiannual installments. However, shorter periods (e.g., monthly payments) may be introduced. The current tax rates for Maseru City Council are given in table 32.1. These rates have remained unchanged since at least 2001. The law allows for the following enforcement mechanisms: interest on arrears; refusal to issue a clearance certificate for a transfer of ownership; and forced sale (not used in practice).

Table 32.1 Property Tax Rates in Maseru, 2015

Category	Tax Rate (%)
Residential property	0.0025
Commercial property	2
Industrial property	2.75
Government	Grant in lieu of rates

Source: Maseru City Council (2015).

The rating system in Maseru is disordered, with extremely low base coverage, an outdated valuation roll, and poor collection and enforcement practices. There is significant scope for improving the system in Maseru and for extending it to other towns and villages in Lesotho. In 2003/2004, revenue from rates in Maseru constituted about LSL 1 million and transfers about LSL 30 million out of total revenues of LSL 33 million (CLGF 2011).

Malawi

Malawi has an area of 118,484 km² and borders Lake Malawi and Mozambique to the east, Mozambique to the south and east, Zambia to the east, and Tanzania in the north. The population is almost 17.2 million, of which only about 16 percent lives in urban areas (United Nations 2014, 2015). The capital is Lilongwe, with a population of about 900,000 (CIA 2016). It was designed on a zonal basis with large open spaces, and even today, few streets and suburbs have names (Franzsen and McCluskey 2005a). Blantyre, with an estimated 810,000 inhabitants, is the second-largest city in Malawi. In 2015, the GDP per capita was estimated at USD 372 (World Bank 2016b).

Malawi is a democratic republic with two spheres of government: national and local. Local government is enshrined in Chapter XIV of the constitution and responsibility for its administration rests with the Minister of Local Government and Community Development. Malawi has a single tier of local government comprising four city councils, 28 district councils, two municipal councils, and one town council.

In Malawi, there are three categories of land holding: customary land, public land, and private land. The customary system of land tenure rests on the premise that land in a village belongs to the community although the individual in the community has the right to cultivate it and uses the land as though he were the owner. Public land is land occupied, used, or acquired by the national government or any other land that is neither customary nor private. Private land is land owned, held, used, or occupied under a freehold title, a leasehold title, or a certificate of claim, which is registered as private land. Customary land is the most common form of tenure in Malawi.

The Property Transfer Tax

A stamp duty is levied on documents pertaining to property transfers. Malawi reduced its stamp duty rate in 2014 (World Bank 2015). The rate is 1.5 percent (Deloitte 2015), while the previous rate was 3 percent.

The Recurrent Property Tax

The property tax (called "rates") is levied and collected from the owners of property under the Local Government Act of 1998. The tax base is the "improved value" of all "assessable properties" (all land and improvements). Specifically excluded are streets, sewers and sewage disposal works, cemeteries, public open spaces, and railway lines used for transit. In practice, however, rates apply only in the three cities of Lilongwe, Blantyre, and Mzuzu; the municipality of Zomba; and eight towns and four district assemblies (Franzsen and McCluskey 2005b). Some assemblies apply split rating, taxing land and improvements at separate tax rates.

A full exemption applies to the following properties, but not to staff residences or properties used for making profit (Franzsen and McCluskey 2005b):

- Properties owned by diplomatic missions (on application only).

- Vacant and unalienated public land.

- Property used exclusively for public worship.

- Public libraries and museums.

- Hospitals and property owned by educational institutions.

- Property owned by a club, society, or institution for the purposes of sport.

Although the government is not exempted, it receives a 50 percent rebate of the tax rate on its assessable land.

Under the law, the value of "land" and the value of "improved property" must be determined separately. The value of improvements constitutes a residual value after the value of the land has been deducted. Valuation rolls must reflect all three of these values. Assemblies may appoint private-sector valuers, but these valuers operate under the supervision of the Ministry of Lands. Before 2002, the Ministry of Lands was responsible for valuations for property tax purposes (Franzsen and McCluskey 2005b). Because there are very few qualified valuers in Malawi, it is challenging to prepare regular general valuation rolls as required by the law. Some valuation rolls are older than the prescribed five years. The valuer must deal with objections. The law does not provide for an appeals procedure.

Assemblies determine tax rates annually. However, the Minister of Finance and Economic Development may set a minimum rate for properties with a minimum value (Franzsen and McCluskey 2005b). Most zones in Lilongwe are known by area numbers only. This makes the task of assessment, billing, collection, and enforcement onerous (Franzsen and McCluskey 2005b), especially in traditional housing areas. Arrears are a serious challenge in Lilongwe, where the council allows for payments to be made in two semiannual installments. In March 2015, it was estimated that arrears in Lilongwe exceeded MWK 8.5 billion.

Payments can be made at banks and building societies; the latter receive a commission on collections (Franzsen and McCluskey 2005b). The following enforcement mechanisms are in the law but are infrequently used in practice: interest at 4 percent per month on arrears after 60 days; attachment of property; and sale in execution after a period of three years.

Swaziland

Swaziland is a small country of 17,364 km^2 that is bordered by South Africa to the south, west, and north and by Mozambique to the east. Most of the population of about 1.29 million lives in rural areas (United Nations 2015). Only about 66,000 live in the capital, Mbabane. The urbanization level is only 21.3 percent (United Nations 2014). In 2015, Swaziland's GDP per capita was estimated at USD 3,200 (World Bank 2016b).

The kingdom of Swaziland is a unitary state with a "Westminster" style government. In Swaziland, local government is divided into rural and urban councils. There are 12 urban councils and 55 rural councils.

Swaziland is characterized by two types of land tenure namely land held under customary tenure, or Swazi Nation land and land held by freehold tenure, or title deed land.

Property-Related Taxes

During the period 2003 to 2011, property taxes as defined by the International Monetary Fund ranged between a low of 0.0376 percent of GDP in 2003 and a high of 0.073 percent in 2011 (IMF 2016).

The Property Transfer Tax

Swaziland is in the process of streamlining its land registration processes, which will increase accuracy and efficiency. However, it is still levying an outdated transfer tax enacted in 1902. This tax is payable by the person who acquires "fixed property" (as defined) at the following tax rates (Deloitte 2015; Franzsen 2003): first SZL 40,000, 2 percent; SZL 40,001–60,000, 4 percent; above SZL 60,000, 6 percent.

The Recurrent Property Tax

The property tax (called "rates") is levied and collected under the Rating Act of 1995 and is the most important source of own revenue for local governments in Swaziland. In Mbabane, its importance increased from 49 percent in 1994/1995 to 78 percent in 2001/2002 (Franzsen and McCluskey 2005a). Presently, only two cities and four towns are designated as rating authorities. The law provides for various possible tax bases: land only; land and improvements; improvements only; or total (improved) value. Tax base coverage in Mbabane and Manzini is apparently good (Franzsen 2003). The owner (as defined) of the property is liable for the tax.

Local authorities appoint a valuer from a panel of eligible valuers appointed by the relevant minister. In practice, private-sector valuers are appointed. A valuation court deals with objections, whereas appeals are adjudicated in the High Court. The law stipulates a valuation cycle of five years.

Local authorities determine tax rates annually. Ministerial approval is required if a local authority wants to introduce differential rates for different use categories. Rates are collected annually, but taxpayers may arrange to pay in monthly installments. Table 32.2 states the tax rates for 2014/2015 and 2015/2016 for the capital, Mbabane.

Table 32.2 City of Mbabane Property Tax Rates, 2014/2015 and 2015/2016

	2014/2015		2015/2016	
Category	Land Value (%)	Improvements (%)	Land Value (%)	Improvements (%)
Developed residential	1.29	0.21	1.49	0.24
Undeveloped residential	1.51	–	1.74	–
Developed commercial	2.53	0.70	2.93	0.81
Undeveloped commercial	2.22	–	2.56	–
Public open spaces	1.82	–	0.15	–

Source: City of Mbabane (2015, 2016).

The law provides for a number of enforcement mechanisms, including interest on arrears and refusal to issue a clearance certificate (indicating that rates are fully paid) before a transfer of ownership can be effected. The law also stipulates that a property in arrears may be seized and sold publicly after a period of three years. Before a transfer of property can be registered, a property tax (rates) clearance certificate must be obtained from the relevant municipal council (World Bank 2014a).

All the countries discussed in this chapter except Seychelles levy a recurrent property tax. In Nigeria, Lesotho, Malawi, and Swaziland, the tax is a local revenue source. The property tax is typically value based in each country; Lesotho and Malawi value land and buildings separately. There is clearly an issue with administration, particularly valuation, where the lack of resources prevents regular revaluations. Coverage of the property tax is a problem in Lesotho, where only a limited number of areas have been declared rating areas; in Malawi, where only three cities and a few other local governments

Table 32.3 Property-Related Taxes in Anglophone Africa

Country	Rental Income Tax[1]	Property Transfer Tax	Capital Gains Tax	Inheritance and Gift Taxes	Recurrent Property Tax
Botswana	No	Yes	Yes	Yes	Yes
The Gambia	No	Yes	Yes	Yes	Yes
Ghana	No	Yes	Yes	Yes	Yes
Kenya	No	Yes	Yes	No	Yes
Lesotho	No	Yes	Yes	Yes	Yes
Liberia	No	Yes	Yes	No	Yes
Malawi	No	Yes	Yes	Yes	Yes
Mauritius	No	Yes	No	No	Yes
Namibia	No	Yes	No	No	Yes
Nigeria	No	Yes	Yes	No	Yes
Seychelles	No	Yes	Yes	No	No
Sierra Leone	No	Yes	Yes	No	Yes
South Africa	No	Yes	Yes	Yes	Yes
South Sudan	No	No	No	No	Yes
Swaziland	No	Yes	No	No	Yes
Tanzania	No	Yes	Yes	No	Yes
Uganda	Yes	Yes	Yes	No	Yes
Zambia	Yes	Yes	Yes	No	Yes
Zimbabwe	Yes	Yes	Yes	Yes	Yes

[1] This is a separate tax from the personal or corporate income tax.

levy the property tax; and in Swaziland, where only two cities and four towns have been declared rating areas.

The property transfer tax legislation in Botswana, Lesotho, Namibia, and Swaziland is generally based on similar legislation in South Africa, although in Swaziland, it dates back more than a century. Property transfer tax rates vary across the countries. In Seychelles, a property transfer incurs a tax of 5 percent of the value, whereas in Malawi, the rate is a fixed 1.5 percent. Swaziland applies a progressive transfer tax rate between 2 and 6 percent.

Tables 32.3 and 32.4 provide an overview of the diversity of property related taxes applied in Anglophone Africa. A continuing issue in many of the countries is the inability to administer the recurrent property tax in accordance with the law. Because many of the systems are value based, there are problems in updating values and expanding the tax base.

Table 32.4 Property Tax Bases in Anglophone Africa

Country	Tax Base(s)
Botswana	Capital values of land and buildings, assessed separately but taxed collectively
The Gambia	Annual rental value (buildings only)
Ghana	Depreciated replacement cost of buildings only
Kenya	Land value only in most instances; area or rental value (for agricultural land) allowed by law
Lesotho	Capital value of land and buildings separately (split-rate system)
Liberia	Capital value of land and buildings separately (split-rate system)
Malawi	Capital value
Mauritius	Annual rental value; land value (for some properties)
Namibia	Capital value of land and buildings separately; land value, building value, land and buildings collectively, and area (used in small rural villages) also allowed by law
Nigeria	Annual rental value in some states; capital value in Lagos State
Seychelles	No recurrent property tax
Sierra Leone	Annual rental value (buildings only)
South Africa	Market value (capital value)
South Sudan	Area
Swaziland	Capital value of land and buildings separately; land value, building value, and land and buildings collectively also allowed by law
Tanzania	Depreciated replacement cost of buildings only
Uganda	Annual rental value
Zambia	Capital value
Zimbabwe	Land only (Harare); land and buildings separately with collective capital value as a further option

International ranking data on doing business and registering property (World Bank 2015), corruption (Transparency International 2015), and property rights (International Property Rights Index 2015) are presented in table A.8 in the appendix. Apart from Botswana, Mauritius, Seychelles, and South Africa, most Anglophone countries in Africa perform rather poorly in these rankings.

Notes

1. The section on Nigeria is largely based on Lincoln Institute of Land Policy working papers by Jibao (2009a, 2009b).
2. The other SACU member states are Botswana, Namibia, South Africa, and Swaziland.

References

CIA (Central Intelligence Agency). 2016. *The World Factbook.* https://www.cia.gov/library /publications/the-world-factbook/geos/.html.

City of Mbabane. 2015, 2016. Property Tax Rates.

———. 2016. "Rates Calculator." http://www.mbabane.org.sz/calculate.php.

CLGF (Commonwealth Local Government Forum). 2011. "The Local Government System in Lesotho." http://www.clgf.org.uk/userfiles/1/files/Lesotho%20local%20 government%20profile%202011-12.pdf.

Deloitte. 2015. *Guide to Fiscal Information—Key Economies in Africa, 2014/15.* http://www2 .deloitte.com/za/en/services/tax/tools-and-publications.html.

Fatimilehin, G. 2003. "Land Taxation in Nigeria: Issues, Opportunities and Threats in Land Management and Property Tax Reform in Nigeria." Paper presented at the Department of Estate Management, University of Lagos, Nigeria.

Franzsen, R. C. D. 2003. "Property Taxation Within the Southern African Development Community (SADC): Current Status and Future Prospects of Land Value Taxation, Botswana, Lesotho, Namibia, South Africa, and Swaziland." Working paper WP03RF1. Cambridge, MA: Lincoln Institute of Land Policy.

Franzsen, R. C. D., and W. J. McCluskey. 2005a. "Ad Valorem Property Taxation in Sub-Saharan Africa." *Journal of Property Tax Assessment and Administration* 2(2): 5–14.

———. 2005b. "An Exploratory Overview of Property Taxation in the Commonwealth of Nations." Working paper. Cambridge, MA: Lincoln Institute of Land Policy. http://www.lincolninst.edu/pubs/pub-detail.asp?id=1069.

IMF (International Monetary Fund). 2016. "IMF World Longitudinal Data (WoRLD)." IMF e-Library Data. http://data.imf.org/?sk=77413F1D-1525-450A -A23A-47AEED40FE78&sId=1390030109571.

Ipaye, A. 2007. "Property Taxation and Revenue Generation in Nigeria." CITN Tax Practice Series no. 27. Lagos, Nigeria: Chartered Institute of Taxation of Nigeria.

Jibao, S. 2009a. "Property Taxation in Anglophone West Africa Appendix 4: Nigeria." Working paper WP09AWA10. Cambridge, MA: Lincoln Institute of Land Policy.

———. 2009b. "Property Taxation in Anglophone West Africa: Regional Overview." Working paper WP09AWA8. Cambridge, MA: Lincoln Institute of Land Policy.

LAA (Land Administration Authority). 2015. "Land Administration Authority." *http://www.laa.org.ls/.*

Maseru City Council. 2015.

MLUH (Ministry of Land Use and Housing). 2016. "Ministry of Land Use and Housing." *http://www.luh.gov.sc/default.aspx?PageId=61.*

Transparency International. 2015. "Corruption Perception Index in 168 Countries." *http://www.transparency.org.*

United Nations. 2014. *World Urbanization Prospects.* Washington, DC: Department of Economic and Social Affairs, Population Division.

United Nations, Department of Economic and Social Affairs, Population Division. 2015. World Population Prospects: The 2015 Revision. *https://esa.un.org/unpd/wpp/Publications/Files/World_Population_2015_Wallchart.pdf.*

World Bank. 2014a. *Comparing Business Regulations for Domestic Firms in 189 Countries.* Washington, DC.

———. 2014b. *World Development Indicators.* Washington, DC.

———. 2015. "Registering Property." *http://www.doingbusiness.org/data/exploretopics/registering-property/reforms.*

———. 2016a. "Country and Lending Groups." *http://data.worldbank.org/about/country-and-lending-groups.*

———. 2016b. "GDP per Capita (Current US%)." *http://data.worldbank.org/indicator/NY.GDP.PCAP.CD.*

Legislation

Lesotho

Local Government Act, 1997.

Local Government (Amendment) Act, 2002.

Valuation and Rating Act, 1980.

Seychelles

Business Tax Act of 2009.

Malawi

Local Government Act of 1998.

Nigeria

Land Use Decree of 1978.

Swaziland

Rating Act of 1995.

33

Francophone Africa

RIËL FRANZSEN AND WILLIAM McCLUSKEY

Specific country reports are provided in earlier chapters on eleven Francophone countries: Benin, Cameroon, the Central African Republic, Côte d'Ivoire, the Democratic Republic of the Congo, Equatorial Guinea, Gabon, Madagascar, Niger, Rwanda, and Senegal. This chapter provides a brief overview of property related-taxes in a further eight Francophone countries: Burkina Faso, Burundi, Chad, the Comoros, the Congo, Guinea, Mali, and Togo.[1] The conclusions at the end of this chapter focus primarily on the countries discussed here, although more general comments regarding Francophone Africa may also include references to the countries discussed in individual chapters. These countries are also included in the comparative tables in this chapter.

Burkina Faso

Burkina Faso, formerly known as Upper Volta, gained independence from France in 1960. It has an area of 274,200 km² and is bordered by Mali to the west and north, Niger and Benin to the east, and Togo, Ghana, and Côte d'Ivoire to the south. The population is estimated at 18.1 million (United Nations 2015), of which about 2.75 million live in the capital,

---

This chapter benefited from the country reports prepared by Dobingar Allassembaye (research fellow in 2008 for Burkina Faso, Chad, and Mali) and Jean-Jacques Nzewanga (research fellow in 2008 and 2009 for Burundi, the Comoros, and Congo).

Ouagadougou (CIA 2016). Approximately 30 percent of the population lives in urban areas (United Nations 2014). The legal system is based on French civil law and customary law (CIA 2016). The GDP per capita in 2015 was estimated at USD 590 (World Bank 2016b).

The Property Transfer Tax

In 2009, Burkina Faso reduced the rate of the property transfer tax from 10 to 8 percent (Deloitte 2015), which is still relatively high by international standards. In 2010, it merged the payment of two previous transfer taxes. The new, consolidated tax can now be paid at the land registry rather than the tax authority (World Bank 2015b). The valuation of property by government officials has also been simplified by the implementation of valuation tables (World Bank 2015b).

The Recurrent Property Tax

Burkina Faso is one of only two African countries that do not levy a recurrent property tax.[2] However, a tax on the occupation and use of public land (*taxe de jouissance*) and a tax on rental income from buildings and unimproved properties (*impôt sur les revenus fonciers*) are levied (Monkam 2010). As Monkam (2010) points out, neither of these two taxes is a property tax in the strict sense of the term.

Burundi

Burundi (officially the Republic of Burundi) is located in the Great Lakes region in central Africa. Of all the neighboring countries, Rwanda is the closest to Burundi because they share geographic, ethnic, and historic identities. Burundi, Rwanda, and the Democratic Republic of the Congo are former Belgian colonies and therefore have the same institutional background and hybrid legal systems (Nzewanga 2009a). Burundi, which has a land area of only 27,830 km², is bordered by Lake Tanganyika and the Democratic Republic of the Congo to the west, Rwanda to the north, and Tanzania to the east and southeast. The capital, Bujumbura, has a population estimated at 750,000 (CIA 2016). Although Burundi is one of the smallest countries on the continent, its population density is one of the highest. The estimated population was in 2015 11.2 million, of which about 88 percent lives in rural areas (United Nations 2014, 2015). It is one of the poorest countries in the world, with an estimated GDP per capita in 2015 of only USD 277 (World Bank 2016b). The official languages are Kirundi and French.

Burundi gained independence from Belgium on July 1, 1962. After independence, the country experienced 30 years of political instability during which there were various coups by Tutsi soldiers and Hutu insurrections (CIA 2016). The 1992 constitution was suspended in 1996 and replaced by Decree Law No. 1/001/96 of September 13, 1996, relating to the organization of a transitional institutional system. Despite the approval of a new constitution in February 2005, the country remains plagued by political unrest, especially after the president was reelected for a third term after a controversial amendment of the constitution in 2016.

Government

Burundi is subdivided into 18 provinces. There are 117 *communes*, which are administered by communal councils and communal administrators. Article 263 of the constitution describes communes as "decentralized administrative units" that can be further subdivided into any other subdivision provided for by the law.

Land Tenure

In Burundi, land has posed serious problems for successive governments, which have offered only temporary solutions. The problems have been exacerbated by the progressive return of refugees, the resettlement of displaced, regrouped, and dispersed persons, the demobilization of soldiers, and the rehabilitation of vulnerable persons (CIA 2016; Nzewanga 2009a).

The original Burundi Land Code (Law No. 1/008 of September 1, 1986) has been amended several times, most recently in 2011. The Land Code of 2011 contains provisions to recognize rights to all land in the country. Article 254 of the Land Code states the authorities that may allocate land and the scope of their power to do so:

- The provincial governor: up to 4 hectares.

- The minister of agriculture and livestock (rural lands): up to 50 hectares.

- The minister of the environment, responsible for urban planning: up to 10 hectares (urban land).

- The president of the republic: more than 50 hectares (rural land) and more than 10 hectares (urban land).

Mayors and traditional chiefs are not included in the list of persons with the authority to allocate land. Several ministries are involved in land management in Burundi, including the Office of Titles and Registration (Ministry of Justice); Land Use Planning, the Cadastre, and Urban Planning (Ministry of Environment, Land Management, and Public Works).

The Land Code recognizes the legitimacy of land rights acquired and held under customary law. However, it also states that all asserted rights must be registered. Unregistered customary rights do not have the protection of the formal law. However, registration has been uncommon because the process is complex and costly. Consequently, local tenure systems with *actes de notoriété* (*acts of notoriety*) tend to have quasi-legal status. There is evidence that sometimes, competing documentation exists for the same piece of land. This produces a great deal of confusion over the legitimacy of documents in the event of transactions or disputes in both rural and urban areas.

The Land Code (2011) provides for a land certificate as an alternative way to record land rights in rural areas. Nationally, investments are being made to improve capacity and strengthen the land administration system through archiving paper records, digitizing titles, training, and building capacity.

Current land titling procedures originated in colonial times and were continued after independence. The registrar of land titles or the Directorate of Deeds within the Ministry of Justice issues land titles (*titres de propriété*). The majority of land titles concern urban land (residential or business), but holders of large tracts of rural land also have titles. The Direction des Titres Fonciers (Land Titling Directorate, DTF) estimates the total number of titles in Burundi at 62,000, of which 58,000 have been issued in Bujumbura. The DTF estimates that only 1 percent of rural land is titled. Titling through the classic land administration system tends to be a lengthy and expensive process, particularly because of precise land surveying requirements, as well as the lack of administrative capacity.

Taxation

Under Article 159(5) of the constitution, national law determines tax bases and rates. In 2012, total taxes constituted only 13.6 percent of GDP (IMF 2015a). No data are available for property taxes as defined by the International Monetary Fund. The Tax Procedure Code was enacted in 2013 and governs property taxes along with all other national taxes.

The Property Transfer Tax

A real estate transaction tax is levied at a rate of 3 percent on the value or price of property and is payable to the Land Registry (Département des Titres Fonciers). This tax is regulated by the Finance Act 2007, which sets the taxable base for property transactions.

The Tax on Rental Income from Real Property

As is common in other Francophone African countries, Burundi levies a tax on the rental income from real property. This tax is based on the net income received from rental buildings. To finance the needs of the population, particularly in the areas of health and urban development, the revenue from this tax was ceded to the city of Bujumbura in 1984 and to the communes in 1987 on the basis of the location of a property (Ntibatingeso 2015). Generally, the net income is determined by deducting 40 percent from the gross income as defined by law.

Taxes on Developed and Undeveloped Land

The Burundi Revenue Authority assesses and has the authority to collect the two recurrent property taxes: the tax on developed land and the tax on undeveloped land. However, it currently does not collect these taxes because this function has been devolved to communes. Only undeveloped lands located in communes as determined by the minister of finance are taxable. Table 33.1 illustrates the insignificance of these two taxes in the capital city, Bujumbura.

Exemptions

If a property is declared exempt or an exemption is removed, the owner is obliged to make a declaration to the Tax Department within one month from the date of award or risk loss of the exemption. The following properties are exempt from both taxes:

- Properties belonging to the state or communes.

- Properties affected by an international agreement ratified by Burundi. This exemption is granted only subject to reciprocity.

Table 33.1 The Revenue Importance of Various Property Taxes in Bujumbura

City of Bujumbura	2012		2013	
	BIF	%	BIF	%
Real estate transfer tax	160,561,658	4.3	253,335,829	3.7
Undeveloped land tax	5,980,878	0.2	10,655,943	0.2
Developed land tax	78,039,275	2.1	188,340,420	2.7
Tax on rental income	1,820,195,790	49.0	3,176,216,623	46.4
Total taxes on real property	2,064,777,601	55.6	3,628,548,815	53.0
Total revenues	3,711,866,819	100	6,850,474,752	100

Source: Municipality of Bujumbura as reported by Ntibatingeso (2015).

- Properties belonging to individuals whose annual taxable income is below BIF 36,000.

The following developed properties (or parts of developed properties) are exempt from the tax on developed land:

- Properties that are exclusively used for legally recognized public worship or as residences for ministers of that religion. In order to benefit from the exemption, a residence must belong to a nonprofit religious association and must be less than 500 meters from the building used for worship, and no commercial activity may take place there.

- Properties used exclusively for education, scientific or technical research, or social, cultural, or sporting activities.

- Properties used exclusively for the normal operations of chambers of commerce and fraternal societies that have obtained legal status.

- Properties used for water catchment or purification.

- Recently constructed buildings for at least two calendar years after the year of their completion, up to a maximum of four years. The Ministry of Finance sets by order the exemption period granted to each category of building depending on the use for which it is intended (Ministerial Order No. 540/176 of August 26, 1978).

The following undeveloped properties are exempt from the tax on undeveloped land:

- Land forming the immediate and essential appurtenances of exempt properties within close proximity (three meters) of the developed surface area.

- Land allocated for agricultural and livestock-raising purposes.

- Land allocated to scientific or sporting activities.

Persons Liable for the Property Tax

The Property tax is payable by the owner or the holder of limited real rights, such as *emphyteosic leases*,[3] a building lease, or the right of usufruct on the taxable property. The authorities will not intervene to effect any sharing of the tax between owners and lessees, even if the lease agreement states that the lessee is obliged to pay. If a property is transferred, the owner is obliged to make a declaration to the Tax Department within one month from the date of the transfer. By default, the new owner is obliged to pay the property tax still owing on the property jointly and severally with the previous owner.

Tax Rates

For land on which buildings or structures are erected, the taxable surface area is determined by the difference between the surface area of the land and the surface area covered by the buildings or structures. The taxable surface area is the area within the external walls of the building or structure but also includes the area of verandas, porches, galleries, balconies, and terraces. The tax rates applicable within the communes depend on the nature of the structure and are as follows:

- Permanent structure: BIF 36/m^2.

- Semipermanent structure: BIF 24/m^2.

- Nonpermanent structure: BIF 15/m^2.

Tax rates for the tax on undeveloped land, applicable only in the city of Bujumbura, are as follows:

- BIF 2/m^2 for minimally serviced areas.

- BIF 3/m^2 for averagely serviced areas.

- BIF 4/m^2 for well-serviced areas.

Collection

Property tax liability is determined by the tax inspectors of the Tax Department. The property tax is due for the full year on the taxable surface area existing on January 1 of the tax year (which coincides with the calendar year). Any transfer of ownership during that year will not result in a rebate. Properties that are rebuilt or substantially modified are taxable according to their new surface area from January 1 of the year after the completion of the reconstruction or modification.

The owner is obliged to make a declaration to the tax inspector regarding the occupation or construction of new buildings or rebuilt or substantially modified buildings within one month from the date of occupation or construction. The owner must attach the plans for the newly constructed or modified building to the declaration. Modifications leading to an increase or decrease in the taxable surface area of the building by at least 20 percent are deemed to be substantial and therefore must be declared.

A proportional reduction in the property tax may be granted at the request of the taxpayer if an unfurnished building has remained completely unoccupied and has produced no revenue for at least 90 days during the taxable year, and if the request is submitted before the expiration of the period allowed for objections. The term *property* must be interpreted to mean an "independent part of the building which may be subject to a separate rental contract." This primarily refers to semidetached houses and apartment blocks.

If there is a change of ownership during the year (e.g., through sale, donation, or inheritance), any periods of vacancy or nonproductivity for each of the owners can be added together. The holder of the ownership right as of January 1 is the only person authorized to contest the tax, which may cover the period of the year during which the person no longer held a right over the property. Any rebates are to be ordered in his favor, even if the causes for rebate have been evaluated, totally or partially, under the new property owner.

Enforcement

Individuals and legal entities are obliged to declare all taxable property to the Tax Department annually. Declaration forms are distributed to taxpayers at the appropriate time. Nonreceipt of forms does not exempt taxpayers from submitting the required declarations within the prescribed time frames. If they do not receive the necessary forms, they should request them from the Tax Department. Property taxpayers must submit one declaration per commune. This declaration must specifically mention all taxable buildings, buildings not situated on a single plot, and the surface area of each plot and must be submitted to the tax inspector before April 1 of the tax year for property owned by the taxpayer on January 1. In the absence of contrary notification by the taxpayer before January 1 of the next tax year, the most recent declaration remains valid for that following year. However, the Tax Department may initiate a partial or general renewal of the declarations on an annual basis. Officers of the Tax Department are responsible for checking the accuracy of declarations.

Taxes, with some exceptions, are subject to the tax roll drawn up by the collector of taxes. An excerpt notice from the tax roll, indicating the assessed amount, is sent to each taxpayer. The tax must be paid in full to the Burundi Revenue Authority by the first day of the month after the month in which the notice was sent. If ownership of a bulding is transferred, the property tax must be paid immediately.

Proceedings for enforced collection of taxes for properties included in the tax roll are carried out by bailiffs at the request of the collector of taxes. Bailiffs exercise writs and attachments. Proceedings take place through enforcements issued by the collector of taxes. All claims relating to the payment of taxes and proceedings are within the jurisdiction of this official. Enforcement mechanisms include collection of the tax from rent paid by third parties, such as lessees; and attachment and sale at auction of the property.

A report by the World Bank (2014) emphasizes the low tax base and weak financial viability of communes, which deny subnational authorities the resources required to generate economies of scale that would enable them to provide goods and services more efficiently. The main revenue sources assigned to communes include the local property tax, business taxes, taxes on bicycles and motorcycles, taxes on cattle, and a variety of small revenue-generating fees and charges. In 2012, the communes in Burundi collected only about 3 percent of total government revenues. Weaknesses in tax collection by the communes include the lack of lists of taxpayers, rarely used unique tax identifiers for taxpayers, the poor knowledge of tax laws by tax collectors, and poor enforcement of penalties against tax delinquents.

Chad

Chad is a vast country with an area of 1.284 million km^2, bordered by Libya to the north, Sudan to the east, the Central African Republic to the south, and Cameroon, Nigeria, and Niger to the west. It is a former French colony and gained its independence in 1960. Only about 22 percent of the population of 14 million is urbanized (United Nations 2014, 2015), and 1.3 million live in N'Djamena, the capital (CIA 2016). The per capita GDP in 2015 was estimated at USD 776 (World Bank 2016b). Its legal system is a hybrid based on French civil law and customary law. The General Tax Directorate administers taxes.

The Property Transfer Tax

The property transfer tax must be paid on the transfer of ownership of real estate. Chad reduced the rate of its property transfer tax in 2014 (World Bank 2015b). A 10 percent flat tax is charged on transfers of developed real estate and 15 percent on transfers of undeveloped real estate (Allassembaye 2010). Other transfer fees are as follows (PWC 2015):

- Transfer of the right to lease or of the benefit of a promise to lease real estate: 10 percent.

- Transfer of leases of real estate: 10 percent.

- Transfer of undivided shares and portions of real property acquired by bidding: 10 percent.

- Real estate returns: 10 percent.

- Transfer of ownership for consideration of movable property: 6 percent.

- Judicial transfer (against payment) of ownership or usufruct of both developed and undeveloped land: 10 percent.

An inheritance tax may also be payable.

The Recurrent Property Tax

The annual real property tax is imposed by the municipality where the property is located. The tax differs depending on whether the property is developed or undeveloped and whether it is located in N'Djamena or elsewhere (Allassembaye 2010). The tax base is the potential revenue of the property, which is 80 percent of the rental value. The rental value is deemed to be 10 percent of the property's market value. The tax rate on developed property in N'Djamena is 10 percent; elsewhere in the country, it is 8 percent. The tax rate on undeveloped property is 21 percent in N'Djamena and 20 percent in other municipalities (Allassembaye 2010; PWC 2015). The market value of undeveloped property in rural areas is determined as a fixed amount of XAF 50,000 per hectare (PWC 2015). Valuations are supposed to be undertaken every three years for developed property and every five years for undeveloped property. However, Allassembyae (2010) reported that no revaluation had occurred in N'Djamena since 2001.

A newly constructed or significantly renovated building is exempted for two years if it is owned by a corporation, is owned by an individual but is rented to someone else, or if it is built or rebuilt for commercial and industrial use. Newly constructed or renovated buildings to be used as a holiday resort or furnished for rent do not qualify for this exemption. An occupancy tax is payable annually by a person occupying a building, whether the owner or the tenant, as set out in table 33.2.

The Comoros

The Comoros is an archipelago of small islands located at the northern end of the Mozambique Channel in the Indian Ocean to the east of northern Mozambique and to the west of the northern tip of Madagascar. It is the most southerly country with Arabic as an official language. It declared its independence from France in 1975 but was plagued by political unrest

Table 33.2 The Occupancy Tax in Chad

Type of Construction	N'Djamena (XAF)	Other Municipalities (XAF)
Local materials	3,000	1,500
Semihard materials	10,000	5,000
Hard and durable materials	10,000[1]	5,000[2]

Source: PWC (2015).

[1] A further surcharge of XAF 10,000 per additional level (story) is payable.

[2] A further surcharge of XAF 10,000 per additional level (story) is payable.

and coups until 2009. Its area is a mere 2,235 km², and its population is only about 790,000 (United Nations 2015), of which 56,000 live in the capital, Moroni, located on the island of Grand Comore. Only 28 percent of the population is urbanized (United Nations 2014). The GDP per capita in 2015 was estimated at USD 717 (World Bank 2016b). All taxes are levied and collected under the General Code of Taxes of 1985.

The Property Transfer Tax and the Rental Income Tax

The tax on real estate transfers is charged at different rates depending on the type of transfer. Tax rates for the property transfer tax were reduced in 2013 (World Bank 2015b). For a sale, the tax rate now ranges between 2 and 9 percent (Lowtax 2014); for a donation or inheritance, between 5 and 60 percent; and for a judicial act, between KMF 1,000 and KMF 20,000 (Ernst and Young 2009). A property recording fee on real estate transactions is levied at 2 percent of the value for property rights and mortgages and 1 percent of the cumulative value for leases (Ernst and Young 2009; Lowtax 2014). A real estate capital gains tax is levied at a flat rate of 20 percent. As in many other African countries, a tax on rental income from real estate is also levied under the General Code of Taxes.

The Recurrent Property Tax

There is an annual tax on the rental value of a property at a rate of 20 percent for residential units and farms and 30 percent on industrial and commercial units. Furthermore, there is also a tax of up to KMF 10,000 per hectare on agricultural land (Nzewanga 2009c). The actual tax rate depends on the type of land use (Lowtax 2014) according to the scale set out in table 33.3.

Table 33.3 The Tax on Agricultural Land in the Comoros

Land Category	Description	Tax Rate (KMF/Ha)
1st category	Land used for poultry farm	10,000
2nd category	Land cultivated for commercial crops	5,000
3rd category	Land cultivated for vegetable crops	3,000
4th category	Arable land not developed	2,000
5th category	Land devoted to cultivation of food crops	1,000
6th category	Forest land and pastures	500

Source: Ernst and Young (2009), with reference to the General Code of Taxes and Amendments.

The Republic of the Congo

The Republic of the Congo is located in central Africa and borders the Atlantic Ocean and Gabon to the west, Cameroon and the Central African Republic to the north, the Democratic Republic of the Congo (from which it is largely separated by the Congo River) to the east and south, and the Cabinda region of Angola to the south. The land area is 342,000 km², and the capital city is Brazzaville. The Congo is sometimes referred to as Congo-Brazzaville to avoid confusion with the Democratic Republic of the Congo, its giant neighbor to the east and south. The country is richly endowed with natural resources (water, natural forests, and various minerals), but because of the small population of approximately 4.6 million (United Nations 2015) and political conflict and turmoil over many years, these have not yet been fully exploited. The urbanization level is 65.4 percent (United Nations 2014), and the 2015 estimated GDP per capita was USD 1,851 (World Bank 2016b).

Since its independence from France in 1960, the Congo has experienced three coups and the assassination of one president. In 1968, a military regime came to power and subsequently installed a Marxist-Leninist government. The National Sovereignty Conference that took place during 1991 reestablished democracy in the country, giving rise to free and transparent elections. However, between 1993 and 1999, the country was shaken by three civil wars. A process of political liberalization occurred in November and December 1999 (the cease-fire agreement made provision for the reestablishment of political parties), and a new constitution was adopted in January 2002, followed by presidential, parliamentary, local, and senatorial elections (Nzewanga 2009b).

Government

The Congo is divided into 12 administrative areas (*départements*) and 5 urban districts (*communes urbaines*), which are divided into 86 smaller administrative areas (*sous-préfectures*). Brazzaville, the capital, comprises 7 districts (*communes*). Although there have been attempts to decentralize the government since 1973, the most recent legal text establishing decentralization is Article 175 of the Constitution of the Congo, 2001. The powers and resources of the decentralized bodies (départements and communes) are determined under a single act. The constitution also specifies that any taxation by decentralized corporate bodies of items that are the responsibility of the state is forbidden. Decentralization in the Congo faces a significant challenge, the inability of local authorities to exercise their powers. The financial resources available to them are limited, and the laws on decentralization are concerned mainly with the devolution of administration rather than fiscal authority (Nzewanga 2009b). About 70 percent of national-government revenue is spent on servicing public debt, which leaves almost no scope for enabling local government to develop infrastructure and provide sufficient public services in their communities. Not surprisingly, decentralized government entities depend heavily on the central government.

Land Tenure

To understand the Congo's land problems, it is necessary to understand the mechanisms used by the different players involved and those responsible for managing the urban land sector. Since colonization, two countervailing legal systems have governed land rights in the Congo, customary law and practice and the French civil law. Although the assumption is that there should be no conflict between these systems, socioeconomic realities and political factors have complicated the situation. For example, the occupation of land in Pointe-Noire is a direct consequence of the duality of the Congolese legal system (Nzewanga 2009b).

According to Congolese customary law, land is owned communally. However, the concept of land within this customary system is narrow and does not apply to land that has been allocated to a person for settlement, agricultural, or pastoral use. Land allocated to and occupied by a person may be enjoyed and used as that person sees fit, but it may not be alienated. Only developed plots of land may be leased without title. To preserve this enjoyment, the land must be developed and maintained. The question of private ownership therefore does not arise in the same way as it does under the civil law.

The Civil Code, however, favors private ownership. The right to alienate property by inheritance or contract is fundamental. Concepts such as *land ownership* or *land title* have been imported into the Congo. Colonists, who were in the minority and had no interest in stirring up opposition among the indigenous peoples by despoiling them of their property, settled in swampy areas that remained open to anyone wishing to occupy them. In these settlements, they enforced their regulations regarding land rights. This partly explains how two legal systems gave rise to two parallel types of land settlement, each with its own laws. In the rural villages, customary laws and practices prevailed; in the colonial towns, the rules based on French law predominated. However, the settlement of some towns, such as Pointe-Noire, bears the marks of both legal systems.

Property-Related Taxes

The tax system of the Republic of the Congo was inherited from the French and is essentially administered by the Customs and Tax Department. The system is based on self-assessment and draws its resources from three main taxes: the income tax on individuals, the corporate income tax, and the value-added tax. These taxes account for more than 80 percent of receipts from all taxes except crude oil and customs receipts. The tax system has undergone significant changes during the past 20 years because of the national and international economic environment.

One feature of the tax system is a tax on rental income of 1/12 of the rent charged. Where appropriate, this is deductible from the income tax on individuals. The taxes and fees on real estate transfers are high by international standards and perhaps very high in comparison with those of similarly situated countries. A registration fee of 15 percent based on the property value is payable. In addition, there are a 0.5 percent transfer tax and a 0.2 percent conservation fee (*frais de conservation*), also based on the property value (World Bank 2015b). The registration fee was reduced in 2009 and then increased again in 2012 (World Bank 2015b).

Property Taxes

There are three recurrent taxes on immovable property. The tax on buildings is set at between 15 and 20 percent of the rental value after a deduction of 25 percent for maintenance; in other words, the tax basis is net annual value. The taxable base for the tax on undeveloped urban land is 50 percent of the land registry value. The land tax in rural areas is based on the surface area of the land. In this regard, the system of property taxation is quite similar to that in the Central African Republic (chapter 7).

The following properties are exempt from the tax on buildings:

- Buildings used for worship.

- Government buildings (owned by municipalities, districts, or communes).

- Public buildings (noncommercial or nonindustrial).

- Properties of cultural associations and charitable associations.

- Properties of diplomatic missions (on the basis of reciprocity).

- Properties of international organizations (by agreement).

The Treasury can demand payment from a third party (e.g., tenants or employers) and may also attach movable and immovable property for sale at a public auction.

Property-related problems in the Congo include disputes over land rights under both customary law and civil law, which are due to the absence of proper management and oversight in the land sector; the level of poverty; fraud and corruption; unrestrained urban sprawl; the lack of utility services for land plots; and the failure to observe town-planning laws. All these issues affect the property market and property values and therefore also the value-based property taxes (Nzewanga 2009b). The government of the Congo and local-government entities face serious challenges regarding urban and rural development.

Guinea

Guinea is a former French colony that gained its independence in 1958 and has been experiencing political turmoil ever since. It borders the Atlantic Ocean to the west, Guinea-Bissau, Senegal, and Mali to the north, Côte d'Ivoire to the east, and Liberia and Sierra Leone to the south. Its area is only 245,857 km², and its population is approximately 12.6 million (United Nations 2015), of which almost 2 million live in the capital, Conakry. The population is 37 percent urbanized (United Nations 2014). The GDP per capita was estimated at USD 531 in 2015 (World Bank 2016b). The legal system is based on French civil law (CIA 2016). The National Tax Authority (Service des Impôts) administers all taxes.

The Property Transfer Tax

Parties to a sale must register a contract of sale with the National Directorate of Taxes and pay the property transfer tax of 5 percent of the value of the property (World Bank 2015b). The General Tax Code 2005 (Article 559) provides for a right of first refusal in favor of the public treasury. This means that if, within six months after the date of registration, the National Directorate of Taxes considers the selling price insufficient, it may exercise this right, under which the state becomes the purchaser. Furthermore, before any transfer is processed, the National Directorate of Taxes must first issue a tax clearance certificate (World Bank 2015b). The property transfer fee was reduced in 2014 (World Bank 2015b). The current fee is 10 percent (Deloitte 2015), which is still very high by international standards.

The Recurrent Property Tax

The real property tax in Guinea is called the unique property tax (*contribution foncière unique*) (Vaillancourt 2004). It is payable by the owner of the property on January 1 of the tax year. The tax rates are 10 percent of the annual rental value for buildings used and occupied by the owners and 15 percent of the annual rental value for rented buildings (Deloitte 2015).

Mali

Mali is located in the Sahel region of northwestern Africa and is bordered by Algeria to the north, Niger to the east and south, Burkina Faso, Côte d'Ivoire, and Guinea to the south, and Senegal and Mauritania to the east. It gained its independence from France in 1960 and has a legal system based on French civil law and customary law. Its area is 1,240,192 km², and the population, of which 40 percent is urbanized, is about 17.6 million (United Nations 2014, 2015). About 2.5 million live in the capital, Bamako (CIA 2016). The 2015 GDP per capita was estimated at USD 724 (World Bank 2016b).

The Property Transfer Tax

The property transfer tax was reduced from 15 percent to 7 percent in 2011 (World Bank 2015b). Although this is a significant reduction, the rate remains high by international standards and has considerable potential to distort market evidence because of the common practice of underreporting to evade tax liability. Because of the high transfer taxes, property taxes as broadly defined by the International Monetary Fund ranged between 0.86 percent and 0.95 percent of GDP for the period 2003 to 2006, when there was no recurrent property tax in Mali (IMF 2015b).

The Tax on Rental Income

Mali levies a tax on the gross annual rental income (*impôt sur les revenus fonciers*), which by definition is classified as a tax on income and profits. It does not constitute a property tax in the strict sense (Monkam 2010).

The Recurrent Property Tax

The recurrent property tax was established by Law 034 (in 2011) and is assessed at 3 percent of the rental value of buildings or unimproved land that has been held for more than three years. It applies to both individuals and legal entities. Property tax receipts collected by the Directorate of General Taxes are particularly low.

The problems with the property tax are an inappropriate tax base (annual rental value) and extensive exemptions. Property tax exemptions apply to buildings occupied by the owner or dependent family members and to agricultural land. The functioning property market in Mali is limited (Durand-Lasserve, Durand-Lasserve, and Selod 2015). Property rights, particularly in rural areas, raise a number of difficulties. Because of the problems with title registration, the Ministry of Government Lands plans to implement a national cadastre.

Mali could benefit from a simplified property tax based on area or the size of the land and buildings. Adjusted or calibrated area approaches are a solution where the property market cannot support a value-based system.

Togo

Togo gained its independence from France in 1960. It borders the Bight of Benin to the south, Benin to the east, Ghana to the west, and Burkina Faso to the north. Its area is 56,785 km^2. About 40 percent of the 7.3 million inhabitants are urbanized (United Nations 2014, 2015). Approximately 960,000 live in the capital, Lomé. In 2015, the GDP per capita was estimated at USD 557 (World Bank 2016b). The legal system is predominantly customary law (CIA 2016). Property taxes as broadly defined by the International Monetary Fund constituted only 0.038 percent of GDP in 2004 and 0.047 percent in 2005. However, in 2006, the percentage increased to 0.182 percent (IMF 2016), and in 2010 it amounted to 0.24 percent (IMF 2015a). In 2012, total taxes amounted to only 15.4 percent of GDP (IMF 2015a).

The Property Transfer Tax

A 6 percent registration tax is payable on the value of a sale, as well as a fixed stamp duty of XOF 1,000 per page (a contract is usually about five pages). The Tax Authority (Service des Impôts) administers this tax and uses different criteria to determine the value of property, such as the zone (location) and the characteristics of the land. It can request a higher registration tax amount if it determines that the value of the transaction was understated (World Bank 2015b). The property registration tax rate was decreased to the current 6 percent rate in 2015 (World Bank 2015b).

The Recurrent Property Tax

The property tax on developed properties is assessed on the basis of the annual value at a rate of 15 percent. The property tax on undeveloped property is calculated on the basis of the market value on January 1 each year and is levied at a tax rate of 2 percent. There is also a property surcharge based on the rental value of buildings and levied at a rate of 1 percent, as well as a garbage-collection fee of 2.02 percent on the rental value of land and buildings (World Bank 2015b).

Although democratization has progressed since the 1990s, the postcolonial era in almost all the countries of Francophone Africa has been characterized by military uprisings (the Central African Republic), coups (Burkina Faso, the Comoros, Mali, and Niger), or attempted coups (Burundi). Multiparty democracies have supplanted the one-party systems that marked the onset of independence in many countries. Political instability or even civil war still prevails in Burundi, the Central African Republic, Chad, the Comoros, Côte d'Ivoire, the Democratic Republic of the Congo, Guinea, Madagascar, Mali, and Niger. This has a direct impact on property markets and indirectly affects value-based property taxes.

Property rights to land play a fundamental role in governing the patterns of its use, management, and taxation. Both customary and modern systems of land tenure operate in parrallel in most Francophone countries, and there are some overlapping or hybrid systems (Durand-Lasserve, Durand-Lasserve, and Selod 2015). Hence, customary law and practices are formally sanctioned or simply allowed to continue in land tenure and management alongside statutory law (e.g., Burundi and the Democratic Republic of the Congo). The colonial legacy still deeply influences current land policies and laws in the region.

Both informal and formal land tenure security are weak in several of the countries (the Congo, Côte d'Ivoire, and Equatorial Guinea). One of the primary causes of tenure insecurity is postwar conflict, which creates disputes between returnees and current occupiers (Burundi and Rwanda). Refugees are a major challenge not only for the host countries but also for their country of origin when they return (the Democratic Republic of the Congo and Rwanda). Land grabbing, illegal occupation, and conflicts over land also create a difficult environment in which to establish proper and defensible rights to land (the Congo).

Customary land use tends to predominate in Burundi, Chad, Côte d'Ivoire, Niger, and Togo. In the Central African Republic, traditional land tenure is restricted to land use rights as opposed to ownership. Land can either be state owned or freehold in Côte d'Ivoire, whereas in Equatorial Guinea and Gabon, all land is state owned, but land can be "owned" by individuals provided it is put to productive use. Land ownership security is also affected by the fact that many land parcels are undocumented, and many of the existing land records are out of date, for example, in Chad and Côte d'Ivoire. Some countries, such as Burundi and Niger, have a land code or similar legislation that seeks to address ownership and occupation rights to land while in some instances also recognizing the legitimacy of customary and legal rights, as is the case in the Congo.

In several countries, such as the Congo and Madagascar, only registered land has the protection of the law. However, registration processes tend to be centralized, complex, and cumbersome (Allassembaye 2010; Durand-Lasserve, Durand-Lasserve, and Selod 2015; Monkam 2010) and are often associated with high transfer taxes and fees, for example, in Chad, Equatorial Guinea, Mali, and Togo. The costs associated with the formal property market make people reluctant to engage in the process (Monkam 2010). Burundi, Côte d'Ivoire, and Madagascar are examples. This reluctance also affects the property tax because ownership rights are indeterminate, and in some countries, such as Equatorial Guinea, only registered land is liable for the property tax.

Generally, recording fees, transaction taxes, and stamp taxes are detrimental to transactions that facilitate efficient allocation of resources among economic actors (Fossat et al. 2013). However, many Francophone countries have been decreasing transfer taxes and related recording fees, for example, Benin, Chad, the Comoros, Guinea, Madagascar, Mali, and Senegal (World Bank 2015b). On the other hand, increases have been enacted in the Congo and Gabon (World Bank 2015b). Senegal reduced recording fees for several types of transactions in connection with its 2012 reforms, particularly the fees on real estate transactions, which were reduced from 15 percent to 10 percent. Senegal also overhauled its stamp tax in 2012. The Central African Republic did the same in 2011, reducing the rate from 15 percent to 7.5 percent (Fossat et al. 2013).

Additionally, there are often several ministries involved in land-related matters, again creating complexity and confusion. Burundi is one example. A further property-related issue that significantly affects property taxation is the lack of street addresses in some countries, which makes it very difficult to match taxable properties with owners or occupiers. In several countries, significant progress has been made in some pilot cities, such as Quagadougou (Burkina Faso), Bobo-Dioulasso (Mali), and Lomé (Togo) (Farvacque-Vitcovic and Kopanyi 2014). Programs to upgrade and digitize land registers and cadastres and other projects to increase efficiency have been ongoing in various Francophone countries, including Burkina Faso, Burundi, Cameroon, Côte d'Ivoire, Guinea, Madagascar, Niger, Rwanda, and Senegal (World Bank 2015b).

In Francophone Africa, the legislation under which the property tax is levied and administered is typically a general or national tax code (Burundi, the Central African Republic, Chad, Côte d'Ivoire, Equatorial Guinea, Madagascar, and Niger). In many countries, the legislation is comprehensive, particularly regarding collection and enforcement, but application of the law in practice is weak (Monkam 2010), as in Burundi, Chad, Equatorial Guinea, and Madagascar.

In some countries, such as the Central African Republic, the Comoros, the Congo, and Equatorial Guinea, urban property and rural property are treated differently. In Chad and the Comoros, taxation of rural land is area based. Even more common is different treatment of developed land and undeveloped land (Burundi, Chad, the Central African Republic, the Congo, Côte d'Ivoire, Niger, and Togo).

All countries in Francophone Africa use self-declaration to a greater or lesser extent. Self-declaration primarily focuses on requiring taxpayers to submit information on the properties they either own or occupy. Declaration is normally mandatory and must be completed within prescribed time limits; failure to do so can result in fines. In some countries, such as Madagascar and Rwanda, declarations are due annually.

Francophone African countries typically have fairly standard general exemptions for property occupied by governments, foreign embassies, re-

Table 33.4 Property-Related Taxes in Francophone Africa

Country	Rental Income Tax[1]	Property Transfer Tax	Capital Gains Tax	Inheritance and Gift Taxes	Recurrent Property Tax
Benin	N/d	Yes	Yes	Yes	Yes
Burkina Faso	Yes	Yes	Yes	No	No
Burundi	N/d	Yes	Yes	No	Yes
Cameroon	N/d	Yes	Yes	Yes	Yes
Central African Republic	N/d	Yes	Yes	No	Yes
Chad	N/d	Yes	Yes	Yes	Yes
Comoros	Yes	Yes	Yes	Yes	Yes
Congo	Yes	Yes	Yes	No	Yes
Côte d'Ivoire	N/d	Yes	Yes	Yes	Yes
Democratic Republic of the Congo	N/d	Yes	Yes	No	Yes
Equatorial Guinea	N/d	Yes	Yes	No	Yes
Gabon	N/d	Yes	Yes	Yes	Yes
Guinea	N/d	Yes	Yes	Yes	Yes
Madagascar	N/d	Yes	Yes	No	Yes
Mali	Yes	Yes	Yes	No	Yes
Niger	N/d	Yes	Yes	Yes	Yes
Senegal	N/d	Yes	Yes	Yes	Yes
Togo	N/d	Yes	Yes	No	Yes

[1] This is a separate tax from the personal and corporate income tax.

Table 33.5 Property Tax Bases in Francophone Africa

Country	Tax Base(s)
Benin	Annual rental value for developed property; capital value for undeveloped land
Burkina Faso	No recurrent property tax, only minor property-related charges
Burundi	Area-based system with some differentiation
Cameroon	Capital value in major cities; area-based system elsewhere (in practice)
Central African Republic	Annual rental value for developed and undeveloped land in urban areas; fixed amount per hectare (with reference to the crop grown or whether land is idle) in rural areas
Chad	Annual rental value
Comoros	Annual rental value; area for agricultural land
Congo	Annual rental value for developed urban land; capital/assessed value for undeveloped urban land; area for rural land
Côte d'Ivoire	Annual rental value for developed property; capital value for undeveloped land
DRC	Area with some differentiation based on location
Equatorial Guinea	Rental value for urban property; area (and income potential) for rural property
Gabon	Annual rental value (law); area (in practice)
Guinea	Annual rental value
Madagascar	Adjusted area
Mali	Annual rental value
Niger	Annual rental value (residential); book value (nonresidential)
Rwanda	Self-declared capital value of buildings; land values determined by the central government
Senegal	Annual rental value
Togo	Annual rental value for developed land; capital value for undeveloped land

ligious organizations, and medical, educational, and charitable establishments. However, temporary exemption (a tax holiday) of new or refurbished buildings is common in fewer countries, for example, Chad, Equatorial Guinea, Madagascar, and Niger.

The property tax is a minimally important revenue source for local governments across all the Francophone countries (Monkam 2010). Various factors contribute to the poor performance of the tax, including poor identification of properties and collection of data on them, poor billing and collection of the tax, weak enforcement, and generally ineffective administration. Liberal and broad exemptions also narrow the tax base and erode potential income. In most instances, the tax is administered by the central government, which may not view it as a priority. This could be an issue in, for example, Burundi, Cameroon, the Central African Republic, the Congo, and the Democratic Republic of the Congo. It is especially an issue where the revenue must be shared with local governments, as is the case in Cameroon and Niger, or entirely devolved to local governments, as is legislated in Côte d'Ivoire and Equatorial Guinea. The property tax is a true local tax in only a few Francophone countries, such as Madagascar. There are minor occupancy taxes at the municipal level in Burkina Faso (Monkam 2010) and Chad (Allasambaye 2010).

Tables 33.4 and 33.5 provide comparative data on the use of property-related taxes in Francophone countries and on the use of various property tax bases for recurrent property taxes.

International ranking data on doing business and registering property (World Bank 2015a, 2015b), the corruption perception index (Transparency International 2015), and the property rights index (IPRI 2015) are presented in table A.8 in the appendix. Francophone countries in Africa tend to perform rather poorly in these rankings.

Notes

1. Although French is one of the official languages in Djibouti and is widely spoken in Mauritania and Tunisia, these countries are discussed in chapter 35 with the predominantly Arabic-speaking countries of North and Northeast Africa.

2. The other country is Seychelles; see chapter 32.

3. *Emphyteosis* is the right to full usage of uncultivated land belonging to the state on condition of improving and maintaining the land and payment to the state of a fee in cash or in kind.

References

Allasembaye, D. 2010. "North Central Africa Appendix 1: Chad." Working paper WP10NCA2. Cambridge, MA: Lincoln Institute of Land Policy.

CIA (Central Intelligence Agency). 2016. *The World Factbook.* https://www.cia.gov/library/publications/the-world-factbook/geos/.html.

Deloitte. 2015. *Guide to Fiscal Information: Key Economies in Africa, 2014/15.* http://www2.deloitte.com/content/dam/Deloitte/et/Documents/tax/ZA_Fiscal_Guide_2015_29012015.pdf.

Durand-Lasserve, A., M. Durand-Lasserve, and H. Selod. 2015. *Land Delivery Systems in West African Cities: The Example of Bamako, Mali.* Washington, DC: Agence Française de Dévellopement and the World Bank Group.

Ernst and Young. 2009. "Doing Business in the Comoros." www.comoros-islands.com/PublicFiles/Doing%20business%20in%20Comoros%20(English).pdf.

Farvacque-Vitkovic, C., and M. Kopanyi. 2014. *Municipal Finances: A Handbook for Local Governments.* Washington, DC: World Bank. https://openknowledge.worldbank.org/handle/10986/18725.

Fossat, P., G. Montagnat-Rentier, P. Petit, G. Parent, G. Chambas, and J. Russell. 2013. "Continued Modernization of the Malian Tax System and Administration August."

International Monetary Fund Technical Report. Washington, DC: IMF. *https://www.imf.org/external/pubs/ft/scr/2013/cr13355.pdf.*

IMF (International Monetary Fund). 2015a. *2014 IMF Government Finance Statistics Yearbook.* Washington, DC.

———. 2015b. *Mali: Technical Assistance Report—Local Taxation and Decentralization.* IMF Country Report No 15/291. Washington, DC.

———. 2016. "IMF World Longitudinal Data (WoRLD)." IMF e-Library Data. *http://data.imf.org/?sk=77413F1D-1525-450A-A23A-47AEED40FE78&sId=1390030109571.*

IPRI (International Property Rights Index). 2015. "International Property Rights Index." Property Rights Alliance. *http://internationalpropertyrightsindex.org.*

Lowtax. 2014. "The Comoros Islands." *www.lowtax.net/features/The-Comoros-Islands-572737.html.*

Monkam, N. 2010. "Mobilising Tax Revenue to Finance Development: The Case for Property Taxation in Francophone Africa." Economic Research Southern Africa (ERSA) Working Paper Series, no. 195 (November). Pretoria: University of Pretoria.

Ntibatingeso, D. 2015. "Property Taxes in Burundi." Draft background paper prepared for the World Bank's Land Governance Assessment Framework (LGAF).

Nzewanga, J. J. 2009a. "Property Taxation in Francophone Africa: Case Study of Burundi." Working paper WP09FAB12. Cambridge, MA: Lincoln Institute of Land Policy.

———. 2009b. "Property Taxation in Francophone Africa: Case Study of Republic of Congo." Working paper WP09FAB2. Cambridge, MA: Lincoln Institute of Land Policy.

———. 2009c. "Property Taxation in Francophone Africa: Case Study of the Comoros." Working paper WP09FAB1. Cambridge, MA: Lincoln Institute of Land Policy.

PWC (Price Waterhouse Coopers). 2015. "Worldwide Tax Summaries." *http://taxsummaries.pwc.com/uk/taxsummaries/wwts.nsf/ID/Chad-Corporate-Other-taxes.*

Transparency International. 2015. "Corruption Perception Index in 168 Countries." *http://www.transparency.org.*

United Nations. 2014. *World Urbanization Prospects.* Washington, DC: Department of Economic and Social Affairs, Population Division.

United Nations, Department of Economic and Social Affairs, Population Division. 2015. World Population Prospects: The 2015 Revision. *https://esa.un.org/unpd/wpp/Publications/Files/World_Population_2015_Wallchart.pdf.*

Vaillancourt, F. 2004. "Land and Property Taxation in Guinea." In *International Handbook of Land and Property Taxation,* ed. R. M. Bird and E. Slack, 205–209. Northampton, MA: Edward Elgar.

World Bank. 2014. "Republic of Burundi Fiscal Decentralization and Local Governance—Managing Trade-offs to Promote Sustainable Reforms." Washington, DC.

———. 2015a. "Doing Business." *www.doingbusiness.org/data/exploreeconomies/guinea/registering-property/.*

———. 2015b. "Registering Property." *www.doingbusiness.org/data/exploretopics/registering-property/reforms.*

———. 2016a. "Country and Lending Groups." *http://data.worldbank.org/about/country -and-lending-groups.*

———. 2016b. "GDP per Capita (Current US%)." *http://data.worldbank.org/indicator /NY.GDP.PCAP.CD.*

Legislation

Burundi

Burundi's Constitution of 2005.

Decree Law No. 1/001/96 (of September 13, 1996).

Finance Act of 2007.

Land Code Law No. 1/008 (of September 1, 1986).

Ministerial Order No. 540/176 (of August 26, 1978).

Tax Procedure Code of 2013.

Comoros

General Code of Taxes Law No. 85-018/AF (of December 24, 1985).

Congo

Constitution of the Congo, 2001.

Guinea

General Tax Code of 2005.

Mali

Law 034 (in 2011).

34

Lusophone Africa

WILLIAM McCLUSKEY, RIËL FRANZSEN,
AND VASCO NHABINDE

A ngola, Cabo Verde, Guinea-Bissau, Mozambique, and São Tomé and Príncipe are former Portuguese colonies, and Portuguese is still the official language in these countries. This chapter briefly discusses property taxes in Angola, Guinea-Bissau, and São Tomé and Príncipe. Cabo Verde and Mozambique are discussed in more detail in chapters 5 and 20, respectively.

Angola

Angola gained its independence from Portugal in 1975 but was plagued by a prolonged civil war until 2002. It borders the Democratic Republic of the Congo to the north and east, Zambia to the east, Namibia to the south, and the Atlantic Ocean to the west and is richly endowed with natural resources, including oil and diamonds. Its area is 1,246,700 km². The population is estimated at 25 million (United Nations 2015). About 44 percent of the population is urban, and approximately 5.5 million people live in the capital, Luanda (CIA 2016). The GDP per capita in 2015 was estimated at USD 4,102 (World Bank 2016b). Angola is an upper-middle-income country (World Bank 2016a).

The country reports prepared by Vasco Nhabinde, research fellow from 2007 to 2008 (Nhabinde 2009a, 2009b, 2009c, 2009d), were used to prepare this chapter.

The Property Transfer Tax and the Tax on Rental Income

A property transfer tax of 2 percent is payable by the person who acquires real estate (land or buildings). A 0.3 percent stamp duty is also payable to the notary. Gift and inheritance taxes are levied in Angola on a sliding scale ranging from 10 to 30 percent (KPMG 2014). The tax rate on rental income is 15 percent (KPMG 2014).

The Recurrent Property Tax

The property tax was important during colonial times (Nhabinde 2009d). It is a national-government tax (there have been no formal local-government structures since independence) and is levied on the value of buildings, determined according to actual rentals or potential rental income. There is also a tax on unleased properties. This real estate tax rate is 0.5 percent of the value of the property that exceeds AOA 5 million (KPMG 2014). The owners of properties are liable for the property tax. However, the following properties may be exempted:

- Buildings occupied by taxpayers paying the industrial tax.

- Residential property when the rent does not exceed a specified limit.

- Properties of charitable institutions, schools, and museums, and properties made available to the public free of charge.

- Properties used exclusively for public worship.

- Embassies and consulates on the basis of reciprocity.

- Properties of nonprofit organizations.

- New housing construction for a period of five to fifteen years (Nhabinde 2009d).

Guinea-Bissau

Guinea-Bissau is a small country in West Africa, bordered by Senegal to the north, Guinea to the east, and the Atlantic Ocean to the southwest. It has been plagued by political instability since independence in 1974. It has an area of only 36,125 km² and a population of approximately 1.8 million, of which 49 percent is urbanized (United Nations 2014, 2015). The capital city, Bissau, has a population of nearly 490,000. Guinea-Bissau is a low-income country (World Bank 2016a) with a 2015 GDP per capita estimated at USD 573 (World Bank 2016b). The country has nine administrative regions.

Property-Related Taxes

The first reference to property taxes in Guinea-Bissau dates to 1946. Extensive reforms were effected after independence in 1974. The devastating civil war of 1998 destroyed many property records and much information on tax revenues (Nhabinde 2009c).

The tax rate on rental income from buldings in urban areas is fixed at 30 percent of taxable rental income. A property transfer tax is levied at 10 percent on the transfer of buildings for consideration or by succession. In 1993, the government amended the law with the aim of increasing revenue from property taxes. The new law provides that municipal councils must submit a monthly list to the Department of Finance that contains the number of permits issued during the previous month for construction, renovation, extension, or modifications of urban buildings. They also must provide details on the state of buildings, as well as the identity of the owners, occupiers, or administrators (Nhabinde 2009a).

Buildings exempted from the property tax include the following:

- All government buildings.
- Buildings that are considered national memorials.
- Buildings operated by political parties.
- Schools and hospitals if they are not generating rent.
- Buildings belonging to public institutes.
- Buildings belonging to, or used by, public utilities.
- Buildings used by cultural associations and recreation and sports clubs if they are not used for commercial purposes.
- Buildings used for religious activities.
- Buildings in cemeteries.

Although these buildings are exempt, they must still be recorded in the valuation roll (Nhabinde 2009c).

The National Government Tax Authority is responsible for the administration of the urban building tax, which is collected annually in March. Tax bills are mailed to property owners. However, the local media are also used to inform taxpayers that property taxes are due. This makes the administration of property taxes more transparent (Nhabinde 2009c). In practice, this tax is not necessarily administered as provided for in the law.

One of the issues regarding the property tax is the interpretation of the legislation by the tax authorities. For example, it is uncertain whether urban buildings built for owner occupation are liable for the property tax (Nhabinde 2009c). However, the legislation clearly prescribes how to calculate taxable income for buildings used by their owners.

São Tomé and Príncipe

São Tomé and Príncipe is the smallest of the five Lusophone countries in Africa and consists of two islands (São Tomé and Príncipe) with a total land area of 964 km^2, located off the equatorial western coast of central Africa. It became independent in 1975. The population of the country is less than 200,000, of which about one-third lives in the capital, São Tomé, and about 65 percent lives in urban areas (United Nations 2014, 2015). There are seven regions, six on São Tomé and one on Príncipe. In principle, the country has a multiparty system of government (CIA 2016). In 2015, the GDP per capita was estimated at USD 1,669 (World Bank 2016b). The country is classified as a lower-middle-income country (World Bank 2016a).

Property Transfer Taxes

The first property taxes in São Tomé and Príncipe were introduced during the colonial period and were levied by 1942. The important taxes are a property transfer tax (*sisa*, as in all the former African Portuguese colonies), levied at 8 percent, and an inheritance and gift tax ranging between 7 and 25 percent.

The Recurrent Property Tax

The urban property tax (*contrabuicão predial urbana*) is a recurrent tax. The tax rate for the urban property tax is 15 percent of the registered value (Farhan 2009; Santos and Tiny 2005). However, the value is adjusted by a factor of 8 if the property was registered before December 31, 1970; a factor of 4 if it was registered between 1971 and 1980; a factor of 2 if it was registered between 1981 and 1990; a factor of 1.5 if it was registered between 1991 and April 1993; and a factor of 1 if it was registered in or after May 1993.

A committee called the permanent commission of valuation values property for the urban property tax. It is composed of three members. The chairperson is nominated by the chief of treasury and account, the second member by the municipality or the administrator of the county where the property is located, and the third by the secretary of the Treasury. The first two members must be selected from appropriately qualified professionals, such as engineers, architects, or engineer assistants. Members are nominated annually in December for the valuation of the following year. The secretary of the Treasury oversees the work of the commission.

There are numerous exemptions from the urban property tax, including the following:

- Buildings belonging to the state, local administrations, and public institutes.

- Hospitals, fraternities, and asylums.

- Schools and sports facilities.

- Buildings used for religious activities.

- Buildings of public benefit organizations and charities authorized and supervised by the state unless they are rented to a third party for profit.

- Houses that serve as places for hosting the poor and orphans.

- Buildings declared to be public utilities.

- All "grass houses" and other buildings constructed with inferior materials if the value is less than STD 5 million.

Taxpayers must apply for an exemption by sending a request to the director of taxes, who then sends the permanent commission of valuation to inspect the building and determine whether it is entitled to the exemption. The value-threshold exemption, primarily of residential properties, is the most common exemption. Buildings under construction and to be used for residential purposes by the owners are exempted for two years. Property owners whose income is less than STD 2,000 per day are also exempt.

Data on property tax revenues in São Tomé and Príncipe have been available only since 2001. Table 34.1 shows that the revenue from property transfer taxes is significantly higher than the revenue from the urban property tax. This is an indication that the recurrent property tax is still underused in

Table 34.1 Revenues from the Urban Property Tax and Transfer Taxes in São Tomé and Principe, 2001–2007

Fiscal Year	Urban Property Tax	Property Transfer Tax (Sisa)
2001	77,281	350,582
2002	178,416	212,108
2003	233,651	477,060
2004	279,941	1,458,766
2005	677,162	1,469,027
2006	717,473	1,122,504
2007	818,424	3,837,216

Source: Nhabinde (2009b) (from the National Directorate of Taxes).

São Tomé and Príncipe and can also suggest that the market values used for the transfer tax are generally much higher than the values determined for the same buildings by the permanent commission of valuation. The permanent commission of valuation could assign lower values to buildings than the market values because of lack of valuation expertise, a deliberate intent to benefit influential groups of property owners (Nhabinde 2009b), or both.

The current political instability undermines the development of appropriate property and tax legislation. This became especially apparent after the discovery of oil fields in their territorial waters. In 2008, São Tomé and Príncipe had three different governments (Nhabinde 2009a). Under such circumstances, no coherent program to systematically develop government finances can be designed and implemented.

During the colonial period, property tax laws were published collectively for all Portuguese colonies and largely did not reflect differences in the level of economic development and the capacity of colonies to generate their own revenue (Nhabinde 2009a). Therefore, substantial changes could be expected after they became independent. Political instability was a significant problem in all five countries after independence and is still a factor in Guinea-Bissau and São Tomé and Príncipe.

The adoption of policies more oriented toward a centrally planned economy with more emphasis on collective action, such as publicly owned agricultural enterprises, prevented the use of the private sector as an engine of the economy. Therefore, taxes as a source of revenue did not receive the necessary attention. Property taxes were especially neglected in the context of the nationalization of land and uncertainty regarding land tenure. However, in contrast to Angola, Guinea-Bissau, and Mozambique, Cabo Verde soon understood that property taxes were important. The fact that Cabo Verde is a country with very limited resources compared with Angola, Guinea-Bissau, and Mozambique probably also played an important role in this regard.

Cabo Verde has been undertaking reforms to its land registration process to provide a more effective and efficient system, which to some extent reflects the requirements of international investors acquiring property in the country. In Mozambique, land is owned by the state, and therefore, freehold ownership is not possible. Land is generally held under 50-year leasehold interests.

Cabo Verde has developed self-declaration of value as the basis of the property tax. Because land registration is becoming more comprehensive, the authorities have good information on properties. In Mozambique, municipalities undertake assessment. Coverage of the property tax in Mozambique is a problem because many leasehold properties are not registered and therefore are not included on the valuation rolls. Too many exemptions are granted, such as the five- to ten-year exemption of newly constructed residential buildings in Angola.

Although a tax on urban buildings exists in both Angola (KPMG 2014; Nhabinde 2009a, 2009b) and Guinea-Bissau (Nhabinde 2009a, 2009c) the tax on rental income from buildings is the most important property-related tax.[1] Property transfer taxes are also important in all five Lusophone countries, with Guinea-Bissau and São Tomé and Príncipe levying the sisa at high rates of 10 percent and 8 percent, respectively. Unlike Mozambique, however, Guinea-Bissau collected much more revenue from recurrent property taxes than from the property transfer tax (the sisa) in the period from 2002 to 2007 (Nhabinde 2009a). Given the state of affairs in all the Lusophone countries, with the possible exception of Cabo Verde, it is unreasonable to expect these countries to achieve 0.6 percent of GDP from the recurrent property tax (Bahl and Martinez-Vazquez 2008; Norregaard 2013) any time soon.

Tables 34.2 and 34.3 provide comparative data on property-related taxes and property tax bases in African Lusophone countries. International ranking data on doing business and registering property (World Bank 2015), the corruption perception index (Transparency International 2015), and the property rights index (IPRI 2015) are provided in table A.8 in the appendix.

Table 34.2 Property-Related Taxes in Lusophone Africa

Country	Rental Income Tax[1]	Property Transfer Tax	Capital Gains Tax	Inheritance and Gift Taxes	Recurrent Property Tax
Angola	Yes	Yes	Yes	Yes	Yes
Cape Verde	Yes	Yes	Yes	No	Yes
Guinea-Bissau	Yes	Yes	No	Yes	Yes
Mozambique	Yes	Yes	Yes	Yes	Yes
São Tomé and Príncipe	Yes	Yes	Yes	Yes	Yes

[1] The rental income tax is levied separately from the personal or corporate income tax.

Table 34.3 Property Tax Bases in Lusophone Africa

Country	Tax Base(s)
Angola	Annual rental value
Cabo Verde	Capital value
Guinea-Bissau	Annual rental value
Mozambique	Capital value (buildings only)
São Tomé and Príncipe	Capital value

Note

1. The tax on rental income from real estate is essentially an income tax. It is, however, treated as a separate tax in various African countries and often listed and discussed as a type of recurrent property tax (see chapter 2). In some of these countries, the tax is administered by local governments; in others, the central government administers the tax but distributes the revenue to local governments.

References

Bahl, R. W., and J. Martinez-Vazquez. 2008. "The Determinants of Revenue Performance." In *Making the Property Tax Work*, ed. R. W. Bahl, J. Martinez-Vazquez, and J. M. Youngman, 35–57. Cambridge, MA: Lincoln Institute of Land Policy.

CIA (Central Intelligence Agency). 2016. *The World Factbook. https://www.cia.gov/library /publications/the-world-factbook/geos/.html.*

Farhan, N. H. 2009. "São Tomé & Príncipe: Domestic Tax System and Tax Revenue Potential." IMF working paper. Washington, DC: International Monetary Fund.

IPRI (International Property Rights Index). 2015. "International Property Rights Index." Property Rights Alliance. *http://internationalpropertyrightsindex.org/countries? f=country&o=asc&r.*

KPMG. 2014. "Angola Fiscal Guide, 2013/14." *https://www.kpmg.com/Africa/en/KPMG -in-Africa/Documents/2014%20Fiscal%20Guides/Fiscal%20Guide%20Angola.pdf.*

Nhabinde, V. C. 2009a. "An Overview of Property Taxation in Lusophone Africa." Working paper WP09LA1. Cambridge, MA: Lincoln Institute of Land Policy.

———. 2009b. "Property Taxation in Lusophone Africa: Appendix 3, São Tomé & Príncipe." Working paper WP09LA9. Cambridge, MA: Lincoln Institute of Land Policy.

———. 2009c. "Property Taxation in Lusophone Africa: Appendix 4, Guinea-Bissau." Working paper WP09LA10. Cambridge, MA: Lincoln Institute of Land Policy.

———. 2009d. "Property Taxation in Lusophone Africa: Appendix 5, Angola." Working paper WP09LA11. Cambridge, MA: Lincoln Institute of Land Policy.

Norregaard, J. 2013. "Taxing Immovable Property—Revenue Potential and Implementation Challenges." IMF working paper. Washington, DC: International Monetary Fund.

Santos, R. M., and K. Tiny. 2005. "Main Taxes of Sao Tome and Principe." JuriSTEP. *www.juristep.com/doc/taxes.pdf.*

Transparency International. 2015. "Corruption Perception Index in 168 Countries." *http://www.transparency.org.*

United Nations, Department of Economic and Social Affairs, Population Division. 2015. World Population Prospects: The 2015 Revision. *https://esa.un.org/unpd/wpp /Publications/Files/World_Population_2015_Wallchart.pdf.*

World Bank. 2015. "Registering Property." *www.doingbusiness.org/data/exploretopics /registering-property/reforms.*

———. 2016a. "Country and Lending Groups." *http://data.worldbank.org/about/country -and-lending-groups.*

———. 2016b. "GDP per Capita (Current US%)." *http://data.worldbank.org/indicator /NY.GDP.PCAP.CD.*

35

North and Northeast Africa

RIËL FRANZSEN AND WILLIAM McCLUSKEY

The countries discussed in this chapter are Algeria, Djibouti, Eritrea, Ethiopia, Libya, Mauritania, Somalia, South Sudan, and Tunisia. Arabic is an official language in all these countries except Ethiopia, Somalia, and South Sudan, which are included for geographic reasons. Detailed discussions are provided only for the property tax systems of Eritrea and Ethiopia. All the countries in this region, including Egypt, Morocco, and Sudan (which are discussed in country chapters) are reflected in the tables at the end of this chapter, as well as the comparative tables in the appendix.

Algeria

Algeria is a former French colony that borders the Mediterranean Sea to the north, Morocco to the north and west, Tunisia and Libya to the east, and Mauritania, Mali, and Niger to the south. The surface area is 2,381,741 km². The population is estimated at 39.7 million (United Nations 2015), of which about 2.6 million live in the capital, Algiers (CIA 2016). An estimated 71 percent of the population is urbanized (United Nations 2014). In 2015, the GDP per capita was estimated at USD 4,206 (World Bank 2016b), and therefore, Algeria is classified as an upper-middle-income country (World

This chapter benefited from the country reports prepared by Khaled Amin (for Libya), Alemayehu Negash Soressa and Bekalu Tilahun Gebreslus (for Ethiopia), and Berhane Tecle (for Eritrea).

Bank 2016a). The legal system is based on French civil law, and the official language is Arabic.

Property Transfer Taxes

Property taxes, as broadly defined by the International Monetary Fund, constituted only 0.001 percent of GDP in 2011 (IMF 2016). The law dealing with property registration provides for a transfer tax on the transfer of land and buildings at a rate of 5 percent (2.5 percent to be paid by each party), with a further 1 percent for the "land publication fee" (Deloitte 2015b). Investors may be granted an exemption from the transfer tax on all real estate purchases for investment, as well as an exemption for 10 years from the date of purchase from the land tax on real estate that is directly involved in investment. There are also inheritance and gift taxes in Algeria that may be levied on property.

The Recurrent Property Tax

The tax base of the recurrent property tax is annual rental value. For developed property, the tax rate is 3 percent; for undeveloped land, the tax rate is 7 percent. As an incentive to attract foreign investment, new construction in specified development areas may receive a tax holiday.

Djibouti

Djibouti gained independence from France in 1977. It is a small country, with an area of only 23,200 km^2, but is strategically located on the Red Sea and the Gulf of Aden. It also borders Eritrea to the north, Ethiopia to the east, and Somalia to the south. An estimated 77 percent of the population of approximately 890,000 lives in urban areas (United Nations 2014, 2015). The population of the capital, Djibouti, is approximately 530,000 (CIA 2016). In 2015, the GDP per capita was estimated at USD 1,945 (World Bank 2016b). Djibouti is classified as a lower-middle-income country (World Bank 2016a). The official languages are Arabic and French.

Djibouti levies a property transfer tax of 10 percent. The tax base for the recurrent property tax is annual rental value. For undeveloped property, the tax rate is 25 percent; for developed property, it is 4.5 percent.

Eritrea

Eritrea is located on the Red Sea and covers an area of 117,600 km^2. Sudan lies to the east, Ethiopia to the southeast, and Djibouti to the south. Eritrea is a former Italian colony that was administered by the British from

1941 until it was placed under Ethiopian control by the United Nations in 1952. In 1962, it was annexed by Ethiopia and gained its independence only in 1993 (CIA 2016). The population is estimated at 5.2 million (United Nations 2015), of which about 800,000 live in the capital, Asmara (CIA 2016). Only about 23 percent of the population is urbanized (United Nations 2014). Eritrea is a low-income country with a GDP per capita estimated in 2011 at USD 544 (World Bank 2016a).

Land Tenure

The Ethiopian government confiscated all land and private property in 1975. Present Eritrean land law provides that all land belongs to the government. There are three basic forms of land rights:

- A rural residential land use right.

- A usufructuary right for rural agricultural land.

- Land leasehold rights for urban land used for residential, commercial, or agricultural purposes.

The property market is highly informal (Tecle 2010).

The Property Transfer Tax and Land Rent

A 4 percent transfer tax is levied on the capital value of the property, which is determined by a committee (World Bank 2015c). Tax clearance certificates are required before property can be transferred. Land leasehold charges (land rent) are collected under Proclamation 58 of 1994.

The Recurrent Property Tax

Eritrea has an area-based property system for both land and buildings. The tax rates are ERN 1.85 per square meter for land and ERN 1.75 per square meter for buildings. There is also a garbage fee of ERN 0.45 per square meter, based on the building area (World Bank 2015b). A rural agricultural land tax is charged under Proclamation 63 of 1994 (Tecle 2010). Tecle (2010) mentions that there have been uncoordinated efforts and initiatives to strengthen Eritrea's rather rudimentary property tax system.

The property tax practices of the municipality of Asmara still reflect the colonial municipality administration (Tecle 2010). The use categories and tax rates for land and buildings in Asmara are set out in tables 35.1 and 35.2. Properties owned by the government and religious institutions are exempt.

Table 35.1 Land Tax Rates in Asmara

Land Category	Zone 1 (ERN/M²)	Zone 2 (ERN/M²)	Zone 3 (ERN/M²)	Zone 4 (ERN/M²)
Residential land	2.00	1.85	1.70	N/A
Commercial and business land	2.50	2.50	2.50	1.50
Commercial agricultural land	0.01–0.15	0.01–0.15	0.01–0.15	0.01–0.15

Source: Tecle (2010).

Table 35.2 Building Tax Rates in Asmara

Building (Covered Area)	Zone 1 (ERN/M²)	Zone 2 (ERN/M²)	Zone 3 (ERN/M²)
Residential buildings:			
1st level: up to 500 m²	2.00	1.75	1.50
2nd level: 500–1,000 m²	1.75	1.50	1.30
3rd level: 1,000–5,000 m²	1.50	1.30	1.20
4th level: above 5,000 m²	1.25	1.10	1.00
Privately owned commercial and business buildings	2.50	2.50	2.50

Source: Tecle (2010).

Ethiopia

The Federal Democratic Republic of Ethiopia is a large country located in the Horn of Africa.[1] It covers 1,104,300 km² and is bordered by Eritrea to the north and northeast, Djibouti and Somalia to the east, Sudan and South Sudan to the west, and Kenya to the south. The country has a population of 99.4 million (United Nations 2015). The estimated 2015 per capita GDP was USD 619 (World Bank 2016b), and Ethiopia is therefore classified as a low-income country (World Bank 2016a). Addis Ababa, which is self-governing under Article 49 of the constitution (Soressa and Gebreslus 2009), is the federal capital and has a population of approximately 3.2 million (CIA 2016). Only 19 percent of the country's population is urbanized (United Nations 2014). Ethiopia is the oldest independent country in Africa. The constitution of 1995 provides for a federal form of government with nine states and two self-governing territories (CIA 2016). The official language is Amharic, although various other languages are acknowledged as official languages at the state level.

Land Tenure

Ethiopia has a long legacy of government intervention in land tenure relations. The Ethiopian government has exerted considerable influence on local land tenure regimes throughout different political regimes. The country's property rights system also differs in some respects from those of most other African countries. Because Ethiopia was never colonized, except for a brief Italian occupation from 1936 to 1941, there is little of the colonial heritage or legacy that is a factor in other sub-Saharan African countries.

Ethiopia has accommodated a land tenure system that is described as one of the most complex compilations of different land use systems in Africa (Joireman 2000). The system of land ownership was of crucial importance to the country's economic and social life (Pankhurst 1968; Wibke, Ayalneh, and Benedikt 2008). Major provisions related to property and taxation are contained in the 1995 Constitution of the Federal Democratic Republic of Ethiopia. For example, every Ethiopian citizen has the right of ownership of private property. Unless prescribed otherwise by law because of the public interest, this right includes the right to acquire, use, and, in a manner compatible with the rights of other citizens, dispose of property by sale or bequest or to transfer it. The term *private property* is taken to mean any tangible or intangible product that has value and is produced by the labor, creativity, enterprise, or capital of an individual citizen. It therefore includes buildings.

The right of ownership of rural and urban land, as well as of all natural resources, is exclusively vested in the state. Land is the common property of the "Nations, Nationalities and Peoples of Ethiopia" and shall not be subject to sale or to other means of exchange (Soressa and Gebreslus 2009). Therefore, land can only be leased, whereas buildings can be owned.

Land and Property Taxes

The Property Transfer Tax and the Stamp Duty

There is a legal requirement that a stamp duty be paid for transfer of property by sale or gift. The Stamp Duty Proclamation No. 110/1998 specifies that the buyer of immovable property shall pay the stamp duty at the rate of 2 percent of the transaction price (KPMG 2014a). Transfers of titles on buildings are effected through the land administration system after the stamp duty is collected on the sale.

The property transfer tax, levied at 4 percent, is based on the sale price of the property agreed between the transacting parties. However, the government can estimate the price for buildings, and if the negotiated price is below the estimated price, the tax is based on the government estimate.

This measure is designed to discourage underestimation of transaction prices to avoid tax obligations (Soressa and Gebreslus 2009). Title transfer of buildings is valid only upon registration and payment of the property transfer tax by the buyer.

The Annual Property Tax and Land Rent

THE TAX BASE

The tax base of the annual property tax reflects the size of the plot under possession and the annual rental value of the privately owned property (Urban Land Rent and Urban Houses Tax Proclamation No. 80/1976). The law recognizes that only property owners, not lessees, public or private, are required to pay the property tax (Soressa and Gebreslus 2009).

According to the proclamation, a legal possessor of urban land is required to pay an annual land rent that is to be assessed on the basis of the size of the plot and the quality of its location within the city (categorized as Grade 1, 2, or 3). The proclamation also indicates that a land plot used for the construction of residential or commercial buildings is assessed differently. For urban houses, the proclamation stipulates that a percentage of the annual rental value of the house is to be used as the basis for assessment. For an annual rental value of up to ETB 600, a tax rate of 1 percent applies. The tax rates are progressive, increasing to 4.5 percent on values that exceed ETB 6,000 (Soressa and Gebreslus 2009).

EXEMPTIONS

The proclamation states the following exemptions from land rent and the property tax:

- Public roads, squares, recreation and sports centers, and cemeteries.
- Places of worship and their compounds, nonprofit private schools, hospitals, and charitable institutions.
- Government institutions.
- Properties with an annual rental value of less than ETB 300.

VALUATION AND ASSESSMENT

The valuation and assessment of the annual property tax begin with the assumption that land rent is a nominal amount. The proclamation takes the view that rent is exploitative. Thus, the annual assessed rental value of properties for tax purposes is far below the market rate.

RATE SETTING

Rate setting depends on two factors: the plot size for the land rate and the assessment of annual rental values for the building tax. Article 6 of Proclamation 80/1976 stipulates that the land rate is to be based on the grade or quality of the land. Cities define the grading of urban land in terms of the infrastructure and urban growth profiles. The Ministry of Public Works and Housing or other persons or organizations designated by the ministry estimate the annual rental value of buildings. The national government sets the tax rates, usually after discussions with local governments. Differential rates are normally prescribed for land and buildings.

TAX ADMINISTRATION

Tax administration covers the tasks of billing, collection, and enforcement. Proclamation 80/1976 states that the city administration must notify taxpayers of the assessed property tax through registered mail or in person. Because of the lack of street-based postal addresses and an efficient postal system linked to property owners, notification through direct delivery is a practical, if expensive, option. The law requires that the receiver of the notice (either the owner or a substitute) shall sign a receipt to verify delivery. This document serves as evidence if receipt of the notice is contested. If a taxpayer or his substitute refuses to accept the notice, the tax administrator has the power to affix the notification at the entrance of the property or publish a notice in official newspapers requiring the taxpayer to attend the tax office to receive the notification. The law clearly indicates that the taxpayer shall bear the costs incurred for publication. However, there is a wide gap between the detailed property tax administration procedures and practice (Soressa and Gebreslus 2009).

Constraints on Legal and Administrative Practices in Property Taxation

After the February Revolution of 1974, all rural land was nationalized by a proclamation of March 4, 1975 (Public Ownership of Rural Lands Proclamation No. 31/1975). This was soon followed by the nationalization of all urban land and extra houses by a proclamation of July 26 of the same year (Government Ownership of Urban Lands and Extra Houses Proclamation No. 47/1975). The rural lands nationalization proclamation declared that all rural lands are "the common property of the Ethiopian People," and that no person, business, or other organization may hold rural land in private ownership. In the same vein, the Government Ownership of Urban Lands and Extra Houses Proclamation stated that all urban land is the property of the government, and that no person, family, or business organization may hold urban land in private ownership.

The Urban Lands Lease Holding Proclamation No. 272/2002 created the leasehold system of land holding. Urban land may be held by lease acquired by auction or through private transactions. The leasehold possessor may transfer or mortgage his leasehold right. The leasehold is thus equivalent to ownership of the land for a limited time. In response to the acute housing shortage in urban areas, Condominium Proclamation No. 370/2003 was enacted with the aim of creating favorable conditions for individuals to build their own houses by pooling their limited resources.

The notion that land belongs to the people, whereas buildings are objects of private ownership, is creating a legal problem (Heroui 2008; Soressa and Gebreslus 2009). The legal issue of a separation of land from the structure built on it is controversial. This anomaly ignores the socioeconomic factor of location in determining property values. The subject of any transfer is the land and the buildings combined. Their fictitious separation adversely affects transparent property taxation.

A significant problem for property taxation is the sheer magnitude of informal property ownership in urban centers. Transactions in this market are currently outside the domain of the tax authorities. The proliferation of informal property ownership is directly attributed to the vague legal definition that attempts to separate the land from the buildings on it (Soressa and Gebreslus 2009). The very high transfer taxes are likely a further reason that informal transactions are common. Houses are freely bought and sold in the informal sector and presently fall outside the land and property registration system. In addition, what is being sold is land and building even though land is still legally deemed to be public property. According to data obtained by Soressa and Gebreslus (2009) from the Urban Information Center of the Addis Ababa city administration, 172,061 of 380,318 buildings, or 45.2 percent, are not included on the valuation rolls. It is reasonable to assume that percentages in other urban centers are similar. Table 35.3 shows that Addis Ababa collected less than 2 percent of its revenue from the property tax from 2000 to 2004, suggesting that there is much room for improvement (Soressa and Gebreslus 2009). The downward trend in revenue, as a percentage, from 2000 to 2003 is also noteworthy.

Urban local governments in Ethiopia are not sufficiently assertive in identifying taxpayers and serving tax notices. Land rent, which is calculated on the basis of plot size and location grade, is directly linked to property market values. However, the assessed annual rental values of properties bear little relationship to current market values. Informality in the property market is also a huge challenge. As suggested earlier, high transfer taxes and outdated laws pertaining to land and buildings play an important role in this regard.

Table 35.3 Revenue Statistics for Addis Ababa, 2000–2004

Fiscal year	Total Revenue (ETB Millions)	Revenue from Property Tax (ETB Millions)	Property Tax as a Percentage of Total Revenue
2000	729.47	14.12	1.92
2001	830.50	13.76	1.68
2002	879.02	13.69	1.59
2003	905.53	12.03	1.32
2004	1642.94	16.17	0.97

Source: Adapted from Soressa and Gebreslus (2009); original data provided by the Finance and Economic Development Bureau of Addis Ababa.

The lack of an integrated approach and the absence of assertive management to maximize revenue from property taxes are major problems in Ethiopia. There are clear property tax policy gaps with respect to the property tax, as well as an absence of administrative capacity in regions and local governments. The only guiding legislation for property taxation is the Urban Land Rent and Urban Houses Tax Proclamation No. 80/1976. This legislation is out of date and needs to be significantly revised to reflect the legal, political, economic, and social changes that have occurred in Ethiopia. Not surprisingly, Ethiopia is currently undertaking reforms and planning extensive modernization of legislation, registration, and revaluation.

Lack of transparency in the administration of property taxes and their weak enforcement contribute to the low level of compliance with the law, which results in the limited contribution of the property tax to local-government total revenue. The property tax is largely ineffectual as a revenue source for local governments to fund the provision of urban services, principally because of the unbalanced tax policy, which includes outdated legislation, broad exemptions, and low assessed values.

Libya

Libya is another vast and arid North African country, with a total surface area of 1,759,540 km^2. It borders the Mediterranean Sea to the north, Tunisia and Algeria to the west, Niger and Chad to the south, and Sudan and Egypt to the east. Almost 79 percent of the population of approximately 6.3 million inhabitants is urbanized (United Nations 2014, 2015). Most people live along the coast, notably in the capital, Tripoli (with an estimated population of about 1.3 million), and Benghazi. The 2011 GDP per capita was estimated at USD 5,518 (World Bank 2016b), and therefore, Libya is classified as an upper-middle-income country (World Bank 2016a). Libya has been subject to extensive political upheaval since 2011. The facts given here generally relate to the established position before the Arab Spring in 2011. There has since been a considerable breakdown in the rule of law and a considerable restructuring of civil society. Arabic is the official language.

The Property Transfer Fax

Capital gains on the transfer of property are taxed as part of income under the income tax (Deloitte 2015a), and a stamp duty may also be payable when real property is transferred.

The Recurrent Property Tax

In principle, an owner of property is liable for a tax on all buildings and their annexed lands within urban jurisdictions as identified by Law 5 of 1969, which deals with the planning of cities and villages (Amin 2010). The Central Government Tax Authority administers the tax. The system is based on self-declaration and self-assessment of property by owners. Land parcels that do not exceed 500 m^2 are exempt. For buildings, exemptions are based on the size of the building and the number of occupants under the following scale:

- 150 m^2 for a building occupied by three individuals.
- 270 m^2 for a building occupied by four to seven individuals.
- 320 m^2 for a building occupied by eight to ten individuals.
- 500 m^2 for a building occupied by more than ten individuals (Amin 2010).

The tax is payable as a lump sum, although taxpayers can apply for payment in four installments if the tax amount exceeds LYD 100 (Amin 2010). Property tax reforms were contemplated in 2008–2010 (Amin 2010), but because of the present political instability in Libya, it is unlikely that any of the new regulations have been implemented.

Mauritania

Mauritania, located on the northwestern coast of Africa, gained its independence from France in 1960. It is a vast country with a surface area of 1,030,700 km^2 and is bordered by Western Sahara (occupied by Morocco) to the northwest, Algeria to the north, Mali to the east and south, and Senegal to the south. The majority of the population of 4.1 million lives in the capital, Nouakchott (almost 1 million people), and in the southern regions of the country (CIA 2016; United Nations 2015). About 60 percent of the population is urbanized (United Nations 2014). The 2011 GDP per capita was estimated at USD 1,370 (World Bank 2016b), and therefore, Mauritania is classified as a lower-middle-income country (World Bank 2016a). The official language is Arabic.

Property transfer tax

A property transfer tax is chargeable at rates that vary between 0.25 and 15 percent (Deloitte 2015a; KPMG 2014b).

The Recurrent Property Tax

There is a tax on annual rental value of built properties. Built properties are all constructions of masonry, iron, wood, or other materials that are permanently fixed to the ground (so that it is impossible to move them without destroying them). The tax is based on the value after an abatement of 20 percent for buildings and 14 percent for equipment tools and installations. The tax rate is between 3 percent and 10 percent of net annual value (Deloitte 2015a).

Somalia

Somalia was formed by the merger of British Somaliland and Italian Somaliland in 1960. It is located in the Horn of Africa, bordering the Indian Ocean to the north, east, and south, Djibouti to the north, and Ethiopia and Kenya to the west. Its surface area is 637,657 km², and the population is approximately 10.8 million. Only about 40 percent of the population lives in urban areas (United Nations 2014). The population of Mogadishu, the capital, is approximately 2 million (CIA 2016). In 2015, the GDP per capita was estimated at USD 549 (World Bank 2016b), which classifies Somalia as a low-income country (World Bank 2016a). It is one of the most politically unstable countries in the world. Some areas of the country are still under relatively independent control, including the self-declared Republic of Somaliland in northwestern Somalia and the semiautonomous state of Puntland in northeastern Somalia (CIA 2016). Although Somali is the official language, Arabic also is widespread.

Taxes were reintroduced in 2014 after 23 years. The new tax system also provides for property taxes. A property transfer tax is levied at 3 percent in the semiautonomous region of Somaliland.

The UN-Habitat Somalia Program has developed an innovative program that combines spatial urban property data and information with improved revenue systems. This program established efficient tax collection systems in three Somali cities where existing information on land and urban properties was at best incomplete, institutional arrangements were weak, and the capacity of local professionals and officials required substantial development (Urban Gateway n.d.).

In 2010, after successful interventions of this kind in three cities in Somaliland, UN-Habitat started to develop a geographic information system for urban properties in Garowe, the capital of the semiautonomous region of Puntland. This city still relied on outdated and incomplete paper-based land records, and very few of its properties were formally registered and included in the property tax roll. This exercise, completed in 2011, captured comprehensive spatial information on land and building characteristics in a digital format (Urban Gateway n.d.). The outcome of the property survey was the creation of a database that combines georeferenced spatial data and property attributes, hyperlinked to photos of individual properties, which will assist municipal staff to verify the database, communicate with property owners and occupants, and match bills to the correct buildings. The database can then be used to print out the complete set of annual property tax bills, which are delivered to individual households. The accurate database (backed up by photographs) is affecting compliance positively. Many owners or occupants feel assured that the tax bills they receive indeed pertain to their property (Urban Gateway n.d.). The spatial database will also be used for, among other things, urban planning and improved service delivery, while the enhanced property tax revenues should enable the local council to identify public infrastructure priorities and improve service delivery.

South Sudan

After a prolonged period of conflict (1983–2005), peace talks between the factions in the south of Sudan and the Sudanese government finally resulted in a comprehensive peace agreement, signed in January 2005. The South was granted a six-year period of autonomy, to be followed by a referendum on its final status. In January 2011, 98 percent of the participants in the referendum voted in favor of secession, resulting in South Sudan's independence on July 9, 2011 (CIA 2016).

South Sudan covers an area of 644,329 km^2 and has a population of about 12 million (United Nations 2015). The capital is Juba, with about 325,000 inhabitants (CIA 2016). South Sudan is a predominantly rural country; only about 19 percent of the population is urbanized (United Nations 2014). In 2015, the GDP per capita was estimated at USD 731 (World Bank 2016b); thus, South Sudan is classified as a lower-middle-income country (World Bank 2016a). English is the official language.

Since its independence, South Sudan has been struggling with governance and nation-building issues, including the establishment of a new tax system and local governments. According to South Sudan's constitution of 2011, state land, the property tax, and royalties are sources of revenue for the 10 states. A rudimentary calibrated area-based system appears to be operating in Juba.

Tunisia

Tunisia is located at the northernmost tip of Africa, bordering the Mediterranean Sea to the north and east, Libya to the southeast, and Algeria to the west. It gained independence from France in 1956. It covers an area of 163,610 km² and has a population of approximately 11.3 million (United Nations 2015), of which almost 2 million live in the capital, Tunis (CIA 2016). About 67 percent of the population is urbanized (United Nations 2014). The 2015 GDP per capita was estimated at USD 3,873 (World Bank 2016b), which classifies Tunisia as an upper-middle-income country (World Bank 2016a). Arabic is the official language.

Property Transfer Taxes

A transfer tax is levied at 5 percent of the property's value. The Local Tax Office levies and collects a further 1 percent registration fee, also based on the value of the property. Tunisia also levies and collects a capital gains tax, as well as inheritance and gift taxes (PWC 2016).

Recurrent Property Taxes

Individuals owning buildings are subject to a local real estate tax, which is levied in proportion to the area (size) of the building. In addition, individuals are also subject to a property tax on their immovable properties, equal to 1.5 percent of the real estate value. The following properties are exempted from this tax:

- Primary residences.

- Buildings exploited for industrial, commercial, or professional activities.

- Agricultural land located in agricultural areas, on the basis of a certificate delivered by the relevant authorities.

- Buildings that generate rental income.

All countries in North and Northeast Africa levy a tax (or taxes) on the transfer of real property. Egypt has the lowest tax rate on property transfers in this region, only 2.5 percent. Most of these countries, especially Algeria, Morocco, and Tunisia (former French colonies or protectorates with similar transfer tax systems), levy taxes in excess of 5 percent. The rate in

Djibouti is 10 percent, while the rate in Mauritania can be as high as 15 percent. A tax on rental income of real property is also encountered in some countries (e.g., Eritrea and Ethiopia).

Significant property tax reform projects are in place in Ethiopia, but little is happening in Libya, Somalia, and Sudan, where property taxes are generally still insignificant (Fjeldstad 2016). Transparency of ownership rights to land and property is an issue in most of the countries. In Egypt, a parcel-based deeds registry project was begun in 2008 in an attempt to increase the number of properties within the registration system (only 5 percent of Cairo's estimated 3 million properties were registered in 2008). In Eritrea, Ethiopia, South Sudan, and Sudan, traditionally held land and state land predominate. Land titling and registration programs are planned or under way in various countries, including Djibouti, Somalia, South Sudan, and Sudan.

To the extent that the property tax still exists in Libya, it is administered centrally through self-declaration by owners. In Ethiopia and Sudan, administration is devolved to the local level. Undeveloped land is taxed at higher rates than developed land in Algeria and Djibouti. Ethiopia and Morocco base the property tax on rental value but set progressive tax rates.

Table 35.4 shows the use of property-related taxes across the twelve countries of North and Northeast Africa. Eritrea is the weakest country

Table 35.4 Property-Related Taxes in North and Northeast Africa

Country	Rental Income Tax[1]	Property Transfer Tax	Capital Gains Tax	Inheritance and Gift Taxes	Recurrent Property Tax
Algeria	No	Yes	Yes	Yes	Yes
Djibouti	No	Yes	Yes	Yes	Yes
Egypt	No	Yes	Yes	No	Yes
Ethiopia	Yes	Yes	Yes	No	Yes
Eritrea	No	Yes	No	No	Yes[1]
Libya	No	No	Yes	No	Yes
Mauritania	No	No	Yes	No	Yes
Morocco	No	Yes	Yes	No	Yes
Somalia	No	Yes	No	No	Yes
South Sudan	No	No	Yes	No	Yes
Sudan	No	Yes	Yes	No	Yes
Tunisia	No	Yes	Yes	Yes	Yes

[1] The rental income tax is primarily an agricultural land use tax along with a land rental charge for urban property.

Table 35.5 Property Tax Bases in North and Northeast Africa

Country	Tax Base(s)
Algeria	Annual rental value
Djibouti	Annual rental value
Egypt	Annual rental value
Eritrea	Area for urban and rural land
Ethiopia	Annual rental value; area
Libya	Area (with some coefficients based on size and occupancy)
Mauritania	Annual rental value
Morocco	Annual rental value; area for undeveloped land
Somalia	Adjusted area (in Puntland)
South Sudan	Area
Sudan	Area with some adjustment for size, location, and use
Tunisia	Annual rental value

in this regard. Table 35.5 highlights the various bases of the property tax. Annual rental value tends to dominate, but an area-based tax is typically charged for agricultural land. Table A.8 in the appendix provides international ranking data on doing business and registering property (World Bank 2015a, 2015c), the corruption perception index (Transparency International 2015), and property rights (IPRI 2015).

Note
1. The discussion of Ethiopia is based on Soressa and Gebreslus 2009.

References

Amin, K. 2010. "Property Tax System in Libya." Paper presented at the Fellowship Workshop of the African Tax Institute/Lincoln Institute of Land Policy Project on Property Taxation in Africa, Stellenbosch, South Africa (December 4–5).

CIA (Central Intelligence Agency). 2016. *The World Factbook. https://www.cia.gov/library /publications/the-world-factbook/.*

Deloitte. 2015a. *Guide to Fiscal Information: Key Economies in Africa, 2014/15. http://www2 .deloitte.com/content/dam/Deloitte/et/Documents/tax/ZA_Fiscal_Guide_2015 _29012015.pdf.*

———. 2015b. *International Tax: Algeria Highlights, 2015. http://www2.deloitte.com /content/dam/Deloitte/global/Documents/Tax/dttl-tax-algeriahighlights-2015.pdf.*

Fjeldstad, O.-H. 2016. "Revenue Mobilization at Sub-national Levels in Sudan." Report SR 2016:1. Bergen: CMI and University of Bergen.

Heroui, Y. 2008. "Registration of Immovable Property: An Overview in Comparative Perspective." *Ethiopian Bar Review* 2(2).

IMF (International Monetary Fund). 2016. "IMF World Longitudinal Data (WoRLD)." IMF e-Library Data. *http://data.imf.org/?sk=77413F1D-1525-450A -A23A-47AEED40FE78&sId=1390030109571.*

IPRI (International Property Rights Index). 2015. "International Property Rights Index." Property Rights Alliance. *http://internationalpropertyrightsindex.org/countries? f=country&o=asc&r.*

Joireman, S. 2000. *Property Rights and Political Development in Ethiopia and Eritrea.* Oxford: James Currey.

KPMG. 2014a. *Ethiopia Fiscal Guide, 2013/2014. https://www.kpmg.com/Africa/en/KPMG -in-Africa/Documents/2014%20Fiscal%20Guides/Fiscal%20Guide%20Ethiopia.pdf.*

———. 2014b. *Mauritania Fiscal Guide, 2013/2014. https://www.kpmg.com/Africa/en/KPMG -in-Africa/Documents/2014%20Fiscal%20Guides/Fiscal%20Guide%20Mauritania.pdf.*

Pankhurst, R. 1968. *Economic History of Ethiopia.* Addis Ababa: HIS University Press.

PWC (Price Waterhouse Coopers). 2016. *PWC Tax Summaries. http://taxsummaries.pwc .com/uk/taxsummaries/wwts.nsf/ID/Tunisia-Individual-Other-taxes.*

Soressa, A. N., and B. T. Gebreslus. 2009. "Property Taxation in North-east Africa: Case Study of Ethiopia." Working paper WP09NEA1. Cambridge, MA: Lincoln Institute of Land Policy.

Tecle, B. 2010. "A Comprehensive Review of Land and Property Taxes System of Eritrea." Paper presented at the Fellowship Workshop of the African Tax Institute/ Lincoln Institute of Land Policy Project on Property Taxation in Africa, Stellenbosch, South Africa (December 4–5).

Transparency International. 2015. "Corruption Perception Index in 168 Countries." *http://www.transparency.org.*

United Nations. 2014. *World Urbanization Prospects.* Washington, DC: Department of Economic and Social Affairs, Population Division.

United Nations, Department of Economic and Social Affairs, Population Division. 2015. World Population Prospects: The 2015 Revision. *https://esa.un.org/unpd/wpp /Publications/Files/World_Population_2015_Wallchart.pdf.*

Urban Gateway. No date. "Urban Geographic Information System and Property Database Come to Garowe." *www.urbangateway.org/document/urban-geographic -information-system-and-property-database-come-garowe-somalia.*

Wibke, C., B. Ayalneh, and K. Benedikt. 2008. "Land Tenure in Ethiopia—Continuity and Change, Shifting Rulers and the Quest for State Control." CAPRi working paper no. 91. Washington, DC.

World Bank. 2015a. *Comparing Business Regulations for Domestic Firms in 189 Countries.* Washington, DC.

———. 2015b. "Doing Business: Paying Taxes in Eritrea." *http://www.doingbusiness.org /data/exploreeconomies/eritrea/paying-taxes/.*

———. 2015c. "Registering Property." *http://www.doingbusiness.org/data/exploretopics /registering-property/reforms.*

———. 2016a. "Country and Lending Groups." *http://data.worldbank.org/about/country -and-lending-groups.*

———. 2016b. "GPD per Capita (Current US%)." *http://data.worldbank.org/indicator /NY.GDP.PCAP.CD.*

Legislation

Eritrea

Proclamation 58 of 1994.

Proclamation 63 of 1994.

Ethiopia

Condominium Proclamation No. 370/2003.

Constitution of the Federal Democratic Republic of Ethiopia, 1995.

Government Ownership of Urban Lands and Extra Houses Proclamation No. 47/1975.

Public Ownership of Rural Lands Proclamation No. 31/1975.

Stamp Duty Proclamation No. 110/1998.

Urban Land Rent and Urban Houses Tax Proclamation No. 80/1976.

Urban Lands Lease Holding Proclamation No. 272/2002.

Libya

Law 5 of 1969 (dealing with the planning of cities and villages).

South Sudan

Constitution of the Republic of South Sudan, 2011.

PART IV

The Future of the Property Tax
in Africa

36

Challenges, Prospects, and Recommendations

WILLIAM McCLUSKEY, RIËL FRANZSEN, AND ROY BAHL

The best approach to reforming tax in a developing country—indeed in any country—is one that takes into account taxation theory, empirical evidence, and political and administrative realities and blends them with a good dose of local knowledge and a sound appraisal of the current macroeconomic and international situation to produce a feasible set of proposals sufficiently attractive to be implemented and sufficiently robust to withstand changing times, within reason, and still produce beneficial results.

—Bird and Oldman (1990, 3)

Almost every country in Africa levies a recurrent property tax, and many have been trying to improve it. During the past 25 years, there have been many efforts to reform existing property tax systems that in some instances date back to colonial times (Egypt, Gabon, Mozambique, Senegal, and Uganda) or to introduce a new property tax system (Namibia), often as part of a more comprehensive decentralization reform (Kenya and South Africa). Some of these reform efforts have been initiated and strongly supported by international funding and donor agencies, which hope to help stimulate revenue mobilization, develop land markets, and improve transparency in government.

Most of these efforts have not been very successful. Property tax revenue performance is near the lowest in the world in almost all African countries; tax administration is characterized by inadequate valuation practices, poor property coverage, and low rates of compliance; and property markets remain underdeveloped. Few African countries have shown a willingness to vigorously enforce their property tax laws. This is not to say that there are no success stories. South Africa has developed a well-administered, revenue-producing property tax. Some countries have seen meaningful increases in their revenues (Liberia and Sierra Leone), although in most cases, these increases were from a very low base. In other countries, revenue increases were realized but could not be sustained (Tanzania). There are some good success stories about property tax reform, but they are often found in individual jurisdictions (McCluskey and Franzsen 2016; Moore 2013). But mostly, there has been little progress in improving the property tax as a revenue instrument.

Nevertheless, there are reasons to be optimistic about the future. Africa is urbanizing rapidly, and the number of large and middle-sized cities is growing. This will both increase the demand for local public services and drive up real estate values. Especially if more African countries embrace fiscal decentralization, demand for a viable property tax will be increased. Property markets are becoming more formal and transparent, which should improve the chances for better administration. Although progress has been slow in this area, it should be boosted by urbanization and, one hopes, by more direct foreign investment. Technology improvements can also enable stronger property tax administration. The movement from manual to automated systems has been slow but steady and already is leading to administrative improvements in some places.

The problems and attitudes to be overcome in creating a strong property tax are formidable, but some good opportunities are coming into view. The question to be addressed now is, how do African countries get to the next step in improving property taxation?

Challenges

The African Environment

African countries are among the poorest in the world, and the resulting low taxable capacity is ultimately the greatest constraint to developing a stronger property tax. But there are other environmental factors that are hostile to implementing a productive tax on real property. The postcolonial era in Francophone Africa has been characterized in almost all of the region's countries by military uprisings (the Central African Republic) and coups or attempted coups (Burkina Faso, Burundi, the Comoros, Mali, and Niger). Political instability or even civil war is under way in Burundi, the Central African Republic, Chad, the Comoros, Côte d'Ivoire, the Democratic Republic of the Congo, Guinea, Madagascar, Mali, and Niger. The Somalian government has collapsed, Nigeria is dealing with serious insurgency problems, Egypt and Libya have gone through a period of political upheaval, and there is a refugee crisis across much of the continent. The constitutions of some countries (e.g., Burundi, Uganda, and Zimbabwe) have been amended to afford current presidents a further term or terms in office. The physical infrastructure in some countries—the object of property taxes—has been badly damaged in some places (Liberia and Sierra Leone) and has fallen into disrepair in others.

In this setting, it is no wonder that property tax reform is not a high priority. But even if it were, governance in many African countries is in crisis and incapable of leading effectively. Audit reports for local governments often express reservations, and procurement of public contracts is riddled with corruption. Moreover, many central governments and local councils lack the political will to enforce the collection of property taxes. Institutions are also a roadblock to reform of real estate taxes. Although the laws pertaining to property taxes may seem adequate, they are often out of step with the capacities of the governments administering the tax. Other causes of a weak property tax are poor institutional networks and intergovernmental collaboration, inadequate databases and logistics, limited capacity, poorly motivated staff, outmoded technology, and political interference. The result continues to be inadequate revenue mobilization and inadequate institutional and financial capacity to implement and maintain the property tax.

The Politics of Property Taxation in Africa

"Tax policy is the product of political decision making, with economic analysis playing only a supporting role" (Holcombe 1998, 359). This certainly describes the practice of property taxation in much of Africa. First, it is a tax on unearned income that is assessed judgmentally and is payable in response to a highly visible annual tax bill. Second, the services purported to be financed by the property tax are usually deficient, and the taxes are collected by governments in which taxpayers have little or no trust (Fjeldstad and Semboja 2001). Last, the property tax in general and the relation between the tax base and the tax rate in particular seem to be poorly understood. Persuading politicians to sell the property tax and voters to buy it is an uphill battle.

As if the natural disadvantages and capacity limits were not enough, national and local politicians have found ways to compromise the workings of the property tax even more. They find favor with voters and constituents by reducing the tax burden through exemptions and value thresholds (Egypt), amnesties (Zimbabwe), forgiveness of the interest on late payments (Nairobi, Kenya), and more. Tax rates are determined by politicians, either in the central government (Cameroon and Egypt) or in local governments (Kenya, Namibia, South Africa, and Zambia). In some instances, rates are set so low that the cost of assessment and collection cannot or can barely be recouped (Franzsen and Welgemoed 2011; McCluskey and Franzsen 2005). Politicians also interfere with the property tax in less visible ways, through the tax administration. There are subjective valuation preferences for certain types of properties, and there are cases of political interference with the preparation of valuation rolls. Collection efforts may be lax and uneven, and the penalties for evading the tax may not be enforced. Even central governments often are delinquent in their property tax payments to local governments.

Politicians may have little incentive to reform the system. The amount of revenue sacrificed is usually quite small because the property tax rarely accounts for a large share of tax collections. Moreover, pressures from constituents can be hard to resist. The disruptive impact of vested interests should not be underestimated. Influential individuals who benefit from the status quo will go to great lengths to undermine reforms that are likely to harm their interests, even if a tax is low. In the eyes of some politicians, the benefits of the announcement of a tax reduction may far outweigh the budget cost.

There are ways to reduce undesirable political interference with property taxation. An increase in the amount of revenue raised would make the property tax more consequential, and reducing it would be more likely to require higher taxes elsewhere. Another tactic could be to require documentation of the cost of preferential property tax treatments and to identify the source of funding for these preferences. A third tactic could be to raise the statutory rate, albeit on a broader base.

Politics is not always bad for the property tax. There are property tax success stories that have much to do with politics. What these stories have in common is strong local political leadership, either during the reform phase (South Africa) or during the implementation phase (Cape Town, South Africa). Implementation of fundamental property tax reform requires political champions who can support the reforms, can help communicate the rationale for the reforms, and are prepared to put their reputations on the line (Bird 2004). Four instances where mayors or ruling parties have provided strong leadership are Bangalore (India), Belo Horizonte (Brazil), Bogotá (Colombia), and Cape Town (South Africa) (McCluskey and Franzsen 2013b). The Bangalore story is described in box 36.1.

The Institutional Environment

The proper institutional infrastructure for a well-functioning property tax is not in place in most of Africa. A value-based property tax system

---

**Box 36.1 POLITICAL LEADERSHIP IN BANGALORE:
A PRAGMATIC APPROACH TO PROPERTY TAXATION**

The property tax system of Bangalore, the capital of Karnataka State in India, can be described as a hybrid of an area-based system and a value-based system. In response to challenges (e.g., rent control) presented by the dysfunctional annual rental value system, the city introduced the Self Assessment Scheme (SAS) in 2000. Under the SAS system, property owners were required to declare the physical characteristics of their property. The process was transparent, and the mayor had the backing of opposition-party politicians, the media, and, most important, the majority of taxpayers. More than 60 percent of taxpayers filed their declarations within the prescribed 45-day period—an indication of taxpayer acceptance. When a capital value system was introduced in Karnataka State in 2005, Bangalore retained the SAS, thus keeping a promise politicians had made to taxpayers when the system was first introduced. In 2008, the SAS was revised with the introduction of unit area values. Unit area values are determined with reference to the average rate of expected returns from a property per square foot per month, depending on the location and use of the property. The municipal corporation was classified into value zones based on published guidance values produced by the Department of Stamps and Registration. These value zones are adjusted regularly. Over a three-year cycle, the value increase must be at least 15 percent. This ensures some buoyancy in the tax base, which would otherwise be rather static because it is based primarily on area, and resulted in property tax revenues increasing between 2000 and 2011.

Sources: McCluskey and Franzsen 2013b; Rao 2008.

---

requires a mature and active property market. This means that there should be a clear definition of tenure rights and an efficient land administration system that guarantees the formal exchange of land and a process for determining, recording, and disseminating information about tenure, value, and the use of land. Reforms should concentrate on improving the system of land administration to formalize land markets, clearing up the intergovernmental and interministerial impediments to expanded coverage of the property tax base, finding an effective way to manage the responsibility for valuation, and addressing the serious shortage of valuers.

Land Administration and Informal Property Markets
Central to the effective administration of a mature property tax system is the registration of titles or deeds and the availability of fiscal and legal cadastres. Further development of these would instill confidence in the

ownership, occupation, and other limited rights pertaining to land and buildings, thus providing increased tenure security. More secure tenure rights and the recording and publicizing of transaction data should result in improved levels of transparency in property markets. Property registration exists in all African countries, but the systems require major technological improvements and more thorough coverage. The deficiencies in ensuring that all transactions are recorded and appropriate titles are issued adversely affect the coverage of the property tax. Both Mauritius and Zambia are implementing programs to modernize their property registers.

Only a few countries in Africa have mature, well-functioning land and property titling systems. However, progress is being made. Many countries are instituting major reforms through full-scale design (Equatorial Guinea), implementing land management modernization programs (Malawi, Uganda, and Zambia), or upgrading or extending geographic coverage (Mozambique). Other countries, such as Eritrea, Mali, and Somalia, are just embarking on this costly but critically important journey. Significant property tax reform projects are in place in Ethiopia and Somalia, but little is occurring in Sudan and South Sudan. On the other hand, as part of its decentralization drive, Kenya seems to be fragmenting its land management system.

Many African countries are discovering appropriate technology and using it to good purpose. A fully digitized property register that records legal ownership is essential; a land information system enabled by a geographic information system (GIS) is equally essential. Several countries have begun their land reforms in urban areas (Benin), followed by extensions into rural areas (Côte D'Ivoire and Mozambique). Digital scanning of deeds and titles is well advanced in many countries; Zambia is only one example.

However, a key challenge facing many countries is sharing of the data contained in legal registers since the register may be in, say, the Ministry of Justice, while property tax administration and valuation are the responsibility of a different ministry. As computerization of land registries gains ground across the countries in Africa, data sharing should become easier. There are still issues, however, when the land registry is a national system, but property tax administration is a local responsibility (The Gambia, Kenya, Lesotho, Mozambique, and Tanzania). Obtaining the data remains problematic. Registration of property has been established in many countries, but the recording of accurate transaction prices and rents is still a problem. This information is essential for a value-based property tax, and it should be recorded in such a way that the data can be regularly reported to the valuation department.

Tax Base Coverage and Property Identification

Ideally, all properties should be covered in a land registration system. With cooperation among the various offices involved, such as titling and deeds, mapping, and the cadastre, preparation and updating of the property tax roll should be relatively easy. However, as noted earlier, there is a great deal of variation in the extent to which individual properties are registered. Compounding the problem, the identification process does not always benefit from intergovernmental and interministerial cooperation.

In most Francophone and Lusophone countries, as well as countries in North and Northeast Africa, central-government entities are most important in the identification process and often rely to a large extent on property owners to self-declare their property holdings regularly, if not annually. Tax departments play a key role in all aspects of the property tax, but it is unclear from the country studies to what extent data are necessarily shared with other ministries and with local authorities. However, it appears that the lack of connectivity between ministries is a constraint. One must also reckon with the silo mentality, which often precludes data sharing.

In Anglophone countries, local authorities play a crucial role in some, if not all, aspects of the property tax, but often with little input from property owners. Data sharing between local authorities and relevant central-government ministries or entities is limited, as is data sharing among departments or divisions within individual local authorities. In the more successful local authorities, one typically finds that municipal valuers receive information on new building permits, rezoning applications, and the issuance of business licenses and occupation permits, which enables them to undertake field visits or interim valuations (Nairobi, Kenya, and South Africa). The updated data are then shared with the finance department, which can bill and collect the property tax accordingly.

Mandating or legislating the sharing of information is no small challenge. It is even more difficult to form new comprehensive departments. There are many players in a highly fragmented environment, such as ministries responsible for land, finances, justice, urban and rural planning, land titling or deeds offices, and the cadastre, and the political infighting can be fierce. But information sharing is important if there is to be an effective property tax. Information sharing can expand the property tax roll significantly. For example, De Cesare (2004, 16) reports that in the city of Guayaquil, Ecuador, an online integration of the public registry of properties and the cadastre made it possible to increase the number of recorded properties from 165,000 in 1993 to 418,474 in 2001.

It is possible to get past intergovernmental and interministry differences. African countries may learn from recent rationalization and streamlining of all the offices or entities involved in the recording and management of land in Northern Ireland and Jamaica, as discussed briefly in box 36.2.

Valuation

In countries where a value-based property tax exists, there will be an institution that by law is responsible for carrying out valuations. The choices are few: either the national government or local governments. The private sector can also play a role in assisting the government. In theory, centralized, decentralized, or shared responsibility for valuation can work. There are many good examples from around the world where different approaches work well. But no system will work well if the institutional framework is not supportive.

In Africa, valuation is one of the weakest links in the property tax chain. Depending on the country, the failures can be attributed to an inappropriate legal framework for the tax, the absence of an adequate fiscal cadastre, the shortage of professional valuation staff, and lack of interministerial coordination and cooperation.

In countries where local governments are responsible for valuation, the problems seem to be worse. Fiscal decentralization programs have directly or indirectly pushed valuation administration down to the local level (Kenya, Mozambique, Tanzania, Uganda, and Zambia) but have not provided the necessary resources to discharge the responsibility. One way to resolve this problem without compromising fiscal decentralization objectives could be to have a centralized national valuation department deliver valuation services to local governments that require them, or at least oversee the work undertaken locally. A model for doing this exists in Botswana and Kenya, but it is not effective in practice. However, such a model seems quite successful in Zambia. There are, of course, some successful experiences with local leadership of valuation. For example, initiatives implemented by the valuation departments in the three Dar es Salaam municipalities in Tanzania (Ilala, Kinondoni, and Temeke) have achieved excellent results in increasing coverage. Good practices are also observed at the local-government level in South Africa (City of Cape Town) and Zambia (Kitwe City Council). But it is difficult to generalize from these few places even to urban local governments in Africa.

The results from placing primary responsibility for valuation at the national level seem to be better, but the improvement is marginal. Examples of poor practice include Gabon, The Gambia, Kenya, Lesotho, and Uganda. In contrast, Botswana, Mauritius, and Namibia (for the

Box 36.2 Rationalizing Land Management: Examples from Northern Ireland and Jamaica

Northern Ireland

Land and Property Services (LPS) is an agency of the Department of Finance and Personnel that was created in 2008 and is responsible for mapping, land registration, valuation, and property tax collection for Northern Ireland. LPS was a merger of four separate government agencies: the Valuation and Lands Agency (VLA), Ordnance Survey Northern Ireland (OSNI), the Land Registry for Northern Ireland (LRNI), and the Rates Collection Agency (RCA). LPS demonstrates the powerful synergies that can be released from merging government organizations involved in land and property services.

The VLA was part of the Department of Finance and was responsible for property tax valuations. OSNI was responsible for mapping services and was an agency within the Department of Culture, Arts and Leisure. The LRNI, within the Department of Finance and Personnel, managed three registers: the Land Register, containing about 60 percent of titles to land; the Register of Deeds; and the Statutory Charges Register. The RCA was formed in 1991 within the Department of Finance and was the largest property tax collection authority in the United Kingdom. It was responsible for collecting approximately £1 billion of property tax annually. The VLA and the RCA merged on April 1, 2007, and the LRNI and OSNI joined on April 1, 2008. On full creation in 2008, LPS employed approximately 1,200 staff.

Source: Greenway 2010.

Jamaica

The National Land Agency (NLA) was established as a result of the Public Sector Modernization Program of the government of Jamaica, which underscored the government's commitment to streamline the administration and management of land. It brought together the core land information functions of government under one agency and included the former Office of Titles, the Survey Department, the Land Valuation Department, and the Lands Department. This merger has enabled the government to build on the synergy of these combined functions and create a modern national land (spatial) information system to support sustainable development. The NLA commenced operation in 2001. Its mission is to ensure (1) an efficient and transparent land titling system that guarantees security of tenure; (2) a national land valuation database that supports equitable property taxation; (3) optimal use of government-owned lands; and (4) basic infrastructure on which to build a modern spatial information system.

Source: Allen 2016.

agricultural land tax) have had some success. The challenge is how to address these problems. Creating an appropriate and dedicated national valuation department, particularly in smaller countries, such as The Gambia, Lesotho, Malawi, Rwanda, Sierra Leone, and Swaziland, could lead to benefits from economies of scale and achieving other institutional gains, such as setting uniform standards. The middle ground might be central oversight. Some countries with national valuation departments, such as Botswana, Kenya, Namibia, Uganda, and Zambia, where typically a division or department in the Ministry of Lands is responsible for or oversees public-sector valuations, might be a good model. However, the mere existence of these divisions or departments does not imply that they are operating effectively. It must be kept in mind that in principle, the responsibility for valuation in Botswana, Kenya, Lesotho, Malawi, and Uganda was previously centralized in the relevant land ministry and was either decentralized (Botswana, Malawi, and Uganda) or simply abdicated to in-house municipal valuers (Kenya and Lesotho) or private-sector valuers contracted by local governments (Botswana and Malawi). In Lesotho, the Maseru City Council appointed its own in-house valuer because it stated that municipal valuation was not viewed as a national-government priority (Franzsen 2003). This was apparently also the case in Kenya, Tanzania, and Uganda.

Other institutions could assist in ensuring that suspicious or corrupt valuation contracts and practices are investigated and eliminated. For example, in 2001, the Anti-corruption Board in Malawi investigated the contract that the city of Blantyre concluded with a private-sector valuation firm for the preparation of a new valuation roll (Franzsen and McCluskey 2005). South Africa created the office of valuer general in 2015 but has excluded municipal valuation from this office's functions and responsibilities—a missed opportunity. Because municipal valuations are excluded from the ambit of the valuer general, the office of the public protector could be requested to undertake a review of the procurement of municipal valuation services.

The Shortage of Valuers

In most African countries, national and local (in-house) valuation departments have too few professionally qualified valuers. Large cities typically have tens or hundreds of thousands of properties to be valued. Because there are not enough in-house valuers, revaluations are not undertaken, and current valuation rolls are not properly maintained. For example, in Nairobi, Kenya, the valuation roll currently in use dates back to 1982. The situation is worse in smaller urban municipalities, for example, in

Tanzania, where a municipality may have only one valuer, and in Uganda, where there is simply no valuation capacity. Furthermore, most African countries have few, if any, institutions capable of providing this training.

In many Francophone, Lusophone, and North African countries, officials in the central government loosely administer value-based property taxes. Tax directorates apply questionable market values to determine assessed values (the Central African Republic, the Democratic Republic of the Congo, Gabon, Libya, and Madagascar). These systems are largely based on annual self-declarations by owners. In reality, they are essentially area-based approaches with basic adjustments to reflect value. However, the approaches adopted are pragmatic where there is a very thin or nonexistent property market, and there are no credible data on market values.

What to do? After all, valuation is the centerpiece of a value-based property tax. One solution is to lessen the dependence on government valuers through administrative measures. A positive development in the valuation departments in some large metropolitan areas is the employment of GIS specialists and others with specific analytical skills, such as statisticians, who complement valuers and reduce reliance on them (Cape Town, Durban, and Nairobi). Another positive development is the use of data collectors to assist with the collection of property and ownership details (Arusha and Cape Town). These developments enhance rather than detract from the important role of valuers and do not infringe the legal requirement that valuations be performed by qualified valuers.

Another possibility is to use the private sector on a consultancy basis. This model has been applied in several African countries. It can be expensive, but in some countries, it can achieve the objective of updating the valuation rolls. If private-sector valuers undertake most or all of the actual valuation work, the government will need to deal with project management and address issues such as uniform standards and proper oversight. Cape Town, South Africa, is an excellent example of how this can be done professionally and efficiently. In some African countries (Sierra Leone and Uganda), however, even the private sector may not have the capacity to take on this task.

A third approach is to look to technology and mass appraisal to help reduce the demand for valuers. But simplified mass valuation approaches also require inputs from valuers. Moreover, the absence of reliable data on property transfers leaves computerized mass appraisal out of the reach of almost all African governments. The City of Cape Town is all but unique in Africa in its use of computer-assisted mass appraisal (CAMA) (box 36.3).

Box 36.3 Cape Town: A CAMA Success Story

The general valuation of 2015 for the City of Cape Town had the purpose of updating the valuation roll to incorporate value changes since the last general revaluation in 2012. The 2015 valuation roll was produced under the Local Government: Municipal Property Rates Act of 2004, which is the national legislation governing the valuation of properties for rating purposes. The act prescribes that all properties on the valuation roll must be valued at market value as of the date of valuation. The market value is defined as "the amount the property would have realised if sold on the date of valuation in the open market by a willing seller to a willing buyer."

By law, metropolitan municipalities in South Africa must produce a general valuation roll at least once every four years. The City of Cape Town elects to produce a general valuation roll once every three years because long periods between general valuations can result in significant changes in property values. Some 830,000 valuations were prepared.

The city gathered information about property sales that took place around the date of valuation (August 1, 2015). These sales were scrutinized and then formed the basis of the property value assessments. The valuation employed CAMA based on sales data, aerial imagery, and other property information (e.g., location, size, number of rooms, outbuildings, general condition and quality, and view) to determine the value of a property. The results were then reviewed by property valuers and adjusted if required.

Source: City of Cape Town Valuation Department 2016.

Urbanization and the Property Tax

Africa is urbanizing faster than any other continent (UN-Habitat 2004). There are already more than 20 urban agglomerations in Africa with more than 2.5 million inhabitants, and in 2014 there were three megacities (Cairo, Kinshasa, and Lagos each have more than 10 million inhabitants) on the continent (United Nations 2014). Dar es Salaam (Tanzania), Johannesburg (South Africa), and Luanda (Angola) are projected to surpass the 10 million mark by 2030 (Viruly and Hopkins 2014). The number of large cities with populations between 5 and 10 million in Africa is also expected to increase from three in 2014 to twelve by 2030 (United Nations 2014). However, the fastest-growing urban agglomerations are medium-sized cities and cities with fewer than 1 million inhabitants.

Because of the pace of urbanization in Africa, sustainable development challenges will be increasingly concentrated in cities, particularly those in the lower-middle-income countries, where the pace of urbanization is fastest (United Nations 2014). Without ignoring the plight of rural dwellers, well-designed and integrated planning policies will be needed to improve the lives of urban dwellers. Africa is expected to be the fastest-urbanizing region from 2020 to 2050 (Durand-Lasserve 2016; United Nations 2014). For example, in 1995, Lagos was estimated to have 6.5 million inhabitants, and in 2000 the population grew to 8.8 million. In 2002, it passed 10 million and continued its astronomical growth to surpass 16 million by 2015—the world's 11th-largest urban agglomeration (UN-Habitat 2004). Durand-Lasserve (2016) provides even more startling projections regarding urbanization, stating that between 2015 and 2050, urbanization in Africa will grow from 38 percent to 55 percent, which implies an additional 790 million urban inhabitants.

If African urban areas are to enjoy the economic growth that can go with this population growth, they will need to increase the level and quality of public expenditures. An expected growth of nearly 800 million urban dwellers will significantly increase the demand for housing, social services, and public utilities. It will also require significant expenditures for infrastructure to support business development and to keep these businesses competitive in international markets.[1] One estimate is that annual new infrastructure needs in developing countries will require about 5 percent of GDP over the next 20 years (Ingram, Liu, and Brandt 2013). By contrast, the level of total central- and local-government revenue in sub-Saharan Africa is only about 13 percent of GDP. At the same time, economic growth and increased public investment in infrastructure will drive up property values. Almost certainly, this will generate increased demand for property taxation in African urban areas, and the premium on improving the administration of the property tax will continue to grow.

Property-Related Taxes and Charges

Property Transfer Taxes, the Stamp Duty, and the Capital Gains Tax

There is evidence that high taxes on real estate transactions undermine the regularization of land registration or titling and discourage transactions, which might ultimately make the market thinner, and encourage underdeclaration of property values. Underdeclaration is detrimental to a value-based recurrent property tax and almost fatal to the possibility of a credible CAMA system. As argued in chapter 2, there are several potentially good reform directions. The best practice in this area would be to remove disincentives to a functioning real estate market and to accurately report sales values for property transactions. This suggests three pathways to reform. The first is to abolish the property transfer tax and make up the revenue loss by increasing the levels of the annual property tax. A nominal duty or fee could be levied to cover the cost of transferring ownership. Perhaps this fee could be redesigned as a user charge or fee for the maintenance of the cadastre and a titling or deeds register.

The second reform direction would retain the property transfer tax but significantly lower its rates where they are high, and aggressively monitor declared values for transactions. This might be done by requiring certified appraisals on high-value properties at the expense of buyers and sellers, upgrading and expanding the valuation staff at the local-government level, and imposing significant penalties for underdeclaration. The administration of the property transfer tax could be merged with that of the annual property tax. There are, however, constraints on this proposal. First, cooperation and coordination of officials are often lacking where these taxes are levied at different government levels, as is often the case. Cabo Verde may provide some guidance in this regard. Second, finding the valuers necessary to do this job is difficult and almost certainly will incur significant cost increases.

The third reform path would be to replace the property transfer tax with a tax on capital gains from sales of real property. Administration would need to be phased in and would require estimated amounts for current values, but this would arguably be no more difficult than verification of declared values under the current transfer tax. Moreover, there would be an incentive for buyers to force an accurate declaration of the transfer price.

Ground Rent

Where land remains in public ownership in many African countries, the system of ground rent should be retained. It could be significantly better managed in many countries, although there are recent examples, most notably Lesotho, where administration has been improved with a positive effect on revenue. However, since ground rent is a rent for the right to occupy land, not a tax, it should be set as close to market rents as feasible.

Value Capture Mechanisms

Land value capture is a concept that describes several land-based finance tools whose use is growing. In essence, land value capture constitutes "a public claim to some portion of the increase in property value due to public investment, such as infrastructure improvements" (Youngman 2016, 13). Among the techniques that are used to capture these costs (or increments in value) are betterment levies, special assessments, land adjustment, and tax increment financing.

These instruments of land value capture may be seen as a way to defray part of the cost of infrastructure investment that goes with urbanization. They have been successful in Latin America (Smolka 2013). One of the great advantages of this approach is that the cost recovery can be assigned in large part to direct beneficiaries. In most African countries, current laws will require amendment, or new laws will have to be passed to enable the use of one or more of these mechanisms. Land value capture does have great potential in growing urban areas of low-income countries, but it may be some time before most African countries can absorb this approach.

Property Tax Reform

Property tax reform involves (1) an in-depth evaluation of the current system that highlights its strengths and weaknesses; (2) identification of the primary objectives of the reform; and (3) a review of the tax policy and administration options that might lead to achieving the objectives (Bahl 2009; Bahl and Bird 2008; Bird and Slack 2004). It is noteworthy that property tax reform is happening not only in developing and transition countries but also in industrialized countries, such as Australia, Ireland, New Zealand, and the United Kingdom (Franzsen 2014). But industrialized countries can take advantage of many more reform options, while African countries are at a much earlier stage in property tax development. The question we raise here is, what appear to be the best reform options for African countries?

The caveat to this discussion, of course, is that not all African countries are alike, not all political settings are alike, and not all capacities to implement a property tax are alike. Specific policy and administrative reform options will not likely be on the mark. But there are enough commonalities in the problems and the setting for us to reach some general conclusions about possible good reform directions.

Clarify the Objectives

The first important question for a country to answer is what property tax reform is to accomplish. In almost all cases, the primary purpose of the reform is to generate revenue (Bird and Slack 2003; Dillinger 1991; Rosengard 2012). But even this objective is problematic because the property tax starts from such a low base in Africa, perhaps an average of only about 0.3 percent of GDP. Even a doubling of the effective rate in most countries, which would risk taxpayer shock, would probably do little to address the revenue gap. Perhaps equally important is to increase the income elasticity of the property tax so that its revenues grow in step with GDP.

A second overall objective could be more fairness (horizontal equity) in the property tax so that families and businesses in similar circumstances would pay roughly the same property taxes. The general strategy is usually to broaden the base and lower the rate through specific initiatives, such as limiting exemptions and preferential treatments, increasing coverage, keeping valuations accurate and up to date, and enforcing the tax to achieve a high collection rate. But oddly enough, an apparently fairer property tax can be politically the most difficult to sell. When tax burdens are rearranged, there are invariably winners and losers. Those who benefit from reform often tend to remain silent, but those who lose tend to be vocal (Kelly 2014). And the losers may be politically powerful.

Although the reform advice here is to stick to fixing the basics, there are other objectives that might be good candidates for emphasis. These include increasing the progressivity of the tax and improving the land use impacts. Although these might eventually be on the table, the right reform now in most African countries is more fundamental structural and administrative change to broaden the base and administer the tax more efficiently. The United Kingdom's Department of the Environment (DoE 1991), the Institute of Revenues, Rating and Valuation (IRRV 1997), and Northern Ireland's Rating Policy Division of the Department of Finance and Personnel's Rating Policy (DFPNI 2002) have indicated several criteria as being worthy of consideration in holistically viewing reform issues. Table 36.1 illustrates some of the models that have been recommended.

Include All the Fiscal Instruments Necessary for Reform

The revenue productivity and horizontal equity of the property tax are the products of several different policy instruments and administrative actions. Unless all these fiscal policy and administrative action instruments are part of the reform program, the objectives are not likely to be realized.

Table 36.1 Proposed Criteria for a Local Property Tax System

United Kingdom Department of the Environment (1991)	Institute of Revenues, Rating and Valuation (1997)	DFPNI Rating Policy (Northern Ireland) (2002)
Practicability	Ability to pay	Adequate yield
Fairness	Ease of understanding	Equity
Accountability	Administratively efficiency	Interference in markets
Cost of administration	Difficulty of evading and avoiding	Stability and certainty
Fiscal dimensions	Impartiality	Policy objectives
Financial control	Benefit principle	Administration
Suitability	Accountability	Transparency
		Compliance costs
		Difficulty of evading

Sources: DFPNI (2002); DoE (1991); and IRRV (1997).

There are many examples of reforms that have stumbled because they failed to get all the pieces on the table, for example, countries that raised the legal tax rate but continued to increase exemptions, or countries that embarked on an aggressive identification campaign but failed to properly revalue the new properties.

One frequent problem in the design of reforms is an excessive concentration on the upstream stages of property tax administration, such as property identification and valuation, to the neglect of collection. Given the extremely low level of collection efficiency in developing countries, much of the effort spent on mapping and valuation is likely to be wasted if corresponding efforts are not made to improve collection administration. Newly identified and valued property does not yield revenue if collection administration is dysfunctional. Roy Kelly (2014) was led to his now well-known "collection-led" strategy of property tax reform by an Indonesian program that at first focused on valuation but ignored collection. The collection focus of the Kampala Capital City Authority in Uganda since its establishment in 2011 is an excellent African example of revenue enhancement through applying the basics of collection. The following are the most important fiscal instruments that might be a target for property tax reform:

The statutory tax rate: In a fiscally decentralized system, tax rates should be determined by the local government in order to foster accountability of the local council to the population. In this way, the tax rate can vary across jurisdictions depending on affordability and the demand for public services. If the property tax is to finance services provided by local governments, then local governments should have the right to change the tax rate annually depending on budget needs, although it may be necessary to limit increases or decreases via applying differential tax rates through central-government oversight, as happens in South Africa. In centralized systems, the national government will set rates, but some method of allowing for differentiation among local governments is probably desirable because the cost of providing local public services may vary from place to place. To preserve accountability, preferential tax rates should be set by the level of government that is responsible for providing local public services. Ideally, the property tax rate should be flexible enough to rise with the increased cost and demand for local public services that it supports. Preferential tax rates other than the zero rate below the value threshold should be discouraged.

Exemptions: Most, if not all, countries in Africa could benefit from a thorough review of their current exclusions and exemptions from the property tax base. Especially, relief for owner-occupied residential property, government-owned property, and newly completed buildings could usefully be reexamined. If the property tax is used to finance local government services in a fiscally decentralized system, the local government should decide most exemptions. In every case, however, a fiscal note should be required that will identify the revenue loss from the exemption, the plan for recouping this loss, the beneficiaries, and the sunset period when the exemption will next be reviewed. Higher-level governments might provide technical assistance for local governments that cannot carry out the necessary analysis. Excessive exemptions could be guarded against in three ways: first, restructure the intergovernmental transfer system to penalize property tax exemptions; second, require public hearings to vet all exemption proposals; and third, impose a finite life for each exemption and require a review and a revote before the preferential treatment can be continued.

In more centralized fiscal systems, the national government usually decides property tax exemptions. Where this is the case, intergovernmental transfer systems should compensate subnational governments for the loss of property tax revenue. In this way, accountability of national politicians could be increased.

Identification of properties: An important problem for the revenue potential of the property tax is that large numbers of properties are not on the tax roll. In some African countries, less than 50 percent of properties have been identified (The Gambia, Kenya, Tanzania). The identification of properties can follow the traditional approach of "feet on the ground," that is, a manual identification and survey, but a modern approach would employ "eyes in the sky" technology, such as aerial photography, satellite imagery, and drones. This approach identifies properties and through a GIS creates a digital map that can be followed up by an actual inspection.

Record keeping: Property tax records, which are essential for assessment and collection, typically include many thousands of properties. Manual approaches to record keeping are not viable and in many cases are being phased out, for example, in Tanzania, where the computerized Local Government Revenue Collection Information System (LGRCIS) was developed to manage all own-source revenues, including the property tax. Early indications are that the LGRCIS has had a positive impact on revenue collections in many cities and municipalities.

Continued modernization and the automation of systems and procedures are important. Countries can gain significantly from the greater use of GISs because they can provide the required data-management capabilities for proper land use administration, as well as property taxation. Cape Town (South Africa), Bangalore (India), Belo Horizonte (Brazil), and Bogotá (Colombia) are examples of cities in developing countries that have made huge strides in enhancing revenue from their property taxes by integrating a comprehensive GIS with their property tax systems (McCluskey and Franzsen 2013b).

Valuation or assessment: Valuation (or assessment) is the core of the property tax system because it provides the mechanism to translate an abstract quantity, the defined tax base, into an amount (of value, size, or extent) that can then be multiplied by a tax rate to determine tax liability. Accurate valuation or assessment is therefore critical in distributing the tax burden fairly among taxpayers. As elsewhere in the developing world, many of the shortcomings in African property tax systems are due to the failure to value accurately (assessment ratios as low as 50 percent are not uncommon) and to revalue at the intervals required by the law.

There are two reform directions that countries might take to address this problem. One is to invest significant resources in correcting the present undervaluation and addressing the irregular revaluations. The other is to rethink whether a value-based tax is feasible if they do not have adequate valuation capacity. The latter has particular appeal as a short-term solution.

Collection rate and enforcement: As Keen (2012, 23) points out, the "fundamental strengthening of revenue collection will be largely a matter of persistent and unspectacular effort." In many African countries, the low rate of revenue mobilization can be directly linked to low collection rates (20 percent for residential properties in Niamey, Niger, in 2007; less than 50 percent in Lusaka, Zambia, in 2011; and less than 70 percent in Dar es Salaam, Tanzania, between 2006 and 2011). Not surprisingly, any meaningful mobilization of the property tax will require that the primary focus of attention be on administration generally and on enforcement more specifically. Tax collection needs to be improved, whether the property tax is a local tax (as in most Anglophone countries) or a central-government tax (as in most Francophone and Lusophone countries).

An efficient, honest tax administration is both a cornerstone and an outcome of good governance and is likely to result in improved voluntary compliance (Fjeldstad and Semboja 2001; Mikesell and Birskyte 2007). Improved administration and compliance should result in increased revenue. Significant progress in billing and collection has been made in most countries in Africa. Improved payment options have reduced administration and especially taxpayers' compliance costs. Focusing on administration does not mean that policy choices are unimportant; policy and administration are inextricably linked. Important concerns such as political will, good governance, and voluntary compliance must be addressed from both policy and administration angles. But "due attention must be paid to the extent to which revenue is attributable to enforcement (the active intervention of the administration) rather than compliance (the relatively passive role of the administration as the recipient of revenues generated by other features of the system)" (Bird 2004, 135). In the end, it is the willingness of the government to enforce the tax that matters most in determining the revenue and the fairness of the tax. First and foremost, collection and enforcement are statutory obligations, as is clear from the example in box 36.4.

Lack of enforcement is the single most important reason that the property tax is not reaching its potential in most African countries. Collection levels are often appalling, and in some instances, councilors and officials are unwilling to pay the property taxes due on their own accounts. The instruments for tough enforcement are in place in nearly all African countries, but so far, most governments have been unwilling to use them. Especially the harsher enforcement mechanisms, even if they are on the statute book, are not used in practice. Governments in Africa need to become as enthusiastic about using enforcement measures as they are about giving preferential treatments. Although there may be administrative challenges in regard to some or all of the available mechanisms, the real solutions to the problem seem to have more to do with governance and trust. Strict enforcement against noncompliance is essential. If existing legislation does not provide for appropriate enforcement mechanisms, these should be introduced. However, local culture and political economy are relevant and need to be considered. Even in countries where collection levels have traditionally been very high, such as Namibia and South Africa, there seems to be cause for concern. Relevant bylaws, if any, should be amended, or bylaws should be introduced to facilitate enforcement through such measures as allowing for the issuance of tax liens, refusal to issue tax clearance certificates, cancellation of leasehold titles, foreclosure on the property of defaulters, seizure, and, as a last resort, public auction of the property in arrears.[2]

Last, the importance of communication between government (at all levels) and taxpayers cannot be overemphasized, as is illustrated by the smooth implementation of the land tax on commercial farmers in Namibia and the problematic aftermath of the 2012 revaluation. The lack of transparency and proper communication also bedeviled the implementation of the new property tax in Egypt and eventually resulted in significant base erosion through a value threshold in response to taxpayer concerns.

Recognize That a One-Size Property Tax Will Not Fit All Local Governments

The "one country, one tax base" model for the property tax is unsustainable. Reforms in Great Britain (1991), Northern Ireland (2007), and the Republic of Ireland (2013) have moved away from having only one base for the property tax. These reforms introduced capital value for residential property while retaining annual rental value for commercial and industrial properties. Clearly, in Africa, there are strong arguments for the use of more than one tax base. There may be active property markets in large urban areas but no

Box 36.4 Debt Collection and Credit Control in South Africa

A municipality has the responsibility to collect all money that is due and payable to it, subject to the law, and for this purpose it must adopt, maintain, and implement a credit-control and debt-collection policy that is consistent with its property tax and tariff policies and complies with the provisions of the law. A credit-control and debt-collection policy must provide for the following:

- Credit-control and debt-collection procedures and mechanisms.
- Provisions for indigent debtors that are consistent with its property tax and tariff policies and any national policy on indigents.
- Realistic targets consistent with generally recognized accounting practices and collection ratios and with revenue estimates set in the budget (less an acceptable provision for bad debts).
- Interest on arrears, where appropriate.
- Extensions of time for payment of accounts.
- Termination of services or restriction of the provision of services when payments are in arrears.
- Matters relating to unauthorized consumption of services, theft, and damages.
- Any other matters that may be prescribed by regulation.

A credit-control and debt-collection policy may differentiate between different categories of taxpayers, users of services, debtors, taxes, services, service standards, and other matters as long as the differentiation does not amount to unfair discrimination.

A municipality may (1) consolidate any separate accounts of a person liable for payments to the municipality; (2) credit a payment by such a person against any account of that person; and (3) implement any of the debt-collection and credit-control measures in relation to any arrears on any of the accounts of such a person.

A municipality may with the consent of a person liable to the municipality for the payment of property tax or other taxes, or fees for municipal services, enter into an agreement with that person's employer to deduct from the salary or wages of that person (1) any outstanding amounts due by that person to the municipality; or (2) such regular monthly amounts as may be agreed; and (3) provide special incentives for employers to enter into such agreements and employees to consent to such agreements.

The minister may make regulations or issue guidelines to provide for or regulate the action that may be taken by municipalities and service providers to secure payment of accounts that are in arrears, including (1) the termination of municipal services or the restriction of the provision of services; (2) the seizure of property; (3) the attachment of rent payable on a property; and (4) the extension of liability to a director, a trustee, or a member if the debtor is a company, a trust, or a close corporation.

Source: Local Government: Municipal Systems Act 32 of 2000.

market in smaller urban and rural areas (Botswana, Kenya, Mozambique, Namibia, and Tanzania). This argues for basing the property tax on value in large urban areas while using less sophisticated nonvalue bases in rural areas, as is already done in many Francophone countries.

Differentiation is already beginning to take place. The law in Kenya allows for up to four bases, although it is uncertain whether it still applies after the 2013 county elections. Niger values residential property on a different basis than commercial property. Most Francophone countries have different taxes (in most instances with different bases) for developed and undeveloped land. Agricultural and rural land provides a good example of property where an area basis could be used. However, where the law does not presently allow for different options (e.g., South Africa and Uganda), new legislation would be required to enable local governments to choose among various options.

Even in rural areas, land titling and registration processes are making significant inroads to provide security of tenure (Mozambique and Rwanda are good examples). However, although first registrations are being achieved, it is essential that subsequent changes in ownership also be captured and registered. The high costs of registration (including high transfer taxes in many instances) and lack of accessibility to land registry offices are impediments to ensuring that registries are properly maintained and remain current. From a property tax perspective, rural areas with high levels of traditional and customary land holdings should be treated differently from urban areas. These are generally areas of low property value where subsistence agriculture predominates. If a property tax is deemed feasible and justifiable in rural areas, it should be based on a structure with low administrative costs, probably area or rudimentary land value zones.

Monitor Property Tax Performance

Fiscal systems in many African countries are centralized. There is a trend toward fiscal decentralization in the Anglophone countries, but it is still in an early stage. The move toward a more viable property tax supports this fiscal decentralization strategy because the tax is so suitable for local governments. But until local-government fiscal autonomy is more developed, the central government will need to monitor the performance of the property tax. This monitoring will serve two purposes. First, it will track the performance of the property tax for all local governments; that is, it will evaluate revenue performance and various aspects of tax administration, such as collection rates, arrears, and coverage rates. This performance evaluation will also track exemptions and other preferences and their costs. Second, it will identify areas where local authorities (and some central-government departments) need technical assistance in improving property tax performance. This might include troubleshooting with respect to administrative procedures, training, automation, and the like.

Successful property tax monitoring will require a unit, probably in the Ministry of Finance, with a small staff that has expertise in property taxation. This unit can then draw on a network of academics, valuers, tax administrators, and other experts to carry out monitoring and technical assistance. It will also be responsible for preparing and updating statistics on property tax performance for all local governments in order to conduct and publish an annual benchmarking exercise.

The Valuation Problem

A sustainable value-based property tax requires a functioning property market and a capacity to value property. Most African countries have neither. A value-based property tax relies on evidence from market transactions to determine assessed values. Property markets in many African countries are immature, lack transparency, and usually operate only in the more developed urban areas. The lack of property registration affects the number of formal transactions and reduces the evidence base used to assess property. There is progress in developing property markets across the continent, but it is slow. Even where the transactions base is present, valuers usually are not. Professional institutions such as those in Zimbabwe and South Africa are active in setting and enforcing professional standards, but little is being done to produce more professional valuers. A few countries are making progress in this area (e.g., Kenya and Tanzania), but here also, the going is slow.

What is abundantly clear is that many value-based property tax systems are in serious administrative decline. To capitalize on the revenue potential of the property tax, more innovative, pragmatic solutions need to be found. The discrete parcel-by-parcel valuation of each parcel often prescribed by law is unsustainable, as is shown by the long intervals between revaluations (Ghana, Kenya, Tanzania, and Uganda). In many countries, valuation rolls are often extremely out of date (The Gambia, Kenya, Lesotho, Uganda, and Zambia; South Africa is an exception). This undermines the buoyancy of the tax base and also the fairness and legitimacy of the property tax (Franzsen and McCluskey 2005; Mutema 2016). A value-based property tax is ideal in theory, but in some instances, it may be necessary for theory to take a back seat and to allow for pragmatism to assist in shaping an appropriate tax base. Simpler solutions are required that can be practically administered, particularly by subnational governments.

Simplified valuation approaches should be adopted for property tax purposes to account for the paucity of valuation skills, to minimize costs, and to produce tax rolls more regularly (Franzsen and McCluskey 2016). Councilors and finance officers should be trained in the new procedures for property assessment, and all stakeholders need a better understanding of the relationship among the tax base, the tax rate, and tax revenue.

In light of the problems with the current practice, one might ask why there is so much reliance on value-based taxes in Africa. The answer is probably somewhere between inertia and "this is the devil we know." Old habits and laws die slowly. Despite some obvious problems and the need for reform, many property tax systems still retain the legacies of colonial administrations (Gabon, Lesotho, and Uganda). However, there are countries, such as Cameroon, that have reformed their system to adopt a value-based property tax.

Area-Based Systems

Legislation in several countries provides for a value-based property tax, but in practice, a system that is not based on value can be a pragmatic solution. The area of land or buildings serves as the tax base in some districts in Sierra Leone and some municipalities in Tanzania (so-called flat rates). In The Gambia, building costs are preferred to property values as the tax base. In Tanzania and Ghana, where only buildings are taxable, depreciated replacement costs are used. This is an example of a solution for the lack of valuation resources. Area-based approaches are also used in Burundi, the Democratic Republic of the Congo, Eritrea, and Sudan.

The land use charge (LUC) in Mozambique recognizes that the use of land has economic value. Although land, according to government policy, has no value, what clearly has monetary value is the use of the land, either existing or potential, and its location. The assessment methodology of the LUC is very simple. Only three objective variables are taken into account: the use of the land, its location, and its area (table 36.2).

Table 36.2 The Land Use Charge in Mozambique

Parcel Use	LUC (MZN)/Hectare
Nonagricultural land	75
Agricultural land	37.5
Cattle farming	5
Wildlife farming	5
Permanent crops	5
Land up to 1 ha within 3 km of coastline	500

Source: Based on Ministerial Diploma 144/2010 and Land Law of Mozambique, 1997.

Such adjusted area-based systems could provide the short- to medium-term answer for countries with poorly developed property markets and limited capacity and skills. Buoyancy under these two options could be addressed by regular revision and adjustments of the multipliers for characteristics such as location, size, age, and quality. Neither requires individual parcel valuation or frequent revaluations. These approaches can produce revenues, but they also can present challenges. One challenge is determining the area or size of the building or parcel. There are different codes of measuring practice applied to different property types (RICS 2007). The adjustment factors should also be based on some objective measure that can be tested. Unit-area values and flat rates are discussed in box 36.5 and box 36.6.

Box 36.5 The Unit-Area Approach in New Delhi, India

The New Delhi Municipal Corporation uses a unit-area assessment approach. The corporation moved to this simplified methodology in response to problems in applying its previous value-based property tax, based on annual rental value. The New Delhi Municipal Corporation uses the following formula to calculate annual value:

Annual value = unit-area value × covered area × multiplicative factors.

Unit-area values are determined in reference to eight categories (zones) from A to H. Category D constitutes the base unit-area value. For categories E to H, multiplicative factors of less than 1.0 are used; for categories A to C, these factors are greater than 1.0. The prescribed unit-area values for Delhi are provided in the table below.

Unit-Area Values

Category	Unit-Area Value (Rupees per M²)	Category	Unit-Area Value (Rupees per M²)
A	630	E	270
B	500	F	230
C	400	G	200
D	320	H	100

The 2011 tax rates on the annual value of vacant land or covered space of the building for the respective categories were as follows: for residential property, 10 percent for categories A to E and 6 percent for categories F to H; for nonresidential property, 10 percent for all categories.

The assessment value is based on specific physical characteristics of the property, such as location, size, use, and age (of buildings). The data requirements for administering an area-based system are less than for a value-based approach. Additional property characteristics can be incorporated as adjustment factors in order to try to have a closer proxy to value.

The Multiplicative Adjustment Factors

Occupancy Factor (Residential)	Factor	Structure	Factor	Age	Factor	Use	Factor
Owner-occupied	1.0	Pucca	1.0	After 2000	1.0	Medical institutions, religious purposes, schools	1.0
Tenanted	2.0	Semipucca	0.7	1990–2000	0.9	Industrial (vacant), utilities, telecommunication	2.0
		Kutcha	0.5	1980–1990	0.8	Industrial (occupied), museums, theaters	3.0
				1970–1980	0.7	Business, retail	4.0
				1960–1970	0.6	Hotels, towers	10.0
				Before 1960	0.5		

For example, in 2011, an owner-occupied 200 m² business property of good-quality material built in 1995 with a unit-area value of 500 rupees per m² would pay property tax as follows:

$$\text{Annual value} = 500 \times 200 \times [1.0 \text{ (occupation)} \times 1.0 \text{ (quality)} \times 0.9 \text{ (age)}$$
$$\times 4.0 \text{ (use)}] \times 10\%$$
$$= 360{,}000 \times 10\%$$
$$= 36{,}000.$$

Sources: The Delhi Municipal Corporation (Amendment) Act, 2003, read with the Delhi Municipal Corporation (Property Tax) Bye-laws, 2003.

Box 36.6 Flat-Rate Taxation in Tanzania: An Interim Solution?

If a property is not valued and included on a valuation roll, it is liable for flat rates. In this context, flat rates are a simplified property-based tax used by some local-government areas and implemented through a bylaw. Properties liable to flat rates are not valued as such but are assessed a tax amount based on such factors as property use, location, and size. The process of applying flat rates is nontechnical.

Given the large number of properties and the lack of valuers within some local-government authorities, flat rates are seen as a viable alternative to value-based taxation. The Arusha City Council and the Temeke Municipal Council use both value rating and flat rating. The table illustrates how the flat rating system works in Temeke. The bylaw specifies the various property types of varying sizes and the prescribed flat rates that are levied. Only two variables need to be obtained, the use of the property and some measure of size, such as square meters, the number of beds (for hotels and guesthouses), or the number of seats (for cinemas).

Description of Ratable Property	Gross External Area	Flat-Rates Assessment
Commercial–prime	Up to 50 m²	75,000
Commercial–prime	Over 50 m²	45,000
Hotel	Up to 10 beds	75,000
Hotel	Over 20 beds	200,000
Bank	Main branch	1,000,000

In Arusha, only 7,000 properties of an estimated total of 80,000 are on the valuation roll. The city has been using students to inspect properties for flat rates and increased the number of properties on the tax roll to over 25,000 in only two months. The program began in January 2016, and the city council was confident that full coverage would be achieved by June 2016.

It is estimated that a property liable to flat rates will have a tax bill approximately 50 percent lower than that which could be charged if the property were to be valued. Thus, operating a flat-rate system in parallel with a value-based system violates the principle of horizontal equity. In the long run, there is a financial benefit to valuing all taxable properties and to moving all flat-rate properties to the valuation roll. However, the flat-rate system seems to be a pragmatic short-term measure to identify and record taxable properties and thereby broaden the tax base.

Value Banding

Another option that countries with functioning property markets could consider, at least in urban areas, is value banding (McCluskey and Franzsen 2013a). It is currently used only in Great Britain (since 1993) and the Republic of Ireland (since 2013). Under this approach, each property is placed in a value band (interval) based on available evidence about that property. All properties in a band have the same tax liability, and a property moves to another band only at the time of a general revaluation. Value banding has a number of advantages. It requires less information and less expertise on the part of tax administrators. Consequently, it is less expensive to implement and maintain than a fully discrete capital market value system. Because there is less precision in valuation, there are fewer grounds to dispute a valuation and therefore fewer objections and appeals from taxpayers (UN-Habitat 2011). Because properties are not individually valued, revaluations are needed less frequently. Depending on the width of the bands, a property value can often increase or decrease within the same band. It is only when values have moved beyond the upper or lower limit of the band or across several bands that a revaluation should be considered, but the revaluation process is relatively quick and inexpensive because it does not require the discrete valuation of all parcels. Another advantage is that the political role of assigning the legal tax rate is separated from the valuation question. The banding approach may be well suited for African countries with limited valuation capability. The major problem is whether there is enough evidence to assign all properties to a specific value band. It is noteworthy that although value banding is not used in practice in Africa, it is at least mentioned in the property tax laws of South Africa and Uganda.

Self-Declaration

Where there is a paucity of valuation expertise, self-declaration may be a pragmatic option. The government's role then becomes the traditional tax authority role of auditing rather than assessing. However, subjectivity in the declarations, and therefore horizontal equity, will be a problem. The limited valuation capacity in the government may also hinder oversight. Liberia and Rwanda have started down this road, and their progress should be watched. Self-assessment has been quite successful in some Indian cities, notably Bangalore and New Delhi (Rao 2008), as well as in Ireland. Self-declaration of property holdings is common across Francophone Africa, but self-declaration of values is less common. The basic problem is how governments are to verify the accuracy of the self-declared values.

Mass Appraisal

Mass assessment that is based on a simplified database algorithm can be an effective methodology to reassess many properties at the same time. It is not a direct value-based approach but uses tables that contain the assessment parameters, such as size, use, age, and location. Each property is linked to a table that gives the relative value for a particular parameter. The final computation is the assessed value of the property. This system is used in Mozambique and Tanzania.

Computer-Assisted Mass Appraisal

The appraisal community has developed computer-assisted mass appraisal (CAMA), which uses statistically based predictive models to determine assessments. A CAMA model can be more accurately described as an automated valuation model. A hedonic index of prices for real properties is developed by linking actual sales prices to the location and physical characteristics of the property. A regression equation is used to develop the index and then to calculate an estimated price for all properties that have not sold (Eckert 2008). This approach is used to assist assessments in North America and is also used to a limited extent in some middle-income and low-income countries. In Africa, it is encountered in Cape Town, South Africa, and in two pilot areas in Cairo, Egypt.

It is easy to see why some low-income countries have become so excited about CAMA. It appears to bypass much of the expensive legwork involved in developing a cadastre and assessing all properties. But for most low-income countries in Africa, CAMA may be an idea that is too good to be true. The basic problem is that the model requires accurate data on sales prices for real property, which few African countries have. The dependent variable that most analysts use (or propose to use) in developing a CAMA system is owner declaration of the sales price at the time of transfer, but this declaration varies according to the seller's subjective determination of how much he can understate the sales price without being audited.[3] In most low-income countries, there is no reason to expect that this is a good proxy for market value. The second problem is that these estimated values are used only to assist the process and do not fully replace the need for trained valuers.

Prospects

If African countries do what is required to improve the practice of property taxation, the result will likely be more revenue mobilization and more efficient property markets, both of which will stimulate economic growth. But the track record of tax reform in Africa has not been good, overall revenue mobilization lags behind that in other regions, and revenues raised from the property tax are very low. Time and urbanization might eventually heal these problems, but well-thought-out reform programs can speed up progress. The prospects for successful reform of the property tax can be evaluated by asking three questions:

- What incentives would make African countries willing to bear the political and economic costs of property tax reform?

- What would be the elements of successful property tax reform in Africa?

- Have past reforms of the property tax been successful?

Incentives

There are a number of incentives for African countries to reform their property tax regimes. The costs of urbanization are high and growing. Central and subnational governments need more revenue to cope with these costs, and central governments want to reduce transfers to local governments. The mobilization of increased property tax revenues to finance local public services can achieve both of these goals. The property tax has good potential for revenue mobilization, especially in rapidly growing urban areas in many African countries. Growth in the property tax base also can recapture some of the value of location-specific capital investments and benefits from government programs and services not captured otherwise through various fees, user charges, and taxes (Kelly 2014).

The creation of a modern property tax will also entail identification and registration of all properties, which will be a big step toward formalizing the land market. If land markets work well, land will be mobile between uses and will be allocated more efficiently (World Bank 2009, 22–23). This can help remove important impediments to urban economic growth, housing, and finance and can facilitate effective urban planning. Finally, a well-functioning property tax is a natural choice for a local-government revenue source in a fiscally decentralized system and can spur the devolution of functions.

The benefits seem clear enough, but they may not be sufficient to stimulate reform. There are also negative aspects of property taxes that work against reform. In Africa, as in the rest of the world, they are unpopular with taxpayers and therefore with politicians. They are expensive to administer properly and demand skills in valuation that many African countries do not have. In some cases, the costs of good administration may outweigh the revenue to be realized. Finally, the availability of significant intergovernmental transfers to subnational governments can dampen the demand for property tax reform by local government taxpayers and politicians. In any case, revenue decentralization has not been a major policy thrust in African countries.

The Elements of Property Tax Reform

Property tax reform can mean many things, ranging from large structural and administrative changes to small tweaks of the operation of property tax systems. Some of these changes directly affect revenues and tax burdens (reduction in legal exemptions and the use of stronger enforcement measures), but others are only intermediate steps to increased revenues (training of valuers, better valuation practices, registration of properties). In a sense, any changes in the property tax regime currently mandated in the law or regulations constitute reform.

Property tax reform is reminiscent of the old saying about pornography: we cannot define it, but we know it when we see it. No doubt, the introduction of a recurrent property tax in Burkina Faso and Seychelles would constitute reform. At the other end of the scale, a general revaluation or an amendment of the tax rate(s) is already provided for in the tax law and has more to do with implementation than reform. In contrast, changing the statutory valuation cycle from five to ten years, as has been done in Kenya and Zimbabwe, may be perceived as a procedurally minor amendment of the law, but it has significant implications, both positive and negative, and can be seen as a policy reform. There are other gray areas, such as a more efficient registration system for properties, university programs for valuation, replacing manual records with computerized systems, and properly codifying enforcement measures.

Reforms do not always improve the property tax. Some may be quite good, some may be quite poor, and some may be a mixed bag. The 2004 national law in South Africa heralded a new regime, replacing provincial laws allowing local municipal choice of one of three possible tax bases with a single, uniform tax base across all municipalities, whether large or small and whether predominantly urban or rural. The result has been increased revenues but less local choice in property tax practice. In contrast, the 2005 law in Uganda retained most of the important principles of the law it replaced; the changes were cosmetic rather than reconstructive. Reforms can also be reversed. Egypt improved its system with reforms in 2008 but dismantled these reforms in 2014.

If we interpret the term broadly, property tax reform has occurred in more than half of the 54 African countries since 1995 (table 36.3). In many instances, these reforms were quite extensive, for example, in Egypt, Mauritius, Mozambique, Rwanda, Senegal, Sierra Leone, and South

Table 36.3 Property Tax Reforms in Africa

1995-2000	2001-2010	2011-2016
Cape Verde	Cameroon	Ethiopia
Gabon	Central African Republic	Lesotho
Liberia	Congo	Kenya[1]
Malawi	Egypt	Nigeria (Abuja Capital Territory)
Swaziland	Gabon	Rwanda[2]
Zambia	Madagascar	Somalia (Puntland)
	Mauritius	South Africa[3]
	Mozambique	Zimbabwe (Harare)
	Namibia	
	Nigeria (Lagos State)	
	Rwanda[2]	
	Senegal	
	Sierra Leone	
	South Africa[3]	
	Tanzania[4]	
	Uganda	

Sources: Fjeldstad and Heggstad (2012); Franzsen (2014).

[1] The creation of new local government structures in Kenya in 2013 and the lack of constitutional clarity regarding legislative responsibility for property taxation will likely have far-reaching implications.

[2] After the decentralization of the property tax in Rwanda in 2005, the base was effectively changed, and self-assessment was introduced in 2015.

[3] In South Africa, a new law comprehensively reforming the property tax system was implemented in 2005. Significant amendments amounting to further reform were implemented in 2015.

[4] The amendments in Tanzania were mostly administrative.

Africa. Less extensive reforms occurred in Cabo Verde, Tanzania, Uganda, and Zambia, although in some cases (e.g., Uganda), a new law was passed.

Evaluation of Property Tax Reforms in Africa

Property tax reforms have multiple outcomes. The shift to a new base may enable easier and more frequent revaluations, but it can lead to unfairness in taxing smaller, more expensive residences at a lower rate than larger, less expensive residences. Lowering the threshold value for property taxation may increase revenues but also increase the regressivity of the property tax. This raises the difficult question of how the impact of property tax reform can be evaluated.

We offer three guidelines for determining whether a property tax reform is successful. The first is whether the goals or targets of the reform were clear, and whether they were achieved. Examples of successes and failures in Africa can illustrate the importance of clear objectives.

Rwanda introduced a universal registration system with the goal of improving the formality of the land market. Full registration of titles (leasehold and freehold) has been achieved, even though property tax revenue will not directly increase. A program in Arusha, Tanzania, stated the goal of increasing the number of properties liable to both rates and flat rates in order to achieve full coverage of all properties by July 2016.

In contrast, the property tax in Egypt has been the subject of reform since the early years of the 21st century, but the objectives have not necessarily been clear or generally agreed to. The government successfully rationalized several outdated property-related taxes when it enacted the real estate tax in 2008. However, because of a lack of transparency, political pressures, and internal civil conflicts, implementation of the reform package was stalled. New legislation was passed in 2014 that introduced significant exemptions, including hotels, and raised the threshold for taxable residential property. Most of the revenue gains foreseen in the 2008 policy change were lost.

The second marker for success is whether all the related elements of the reform were included in the package of changes to be implemented. Success in improving the mobilization of property tax revenue requires getting all the pieces on the table: coverage of the base, automated record keeping, valuation, and collection. If one step is missing, the revenue objective will be compromised.

There are many examples of African countries that have missed a step, notably The Gambia and Kenya. Francophone countries generally rely on self-declaration of property values, with the result that the tax base is greatly understated and revenues underperform. But there is no effective monitoring system to verify the accuracy of declared values. Arusha and Mtwara, Tanzania, have taken pragmatic steps to get as many properties as possible recorded in the property tax system by assessing flat rates (see box 36.6). However, enforcement continues to be lax, and collection rates are low.

Third, a property tax reform can be viewed as successful if taxpayers understand it and accept it as fair. The result may be an increase in revenues and in voluntary compliance.

South Africa's property tax reform, unlike Egypt's, was managed in a transparent and politically accountable manner. The tax base eventually chosen was market value, to be applied uniformly across all property use categories in urban and rural areas. The broad base extended to many properties not formerly taxed, most noticeably commercial farms. Effective measures were enacted to mitigate the impact on bona fide farmers and other vulnerable use or ownership categories. Revenues increased dramatically, so seemingly the reform was successful. However, there are still concerns. Was the extension of a market value tax to local municipalities with predominantly communal land a success? This is an important policy matter that needs to be reexamined. On the administrative side, the procurement of private-sector valuation services and the lack of professional oversight are issues to be revisited.

The introduction of an earmarked land tax on commercial farms in Namibia was a resounding success. Policies were well designed, property owners were consulted and kept informed, and the eventual legislation was professionally drafted. The small numbers of objections to the first (2002) and second (2007) provisional valuation rolls suggest broad acceptance of the quality of the valuations, and the tax rates that were set resulted in tax liabilities that the commercial farming community generally accepted. Problems emerged when the 2012 provisional valuation roll was published. Values of farms increased dramatically, and there was no indication that the government was going to adjust the tax rates accordingly. Objections increased from less than 2 percent in 2007 to more than 21 percent. The High Court ruled that because of various administrative lapses, the valuation court was not lawfully constituted, and somewhat abruptly, the whole process was put on hold. The important lesson is that the government cannot rest on its laurels once the tax has seemingly been implemented successfully. The system's credibility must be maintained through proper administrative practices, but more important, politicians need to remain cognizant of realities and respond accordingly.

Finally, property tax policy may be affected by other reforms. Kenya did not embark on property tax reform as such. However, this country's far-reaching constitutional and institutional reforms by default significantly affect a property tax system that is regulated by two national laws, the Rating Act and the Valuation for Rating Act. There is uncertainty, rooted in the 2010 constitution, whether these acts still apply to the 47 new counties, or whether counties can enact their own property tax laws. Meanwhile, the Nairobi City County has passed its own property tax law, largely based on the two national acts. In short, Kenya's property tax was already beset by serious administrative problems and political interference, but it now faces a much more severe and potentially damaging policy challenge: deciding who has the power to determine the tax base and who has the responsibility to regulate and oversee municipal valuations.

Recommendations

The property tax has been maligned for years (in most cases rightfully so) as a badly administered tax that has not lived up to its potential in developing countries.[4] In African countries, this may have been a self-fulfilling prophecy. The property tax raises little revenue because it is badly structured and administered. Governments have continued to neglect administration of the property tax and have ravaged its base by preferential treatments, with the result that it has fallen into even more disrepair. Taxpayers have lost confidence that it is a fair tax, and few politicians are interested in championing it. Most of the proposals for reform that are seen nowadays are the same tired and safe recommendations that have been around for years: revalue more accurately and collect better. This remains good advice, but it does not seem to go anywhere. Almost everybody says it, but few do it.

Is there a way out of this state of affairs, or is the best course to move to other sources of financing local public services? We take the view that there is a way forward for the property tax. Although there is no one size that fits all in property tax reform in Africa, there are some basic principles that, in many African countries, might show the way to a more sustainable property tax. There are also a few bad practices where one size really does fit all. Steps toward sustainable property tax reform include the following.

Decide what roles the property tax will play in national development policy. Should it emphasize revenue mobilization, focus on horizontal equity, tax property wealth, stimulate more intensive use of land, form an integral part of a fiscal decentralization strategy, or promote some combination of these? The government should begin the effort by thoroughly analyzing the existing property tax and determining how it is out of step with the economic development goals of the country.[5] The result could be a white paper on property tax reform that provides a road map for policy and administrative actions.

Find a champion. Not many politicians will want to play this part, but those who are strong advocates of fiscal decentralization will be more sympathetic to strengthening the property tax as a source of local-government revenue. As urbanization increases public expenditure needs, the property tax may find more advocates than it has had in the past. Property tax reform as a plank in the decentralization strategy should be a less difficult sell than simply stating that the property tax is a good local tax (Kelly 2014).

Audit the legal underpinnings of the property tax—the constitution, the property tax laws, and the implementing regulations—to make sure that the definition and coverage of the tax base and the tax rate structure are clear and appropriate. Redrafting the laws may be required.[6]

If the goal is to support fiscal decentralization, develop an overall strategy, including laws and incentives that will cause local governments to make more intensive use of the property tax. The most powerful way to do this is to reduce intergovernmental transfers to local governments with significant property tax revenue potential. This might be accompanied by a combination of revisions in the intergovernmental transfer formula and significant rewards in the transfer system for local governments that raise their property tax revenues above a threshold level.

Divide property tax administration appropriately between the higher and lower levels of government. This division should be based on comparative advantage, particularly with respect to who handles the maintenance and upgrading of the cadastre, property transfers, and valuation. The weaker the local-government capacity, the stronger the case for centralizing these responsibilities.

Upgrade the infrastructure of property tax administration. Governments should develop a system that generates and records accurate information on property transactions. This information is essential for developing the value map that underlies good assessment practice. Advances in technology, such as CAMA and GISs, can be especially useful for valuation and assessment. Replacing the property transfer tax with a capital gains tax on real property could remove an impediment to accurate self-reporting of transaction amounts. An alternative approach is to lower the rate of the transfer tax and aggressively check declared sales values. It may also be feasible to merge the administration of the recurrent property tax and the property transfer tax.

Align the structure of the property tax with the goals that have been set for it. The reform should focus on broadening the tax base, removing preferential treatments, and simplifying the tax. In most cases, this will require a new law. Exemption policy should be reviewed and revised. Exemptions should be minimized because a broad-based property tax better serves equity goals. Low-income housing might usefully be exempt or assigned a lower burden, but the practice of exempting owner-occupied property and government property and providing special exemptions should be rethought. At a minimum, all exemptions should be reviewed periodically, the revenue forgone should be annually calculated and reported, and a sunset period should be set to review every exemption. Preferential treatments become entitlements that are hard to get rid of. Beware of fiscal engineers who have plans to stimulate desired actions by reducing property tax liability. Graduated property tax rate structures and classification systems complicate the administration of the tax and can introduce unwanted distortions. A better approach would be a flat rate with a floor exemption, no classification, and accurate valuation of the base.

Review collection and enforcement practices. Low collection rates are an important constraint on revenues. Tougher enforcement and a more realistic set of penalties are likely to be more effective in raising property tax revenues than attempts to create a more "friendly" property tax.

In most African countries, concentrate reform and revenue-mobilization efforts on the largest cities. The tax base is larger there, the administrative machinery is usually better, and the local public financing needs are greater. Smaller governments and rural areas are important, but a more rudimentary form of the property tax can be more successful in them. These governments will in any case remain more dependent on intergovernmental transfers.

A more far-reaching idea: change the focus of the reform to the creation of a comprehensive system for taxing all land and real property. In the present system of property and land taxation in most developing countries, the annual use of urban property is subject to one rate schedule, agricultural use to another, gains from the sale of property to a third, and so on. A plausible idea is to begin moving this system toward one that taxes a more uniform base. The result could be an increase in the revenue yield from property taxes to a level that could justify significant increases in administrative expenditures.

Finally, recognize that developing and transitioning countries cannot move immediately to the practices of industrialized countries. They need to develop a long-term plan for improved property taxation and implement it over a period of years. The timing of changes is important. The best route to success is to plan a transition that allows the tax administration to catch up and taxpayers to get used to the new system.

Conclusions

Theory suggests that the property tax is a good local tax. Moreover, almost all countries across the world use it (Almy 2016). However, the property tax is notoriously difficult to administer and maintain and is wildly unpopular. This raises the question: Should we bother with it at all? Our short answer is yes, but the medium-term focus should be on urban centers, higher-value properties, and more affluent taxpayers. Well-targeted relief must ensure that valuers and tax collectors do not waste time and effort on thousands of low-value properties and poor taxpayers, but it also must ensure that the relief is counterbalanced by taxing those with the ability to pay for local public services.

The priority must be to improve collection, tax base coverage, and valuation, preferably in that order. In most, if not all, of the countries reviewed, collection and enforcement were the weakest links in property tax administration. A collection-led strategy deserves special consideration (Kelly 2000, 2014), such as the revenue-enhancement reform in Kampala, Uganda. Strategies that focus on valuation have generally not been successful in Africa and elsewhere (Kelly 2014). Without an effective collection and enforcement system, there is little to be gained from increasing the coverage and valuation components, both of which can be costly, as is clear in Egypt, South Africa, Tanzania, and Uganda.

Enforcing a tax system, is difficult, especially in the dynamic environments in developing countries. However, unless this task is approached fairly, efficiently, and consistently, even a well-designed tax system will fail to produce good results (Bird and Zolt 2003). Arguably the greatest failing of the property tax in Africa is the unwillingness of governments to enforce it. Implementing a well-designed and well-administered property tax is an investment that the countries of Africa can ill afford to ignore.

Notes

1. However, a serious concern is that although urbanization in developing countries has proceeded faster than in developed countries, the correlation of the rate of urbanization with economic growth has been weaker (United Nations 2014).

2. Bylaws can deal only with issues provided for in the law. In countries where the property tax is contained in the tax code or the revenue code, which is often the case in Francophone Africa, all the enforcement mechanisms mentioned in the code may be available to the authority (be it the local government or the central government's revenue authority) responsible for collecting the tax and enforcing its payment.

3. Declared transaction values supplied to the stamp duty office could be supplemented with expert judgment and other evidence of land values (e.g., bank mortgage information and real estate listings), just as they are when property values are assessed under an improved capital value system. However, there is limited evidence, except in South Africa and Zambia, that this happens in practice. The expectation in most countries is considerable underassessment.

4. This section has benefited from the discussion in Bahl and Bird (forthcoming).

5. Some examples of property tax reviews are those sponsored in Pakistan (Bahl, Cyan, and Wallace 2015) and Tanzania (McCluskey et al. 2003) by the World Bank, in Macedonia and Montenegro by the U.S. Agency for International Development (USAID 2006), in Jamaica by Inter-American Development Bank (IADB) (Sjoquist 2005), and in India (Mathur, Thakur, and Rajadhyasksha 2009). See also Bird and Slack (2004, chapter 3), and Bahl and Bird (forthcoming).

6. The property tax reform in South Africa is an example. Giving effect to the 1993 constitution, the *White Paper on Local Government* (Government of South Africa 1998) was drafted, which eventually culminated in the current property tax law.

References

Allen, E. 2016. "How the Merger of Four Land Related Departments Improved Land Governance in Jamaica." Paper presented at the CARTAC Seminar on Property Taxation in the Caribbean Region (February 15–18).

Almy, R. 2016. "Effective and Sustainable Systems for Valuing Property for Taxation: A Comparison." Paper for the 17th Annual World Bank Conference on Land Policy and Poverty, Washington, DC (March 14–17).

Bahl, R. W. 2009. "Property Tax Reform in Developing and Transition Countries." Working paper. Washington, DC: USAID.

Bahl, R. W., and R. Bird. 2008. "Subnational Taxes in Developing Countries: The Way Forward." *Public Budgeting and Finance* 28(4): 1–25.

———. Forthcoming. *Fiscal Decentralization in Developing Countries.* Cheltenham, UK: Edward Elgar.

Bahl, R. W., M. Cyan, and S. Wallace. 2015. "Underutilized Land and Property Taxes." In *The Role of Taxation in Pakistan's Economic Revival*, ed. J. Martinez-Vazquez and M. Cyan, chapter 8. Oxford: Oxford University Press.

Bird, R. M. 2004. "Administrative Dimensions of Tax Reform." *Asia-Pacific Tax Bulletin*, March, 134–150.

Bird, R. M., and O. Oldman. 1990. *Taxation in Developing Countries.* Baltimore: Johns Hopkins University Press.

Bird, R. M., and E. Slack. 2003. "Land and Property Taxation Around the World: A Review." *Journal of Property Tax Assessment and Administration* 7(3): 31–79.

———, eds. 2004. *International Handbook of Land and Property Taxation.* Cheltenham, UK: Edward Elgar.

Bird, R. M., and E. Zolt. 2003. "Introduction to Tax Policy Design and Development." Notes for the course Practical Issues of Tax Policy in Developing Countries, World Bank. *http://www1.worldbank.org/publicsector/LearningProgram/PracticalIssues/papers /introduction%20to%20tax%20policy/WBI%20Module%201(Bird&Zolt)April10.doc.*

City of Cape Town. 2016. Valuation Department.

De Cesare, C. 2004. "General Characteristics of Property Tax Systems in Latin America." Paper presented at the Seventh International Conference of the International Property Tax Institute on Optimizing Property Tax Systems in Latin American, Guadalajara, Jalisco, Mexico (September 28–October 1).

DFPNI (Department of Finance and Personnel, Northern Ireland). 2002. *Review of Rating Policy.* Department of Finance and Personnel, Rating Policy Division, Belfast, Northern Ireland.

Dillinger, W. 1991. "Urban Property Tax Reform: Guidelines and Recommendations." Urban Management and Municipal Finance. Washington, DC: World Bank.

DoE (Department of the Environment). 1991. *The New Tax for Local Government: A Consultation Paper.* London.

Durand-Lasserve, A. 2016. "Why Should Urban Issues Be Integrated in African Land Policies?" Paper for the 17th Annual World Bank Conference on Land Policy and Poverty, Washington, DC (March 14–17).

Eckert, J. 2008. "Computer Assisted Mass Appraisal Options for Developing Countries." In *Making the Property Tax Work: Experiences in Developing and Transitional*

Countries, ed. R. W. Bahl, J. Martinez-Vazquez, and J. M. Youngman, 207–228. Cambridge, MA: Lincoln Institute of Land Policy.

Fjeldstad, O.-H., and K. Heggstad. 2012. "Local Government Revenue Mobilisation in Anglophone Africa." CMI Working Paper WP 2012:6. Bergen, Norway: Chr. Michelsen Institute.

Fjeldstad, O.-H., and J. Semboja. 2001. "Why People Pay Taxes: The Case of the Development Levy in Tanzania." *World Development* 29(12): 2059–2074.

Franzsen, R. C. D. 2003. "Property Taxation Within the Southern African Development Community (SADC): Current Status and Future Prospects of Land Value Taxation, Botswana, Lesotho, Namibia, South Africa and Swaziland." Working paper WP03RF1. Cambridge, MA: Lincoln Institute of Land Policy.

———. 2014. "Recurrent Property Taxes in Africa: Policy Issues and Administrative Challenges." Guest lecture presented at Stellenbosch University (September 1).

Franzsen, R. C. D., and W. J. McCluskey. 2005. "Ad Valorem Property Taxation in Sub-Saharan Africa." *Journal of Property Tax Assessment & Administration* 2(2): 63–72.

———. 2016. "Alternative Approaches to Value-based Property Tax in Africa: An Exploratory View of Options." Paper for the Africa Tax Research Network Conference on Revenue Mobilisation, Seychelles (September 7–9).

Franzsen, R. C. D., and W. Welgemoed. 2011. "Submission on Proposed Amendments to the Municipal Property Rates Act (MPRA)." Unpublished report for the South African Local Government Association (June).

Government of South Africa. 1998. *White Paper on Local Government*. Pretoria: Government Printers.

Greenway, I. 2010. "Transforming Land and Property Services—Northern Ireland Learns from and Builds on the Australian Experience." Paper presented at the FIG Congress 2010, "Facing the Challenges—Building the Capacity," Sydney, Australia (April 11–16, 2010).

Holcombe, R. G. 1998. "Tax Policy from a Public Choice Perspective." *National Tax Journal* 51(2): 359–371.

Ingram, G., Z. Liu, and K. Brandt. 2013. "Metropolitan Infrastructure and Capital Finance." In *Metropolitan Government Finance in Developing Countries*, ed. R. Bahl, J. Linn, and D. Wetzel, 339–365. Cambridge, MA: Lincoln Institute of Land Policy.

IRRV (Institute of Revenues Rating and Valuation). 1997. *Principles for Local Government Finance*. London.

Keen, M. 2012. "Taxation and Development—Again." IMF working paper 12/220. Washington, DC: IMF.

Kelly, R. 2000. "Designing a Property Tax Strategy for Sub-Saharan Africa: An Analytical Framework Applied to Kenya." *Public Budgeting and Finance* 20(4): 36–51.

———. 2014. "Implementing Sustainable Property Tax Reform in Developing Countries." In *Taxation and Development: The Weakest Link? Essays in Honor of Roy Bahl*, ed. R. M. Bird and J. Martinez-Vazquez, 326–363. Cheltenham, UK: Edward Elgar.

McCluskey, W. J., and R. C. D. Franzsen. 2005. "An Evaluation of the Property Tax in Tanzania: An Untapped Fiscal Resource or Administrative Headache?" *Property Management* 23: 45–69.

———. 2013a. "Non–Market Value and Hybrid Approaches to Property Taxation." In *A Primer on Property Tax: Administration and Policy*, ed. W. J. McCluskey, G. C. Cornia, and L. C. Walters, 287–305. West Sussex: Wiley-Blackwell.

———. 2013b. "Property Taxes in Metropolitan Cities." In *Metropolitan Government Finance in Developing Countries*, ed. R. Bahl, J. Linn, and D. Wetzel, 159–181. Cambridge, MA: Lincoln Institute of Land Policy.

———. 2016. "Property Tax Reform in Africa: Challenges and Potential." Paper for the 17th Annual World Bank Conference on Land Policy and Poverty, Washington, DC (March 14–17).

McCluskey, W. J., R. Franzsen, T. Johnstone, and D. Johnstone. 2003. "Property Tax Reform: The Experience of Tanzania." *Our Common Estate*. London: RICS Foundation.

Mikesell, J. L., and L. Birskyte. 2007. "The Tax Compliance Puzzle: Evidence from Theory and Practice." *International Journal of Public Finance* 30: 1045–1081.

Moore, M. 2013. "Wanted Worldwide: Sensible Property Taxes, and a Property Tax Champion." *IDS Governance and Development Blog*. *www.governanceanddevelopment .com/2013/10/wanted-worldwide-sensible-property.html?utm_source=feedburner&utm _medium=email&utm_campaign=Feed%3A+GovernanceAndDevelopment+%28Gove rnance+and+Development%29*.

Mutema, M. 2016. "Property Valuation Challenges in Africa: The Case of Selected African Countries." Paper for the 17th Annual World Bank Conference on Land Policy and Poverty, Washington, DC (March 14–17).

Rao, U. A. V. 2008. "Is Area-Based Assessment an Alternative, an Intermediate Step, or an Impediment to Value-Based Taxation in India?" In *Making the Property Tax Work*, ed. R. W. Bahl, J. Martinez-Vazquez, and J. M. Youngman, 241–267. Cambridge, MA: Lincoln Institute of Land Policy.

RICS (Royal Institution of Chartered Surveyors). 2007. *Code of Measuring Practice*. 6th ed. London.

Rosengard, J. K. 2012. "The Tax Everyone Loves to Hate: Principles of Property Tax Reform." Cambridge, MA: Harvard University Kennedy School of Government.

Sjoquist, D. 2005. "The Land Value Tax in Jamaica: An Analysis and Options for Reform." *Bulletin for International Fiscal Documentation*, November, 489–497.

Smolka, M. 2013. "Implementing Value Capture in Latin America: Policies and Tools for Urban Development." Policy Focus Report. Cambridge, MA: Lincoln Institute of Land Policy.

UN-Habitat. 2004. "State of the World's Cities: Trends in Sub-Saharan Africa; Urbanization & Metropolitanization." *http://mirror.unhabitat.org/documents/media _centre/sowc/RegionalAfrica.pdf*.

———. 2005. "State of the World's Cities: Trends in Sub-Saharan Africa—Urbanization & Metropolitanization."

———. 2011. *Land and Property Tax—A Policy Guide*. Nairobi: United Nations Human Settlement Programme (Principal author: Lawrence Walters).

United Nations. 2014. World Urbanization Prospects. *https://esa.un.org/undp/wup/ Publications/Files/WUP2014-Report.pdf*.

USAID (U.S. Agency for International Development). 2006. *Reforming Property Taxation in Southeast Europe: A Comparative Review.* Fiscal Decentralization Initiative for Central and Eastern Europe. Budapest: Open Society Institute.

Viruly, F., and N. Hopkins. 2014. *Unleashing Sub-Saharan Africa Property Markets.* Report prepared for the Royal Institute of Chartered Surveyors. London: rics.org /research.

World Bank. 2009. *Reshaping Economic Geography.* World Development Report. Washington, DC.

Youngman, J. M. 2016. *A Good Tax.* Cambridge, MA: Lincoln Institute of Land Policy.

Legislation

Delhi Municipal Corporation (Amendment) Act, 2003 (India).

Delhi Municipal Corporation (Property Tax) Bye-laws, 2003 (India).

Land Law of Mozambique, 1997 (Mozambique).

Local Government: Municipal Property Rates Act of 2004 (South Africa).

Local Government: Municipal Systems Act 32 of 2000 (South Africa).

Ministerial Diploma 144/2010 (Mozambique).

Rating Act (Chapter 267) (Kenya).

Valuation for Rating Act (Chapter 266) (Kenya).

Appendix: Comparative Tables

Table A.1 Basic Country Statistics

Country	Capital City	Area (Km²)	Independence	Official Language(s)
Algeria	Algiers	2,381,741	1962	Arabic
Angola	Luanda	1,246,700	1975	Portuguese
Benin	Porto-Novo	112,622	1960	French
Botswana	Gaborone	581,730	1966	English
Burkina Faso	Ouagadougou	274,200	1960	French
Burundi	Bujumbura	27,830	1962	Kirundi and French
Cabo Verde	Praia	4,033	1975	Portuguese
Cameroon	Yaoundé	475,440	1960	English and French
Central African Republic	Bangui	622,984	1960	French
Chad	N'Djamena	1,284,000	1960	French and Arabic
Comoros	Moroni	2,235	1975	Arabic and French
Congo	Brazzaville	342,000	1960	French
Côte d'Ivoire	Yamoussoukro	322,463	1960	French
Democratic Republic of the Congo	Kinshasa	2,344,858	1960	French
Djibouti	Djibouti	23,200	1977	Arabic and French
Egypt	Cairo	1,001,450	1922	Arabic
Equatorial Guinea	Malabo	28,051	1968	Spanish and French
Eritrea	Asmara	117,600	1993	Tigrinya, Arabic, and English
Ethiopia	Addis Ababa	1,104,300	Est. first century B.C.	Amharic

Country	Capital	Area	Year	Language
Gabon	Libreville	267,667	1960	French
The Gambia	Banjul	11,295	1965	English
Ghana	Accra	238,533	1957	English
Guinea	Conakry	245,857	1958	French
Guinea-Bissau	Bissau	36,125	1973	Portuguese
Kenya	Nairobi	580,367	1963	English and Kiswahili
Lesotho	Maseru	30,355	1966	English and Sesotho
Liberia	Monrovia	111,369	1847	English
Libya	Tripoli	1,759,540	1951	Arabic
Madagascar	Antananarivo	587,041	1960	French and Malagasy
Malawi	Lilongwe	118,484	1964	English
Mali	Bamako	1,240,192	1960	French
Mauritania	Nouakchott	1,030,700	1960	Arabic
Mauritius	Port Louis	2,040	1968	English
Morocco	Rabat	446,550	1956	Arabic and Tamazight
Mozambique	Maputo	799,380	1975	Portuguese
Namibia	Windhoek	824,292	1990	English
Niger	Niamey	1,267,000	1960	French
Nigeria	Abuja	923,768	1960	English
Rwanda	Kigali	26,338	1962	Kinyarwanda
São Tomé and Príncipe	São Tomé	964	1975	Portuguese
Senegal	Dakar	196,722	1960	French
Seychelles	Victoria	455	1976	Seychellois Creole
Sierra Leone	Freetown	71,740	1961	English
Somalia	Mogadishu	637,657	1960	Somali

(continued)

Table A.1 Basic Country Statistics (*continued*)

Country	Capital City	Area (Km²)	Independence	Official Language(s)
South Africa	Pretoria	1,219,090	1961	Afrikaans, English, IsiNdebele, IsiXhosa, IsiZulu, Sepedi, Sesotho, Setswana, siSwati, Xitsonga, and Tshivenda
South Sudan	Juba	644,329	2011	English
Sudan	Khartoum	1,861,484	1956	Arabic and English
Swaziland	Mbabane	17,364	1968	English and siSwati
Tanzania	Dodoma	947,300	1964	Kiswahili and English
Togo	Lomé	56,785	1960	French
Tunisia	Tunis	163,610	1956	Arabic
Uganda	Kampala	241,038	1962	English
Western Sahara[1]	El Aarun	266,000	N/A	Arabic
Zambia	Lusaka	752,618	1964	English
Zimbabwe	Harare	390,757	1980	English

Source: Central Intelligence Agency, *The World Factbook 2016.*

[1] Western Sahara is included to provide a comprehensive overview of the whole African continent.

Table A.2 Population Statistics

Country	Population in millions (July 2015 Est.)	Urbanized Population Percentage (2014 Est.)	Per Capita GDP in USD (2015 Est.)	Income Level Based on GNI Per Capita (2016 Est.)
Algeria	39.67	71	4,206	Upper-middle-income
Angola	25.02	44	4,102	Upper-middle-income
Benin	10.88	44	762	Low-income
Botswana	2.26	57	6,360	Upper-middle-income
Burkina Faso	18.11	30	590	Low-income
Burundi	11.18	12	277	Low-income
Cabo Verde	0.52	66	3,080	Lower-middle-income
Cameroon	23.34	54	1,217	Lower-middle-income
Central African Republic	4.90	40	323	Low-income
Chad	14.04	22	776	Low-income
Comoros	0.79	28	717	Low-income
Congo	4.62	65	1,851	Lower-middle-income
Côte d'Ivoire	22.70	54	1,399	Lower-middle-income
Democratic Republic of the Congo	77.27	42	456	Low-income
Djibouti	0.89	77	1,945	Lower-middle-income
Egypt	91.51	43	3,615	Lower-middle-income
Equatorial Guinea	0.85	40	14,440	Upper-middle-income
Eritrea	5.23	22	544 (2011)	Low-income
Ethiopia	99.39	19	619	Low-income
Gabon	1.73	87	8,266	Upper-middle-income

(continued)

Table A.2 Population Statistics (*continued*)

Country	Population in Millions (July 2016 Est.)	Urbanized Population Percentage (2016 Est.)	Per Capita GDP in USD (2016 Est.)	Income Level Based on GNI Per Capita (2016 Est.)
The Gambia	1.99	60	472	Low-income
Ghana	27.41	54	1,370	Lower-middle-income
Guinea	12.61	37	531	Low-income
Guinea-Bissau	1.84	49	573	Low-income
Kenya	46.05	26	1,377	Lower-middle-income
Lesotho	2.14	27	1,067	Lower-middle-income
Liberia	4.50	50	456	Low-income
Libya	6.28	79	5,518 (2011)	Upper-middle-income
Madagascar	24.24	35	402	Low-income
Malawi	17.22	16	372	Low-income
Mali	17.60	40	724	Low-income
Mauritania	4.07	60	1,370 (2011)	Lower-middle-income
Mauritius	1.27	40	9,252	Upper-middle-income
Morocco	34.38	60	2,878	Lower-middle-income
Mozambique	27.98	32	529	Low-income
Namibia	2.46	47	4,677	Upper-middle-income
Niger	19.90	19	359	Low-income
Nigeria	182.20	48	2,640	Lower-middle-income

Rwanda	11.61	29	697	Low-income
São Tomé and Príncipe	0.19	65	1,669	Lower-middle-income
Senegal	15.13	44	900	Low-income
Seychelles	0.10	54	15,476	High-income
Sierra Leone	6.45	40	653	Low-income
Somalia	10.79	40	549	Low-income
South Africa	54.49	65	5,724	Upper-middle-income
South Sudan	12.34	19	731	Low-income
Sudan	40.24	34	2,415	Lower-middle-income
Swaziland	1.29	21	3,200	Lower-middle-income
Tanzania	53.47	32	879	Low-income
Togo	7.31	40	557	Low-income
Tunisia	11.25	67	3,873	Lower-middle-income
Uganda	39.03	16	705	Low-income
Zambia	16.21	41	1,305	Lower-middle-income
Zimbabwe	15.60	32	924	Low-income

Sources: United Nations, Department of Economic and Social Affairs, Population Division, 2015, "World Population Prospects: The 2015 Revision," https://esa.un.org/unpd/wpp/Publications/Files/World_Population_2015_Wallchart.pdf; United Nations, 2014, "World Urbanization Prospects," https://esa.un.org/unpd/wup/Publications/Files/WUP2014-Report.pdf; World Bank, 2016a, "Country and Lending Groups," http://data.worldbank.org/about/country-and-lending-groups; World Bank, 2016b, "GDP per Capita (Current US%)," http://data.worldbank.org/indicator/NY.GDP.PCAP.CD.

Note: Discrepancies between the level of GDP per capita and the income classifications (as measured in GNI per capita) may be due to the variation in the calculation of these figures.

Table A.3 Currencies and Exchange Rates

Country	Currency	Currency Initialism	USD Exchange Rate (June 15, 2016)
Algeria	Dinar	DZD	110.169
Angola	Kwanza	AOA	165.731
Benin	Franc	XOF	584.613
Botswana	Pula	BWP	11.0497
Burkina Faso	Franc	XOF	584.613
Burundi	Franc	BIF	1,605.81
Cabo Verde	Escudo	CVE	98.3640
Cameroon	Franc	XAF	584.924
Central African Republic	Franc	XAF	584.613
Chad	Franc	XAF	584.613
Comoros	Franc	KMF	438.647
Congo	Franc	CDF	928.755
Côte d'Ivoire	Franc	XOF	584.613
Democratic Republic of the Congo	Franc	CDF	928.755
Djibouti	Franc	DJF	177.868
Egypt	Pound	EGP	8.87650
Equatorial Guinea	Franc	XAF	584.613
Eritrea	Nakfa	ERN	10.4700
Ethiopia	Birr	ETB	21.7482
Gabon	Franc	XAF	584.613
The Gambia	Dalasi	GMD	42.4271
Ghana	Cedi	GHS	3.95960
Guinea	Franc	GNF	7,336.76
Guinea-Bissau	Franc	XOF	584.613
Kenya	Shilling	KES	101.126
Lesotho	Loti	LSL	15.2772
Liberia	Dollar	LRD	90.0000
Libya	Dinar	LYD	1.37348
Madagascar	Malagasy ariary	MGA	3,285.26
Malawi	Kwacha	MWK	710.712
Mali	Franc	XOF	584.613
Mauritania	Ouguiya	MRO	312.500
Mauritius	Rupee	MUR	35.2000
Morocco	Dirham	MAD	9.73340
Mozambique	Metical	MZN	60.2891
Namibia	Dollar	NAD	15.2723
Niger	Franc	XOF	584.613
Nigeria	Nira	NGN	199.000
Rwanda	Franc	RWF	783.705
São Tomé and Príncipe	Dobra	STD	21,739.13

Table A.3 Currencies and Exchange Rates (*continued*)

Country	Currency	Currency Initialism	USD Exchange Rate (June 15, 2016)
Senegal	Franc	XOF	584.613
Seychelles	Rupee	SCR	13.1488
Sierra Leone	Leone	SLL	3,944.31
Somalia	Shilling	SOS	586.937
South Africa	Rand	ZAR	15.2771
South Sudan	Pound	SSP	31.2301
Sudan	Pound	SDG	6.07710
Swaziland	Lilangeni	SZL	15.2808
Tanzania	Shilling	TZS	2,195.25
Togo	Franc	XOF	584.613
Tunisia	Dinar	TND	2.16154
Uganda	Shilling	UGX	3,344.93
Zambia	Kwacha	ZMW	10.8250
Zimbabwe	Dollar	ZWD	361.900

Sources: For all countries excluding South Sudan, XE Currency Converter. *www.xe.com/currencyconverter/*; for South Sudan, Mataf.net. *https://www.mataf.net/en/currency/converter-USD-SSP.*

Table A.4 Property-Related Taxes

Country	Recurrent Tax	Transfer Tax or Stamp Duty	Capital Gains Tax	Gift or Death Taxes
Algeria	Yes	Yes	Yes	Yes
Angola	Yes	Yes	Yes	Yes
Benin	Yes	Yes	Yes	No
Botswana	Yes	Yes	Yes	Yes[1]
Burkina Faso	No	Yes	Yes	No
Burundi	Yes	Yes	Yes	No
Cabo Verde	Yes	Yes	Yes	No
Cameroon	Yes	Yes	Yes	Yes
Central African Republic	Yes	Yes	Yes	No data
Chad	Yes	Yes	Yes	No
Comoros	Yes	Yes	Yes	Yes
Congo	Yes	Yes	Yes	No
Côte d'Ivoire	Yes	Yes	Yes	Yes
Democratic Republic of the Congo	Yes	Yes	Yes	No
Djibouti	Yes	Yes	Yes	No

(continued)

Table A.4 Property-Related Taxes (*continued*)

Country	Recurrent Tax	Transfer Tax or Stamp Duty	Capital Gains Tax	Gift or Death Taxes
Egypt	Yes	Yes	Yes	No
Equatorial Guinea	Yes	Yes	Yes	Yes
Eritrea	Yes	Yes	Yes	No
Ethiopia	Yes	Yes	Yes	No
Gabon	Yes	Yes	Yes	No
The Gambia	Yes	Yes	Yes	No
Ghana	Yes	Yes	Yes	Yes
Guinea	Yes	Yes	Yes	Yes
Guinea-Bissau	Yes	Yes	No data	No data
Kenya	Yes	Yes	No	No
Lesotho	Yes	Yes	Yes	No
Liberia	Yes	Yes	Yes	No
Libya	Yes	Yes	Yes	No
Madagascar	Yes	Yes	Yes	No
Malawi	Yes	Yes	Yes	Yes
Mali	Yes	Yes	Yes	No
Mauritania	Yes	Yes	Yes	No
Mauritius	Yes	Yes	No	No
Morocco	Yes	Yes	Yes	Yes
Mozambique	Yes	Yes	Yes	Yes
Namibia	Yes	Yes	No	No
Niger	Yes	Yes	Yes	Yes
Nigeria	Yes	Yes	Yes	No
Rwanda	Yes	Yes	Yes	No
São Tomé and Príncipe	Yes	Yes	No data	No data
Senegal	Yes	Yes	Yes	Yes
Seychelles	No	Yes	No	No
Sierra Leone	Yes	Yes	No	No
Somalia	Yes	No data	No data	No data
South Africa	Yes	Yes	Yes	Yes
South Sudan	Yes	No data	Yes	No
Sudan	Yes	Yes	Yes	No
Swaziland	Yes	Yes	No	No
Tanzania	Yes	Yes	Yes	No
Togo	Yes	Yes	Yes	No data
Tunisia	Yes	Yes	Yes	Yes
Uganda	Yes	Yes	Yes	No
Zambia	Yes	Yes	No	No
Zimbabwe	Yes	Yes	Yes	Yes

[1] An inheritance or donations tax is imposed in the form of a capital gains tax.

Table A.5 Taxes on the Transfer of Real Property

Country	Transfer Tax or Stamp Duty	Tax Rate
Algeria	Transfer tax	5%
	Land publication fee	1%
Angola	Transfer tax (sisa)	2%
	Stamp duty	0.3%
Benin	Transfer tax	8%
Botswana	Transfer tax	5%; 30% for noncitizens acquiring agricultural land
Burkina Faso	Yes	1%
Burundi	Transfer tax	3%
Cabo Verde	Transfer tax (sisa)	3%
	Stamp duty	1%
Cameroon	Stamp duty	From 5% to 15%
Central African Republic	Transfer tax	7.5%
	Registration fee	1%
	Stamp duty	XAF 5,000
Chad	Transfer tax	10% for developed and undeveloped land
	Stamp duty	XAF 1,000
Comoros	Transfer tax	2% to 9% (of selling price)
	Recording fee	2%
Congo	Registration fee	15%
	Transfer tax	0.5%
	Conservation fee	0.2%
Côte d'Ivoire	Transfer tax	7.5% (juristic persons); 4% (all other property)
Democratic Republic of the Congo	Registration fee	From 5% to 10%
Djibouti	Transfer tax	10% of property value
Egypt	Transfer tax	2.5%
Equatorial Guinea	Transfer tax	Between residents: between 1% and 9% (usually 5%); between residents and nonresidents or between nonresidents: between 10% and 25%; on all legal documents (e.g., registration), between 1% and 10%
	Stamp duty	
Eritrea	Transfer tax	4%
	Stamp duty	ERN 340 (maximum)
Ethiopia	Transfer tax	4%
	Stamp duty	2%
		ETB 10 for the service charge and ETB 55 for the power of attorney

(continued)

Table A.5 Taxes on the Transfer of Real Property (*continued*)

Country	Transfer Tax or Stamp Duty	Tax Rate
Gabon	Transfer tax	6%
The Gambia	Transfer tax	5%
	Stamp duty	GMD 1,000
Ghana	Stamp duty	0.25%, 0.5%, or 1% on a sliding scale determined by value
Guinea	Transfer tax	5%
	Stamp duty	0.25% to 1%
Guinea-Bissau	Transfer tax (sisa)	10%
	Stamp duty	(XOF 2,000 per page + 0.5% of half of property value) + (XOF 2,000 for the stamps to register new ownership)
Kenya	Stamp duty	2% (rural property); 4% (urban property)
Lesotho	Transfer duty	3% and 4%, sliding scale
	Stamp duty	1% and 3%, sliding scale
Liberia	Stamp duty	LRD 100 fixed fee
Libya	Stamp duty	5%, 8%, and 10%
Madagascar	Transfer tax	6% upon registration of the contract of sale
	Recording fee	2% upon recording the transfer at the Registry
Malawi	Stamp duty	1.5%
Mali	Registration fee	7%
	Fixed registry tax	XOF 12,500
	Transfer fee	1.5%
	Stamp duty	XOF 14,000
Mauritania	Transfer tax	From 0.25% to 15%
Mauritius	Registration duty	From 0.1% to 12%
	Land transfer tax	5%
Morocco	Registration fee	From 1.5% to 6% registration duty and 1% real estate tax at time of acquisition
	Stamp duty	MAD 20 per page, 5-page sale contract, 6 copies (signing and notarizing sale contract) + 1% of property value (inscription of the registered deed on the land registers)
Mozambique	Transfer tax (sisa)	2%
	Stamp duty	0.2%
Namibia	Transfer duty	Individuals: 0%, 1%, 5%, and 8%, sliding scale. Juristic persons: 12%
	Stamp duty	Individuals: ((purchase price–NAD 600,000)/1,000) × 10 Juristic persons: (purchase price/1,000) × 12

Table A.5 Taxes on the Transfer of Real Property (*continued*)

Country	Transfer Tax or Stamp Duty	Tax Rate
Niger	Transfer tax	3%
Nigeria	Stamp duty	0.75%
Rwanda	Transfer fee	RWF 20,000, fixed fee
São Tomé and Príncipe	Transfer tax (sisa)	8%
Senegal	Transfer tax	10%
Seychelles	Stamp duty	5%
Sierra Leone	Stamp duty	0.1%
Somalia	Transfer tax	3% in semiautonomous Somaliland
South Africa	Transfer duty	0%, 3%, 5%, 8%, 11%, 13%
South Sudan	Yes	No data
Sudan	Yes	2%
Swaziland	Transfer duty	2%, 4%, or 6%, sliding scale
	Stamp duty	For some documents, ad valorem; for others, a fixed amount
Tanzania	Stamp duty	1%
Togo	Registration fee	6%
	Stamp duty	XOF 1,000 per page on, e.g., a contract of sale
Tunisia	Transfer tax	5%
	Registration fee	1%
Uganda	Stamp duty	0.5%, 1%
Zambia	Transfer tax	5%
Zimbabwe	Transfer tax	2%, 3%, 4%
	Stamp duty	0.05%, 0.25%, 0.4%, 1%, 2%

Source: Authors' compilation.

Table A.6 Property Tax Bases Used in Practice

Country	Tax Base(s)
Algeria	Annual rental value
Angola	Annual rental value
Benin	Annual rental value for developed property; capital value for undeveloped land
Botswana	Capital value of land and buildings, assessed separately but taxed collectively
Burkina Faso	No recurrent property tax, only minor property-related charges
Burundi	Area-based system with some differentiation
Cabo Verde	Capital value
Cameroon	Capital value in major cities; area-based system elsewhere (in practice)
Central African Republic	Annual rental value for developed and undeveloped land in urban areas; a fixed amount per hectare (with reference to the crop grown or whether land is idle) in rural areas
Chad	Annual rental value
Comoros	Annual rental value; area for agricultural land
Congo	Annual rental value for developed urban land; capital/assessed value for undeveloped urban land; area for rural land
Côte d'Ivoire	Annual rental value for developed property; capital value for undeveloped land
Democratic Republic of the Congo	Area with some differentiation based on location
Djibouti	Annual rental value
Egypt	Annual rental value
Equatorial Guinea	Rental value for urban property; area (and income potential) for rural property
Eritrea	Area for urban and rural property
Ethiopia	Annual rental value; area
Gabon	Annual rental value (law); area (in practice)
The Gambia	Annual rental value (buildings only)
Ghana	Capital value (buildings only)
Guinea	Annual rental value
Guinea-Bissau	Annual rental value
Kenya	Land value only in most instances; area or rental value (for agricultural land) also allowed by law
Lesotho	Capital value of land and buildings separately (split-rate system)

Table A.6 Property Tax Bases Used in Practice (*continued*)

Country	Tax Base(s)
Liberia	Capital value of land and buildings separately (split-rate system)
Libya	Area (with some coefficients based on size and occupancy)
Madagascar	Adjusted area
Malawi	Capital value
Mali	Annual rental value
Mauritania	Annual rental value
Mauritius	Annual rental value; land value (for some properties)
Morocco	Annual rental value; area for undeveloped land
Mozambique	Capital value (buildings only)
Namibia	Capital value of land and buildings separately; land value, building value, land and buildings collectively, and area (used in small rural villages) allowed by law
Niger	Annual rental value (residential); book value (nonresidential)
Nigeria	Annual rental value in some states; capital value in Lagos State
Rwanda	Self-declared capital value of buildings and land values determined by central government
São Tomé and Príncipe	Capital value
Senegal	Annual rental value
Seychelles	No recurrent tax
Sierra Leone	Annual rental value (buildings only)
Somalia	Adjusted area (in Puntland)
South Africa	Market value (capital value)
South Sudan	Area
Sudan	Area with some adjustment for size, location, and use
Swaziland	Capital value of land and buildings separately; land value, building value, and land and buildings collectively also allowed by law
Tanzania	Depreciated replacement cost of buildings only
Togo	Annual rental value for developed land; capital value for undeveloped land
Tunisia	Annual rental value
Uganda	Annual rental value
Zambia	Capital value
Zimbabwe	Land only (Harare); land and buildings separately with collective capital value as a further option

Table A.7 Property Tax Base Coverage, Assessment, and Administration

Country	Base Coverage		Assessment Responsibility	Collection	Revenue
	Urban	Rural			
Algeria	Yes	No data	No data	No data	No data
Angola	Yes (limited)	No	Central	Central	Central
Benin	Yes	No	Central	Central	Central and local
Botswana	Yes (limited)	No	Central and local	Local	Local
Burkina Faso	No	No	Not applicable	Not applicable	Not applicable
Burundi	Yes	No	Taxpayer	Central and local	Local
Cabo Verde	Yes	No data	Central and taxpayer	Local	Local
Cameroon	Yes	Exempted	Central	Central	Local
Central African Republic	Yes (limited)	In principle	Central	Central	Central
Chad	Yes (limited)	In principle	Local	Local	Local
Comoros	Yes	Yes	No data	No data	No data
Congo	Yes (limited)	In principle	Central	Central	Central
Côte d'Ivoire	Yes	In principle	Central	Central	Central and local
Democratic Republic of the Congo	Yes (limited)	No	Central	Central	Central and local
Djibouti	Yes	No data	No data	No data	No data
Egypt	Yes	Yes	Central and local	Central	Local
Equatorial Guinea	Yes	Yes	Tax administration	Central	Local
Eritrea	Yes	Yes	Central and local	Local (Asmara)	Local (Asmara)
Ethiopia	Yes (limited)	In principle	Central	Local	Local

Gabon	Yes	Yes	Central and taxpayer	Local	Local
The Gambia	Yes	No	Central and local	Local	Local
Ghana	Yes	No	Central and local	Local	Local
Guinea	Yes (limited)	No data	Central and taxpayer	Central	Central and local
Guinea-Bissau	Yes (limited)	No	Central	Central	Local
Kenya	Yes	In principle	Central and local	Local	Local
Lesotho	Yes (limited)	No	Central and local	Local	Local
Liberia	Yes (limited)	No	Central and taxpayer	Central	Local
Libya	Yes (limited)	No	Central and taxpayer	Central	Central
Madagascar	Yes	Limited	Local committees	Local	Local
Malawi	Yes	No	Local	Local	Local
Mali	Yes (limited)	No data	No data	Central	No data
Mauritania	Yes	No data	No data	No data	No data
Mauritius	Yes	No	Central	Local	Local
Morocco	Yes	No	Central and local	Central and local	Local
Mozambique	Yes (limited)	No	Local	Local	Local
Namibia	Yes	Yes (limited)	Central and local	Central and local	Central and local
Niger	Yes	No	Central and taxpayer	Central	Central and local
Nigeria	Yes	No data	State (Lagos)	Local	Local
Rwanda	Yes	No	Taxpayer	Central	Local
São Tomé and Príncipe	Yes	No data	Central and local	Central	No data
Senegal	Yes	No	Central	Central	Local
Seychelles	No	No	Not applicable	Not applicable	Not applicable
Sierra Leone	Yes (limited)	No	Local committees	Local	Local
Somalia	Yes (limited)	No	Local	Local	Local

(continued)

Table A.7 Property Tax Base Coverage, Assessment, and Administration (*continued*)

| Country | Base Coverage | | Assessment Responsibility | Collection | Revenue |
	Urban	Rural			
South Africa	Yes	Yes	Local	Local	Local
South Sudan	No data	No data	No data	No data	No data
Sudan	Yes (limited)	No data	Not applicable	Local	Local
Swaziland	Yes (limited)	No	Local	Local	Local
Tanzania	Yes	No	Local	Local	Local
Togo	Yes	No data	No data	No data	No data
Tunisia	Yes	Limited	Central and taxpayer	Central	Central and local
Uganda	Yes (limited)	In principle	Local	Local	Local
Zambia	Yes	No	Central and local	Local	Local
Zimbabwe	Yes	Limited	Local	Local	Local

Table A.8 Comparative Indexes

Country	Ease of Doing Business (190 Jurisdictions)	Registering Property (190 Jurisdictions)	Corruption Perception Index (176 Jurisdictions)	International Property Rights Index (128 Countries) (2016)
Algeria	156	162	108	108
Angola	182	170	164	127 (2015)
Benin	155	173	95	96
Botswana	71	70	35	44
Burkina Faso	146	136	72	101 (2015)
Burundi	157	94	159	123
Cabo Verde	129	73	38	–
Cameroon	166	177	145	111
Central African Republic	185	167	159	–
Chad	180	157	159	118
Comoros	153	90	153	–
Congo	177	171	159	–
Côte d'Ivoire	142	113	108	82
Democratic Republic of the Congo	184	156	156	–
Djibouti	171	168	123	–
Egypt	122	109	108	98
Equatorial Guinea	178	160	–	–
Eritrea	189	178	164	–
Ethiopia	159	133	108	103
Gabon	164	175	101	84
The Gambia	145	124	145	–
Ghana	108	77	70	53
Guinea	163	140	142	–
Guinea-Bissau	172	149	168	–
Kenya	92	121	145	88
Lesotho	100	108	83	–
Liberia	174	179	90	73
Libya	188	187	170	124 (2015)
Madagascar	167	159	145	116
Malawi	133	95	120	89
Mali	141	135	116	93
Mauritania	160	102	142	119
Mauritius	49	98	50	34

(continued)

Table A.8 Comparative Indexes (*continued*)

Country	Ease of Doing Business (190 Jurisdictions)	Registering Property (190 Jurisdictions)	Corruption Perception Index (176 Jurisdictions)	International Property Rights Index (128 Countries) (2016)
Morocco	68	87	90	58
Mozambique	137	107	142	99
Namibia	108	174	53	–
Niger	150	125	101	–
Nigeria	169	182	136	122
Rwanda	56	4	50	33
São Tomé and Príncipe	162	161	62	–
Senegal	147	142	64	74
Seychelles	93	66	40 (2015)	–
Sierra Leone	148	163	123	102
Somalia	190	148	176	–
South Africa	74	105	64	30
South Sudan	186	181	175	–
Sudan	168	89	170	–
Swaziland	111	117	–	75
Tanzania	132	132	116	92
Togo	154	183	116	–
Tunisia	77	92	75	72
Uganda	115	116	151	86
Zambia	98	145	87	77
Zimbabwe	161	111	154	124

Sources: "Doing Business," World Bank, 2017, *www.doingbusiness.org/*; corruption perception index: Transparency International, "Corruption Perception Index in 168 Countries," 2016, *www.transparency.org*; international property rights index: Property Rights Alliance, "The International Property Rights Index 2016," 2016, *http://international propertyrightsindex.org/countries?f=country&o=asc&r.*

Notes:

[1] Countries with identical scores will have the same ranking (e.g., Ghana and Namibia in column 1).

[2] Some countries were removed from the relevant indexes in 2016. In these cases the relevant 2015 position is provided.

Contributors

Editors

RIËL FRANZSEN
South African Research Chair in Tax Policy and Governance
African Tax Institute
University of Pretoria, South Africa

WILLIAM McCLUSKEY
Extraordinary Professor
African Tax Institute
University of Pretoria, South Africa

Chapter Authors

KHALED AMIN
Professor
School of Economics and Political Science
Cairo University, Egypt

ROY BAHL
Professor Emeritus, Georgia State University;
Extraordinary Professor, African Tax Institute
University of Pretoria, South Africa

JOHN CHAKASIKWA
Zimbabwe Revenue Authority
Harare, Zimbabwe

MARIA ELKHDARI
Ph.D. candidate in economics
Centre d'Études et de Recherches sur le Développement International
Université d'Auvergne, France

SHAHENAZ HASSAN
Architect
Dresden, Germany

BOUBACAR HASSANE
Lecturer
Faculty of Economics and Law
Abdou Moumouni University
Niamey, Republic of Niger

SAMUEL JIBAO
Director
Centre for Economic Research and Capacity Building
Sierra Leone;
Senior Lecturer
African Tax Institute
University of Pretoria, South Africa

MUNDIA KABINGA
Senior Lecturer
Graduate School of Business
University of Cape Town, South Africa

CHABALA KASESE
Legal Officer
Zambia Revenue Authority
Zambia

NARA MONKAM
Director of Research
African Tax Administration Forum
Pretoria, South Africa

VASCO NHABINDE
Director of Economic and Finance Studies
Ministry of Economy and Finance
Mozambique

JEAN-JACQUES NZEWANGA
Consultant Economique
Coordonateur Principal du CANECO
Kinshasa, Democratic Republic of the Congo

WASHINGTON OLIMA
Professor
Department of Land Development
University of Nairobi, Kenya

BERNARD TAYOH
Adviser on Trade Policy
Deutsche Gesellschaft für Internationale Zusammenarbeit (GIZ)
Abuja, Nigeria

Research Fellows

DOBINGAR ALLASSEMBAYE
Ministry of Land Management
Urban Development
N'Djamena, Chad

KHALED AMIN
Professor
School of Economics and Political Science
Cairo University, Egypt

BEKALU TILAHUN GEBRESLUS
Addis Ababa, Ethiopia

SHAHENAZ HASSAN
Architect
Dresden, Germany

BOUBACAR HASSANE
Lecturer
Faculty of Economics and Law
Abdou Moumouni University
Niamey, Republic of Niger

SAMUEL JIBAO
Director
Centre for Economic Research and Capacity Building
Sierra Leone;
Senior Lecturer
African Tax Institute
University of Pretoria, South Africa

MUNDIA KABINGA
Senior Lecturer
Graduate School of Business
University of Cape Town, South Africa

NARA MONKAM
Director of Research
African Tax Administration Forum
Pretoria, South Africa

VASCO NHABINDE
Director of Economic and Finance Studies
Ministry of Economy and Finance
Mozambique

JEAN-JACQUES NZEWANGA
Consultant Economique
Coordonateur Principal du CANECO
Kinshasa, Democratic Republic of the Congo

WASHINGTON OLIMA
Professor
Department of Land Development
University of Nairobi, Kenya

ALEMAYEHU NEGASH SORESSA
Senior Consultant
AG Consult
Addis Ababa, Ethiopia

BERNARD TAYOH
Adviser on Trade Policy
Deutsche Gesellschaft für Internationale Zusammenarbeit (GIZ)
Abuja, Nigeria

BERHANE TECLE
Formerly from the Ministry of Finance
Asmara, Eritrea

Index

ad valorem property tax, 66
adobe buildings, 332, 335*n*1
Africa, xv; languages, xv. *See also specific
countries*
African countries: basic statistics,
594–597; comparative indexes, xvi,
xviii*n*7, *611–612*; currencies and
exchange rates, xvi, xviii*n*10, *600–601*;
governments, xvi; political
instability, xvi, xviii*nn*6–7; population
statistics, *597–599*; property transfer
taxes in, 46–47; property-related taxes
overview, *601–602*; real property
transfer taxes overview, *603–605*;
tax base coverage overview, *608–610*.
See also specific topics
African countries, property tax:
administration overview, *608–610*;
assessment overview, *608–610*; base
overview, *606–607*; challenges of,
96–98; research overview, xv–xvii,
xvii*n*1, xvii*n*3, xviii*n*5, xviii*n*9. *See also*
African property tax
African land administration, 12. *See also*
land administration
African property tax, 3–4, 11–12;
importance of cities, 36, *37*; overview,
588; ownership of, 39–42, 98*n*5; policy
and practice overview, 29–30; politics
and, 97. *See also* property tax; *specific
issues*
African property tax, challenges, 96–98;
African environment, 552–553;
institutional environment, 554–561;

politics, 553–554; property tax reform,
565–573; property-related taxes,
563–565; urbanization and property
tax, 562–563, 588*n*1; valuation
problem, 573–579
African property tax, institutional
environment: land administration
and informal property markets,
555–556; overview, 554–555;
shortage of valuers, 560–561; tax
base coverage and property
identification, 557–558; valuation,
558, 560–562
African property tax, prospects:
elements of property tax reform,
581–582; evaluation of reforms,
582–584; incentives, 580–581;
overview, 579–580
African property tax, valuation
problem: area-based systems,
574, 574–577; computer-assisted mass
appraisal, 579; mass appraisal, 579;
overview, 573–574; self-declaration,
578, 579, 588*n*3; value banding, 578
African property tax reform, 3, 21*n*6;
clarifying objectives, 565–566, *566*;
including all fiscal instruments,
566–570; monitoring performance,
572–573; one-size tax and local
governments, 570, 572; overview, 565,
581–582, *582*; problems, 551–552;
recommendations, 585–588; reviews,
585, 588*n*5. *See also* African property
tax, challenges

About the Lincoln Institute of Land Policy

The Lincoln Institute of Land Policy is an independent, nonpartisan organization whose mission is to help solve global economic, social, and environmental challenges to improve the quality of life through creative approaches to the use, taxation, and stewardship of land. As a private operating foundation whose origins date to 1946, the Lincoln Institute seeks to inform public dialogue and decisions about land policy through research, training, and effective communication. By bringing together scholars, practitioners, public officials, policy makers, journalists, and involved citizens, the Lincoln Institute integrates theory and practice and provides a forum for multidisciplinary perspectives on public policy concerning land, both in the United States and internationally. The Lincoln Institute's work is organized in five major areas: Planning and Urban Form, Valuation and Taxation, International and Institute-Wide Initiatives, the People's Republic of China, and Latin America and the Caribbean.

LINCOLN INSTITUTE
OF LAND POLICY

113 Brattle Street
Cambridge, MA 02138-3400 USA
P 1.617.661.3016   1.800.526.3873
F 1.617.661.7235   1.800.526.3944
help@lincolnist.edu
lincolninst.edu